GERMAN HISTORY AND CIVILIZATION, 1806-1914,

A Bibliography of Scholarly Periodical Literature

compiled by
JOHN C. FOUT, *1937-*

The Scarecrow Press, Inc.
Metuchen, N.J.   1974

Library of Congress Cataloging in Publication Data

Fout, John C   1937-
    German history and civilization, 1806-1914.

    1. Germany--History--1789-1900--Bibliography.
2. Germany--History--William II, 1888-1918--Bibliogra-
phy. 3. Germany--Intellectual life--History--Biblio-
graphy. I. Title.
Z2239.F68   016.9143'03   74-10803
ISBN 0-8108-0742-4

FOR

JUSTINE, ELIZABETH, AND JOHN

TABLE OF CONTENTS

INTRODUCTION

As everyone in the historical profession knows, some of the most important literature, both primary and secondary, is to be found in the scholarly journals. Just as well known is the fact that this literature is consistently the most difficult to locate. In recent years some steps have been taken to remedy that situation. At least it is now possible to use the Union List of Serials in conjunction with the wonders of photoduplication and interlibrary loan to obtain a copy of an article, no matter how obscure the journal. Likewise, Historical Abstracts and similar guides in related disciplines (economics, religion, etc.) now make the arduous task of searching out recent literature somewhat less tedious. In addition, many journals provide us with a list of articles as they appear, e. g., the American Historical Review and the Historische Zeitschrift, to name only two of the most obvious on a list which ranges into the dozens. Many of the "standard" bibliographies, such as Gebhardt's Handbuch der deutschen Geschichte, cite articles in connection with extensive lists of monographs. Finally, in the decades since 1945 especially, a number of specialized bibliographies have appeared which provide us with bibliographic help in a very detailed fashion; for example, Alfred Milatz, Friedrich-Naumann-Bibliographie and Karl Eric Born, et al., Bismarck-Bibliographie, to name two of many.

Despite the lengthy list of bibliographies which have appeared, they are nonetheless weighted in favor of monographic literature. There have been few systematic attempts to search out a broad survey of periodical literature, and thus, even with all the guides now available to the historian, the bibliographic challenge is still a formidable one when a new research problem is approached. This bibliography is an attempt to bridge the gap, at least in terms of nineteenth century German history. Since the journals which contain significant articles number in the hundreds, the dimensions of such an undertaking are gargantuan. Essentially this compilation represents a survey of approximately one hundred and fifty journals (a few journals marked with an "x" indicate only a substantial partial run) encompassing over 5,500 volumes dating from the 1840's to 1973 in some cases. Major historical journals in English, German and French and a number of local history journals from Germany were used. Journals from related disciplines which are helpful to the historian were also included, for example, over twenty journals dealing with church history and religious thought, a dozen dealing with the history of ideas and philosophy, a score concerning economic history, thought and development and yet another dozen on politics and political thought. It should be noted that there is a section in the bibliography on intellectual and cultural history and articles on literary figures are included but not studies dealing with literary criticism. Therefore, there are articles on Goethe in politics but not on Faust or other literary works.

To make the bibliography useful to a wide variety of scholars, I have provided an unusually detailed Table of Contents. Besides the standard categories to be found in an historical bibliography of this type, there are numerous sub-categories, including over two hundred individuals. These categories were not chosen in advance but came about as a result of the material I found. It is unfortunately quite clear that a core of individuals have been "researched to death" and many others, some of considerable importance, have been scarcely dealt with--this seemingly is quite consistent with the monographic literature on the same figures. Adhering to the limits of the 1806- 1914 dates was sometimes difficult. In the case of someone like Karl Theodor von Dalberg only material on his later years was included. In the instance of Matthias Erzberger, only articles on his activities before 1914 were cited.

The method of citation and the abbreviation of journal titles I have devised is at best a compromise between American and European forms on the one hand and historians and social scientists in general on the other. The day when there will be a uniform system seems yet to be a long way off. As to citation here, I have found the pattern followed in the Historische Zeitschrift the most adequate for bibliographic purposes and it is the one generally adhered to. Author, title of the article, abbreviated journal title, volume number, year, and inclusive pages follow in that order. For example: Otto P. Pflanze, "Bismarck and German Nationalism," AHR, 60, 1955, 548-66. In a few cases where issue numbers are not consecutive, the issue number follows the volume number in parenthesis: Franz Schnabel, "Friedrich Meinecke und die deutsche Geschichtsschreibung," Hochland, 34 (2), 1936/1937, 157-62. In the overwhelming majority of the cases, each article is followed by a complete citation. In a relatively few instances journals do not have volume numbers, or a reference was culled from another source than the journals searched, and the citation is incomplete. When no author is indicated, the article is alphabetized by title.

The list of abbreviated journal titles that follows reflects only the journals I searched completely. If a journal is cited but not listed in the abbreviations, this indicates a random citation from that journal. The system of abbreviating the journal titles generally follows the Historische Zeitschrift for non-English titles and the American Historical Review for English language periodicals. The same rules apply for journals not on the list.

The bibliography is regrettably not annotated in any way. It would, of course, have been helpful to point out some of the seminal articles. But I felt it was more important to put the emphasis on making available a lengthy list rather than a select one whose significance might lessen with time and changing research interests.

ACKNOWLEDGMENTS

I am indebted to the New York Public Library, Columbia University Libraries and the Union Theological and Vassar College Libraries. I am especially indebted to the entire staff of the Bard College Library. I would like to thank Dr. Arnold Price of the Library of Congress for his help and advice. Many of my colleagues at Bard should be thanked and I would single out John Toomey, Associate Professor of History, and Richard Wiles, Associate Professor of Economics, for my special thanks. I am also indebted to Dr. Reamer Kline, President of Bard College, for his enthusiasm and financial support. My thanks to my many student assistants, especially Hilaria Winkfield and Amalia Choman, to whom fell most of the terrible burden of typing. Finally, my gratitude is expressed to Mary Jane Fout for her help in the research and the task of typing as well.

John C. Fout
Assoc. Prof. of History
Bard College
Annandale-on-Hudson, New York
December, 1973

ABBREVIATIONS

Ag. Hist.	Agricultural History
AHR	American Historical Review
Ann. Niederrhein	x Annalen des historischen Vereins für den Niederrhein
Annales	Annales Economies, Sociétés, Civilisations
Annals Med. Hist.	Annals of Medical History
Arch. d. Soc. d. Rel.	Archives de Sociologie des Religions
Arch. f. d. Gesch. d. Soz.	Archiv für die Geschichte des Sozialismus und der Arbeiterbewegung
(Zs. f. Sozialforschung)	(Zeitschrift für Sozialforschung)
Arch. f. dt. Postgesch.	Archiv für Deutsche Postgeschichte
Arch. f. Frankfurts Gesch.	x Archiv für Frankfurts Geschichte und Kunst
Arch. f. Gesch. d. Phil.	Archiv für Geschichte der Philosophie
Arch. f. hessische Gesch.	Archiv für hessische Geschichte und Alterthumskunde (Neue Folge)
Arch. f. KuG.	Archiv für Kulturgeschichte
Arch. f. mrh. KiG.	Archiv für Mittelrheinische Kirchengeschichte
Arch. f. Sozialgesch.	Archiv für Sozialgeschichte
Arch. f. Sozialw. u. Sozialpol.	Archiv für Sozialwissenschaft und Sozialpolitik
Aussenpol.	Aussenpolitik
Bär v. Ber.	Bär von Berlin
Beitr. z. Gesch. d. dt. Arbeiterbeweg.	Beiträge zur Geschichte der Deutschen Arbeiterbewegung
Bremisches Jb.	x Bremisches Jahrbuch
Bus. Hist.	Business History
Bus. Hist. Rev.	Business History Review
Can. J. Hist.	Canadian Journal of History
Cath. Hist. Rev.	Catholic Historical Review
Cen. Eur. Hist.	Central European History
Church Hist.	Church History
Comp. Stud. Soc. Hist.	Comparative Studies in Society and History

---

x indicates only a partial run indexed.

Dt. Zs. f. KiR.	Deutsche Zeitschrift für Kirchenrecht (Dritte Folge)
Dt. Zs. f. Phil.	Deutsche Zeitschrift für Philosophie
Econ. Hist. Rev.	Economic History Review
Econ. J.	Economic Journal
EEH	Explorations in Economic History
EHR	English Historical Review
Ethics	Ethics
Eur. J. Soc.	European Journal of Sociology
Eur. Stud. Rev.	European Studies Review
Ev. Theol.	Evangelische Theologie
Evan. Q.	Evangelical Quarterly
FBPG	Forschungen zur Brandenburgischen und Preussischen Geschichte
Freiburger Zs. f. Phil.	Freiburger Zeitschrift für Philosophie und Theologie
Gelbe Hefte	Gelbe Hefte Historische und Politische Zeitschrift für das Katholische Deutschland
Ger. Econ. Rev.	German Economic Review
Ger. Life Letters	German Life and Letters
Ger. Rev.	The Germanic Review
GiWuU	Geschichte in Wissenschaft und Unterricht
H. Jb.	Historisches Jahrbuch der Görres Gesellschaft
Hamb. Mittel- u. ostdt. Forsch.	Hamburger Mittel- und Ostdeutsche Forschungen
Har. Theol. Rev.	Harvard Theological Review
Hist. J.	Historical Journal (Cambridge Historical Journal)
Hist. Judaica	Historia Judaica
Hist. Pol. Econ.	History of Political Economy
Hist. Sci.	History of Science
Hist. Stud.	Historical Studies
Hist. Theor.	History and Theory
Hist. Vjschr.	Historische Vierteljahrsschrift (Deutsches Zeitschrift für Geschichtswissenschaft)
Historian	The Historian
History	History
Hochland	x Hochland
HZ	Historische Zeitschrift
Int. Rev. Soc. Hist.	International Review of Social History
Isis	Isis
J. Cen. Eur. Aff.	Journal of Central European Affairs
J. Church State	Journal of Church and State

J. Contemp. Hist.	Journal of Contemporary History
J. Eccl. Hist.	Journal of Ecclesiastical History
J. Econ. Hist.	Journal of Economic History
J. Hist. Ideas	Journal of the History of Ideas
J. Hist. Med. Allied Sci.	Journal of the History of Medicine and Allied Sciences
J. Hist. Phil.	Journal of the History of Philosophy
J. Interdis. Hist.	The Journal of Interdisciplinary History
J. Jew. Stud.	Journal of Jewish Studies
J. Mod. Hist.	Journal of Modern History
J. Pol.	Journal of Politics
J. Rel.	The Journal of Religion
J. Sci. Stud. Rel.	Journal of the Scientific Study of Religion
J. Soc. Hist.	Journal of Social History
Jb. d. Schles. -Fried. - Wilh. Univ. z. Breslau	Jahrbuch der Schlesischen Friedrich-Wilhelms-Universität zu Breslau
Jb. f. Ber. -Brandenburg. KiG	x Jahrbuch für Berlin-Brandenburgische Kirchengeschichte
Jb. f. Gesch.	Jahrbuch für Geschichte
Jb. f. Gesch. Kunst d. MRh.	Jahrbuch für Geschichte und Kunst des Mittelrheins und seiner Nachbargebiete
Jb. f. Gesch. M. O. Dtschl.	Jahrbuch für die Geschichte Mittel-und Ostdeutschlands
Jb. f. Regionalgesch.	Jahrbuch für Regionalgeschichte
Jb. f. Sozialw.	Jahrbuch für Sozialwissenschaft
Jb. f. Wgesch.	Jahrbuch für Wirtschaftsgeschichte
Jbb. f. Gesch. Osteur.	Jahrbücher für Geschichte Osteuropas
Jbb. f. Nationalökon. u. Stat.	Jahrbücher für Nationalökonomie und Statistik
Jew. Soc. Stud.	Jewish Social Studies
Judaica	Judaica
Leo Daeck Inst. Yrbk.	The Leo Baeck Institute Yearbooks
Luth. Q.	The Lutheran Quarterly
Med. Hist.	Medical History
Militärgesch. Mitt.	Militärgeschichtliche Mitteilungen
Mitt. d. Ver. f. Gesch.	x Mitteilungen des Vereins für die Geschichte Berlins
Neue Zs. f. system. Theol. u. RP.	Neue Zeitschrift für Systematische Theologie und Religionsphilosophie
Past and Present	Past and Present
Phil. Rev.	The Philosophical Review
Philosophy	Philosophy
Pol. Mein.	Politische Meinung
Pol. Sci. Q.	Political Science Quarterly
Pol. Soc.	Politics and Society
Pol. Stud.	Politische Studien
Pol. Vjschr.	Politische Vierteljahresschrift
Pr. Jbb.	Preussische Jahrbücher

Rev. d. Etud. Juives	x Revue des Etudes Juives
Rev. d'hist. dipl.	Revue d'histoire diplomatique
Rev. d'hist. econ. soc.	Revue d'histoire des Doctrines economique et sociale
Rev. d'hist. mod.	Revue d'histoire moderne et contemporaine
Rev. Metaphysics	Review of Metaphysics
Rev. Pol.	Review of Politics
RH	x Revue Historique
Rhein. Vjsbll.	Rheinische Vierteljahrsblätter
Röm. Qu. -Schr.	Römische Quartalschrift für Christliche Altertumskunde und Kirchengeschichte
Saec.	Saeculum Jahrbuch für Universalgeschichte
Schmoll. Jb.	Schmollers Jahrbuch für Gesetzgebung, Verwaltung und Volkswirtschaft im Deutschen Reiche
Schw. Zs. f. Gesch. (Zs. f. Schw. Gesch.)	Schweizerische Zeitschrift für Geschichte (Zeitschrift für Schweizerische Geschichte)
Sci. Soc.	Science and Society
Scott. J. Theol.	Scottish Journal of Theology
Staat	Der Staat
Theol. Qu. -Schr.	Theologische Quartalschrift
Theol. Rs.	Theologische Rundschau
Theol. Zs.	Theologische Zeitschrift
Thomist	The Thomist
Tradition	Tradition
VjHZG	Vierteljahrshefte für Zeitgeschichte
Vjschr. f. Litw.	Deutsche Vierteljahrsschrift für Literaturwissenschaft und Geistesgeschichte
VSW	Vierteljahrschrift für Sozial- und Wirtschaftsgeschichte
WaG	Die Welt als Geschichte
Wehrw. Rs.	Wehrwissenschaftliche Rundschau
Weltwirtsch. Arch.	Weltwirtschaftliches Archiv
Westf. Zs.	x Westfälische Zeitschrift (Zeitschrift für vaterländische Geschichte und Altertumskunde)
Zeitwende	Zeitwende
ZgesStw.	Zeitschrift für die Gesamte Staatswissenschaft
ZGORh.	Zeitschrift für die Geschichte des Oberrheins
ZRG (Kan. Abt.)	Zeitschrift der Savigny Stiftung für Rechtsgeschichte (Kanonistische Abteilung)

ZRGG	Zeitschrift für Religions und Geistes- geschichte
Zs. f. Armenwesen	Zeitschrift für Armenwesen, Armen- und Krankenpflege
Zs. f. Bayer. LG.	Zeitschrift für Bayerisches Landes- geschichte
Zs. f. d. Armenwesen	Zeitschrift für das Armenwesen
Zs. f. d. Gesch. d. Juden	Zeitschrift für die Geschichte der Juden
Zs. f. d. Gesch. d. Juden in Dtschl.	Zeitschrift für die Geschichte der Juden in Deutschland
Zs. f. evan. KiR.	Zeitschrift für Evangelisches Kirchen- recht
Zs. f. Geschw.	Zeitschrift für Geschichtswissenschaft
Zs. f. KiG.	Zeitschrift für Kirchengeschichte
Zs. f. MilitärG.	Zeitschrift für Militärgeschichte
Zs. f. Ostforsch.	Zeitschrift für Ostforschung
Zs. f. Pol.	Zeitschrift für Politik
Zs. f. Theol. u. K.	Zeitschrift für Theologie und Kirche
Zs. f. Württbg. LG.	Zeitschrift für Württembergische Landesgeschichte (Württembergische Vierteljahrshefte für Landesgeschichte)

CHURCH HISTORY (RELIGION)

General Studies

1. BÄUMER, P. Suitbert, "Blick auf die Geschichte der Liturgie und deren Literatur im 19. Jahrhundert," H. Jb., 11, 1890, 44-76.

2. BAIER, Hermann, "Die Beziehungen Badens zur Eidgenossenschaft und die Säkularisation," ZGORh, 89, 1936-37, 531-91.

3. BAINTON, Roland H., "Yale and German Theology in the middle of the nineteenth century," Zs. f. KiG, 66, 1954/55, 294-302.

4. BALAN, C., "Der Einfluss des juristischen Elements in den Behörden der preussischen Landeskirchen," Pr. Jbb., 77, 1894, 61-83.

5. BAUDISSIN, Wolf W. Grafen, "Die alttestamentliche Religion und die Armen," Pr. Jbb., 149, 1912, 193-231.

6. BECKER, Josef, "Staat und Kirche in Baden in der zweiten Hälfte des 19. Jhs," ZGORh, 111, 1963, 579-87.

7. BENRATH, Adolf, "Evangelische und katholische Kirchenhistorie im Zeichen der Aufklärung und der Romantik," Zs. f. KiG, 82, 1971, 203-17.

8. BERNARDS, Matthäus, "Zur Geschichte des theologischen Konvikts in Bonn 1827-1875," Ann. Niederrhein, 153/154, 1953, 201-35.

9. BÖTTICHER, V., "Ein Beitrag zur Frage nach der rechtlichen Natur der Kirchenlasten in der hannoverschen Landeskirche," Dt. Zs. f. KiR., 3, 1893, 308-33.

10. BRÜCK, Anton Ph., ed., "Briefe des Religionswissenschaftlers Edmund Hardy (1852-1904) nach Mainz," Arch. f. mrh. KiG, 21, 1969, 259-82.

11. BRÜNE, Friedrich, "Staaten und Kirchen im Raum Westfalen zu Beginn des 19. Jahrhunderts," Jb. Ver. Westfäl. Kirchengesch., 68, 1970.

12. CASE, Shirley Jackson, "The Ethics of Jesus from Strauss to Barth," J. Rel., 15, 1935, 389-99.

13. CASELMANN, August, "Wilhelm Raabe und das Christentum," Zeitwende, 5(1), 1929, 245-59.

14. CHICKERING, Roger P., "The Peace Movement and the Religious Community in Germany, 1900-1914," Church Hist., 38, 1969, 300-11.

15. CONRATH, Hanns R., "Die Stellung des Gottesdienstes im bayerischen Staatskirchenrecht," Dt. Zs. f. KiR, 24, 1914, 205-306.

1

16. DEEGAN, Daniel L., "Martin Kähler Kerygma and Gospel History," Scott. J. Theol., 16, 1963, 50-67.

17. DICKERHOF, H., "Kirchenbegriff Wissenschaftsentwicklung Bildungssoziologie und die Formen kirchlicher Historiographie Gedanken und Exkurze zu Peter Meinholds 'Geschichte der kirchlichen Historiographie,'" H. Jb., 89, 1969, 176-202.

18. DIEHL, Wilhelm, "Zur Geschichte des theologischen Fakultätsexamens in Giessen," Arch. f. hessische Gesch., 9, 1913, 65-133.

19. DRU, Alexander, "The Reformation of the 19th Century Christianity in Germany from 1800 to 1848," The Dublin Review, 116, 1952, 34-45.

20. FISCHER, Hermann and Theodor WOHNHAAS, "Die Speyerer Domorgeln im 19. Jahrhundert," Arch. f. mrh. KiG, 24, 1972, 223-42.

21. FLAMM, Hermann, "Kirchliches Lehramt und soziale Frage zum Stand der Gewerkschaftsfrage," Zs. f. Pol., 7, 1914, 456-70.

22. FOERSTER, Erich, "Die Aufklärung in der Theologie des 19. Jahrhunderts," Theol. Rs, 10, 1938, 329-57.

23. FUCHS, Walther Peter and Wolfgang MÜLLER, "Staat und Kirche im 19. Jahrhundert," ZGORh, 110, 1962, 405-16.

24. GAREIS, Carl, "Das neue kirchenpolitische Gesetz Preussens," Schmoll. Jb., 4, 1880, 521-37.

25. GRÄF, Gerhard, "Albert Hauck über Jan Hus Zur Selbstkritik der Reformationshistoriographie," Zs. f. KiG., 83, 1972, 34-51.

26. HECKEL, Martin, "Zum Sinn und Wandel der Freiheitsidee im Kirchenrecht der Neuzeit," ZRG, 55, 1969, 395-436.

27. _____, "Zur Entwicklung des deutschen Staatskirchenrechts von der Reformation bis zum Schwelle der Weimarer Verfassung," Zs. f. evan. KiR., 12, 1966-67, 1-39.

28. HELLMUTH, H., "Die bayerische Kirchengemeindeordnung vom 24 September 1912," Theol. Qu.-Schr., 97, 1915, 250-82.

29. HERZOG, Heinrich, "Beitrag zur Geschichte des sächsischen Konsistorialgesetzes vom 15. April 1873," Beitr. Kirchengesch. Deutschlands, 7, 1969.

30. JEDIN, Hubert, "Gustav Hohenlohe und Augustin Theiner 1850-1870," Röm. Qu.-Schr, 66, 1971, 171-86.

31. KAMMRADT, Friedrich, "Die psychischen Wurzeln der frühromantischen Frömmigkeit," Zs. f. Theol. u. K., 25, 1915, 124-55; 181-274.

32. KANTZENBACH, Friedrich Wilhelm, "Das Phänomen der Ent kirchlichung als Problem kirchengeschichtlicher Forschung und theologischer Interpretation," Neue Zs. f. system. Theol. u. RP, 13, 1971, 58-87.

33. _____, "Zur geistig-religiösen Situation der christlichen Konfessionen zwischen 1850 und 1860," ZRGG, 18, 1966, 193-219.

34. KATEIN, Werner, "Das Verhältnis von Staat, Kirche, und Volksschule im Königreich Württemberg," Zs. f. Württbg. LG, 15, 1956, 53-117.

35. "Die KIRCHLICHE Reaction in Preussen während der letzten zehn Jahre," Pr. Jbb., 5, 1860, 281-94.

36. KUHN, Annette, "Der Herrschaftsanspruch der Gesellschaft und die Kirche," HZ, 201, 1965, 334-58.

37. _____, "Kirche und soziale Frage Geschichtliche Entwicklungaktuelle Bedeutung," Zs. f. Pol., 13, 1966, 421-28.

38. _____, "Was Heisst 'Christlich-Sozial'?" Zs. f. Pol., 10, 1963, 102-22.

39. KUPISCH, Karl, "Bürgerliche Frömmigkeit im Wilhelminischen Zeitalter," ZRGG, 14, 1962, 123-43.

40. LAUBERT, Manfred, "Die provisorische Regelung der geistlichen Gerichtsbarkeit und die Entschädigung des Klerus in der Provinz Posen nach 1815," H. Jb., 47, 1927, 367-77.

41. LEMPP, Richard, "Present Religious Conditions in Germany," Har. Theol. Rev., 3, 1910, 85-124.

42. LENHART, Ludwig, "Mainz-Prager kirchlich-religiöse Kontakte im neunzehnten Jahrhundert," Arch. f. mrh. KiG., 20, 1968, 141-63.

43. LENZ, Max, "Nationalität und Religion," Pr. Jbb., 127, 1907, 385-408.

44. LÖHR, Joseph, "Die Streitfrage betreffend das Mitwirkungsrecht der Reichsregierung bei der Ernennung der Kantonspfarrer in Elsass-Lothringen in den Jahren 1871/72," Theol. Qu.-Schr., 111, 1930, 161-89.

45. LÖWITH, Karl, "Die philosophische Kritik der christlichen Religion im 19. Jahrhundert," Theol. Rs, 5. 1933, 131-72; 201-26.

46. LOHMANN, Landrat, "Die Staatsgenehmigung zur Errichtung von Kirchengebäuden in Preussen," Dt. Zs. f. KiR, 10, 1900/01, 341-67; 11, 1901/02, 62-115.

47. LOSCH, Ph., "Zur Geschichte der hessischen Renitenz," Zs. f. KiG, 27, 1906, 209-19.

48. MARTIN, Alfred v., "Das Wesen der romantischen Religiosität," Vjschr. f. Litw., 2, 1924, 367-417.

49. MAURER, W., "Bekenntnis und Recht in der Kurhessischen Kirche des 19. Jahrhunderts," Zs. f. Theol. u. K., 45, 1937, 112-31.

50. MEIER, O., "Landesherrliches Kirchenregiment," Pr. Jbb., 58, 1886, 467-88.

51. NIEDER, Johannes, "Die Bedeutung des Militärkirchenwesens für das Verhältnis von Staat und Kirche," Zs. f. Pol., 1, 1907-08, 471ff.

52. NITZE, E., "Die religiöse Erziehung der Kinder und deren Theilnahme am Schulreligionsunterricht," Dt. Zs. f. KiR., 8, 1898, 159-85.

53. NITZSCH, Friedrich, "Die romantische Schule und ihre Einwirkung auf die Wissenschaften, namentlich die Theologie," Pr. Jbb., 75, 1894, 321ff.

54. OETKER, Fr., "Die Kurhessische Kirchenfrage," Pr. Jbb., 27, 1871, 427-59.

55. ORTLOFF, Herm., "Die Konfession der Kinder aus gemischten Ehen zwischen Evangelischen und Katholiken und deren

Konfessionswechsel, " [Sachsen-Weimar-Eisenach], Dt. Zs.
f. KiR., 6, 1896/7, 51-105.

56. PAULS, Wilhelm, "Die Fürsorge für die Armen in der
Geschichte der Braunschweigischen Landeskirche, " Jahrb.
d. Gesell. f. niedersächsische Kirchengesch., 68, 1968.

57. RATH, R. John, "Early Nineteenth Century Bavarian Religious
Laws, " Social Education, 1950, 263-66.

58. RIEKER, Karl, "Die Krisis des landesherrlichen Kirchenregi-
ments in Preussen 1848-50 und ihre Kirchenrechtliche Bedeutung, " Dt. Zs. f. KiR., 10, 1900/01, 1-60.

59. _____, "Das landesherrliche Kirchenregiment in Bayern, "
Dt. Zs. f. KiR., 23, 1913, 1-53.

60. _____, "Staat und Kirche nach lutherischen, reformierter,
moderner Anschauung, " Hist. Vjschr., 3, 1893, 370-416.

61. SASSE, Hermann, "Das Jahrhundert der preussischen Kirche
Zur Erinnerung an der Weihnachtsfest 1834 in Hönigern, "
Zeitwende, 11(1), 1934/35, 129-40.

62. _____, "Die Reichskirche im 19. Jahrhundert, " Zeitwende,
14, 1937/38, 223-34.

63. SCHÄFER, Gerhard, "Die Württembergische Landeskirche und
die Deutsche Einigung 1864-1871, " Zs. f. Württbg. LG, 26,
1967, 421-31.

64. SCHERER, Karl, "Zur pfälzischen Kirchengeschichte des 19.
Jahrhunderts-theologischer Rationalismus und politischer
Liberalismus im pfälzischen Vormärz, " Bl. f. Pfälz. KiG.
u. rel. Volksk., 32, 1965, 146-75.

65. SCHMIDT, Georg, "Die Kirchengemeinde im rechtsrheinischen
Bayern, " Dt. Zs. f. KiR., 3, 1893, 334-54.

66. SCHMIDT, Martin, "Die Entchristlichung in der neuzeitlichen
Kirchengeschichte im deutschsprachigen Gebiet, " Zs. f.
KiG, 79, 1968.

67. SCHOEPS, Hans-Joachim, "Die Erfurter Konferenz von 1860
(Zur Geschichte des katholisch-protestantischen Gesprächs)"
ZRGG, 5, 1953, 135-59.

68. SCHREY, Heinz-Horst, "Die Kirche und die soziale Frage, "
Theol. Rs, 21, 1953, 15-62.

69. SELL, Karl, "Die allgemeinen Tendenzen und die religiösen
Triebkräft in der Kirchengeschichte des neunzehnten Jahrhunderts, " Zs. f. Theol. u. K., 16, 1906, 347-85.

70. _____, "Landeskirche und Freikirche nach ihrem Wert für
christliche Volkserziehung und innere Mission, " Zs. f.
Theol. u. K., 8, 1898, 382-405.

71. _____, "Uebertritte von der evangelischen zur Katholischen
Kirche in der ersten Hälfte des 19. Jahrhunderts, " Pr.
Jbb., 121, 1905, 26-48.

72. SERING, Max, "Die sociale Frage in England und Deutschland, "
Schmoll. Jb., 14, 1890, 373-91.

73. SIMON, Matthias, "Ein Kirchenschatz als Reformationsgedächt-
nisstiftung, " Zs. f. bayer. LG., 27, 1904, 409-30.

74. SIMONS, Prof. D., "Kirchliche Armenpflege, " Pr. Jbb., 132,
1908, 1-14.

75. SMEND, Rudolf, "Universalismus und Partikukrismus in der Alttestamentlichen Theologie des 19. Jahrhunderts, " Ev. Theol., 22, 1962, 169-79.
76. SPAHN, Martin, "Die christsoziale Bewegung, " Hochland, 26 (2), 1928/29, 164-82.
77. SPINDLER, Max, "Die kirchlichen Erneuerungs Bestrebungen in Bayern im 19. Jahrhundert, " H. Jb., 71, 1951, 197-211.
78. "STAATLICHE und kirchliche Zustände im Grossherzogthum Hessen von 1850-1869, " Pr. Jbb., 24, 1869, 22-42.
79. STEINHAUER, L., "Zur Geschichte des Paderborner Dom-kapitels von 1800 bis 1830, " Westf. Zs., 61(2), 1903, 179-201.
80. STEPHAN, Horst, "Die religiöse Frage--die Schichsals Frage des deutschen Idealismus, " Zs. f. Theol. u. K., 34, 1926, 243-67.
81. STRUCK, Wolf-Heino, "Die Säkularisation im Lande Nassau, " Hessisches Jahrb. f. L.G., 13, 1964, 280-309.
82. URNER, Hans, "Gerhart Hauptmann und Wilhelm Bölsche in ihren Aufängen (1885-1889), " Jb. f. Ber.-Brandenburg. KiG, 45, 1970, 150-76.
83. WEHRUNG, Georg, "Theologie und deutscher Idealismus, " Zs. f. systematische Theol., 9, 1932, 179-210.
84. WEICHERT, Friedrich, "Hintergründe des letzten Berlin Dom-baues, " Jb. f. Ber.-Brandenburg. KiG., 46, 1971, 117-30.
85. _____, "Die Plannung des letzten Berliner Domes, " Bär v. Ber., 20, 1971.
86. WENDLAND, Johannes, "Die Wandlung religiöser Stimmung im Laufe des 19. Jahrhunderts, " Pr. Jbb., 121, 1905, 434-46.
87. WIESNER, Werner, "Dialektischer Materialismus und christ-licher Glaube, " Theol. Zs., 17, 1961, 40-63.
88. WINKEL, H., "Die Bedeutung der Ablösungsgesetzgebung im 19. Jh. für die Finanzierung der Kirchen, " Zs. f. Agrar-gesch., 18, 1970, 43-61.
89. WITETSCHEK, Helmut, "Die Bedeutung der theologischen Fakul-tät der Universität München für die kirchliche Erneuerung in der ersten Hälfte des 19. Jahrhunderts, " H. Jb., 86, 1966, 107-37.
90. ZEEDEN, Ernst W., "Die katholische Kirche in der Sicht des deutschen Protestantismus im 19. Jahrhundert, " H. Jb., 72, 1952, 433-56.

The Catholic Church

91. ADAM, Karl, "Die katholische Tübinger Schule, " Hochland, 24 (2), 1926-27, 581-601.
92. APEL, Dr., "Die Versuche zur Errichtung eines katholischen Bistums für Kurhessen in den ersten Jahrzehnten der 19. Jahrhunderts, " ZRG, 10, 1920, 51-83.
93. AUBERT, Rogert, "Das schwierige Erwachen der katholischen Theologie in Zeitalter der Restauration Zur Würdigung der

Katholischen Tübinger Schule," Theol. Qu.-Schr., 148, 1968, 9-38.

94. BAIER, Hermann, "Die Exkommunikation des badischen Ober-kirchenratsdirektors Prestinari," H. Jb., 55, 1935, 410-22.

95. BASTGEN, Hubert, "Die ersten Bischofskandidaten der Oberrheinischen Kirchenprovinz in den Berichten an die Nuntien von Wien und München (1823)," Theol. Qu.-Schr., 116, 1935, 485-543.

96. BECKER, Hans, "Die Domdekane von Limburg," Arch. f. mrh. KiG, 22, 1970, 211-26.

97. _____, "Die Säkularisation des Kapuzinerklosters in Königstein 1813," Arch. f. mrh. KiG, 9, 1957, 283-89.

98. DEITE, Hermann, "Die Katholische-soziale Bewegung in Deutschland nach ihrer Literatur geschildert," Schmoll. Jb., 32, 1908, 957-82.

99. DEUERLEIN, E., "Das Bistum Augsburg zwischen Säkularisation und Wiederrichtung," Jb. d. Ver. f. Augsburgr Bistumgesch., 2, 1968, 107-27.

100 FASSBENDER, Prof. Dr., "Die deutschen Jesuiten und die deutschnationalen Interessen," Pr. Jbb., 154, 1913, 511-22.

101. FLEISCHER, Manfred, "Luther and Catholic Reunionists in the Age of Bismarck," Church Hist., 38, 1969, 43-66.

102. FRANTZ, Adolf, "Preussen und die katholische Kirche zu Anfang dieses Jahrhunderts," Dt. Zs. f. KiR., 1, 1892, 19-44.

103. GATZ, Erwin, "Kaplan Josef Istas und der Aachener Karitaskreis," Rhein. Vjsbll., 36, 1972, 207-28.

104. GEISELMANN, Josef Rupert, "Das Übernatürliche in der katholischen Tübinger Schule," Theol. Qu.-Schr., 143, 1963, 422-53.

105. GESCHER, Franz, "Die erzbischöfliche Kurie in Köln von ihren ersten Aufängen bis zur Gegenwart, eine rechtgeschichtliche Skizze," Ann. Niederrhein., 118, 1931, 1-31.

106. GOEBEL, Klaus, "Diesterwegs Nachfolger in Moers--die politische Vorgeschichte der Berufung Franz Ludwig Zahns zum Seminardirektor, 1832," Rhein. Vjsbll., 36, 1972, 229-44.

107. HEGEL, Eduard, "Thaddaeus Anton Deresers Studium und Lehrtätigkeit an der Universität Heidelberg Ein Beitrag zur Geschichte der Katholische-Theologischen Fakultät der Ruperto-Carola," Arch. f. mrh. KiG., 4, 1952, 229-53.

108. HERKNER, Heinrich, "Die soziale Frage und der Katholizismus," ZgesStw., 93, 1932, 1-23.

109. HERMESDORF, Herbert, "Die Stellung des Katholizismus in der politischen und sozialen Entscheidungen des 19. Jahrhunderts als Unterrichtsthema," GiWuU., 4, 1953, 616-23.

110. HINSCHIUS, Paul, "Die Orden und Kongregationen der katholischen Kirche in Preussen," Pr. Jbb., 34, 1874, 117-48.

111. HIRSCH, Helmut, "Carl Heinrich Marx als Prediger der Krefelder Deutschkatholiken (1847-1851), Arch. f. Sozialgesch., 3, 1963, 119-39.

112. HÖFFER, Josef, "Zum Ausbruch der Neuscholastik im 19. Jh.--Chrostoph Bernhard Schlüter, Franz von Baader und Hermann Ernst Plassmann," H. Jb., 72, 1952, 410-32.

113. HÖFFNER, Joseph, "Die Stellung des deutschen Katholizismus in den sozialen Entscheidungen des 19. Jahrhunderts," GiWuU., 4, 1953, 601-16.

114. HOFFMANN, Alfons, "Die katholischen geistlichen Abgeordneten der Pfalz in der bayerischen Ständeversammlung 1819 bis 1848," Zs. f. bayer. LG., 32, 1969, 767-812.

115. J., R., "Das staatliche Veto bei Bischofswahlen nach dem Rechte der oberrheinischen Kirchenprovinz," Pr. Jbb., 23, 1869, 234-41.

116. JUNG, H. W., "Der Saint-Simonismus und das katholische Deutschland," Arch. f. mrh. KiG., 23, 1971, 189-207.

117. KAAS, Ludwig, "Das Trierer Apostolische Vikariat in Ehrenbreitstein (1816-1824)," ZRG, 7, 1917, 135-283.

118. KEINEMANN, Fr., "Militärgottesdienst und Parität. Bemühungen der westf. und rheinischen Provinziallandtage um eine verbesserte Fürsorge für den kathol. Militärgottesdienst in der 1. Hälfte des 19. Jahrhunderts," Jb. f. westf. KiG., 63, 1970, 107-25.

119. KOLBE, Günter, "Demokratische Opposition in religiösem Gewande Zur Geschichte der deutschkatholischen Bewegung in Sachsen am Vorabend der Revolution von 1848/49," Zs. f. Geschw., 20, 1972, 1102-12.

120. KRÜGER, Prof. Dr. Gustav, "Der Mainzer Kreis und die katholische Bewegung," Pr. Jbb., 148, 1912, 395-414.

121. LANG, Hugo, "Die Versammlung katholischer Gelehrter in München-St. Bonifaz vom 28. IX bis 1. X 1863," H. Jb., 71, 1951, 246-58.

122. LENHART, Ludwig, "Dr. Georg Heinrich Kirstein (1859-1921) Der Volkstümliche Seelsorgsbischof auf dem Mainzer Bonifatisstuhl (1903-1921)," Arch. f. mrh. KiG., 17, 1965, 121-91.

123. _____, "Der Mainzer Bischofseid vor dem Grossherzzog von Hessen und bei Rhein (1830/1904)," Arch. f. hessische Gesch., 28, 1963, 357-82.

124. _____, "Der Streit um die Abgrenzung des Präsentations- und Collatur-Rechtes auf die Pfarrei Weiskirchen zwischen Kurhessen-Hessen-Kassel und dem Bistum Mainz im 19. Jahrhundert," Arch. f. mrh. KiG., 21, 1969, 119-31.

125. LEONHARD, Ludwig, "Die Dotationsurkunde des Grossherzogs Ludwig I. von Hessen für das 1821/27 neu umschriebene Bistum Mainz," Arch. f. mrh. KiG., 16, 1964, 378-93.

126. LEPPER, Herbert, "Die Generalversammlung der Katholiken Deutschlands vom 8. bis 11. September 1879 in Aachen," Z. Aachener Geschichtsver., 80, 1970.

127. _____, "Die kirchenpolitische Gesetzgebung der Jahre 1872

und ihre Auswirkung im Regierungsbezirk Aachen, " <u>Ann.</u> <u>Niederrhein</u>, 171, 1969.

128. LICHTER, Eduard, "Die Rückkehr des Hl. Rockes aus Augsburg im Jahre 1810, " <u>Kurtierisches Jahrb.</u>, 8, 1968; 9, 1969.

129. LILL, Rudolf, "Die ersten deutschen Bischofskonferenzen, " <u>Röm. Qu.-Schr.</u>, 60, 1965, 1-75, 59, 1964, 127-85.

130. LÖSCH, Dr. St., "Die Katholische-theologischen Fakultäten zu Tübingen und Giessen (1830-1850), " <u>Theol. Zs.</u>, 108, 1927, 159-208.

131. MAIER, Hans, "Katholizismus, nationale Bewegung und Demokratie in Deutschland, " <u>Hochland</u>, 57, 1964/65, 318-33.

132. MARTIN, Alfred von, "Romantischer Katholizismus und katholische Romantik, " <u>Hochland</u>, 23(1), 1925-26, 315-37.

133. MAY, Georg, "Mit Katholiken zu besetzende Professuren an der Universität Breslau von 1811 bis 1945. Ein Beitrag zu dem Ringen um Parität in Preussen, " <u>ZRG</u>, 53, 1967, 155-272; 54, 1968, 200-68.

134. MERKLE, Sebastian, "Der Hermesische Streit im Lichte neuer Quellen, " <u>H. Jb.</u>, 60, 1940, 179-220.

135. _____, "Zum württembergischen Mischehenstreit, " <u>Theol.</u> <u>Qu.-Schr.</u>, 119, 1938, 60-108.

136. MEYER, Christian, "Preussen und die katholische Kirche, " <u>Pr. Jbb.</u>, 44, 1879, 294-313; 371-403.

137. MIKO, Norbert, "Zur Frage der Publikation des Dogmas von der Umfehlbarkeit des Papstes durch den deutschen Episkopat im Sommer 1870, " <u>Röm. Qu.-Schr.</u>, 58, 1963, 28-50.

138. MILLER, Max, "Die römische Kurie, die württembergische Königwürde und der Beginn der Kondordatspolitik, " <u>Theol.</u> <u>Qu.-Schr.</u>, 112, 1931, 223-35.

139. MÜLLER, Franz, "Katholizismus und Sozialismus, " <u>Gelbe</u> <u>Hefte</u>, 2, 1925/26, 111-29.

140. NEUMANN, Johannes, "Vom Geist der katholischen Tübinger Theologie, " <u>Theol. Qu.-Schr.</u>, 148, 1968, 1-8.

141. NORRENBERG, P., "Joseph Hubert Mooren, " <u>Ann. Niederrhein</u>, 48, 1889, 1-8.

142. PHILIPPI, Hans, "Kronkardinalat oder Nationalkardinalat Preussische und bayerische Bemühungen an der Kurie 1900-1914, " <u>H. Jb.</u>, 80, 1960, 185-217.

143. POLL, Bernhard, "Joseph Reinkens Ein Jugendbild in Briefen, " <u>Ann. Niederrhein</u>, 155/56, 1954, 392-410.

144. POUPARD, Paul, "Abbé-Bautain und die Katholisch-Theologische Fakultät Tübingen, " <u>Theol. Qu.-Schr.</u>, 138, 1958, 460-70.

145. RAAB, Heribert, "Zur Geschichte und Bedeutung des Schlagwortes 'Ultramontan' im 18. und frühen 19. Jahrhundert, " <u>H. Jb.</u>, 81, 1961, 159-73.

146. REHM, Dr. Hermann, "Der katholische Konservatismus, " <u>Zs. f. Pol.</u>, 6, 1913, 151-58.

147. REINHARDT, Rudolf, "150 Jahre Katholisch-Theologische Fakultät, " <u>Tübinger Blätter</u>, 54, 1967, 37-40.

148. RICHTER, A. L., "Die Entwicklung des Verhältnisses zwischen

dem Staate und der katholischen Kirche in Preussen seit
der Verfassungs-Urkunde vom 5. December 1848," Zs. f.
KiR, 1, 1861, 100-22.

149. SÄGMÜLLER, Joh. B., "Der Rechtsanspruch der katholischen
Kirche in Deutschland auf finanzielle Leistungen seitens
des Staates," Theol. Qu.-Schr., 95, 1913, 204-34.

150. SCHABERT, Joseph A., "The Ludwig-Missionverein," Cath.
Hist. Rev., 9, 1923, 23-41.

151. SCHARNAGL, Anton, "Das königliche Nominationsrecht für
die Bistümer in Bayern 1817-1918," ZRG, 17, 1928, 228-
63.

152. SCHARWATH, Alfred G., "Eine staatliche 'Nachweisung'
geeigneter Bischofs- und Domherrenkandidaten der Diözese
Trier aus dem Jahre 1902," Arch. f. mrh. KiG., 20,
1968, 335-46.

153. _____, "Die Geheim-Acta der Stadt Trier betr. Ultra-
montane, Kirchenangelegenheiten, 1873-1903," Kurtrie-
risches Jahrb., 9, 1969.

154. SCHEFFEZYK, Leo, "Der Weg der deutschen katholischen
Theologie im 19. Jahrhundert," Theol. Qu.-Schr., 145,
1965, 273-306.

155. SCHITTERER, Richard, "Professor Andreas Benedikt Feil-
moser (1777-1831) in Tübingen," Theol. Qu.-Schr., 148,
1968, 199-222.

156. SCHMIDLIN, Josef, "Quellen und Literatur über Pius IX und
Leo XIII," Röm. Qu.-Schr., 41, 1933, 101-23.

157. SCHNABEL, Franz, "Die Katholische Kirche und die Grundzüge des 19. Jahrhunderts," Hochland, 33(1), 1935/36,
193-204.

158. SCHNEIDER, B., S.J., "Der Syllabus Pius IX. und die
deutschen Jesuiten," Arch. hist. pont., 6, 1968, 371-92.

159. SCHNEIDER, P. Ambrosius, "Die Cistercienserabtei Him-
merod zwischen Aufhebung und Neugründung (1802-1919),"
Arch. f. mrh. KiG., 10, 1958, 241-96.

160. SCHNITZER, Dr. Joseph, "Der katholische Modernismus,"
Zs. f. Pol., 5, 1911-12, 1-218.

161. SCHNÜTGEN, A., "Ein Deutschland eng verbundener römi-
scher Kurialbeamter zur kirchlichen Lage insbesondere im
deutschen Süden zwischen Wiener Kongress und bayer-
ischem Konkordat," H. Jb., 36, 1915, 820-44.

162. SCHÖNINGH, Franz Josef, "Der deutsche Katholizismus im
Zeitalter der Kapitalismus," Hochland, 29(2), 1931/32,
551-58.

163. SCHOLZ, Alfons, "Materialien zur Biographie Franz Anton
Staudemaiers (1800-1856)," Theol. Qu.-Schr., 147, 1967,
210-39.

164. SCHRÖRS, Heinrich, "Der Bonner Professor Heinrich Klee
und die Hermesianer Eine Episode aus den theologischen
Kämpfen des vorigen Jahrhunderts," Ann. Niederrhein, 81,
1906, 140-44.

165. _____, "Hermesianische Pfarrer," Ann. Niederrhein, 103,
1919, 76-183.

166.   _____, "Neue Quellen zur kölnischen Kirchengeschichte in
        der ersten Hälfte des 19. Jahrhunderts (1835-1850), " Ann.
        Niederrhein, 104, 1920, 1-85.
167.   _____, "Die Kölner Erzbischofswahl nach Geissels Tode
        (1864-1865), " Ann. Niederrhein, 108, 1926, 103-40.
168.   _____, "Zur Ehrenrettung eines hermesianischen Pfarrers, "
        Ann. Niederrhein, 110, 1927, 202-09.
169.   SCHUTH, Johannes, "Aus der Frühzeit der katholischen
        Presse der Rheinlande, " Arch. f. mrh. KiG., 9, 1957,
        148-65.
170.   "Der STAAT und die Hierarchie, " Pr. Jbb., 1, 1858, 382-93.
171.   STAMER, Ludwig, "Der Streit zwischen Staat und Kirche um
        den Ausbau des Speyerer Priesterseminars vor hundert
        Jahren, " Arch. f. mrh. KiG., 16, 1964, 249-80.
172.   "Die STIMMUNGEN und Bestrebungen der Katholiken in Rhein-
        preussen, " Pr. Jbb., 9, 1862, 249-71.
173.   THOMAS, Alois, "Archivalische und historische Arbeiten in
        Bistum Trier unter Bischof Josef von Hommer (1824-
        1836), " Arch. f. mrh. KiG., 1, 1949, 183-208.
174.   _____, "Das Priesterseminar in Trier in der ersten Hälfte
        des 19. Jahrhunderts, " Arch. f. mrh. KiG., 24, 1972,
        195-222.
175.   _____, "Professor Franz Xaver Scholl (1801-1860), " Arch.
        f. mrh. KiG., 19, 1967, 95-155.
176.   THUN, Alphons, "Die Sozialpolitik des deutschen Katholizis-
        mus, " Schmoll. Jb., 6, 1882, 821-57.
177.   TRZOCIAKOWSKI, Lech, "The Prussian State and the Catholic
        Church in Prussian Poland 1871-1914, " Slavic Review, 26,
        1967, 618-37.
178.   VAHLE, Hans, "Der Streit um die münsterische Domelemosyne
        1810-1834, " Westf. Zs., 80, 1922, 36-54.
179.   VIGENER, Fritz, "Die Mainzer Bischofswahl von 1849/50, "
        ZRG, 11, 1921, 351-427.
180.   WALTER, Paula, "Isabella Braun Eine katholische Jugend-
        shriftstellerin, " Gelbe Hefte, 4, 1927-28, 814-21.
181.   WELTE, Bernhard, "Beobachtungen zum Systemgedanken in
        der Tübinger Katholischen Schule, " Theol. Qu.-Schr., 147,
        1967, 40-59.
182.   WIESEOTTE, Hermann Josef, "F. J. Sausen und die Gründung
        des 'Mainzer Journal'," Arch. f. mrh. KiG., 5, 1953, 267-
        98.
183.   ZELLER, Josef, "Die Errichtung der katholisch-theologischen
        Fakultät in Tübingen im Jahre 1817, " Theol. Qu.-Schr.,
        108, 1927, 77-158.
184.   _____, "Das Generalvikariat Ellwangen (1812-1817) und sein
        erster Rat Dr. Joseph von Mets, " Theol. Qu.-Schr., 109,
        1928, 3-160.
185.   "ZUR Geschichte der Folgen des Vaticanischen Concils, "
        HZ, 30, 1873, 324-46.

Hermann A. Daniel (1812-1871)

186. CONZEMIUS, Victor, "Hermann Adalbert Daniel (1812-1871), "
      Zs. f. KiG., 76, 1965, 64-111.
187. _____, "Hermann Adalbert Daniel ein vergessener Hallen-
      ser Ireniker und Vertreter des anderen Preussens,"
      ZRGG, 16, 1964, 332-53.
188. WEYMAR, Ernst, "Hermann Adalbert Daniel Ein patriotischer
      Schwärmer," ZRGG, 17, 1965, 235-50.

Melchior von Diepenbrock (1798-1853)

189. DOEBERL, Anton, "Fürstbischof Melchior von Diepenbrock
      (1798-1853) Ein jünger Sailers," Gelbe Hefte, 4, 1927-28,
      346-47.
190. FINKE, Heinrich, "Erinnerung an Kardinal Melchior von
      Diepenbrock (1798-1898) Nach ungedruckten Briefen u.s.w.,"
      Westf. Zs., 55, 1897, 218-58.

Ignaz Döllinger (1799-1890)

191. ACTON, Lord, "Doellinger's Historical Work," EHR, 5,
      1890, 700-44.
192. CONZEMIUS, Victor, "Die 'Römischen Briefe vom Konzil'
      Eine entstehungsgeschichtliche und quellenkritische Unter-
      suchung zum Konzilsjournalismus Ignaz v. Döllingers und
      Lord Actons," Röm. Qu.-Schr., 59, 1964, 186-229; 60,
      1965, 76-119.
193. DENZLER, Georg, "Neuentdeckte Briefe des Ignaz von Döl-
      linger an Chlodwig von Hohenlohe," Röm. Qu.-Schr., 67,
      1972, 212-31.
194. DÖBERL, Anton, "Döllinger und Newman," Gelbe Hefte, 1,
      1924/25, 58-66.
195. DRU, Alexander, "Lord Acton, Döllinger und der Münchner
      Kongress," Hochland, 56, 1963/64, 49-58.
196. REINHARDT, Rudolf, "Johannes Joseph Ignaz von Döllinger
      und Carl von Hefele," Zs. f. bayer. LG., 33, 1970, 439-
      46.
197. SCHWAIGER, Georg, "Ignaz von Döllinger," Hochland, 56,
      1963/64, 294-309.
198. WENDT, Heinrich, "Ignaz von Döllingers innere Entwicklung,"
      Zs. f. KiG., 24, 1903, 281-309.

Johann Sebastian von Drey (1777-1853)

199. GEISELMANN, J., "Die Glaubenswissenschaft der katholischen
      Tübinger in ihrer Grundlegung durch Johann Sebastian v.
      Drey," Theol. Qu.-Schr., 111, 1930, 49-117.

200.   MILLER, Max, "Professor Dr. Johann Sebastian Drey als
        württembergischer Bischofskandidat (1822-1827), " Theol.
        Qu.-Schr., 114, 1933, 363-405.
201.   _____, "Die Tübinger kath.-theologische Fakultät und die
        württembergische Regierung von Weggang J. A. Möhlers
        (1835) bis zur Pensionierung J. S. Dreys (1846) Ein Bei-
        trag zur württembergischen Staatskirchenpolitik im Vor-
        märz, " Theol. Qu.-Schr., 132, 1952, 22-45; 213-34.

                    Karl Josef von Hefele (1809-1893)

202.   FUNK, Ph., "Ein literarisches Porträt von Kuhn, Hefele und
        Aberle in zeitgenössischen Briefen, " Theol. Qu.-Schr.,
        108, 1927, 209-20.
203.   LÖSCH, Stephan, ed., "Briefe des jungen Karl Joseph Hefele
        (1834-1846), " Theol. Qu.-Schr., 119, 1938, 3-59.
204.   REINHARDT, Rudolf, "Der Nachlass des Kirchenhistorikers
        und Bischofs Karl Joseph v. Hefele (1809-1893), " Zs. f.
        KiG., 82, 1971, 361-72.
205.   STOCKMEIER, Peter, "Die Causa Honorii und Karl Josef von
        Hefele, " Theol. Qu.-Schr., 148, 1968, 405-28.

              Wilhelm Emanuel Freiherr von Ketteler (1811-1877)

206.   BUCHHEIM, Karl, "Kettelers Gegenkandidat Ein Beitrag zur
        deutschen Parteigeschichte um 1848, " H. Jb., 74, 1954,
        473-84.
207.   HERTLING, Georg von, "Bischof Ketteler und die katholische
        Sozialpolitik in Deutschland, " Historisch-politische Blätter,
        120, 1897, 873-900.
208.   KETTELER, Bischof v., "Über die Lage der Kirche in der
        Gegenwart, " Der Katholik, 41(1), 1867, 239-56.
209.   REINARZ, Heinrich, "Wilhelm Emmanuel von Ketteler Ein
        katholischer Sozialpolitiker auf dem Bischofsstuhle, " Gelbe
        Hefte, 1, 1924/25, 752-78.
210.   RIED, Dr. U., "Studien zu Kettelers Stellung zum Infalli-
        bilitätsdogma bis zur Definition am 18. Juli 1870, " H. Jb.,
        47, 1927, 657-726.
211.   RITTHALER, A., "Ketteler Ein deutscher Bischof, " Gelbe
        Hefte, 13, 1936-37, 501-18.
212.   SCHÖNINGH, Franz Josef, "Ketteler, " Hochland, 31(1), 1933/
        34, 1-18.
213.   SPAHN, Martin, "Bischof Ketteler, " Hochland, 22(2), 1924-
        25, 129-51.
214.   VIGENER, Fritz, "Ketteler vor dem Jahre 1848, " HZ, 121,
        1921, 398-479.
215.   "W. E. Frhr. von Ketteler, Bischof von Mainz, " Der Katho-
        lik, 57 (2), 1877, 113-34, 224-41.

The Kölner Wirren

Ferdinand August von Spiegel (1764-1906)
Johannes von Geissel (1796-1864)

216. BASTGEN, Hubert, "Ein Briefwechsel zwischen Bischof
Reisach und Kardinal Lambruschini (Über das 'Kölner
Ereignis' Hermesianismus, Hüsgen, Münchener Nunziatur),"
Röm. Qu.-Schr., 34, 1926, 199-241.
217. _____, "Erzbischof Graf Spiegel von Köln und der Heilige
Stuhl," Röm. Qu.-Schr., 39, 1931, 507-605.
218. _____, "Vatikanische Akten aus den Jahren 1835/36 zum
Beginn des Konflikts zwischen des Katholischen Kirche und
Preussen," Röm. Qu.-Schr., 33, 1925, 111-49.
219. BIBL, Viktor, "Der Kölner Kirchenstreit und Metternich,"
FBPG, 42, 1929, 78-92.
220. GOTZEN, Jos., "Welche Schriften hat Ellendorf bei Gelegen-
heit der Kölner Wirren verfasst?" Ann. Niederrhein, 108,
1926, 141-46.
221. GRISAR, Joseph, "Das Kölner Ereignis nach Berichten
italienischer Diplomaten," H. Jb., 74, 1954, 727-39.
222. "JOHANNES von Geissel, Cardinal und Erzbischof von Köln,"
HZ, 31, 1874, 136-48.
223. JOLLY, Dr. Ludwig, "Der Kirchenstreit in Preussen," Pr.
Jbb., 50, 1882, 107-64.
224. KEINEMANN, F., "Preussische Erkundigungen über den
Speyrer Bischof Johannes von Geissel im Hinblick auf
eine Berufung zum Koadjutor der Erzdiözese Köln (1841),"
Arch. f. mrh. KiG., 22, 1970, 241-46.
225. LIPGENS, Walter, "Beiträge zur Lehrtätigkeit von Georg
Hermes Seine Briefe an den späteren Kölner Erzbischof
Ferdinand August Graf Spiegel 1812-24," H. Jb., 81,
1961, 174-222.
226 _____, "Zum Driefwechsel des Grafen Ferdinand August
Spiegel mit Ignaz Heinrich von Wessenberg (1815-18),"
ZGORh, 109, 1961, 88-132.
227. NIPPOLD, Dr., "Die verschiedenen Stadien des sogenannten
preussischen Kirchenstreites nach Bunsen's Papieren,"
Pr. Jbb., 23, 1869, 325-55, 423-48; 24, 1869, 381-422.
228. SCHNÜTGEN, Alexander, "Beitrage zur Ära des Kölner
Erzbischofs Graf Spiegel," Ann. Niederrhein, 110, 1927,
1-59; 119, 1931, 121-63; 125, 1934, 38-107.
229. _____, "Geissel und die Anfänge einer periodischen kirchlichen Publizistik in Kölner Erzbistum," Ann. Niederrhein,
112, 1928, 156-68.
230. SCHRÖRS, Heinrich, "Rheinische Katholiken und belgische
Parteien zur Zeit der Kölner Wirren (1837)," Ann. Niederrhein, 107, 1923, 1-91; 108, 1926, 1-66.
231. STRUCK, W., "Kardinal v. Geissel und die katholische Bewegung 1848/49," Pr. Jbb., 111, 1903, 98-125.
232. WILBRAND, Wilhelm, "Briefe des Kölner Erzbischofs Graf

Spiegel an den Giessener Professor J. B. Wilbrand," <u>Ann.</u>
<u>Niederrhein,</u> 125, 1934, 119-26.

Adolf Kolping (1813-1865)

233. CONZEMIUS, Viktor, "Adolf Kolping and Ignaz von Döllinger,"
      <u>Ann. Niederrhein,</u> 164, 1962.
234. WOTHE, Fr. Jos., "Ein deutscher Priester und Erzieher,"
      <u>Gelbe Hefte,</u> 15, 1938/39, 568-82.

Franz Xaver Kraus (1840-1901)

235. BAUER, Clemens, "Die Selbstbildnisse des Franz Xaver
      Kraus," <u>Hochland,</u> 52, 1959/60, 101-21.
236. BRAUBACH, Max, "Die Tagebücher von Franz Xaver Kraus,"
      <u>Rhein. Vjsbll.,</u> 22, 1957, 266-85.
237. FINK, Karl August, "Zu den Tagebüchern von Franz Xaver
      Kraus," <u>Theol. Qu.-Schr.,</u> 138, 1958, 471-80.
238. SCHIEL, Hubert, "Franz Xaver Kraus, sein Lebenswert und
      sein Charakter im Spiegel der Briefe an Anton Stöck,"
      <u>Arch. f. mrh. KiG.,</u> 3, 1951, 218-39.
239. _____, "Ludwig von Pastors Briefwechsel mit Franz
      Xaver Kraus," <u>Rhein. Vjsbll.,</u> 19, 1954, 191-241.
240. _____, "Tübinger Theologen in Verbindung mit Franz
      Xaver Kraus," <u>Theol. Qu.-Schr.,</u> 137, 1957, 18-57, 168-
      86, 289-323.
241. WEBER, Christoph, "Eine kirchenpolitische Denkschrift von
      F. X. Kraus (1874) und der Streit um die Rechtsnatur der
      Konkordate," <u>Röm. Qu.-Schr.,</u> 67, 1972, 83-116.

Kulturkampf

242. ARLINGHAUS, Francis A., "The Kulturkampf and European
      Diplomacy 1871-1875," <u>Cath. Hist. Rev.,</u> 28, 1942, 340-
      75.
243. BRANDMÜLLER, W., "Die Publikation des 1. Vatikanischen
      Konzils in Bayern. Aus den Anfängen des bayrischen
      Kulturkampfes," <u>Zs. f. bayer. LG,</u> 31, 1968, 197-258,
      575-634.
244. BRIEGER, Dr. Theodor, "Der erste Waffengang des römischen
      Kirchentums mit dem preussischen Staate," <u>Pr. Jbb.,</u> 29,
      1872, 669-90.
245. FOERSTER, Erich, "Liberalismus und Kulturkampf," <u>Zs. f.</u>
      <u>KiG.,</u> 47, 1929, 543-59.
246. GALL, Lothar, "Die partei- und sozialgeschichtliche Prob-
      lematik des badischen Kulturkampfes," <u>ZGORh,</u> 113, 1965,
      151-96.
247. HECKEL, Johannes, "Die Beilegung des Kulturkampfes in
      Preussen," <u>ZRG,</u> 19, 1930, 215-53.

248.   LOUGEE, R. W., "Kulturkampf and historical positivism,"
       Church Hist., 23, 1954, 219-35.
249.   MORSEY, Rudolf, "Probleme der Kulturkampf-Forschung,"
       H. Jb., 83, 1963, 217-45.
250.   TRAUTH, Sister Mary Philip, "The Bancroft Dispatches on
       the Vatican Council and the Kulturkampf," Cath. Hist.
       Rev., 40, 1954, 178-90.
251.   W., "Die Ultramontanen im Reichstag und die römische
       Kirche," Pr. Jbb., 27, 1871, 492-505.

                   Johann Adam Möhler (1796-1838)

252.   FRANZEN, A., "Die Zölibatsfrage im 19. Jahrhundert. Der
       'Badische Zölibatssturm' (1828) und das Problem der
       Priesterehe im Urteile Johann Adam Möhler und Johann
       Baptist Hirschers," H. Jb., 91, 1971, 345-83.
253.   FUNK, Philipp, "Die geistige Gestalt Johann Adam Möhlers,"
       Hochland, 27(1), 1929/30, 97-110.
254.   GEISELMANN, J., "Johann Adam Möhler und die Entwicklung
       seines Kirchenbegriffs," Theol. Qu.-Schr., 112, 1931, 1-
       91.
255.   _____, "Johann Adam Möhler und das idealistische Ver-
       ständnis des Sündenfalls," Theol. Qu.-Schr., 125, 1944,
       19-37.
256.   GÜNTHÖR, Anselm, "Johann Adam Möhler und das Mönch-
       tum," Theol. Qu.-Schr., 121, 1940, 168-83.
257.   HAUSSLER, Bernhard, "Johann Adam Möhler, Theologe der
       Kirche," Hochland, 35(2), 1937/38, 17-26.
258.   KANTZENBACH, Friedrich Wilhelm, "Vilmars 'Theologie der
       Tatsachen' und die 'Symbolik' Johann Adam Möhlers," Zs.
       f. KiG., 70, 1959, 253-77.
259.   KÖNIG, Herman, "Die Einheit der Kirche nach Joseph de
       Maistre und Johann Adam Möhler," Theol. Qu.-Schr., 115,
       1934, 38-140.
260.   LÖSCH, Stephan, "J. A. Möhler im Jahre 1834/35," Theol.
       Qu.-Schr., 106, 1925, 66-99.
261.   _____, "J. A. Möhler und die Lehre von der Entwicklung
       des Dogmas," Theol. Qu.-Schr., 99, 1917/18, 129-52.
262.   MATHÄSER, Willibald, ed., "Fünf Briefe der Freundschaft
       von Johann Adam Möhler," H. Jb., 91, 171, 394-400.
263.   REINHARDT, Rudolf, "Der Briefwechsel zwischen Johann
       Heinrich Schlosser und Johann Adam Möhler im Jahre
       1837," Gesch. Landesk., 5, 1969.
264.   _____, ed., "Johann Adam Möhler über Heinrich Klee
       (1828)," Arch. f. mrh. KiG., 21, 1969, 255-58.
265.   SÄGMÜLLER, Johannes B., "Die Kirchenrechtliche Anstoss
       zu Johann Adam Möhlers theologischer Entwicklung," Theol.
       Qu.-Schr., 122, 1941, 1-13.
266.   SCHMID, Alois von, "Die geistige Entwicklungsgang Johann
       Adam Möhlers," H. Jb., 18, 1897, 322-56, 572-99.
267.   VIERNEISEL, Emil J., "Aus Möhlers handschriftlichem Nach-

lass," Theol. Qu.-Schr., 119, 1938, 109-17.

Christoph Moufang (1817-1890)

268. LENHART, Ludwig, "Moufangs Ablehnung als Kapitelsvikar
      durch den hessischen Staat und die dadurch verursachte
      Mainzer Sedisvakanz von 1871-1886," Arch. f. mrh. KiG.,
      19, 1967, 157-91.
269. MAY, Georg, "Christoph Moufang (1817-1890)," Arch. f.
      mrh. KiG., 22, 1970, 227-36.

Johann Michal von Sailer (1751-1832)

270. DOEBERL, Anton, "Johann Michael Sailer (1751-1832) Ein
      altbayrischer Kirchenfürst in der Zeit der Aufklärung und
      der Romantik," Gelbe Hefte, 4, 1927-28, 100-21.
271. HAMMERMAYER, Ludwig, "Katholikenemanizipation in Gross-
      britannien ... Seminar der Schotten in Regensburg (1826/
      29) Zur Kloster- und Kirchenpolitik unter Ludwig I von Ba-
      yern und Bischof Johann Michael Sailer," Zs. f. bayer LG.,
      28, 1965, 392-459.
272. HUBER, Georg Brand, C.S.S.R., "J. M. Sailers Rechtferti-
      gung gegen die Anklagen des hl. Klemens Maria Hofbauer,"
      H. Jb., 52, 1932, 72-78.
273. SCHIEL, Hubert, "Der unbekannte Sailer," Hochland, 26(2),
      1928/29, 415-32.

Ignaz Heinrich von Wessenberg (1774-1860)

274. BAIER, Hermann, "Wessenbergs Romreise 1817," ZGORh.,
      79, 1927, 207-35.
275. ENGELMANN, Ursmar, "Ignaz Heinrich von Wessenberg und
      die Kirche," H. Jb., 91, 1971, 46-69.
276. MILLER, Max, "I. H. Frhr. v. Wessenberg als württem-
      bergischer Bischofskandidat i. j. 1822," Württemb. Vtljhefte
      f. Landesgesch., 38, 1932, 369-400.

The Protestant Church

277. A., "Das Evangelium und die Armen," Zs. f. Armenwessen,
      2, 1865, 2-15.
278. ALTHAUSEN, Johannes, "Aus dem Anfängen der Berliner
      Missionsgesellschaft," Jb. f. Ber.-Brandenburg. KiG., 43,
      1968, 112-50.
279. ALTMÜLLER, F., "Ueber das Diakonenamt in der evange-
      lischen Kirche," Zs. f. Armenwessen, 1, 1864, 33-41.
280. ANDERSON, H. George, "Challenge and Change within German
      Protestant Theological Education during the Nineteenth Cen-

tury," Church Hist., 39, 1970, 36-48.

281. BENN, Ernst Viktor, "Entwicklungsstufen des evangelischen
      Kirchenrechts im 19. Jahrhundert," Zs. f. evan. KiR.,
      15, 1970, 1-19.

282. BEYER, Hans, "Der Breslauer Jurist. Ph. E. Huschke
      (1801-1886) und die Grundprobleme einer lutherischen
      Kirchenverfassung," H. Jb., 77, 1957, 270-97.

283. BLANKE, Fritz, "Evangelische Missionskritik im 19. Jahr-
      hundert Die Auseinandersetzung zwischen Ernst Friedrich
      Langhans und Hermann Gundert (1864-65)," Zs. f. KiG.,
      72, 1961, 87-105.

284. BRAMSTED, E., "The Position of the Protestant Church in
      Germany 1871-1933," J. Rel. Hist., Pt 1: 2, 1963, 314-
      34; Pt 2: 3, 1964, 61-79.

285. CHADWICK, Henry, "Der Einfluss der deutschen protestant-
      ischen Theologie auf die englische Kirche im 19. Jahr-
      hundert," Ev. Theol., 16, 1956, 556-71.

286. DAHM, Karl-Wilhelm, "Der Staat und die Pastoren," Zs. f.
      Pol., 13, 1966, 429-50.

287. DIEHL, Wilhelm, "Zur Geschichte der Staatsgehalte der rhein-
      hessischen evangelischen Pfarreien," Arch. f. hessische
      Gesch., 12, 1917/19, 147-412.

288. DORNER, "Katholisirende Neigungen in der Protestantischen
      Ethik," Pr. Jbb., 95, 1899, 208-30.

289. DRUMMOND, A. L., "Church and State in Protestant Ger-
      many before 1918 with special reference to Prussia,"
      Church Hist., 13, 1944, 210-29.

290. FISCHER, Fritz, "Der deutsche Protestantismus und die
      Politik im 19. Jahrhundert," HZ, 171, 1951, 473-518.

291. _____, "Zur Geschichte des deutschen Luthertums im 19.
      Jahrhundert," Zs. f. evan KiR., 6, 1957/58, 240-49.

292. FOERSTER, Pfarrer, "Die Kirchengemeinde- und Synodal
      Ordnung für die evangelischen Kirchengemeinschaften des
      Consistorialbezirks Frankfurt a. Main," Dt. Zs. f. KiR.,
      9, 1899-1900, 253-302.

293. FROHNES, Heinzgünter, "Der Nachlass von Martin Kähler
      (1835-1912), Zs. f. KiG., 80, 1909, 79-99.

294. GAUL, Willy, "Zur Geschichte des evangelischen Katechis-
      mus im Grossherzogtum Hessen während des 19. Jahr-
      hunderts," Arch. f. hessische Gesch., 12, 1917/19, 86-
      146.

295. GEIGER, Max, "Das Problem der Erweckungstheologie,"
      Theol. Zs., 14, 1958, 430-50.

296. _____, "Roxandra Scarlatovna von Stourdza (1786-1844)
      Zur Erweckungsbewegung der Befreiungskriege," Theol.
      Zs., 12, 1956, 393-408.

297. GOLLWITZER, Heinz, "Graf Carl Giech 1795-1863 Eine
      Studie zur politischen Geschichte des Fränkischen Protes-
      tantismus in Bayern," Zs. f. bayer. LG, 24, 1961, 102-
      62.

298. GOLTZ, Eduard Freiherr von der, ed., "Aus der Werdezeit
      von Hermann v. d. Goltz," Zs. f. KiG., 44, 1925, 282-

90, 429-59.
299. GROSSMANN, Friedrich, "Die evangelisch-sociale Bewegung
      in Deutschland," Schmoll. Jb., 16, 1892, 103-26.
300. GRÜN, Hugo, "Die Nassauische Union von 1817. Der Weg
      der getrennten lutherischen und reformierten Konfessionen
      zu einer einheitlichen Landeskirche," Nass. Ann., 79,
      1968, 157-75.
301. HANDRICH, Hans, "Die Pfälzer Union Ein Beitrag zum Kon-
      fessionellen Problem," Ev. Theol., 6, 1946/47, 258-72.
302. HEINTZE, Johannes, "Die erste preussische Generalsynode
      1846," Jb. f. Ber.-Brandenburg. KiG., 41, 1966, 122-41.
303. HERZOG, John., "Das Testament der Christlich-Sozialen
      Englands an unsere deutsche evangelische Kirche," Zs. f.
      Theol. u. K., 11, 1901, 341-406.
304. HEYBEY, Wolfgang, "Die Stellung des Protestantismus in
      den politischen und sozialen Entscheidungen des 19. Jahr-
      hunderts als Unterrichtsthema," GiWuU, 4, 1954, 471-75.
305. HEYDEN, Hellmuth, "Aktenstücke zur Geschichte der Kämpfe
      um Union und Agende in Pommern," Zs. f. KiG., 70, 1959,
      231-52.
306. _____, "Zur Geschichte der Kämpfe um Union und Agende
      in Pommern," Zs. f. KiG., 71, 1960, 287-323.
307. HEYER, Friedrich, "Daniel Amadeus Neander," Jb. f. Ber.-
      Brandenburg. KiG., 45, 1970, 122-49.
308. HINTZE, Otto, "Die Epochen des evangelischen Kirchenregi-
      ments in Preussen," HZ, 97, 1906, 67-118.
309. HOKENSON, Rodney, "The awakening of political responsibility
      among German Protestants," Luth. Q., 8, 1956, 296-318.
310. HOLBORN, Hajo, "Protestantismus und politische Ideen-
      geschichte," HZ, 144, 1931, 15-30.
311. HOLL, Karl, "Thomas Chalmers und die Anfänge der kirch-
      lich-sozialen Bewegung," Zs. f. Theol. u. K., 23, 1913,
      219-65.
312. HUCK, Friedrich, "Gottlob Christian Baltzer, ein Pfarrerle-
      ben des 19. Jahrhunderts," Jb. f. Ber.-Brandenburg. KiG.,
      42, 1967, 133-58.
313. KAHLE, Wilhelm, "Die Orthodoxe Kirche des Ostens im
      Spiegel der deutschen evangelischen Kirchenzeitungen wäh-
      rend der zweiten Hälfte des 19. Jahrhunderts," ZRGG, 12,
      1960, 219-41.
314. KAISER, Gerhard, "L'Eveil du Sentiment National Rôle du
      piétisme dans la naissance du patriotisme," Arch. d. Soc.
      d. Rel., 22, 1966, 59-80.
315. KANTZENBACH, Prof. Dr. Friedrich Wilhelm, "Das Bekennt-
      nisproblem in der lutherischen Theologie des 19. Jahr-
      hunderts," Neue Zs. f. system. Theol. u. RP, 4, 1962,
      243-317.
316. _____, "Die Geschichte der evangelischen Theologie im
      Rahmen der Kirchengeschichtsschreibung des 19. und 20.
      Jahrhunderts," Bl. pfalz Kirchengesch. rel. Volksk., 35,
      1968.
317. _____, "Dr. Karl Krafft, Freund von Anselm Feuerbach,

als Gelehrter und protestantischer Pfarrer in Regensburg, "
Verh. Hist. Ver. Oberpfalz Regensburg, 110, 1970.

318. _____, "Ludwig Jonas, Schüler und Freund Schleiermachers Ein Kämpfer für die Selbständigkeit der Kirche, "
Jb. f. Ber.-Brandenburg. KiG., 44, 1969, 167-91.

319. _____, "Theologie und kirchliche Praxis im evangelischen
Bayern des 19. Jahrhunderts angesichts der Krisis der
Staatskirche," Zs. f. bayer. KiG., 1969.

320. _____, "Wilhelm Tretzels Kampf für die lebendige Gemeinde im Rahmen der fränkischen Erweckungsbewegung, "
Zs. f. bayer. KiG., 1969.

321. KRAMM, H. H., "Organization and Constitution of the German Protestant Churches (prior to 1933), " Church Q. Rev.,
275, 1944, 87-98.

322. KRIMM, Herbert, "Unvollendetes Erbe Der Väter der Diakonie
in Deutschland, " Zeitwende, 22, 1950-51, 391-98.

323. LANKHEIT, Klaus, "Casper David Friedrich und der Neu-
protestantismus, " Vjschr. f. Litw., 24, 1950, 129-43.

324. LAUBERT, Manfred, "Die Anfänge der altlutherischen Bewegung in der Provinz Posen, " Zs. f. KiG., 39, 1921,
44-76.

325. LAUERER, Hans, "Hundert Jahre Weibliche Diakonie, " Zeitwende, 13, 1936/37, 93-102.

326. LERCHE, Otto, "Die lutherische Auswanderung und die Union
(Beispiel Australien), " Zs. f. KiG., 62, 1943/44, 272-94.

327. MÜLLER, Gerhard, "Die Union auf dem Wege zur Ökumene
Zum 150 jährigen Bestehen der Hanauer Union, " Jb. hess.
KiG. Vereinigung, 20, 1969.

328. MÜSEBECK, Ernst, "Die evangelische Kirche und das Volksleben der Gegenwart, " Zs. f. Theol. u. K., 16, 1906,
386-428.

329. NATALE, Herbert, "Beda Webers Briefe nach Sigmaringen
1843-1848 Ergänzungen zur Biographie des späteren Frankfurter Stadtpfarrers, " Arch. f. mrh. KiG., 24, 1972, 277-
304.

330. NAUMANN, Johannes, "Friedrich Ahlfeld Ein Beitrag zum
Verständis der konfesionell-lutherischen Strömung des
vorigen Jahrhunderts, " Zs. f. Theol. u. K., 21, 1911,
61-83.

331. NEBELSIECK, D. Heinrich, "Die kirchliche Union in den
ehemaligen Fürstentümern Waldeck und Pyrmont, " Zs. f.
KiG., 62, 1943/44, 232-71.

332. ORTLOFF, Hermann, "Die Dienstvergehen der evangelischen
Geistlichen und deren Bestrafung im Grossherzogtum Sach-
sen-Weimar-Eisenach, " Dt. Zs. f. KiR., 7, 1897, 1-60.

333. PFLEIDERER, Otto, "Alois Emanuel Biedermann, " Pr. Jbb.,
57, 1886, 53-76.

334. RITSCHL, Otto, "Studien zur Geschichte der protestantischen
Theologie im 19. Jahrhundert, " Zs. f. Theol. u. K., 5,
1895, 486-529.

335. RÖSSLER, Dietrich, "Zwischen Rationalismus und Erweckung
Zur Predigtlehre bei Claus Harms, " Zs. f. KiG., 73,

1962, 62-73.

336. ROGGE, D., "D. Emil Hermann Weil. Präsident des ev. Oberkirchenrathes zu Berlin, gest. den 16. April 1885 zu Gotha," Pr. Jbb., 56, 1885, 107-25.

337. ROHLES, Joachim, "Staat, Nation und Evangelische Kirche im Zeitalter der deutschen Einigung (1848-1871)," GiWuU, 9, 1958, 593-616.

338. SCHÄFER, Rudolf, "Die Geltung des kanonischen Rechts in der evangelischen Kirche Deutschlands von Luther bis zur Gegenwart," ZRG, 5, 1915, 165-413.

339. SCHMID, Eugen, "Karl Grüneisen (1802-1878)," Zs. f. Württbg. LG., 4, 1940, 376-466.

340. SCHMIDT, Ferdinand J., "Die evangelische Kirche und ihre nationale Mission," Pr. Jbb., 153, 1913, 488-514.

341. _____, "Kapitalismus und Protestantismus," Pr. Jbb., 122, 1905, 189-230.

342. _____, "Der mittelalterliche Charakter des kirchlichen Protestantismus," Pr. Jbb., 27, 1907, 193-221.

343. SCHMIDT, Walter, "Die Union in der evangelischen Kirche im Rheinland," Bl. pfälz. Kirchengesch. rel. Volksk., 35, 1968.

344. SCHREINER, Helmuth, "Die Diakonie als Gestalt der Kirche," Zeitwende, 14, 1937-38, 458-67.

345. SCHÜSSLER, Wilhelm, "Die politischen und sozialen Entscheidungen des Protestantismus im 19. Jahrhundert," GiWuU, 4, 1953, 461-71.

346. SCHÜTTLÖFFEL, Friedrich, "Der erste preussische Superintendent von Zeitz, Geheimrat Dr. Delbrück," Beitr. KiG. Dtschl., 5, 1965, 126-35.

347. SEELING, Werner, "Die pfälzische Union von 1818," B. pfälz Kirchengesch. rel. Volksk., 35, 1968.

348. SIMON, Matthias, "Diakonus Hagen in Selb 1809," Zs. f. bayer. LG, 18, 1955, 469-89.

349. STUPPERICH, Robert, "Aus Hermann Cremers Briefwechsel mit Martin Kähler (1860-1865)," Jb. Ver. Westfäl. Kirchengesch., 63, 1970.

350. _____, "Die preussische Union in der Krise des Jahres 1867," Bl. pfälz Kirchengesch. rel. Volksk., 35, 1968.

351. STUTZ, Ulrich, "Des Amt des evangelischen Universitätspredigers an der rheinischen Friedrich-Wilhelms-Universität in Bonn während des ersten Jahrhunderts ihres Bestehens," ZRG, 10, 1920, 1-50.

352. TEICHMANN, Pfarrer, "Die Stellung des evangelischen Theologen zur heutigen psychiatrischen Wissenschaft," Zs. f. Theol. u. K., 4, 1894, 463-88.

353. THEMEL, Karl, "Die Mitglieder und die Leitung des Berlinger Konsistoriums von 1816-1900," Jb. f. Ber.-Brandenburg. KiG., 43, 1968, 55-111.

354. TÖNNIES, Ilse, "Die Arbeitswelt von Pietismus, Erweckungsbewegung und Brüdergemeine Ideen und Institutionen," Jb. f. Gesch. M. O. Dtschl., 20, 1971, 89-133.

355. VORLÄNDER, Karl, "Sozialdemokratische Pfarrer," Arch. f.

Sozialw. u. Sozialpol., 30, 1910, 455-513.

356. VOSSBERG, Herbert, "Adolf Menzel und die evangelische Kirche," Jb. f. Ber.-Brandenburg. KiG., 39, 1964, 140-66.

357. WENDT, Hans Hinrich, "Das Verhältniss der inneren Mission zur kirchlichen Organisation," Zs. f. Theol. u. K., 2, 1892, 146-70.

358. WIEFEL, Wolfgang, "Zur Würdigung William Wredes," ZRGG, 23, 1971, 60-83.

359. WOLF, Hanns-Martin, "Die Darmstädter Erweckung," Jb. hess. KiG. Vereinigung, 20, 1969.

Ferdinand Christian Baur (1792-1860)

360. BARNIKOL, Ernst, "Der Briefwechsel zwischen Strauss und Baur," Zs. f. KiG., 73, 1962, 74-125.

361. BAUER, K., "Die geistige Heimat F. Chr. Baurs," Zs. f. Theol. u. K., 31, 1923-24, 63-73.

362. "FERDINAND Christian Baur," Pr. Jbb., 7, 1861, 495-512; 8, 1861, 187-206, 283-314.

363. HEFNER, Philip, "Baur versus Ritschl on early Christianity," Church Hist., 31, 1962, 259-78.

364. HODGSON, Peter C., "The rediscovery of Ferdinand Christian Baur: A Review of the first two volumes of his Ausgewählte Werke," Church Hist., 33, 1964, 206-14.

365. LANG, Wilhelm, "Ferdinand Baur und David Friedrich Strauss," Pr. Jbb., 160, 1915, 474-504; 161, 1915, 123-44.

366. LIEBING, Heinz, "Historisch-kritische Theologie zum 100. Todestag Ferdinand Christian Baurs am 2. Dezember 1960," Zs. f. Theol. u. K., 57, 1960, 302-17.

367. SCHOLDER, Klaus, "Ferdinand Christian Baur als Historiker," Ev. Theol., 21, 1961, 435-58.

368. SCHUFFELS, Klaus, "Der Nachlass Ferdinand Christian Baurs," Zs. f. KiG., 79, 1968, 375-84.

Friedrich von Bodelschwingh (1831-1910)

369. FRANKFURTH, Hermann, "Friedrich von Bodelschwingh," Zeitwende, 7(1), 1931, 258-69, 356-64.

370. KÄHLER, Walter, "Das Vermächtnis Friedrich von Bodelschwinghs an uns," Zeitwende, 19, 1947-48, 541-50.

371. LEHMANN, Hartmut, "Bodelschwingh und Bismarck Christlich-konservative Sozialpolitik im Kaiserreich," HZ, 208, 1969, 607-26.

372. _____, "Friedrich von Bodelschwingh und das Sedanfest. Ein Beitrag zum nationalen Denken der politish aktiven Richtung im deutschem Pietismus des 19. Jahrhunderts," HZ, 202, 1966, 542-73.

373. MÜLLER, Georg, "Friedrich von Bodelschwingh und das

Sedanfest, " GiWuU, 14, 1963, 77-90.
374.   RORARIUS, Winfried, "Ein evangelischer Franziskus Leben
       und Werk Friedrich von Bodelschwinghs, " Zeitwende, 38,
       1967, 460-70.

Adolf v. Harnack (1851-1930)

375.   BLASER, Klauspeter, "Harnack in der Kritik Overbecks, "
       Theol. Zs., 21, 1965, 96-112.
376.   FOERSTER, Erich, "Harnacks 'Wesen des Christentums' eine
       Bestreitung oder eine Verteidigung des christlichen Glau-
       bens, " Zs. f. Theol. u. K., 12, 1902, 179-201.
377.   GLICK, G. W., "Nineteenth century theological and cultural
       influences on Adolf Harnack, " Church Hist., 28, 1959,
       157-82.
378.   HARNACK, Adolf, "Die ausdrücklichen Selbstzeugnisse Jesu
       über dem Zweck seiner Sendung und seines Kommens, "
       Zs. f. Theol. u. K., 22, 1912, 1-30.
379.   _____, "Der Evangelisch-sociale Congress zu Berlin, "
       Pr. Jbb., 65, 1890, 566-76.
380.   _____, "Die evangelisch-sociale Aufgabe im Lichte der
       Geschichte der Kirche (Vortrag auf dem evangelisch-
       socialen Kongress zu Frankfurt 1894), " Pr. Jbb., 76, 1894,
       502-42.
381.   _____, "Geschichte der Lehre von der Seligkeit allein
       durch den Glauben in der alten Kirche, " Zs. f. Theol. u.
       K., 1, 1891, 82-178.
382.   _____, "Leibnitz und Wilhelm v. Humboldt als Begründer
       der Königlich Preussischen Akademie der Wissenschaften, "
       Pr. Jbb., 140, 1910, 197-208.
383.   _____, "Protestantismus und Katholizismus in Deutsch-
       land, " Pr. Jbb., 127, 1907, 294-311.
384.   _____, "Rede auf August Neander, " Pr. Jbb., 63, 1889,
       179-96.
385.   _____, "Das Urchristentum und die sozialen Fragen, " Pr.
       Jbb., 131, 1908, 443-59.
386.   KANTZENBACH, Friedr. Wilh., "Adolf Harnack und Theodor
       Zahn Geschichte und Bedeutung einer gelehrten Freund-
       schaft, " Zs. f. KiG., 83, 1973, 226-44.
387.   LASSON, Adolf, "Harnack's Dogmengeschichte, " Pr. Jbb., 68,
       1891, 202-49.
388.   MARON, Gottfried, "Harnack und der römische Katholizismus, "
       Zs. f. KiG., 80, 1969, 176-93.
389.   RICHTER, Werner, "Adolf von Harnacks Stellung im Kulturel-
       len Leben seiner Zeit, " Zs. f. KiG., 55, 1936, 295-304.
390.   SASSE, Hermann, "Der Theologe des Zweiten Reiches Gedanken
       über die Lebensbeschreibung Adolf von Harnacks, " Zeit-
       wende, 12, 1935/36, 346-54.
391.   SCHMIDT, Ferdinand J., "Adolf Harnack und die Wiederbele-
       bung der spekulativen Forschung, " Pr. Jbb., 117, 1904,
       1-17.

392.   SCHNEEMELCHER, Wilhelm, "Das Problem der Dogmen-
        geschichte zum 100. Geburtstag Adolf von Harnacks," Zs.
        f. Theol. u. K., 48, 1951, 63-89.
393.   VÖLKER, Walther, "Adolf von Harnack als Kirchenhistoriker,"
        Theol. Zs., 7, 1951, 209-27.
394.   WOBBERMIN, Dr., "Loisy contra Harnack (Das Wesen des
        Christentums in evangelischer und katholischer Beleuch-
        tung," Zs. f. Theol. u. K., 15, 1905, 76-102.

Wilhelm Herrmann (1846-1922)

395.   BILLING, E., "Ethische Grundfragen des evangelischen
        Christentums Einige Betrachtungen beim Studium von Herr-
        manns Ethik," Zs. f. Theol. u. K., 13, 1903, 267ff.
396.   BORNHAUSEN, Karl, "Die Bedeutung von Wilhelm Herrmanns
        Theologie für die Gegenwart," Zs. f. Theol. u. K., 30,
        1922, 161-79.
397.   FISCHER-APPELT, Peter, "Albrecht Ritschl und Wilhelm
        Herrmann Eine Auswahl aus dem Briefwechsel (1875-
        1889)," Zs. f. KiG., 79, 1968, 208-24.
398.   HERRMANN, W., "Die Busse des evangelischen Christen,"
        Zs. f. Theol. u. K., 1, 1891, 28-81.
399.   _____, "Religion und Sozialdemokratie (Vortrag gehalten
        auf dem zweiten evangelisch-sozialen Kongress)," Zs. f.
        Theol. u. K., 1, 1891, 259-86.
400.   TROELTSCH, Ernst, "Grundprobleme der Ethik Erörtert aus
        Anlass von Herrmanns Ethik," Zs. f. Theol. u. K., 12,
        1902, 44-94, 125-78.

Wilhelm Löhe (1808-1872)

401.   LAUERER, Hans, "Wilhelm Löhe," Zeitwende, 5(2), 1929,
        360-65.
402.   OTTERSBERG, Gerhard, "Wilhelm Loehe," Luth. Q., 4,
        1952, 170-90.
403.   TRILLHAAS, Wolfgang, "Wilhelm Löhe--ein unbürgerlicher
        Christ," Zeitwende, 25, 1954, 378-84.

Karl Immanuel Nitzsch (1787-1868)

404.   NEMBACH, Ulrich, "Seelsorge nach Karl Immanuel Nitzsch,"
        Theol. Zs., 28, 1972, 331-46.
405.   WINTZER, Friedrich, "C.I. Nitzschs Konzeption der Prak-
        tischen Theologie in ihren geschichtlichen Zusammenhän-
        gen," Ev. Theol., 29, 1969, 93-109.

Franz Overbeck (1837-1905)

See also entry 375.

406. BAMMEL, Ernst, "Overbeck über seine Freunde, " Theol.
      Zs., 21, 1965, 113-15.
407. BUSKE, Thomas, "Overbecks theologisierte Christlichkeit
      ohne Glauben, " Theol. Zs., 23, 1967, 396-411.
408. SIELHAUER, Philipp, "Franz Overbeck und die neutestament-
      liche Wissenschaft, " Ev. Theol., 10, 1950-51, 193-207.
409. TETZ, Martin, "Adolf Jülichers Briefwechsel mit Franz
      Overbeck, " Zs. f. KiG., 76, 1965, 307-22.

Albrecht Ritschl (1822-1889)

See also entries 363, 397.

410. BOHLIN, Torsten, "Die Reich-Gottes-Idee im letzten halben
      Jahrhundert, " Zs. f. Theol. u. K., 37, 1929, 1-27.
411. DEEGAN, Dan L., "Albrecht Ritschl as critical empiricist, "
      J. Rel., 44, 1964, 149-60.
412. _____, "Albrecht Ritschl on the historical Jesus, " Scott.
      J. Theol., 15, 1962, 133-50.
413. _____, "Critical empiricism in the theology of Albrecht
      Ritschl, " Scott. J. Theol., 18, 1965, 40-56.
414. DE MOOR, Leonard, "The Ritschlian view of revelation, "
      Evan. Q., 42, 1970, 18-29, 93-106.
415. FABRICIUS, Cajus, "Albrecht Ritschl und die Theologie der
      Zukunft, " Pr. Jbb., 141, 1910, 16-31.
416. FOLEY, Grover, "Ritschls Urteil über Zinzendorfs Christo-
      zentrismus, " Ev. Theol., 20, 1960, 314-26.
417. GRABY, James K., "The problem of Ritschl's relationship
      to Schleiermacher, " Scott. J. Theol., 19, 1966, 257-68.
418. GREWEL, H., "Kirche und Gemeinde in der Theologie
      Albrecht Ritschls, " Neue Zs. f. system. Theol. u. RP,
      11, 1969, 292-311.
419. HÄRING, Theodor, "Albrecht Ritschls Bedeutung für die
      Gegenwart, " Zs. f. Theol. u. K., 20, 1910, 165-96.
420. HAMMER, Karl, "Albrecht Ritschls Lutherbild, " Theol. Zs.,
      26, 1970, 109-22.
421. HEFNER, Philip J., "Albrecht Ritschl and his current crit-
      ics, " Luth. Q., 13, 1961, 103-12.
422. _____, "The role of church history in the theology of
      Albrecht Ritschl, " Church Hist., 33, 1964, 338-55.
423. JERSILD, Paul, "The judgment of God in Albrecht Ritschl and
      Karl Barth, " Luth Q., 14, 1962, 328-46.
424. _____, "Natural theology and the doctrine of God in Al-
      brecht Ritschl and Karl Barth, " Luth. Q., 14, 1962, 239-
      57.
425. RADE, Martin, "Unkonfessionalistisches Luthertum Erin-
      nerung an die Lutherfreude in der Ritschlschen Theologie, "

Zs. f. Theol. u. K., 45, 1937, 131-51.

426. RITSCHL, Albrecht, "Prolegomena zu einer Geschichte des Pietismus," Zs. f. KiG., 2, 1878, 1-55.

427. RITSCHL, Otto, "Albrecht Ritschls Theologie und ihre bisherigen Schichsale," Zs. f. Theol. u. K., 43, 1935, 43-61.

428. SCHÄFER, Rolf, "Die Rechtfertigungslehre bei Ritschl und Kähler," Zs. f. Theol. u. K., 62, 1965-66, 66-85.

429. _____, "Das Reich Gottes bei Albrecht Ritschl und Johannes Weiss," Zs. f. Theol. u. K., 61, 1964, 68-88.

430. SCHOLZ, H., "Albrecht Ritschl," Pr. Jbb., 63, 1889, 558-77.

431. SCHÜTTE, Hans Walter, "Die Ausscheidung der Lehre vom Zorn Gottes in der Theologie Schleiermachers und Ritschls," Neue Zs. f. system. Theol. u. RP, 10, 1968, 387-97.

432. STEPHAN, Horst, "Albrecht Ritschl und die Gegenwart," Zs. f. Theol. u. K., 43, 1935, 21-43.

433. TRAUB, Fr., "Die Beurteilung der Ritschl'schen Theologie in Theobald Zieglers Werk: 'Die geistigen und socialen Strömungen des Neunzehnten Jahrhunderts,'" Zs. f. Theol. u. K., 12, 1902, 497-548.

434. _____, "Ritschls Erkenntnis Theorie," Zs. f. Theol. u. K., 4, 1894, 91-129.

435. _____, "Zur Interpretation Ritschls," Zs. f. Theol. u. K., 35, 1927, 269-73.

436. WENDT, Hans H., "Albrecht Ritschls theologische Bedeutung," Zs. f. Theol. u. K., 30, 1922, 3-48.

437. WILLIAMSON, Clark M., "Did Ritschl's critics read Ritschl," Evan. Q., 44, 1972, 159-68, 234-46.

438. WRZECIONKO, Paul, "Der geistesgeschichtliche Horizont der Theologie Albrecht Ritschls," Neue Zs. f. system. Theol. u. RP, 5, 1963, 214-34.

Friedrich Schleiermacher (1768-1834)

439. BACHMANN, Karl, "Der Begriff der Persönlichkeit bei Schleiermacher und in der Gegenwart," Zs. f. Theol. u. K., 27, 1917, 1-18.

440. BAUER, Johannes, ed., "Briefe Schleiermachers an Wilhelmine und Joachim Christian Gass," Zs. f. KiG., 47, 1929, 250-78.

441. _____, ed., "Neue Briefe Schleiermachers aus der Jugendzeit Niesky 1784 und 1785," Zs. f. KiG., 31, 1910, 587-92.

442. BIRKNER, Hans-Joachim, "Beobachtungen zu Schleiermachers Program der Dogmatik," Neue Zs. f. system. Theol. u. RP, 5, 1963, 119-31.

443. BOMMERSHEIM, Paul, "Von der religiösen Welt Schleiermachers," Vjschr. f. Litw., 22, 1944, 278-99.

444. BORNHAUSEN, Karl, "Die Religion als Freiheit Ein Schleiermacher Bekenntnis zu der 100. Wiederkehr seines Todestags 12. Februar 1934," Zs. f. Theol. u. K., 42, 1934,

46-54.
445.   CORDES, Martin, "Der Brief Schleiermachers an Jacobi Ein
        Beitrag zu seiner Entstehung und Überlieferung, " Zs. f.
        Theol. u. K., 68, 1971, 195-212.
446.   DAWSON, Jerry F., "Friedrich Schleiermacher and the sepa-
        ration of Church and State, " J. Church State, 7, 1965,
        214-25.
447.   DELIUS, Walter, "Schleiermacher und die Katechismus-
        frage, " Jb. f. Ber.-Brandenburg. KiG., 38, 1963, 97-
        105.
448.   DILTHEY, Wilhelm, "Schleiermacher's politische Gesinnung
        und Wirksamkeit, " Pr. Jbb., 10, 1862, 234ff.
449.   DOERNE, Martin, "Theologie und Kirchenregiment Eine
        Studie zu Schleiermachers praktischer Theologie, " Neue Zs.
        f. system. Theol. u. RP, 10, 1968, 360-86.
450.   DUPRE, Louis, "Toward a revaluation of Schleiermacher's
        philosophy of religion, " J. Rev., 44, 1964, 97-112.
451.   FAURE, Alexander, "Eine Predigt Schleiermachers in Fon-
        tanes Roman 'Vor dem Sturm, '" Zs. f. system. Theol.,
        17, 1940, 221-79; 19, 1942, 385-413.
452.   _____, "Schleiermacher und die Aufrufe zu Beginn der
        Freiheitskriege 1813, " Zs. f. system. Theol., 17, 1940,
        523-68,
453.   _____, "Tod und Leben nach dem Tode in Predigten
        Schleiermachers," Neue Zs. f. system. Theol. u. RP,
        18, 1941, 436-57.
454.   FOERSTER, Erich, "Der Organismusbegriff bei Kant und bei
        Schleiermacher und seine Anwendung auf den Staat, " Zs. f.
        Theol. u. K., 39, 1931, 407-21.
455.   FUCHS, Emil, "Der Charakter der Frömmigkeit Schleier-
        machers, " Zs. f. Theol. u. K., 22, 1912, 369-78.
456.   GILG, Arnold, "Ein neues Schleiermacherbuch zu Felix
        Flückiger, Philosophie und Theologie bei Schleiermacher, "
        Theol. Zs., 4, 1948, 434-54.
457.   GIRNDT, Helmut, "Kultur und Erziehung bei Schleiermacher, "
        Zs. f. philosophische Forschung, 23, 1969, 550-66.
458.   GRABY, James K., "Reflections on the history of the inter-
        pretation of Schleiermacher, " Scott. J. Theol., 21, 1968,
        283-99.
459.   GROSSMANN, Constantin, "Das Problem der kritischen
        Erklärung Schleiermachers, Kants, Luthers, " Zs. f. Theol.
        u. K., 21, 1911, 405-89.
460.   GUNDOLF, Friedrich, "Schleiermachers Romantik, " Vjschr.
        f. Litw., 2, 1924, 418-509.
461.   HALPERN, I., "Der Entwicklungsgang der Schleiermacher'schen
        Dialektik, " Arch. f. Gesch. d. Phil., 14, 1901, 210-72.
462.   HAMILTON, Kenneth, "Schleiermacher and relational The-
        ology, " J. Rel., 44, 1964, 29-39.
463.   HARTMANN, Hans, "Schleiermachers Stellung zum Berkennt-
        nis, " Zs. f. Theol. u. K., 24, 1914, 285-362.
464.   HARVEY, Van A., "A word in defense of Schleiermacher's
        theological method, " J. Rev., 42, 1962, 151-70.

465. HAYM, R., "Die Dilthey'sche Biographie Schleiermacher's,"
     Pr. Jbb., 26, 1870, 556-604.
466. HEUSER, Pastor Konrad, "Schleiermacher, Goethe und die
     Kirche," Pr. Jbb., 164, 1916, 393-419.
467. HOLLANDS, Edmund H., "Schleiermacher's development of
     subjective consciousness," Phil. Rev., 15, 1906, 293-306.
468. HUPFELD, Renatus, "Schleiermacher in seiner Bedeutung
     für unsere Zeit," Zeitwende, 3(1), 1927, 517-32.
469. JWAND, Hans-Joachim, "Schleiermacher als Ethiker," Ev.
     Theol., 11, 1951-52, 49-64.
470. KAULBACH, Friedrich, "Schleiermacher Idee der Dialektik,"
     Neue Zs. f. system. Theol. u. RP, 10, 1968, 225-60.
471. KEIL, Siegfried, "Die christliche Sittenlehre Friedrich
     Schleiermachers--Versuch einer sozialethischen Aktual-
     isierung," Neue Zs. f. system. Theol. u. RP, 10, 1968,
     310-42.
472. KNEVELS, Wilhelm, "Schleiermacher und die Wirklichkeit
     Gottes," Jb. d. Schles.-Fried.-Wilh. Univ. z. Breslau,
     13, 1968, 108-21.
473. KÖLBING, P., "Schleiermacher's Zeugnis vom Sohne Gottes
     nach seinen Festpredigten," Zs. f. Theol. u. K., 3, 1893,
     277-310.
474. KRÖNERT, Georg, "Schleiermacher und die Gegenwart,"
     ZRGG, 2, 1949-50, 345-57.
475. LEMPP, Otto, "Schleiermachers Gotteslehre," Zs. f. Theol.
     u. K., 21, 1911, 17-60.
476. _____, "Schleiermacher und Jatho," Zs. f. Theol. u. K.,
     22, 1912, 102-31.
477. LICHTENSTEIN, Ernst, "Schleiermachers Pädagogik," Neue
     Zs. f. system. Theol. u. RP, 10, 1968, 343-59.
478. LOEW, Wilhelm, "Die religionsphilosophische Fragestellung
     bei Schleiermacher und die Methode der Glaubenslehre,"
     Zs. f. Theol. u. K., 22, 1912, 203-10.
479. McCLYMONT, A. W., "The theology of Schleiermacher:
     some characteristic elements," Evan. Q., 20, 1948, 108-
     24.
480. McGIFFERT, A. C., "The theology of crisis in the light of
     Schleiermacher," J. Rel., 10, 1930, 362-77.
481. MEISNER, Heinrich and Hermann MULERT, "Schleiermachers
     Briefwechsel mit Friedrich Heinrich Christian Schwarz,"
     Zs. f. KiG., 53, 1934, 255-94.
482. MOORE, Walter L., "Schleiermacher as a Calvinist," Scott.
     J. Theol., 24, 1971, 167-83.
483. MULERT, D., "Neue deutsche Schleiermacher-Literatur,"
     Zs. f. Theol. u. K., 41, 1933, 370-78; 42, 1934, 77-88,
     256-73, 370-78.
484. MULERT, Hermann, "Die Aufnahme der Glaubenslehre
     Schleiermachers," Zs. f. Theol. u. K., 18, 1908, 107-39.
485. _____, "Zwei Briefe Schleiermachers zur Kirchenverfas-
     sungsreform," Zs. f. KiG., 36, 1916-17, 509-33.
486. NIEBUHR, Richard R., "Schleiermacher: Theology as human
     reflection," Har. Theol. Rev., 55, 1962, 21-49.

487. PACHALI, Heinrich, "Schraeder wider Schleiermacher," Zs.
      f. Theol. u. K., 22, 1912, 293-314.
488. PATSCH, Hermann, "Friedrich Schlegels 'Philosophie der
      Philologie und Schleiermachers frühe Entwürfe zur Her-
      meneutik Zur Frühgeschichte der romantischen Hermeneu-
      tik,'" Zs. f. Theol. u. K., 63, 1966, 434-72.
489. PENZEL, Klaus, "A chapter in the history of ecumenical
      quest: Schelling and Schleiermacher," Church Hist., 33,
      1964, 322-37.
490. PERLE, Johannes, "Individualität und Germeinschaft in Den-
      ken des jungen Schleiermacher," Zs. f. system. Theol.,
      12, 1935, 45-79.
491. PIPER, Otto, "Schleiermacher und die neue Universität,"
      Zs. f. Theol. u. K., 41, 1933, 350-69.
492. RAACK, R. C., "A new Schleiermacher letter on the con-
      spiracy of 1808," ZRGG, 16, 1964, 209-23.
493. _____, "Schleiermacher's political thought and activity,
      1806-1813," Church Hist., 28, 1959, 374-90.
494. REBLE, Albert, "Schleiermachers Denkstruktur," Zs. f.
      Theol. u. K., 44, 1936, 254-72.
495. _____, "Der Volksbegriff bei Schleiermacher," Vjschr. f.
      Litw., 13, 1935, 361-81.
496. RENDTORFF, Trutz, "Kirchlicher und freier Protestantismus
      in der Sicht Schleiermachers," Neue Zs. f. system. Theol.
      u. RP., 10, 1968, 18-30.
497. RÖNNAU, Erich, "Schleiermachers Religionsbegriff," Zs. f.
      system. Theol., 6, 1929, 142-87.
498. ROGGE, Joachim, "Schleiermacher und die Union," Jb. f.
      Ber.-Brandenburg. KiG., 44, 1969, 192-217.
499. ROTHERT, Hans Joachim, "Die Dialektik Friedrich Schleier-
      machers," Zs. f. Theol. u. K., 67, 1970, 183-214.
500. "SCHLEIERMACHER," Pr. Jbb., 2, 1858, 210-26.
501. SCHMOLZE, Gerhard, "'Freie Geselligkeit' Ein unausgear-
      beitetes Kapitel der Ethik Schleiermachers," Jb. d. Schles.-
      Fried.-Wilh. Univ. z. Breslau, 16, 1971, 232-61.
502. SCHOLZ, Heinrich, "Analekta zu Schleiermacher," Zs. f.
      Theol. u. K., 21, 1911, 293-314, 490-92.
503. _____, "Schleiermachers Lehre von der Sündlosigkeit
      Jesu," Zs. f. Theol. u. K., 17, 1907, 391-422.
504. SCHULTZ, Dr., "Die theoretische Begründung des Begriffs
      der Individualität in Schleiermachers ethischen Entwürfen,"
      Zs. f. Theol. u. K., 32, 1924, 37-63.
505. SCHULTZ, Werner, "Das griechische Ethos in Schleier-
      machers Reden und Monologen," Neue Zs. f. system.
      Theol. u. RP., 10, 1968, 261-88.
506. _____, "Die Grundlagen der Hermeneutik Schleiermachers,
      ihre Auswirkung und ihre Grenzen," Zs. f. Theol. u. K.,
      50, 1953, 159-84.
507. _____, "Die Idee des Spiels und die Idee der Menschheit
      in der Theologie Schleiermachers," Neue Zs. f. system.
      Theol. u. RP., 4, 1962, 340-72.
508. _____, "Schleiermachers Deutung der Religionsgeschichte,"

Zs. f. Theol. u. K., 56, 1959, 55-82.

509. SEIFERT, Paul, "Zur Theologie des jungen Schleiermacher,"
Neue Zs. f. system. Theol. u. RP, 1, 1959, 184-289.

510. SIEGFRIED, Theodor, "Zur Christologie Schleiermachers,"
Zs. f. Theol. u. K., 40, 1932, 223-35.

511. SOMMER, Wolfgang, "Cusanus und Schleiermacher," Neue
Zs. f. system. Theol. u. RP, 12, 1970, 85-102.

512. STANGE, Carl, "Die geschichtliche Bedeutung Schleiermachers," Zs. f. system. Theol., 11, 1934, 691-706.

513. _____, "Vaterlandsliebe und Weltbürgertum Schleiermachers Predigt über Vaterlandsliebe," Zeitwende, 5(2),
1929, 157-67.

514. STEINMANN, Th., "Wegweisendes in Schleiermachers Lehre
von Erlöser und seinem Erlösertum," Zs. f. Theol. u. K.,
41, 1933, 305-20.

515. STEPHAN, Horst, "Der neue Kampf um Schleiermacher,"
Zs. f. Theol. u. K., 33, 1925, 159-215.

516. _____, "Schleiermachers politische Ethik als Spiegel
seines Denkens," Zs. f. Theol. u. K., 41, 1933, 320-49.

517. _____, "Schleiermachers 'Reden über die Religion' und
Herders 'Religion, Lehrmeinigen und Gebräuche,'" Zs. f.
Theol. u. K., 16, 1906, 484-505.

518. STOLTENBERG, H. L., "Friedrich Schleiermacher als Soziologe," ZgesStw., 88, 1930, 71-113.

519. THIMME, Wilh., "Gottesgedanke und Schlechthinniges Abhän-
gigkeitsgefühl in Schleiermachers Glaubenslehre," Zs. f.
Theol. u. K., 35, 1927, 365-75.

520. TICE, Terrence N., "Schleiermacher's interpretation of
Christmas: 'Christmas Eve,' 'The Christian Faith,' and
the Christmas sermons," J. Rel., 47, 1967, 100-26.

521. TORRANCE, James B., "Interpretation and understanding in
Schleiermacher's theology: some critical questions,"
Scott. J. Theol., 21, 1968, 268-82.

522. TORRANCE, Thomas F., "Hermeneutics according to F. D.
E. Schleiermacher," Scott. J. Theol., 21, 1968, 257-67.

523. TRILLHAAS, Wolfgang, "Der Mittelpunkt der Glaubenslehre
Schleiermachers," Neue Zs. f. system. Theol. u. RP,
10, 1968, 289-309.

524. "UNGEDRUCKTE Briefe und Berichte über Schleiermacher,"
ZRGG, 2, 1949-50, 357-63.

525. UNGERN-STERNBERG, Arthur v., "Die Begegnung von Theologie und Philosophie bei Schleiermacher in seiner Reise-
zeit," Zs. f. Theol. u. K., 41, 1933, 289-304.

526. VERWIEBE, Walter, "Pneuma und Nus in Schleiermachers
christlicher Sitte," Zs. f. Theol. u. K., 20, 1932, 236-
43.

527. WALSEMANN, Dr. Hermann, "Schleiermacher und die Frau-
en," Pr. Jbb., 154, 1913, 451-82.

528. WEERTS, Dr., "Schleiermacher und das Alte Testament,"
Zs. f. system. Theol., 16, 1939-40, 233-49.

529. WEHRUNG, Georg, "Der Durchgang Schleiermachers durch
die Brüdergemeine," Zs. f. system. Theol., 4, 1927,

193-210.
530.   WELLMANN, Gordon B., "Schleiermacher Today," J. Rel.,
       18, 1938, 161-73.
531.   WENDLAND, Johannes, "Friedrich Schleiermacher," Pr.
       Jbb., 149, 1912, 1-29.
532.   ZELLER, E., "Schleiermacher in der ersten Hälfte seines
       Lebens," HZ, 25, 1871, 49-65.

Adolf Stoecker (1835-1909)

533.   BOEHLICH, Walter, "Der Berliner Antisemitismus Streit,"
       Der Monat, 17, 1965, 40-54.
534.   BUCHNER, Max, "Adolf Stoecker," Gelbe Hefte, 5, 1928-29,
       323-48.
535.   D., "Der Process Bäcker-Stoecker," Pr. Jbb., 56, 1885,
       99-102.
536.   DEHN, Günther, "Adolf Stoecker," Zwischen den Zeiten, 8,
       1924, 26-48.
537.   "Der DEUTSCHE Volksmissionar Zeugnisse aus Adolf
       Stoeckers Lebenskampf," Zeitwende, 12(1), 1935/36, 160-
       69.
538.   FRANK, Walter, "Hofprediger Stöcker," Pr. Jbb., 201,
       1925, 56-81.
539.   GILMAN, Sander L., "Hofprediger Stöcker and the Wandering
       Jew," J. Jew. Stud., 19, 1968, 63-69.
540.   HÜBNER, Reinhard, "Adolf Stöcker," Zeitwende, 4(1), 1928,
       204-14.
541.   KAMPMANN, W., and O. St. RÄTIN, "Adolf Stoecker u. d.
       Berliner Bewegung," GiWuU, 13, 1962, 558-79.
542.   MASSANARI, Ronald L., "Christian Socialism: Adolf Stoeck-
       er's formulation of a Christian perspective for social
       change for the Protestant Church in nineteenth century
       Germany, Luth. Q., 22, 1970, 185-98.
543.   RÖSSLER, Johannes, "Die Gründung der 'Christlich-sozialen
       Arbeiterpartei' des Hofpredigers Stöcker Ein Versuch zur
       Errichtung einer offenen Agentur der Reaktion in der
       Berliner Arbeiterbewegung," Berliner Heimat, 1957, 81-91.
544.   STUPPERICH, Robert, "Adolf Stoeckers Anfänge," HZ, 202,
       1966, 309-32.

David Friedrich Strauss (1808-1874)

See also entries 360, 365.

545.   BREUSS, Josef, "Das 'Leben Jesu' von David Friedrich
       Strauss und die Hegelsche Philosophie," Freiburger Zs. f.
       Phil., 19, 1972, 381-409.
546.   GEISSER, Hans, "David Friedrich Strauss als verhinderter
       (Züricher) Dogmatiker," Zs. f. Theol. u. K., 69, 1972,
       214-58.

547. GÜNTHER, Ernst, "Bemerkungen zur Christologie von David Friedrich Strauss," Zs. f. Theol. u. K., 18, 1908, 202-11.
548. HARVEY, Van A., "D. F. Strauss' Life of Jesus Revisited," Church Hist., 30, 1960, 191-211.
549. HEIN, Arnold, "Die Christologie von D. Fr. Strauss," Zs. f. Theol. u. K., 16, 1906, 321-45.
550. KRAUSS, R., "D. Fr. Strauss im Jahre 1848," Zs. f. Württbg. LG, 18, 1909, 161-72.
551. LANG, W., "Das Leben Jesu von Strauss," Pr. Jbb., 13, 1864, 465-84, 587-613.
552. MERK, Otto, "Über David Friedrich Strauss," ZRGG, 23, 1971, 143-46.
553. RAPP, Adolf, "David Friedrich Strauss Ein Bild seiner Persönlichkeit," Zs. f. Württbg. LG, 10, 1951, 182-200.
554. _____, "David Friedrich Strauss in einem bedeutsamen Abschnitt seines Lebens 1835-1842," Zs. f. Württbg. LG, 12, 1953, 147-68, 271-300.
555. _____, "David Friedrich Strauss Sein Lebensleistung und sein Schicksal," WaG, 17, 1957, 213-20.
556. ZIEGLER, Theobald, "David Friedrich Strauss als Vater," Zs. f. Württbg. LG, 20, 1911, 126-38.

Ernst Troeltsch (1865-1923)

See also entries 400, 2825

557. ADAMS, James Luther, "Ernst Troeltsch as analyst of religion," J. Sci. Stud. Rel., 1, 1961, 98-109.
558. BORNHAUSEN, Karl, "Ernst Troeltsch und das Problem der wissenschaftliche Theologie," Zs. f. Theol. u. K., 31, 1923-24, 196-223.
559. DOBRILUGK, Heinrich, "Der Begriff der Entscheidung bei Ernst Troeltsch," Zs. f. Theol. u. K., 39, 1931, 422-42.
560. DRESCHER, Hans-Georg, "Das Problem der Geschichte bei Ernst Troeltsch," Zs. f. Theol. u. K., 57, 1960, 186-230.
561. FISCHER, Hermann, "Luther und seine Reformation in der Sicht Ernst Troeltschs," Neue Zs. f. system. Theol. u. RP, 5, 1963, 132-72.
562. FOERSTER, Erich, "Luthers Kirchenbegriff und die kirchliche Krisis von heute Die Darstellung des lutherischen Protestantismus in Ernst Troeltschs 'Soziallehren,'" Zs. f. Theol. u. K., 28, 1920, 103-23.
563. GETZENY, Heinrich, "Ernst Troeltsch als Theologe und Soziologe," Hochland, 25(2), 1927/28, 582-97.
564. GUSTAFSON, Paul, "UO-US-PS-PO: A restatement of Troeltsch's Church-sect typology," J. Sci. Stud. Rel., 6, 1967, 64-68.
565. HANSON, John R., "Ernst Troeltsch's concept of compromise," Luth. Q., 18, 1968, 351-61.

566.   HINTZE, Otto, "Troeltsch und die Probleme des Historis-
       mus," HZ, 135, 1927, 188-239.
567.   KOLLMAN, Eric C., "Eine Diagnose der Weimarer Republik
       Ernst Troeltschs politische Anschauungen," HZ, 182, 1956,
       291-319.
568.   LE BRAS, G. and J. SEGUY, "Christianismes sociaux et
       sociologie du Christianisme chez Ernst Troeltsch," Arch.
       d. Soc. d. Rel., 11, 1961, 3-34.
569.   LITTLE, H. Ganse, jr., "Ernst Troeltsch on history, deci-
       sion and responsibility," J. Rel., 48, 1968, 205-34.
570.   _____, "Ernst Troeltsch and the scope of historicism,"
       J. Rel., 46, 1966, 343-64.
571.   LYMAN, Eugene W., "Ernst Troeltsch's philosophy of his-
       tory," Phil. Rev., 37, 1928, 443-65.
572.   MILLER, Donald E., "Troeltsch's critique of Karl Marx,"
       J. Sci. Stud. Rel., 1, 1961, 117-21.
573.   MILLER, Lucius Hopkins, "The teaching of Ernst Troeltsch
       of Heidelberg," Har. Theol. Rev., 6, 1913, 426-50.
574.   MÜLLER, Gotthold, "Die Selbstauflösung der Dogmatik bei
       Ernst Troeltsch," Theol. Zs., 22, 1966, 334-46.
575.   NEUMANN, Carl, "Zum Tode von Ernst Troeltsch," Vjschr.
       f. Litw., 1, 1923, 161-71.
576.   QUARBERG, David, "Historical reason, faith and the study
       of Religion," J. Sci. Stud. Rel., 1, 1961, 122-24.
577.   RICHARDS, G. W., "Was Troeltsch right?" Church Hist.,
       2, 1933, 123-38.
578.   RINTELEN, Fritz-Joachim von, "Der Versuch einer Über-
       windung des Historismus bei Ernst Troeltsch," Vjschr. f.
       Litw., 8, 1930, 324-72.
579.   SCHREY, Heinz-Horst, "Ernst Troeltsch und sein Werk,"
       Theol. Rs., 12, 1940, 130-62.
580.   SCHWARZ, G. M., "Deutschland und Westeuropa bei Ernst
       Troeltsch," HZ, 191, 1960, 510-47.
581.   SEGUY, Jean, "Ernst Troeltsch Ou de l'essence de la reli-
       gion à la typologie des christianismes," Arch. d. Soc. d.
       Rel., 25, 1968, 3-11.
582.   TILLICH, Paul, "E. Troeltsch: Historismus und seine Prob-
       leme," J. Sci. Stud. Rel., 1, 1961, 109-14. (Reprinted
       from Theologische Literatur-Zeitung, 49, 1924, 25-30.)
583.   TÖNNIES, Ferdinand, "Troeltsch und die Philosophie der
       Geschichte," Schmoll. Jb., 49, 1925, 147-91.
584.   TRAUB, Friedrich, "Die religionsgeschichtliche Methode und
       die systematische Theologie Eine Auseinandersetzung mit
       Tröltschs theologischen Reformprogramm," Zs. f. Theol.
       u. K., 11, 1901, 301-40.
585.   TROELTSCH, Ernst, "Die christliche Weltanschauung und die
       wissenschaftlichen Gegenströmungen," Zs. f. Theol. u. K.,
       3, 1893, 493-528; 4, 1894, 167-231.
586.   _____, "Geschichte und Metaphysik," Zs. f. Theol. u. K.,
       8, 1898, 1-69.
587.   _____, "Eine Kulturphilosophie des bürgerlichen Liberalis-
       mus," Pr. Jbb., 165, 1916, 353-77.

588. _____, "Naturrecht und Humanität in der Weltpolitik,"
     Weltwirtsch. Arch., 18, 1922, 485-501.
589. _____, "Die Selbständigkeit der Religion," Zs. f. Theol.
     u. K., 5, 1895, 361-436; 6, 1896, 71-110, 167-218.
590. WENDLAND, Johannes, "Philosophie und Christentum bei
     Ernst Troeltsch," Zs. f. Theol. u. K., 24, 1914, 129-65.
591. WERNLE, Paul, "Vorläufige Anmerkungen zu den Soziallehren
     der christlichen Kirchen und Gruppen von Ernst Troeltsch,"
     Zs. f. Theol. u. K., 22, 1912, 329-68; 23, 1913, 18-80.

August Friedrich Christian Vilmar (1800-1868)

592. GUNKEL, Hermann, "A.F.C. Vilmars Auffassung vom Alten
     Testaments," Ev. Theol., 17, 1957, 232-48.
593. LOHSE, Bernhard, "Kirche und Offenbarung bei A.F.C.
     Vilmar," Ev. Theol., 17, 1957, 445-67.
594. RAMGE, Karl, "Vilmar und die Zukunft des deutschen Pro-
     testantismus," Hochland, 32(1), 1934/35, 303-23.
595. SCHLIEBITZ, Alfred, "Die pädagogischen Anschauungen
     A.F.C. Vilmars," Ev. Theol., 5, 1938, 275-302.
596. SCHMOLZE, Gerhard, "Erkenntnisse und Irrtümer August
     Vilmars Ein Beispiel politischer Diakonie im 19. Jahr-
     hundert," Zeitwende, 40, 1969, 173-82.
597. STEINLEIN, Wilhelm, "August Chr. Fr. Vilmar," Zeitwende,
     15, 1938/39, 257-66.

Johann Hinrich Wichern (1808-1881)

598. CHRISTIANSON, Gerald, "J. H. Wichern and the rise of the
     Luthern social Institution," Luth. Q., 19, 1967, 357-70.
599. GERHARDT, Martin, "Aufgaben der Wichernforschung,"
     Neue Kirchliche Zeitschrift, 39, 1928, 432ff.
600. _____, "Innere Mission und christlich-soziale Bewegung,"
     Zs. f. KiG., 51, 1932, 281-304.
601. _____, "Wicherns Stellung zu Staat, staatlicher Wohlfahrts-
     pflege und Gesellschaft," Freie Wohlfahrtspflege, 2, 1927,
     6-13, 49-55.
602. LÜTGERT, W., "Wichern und Mahling," Zs. f. system.
     Theol., 11, 1934, 171-87.
603. OETTINGEN, Alexander v., "J. H. Wicherns Bedeutung für
     die sociale Bewegung unserer Zeit," Pr. Jbb., 61, 1888,
     27-54.
604. SCHRÖDER, Kurt, "Wesen und Recht der christlichen Lie-
     bestätigkeit und der Inneren Mission auf Grund von Bibel
     und Bekenntnis," Zs. f. system. Theol., 14, 1937, 495-
     531.
605. VOELTER, Hans, "Wie verhält sich der dem Wichernschen
     Programm der Innern Mission zugrunde liegende Kirchenge-
     danke zu der Schleiermacherschen Kirchenidee?" Zs. f.
     Theol. u. K., 23, 1913, 104-28, 171-217.

606.   ZSCHARNACK, Leopold, "Wicherns Stellung in der Geschichte der Fürsorgeerziehung und des Rettungshauswesens," Zs. f. d. Armenwesen, 10, 1909, 303-17.

CONSTITUTIONAL, LEGAL, ADMINISTRATIVE HISTORY
(Including Bureaucracy and City Government)

General Studies

607. "ALTE und neue Rechtszustände in Preussen," Pr. Jbb., 5, 1860, 375-92, 417-45, 533-52.
608. ANDREAS, Willy, "Ludwig Winter über eine Reform der Verwaltungsordnung (1817)," ZGORh., 64, 1910, 477-501.
609. _____, "Zu Beurteilung der badischen Verwaltungsorganisation vom 26. November 1809 und ihrer Weiterbildung," ZGORh., 66, 1912, 308-32.
610. ARNDT, Erwin, "Vom markgräflichen Patrionialstaat zum grossherzoglichen Verfassungsstaat Baden Ein Beitrag zur Verfassungsgeschichte Badens zu Beginn des 19. Jahrhunderts mit Berücksichtigung der Verhältnisse in Bayern und Württemberg," ZGORh., 101, 1953, 153-264, 436-531.
611. "Die AUSBILDUNG der preussischen Verwaltungsbeamten und ihre Leistungen," Pr. Jbb., 148, 1912, 54-85.
612. BÄHR, O., "Die Einheit des obersten Gerichtshofs in Preussen," Pr. Jbb., 22, 1868, 621-39.
613. BAUMBACH, Karl, "Die Verwirklichung der deutschen Grundrechte in der Gegenwart," Grenzboten, 1876, 361ff, 453ff.
614. "BAYRISCHES Verfassungsleben während der Jahre 1859 bis 1863," Pr. Jbb., 12, 1863, 567-86.
615. BERGSTRÄSSER, Ludwig, "Ein politisches Stammbuch aus den Anfängen des preussischen Konsitutionalismus," Arch. f. KuG., 14, 1918, 261-78.
616. BERNER, E., "Die Hausverfassung der Hohenzollern," HZ, 52, 1884, 78-121.
617. BINDING, Karl, "Der Kampf um die deutsche Strafgerichtsbank," Pr. Jbb., 32, 1873, 117-75.
618. BÖING, Dr. Heinr., "Die Selbstverwaltung in Berlin im Jahre 1899," Pr. Jbb., 106, 1901, 418-37.
619. BRANIG, Hans, "Die oberste Staatsverwaltung in Preussen zur Zeit des Todes von Hardenberg," Jb. f. Gesch. M. O. Dtschl., 13/14, 1965, 182-99.
620. BRAUN, Karl, "Die Civilrechts-Gesetzgebung des Norddeutschen Bundes," Pr. Jbb., 23, 1869, 191-222.
621. BÜNGER, R., "Die Verhältnisse der höhern Beamten in Preussen," Pr. Jbb., 125, 1906, 427-48.
622. "Die BUNDESCIVILPROJESSORDNUNG und die Organisation der Justiz," Pr. Jbb., 22, 1868, 296-329.
623. CONRAD, Hermann, "Der parlamentarische Kampf um die

Zivilehe bei Einführung des Bürgerlichen Gesetzbuches für das Deutsche Reich," H. Jb., 72, 1952, 474-93.

624. CROON, Helmuth, "Bürgtertum und Verwaltung in den Städten des Ruhrgebiets im 19. Jahrhundert," Tradition, 9, 1964, 23-41.

625. CULLITY, John P., "The Growth of Governmental Employment in Germany, 1882-1950," ZgesStw., 123, 1967, 201-17.

626. DARMSTÄDTER, Paul, "Die Verwaltung des Unter-Elsass (Bas Rhin) unter Napoleon I (1799-1814)," ZGORh, 57, 1903, 286-330, 538-63; 58, 1904, 122-47, 284-309, 631-72.

627. DAUL, Hansjoachim, "Die würzburgischen Landgerichte im Jahre 1810," Jb. f. Gesch. Kunst d. MRh., 21, 1969.

628. DEUERLEIN, Ernst, "150 Jahre kommunale Selbstverwaltung in Nürnberg 1818-1968," Mitteil. Ver. Gesch. Stadt Nürnberg, 57, 1970.

629. DIETRICH, Richard, "Die Verwaltungsreform in Sachsen 1869-1873," Neues Arch. f. Sächs. Gesch., 61, 1940, 49-85.

630. DÖRR, Margarete, "Deutsche Verfassengsgeschichte im Zeitalter Bismarcks," GiWuU, 7, 1956, 667-80.

631. "DREI Capitel über Repräsentativverfassungen," Pr. Jbb., 11, 1863, 349-87.

632. EBERSTADT, Rudolph, "Berliner Communalreform," Pr. Jbb., 70, 1892, 577-610.

633. "EINIGE der gesetzgeberischen Reformen im Königreich Sachsen unter König Johann," Pr. Jbb., 23, 1869, 283-325, 381-406.

634. FABER, Karl-Georg, "Die Entstehung der Grossgemeinden im Oberbergischen Kreis," Rhein. Vjsbll., 25, 1960, 253-99.

635. _____, "Die kommunale Selbstverwaltung in der Rheinprovinz im 19. Jahrhundert," Rhein. Vjsbll., 30, 1965, 132-51.

636. FAUCK, Siegfried, "Die Domänenjustiz in der Kurmark im 18. und 19. Jahrhundert," Jb. f. Gesch. M. O. Dtschl., 13/14, 1965, 110-27.

637. FILBRY, Gerd, "Die Einführung der Revidierten Preussischen Städteordnung von 1831 in der Stadt Münster," Westf. Zs., 107, 1957, 169-234.

638. FORSTHOFF, Ernst, "Zur Rechtsfindungslehre im 19. Jahrhundert," ZgesStw., 96, 1935/36, 49-70.

639. FRAHM, F., "Entstehungs- und Entwicklungsgeschichte der preussischen Verfassung," FBPG, 41, 1928, 248-301.

640. FRAUENDIENST, Werner, "Demokratisierung des deutschen Konstituionalismus in der Zeit Wilhelms II," ZgesStw., 113, 1957, 721-46.

641. _____, "Das preussische Staatsministerium in Vorkonstitutioneller Zeit," ZgesStw., 116, 1960, 104-77.

642. FRENSDORFF, F., "Die verschiedene Stellung der ober- und niederdeutschen Städte zur Reichsgewalt," Pr. Jbb., 34, 1874, 215ff.

643. FRICKE, Hermann, "Die Landesdirektoren der Provinz Brandenburg 1876-1945," Jb. f. Gesch. M. O. Dtschl., 5, 1956, 295-325.

644. FRICKER, C., "Die Entstehung d. württembergischen Verfassung von 1819," ZgesStw., 18, 1862, 139-93.

645. "The GERMAN Emperor and the Federal Council," Pol. Sci. Q., 10, 1895, 656-63.

646. GIERKE, Otto von, "Die Städteordnung von 1808 und die Stadt Berlin," Schmoll. Jb., 36, 1912, 369-78.

647. GILLIS, John R., "Aristocracy and bureaucracy in nineteenth century Prussia," Past and Present, 39, 1968, 105-29.

648. GOLDSCHMIDT, P., "Die oktroyierte preussische Verfassung," Pr. Jbb., 125, 1906, 197-216.

649. GOODNOW, F. J., "Local government in Prussia," Pol. Sci. Q., 4, 1889, 648-66.

650. GROTE, Waldemar, "Der Rechtsgelehrte Ernst Heymann als Jura Student in Breslau (1889-92)," Jb. d. Schles.-Fried.-Wilh. Univ. z. Breslau, 16, 1971, 286-96.

651. GRUPP, G., "Die Verfassungskämpfe, 1815-17, und der hohe Adel, insbesondere Fürst Ludwig v. Ottingen-Wallerstein," Württemb. Vtljhefte f. Landesgesch., 27, 1918, 177-214.

652. GUTENKUNST, Emil, "Der geschichtliche Ursprung der Reallasten in Baden in Beziehung auf das badische Landrecht von 1809," ZGORh., 82, 1929/30, 363-439.

653. HAAKE, Paul, "Die Errichtung des preussischen Staatsrats im März 1817," FBPG, 27, 1914, 247-65.

654. HARTUNG, Fritz, "Verantwortliche Regierung, Kabinette und Nebenregierungen im konstitutionellen Preussen 1848-1918," FBPG, 44, 1932, 1-45, 302-73.

655. HAUSER, Oswald, "Preussischer Verwaltungsstil im 19. Jahrhundert," Staat, 6, 1967, 467-78.

656. HEINEMANN, Reinhard, "Studien zum braunschweigischen Gerichtswesen im 10. Jahrhundert," Braunschweig. Jahrb., 50, 1969.

657. HERMES, Gertrud, "Ein preussischer Beamtenhaushalt 1859-1890," ZgesStw., 76, 1921, 43-92, 268-95, 478-86.

658. HERRMANN, Alfred, "Die Rheinländer und die preussische Verfassungsfrage 1815-23," Ann. Niederrhein, 120, 1932, 95-135.

659. HILL, Henry B., "The constitutions of Continental Europe: 1789-1813," J. Mod. Hist., 8, 1936, 82-94.

660. HINTZE, Otto, "Das monarchische Prinzip und die Konstitutionelle Verfassung," Pr. Jbb., 144, 1911, 381-412.

661. _____, "Preussens Entwicklung zum Rechtsstaat," FBPG, 32, 1919, 385-451.

662. HOMBURG, Herfried, "Politische Äusserungen Louis Spohrs Ein Beitrag zur Opposition Kasseler Künstler während der Kurhessischen Verfassungskämpfe," Zs. d. Vereins f. Hess. Gesch. u. Landeskunde, 75/76, 1964/65, 545-68.

663. HÜBNER, R., "Die Entwicklung der Obergerichte und der obersten Justizverwaltungsbehörden in Preussen," Schmoll. Jb., 14, 1890, 227-58.

38   German History and Civilization

664.   HÜLSMANN, Heinrich, "Geschichte der Verfassung der Stadt
       Münster von den letzten Zeiten der fürstbischöflichen bis
       zum Ende der französischen Herrschaft 1802-1813," Westf.
       Zs., 63, 1965, 1-90.
665.   HÜPEDEN, F., "Die preussischen Städteordnungen und die
       städtischen Finanzen," Pr. Jbb., 133, 1908, 298-321.
666.   JAMMERS, Antonius, "Die Bibliothek des Heidelberger
       Juristen Karl Joseph Anton Mittermaier (1787-1867) und
       ihre Eingliederung in die Universitätsbibliotek Heidelberg,"
       Bibliothek und Wissenschaft, 3, 1966, 156-218.
667.   JASTROW, Hermann, "Der sozialpolitische Inhalt der Civil-
       prozessnovelle," Arch. f. Sozialw. u. Sozialpol., 12,
       1898, 589-625.
668.   JOULIA, Antoinette, "Les institutions administratives des
       départements hanséatiques," Rev. d'hist. mod., 17, 1970,
       880-92.
669.   KAEBER, Ernst, "Das Weichbild der Stadt Berlin seit der
       steinischen Städteordnung," FBPG, 40, 1927, 267-335; 49,
       1937, 289-366.
670.   KAHLENBERG, Friedrich P., "Preussen und die Annexionen
       des Jahres 1866 Nationalstaat und Selbstverwaltung während
       des Übergangsjahres in Kurhessen," Hess. Jb. f. LG, 16,
       1966, 165-214.
671.   KLEIN, August, "Werner von Haxthausen (1780-1842) und sein
       Freundekreis am Rhein," Ann. Niederrhein, 155/56, 1954,
       160-83.
672.   KLEIN, Ernst, "Funktion und Bedeutung des preussischen
       Staatsministeriums," Jb. f. Gesch. M. O. Dtschl., 9/10,
       1961, 195ff.
673.   KNAPP, Theodor, "Der hannoversche Verfassungsbruch von
       1837 und die württembergische Abgeordnetenkammer," Zs.
       f. Württbg. LG, 2, 1938, 206-14.
674.   KOCHENDÖRFFER, H., "Territorialentwicklung und Behörden-
       verfassung von Westfalen 1802-1813," Westf. Zs., 86,
       1929, 97-218.
675.   "Das KÖNIGTHUM und die verfassungsmässige Ordnung," Pr.
       Jbb., 2, 1858, 624-39.
676.   KOPPATZ, Jürgen, "Zu einigen Fragen der Kommunalwahlen
       und der städischen Verwaltung in Potsdam (1808-1946),"
       Beitr. z. Potsdamer Gesch., 1969.
677.   KUNTSCHKE, Horst, "Zur Ausgestaltung der staatsbürgerlich-
       en Rechte im deutschen Kaiserreich von 1871," Marxistische
       Beitr. Rechtsgesch., 1968.
678.   _____, "Die Institution des Reichsgerichts als Ausdruck
       des Kompromisses bei der Gestaltung des deutschen Reiches
       von 1871," Wiss. Zs. der Humboldt-Universität zu Berlin,
       17, 1968, 383-87.
679.   LANDSBERG, Dr. Ernst, "Die Instruktion der preussischen
       Immediat-Justiz-Kommission für die Rheinlande von 1816,"
       Zs. f. Pol., 6, 1913, 171-85.
680.   LAUBERT, Manfred, "Die Ernennung der Marschälle für die
       Posener Provinziallandtage 1827-45," FBPG, 46, 1934,

275-95.

681.   LEHMANN, Max, "Der Ursprung der Städteordnung von 1808,"
       Pr. Jbb., 93, 1898, 471-514.
682.   LETTE, Dr., "Die Reorganisation der Staats- und der Selbst-
       verwaltung in Preussen," Pr. Jbb., 22, 1868, 139-85.
683.   LISSEK, Vincens M., "Die Mediatisierung des Fürstentums
       Wied-Neuwied (1806-1848) Beitrag zur Verfassung der
       Rheinbundstaaten," Nassauische Ann., 80, 1969, 159-239.
684.   LOENING, Edgar, "Die Verwaltung der Stadt Berlin," Pr.
       Jbb., 55, 1885, 511-560; 635-66; 56, 1885, 19-56.
685.   LOHMEYER, Hans, "Die Entwicklung Berlins zum Stadtstaat
       Ein Beitrag zur Geschichte der Selbstverwaltung seit 1850,"
       Bär v. Berlin, 5, 1955, 16-32.
686.   LORENZ, Ottokar, "Reichskanzler und Reichskanzlei in
       Deutschland," Pr. Jbb., 29, 1872, 474-505.
687.   LOTZ, Albert, "Die Behördenorganisation im ehemaligen
       Kurhessen nach der Reform von 1821 und ihre Entwicklung
       in vorpreussischer Zeit," Schmoll. Jb., 28, 1904, 1343-
       69.
688.   MANGOLD, Gustav, "Die ehemalige Reichsritterschaft und die
       Adelsgesetzgebung in Baden vom Wiener Kongress bis zur
       Erteilung der Verfassung (1815-1818)," ZGORh, 85, 1932-
       33, 3-108.
689.   MARKOV, Walter, "Institutions napoléoniennes en Allemagne:
       Les deux faces d'un progrès," Rev. d'hist. mod., 17,
       1970, 893-96.
690.   MARTIN, Paul C., "Die Einbeziehung der Rheinlande in den
       preussischen Währungsraum," Rhein. Vjsbll., 32, 1968,
       482-97.
691.   MEINECKE, Friedrich, "Der Abschluss des preussischen
       Verfassungswerkes im Jahre 1850," HZ, 109, 1912, 148-60.
692.   MEISNER, Heinrich O., "Bundesrat, Bundeskanzler und Bun-
       deskanzleramt (1867-1871)," FBPG, 54, 1943, 342-73.
693.   _____, "Zur neueren Geschichte des preussischen Kabinetts,"
       FBPG, 36, 1924, 38-66, 180-209.
694.   MUTH, Heinrich, "Die Grundrechte in der deutschen Verfas-
       sungsentwicklung des 19. und 20. Jahrhunderts," GiWuU.,
       2, 1951, 654-68.
695.   MUTIUS, Albert v., ed., "Aus dem Nachlass des ehemaligen
       Kaiserlichen Statthalters von Elsass-Lothringen, früheren
       preussischen Ministers des Innern von Dallwitz," Pr. Jbb.,
       214, 1928, 1-22, 147-66, 290-303.
696.   NAUDE, Wilhelm, "Zur Geschichte des preussischen Subaltern-
       beamtentums," FBPG, 18, 1905, 365-86.
697.   OBSER, Karl, ed., "Briefe Friedrich Cäsar Laharpes an
       Johann Ludwig Klüber," ZGORh., 67, 1913, 537-58.
698.   _____, "Reitzensteins Entwurf einer Ministerialorganisation
       von August 1806," ZGORh., 57, 1903, 331-42.
699.   OETKES, Fr., "Zur 'Reform der preussischen Verfassung,'"
       Pr. Jbb., 26, 1870, 172-91.
700.   OPPENHEIM, Karl, "Verzeichnis der Richter und Staatsan-
       wälte der Gerichte des Münsterlandes seit 1815," Westf.

Zs., 109, 1959, 109-42.

701. "PARLAMENTARISCHE Studien," Pr. Jbb., 3, 1859, 153-75.
702. PIKART, E., "Die Rolle der Parteien im deutschen Konstitutionellen System vor 1914," Zs. f. Pol., 9, 1962, 12-32.
703. PREUSS, Hugo, "Verwaltungsreform und Politik," Zs. f. Pol.,
1, 1907-08, 95-126.
704. "Das PREUSSISCHE Recht und das Rechtsstudium, insbesondere auf den preussischen Universitäten," Pr. Jbb., 3,
1859, 29-57.
705. PRÖSSLER, Helmut, "Adolf von Pommer Esche (1804-1871)
Oberpräsident der Rheinprovinz 1858-1871," Jb. f. Gesch.
Kunst d. MRh., 15/16, 1964, 81-93.
706. REAL, Willy, "Der Hannoversche Verfassungskonflikt im
Jahre 1837 und das deutsche Bundesrecht," H. Jb., 83,
1963, 135-61.
707. RECHBERG, Gabrielle Gräfin von, "Der Versuch der Berufung des Grafen Bernhard von Rechberg in den bayerischen
Staatsdienst (1851/52)," Zs. f. bayer. LG., 2, 1929, 319-
28.
708. RICHTER, P., "Aus der schleswig-holsteinischen Verfassungs-
und Verwaltungsgeschichte," Z. d. Ges. f. Schleswig-holsteinische Gesch., 58, 1929, 449ff.
709. RICHTERING, H., "Friedrich Alexander von Hövel (1766-
1826). Lebensbild eines märkischen Adligen, Verwaltungsbeamten und Publizisten," Beitr. zur Gesch. Dortmunds
und der Grafschaft Mark., 66, 1970, 5-43.
710. RÖHL, J. C. G., "Higher civil servants in Germany, 1890-
1900," J. Contemp. Hist., 2, 1967, 101-21.
711. ROMBERG, Hermann, "Die Verwaltung der Stadt Duisburg in
napoleonischer Zeit," Duisburger Forsch., 14, 1970.
712. ROSENBERG, Werner, "Der Bundesrath," Pr. Jb., 109,
1902, 420-43.
713. SCHIEDER, Theodor, "Das Verhältnis von politischer und
gesellschaftlicher Verfassung und die Krise des bürgerlichen Liberalismus," HZ, 177, 1954, 49-74.
714. SCHINKEL, Harald, "Polizei und Staatsverfassung im frühen
19. Jahrhundert. Eine historisch-kritische Interpretation
der preussischen Städteordnung von 1808," Staat, 3, 1964,
315-34.
715. SCHLAICH, Heinz W., "Der bayerische Staatsrat Beiträge
zu seiner Entwicklung von 1808/09 bis 1918," Zs. f.
bayer. LG, 28, 1965, 460-520.
716. SCHMELZEISEM, G. K., "Bundesexekution in Hohenzollern
und preussischer Richtereid 1866," Zs. f. Württbg LG.,
3, 1939, 212-15.
717. SCHNABEL, Franz, "Geschichte der Ministerverantwortlich-
keit in Baden," ZGORh., 75, 1921, 87-110, 171-91, 303-
31.
718. SCHNEIDER, Franz, "Die politische Komponente der Rechts-
staatidee in Deutschland," Pol. Vjschr., 9, 1968, 330-52.
719. SCHOEPS, Hans-Joachim, "Das Pluralwahlrecht," ZRGG, 23,
1971, 117-28.

720. SCHREIBER, Arndt, "Ein 'Stein'sches Papier' Wilhelm von
        Humboldts Altersteins 'Grundzuege für eine ständische
        Verfassung in den Oberpräsidial-Bezirken von Coblenz und
        Coeln,' und 'Grundideen für eine communal-Ordnung,'"
        Ann. Niederrhein, 157, 1955, 147-73.
721. SCHRÖKER, Sebastian, "Ungeschriebenes Verfassungsrecht
        im Bundesstaat Zum 100. Gründungsjahr des deutschen
        Bundesstaats," Staat, 5, 1966, 137-61, 315-40.
722. SCHUBERT, W., "Das Streben nach Prozessbeschleunigung
        und Verfahrensgliederung im Zivilprozessrecht des 19.
        Jahrhunderts," ZRG (Germ. Abt.), 85, 1968, 127-87.
723. SCHULTZ, Dr. Wolfgang M., "Amerikanisches und deutsches
        Verfassungsleben," Pr. Jbb., 128, 1907, 81-133.
724. SEITERICH, Ludwig, "Kreisdirektorium und Kreisregierung
        im ehemaligen Grossherzogtum Baden und die historische
        Entwicklung ihre Zuständigkeiten," ZGORh., 81, 1928-29,
        493-556.
725. SEYDEL, Dr. Max, "Der deutsche Bundesrath," Schmoll. Jb.,
        3, 1879, 273-96.
726. SICHELSCHMIDT, Gustav, "Das bergische Land unter dem
        General-Gouvernement Berg (1813 bis 1815)," Ann. Nieder-
        rhein, 133, 1938, 1-76.
727. "SIEBEN Worte der Verfassung," Pr. Jbb., 11, 1863, 162-81.
728. SIEBURG, Heinz Otto, "Napoléon et la transformation des in-
        stitutions en Allemagne," Rev. d'hist. mod., 17, 1970,
        897-912.
729. SIEGFRIED, R., "Ausblicke auf die künftige preussische
        Wahlreform," Schmoll. Jb., 34, 1910, 1-35.
730. SMITH, Munroe, "Four German Jurists," Pol. Sci. Q., 10,
        1895, 664-92.
731. STENGEL, Karl von, "Staatenbund und Bundesstaat," Schmoll.
        Jb., 22, 1898, 707-97, 1089-1175.
732. _____, "Die preussische Verwaltungsreform und die Ver-
        waltungsgerichtsbarkeit," Schmoll. Jb., 7, 1883, 373-460.
733. STERN, Alfred, "Zur Geschichte der preussischen Verfas-
        sungsfrage 1807-1815," HZ, 48, 1882, 236-304.
734. STIRK, S. D., "Germany and the idea of natural law," In-
        tern. Jl., 5.
735. SYBEL, Heinrich v., "Hans Daniel Hassenpflug," HZ, 71,
        1893, 48-67.
736. SYDOW, R., "Die deutsche Justizreform," Schmoll. Jb., 6,
        1882, 1143-70; 7, 1883, 53-83.
737. THIEME, Horst, "Preussisches geheimes Zivilkabinet ...:
        Übersicht über einen Bestand im Deutschen Zentralarchiv,"
        Zs. f. Geschw., 18, 1970, 90-93.
738. TIDEMANN, Heinrich, "Bremische Verfassungskämpfe von
        1830 bis 1837," Bremisches Jb., 37, 1937, 172-257.
739. TREITSCHKE, Heinrich von, "Der erste Verfassungskampf in
        Preussen (1815-1823)," Pr. Jbb., 29, 1872, 313-60, 409-
        73.
740. _____, "Der Prinz von Preussen und die reichsständische
        Verfassung (1840-47)," FBPG, 1, 1888, 587-98.

741.   _____, "Das Zweikammersystem und das Herrenhaus,"
            Pr. Jbb., 31, 1873, 221-56.
742.   UNRUH, Georg-Christoph von, "Spannungen zwischen Staats-
            und Selbstverwaltung im bürgerlichen und im sozialen
            Rechtsstaat," Staat, 4, 1965, 441-68.
743.   WALKER, Mack, "Home towns and state administrators:
            South German politics, 1815-30," Pol. Sci. Q., 82, 1967,
            35-60.
744.   WEECH, Friedrich von, ed., "Das acht und neunte badische
            Konstitutionsedikt Aus dem Akten des Grossh. General-
            Landesarchivs," ZGORh., 46, 1892, 249-313.
745.   WELKER, August, "Die Gerichtsorganisation des rechtsrhein-
            ischen Teiles des Landgerichtsbezirks Koblenz von 1783
            bis 1945," Jb. f. Gesch. Kunst d. MRh., 12/13, 1960-61,
            55-69.
746.   WELKOBORSKY, Gerhard, "Die hessische Verfassung von
            1820," Arch. f. hessische Gesch., 26, 1958/61, 139-50.
747.   WERNER, Fritz, "Zur Geschichte des Kammergerichts in
            Berlin," Jahrb. Preussischer Kulturbesitz, 6, 1968.
748.   WULFMEYER, R., "Die Einführung der Bezirksräte und die
            Umbildung der inneren Landesverwaltung in Kurhessen
            1821-1848," Hess. Jb. f. Lg., 21, 1971, 160-213.
749.   "ZEHN Jahre bayrischen Verfassungslebens," Pr. Jbb., 3,
            1859, 194-219, 325-42.
750.   ZELLER, Alfred, "Über die Entwicklung Württ. Verwaltungs-
            einrichtungen im XIX. Jahrhundert," ZgesStw., 54, 1898,
            441-66.
751.   ZORN, P. K. L., "The constitutional position of the German
            Emperor," The Annals of the American Academy of Po-
            litical and Social Sciences, 14, 1899, 73-93.
752.   ZURBONSEN, Friedrich, "Aus den Aufzeichnungen eines
            Westfälischen Juristen, 1846," Westf. Zs., 88, 1931, 196-
            207.

Friedrich Carl von Savigny (1779-1861)

753.   CARONI, Pio, "Savigny und die Kodifikation," ZRG (Germ.
            Abt.), 86, 1969, 75-176.
754.   "FRIEDRICH Carl von Savigny," Pr. Jbb., 9, 1862, 121-68.
755.   FUNK, Philipp, "Der geistesgeschichtliche Ort Friedrich Karl
            von Savignys," H. Jb., 50, 1930, 189-204.
756.   LEIST, Alexander, "Savigny und Adam Smith," Schmoll. Jb.,
            41, 1917, 135-51.
757.   REAL, Willy, "Aus dem Leben eines preussischen Diplomaten.
            Karl Friedrich von Savignys Weg bis zum Eintritt in den
            diplomatischen Dienst (1814-1840)," H. Jb., 85, 1965, 84-
            118.
758.   SCHNEIDER, Franz, "Karl Friedrich von Savignys Denkschrift
            über die Reorganisation der Universität Heidelberg 1804,"
            ZGORh, 67, 1913, 609-25.
759.   SCHÖNBERG, Josepha von (geb. von Savigny), "Carl Friedrich

von Savigny Ein katholischer Staatsmann des 19. Jahrhunderts," Gelbe Hefte, 1, 1924/25, 548-74.

760.   SCHOOF, Wilhelm, "Friedrich Karl von Savigny in Berlin Ein Lebens- und Zeitbild," Bär v. Ber., 21, 1972, 7-61.

761.   WOHLHAUPTER, Eugen, "Friedrich Karl von Savigny und Clemens Brentano, unter besonderer Berücksichtigung der Landshuter Universitätsjahre Savignys (1808-1810)," Zs. f. bayer. LG., 14, 1941, 282ff.

DIPLOMACY

1806-1871

762. "1814, Le Roi de Wurtemberg," Rev. d'hist. dipl., 1, 1887, 253-66.

763. ALBERTINI, Rudolf von, "Frankreichs Stellungnahme zur deutschen Einigung während des zweiten Kaiserreiches," Schw. Zs. f. Gesch., 5, 1955, 305-68.

764. BARTLETT, C. J., "Clarendon, the Foreign Office and the Hohenzollern Candidature, 1868-1870," EHR, 75, 1960, 276-84.

765. BAUMGART, W., "Probleme der Krimkriegsforschung. Eine Studie über die Literatur des letzten Jahrzehnts (1961-1970)," Jbb. f. Gesch. Osteur., 19, 1971, 243-64.

766. BLAESE, Hermann, "Zar Alexander I und Baden," ZGORh., 99, 1951, 507-67.

767. BLAYAU, Noël, "Une négociation matrimoniale sans lendemain entre la Bavarière et la France du Second Empire (1856)," Rev. d'hist. dipl., 84, 1970, 267-78.

768. BOBR-TYLINGO, Stanislaw, "Lord Clarendon's Mission to Germany in 1863," Antemurale, 11, 1967, 185-89.

769. BONJOUR, Edgar, "Preussen und Österreich im Neuenburger Konflikt 1856/57," Zs. f. Schw. Gesch., 10, 1930, 52-108.

770. BORRIES, Kurt, "Zur Politik der deutschen Mächte in der Zeit des Krimkrieges und der italienischen Einigung," HZ, 151, 1934-35, 294-310.

771. CLARK, Chester W., "The foreign policy of Prussia 1858-71," J. Mod. Hist., 6, 1934, 444-50.

772. CLÉMENT-SIMON, F., "La politique de la Prusse en Orient (1763-1871)," Rev. d'hist. dipl., 22, 1908, 383-415.

773. DANIELS, Emil, "Oesterreich und Preussen von 1859-1866," Pr. Jbb., 92, 1898, 83-115.

774. DELBRÜCK, Hans, "Der Ursprung des Krieges von 1870," Pr. Jbb., 70, 1892, 729-46.

775. DISCH, Karl, "Der Kabinettsrat Beyme und die auswärtige Politik Preussens in den Jahren 1805/06," FBPG, 41, 1928, 331-66; 42, 1929, 93-134.

776. DUPUIS, Charles, "La Sainte Alliance et la Directoire européen de 1815 à 1818," Rev. d'hist. dipl., 48, 1934, 265-92, 436-69.

777. FESTER, Richard, "Neue Beiträge zur Geschichte der Hohenzollernschen Thronkandidatur in Spanien," Hist. Vjschr.,

15, 1912, 34-55, 222-50.

778. FRAHM, Friedrich, "Frankreich und die Hohenzollernkandidatur bis zum Frühjahr 1869," Hist. Vjschr., 29, 1934-35, 342-70.

779. FRIEDJUNG, Heinrich, "Fürst Felix Schwarzenberg und Graf Albrecht Bernstorff," HZ, 107, 1911, 540-79.

780. GEIGER, Max, "Politik und Religion nach dem Programm der Heiligen Allianz," Theol. Zs., 15, 1959, 107-25.

781. GOLLWITZER, H. v., "Der Cäsarismus Napoleons III im Widerhall der öffentlichen Meinung Deutschlands," HZ, 173, 1952, 23-75.

782. HAMBERGER, Heinrich, "Die preussisch-italienische Allianz von 1866," Pr. Jbb., 27, 1871, 132-59, 217-38, 392-417, 610-40.

783. HAMMEN, Oscar J., "The failure of an attempted Franco-German liberal rapprochement, 1830-1840," AHR, 52, 1946-47, 54-67.

784. HANSEN, R., "Zur Geschichte der dänischen Politik 1840-48," Z. d. Ges. f. schleswig-holsteinische Gesch., 42, 1912, 253ff.

785. HENCHE, Albert, "Die Berichte Ibells an Marschall während des Wiener Kongresses," Jb. f. Gesch. Kunst d. MRh., 2/3, 1950/51, 99-140.

786. _____, "Der erste nassauische Gesandschaftsbericht aus Wien als zeitgenössische Quelle zur Napoleonszeit," Jb. f. Gesch. Kunst d. MRh., 8/9, 1956/57, 104-10.

787. _____, "Die herzoglich-nassauischen Gesandtschaftsberichte aus Wien und Berlin als Beitrag zur Geschichte des Jahres 1866," H. Jb., 75, 1955, 173-201.

788. HENDERSON, Gavin B., "Problems of neutrality, 1854: Documents from the Hamburg Staatsarchiv," J. Mod. Hist., 10, 1938, 232-41.

789. HERKLESS, J. L., "Lord Clarendon's attempt at Franco-Prussian Disarmament," Hist. J., 15, 1972, 455-70.

790. HOFFMANN, P., "Die Politik Württembergs und Bayerns während des italienischen Einheitskrieges 1859," Zs. f. Württ. LG., 29, 1970, 213-93.

791. HUBATSCH, Walther, "Deutsche Grenzprobleme 1813-1815," Die Welt als Geschichte, 16, 1956, 179-95.

792. JACINI, S., "Eine Stimme aus Italien über das preussisch-italienische Bündniss von 1866," Pr. Jbb., 29, 1872, 513-19.

793. JELAVICH, Barbara, "Russland und die Einigung Deutschlands unter preussischer Führung," GiWuU., 19, 1968, 521-38.

794. KAEHLER, S. A., "Realpolitik zur Zeit des Krimkrieges-- Eine Säkularbetrachtung," HZ, 174, 1952, 417-78.

795. KESSEL, Eberhard, "Gastein," HZ, 176, 1953, 521-44.

796. KISSINGER, Henry A., "The Congress of Vienna; A Reappraisal," World Politics, 9, 1956, 264-80.

797. KOEPPEL, Ferdinand, "Bayern und die französische Pfalzpolitik 1866," Zs. f. bayer. LG., 8, 1935, 425-44.

798. KONETZKE, Richard, "Spanien, die Vorgeschichte des Krieges von 1870 und die deutsche Reichsgründung," HZ, 214, 1972, 580-609.

799. KOSER, Reinhold, "Zur Geschichte der preussischen Politik während des Krimkrieges," FBPG, 2, 1889, 233-43.

800. KOSSOK, Manfred, "Preussen, Bremen und die 'Texas-Frage' 1835-1845," Wiss. Zs. d. Karl-Marx Univ. Leipzig, Ges-U. Sprach. Wiss. Reihe, 13, 1964, 183-98.

801. KÜHN, Joachim, "Herzog Karl II. und Napoleon III. nach ihrem ungedruckten Briefwechsel," Braunschw. Jb., 46, 1965, 125-44.

802. _____, "Napoleon im Urteil eines seiner Diplomaten Ein Beitrag zur Bewertung der napoleonischen Politik inbesondere bezüglich Preussens," Zs. f. Pol., 8, 1961, 321-33.

803. LANG, Wilhelm, "Die preussisch-italienische Allianz von 1866," HZ, 94, 1905, 251-86.

804. LEHMANN, Max, "Die Genesis des preussisch-russischen Bündnisses von 1813," HZ, 112, 1914, 284-326.

805. LHERITIER, Michel, "Les Documents diplomatiques austro-allemands sur les origines de la guerre de 1870-1871," Rev. d'hist. mod., 2, 1927, 422-48.

806. MATTER, Paul, "Les Missions de M. Persigny a Berlin (1849-1850)," Rev. d'hist. dipl., 12, 1898, 62-79.

807. MAURENBRECHER, Wilh., "Die deutsche Frage 1813-1815," Pr. Jbb., 27, 1870, 39-60.

808. MAZOUR, Anatole G., "Russian and Prussia during the Schleswig-Holstein Crisis in 1863," J. Cen. Eur. Aff., 1, 1941, 275-87.

809. MEISNER, Heinrich O., "England, Frankreich und die deutsche Einigung," Pr. Jbb., 211, 1928, 67-91.

810. _____, "Die Sendung Knesebecks nach Petersburg (1812) im alten Lichte," FBPG, 34, 1922, 93-103.

811. MEYER, Arnold O., "Die Aktenveröffentlichung über die Auswärtige Politik Preussens 1858-1871," HZ, 153, 1935-36, 322-35.

812. MOSSE, W. E., "The Crown and Foreign Policy. Queen Victoria and the Austro-Prussian conflict March-May, 1866," Cambridge Historical Journal, 10, 1950-52, 205-23.

813. _____, "Queen Victoria and her Ministers in the Schleswig-Holstein Crisis 1863-1864," EHR, 78, 1963, 263-83.

814. NADAILLAC, Col. marquis de, "La Candidature Hohenzollern," Rev. d'hist. dipl., 26, 1912, 549-72.

815. OBSER, Karl, "Die Sendung des Obersthofmeisters Freiherrn Christian von Berckheim nach Paris im J. 1807 und seine Unterredung mit Napoleon," ZGORh., 62, 1908, 328-39.

816. "Ein OSTSEEFELDZUG und die preussische Politik in der polnischen Frage," Pr. Jbb., 11, 1863, 533-51.

817. PFLUGK-HARTTUNG, Julius v., "Die Gegensätze zwischen England und Preussen wegen der Bundestruppen 1815," FBPG, 24, 1911, 447-501.

818. PLATZHOFF, Walter, "Die Anfänge des Dreikaiserbundes (1867-1871) unter Benutzung unveröffentlichen Materials,"

Pr. Jbb., 188, 1922, 283-306.
819. _____, "England und der Kaiserplan von Frühjahr 1870,"
HZ, 127, 1923, 454-75.
820. POLISENSKY, J., "Österreich Preussen und Deutschland
1850-1866," Cesl. Cas. Hist., 15, 1967, 249-62.
821. REAL, Willy, "Österreich und Preussen im Vorfeld des
Frankfurter Fürstentages Ein Beitrag zur Geschichte der
Bundesreform," H. Jb., 86, 1966, 339-93.
822. RIESS, Ludwig, "Abekens politischer Anteil an der Emser
Depesche," HZ, 118, 1917, 449-76.
823. RITTHALER, A., "Napoleon III und der Rhein," Gelbe Hefte,
2, 1925/26, 893-911.
824. RÖDER, Reinhold, "Zur Konvention von Tauroggen," Zs. f.
MilitärG., 1, 1962, 177-93.
825. ROTHAM, G., "L'Allemagne au Lendemain de la Guerre de
1866," Rev. d'hist. dipl., 1, 1887, 578-92.
826. SALOMON, Felix, "Eine neue französische Aktenpublikation
über den Ursprung des Krieges von 1870/71," Hist.
Vjschr., 14, 1911, 396-413.
827. SARING, Hans, "Die Rolle des Geheimen Staatsrats v. Heyde-
breck bei der Durchführung der Kontinentalsperre in Preussen," FBPG, 44, 1932, 84-129.
828. SCHARWATH, Alfred Günther, "Die Fürsten von der Leyen
und der Wiener Kongress," Rhein. Vjsbll., 33, 1969, 139-
54.
829. SCHEEL, Heinrich, "Probleme der deutsch-französischen
Beziehungen 1789-1830," Zs. f. Geschw., 18(2), 1970,
163-71.
830. SCHMITT, Hans A., "Count Beust and Germany, 1866-1870:
Reconquest, Realignment, or Resignation?" Cen. Eur. Hist.,
1, 1968, 20-34.
831. SIMSON, Bernhard von, "Zu dem Aufenthalt der verbündeten
Monarchen in Freiburg i. B. im Winter 1813/14," ZGORh,
53, 1899, 635-64.
832. SOMMERFELDT, Gustav, "Die preussisch-österreichische
Politik des Jahres 1807 bis zur Entsendung Stutterheims
nach Tilsit," FBPG, 18, 1905, 539-73.
833. STERNE, Margaret, "Ein Amateur wird Diplomat Die politische Karriére von William Murphy, amerikanischer
Generlkonsul in Frankfurt am Main 1861-1869," Arch. f.
Frankfurts Gesch., 48, 1962, 119-32.
834. THIEME, Horst, "Die Frankfurter Berichte des letzten nieder-
ländischen Gesandten am Bundestag Friedrich Heinrich Wilhelm von Scherff 1863-1866," Arch. f. Frankfurts Gesch.,
51, 1968.
835. THIMME, Friedrich, "Die Mission Knesebecks nach Petersburg (1812) in neuem Lichte," FBPG, 17, 1904, 535-48.
836. _____, "Zur Vorgeschichte der Konvention von Tauroggen,"
FBPG, 13, 1900, 246-62.
837. TILLOS, H., "L'Allemagne en 1867 Lettres inédites de Henri
Tillos," Rev. d'hist. dipl., 78, 1964, 340-60.
838. TREITSCHKE, H. v., "Preussen auf dem Wiener Congresse,"

Pr. Jbb., 36, 1875, 655-714; 37, 1876, 133-65, 281-326.

839. _____, "Zur Geschichte des preussisch-russischen Bündnisses," Pr. Jbb., 45, 1880, 528-41.

840. ULMANN, H., "Der Beitritt Hessen-Darmstadts zu dem
Wiener Geheimvertrag vom 3. Januar 1815," Arch. f. hessische Gesch., 11, 1916, 309-20.

841. WEIS, Eberhard, "Vom Kriegsausbruch zur Reichsgründung:
Zur Politik des bayerischen Aussenministers Graf Bray-
Steinburg im Jahre 1870," Zs. f. bayer. LG., 33, 1970,
787-810.

842. WIEDEMANN, Franz, "Zur Geshichte des Aufrufs von Kalisch
1813," FBPG, 45, 1933, 262-85.

843. ZAK, L. A., "Die Grossmächte und die deutschen Staaten
am Ende der napoleonischen Kriege," Zs. f. Geschw., 19,
1971, 1536-47.

Christian Karl Josias Freiherr von Bunsen (1791-1860)

844. BASTGEN, Hubert, "Die Antworten Bunsens auf die Note der
Kurie vom 15. März 1836," Röm. Qu.-Schr., 38, 1930,
281-306.

845. _____, "Die Note der Kurie an Bunsen vom 15. März
1836," Röm. Qu.-Schr., 35, 1927, 413-27.

846. "BUNSEN, Ch. K. J.," Pr. Jbb., 7, 1861, 50-66.

847. DRUMMOND, Andrew L., "Baron Bunsen (1795-1860), Pioneer of Pan-Protestantism," Evan. Q., 13, 1941, 46-61.

848. SCHMIDT, Martin, "Der Streit zwischen Karl Josias von
Bunsen und Friedrich Julius Stahl in den Jahre 1855 und
1856 in seiner Kirchengeschichtlichen und grundsätzlichen
Bedeutung," Jb. f. Ber.-Brandburg. KiG., 44, 1969, 113-
66.

1871-1914

849. ANCHIERI, Ettore, "Une nouvelle source pour l'histoire des
années 1870 a 1872: les documents diplomatiques Italiens,"
Rev. d'hist. mod., 19, 1972, 249-55.

850. AURICH, Ernst, "Die deutsch Politik in der ersten Marok-
kokrise," Hist. Vjschr., 30, 1935, 115-63.

851. BÄCHTOLD, Hermann, "Der entscheidende weltpoltische
Wendepunkt der Vorkriegszeit," Weltwirtsch. Arch., 20,
1924, 381-407.

852. BAUER, Clemens, "Der Vatikan im System der europäischen
Bündnispolitik von 1870-1900," Hochland, 30(1), 1932/33,
385-402.

853. BERGSTRÄSSER, Ludwig, "Die diplomatischen Kämpfe vor
Kriegsausbruch," HZ, 114, 1915, 489-592.

854. BERNSTEIN, Samuel, "The First International and the Great
Powers," Sci. Soc., 16, 1951-52, 247-72.

855. BICKFORD, J. D. and E. JOHNSON, "The contemplated

Anglo-German alliance: 1880-1901, " Pol. Sci. Q., 42, 1927, 1-57.

856. BREDT, Joh.-Victor, "Italien als Bundesgenosse, " Pr. Jbb., 216, 1929, 1-16 and Dr. h. e. Graf Manfredi GRAVINA, "Italien als Bundesgenosse, " Pr. Jbb., 216, 1929, 17-29.

857. _____, "Lichnowky und Grey, " Pr. Jbb., 212, 1928, 1-17.

858. _____, "Das 'Missverständnis' des Fürsten Lichnowsky vom 1. August 1914, " Pr. Jbb., 230, 1932, 120-31.

859. CORRIGAN, H. S. W., "German-Turkish relations and the outbreak of war in 1914: a re-assessment, " Past and Present, 1967, 144-52.

860. DANIELS, Emil, "Zur Entstehung des Weltkriegs, " Pr. Jbb., 213, 1928, 253-87.

861. DEHIO, L., "Gedanken über die deutsche Sendung 1900-1918, " HZ, 174, 1952, 479-502.

862. DELAVAUD, L., "Le Mystère D'Agadir, " Rev. d'hist. dipl., 27, 1913, 23-40.

863. DIETRICH, Richard, "Greys Konferenzvorschlag vom 26, Juli 1914, " Hist. Vjschr., 31, 1936-37, 307-42.

864. "Die DIPLOMATISCHE und die Consularvertretung des deutschen Reiches, " Pr. Jbb., 47, 1881, 380-96, 625-41.

865. DONIOL, Henri, "Négociations et negociateurs de la libération du territoire français en 1871, " Rev. d'hist. dipl., 10, 1896, 380-432.

866. EARLE, E. M., "The secret Anglo-German Convention of 1914 regarding Asiatic Turkey, " Pol. Sci. Q., 38, 1923, 24-44.

867. EDWARDS, E. W., "The Franco-German Agreement on Morocco, 1909, " EHR, 78, 1963, 483-513.

868. EKSTEIN, Michael, "Sir Edward Grey and Imperial Germany in 1914, " J. Contemp. Hist., 6(3), 1971, 121-31.

869. ENGELSING, R., "Deutschland und die Vereinigten Staaten im 19. Jahrhundert, " WaG., 18, 1958, 138-56.

870. EPSTEIN, Fritz T., "Die Erschliessung von Quellen zur Geschichte der deutschen Aussenpolitik Die Publikation von Akten des Auswärtigen Amts nach den beiden Weltkriegen-- ein Vergleich der Methoden, " WaG, 22, 1962, 204-19.

871. FISCHER, Eric, "New light on German-Czech relations in 1871, " J. Mod. Hist., 14, 1942, 177-94.

872. FISCHER, Fritz, "Weltpolitik, Weltmachtstreben und deutsche Kriegsziele, " HZ, 199, 1964, 265-346.

873. FRANKE, Bruno W., "Handelsneid und Grosse Politik in den englisch-deutschen Beziehungen 1871-1914, " Zs. f. Pol., 29, 1939, 455-75.

874. FRAUENDIENST, W., "Deutsche Weltpolitik zur Problematik des Wilhelminischen Reichs, " WaG, 19, 1959, 1-39.

875. GAULD, William A., "The 'Dreikaiserbündnis' and the Eastern Question 1871-6, " EHR, 40, 1925, 207-21; 42, 1927, 560-68.

876. GEISS, Imanuel, "The outbreak of the First World War and German war aims, " J. Contemp. Hist., 1, 1966, 75-91.

877. GILLARD, D. R., "Salisbury's African Policy and the Heligo-

land Offer of 1890," EHR, 75, 1960, 631-53.
878. _____, "Salisbury's Heligoland Offer: The case against the 'Witu Thesis.'" EHR, 80, 1965, 538-52.
879. GOTOVITCH, José, "La légation d'Allemagne et le mouvement flamand entre 1867 et 1914," Rev. Belge, 45, 1967, 438-78.
880. GRANFELT, Helge, "Der Dreibund als Same zu einer neuen Staatenbildung," Schmoll. Jb., 54, 1930, 125-34.
881. GUILLEN, P. and J.-L. MIÉGE, "Les débuts de la politique allemande au Maroc (1870-1877)," RH, 234, 1965, 323-52.
882. HAAKE, Paul, "Die deutsche Aussenpolitik von 1871 bis 1890," FBPG, 36, 1924, 97-124.
883. _____, "Die deutsche Aussenpolitik von 1890 bis 1898," FBPG, 37, 1925, 77-123.
884. HAGEN, Dr. Maximilian v., "Die Bündnispolitik des deutschen Reiches Betrachtungen zu den Memoiren des Freiherrn v. Eckardstein," Pr. Jbb., 186, 1921, 145-71.
885. HALEVY, Elie, "Franco-German relations since 1870," History, 9, 1924, 18-29.
886. HALL, Luella J., "The abortive German-American-Chinese Entente of 1907-08," J. Mod. Hist., 1, 1929, 219-35.
887. HALLGARTEN, Wolfgang, "L'Essor et L'Echec de la politique Boer de L'Allemagne (1890-1898)," RH, 177, 1936, 505-29.
888. HASHAGEN, Justus, "Zur Geschichte der amerikanisch-deutschen Beziehungen 1897-1907," Zs. f. Pol., 16, 1926-27, 122-29.
889. HATTON, P. H. S., "Harcourt and Solf: The search for an Anglo-German understanding through Africa, 1912-14," Eur. Stud. Rev., 1, 1971, 123-45.
890. HEFFTER, Heinrich, "Vom Primat der Aussenpolitik," HZ, 171, 1951, 1-20.
891. HERTZ, Richard, "Der Fall Wohlgemuth ein deutsch-schweizerischer Konflikt aus der Bismarck-Zeit," Hist. Vjschr., 31, 1936-37, 734-80.
892. ISAAC, Jules, "Le problème des origines de la guerre Trois solutions Américaines," Rev. d'hist. mod., 7, 1932, 138-78.
893. JOLL, James, "The 1914 debate continues. Fritz Fischer and his critics," Past and Present, 1966, 100-13.
894. KAERGER, Dr. K., "Buren, Engländer und Deutsche in Südafrika," Pr. Jbb., 77, 1894, 397-423.
895. KAPP, Friedrich, "Der deutsch-amerikanische Vertrag vom 22. Februar 1868," Pr. Jbb., 35, 1875, 509-34, 660-83; 36, 1876, 189-228.
896. KOCH, H. W., "The Anglo-German Alliance negotiations: missed opportunity or myth?" History, 54, 1969, 378-92.
897. KRAUSS, Luigi, "L'Evolution de Pangermanisme au dix-neuvième siècle et la diplomatie," Rev. d'hist. dipl., 15, 1901, 453-67, 571-90; 16, 1902, 19-50, 189-230.
898. LANGHORNE, Richard, "The naval question in Anglo-German relations, 1912-14," Hist. J., 14, 1971, 359-70.
899. LEHMANN, Konrad, "Die Ablehnung des englischen Bündnisan-

trags (1898-1901)," Pr. Jbb., 221, 1930, 162-83.
900. LIU, Kwang-Ching, "German fear of a Quadruple Alliance,
     1904-1905," J. Mod. Hist., 18, 1946, 222-40.
901. MARTE, Dr., "Die Weltlage Deutschlands vor einem Men-
     schenalter," Gelbe Hefte, 7, 1930-31, 531-51.
902. MEISNER, Heinrich O., "Der 'Neue Kurs,'" Pr. Jbb., 196,
     1924, 41-70, 261-88.
903. MEURER, Vizeadmiral a. D. Alexander, "'Holland in Not'
     im 17. Jahrhundert und Deutschlands Lage zu Beginn des
     Weltkrieges Ein geschichtlicher Vergleich," Pr. Jbb., 214,
     1928, 65-89.
904. MICHAEL, Wolfgang, "Richard Krauel als deutscher Gesandter
     in Brasilien, 1894-1897," Pr. Jbb., 195, 1924, 62-80.
905. MOMMSEN, Wolfgang J., "The debate on German war aims,"
     J. Contemp. Hist., 1(3), 1966, 47-72.
906. _____, "Domestic factors in German foreign policy before
     1914," Cen. Eur. Hist., 6, 1973, 3-43.
907. MOWAT, R. B., "Great Britain and Germany in the early
     twentieth century," EHR, 46, 1931, 423-41.
908. NOVOTNY, A., "Der Berliner Kongress und das Problem
     einer europäischer Politik," HZ, 186, 1958, 285-307.
909. OHNESSEIT, Wilhelm, "Deutsche Bündnispolitik unter Bis-
     marck und seinen Nachfolgern," Pr. Jbb., 218, 1929, 197-
     221.
910. OPPEL, Bernard F., "The waning of a traditional alliance:
     Russia and Germany after the Portsmouth Peace Con-
     ference," Cen. Eur. Hist., 5, 1972, 318-29.
911. OW, A. Frhr. von, "Frankreichs Beziehungen zu Deutsch-
     land am Vorabend des Weltkrieges," Gelbe Hefte, 11,
     1934-35, 513-40, 577-602.
912. PATTON, P. H. S., "Britain and Germany in 1914.   The
     July Crisis and war aims," Past and Present, 36, 1967,
     138-43.
913. PHILIPPI, Hans, "Beiträge zur Geschichte der diplomatischen
     Beziehungen zwischen dem Deutschen Reich und dem heili-
     gen Stuhl 1872-1909," H. Jb., 82, 1962, 219-62.
914. PICK, Fritz, "Das deutsch-englische Bündnis," Pr. Jbb.,
     239, 1935, 56-65.
915. POIDEVIN, Raymond, "Aspects économiques des négociations
     Franco-Allemandes (Juin-Octobre 1871)," Rev. d'hist. mod.,
     19, 1972, 219-34.
916. POURALES, Friedrich, "Neues über die Ententediplomatie
     vor dem Weltkriege," Pr. Jbb., 185, 1921, 289-320.
917. RACHFAHL, Felix, "Deutschland und die Balkanfrage im
     Wandel der Jahrhunderte," Weltwirtsch. Arch., 5, 1915,
     23-62, 244-91.
918. RALL, Hans, "Der deutsch-russische Rückversicherungsver-
     trag und seine Nichterneuerung," Gelbe Hefte, 10, 1933-
     34, 213-30.
919. RITTER, Moritz, "Deutschland und der Ausbruch des Welt-
     kriegs," HZ, 121, 1920, 23-92.
920. ROLOFF, Gustav, "Die Verhandlungen über ein deutsch-

englisches Bündnis 1898-1901," Pr. Jbb., 177, 1919, 345-64.

921. ROTHAN, G., "L'Alliance de L'Allemagne et L'Autriche en 1879," Rev. d'hist. dipl., 1, 1887, 61-64.

922. ROTHFELS, Hans, "Studien zur Annexionskrisis von 1908/1909," HZ, 148, 1933, 320-48.

923. SANDERSON, G. N., "The Anglo-German agreement of 1890 and the Upper Nile," EHR, 78, 1963, 49-72.

924. SCHMITT, Bernadotte E., "The origins of the war of 1914," J. Mod. Hist., 24, 1952, 69-74.

925. _____, "The origins of the war," J. Mod. Hist., 6, 1934, 160-74.

926. SHIPPEE, Lester B., "German-American relations 1890-1914," J. Mod. Hist., 8, 1936, 479-88.

927. _____, "Germany and the Spanish-American War," AHR, 30, 1924/25, 754-77.

928. SIEBURG, Heinz Otto, "Die Elsass-Lothringen-Frage in der deutsch-französischen Diskussion von 1871 bis 1944," Zs. f. Gesch. d. Saargegend, 17/18, 1969/70, 9-37.

929. SONTAG, Raymond J., "German Foreign Policy 1904-1906," AHR, 33, 1927/28, 278-301.

930. STEINBERG, Jonathan, "Germany and the Russo-Japanese War," AHR, 75, 1970, 1965-86.

931. STOECKER, Helmuth, "Der Eintritt Preussens und Deutschlands in die Reihe der in China bevorrechteten Mächte," Zs. f. Geschw., 5, 1957, 249-63.

932. THIELEN, Peter G., "Die Aussenpolitik des Deutschen Reiches 1890-1914, Literatur- und Forschungsbericht für die Jahre 1945-1960," WaG, 21, 1962, 27-48.

933. TREITSCHKE, Heinrich v., "Deutschland und die orientalische Frage," Pr. Jbb., 38, 1876, 664-75.

934. TRUMPENER, Ulrich, "Liman von Sanders and the German-Ottoman alliance," J. Contemp. Hist., 1(4), 1966, 179-92.

935. URBAS, Ernst, "Zur letzten Phase des Dreibundes," Pr. Jbb., 206, 1926, 269-80.

936. USHER, Roland G., "Austro-German relations since 1866," AHR, 23, 1917/18, 577-95.

937. VAGTS, Alfred, "Hopes and fears of an American-German war, 1870-1915," Pol. Sci. Q., 54, 1939, 514-35; 55, 1940, 53-76.

938. VALENTIN, Veit, "Foreign policy and high finance in the Bismarckian Period," J. Cen. Eur. Aff., 5, 1945, 165-75.

939. _____, "The vicissitudes of Franco-German relations during the last hundred years," Ger. Life Letters, 3, 1938/39, 184-94.

940. VOIGT, Johannes H., "Die Auseinandersetzung zwischen Theodor Mommsen und Max Müller über den Burenkrieg (Ein Beitrag zum deutsch-englischen Verhältnis um die Jahrhundertwende," GiWuU, 17, 1966, 65-77.

941. WALTHER, Heinrich, "Die deutsch-englischen Bündnisverhandlungen von 1901 und ihre Ergebnisse," Hist. Vjschr., 25, 1929-31, 602-35.

942. WENZ, Heinrich, "Kurd von Schlözer Ein Diplomat aus der
      Ära Bismarcks," Zeitwende, 4(2), 1928, 517-34.
943. WINCKLER, Martin, "Zur Bedeutung der Zeitung als Quelle
      für die internationalen Beziehungen in der Bismarckschen
      Epoche," Publizistik, 1971.

Friedrich von Holstein (1837-1909)

944. GOLTZ, Hans v. d., "Holstein," Zs. f. Pol., 27, 1937,
      217-25.
945. HALLGARTEN, G. W. F., "Fritz von Holsteins Geheimnis,"
      HZ, 177, 1954, 75-83.
946. HERZ, Ludwig, "Rätsel um Fritz von Holstein Glossen zu
      seinen Briefen an Ida von Stülpnagel," Pr. Jbb., 231,
      1933, 155-73.
947. LOHMEYER, Hans, "Holstein und Bismarck," WaG, 7, 1941,
      243-58.
948. PAPPENHEIM, Hans E., "Grossbeerenstrasse 40 Fritz von
      Holstein am Viktoriapark," Bär v. Ber., 21, 1972, 62-88.
949. RASSOW, Peter, "Schlieffen und Holstein," HZ, 173, 1952,
      297-313.
950. RICH, Norman, "Holstein and the Arnim Affair," J. Mod.
      Hist., 28, 1956, 35-54.
951. STOLBERG-WERNIGERODE, Otto Graf zu, "Friedrich von
      Holstein und die Krise der Reichsführung," Zeitwende, 31,
      1960, 298-308.
952. VOGEL, C. William, "The Holstein Enigma: A reappraisal
      of its origins," J. Mod. Hist., 14, 1942, 46-63.

Alfred von Kiderlein-Wächter (1852-1912)

953. ANDREAS, W., "Kiderlein-Wächter Randglossen zu seinem
      Nachlass," HZ, 132, 1925, 247-76.
954. BOLEN, C. Waldron, "Kiderlen's policy in Anglo-German
      naval conversations 1909-1912," J. Cen. Eur. Aff., 9,
      1949, 131-49.
955. GOOCH, G. P., "Kiderlen-Wächter," Cambridge Historical
      Journal, 5, 1935-37, 178-92.

Colonies, Imperialism

956. AYDELOTTE, William Osgood, "The first German colony
      and its diplomatic consequences," Cambridge Historical
      Journal, 5, 1935-37, 291-313.
957. BALD, D., "Probleme der Imperialismusforschung am
      Beispiel Deutsch-Ostafrikas," GiWuU, 22, 1971, 611-16.
958. BALLOD, Karl, "Die Bedeutung von Südbrasilien für die
      deutsche Kolonisation," Schmoll. Jb., 23, 1899, 631-55.
959. BAUMGART, W., "Die deutsche Kolonialherrschaft in Afrika.

54 German History and Civilization

Neue Wege der Forschung," VjHZG, 19, 1971, 468-81.
960. _____, "Eine neue Imperialismustheorie? Bemerkungen zu
dem Buche von Hans-Ulrich Wehler über Bismarcks Imperialismus," Militärgesch. Mitt., 2, 1971, 197-207.
961. BRUNSCHWIG, Henri, "Autour de quelques thèses récentes en
allemand sur la colonisation," RH, 244, 1970, 375-86.
962. BUSSE, Dr. Ludwig, "Die Begründung der deutschen Macht-
stellung in Ostafrika," Pr. Jbb., 58, 1886, 253-82.
963. CZAYA, Eberhard, "Interessenverbände und Propagandaorgani-
sationen für die Expansion des deutschen Imperialismus
nach Südafrika," Jb. f. Wgesch., 1970, (3), 57-83.
964. DANIELS, Emil, "Amerikanischer Imperialismus und deutsche
Vorkriegspolitik," Pr. Jbb., 188, 1922, 23-49.
965. ECKERT, Christian, "Die Bevölkerung tropischer Kolonien,
insbesondere Deutsch-Ostafrikas," Schmoll. Jb., 33, 1909,
1161-80.
966. FRANZ, Eckhardt, "Die Deutsch-Ostafrika-Akten im National-
archiv Dar es Salaam," Archivar, 1970.
967. FRICKE, Dieter, "Der deutsche Imperialismus und die Reichstagswahlen von 1907," Zs. f. Geschw., 9, 1961, 538-76.
968. GOSSWEILER, Kurt, "Die Rolle der Grossbanken im Imperialismus," Jb. f. Wgesch., 1971 (3), 35-54.
969. GRABOWSKY, Adolf, "Das Wesen der imperialistischen
Epoche," Zs. f. Pol., 12, 1922-23, 30-66.
970. GREWE, Wilhelm G., "Rechtsformen des ökonomischen Imperialismus im neunzehnten Jahrhundert," Zs. f. Pol., 31,
1941, 231-42.
971. GROOT, Emile de, "Great Britain and Germany in Zanzibar:
Consul Holmwood's papers, 1886-1887," J. Mod. Hist.,
25, 1953, 120-38.
972. GROSSMANN, Henryk, "Eine neue Theorie über Imperialismus und die soziale Revolution," Arch f. d. Gesch. d.
Soz., 13, 1928, 141-92.
973. GUTSCHE, Willibald, "Mitteleuropaplanungen in der Aussenpolitik des deutschen Imperialismus vor 1918," Zs. f.
Geschw., 20, 1972, 533-49.
974. HAGEN, Maximilian von, "Neue Literatur zur Geschichte der
deutschen Kolonialpolitik," Zs. f. Pol., 29, 1939, 121-26.
975. HALLGARTEN, G. F. W., "Wehler, der Imperialismus und
ich. Eine geharnischte Antwort," GiWuU, 23, 1972, 296-
303.
976. HENDERSON, Gavin B., "German colonial projects on the
Mosquito Coast, 1844-48," EHR, 59, 1944, 257-71.
977. HENDERSON, W. O., "British economic activity in the
German colonies 1884-1914," Econ. Hist. Rev., 15, 1945,
56-66.
978. _____, "German Colonization," Ger. Life Letters, 1,
1936/37, 241-54.
979. _____, "Germany's trade with her colonies, 1884-1914,"
Econ. Hist. Rev., 9, 1938-39, 1-16.
980. JERUSSALIMSKI, A. S., "Die Aussenpolitik und Diplomatie
des deutschen Imperialismus zu Beginn des 20. Jahrhun-

derts Probleme und Quellen," Zs. f. Geschw., 10, 1962, 575-97.

981. KENNEDY, P. M., "Bismarck's Imperialism: The case of Samoa, 1880-1890," Hist. J., 15, 1972, 261-83.

982. KIND, D. Aug., "Mission und Kolonialpolitik in den deutschen Schutzgebieten," Pr. Jbb., 142, 1910, 48-61.

983. KLEIN, Fritz, "Zur China-Politik des deutschen Imperialismus im Jahre 1900," Zs. f. Geschw., 8, 1960, 817-43.

984. KÖLLNER, Lutz, "Stand und Zukunft der Imperialismustheorie Anmerkungen zur neueren Beiträgen," Jb. f. Sozialw., 11, 1960, 103-24.

985. LOTH, H., "Das kaiserliche Deutschland und die frühe antikoloniale Bewegung in Afrika," Zs. f. Geschw., 20, 1972, 325-44.

986. MEDICK, Hans, "H. U. Wehler Bismarck und der Imperialismus," Hist. Theor., 10, 1971.

987. MIASKOWSKI, A. von, "Zur deutschen Kolonialpolitik der Gegenwart," Schmoll. Jb., 9, 1885, 271-83.

988. MOMMSEN, Wolfgang J., "Hans-Ulrich Wehler Bismarck und der Imperialismus," Cen. Eur. Hist., 2, 1969, 366-72.

989. MÜLLER, Günther, "Sozialdemokratie und Kolonialpolitik vor 1914," Aus Pol. u. Zeitgesch., 11, 1968, 16-24.

990. NAHMER, Ernst von der, "Deutsche Kolonisationspläne und -erfolge in der Türkei vor 1870," Schmoll. Jb., 40, 1916, 915-76.

991. PENNER, C. D., "Germany and the Transvaal before 1896," J. Mod. Hist., 12, 1940, 31-58.

992. RATHGEN, Karl, "Die Zollbegünstigung des Handels zwischen Deutschland und seinen Kolonien," Schmoll. Jb., 35, 1911, 227-50.

993. RATHMANN, Lothar, "Zur Legende vom 'antikolonialen' Charakter der Bagdadbahnpolitik in der wilhelminischen Ära des deutschen Monopolkapitalismus," Zs. f. Geschw., 9, 1961, 246-70.

994. RENOUVIN, Pierre, "Nationalisme et impérialisme en Allemagne de 1911 à 1914 Déprès un ouvrage récent," RH, 245, 1971, 63-72.

995. RICHTER, Siegfried and Rolf SONNEMANN, "Zur Problematik des Übergangs vom vormonopolistischen Kapitalismus zum Imperialismus in Deutschland," Jb. f. Wgesch., 1963 (II), 39-78.

996. _____, "Zur Rolle des Staates beim Übergang vom vormonopolistischen Kapitalismus zum Imperialismus in Deutschland," Jb. f. Wgesch., 1964 (II/III), 240-55.

997. ROHRBACH, Paul, "Deutsche Kolonial-Vorgeschichte," Zeitwende, 11 (1), 1934/35, 354-65.

998. _____, "Deutsche Welt- und Kolonialpolitik," Pr. Jbb., 152, 1913, 509-27.

999. _____, "Ostafrikanische Studien," Pr. Jbb., 135, 1909, 82-107, 276-317.

1000. SAPPER, Karl, "Deutsche als Kolonialpioniere in den Tropen," Zs. f. Pol., 29, 1939, 39-52.

1001. SCHLEIER, Hans, "Explizite Theorie, Imperialismus, Bismarck und Herr Wehler," Jb. f. Gesch., 6, 1972, 477-500.

1002. SCHRÖTER, Hermann, "Essen und die Kolonialfrage, Gründung und Geschichte der Sigipflanzung in Deutsch-Ostafrika," Tradition, 12, 1967, 526-42.

1003. SCHWERTFEGER, Bernhard, "Das deutsch-österreichische Bündnis vom 7. Oktober 1879 im Lichte der französischen Akten," Hist. Vjschr., 29, 1934-35, 145-76.

1004. STENGEL, Karl von, "Die deutschen Kolonialgesellschaften, ihre Verfassung und ihre rechtliche Stellung," Schmoll. Jb., 12, 1888, 219-84.

1005. STOKES, E., "Late nineteenth-century colonial expansion and the attack on the theory of economic imperialism. A case of mistaken identity?" Hist. J., 12, 1969, 285-301.

1006. STRANDMANN, Hartmut Pogge von, "Domestic origins of Germany's colonial expansion under Bismarck," Past and Present, 40(42), 1969, 140-59.

1007. TREITSCHKE, H. v., "Die ersten Versuche deutscher Kolonialpolitik," Pr. Jbb., 54, 1884, 555-66.

1008. WEBER, Alfred, "Deutschland und der wirtschaftliche Imperialismus," Pr. Jbb., 116, 1904, 298-324.

1009. WEGE, Fritz, "Die Anfänge der Herausbildung einer Arbeiterklasse in Südwestafrika unter der deutschen Kolonialherrschaft," Jb. f. Wgesch., 1969 (I), 183-221.

1010. _____, "Zur Sozialen Lage der Arbeiter Namibias unter der deutschen Kolonialherrschaft in den Jahren vor dem ersten Weltkrieg," Jb. f. Wgesch., 1971 (3), 201-18.

1011. WEHLER, Hans-Ulrich, "Bismarck's Imperialism 1863-1890," Past and Present, 41, 1970, 119-55.

1012. _____, "Noch einmal: Bismarcks Imperialismus," GiWuU., 23, 1972, 226-35.

1013. WERNER, Inge, "Zur Indienpolitik des deutschen Imperialismus seit dem Ende des 19. Jahrhunderts bis zum Ausbruch des ersten Weltkrieges," Zs. f. Geschw., 9, 1961, 271-99.

1014. WIEDEN, Helge Beider, "Wollschcafzuchte in Deutsch-Südwestafrika," VSW, 58, 1971, 67-87.

ECONOMIC AND SOCIAL HISTORY

General Studies

1015.   ADELMANN, Gerhard, "Führende Unternehmer im Rheinland und in Westfalen 1850-1914," Rhein. Vjsbll., 35, 1971, 335-52.

1016.   _____, "Studien zur sozialen Betriebsverfassung des Ruhrbergbaus von der Mitte des 19. Jahrhunderts bis zum Bergarbeiterstreik von 1889," Rhein. Vjsbll., 25, 1960, 1-41.

1017.   _____, "Strukturwandlungen der rheinischen Leinen- und Baumwollgewerbe zu Beginn der Industrialisierung," VSW, 53, 1966, 162-84.

1018.   _____, "Zur Herausgabe von Industriekarten für die Regierungsbezirke Arnsberg (1858) und Düsseldorf?" Rhein. Vjsbll., 29, 1964, 119-23.

1019.   ALBRECHT, Gerhard, "Die Ausgabenverteilung im Haushalte des Arbeiters und des mittleren Beamten," Schmoll. Jb., 38, 1914, 1389-1428.

1020.   ARNSTEIN, Walter L., ed., "A German view of English society: 1851," Victorian Studies, 16, 1972/73, 183-203.

1021.   ASCHER, Abraham, "Baron von Stumm, Advocate of feudal capitalism," J. Cen. Eur. Aff., 22, 1962, 271-85.

1022.   AUGEL, Pierre, "Les structures économiques et sociales de l'Allemagne Bismarckienne," Rev. d'hist. econ. soc., 41, 1963, 374-90.

1023.   BACH, Adolf, "Der Kampf gegen die deutschen Spielbanken des 19. Jahrhunderts," Schmoll. Jb., 46, 1922, 785-811.

1024.   BALLOD, Carl, "Deutschlands wirtschaftliche Entwickelung seit 1890," Schmoll. Jb., 24, 1900, 493-516.

1025.   BARKHAUSEN, Max, "Die sieben bedeutendsten Fabrikanten der Roerdepartements im Jahre 1810," Rhein. Vjsbll., 25, 1960, 100-13.

1026.   BARLEBEN, Ilse, "Ein Industriebetrieb in Klostermauern," Rhein. Vjsbll., 24, 1960, 114-20.

1027.   BAUDIS, Dieter, Horst HANDKE and Rudolf SCHRÖDER, "Der Unternehmer in der Sicht der westdeutschen Firmen- und Wirtschaftsgeschichte," Zs. f. Geschw., 11, 1963, 78-103.

1028.   BEHRENS, Hedwig, "Der erste Kokschochofen des rheinisch-westfälischen Industriegebietes auf der Friedrich-Wilhelms Hütte in Mülheim a. d. Ruhr," Rhein. Vjsbll., 25, 1966, 121-25.

1029.   BETTEX, Albert, "The turn of the century according to
        recent memoirs," Ger. Life Letters, 3, 1938/39, 138-44.
1030.   BEUTIN, Ludwig, "Die Massengesellschaft' im 19. Jahr-
        hundert Eine terminologische Besinnung," WaG, 17, 1959,
        69-89.
1031.   BEUTNER, G. F., "Der Preisbegriff und die soziale
        Frage," Pr. Jbb., 23, 1869, 501-22.
1032.   "BIBLIOGRAPHIE der Schriften von Jürgen Kuczynski," Jb.
        f. Wgesch., 1964 (2-3), 505-50.
1033.   BISSING, Wilhelm Moritz Frhr. v., "Autoritärer Staat und
        pluralistische Gesellschaft in den ersten Jahrzehnten des
        Bismarckischen Reiches," Schmoll. Jb., 83, 1963, 17-45.
1034.   BLESSING, Werner K., "Zur Analyse politischer Mentalität
        und Ideologie der Unterschichten im 19. Jahrhundert,"
        Zs. f. bayer. LG., 34, 1971, 768-816.
1035.   BOEHME, Friedrich, "175 Jahre Isselburger Hütte AG
        Chronik einer Eisengiesserei und Maschinenfabrik am
        Niederrhein," Tradition, 14, 1969, 225-29.
1036.   BÖHMERT, Victor, "Deutschlands wirtschaftliche Neugestal-
        tung," Pr. Jbb., 18, 1866, 269-304.
1037.   BOG, Ingomar, "Wirtschaft und Gesellschaft im Zeitalter der
        industriellen Revolution," GiWuU., 20, 1969, 193-224.
1038.   BONDI, Gerhard, "Zur Vorgeschichte der 'kleindeutschen
        Lösung' 1866-1871 Eine wirtschaftshistorische Betrach-
        tung," Jb. f. Wgesch., 1966 (2), 11-33.
1039.   BORCHARDT, Knut, "Zur Frage des Kapitalmangels in der
        ersten Hälfte des 19. Jahrhunderts in Deutschland," Jbb.
        f. Nationalökon. u. Stat., 173, 1961, 401-21.
1040.   BORST, Otto, "Staat und Unternehmer in der Frühzeit der
        württembergischen Industrie," Tradition, 11, 1966, 105-
        26.
1041.   BRAUN, Dr. Karl, "Gewerbe- Zug- und Verehelichungs-
        Freiheit im Norddeutschen Bunde," Pr. Jbb., 21, 1868,
        435-66.
1042.   BRIEFS, Goetz A., "The economic philosophy of Romanti-
        cism," J. Hist. Ideas, 2, 1941, 279-300.
1043.   BRINKMANN, Carl, "Weltpolitik und Weltwirtschaft im 19.
        Jahrhundert," Weltwirtsch. Arch., 16, 1920-21, 186-211.
1044.   BRODNITZ, Georg, "Bibliography: Recent work in German
        economic history (1900-1927)," Econ. Hist. Rev., 1,
        1927-28, 322-45.
1045.   BUCKENMAIER, Anton Heinrich, "Eugenie Fürstin von Hohen-
        zollern-Hechingen," Zeitsch. f. Hohenzollerische Gesch.,
        1965.
1046.   BÜHRIG, Wilhelm, "Ein Beitrag zur preussischen Wasser-
        wirtschaft und Wassergesetzgebung der letzten hundert
        Jahre," Schmoll. Jb., 38, 1914, 1289-1326.
1047.   BUNDSCHUH, Otto, "Die wirtschaftliche Entwicklung der
        deutschen Kommanditgesellschaften auf Aktien," Schmoll.
        Jb., 38, 1914, 1327-60.
1048.   CAMERON, Rondo E., "Some French contributions to the in-
        dustrial development of Germany, 1840-1870," J. Econ.
        Hist., 16, 1956, 281-321.

1049.	CECIL, Lamar, "The creations of nobles in Prussia, 1871-1918," AHR, 75, 1970, 757-95.

1050.	CHICKERING, Roger, "A voice of moderation in Imperial Germany: The 'Verband für Internationale Verständigung' 1911-1914," J. Contemp. Hist., 8, 1973, 147-64.

1051.	CONZE, Werner, "Staat und Gesellschaft in der Frührevolutionären Epoche Deutschlands," HZ, 186, 1958, 1-34.

1052.	CRONER, Dr. Johannes, "Die Entwicklung der deutschen Börsen von 1870-1914," Pr. Jbb., 192, 1923, 343-56; 193, 1923, 304-14.

1053.	CROON, Helmuth, "Die Einwirkungen der Industriealisierung auf die gesellschaftliche Schichtung der Bevölkerung im rheinisch-westfälischen Industriegebiet," Rhein. Vjsbll., 20, 1955, 301-16.

1054.	DAHRENDORF, Rolf, "Demokratie und Sozialstruktur in Deutschland," Eur. J. Soc., 1, 1960, 86ff.

1055.	"Der DEUTSCHE Handelstag und seine drei Generalversammlungen," Pr. Jbb., 16, 1865, 554-88.

1056.	DÖSSLER, E., "Eisenhandel im südlichen Westfalen und seiner Nachbarschaft in der vorindustriellen Zeit," Westfälische Forsch., 21, 1968.

1057.	DRAHN, Ernst, "George Weerth auf dem internationalen Kongress der Volkswirte in Brüssel 1847," Arch. f. d. Gesch. d. Soz., 11, 1923, 186-95.

1058.	DREYFUS, François-G., "Bilan Économique des Allemagnes en 1815," Rev. d'hist. econ. soc., 43, 1965, 433-64.

1059.	_____, Économie et politique dans les Allemagnes pendant la première moitié du xixe siècle," Annales, 18, 1963, 363-79.

1060.	EAGLY, Robert V., "Business cycle trends in France and Germany, 1869-79: A new appraisal," Weltwirtsch. Arch., 99, 1967, 90-106.

1061.	ENGELSING, Rolf, "Dienstbotenlektüre im 18. und 19. Jahrhundert in Deutschland," Int. Rev. Soc. Hist., 13, 1968, 384-429.

1062.	_____, "Die Häfen an der Südküste der Ostsee und der Ostwestverkehr in der ersten Hälfte des 19. Jahrhunderts," VSW, 58, 1971, 24-66.

1063.	_____, "Das häusliche Personal in der Epoche der Industrialisierung," Jb. f. Sozialw., 20, 1969, 84-121.

1064.	_____, "Probleme der Lebenshaltung in Deutschland im 18. und 19. Jahrhundert," ZgesStw., 126, 1970, 290-308.

1065.	_____, "Die Vorgeschichte der Gründung des Norddeutschen Lloyd," Tradition, 2, 1957, 77-100.

1066.	_____, "Die wirtschaftliche und soziale Differenzierung der deutschen kaufmännischen Angestellten 1690-1900," ZgesStw., 123, 1967, 347-80, 482-514.

1067.	FAY, S. B., "State ownership in Germany," Current History, 18, 1950, 129-33.

1068.	FEDER, Ernest, "La reine Victoria et ses parents de Berlin," Rev. d'hist. mod., 12, 1937, 126-39.

1069.	FEIG, Johannes, "Deutschlands gewerbliche Entwickelung seit dem Jahre 1882," ZgesStw., 56, 1900, 658-95.

1070. FISCHER, Alfred, "Bibliographie von Veröffentlichungen zur Geschichte der Kapitalistischen Unternehmen, die nach 1945 in Westdeutschland und Westberlin erschienen sind," Jb. f. Wgesch., 1960 (2), 355-402; 1962 (3), 207-72.

1071. _____, "Bibliographie von Veröffentlichungen zur Geschichte der Kapitalistischen Unternehmen, die nach 1945 in Westdeutschland und Westberlin erschienen sind," Jb. f. Wgesch., 1968 (2), 407-423.

1072. FISCHER, Ernst, "Meister Lucius und Brüning, die Gründer der Farbwerke Hoechst AG," Tradition, 3, 1958, 65-78.

1073. FISCHER, Wolfram, "Die Anfänge der Fabrik von St. Blasien (1809-1848) Ein Beitrag zur Frühgeschichte der Industrialisierung," Tradition, 7, 1962, 59-78.

1074. _____, "Ansätze zur Industrialisierung in Baden 1770-1870," VSW, 47, 1960, 186-231.

1075. _____, "Karl Mez (1808-1877) Ein badischer Unternehmer im 19. Jahrhundert," Tradition, 1, 1956, 26-34; 2, 1957, 132-43.

1076. _____, "Konjunkturen und Krisen im Ruhrgebiet seit 1840 und die wirtschaftspolitische Willensbildung der Unternehmer," Westfäl. Forsch., 21, 1968, 42-53.

1077. _____, "Social tension at early stages of industrialization," Comp. Stud. Soc. Hist., 9, 1966, 64-83.

1078. _____, "Some recent developments of business history in Germany, Austria and Switzerland," Bus. Hist. Rev., 37, 1963, 416-36.

1079. _____, "Soziale Unterschichten im Zeitalter der Frühindustrialisierung," Int. Rev. Soc. Hist., 8, 1963, 415-35.

1080. _____, "Die Stellung der preussischen Bergrechtsreform von 1851-1865 in der Wirtschafts- und Sozialverfassung des 19. Jahrhunderts," ZgesStw., 117, 1961, 521-34.

1081. FREYER, Hans, "Das soziale Ganze und die Freiheit des Einzelnen unter den Bedingungen des industriellen Zeitalters," HZ, 183, 1957, 97-115.

1082. FRICKE, Rolf, "Die geistigen Voraussetzungen der Industrialisierung im 19. und 20. Jahrhundert," Schmoll. Jb., 85, 1965, 257-72.

1083. FRIEDRICH, Fritz, "Die Prinzessin von Preussen auf Grund ihres literarischen Nachlasses (1840-1850)," Pr. Jbb., 156, 1914, 285-307.

1084. FRIESE, Alfred, "Zwischen Mettnau und Eugensberg unveröffentlichte Briefe Joseph Viktor von Scheffels an Amélie Gräffin von Reichenbach-Lessonitz," ZGORh, 106, 1958, 437-71.

1085. FUCHS, Konrad, "Die Bismarckhütte in Oberschlesien Ein Beitrag zur oberschlesischen Industriegeschichte in der achtziger Jahren des 19. Jahrhunderts," Tradition, 15, 1970, 255-72.

1086. _____, "Ursachen und Auswirkungen des wirtschaftlichen Strukturwandels im westlichen Siegerland in der zweiten Hälfte des 19. und im Anfang des. 20. Jahrhunderts," Jb. f. Gesch. Kunst d. MRh, 11, 1959, 34-41.

1087. _____, "Zur Bedeutung des Herzogtums Nassau als Wirtschaftsfaktor 1815-1866," Nass. Ann., 78, 1967, 167-76.

1088. _____, "Zur Verkehrspolitik des Herzogtums Nassau 1815-1866," Nass. Ann., 77, 1966, 134-41.

1089. FUJISE, Hiroshi, "Deutschlands Entwicklung zum Industrie- und Welthandelsstaat ... 1850 bis 1878," Scripta Mercaturae, 1970.

1090. GAHLEN, Bernhard and Helmut HESSE, "The growth of the net domestic product in Germany 1850-1913. Calculation of macroeconomic production functions," Ger. Econ. Rev., 4, 1966, 328-31.

1091. _____, "Das Wachstum des Nettoinland-Produkts in Deutschland 1850-1913," ZgesStw., 121, 1965, 452-97.

1092. GALL, Lothar, "Staat und Wirtschaft in der Reichsgründungszeit," HZ, 209, 1969, 616-30.

1093. GEBSATTEL, Ludwig von, "Lepold, Prinz von Bayern," Gelbe Hefte, 4, 1927-28, 471-519.

1094. GEHRING, Paul, "Das Wirtschaftsleben unter Koenig Wilhelm I," Zs. f. Württbg. LG., 9, 1949, 196-256.

1095. GERICKE, Hans Otto, "Der Charakter der Produktions Verhältnisse im Messingwerk Niedereuerbach/Vgtl. von 1600 bis zum Mitte des 19. Jahrhunderts," Jb. f. Wgesch., 1963 (3), 162-201.

1096. GEYER, Ph., "Untersuchungen über Quellen und Umfang des allgemeinen Wohlstandes in Deutschland," Schmoll. Jb., 4, 1880, 1-53, 161-89.

1097. GIGNOUX, C.-J., "L'industrialisme de Saint-Simon a Walther Rathenau," Rev. d'hist. econ. soc., 11, 1923, 200-17.

1098. GOLDBECK, Gustav, "Geschichte des Werkes Magirus, Ulm Hundert Jahre im Dienste des Brandschutzes 1864-1951," Tradition, 9, 1964, 241-60; 10, 1965, 8-22.

1099. _____, "Statistische Zahlen zur Geschichtlichen Entwicklung des Verbrennungsmotors," Tradition, 3, 1958, 113-19.

1100. GROH, Dieter, "L'Échec de la 'Fondation interne du Reich' institutions, économie et politique sociale du Deuxième Reich," Rev. d'hist. mod., 19, 1972, 269-82.

1101. GRUMBACH, Franz von and Heinz KÖNIG, "Beschäftigung und Löhne der deutschen Industriewirtschaft 1888/1954," Weltwirtsch. Arch., 79, 1957, 125-55.

1102. GRUNDMANN, Günther, "Das Schicksal eines mitteldeutschen Bergmannes in Oberschlesien (Friedrich Wilhelm Grundmann in Katlowitz)," Hamb. Mittel- u. ostdt. Forsch., 3, 1961, 9-26.

1103. _____, "Schlösser und Villen des 19. Jahrhunderts von Unternehmern in Schlesien," Tradition, 10, 1965, 149-62.

1104. GÜNTHER, Ernst, "Der Haushalt des kleinen Mittelstandes und der Arbeiter," Schmoll. Jb., 34, 1916, 253-77.

1105. _____, "Die internationale Stellung der deutschen Eisenindustrie," Schmoll. Jb., 38, 1914, 1429-94.

1106. GÜNTHER, Wilhelm, "Zur Geschichte der Eisenindustrie in der Nordeifel," Rhein. Vjsbll., 30, 1965, 309-33.

1107. HAAN, Heiner, "Zur historischen Wirtschaftskarte des

62 German History and Civilization

bayerischen Rheinkreises 1820," Gesch. Landesk., 1968.
1108. HAERING, Dr. Hermann, "Zur neueren Geschichte des deutschen Bürgertums," Pr. Jbb., 187, 1922, 80-105.
1109. "HANNOVERS Staatswirthschaft in den letzen zwölf Jahren," Pr. Jbb., 6, 1860, 583-93.
1110. HARRAS, Hans, "Theodor v. Bernhardi und die politische Ökonomie," Schmoll. Jb., 60, 1936, 129-57.
1111. HATZFELD, Lutz, "Der Anfang der deutschen Drahtindustrie," Tradition, 6, 1961, 241-51.
1112. _____, "Der Anfang der deutschen Röhrenindustrie," Tradition, 5, 1960, 241-57.
1113. _____, "Das Phoenix-Rheinrohr-Archiv als Problem industrieller Verwaltung," Duisburger Forschungen, 8, 1965, 130-47.
1114. HAUSER, Oswald, "Einige Grundzüge aus der Entwicklung des Ruhrgebiets," GiWuU, 18, 1967, 449-56.
1115. HELLWIG, Fritz, "Louis Pièttes Entwurf einer Fabrikordnung," Tradition, 7, 1962, 124-40.
1116. HELMREICH, E. C., "Prussian economic policy foundations of German unification," Current History, 16, 1949, 151-55.
1117. HENDERSON, W. O., "England und die Industrialisierung Deutschlands," ZgesStw., 108, 1952, 264-94.
1118. _____, "Peter Beuth and the rise of Prussian industry 1810-1845," Econ. Hist. Rev., 8, 1955-56, 222-31.
1119. _____, "Prince Smith and Free Trade in Germany," Econ. Hist. Rev., 2, 1949-50, 295-302.
1120. _____, "William Thomas Mulvany: An Irish pioneer in the Ruhr," EEH, 5, 1952-53, 107-20.
1121. HENDINGER, H., "Vom Gerberhandwerk zur Lederindustrie. Eine Untersuchung des Bedeutungs- und Strukturwandels der Gerberei in vier Jahrhunderten an Beispielen aus Franken und Schwaben," Jb. f. fränk. Landesforschg., 30, 1970, 15-82.
1122. HERZOG, Bodo, "Wilhelm Lueg, 1792-1864," Tradition, 16, 1971, 49-71.
1123. HINTZE, O., "Roschers politische Entwickelungstheorie," Schmoll. Jb., 21, 1897, 767-811.
1124. _____, ed., "Zwei Denkschriften aus dem Jahre 1800 über die preussische Seidenindustrie," FBPG, 8, 1895, 103-42.
1125. HÖFELE, Karl H., "Selbstverständnis und Zeitkritik des deutschen Bürgertums vor dem ersten Weltkrieg," ZRGG, 8, 1956, 40-56.
1126. HOETZSCH, O., "Kaiserin Maria Alexandrowna von Russland, geb. Prinzessin Maria von Hessen 1824-80," Arch. f. hessische Gesch., 21, 1940, 81ff.
1127. HOFFMANN, Walther G., "Die unverteilten Gewinne der Kapitalgesellschaften in Deutschland 1871-1957," ZgesStw., 115, 1959, 271-91.
1128. HOFMANN, Werner, "Das Phänomen der wirtschaftliche Macht in der neueren Literatur," Jb. f. Sozialw., 13, 1962, 170-95.

1129. HUCK, Jürgen, "Die Kalker Trieurfabrik und Frabrik
       gelochter Bleche Mayer & Cie.," Tradition, 15, 1970,
       296-310.
1130. HUTTER, P.-J., "La Famine de Coton en Westphalie 1861-
       1865," Rev. d'hist. econ. soc., 20, 1932, 392-405.
1131. HYCKEL, Georg, "Die Industrieanlagen der Herrschaft Rati-
       bor (Nach dem Etat von 1823)," Jb. d. Schles.-Fried.-
       Wilh. Univ. z. Breslau, 10, 1965, 138-49.
1132. IPSEN, G., "Landkreis im Sauerland: Meschede 1818-1915.
       Soziale Beharrung am Rande der grossen Industrie," Zs.
       f. Agrargesch., 19, 1971, 197-210.
1133. JANSEN, Heiner, "Zur Geschichte der Fabrikentabelle von
       1820," Rhein. Vjsbll., 30, 1965, 346-50.
1134. JEISMANN, Karl-Ernst, "Staat und Gesellschaft in Preus-
       sen," GiWuU., 21, 1970, 453-70.
1135. KAISER, Wilhelm, "Die Anfänge der fabrikmässig organi-
       sierten Industrie in Baden," ZGORh., 85, 1932-33, 612-
       35.
1136. KEIBEL, Rudolf, "Aus hundert Jahren deutscher Eisen- und
       Stahlindustrie," Schmoll. Jb., 38, 1914, 889-937.
1137. KELLENBENZ, Hermann, "Handelshochschulen--Betriebs-
       wirtschaft-Wirtschaftsarchive," Tradition, 10, 1965,
       301-09.
1138. _____, "Unternehmertum im Südwestdeutschland," Tra-
       dition, 10, 1965, 163-88.
1139. KLEIN, Ernst, "Die Hohenheimer Ackergerätefabrik (1819-
       1904)," Zs. f. Württbg. LG., 22, 1963, 302-76.
1140. _____, "Der Staat als Unternehmer im saarländischen
       Steinkohlenbergbau 1750-1850," VSW, 57, 1970, 323-49.
1141. KOCH, Heinrich, "75 Jahre Röhrenwerke Bous (SAAR),"
       Tradition, 8, 1963, 15-28.
1142. KOCKA, Jürgen, "Industrielles Management: Konzeptionen
       und Modelle in Deutschland vor 1914," VSW, 56, 1969,
       332-72.
1143. KÖTZ, Günter, "Besucherzahlen des Emser Bades in 19.
       und 20. Jahrhundert," Nass. Ann., 82, 1971.
1144. KOLLMANN, Dr. Paul, "Die deutsche Gewerbe-Aufnahme
       vom 1. Dezember 1875 in ihren Hauptergebnissen,"
       Schmoll. Jb., 6, 1882, 443-562.
1145. KRINGS, Wilfried and Wolfgang ZORN, "Nachtrag zur his-
       torischen Wirtschaftskarte um 1820," Rhein. Vjsbll., 35,
       1971, 274-87.
1146. KRUSE, Alfred, "Adolf Weber zum Gedächtnis," Schmoll.
       Jb., 83, 1963, 257-68.
1147. KUBITSCHEK, Helmut, "Zu Tendenzen des staatsmonopolis-
       tischen Kapitalismus in Deutschland vor dem ersten Welt-
       krieg," Jb. f. Wgesch., 1963 (2), 103-42.
1148. KUCZYNSKI, Jürgen, "Zur Geschichte der Bürgerlichen
       Krisentheorie," Jb. f. Wgesch., 1960 (1), 29-52.
1149. _____, "Zum Problem der Industriellen Revolution," Zs.
       f. Geschw., 4, 1956, 501-24.
1150. KUCZYNSKI, Thomas, "Die Stellung der deutschen Teerfar-
       benindustrie zum Stoff- und Verfahrenspatent in der Zeit

         bis ... 1891," Jb. f. Wgesch., 1970 (4), 115-40.

1151.   KÜHN, Joachim, "Aus der preussischen Hofgesellschaft der Biedermeierzeit Briefe aus dem Familienkreis des Kgl. Flügeladjutanten Oberst von Below," Bär v. Ber., 17, 1968, 54-76.

1152.   _____, "Eine Liebesaffäre im preussischen Königshaus Prinz August und Delphine de Custine," Bär v. Ber., 18, 1969, 7-35.

1153.   KUHLMANN, Leopold, "Freundschaft und Liebe vor Hundert Jahren," Arch. f. KuG., 11, 1914, 363-76.

1154.   KULISCHER, Josef, "Die Ursachen des Übergangs vom der Handarbeit zur maschinellen Betriebsweise um die Wende des 18. und in der ersten Hälfte des 19. Jahrhunderts," Schmoll. Jb., 30, 1906, 31-79.

1155.   KURS, Major a. d., "Schiffahrtsstrassen im Deutschen Reich, ihre bisherige und zukünftige Entwickelung und ihre gegenwärtige wirtschaftliche und finanzielle Ausnutzung," Jbb. f. Nationalökon. u. Stat., 65, 1895, 641-705.

1156.   KUSKE, Bruno, "Die Grundzüge der Wirtschaftsentwicklung am Niederrhein vom Mittelalter bis zur Gegenwart," Ann. Niederrhein, 115, 1929, 38-60.

1157.   LAMBI, Ivo N., "The protectionist interests of the German iron and steel industry, 1873-1879," J. Econ. Hist., 22, 1962, 59-70.

1158.   LANDGRAF, Dr., "Industrielle Fachverbände, ihre Entstehung, ihre Aufgaben, ihre Erfolge," Jbb. f. Nationalökon. u. Stat., 77, 1901, 343-65.

1159.   LANGE, Dr. Ernst, "Die Ursuchen der Betriebsunfälle in der deutschen Industrie und Landwirtschaft," Arch. f. Sozialw. u. Sozialpol., 11, 1897, 143-60.

1160.   LANGKAU, Götz, "Die deutsche Sektion in Paris," Int. Rev. Soc. Hist., 17, 1972, 103-50.

1161.   LASLOWSKI, Ernst, "Die Grafen von Ballestrem als oberschlesische Bergherren," H. Jb., 77, 1957, 517-21.

1162.   LASPEYRES, E., "Hamburger Waarenpreise 1851-1863 und die califorinsch-australischen Goldentdeckungen seit 1848," Jbb. f. Nationalökon. u. Stat., 3, 1864, 81-118, 209-36.

1163.   LAUES, Theodor, "Die deutsche Waaren-Ein- und Ausfuhr und die Durchfuhr durch das Deutsche Reich von 1880 bis 1882," Schmoll. Jb., 8, 1884, 1189-1213.

1164.   LEDEBUR, Leopold von, "Die in dem Zeitraum von 1740 bis 1840 erloschenen altadeligen Geschlechter der Mark Brandenburg," Märkische Forschungen, 2, 1843, 374-88.

1165.   LEIPOLDT, Johannes, "Soziale Umschichtungen vor und während der industriellen Revolution in Reichenbach im Vogtland," Jb. f. Regionalgesch., 3, 1968, 230-40.

1166.   LENZ, Friedrich, "Die soziale Geschichte der Schultheiss-Brauerei," Arch. f. Sozialw. u. Sozialpol., 37, 1913, 175-214.

1167.   LEWALD, Ursula, "Die Entwicklung der ländlichen Textilindustrie im Rheinland und in Schlesien," Zs. f. Ostforsch., 10, 1961, 601-30.

1168.   LIEFMANN, Robert, "Die internationale Organisation des
        Frankfurter Metallhandels," Weltwirtsch. Arch., 1, 1913,
        108-22.
1169.   LIERMANN, Hans, "Vom Bau des Ludwig-Kanal vor der
        Donau zum Main," Zs. f. bayer. LG., 33, 1970, 257-71.
1170.   LÖTZKE, Helmut, "Quellen zur wirtschaftsgeschichte in der
        Epoche des Imperialismus im Deutschen Zentralarchiv
        Potsdam," Jb. f. Wgesch., 1961 (1), 239-83.
1171.   LOOSE, Hans-Dieter, "Pläne für ein Hanseatisches 'Elbe-
        Weser-Reich' vom Jahre 1810," Zeitsch. d. Vereins f.
        Hamburgische Gesch., 55, 1969, 189-203.
1172.   LOTZ, W., "The effect of protection on some German in-
        dustries," Econ. J., 14, 1904, 515-26.
1173.   LUNTOWSKI, Gustav, "Lüneburgs Unternehmer im 19. Jahr-
        hundert Zur neueren Wirtschafts- und Sozialgeschichte
        einer Mittelstadt," Tradition, 11, 1966, 201-17.
1174.   MARQUARDT, Ernst, "Das Hotel Marquardt in Stuttgart
        1840-1938 Ein Firma- und familiengeschichtlicher Ver-
        such," Tradition, 10, 1965, 49-66, 127-42; 11, 1966,
        70-89.
1175.   MARTIN, Paul Christoph, "Die Entstehung des preussischen
        Aktiengesetzes von 1843," VSW, 56, 1969, 499-542.
1176.   MARTIN, Paul C., "Monetäre Probleme der Frühhindus-
        trialisierung am Beispiel der Rheinprovinz (1816-1848),"
        Jbb. f. Nationalökon. u. Stat., 181, 1967/68, 117-50.
1177.   MASCHKE, Erich, "Die Industrialisierung Deutschlands im
        Spiegel der Parlamentszusammensetzungen von 1848 bis
        Heute," Tradition, 10, 1965, 230-45.
1178.   MEISEN, Karl, "Rheinisches Volkstum als Forschungsaufgabe
        Rückblick und Ausblick," Ann. Niederrhein, 122, 1933,
        1-50.
1179.   MEITZEN, August, "Die Frage des Kanalbaues in Preus-
        sen," Schmoll. Jb., 8, 1004, 751-821.
1180.   MENDELS, Franklin F., "Proto-industrialization: The first
        phase of the industrialization process," J. Econ. Hist.,
        32, 1972, 241-61.
1181.   MERKLE, J., ed., "Briefwechsel der Grossfürstin Katharina
        Paulowna, Königin Württemberg, mit Johann Georg Müller
        in Schaffhaussen," Württ. Vtljh. f. LG., 5, 1896, 127-
        48.
1182.   METELMANN, Ernst, "J. B. Metzlersche Verlagsbuchhand-
        lung 1682-1957," Tradition, 2, 1957, 247-64.
1183.   MINCHINTON, Walter, "The diffussion of the Tinplate Manu-
        facturer," Econ. Hist. Rev., 9, 1956-57, 349-58.
1184.   MITGAU, Hermann, "Die GewehrFabrik zu Herzberg (Harz)
        (1739-1876) und die Hof-Rüstmeisterfolge der Tanner,"
        Tradition, 6, 1961, 271-84.
1185.   MOHRMANN, Eili, "Johann Friedrich Benzenberg Ein
        Sprecher der frühen rheinischen Bourgeoisie," Jb. f.
        Wgesch., 1970 (1), 75-96.
1186.   MOLL, Ewald, "Die preussische Alaunhüttenindustrie und
        das Alaunsyndikat von 1836-1844," Schmoll. Jb., 29,
        1905, 265-309, 593-645.

1187.   MOOD, Fulmer, "The rise of official statistical cartography
        in Austria, Prussia and the United States, 1855-1872,"
        Ag. Hist., 20, 1946, 209-25.
1188.   MÜLLER, Klaus, "Das Rheinland als Gegenstand der his-
        torischen Wahlsoziologie," Ann. Niederrhein, 167, 1965,
        124-42.
1189.   MÜLLER, Rolf, "1844-1910 Gründer und Unternehmer in
        der deutschen Dynamitindustrie," Tradition, 8, 1963, 84-
        94.
1190.   MÜLLER-CLEMM, Hellmuth, "Hans Clemm," Tradition, 6,
        1961, 22-28.
1191.   NASSE, Erwin, "Die Währungsfrage in Deutschland," Pr.
        Jbb., 55, 1885, 295-345.
1192.   NEHER, Franz Ludwig, "Friedrich Deckel Ein Wegbereiter
        der Photoindustrie," Tradition, 9, 1964, 6-22.
1193.   NEUMANN, Ina, "Bibliographie zur Firmengeschichte und
        Unternehmerbiographie," Tradition, 12, 1967, 441-48,
        545-52; 13, 1968, 48-56, 153-60, 265-72; 14, 1969, 57-
        64, 216-24, 339-46.
1194.   NUSSBAUM, Helga, "Versuche zur Reichsgesetzlichen Rege-
        lung der deutschen Elektrizitätswirtschaft und ihrer Über-
        führung in Reichseigentum 1909 bis 1914," Jb. f. Wgesch.,
        1968 (2), 117-203.
1195.   OBERMANN, Karl, "Zur Frage der unbedingten Übereinstim-
        mung der Produktionsverhältnisse mit dem Charakter der
        Produtivkräfte in Deutschland im 19. Jahrhundert," Zs.
        f. Geschw., 1, 1953, 737-54.
1196.   O'BOYLE, Lenore, "The middle class in Western Europe
        1815-1848," AHR, 71, 1965-66, 826-45.
1197.   OVERBECK, Hermann, "Die Saarwirtschaft," VSW, 27,
        1934, 209-34.
1198.   PACYNA, Günther, "Die Auswirkungen der Kontinentalsperre
        auf die Wirtschaftsstruktur Ostdeutschlands," Alt-Preus-
        sische Forschungen, 16, 1939, 77-110.
1199.   PAPPENHEIM, Max, "Das geltende deutsche Privatseerecht
        und seine Weiterentwicklung," Weltwirtsch. Arch., 2,
        1913, 69-87.
1200.   PARKER, William N., "Entrepreneurship, industrial or-
        ganization, and economic growth: a German example,"
        J. Econ. Hist., 14, 1954, 380-400.
1201.   PERLICK, Alfons, "Hegenscheidt und Caro Zur Geschichte
        der beiden Unternehmergruppen im oberschlesischen In-
        dustrierevier," Tradition, 8, 1963, 172-92.
1202.   PESMAZOGLU, J. S., "A note on the cyclical fluctuations
        of the volume of German home investment, 1880-1913,"
        ZgesStw., 107, 1951, 151-71.
1203.   _____, "Some international aspects of German cyclical
        fluctuations, 1880-1913," Weltwirtsch. Arch., 64, 1950,
        77-110.
1204.   PETTO, W., "Zur Geschichte der Eisenindustrie im
        Schwarzwälder Hochwald und ihrer Unternehmerfamilien
        von ihren Anfängen bis 1870," Zs. f. Gesch. d. Saarge-
        gend, 17/18, 1969/70, 112-70.

1205. PETZINA, Dieter, "Materialien zum sozialen und wirtschaftlichen Wandel in Deutschland seit dem Ende des 19. Jahrhunderts, " VjHZG, 17, 1969, 308-38.

1206. PHILIPPI, Dr. E., "Die Schwankungen des Volkswohlstandes im deutschen Reiche, " Pr. Jbb., 52, 1883, 313-41; 54, 1884, 213-27, 418-44; 55, 1885, 414-32; 56, 1885, 301-10.

1207. PÖNICKE, Herbert, "Friedrich Georg Wieck: Leben und Werk eines Unternehmers und Wirtschaftspolitikers in der ersten Phase der industriellen Revolution, " Hamb. Mittel- u. ostdt. Forsch., 7, 1970, 207-50.

1208. _____ , "Die Geschichte der Textilgewerbe der Stadt Reichenbach im Vogtland im Zeitalter der industriellen Revolution, " Hamb. Mittel- u. ostdt. Forsch., 4, 1963, 268-82.

1209. _____ , "Zwei Entscheidende Jahrzehnte Sächsischer Wirtschaftgeschichte (1850-1870), " Hamb. Mittel- u. ostdt. Forsch., 1, 1957, 189-206.

1210. "PREUSSEN und das Meer, " Pr. Jbb., 1, 1858, 433-44, 577-93; 2, 1858, 7-26, 533-42; 4, 1859, 163-78; 6, 1861, 512-25.

1211. PÜTZ, Theodor, "Karl Knies also Vorbereiter eines politischen Volkswirtschaftstheorie, " Schmoll. Jb., 60, 1936, 1-31.

1212. RADANDT, Hans, "Bibliographie selbstständiger Schriften zur Geschichte der Fabriken und Werke, die nach 1945 im Gebiet der Deutschen Demokratischen Republik erschienen sind, " Jb. f. Wgesch., 1960 (1), 353-64; 1961 (1), 363-71.

1213. REDLICH, Fritz, "Research on German entrepeneurship, " EEH, 2, 1949-50, 100-02; 4, 1951-52, 38-43.

1214. _____ , "Two nineteenth-century financiers and autobiographers. A comparative study in creative destructiveness and business failure, " Economy and History, 10, 1967, 37-128.

1215. REICH, N., "Die Entwicklung des deutschen Aktienrechts im 19. Jahrhundert, " Ius Commune, 2, 1969, 239-76.

1216. RIEDEL, Manfred, "Vom Biedermeier zum Maschinenzeitalter, " Arch. f. KuG., 43, 1961, 100-23.

1217. RIEKER, Karlheinrich, "Die Konzentrationsentwicklung in der Gewerblichen Wirtschaft Eine Auswertung der deutschen Betriebszählungen von 1870 bis 1950, " Tradition, 5, 1960, 116-31.

1218. RJAZANOV, D. B., "Sieben Jahre 'Zur Kritik der politischen Ökonomie, '" Arch. f. d. Gesch. d. Soz., 15, 1930, 1-32.

1219. ROOB, Helmut, "Die Domänen Frage im Gothaer Land, " Jb. f. Regionalgesch., 2, 1967, 50-61.

1220. ROSE, Günther, "Zur Genesis und Funktion der Theorie der 'Industriegesellschaft, '" Zs. f. Geschw., 15, 1967, 20-45.

1221. ROSEN, Heinrich, "Krefeld und die Krefelder Seidenindustrie im Krieg 1870/71, " Heimat (Krefeld), 41.

1222. ROSENBAUM, Eduard, "Albert Ballin: A note on the style of his economic and political activities, " Leo Baeck Inst.

Yrbk., 3, 1958, 257-99.

1223. ROSENBERG, H., R. A. BRADY and M. E. TOWNSEND,
"The economic impact of Imperial Germany," J. Econ.
Hist., 1943, 101-34.

1224. _____, "Political and social consequences of the Great
Depression of 1873-1896 in Central Europe," Econ. Hist.
Rev., 13, 1943, 58-73.

1225. ROTH, Günther D., "Die Grundlagen für eine optische Industrie in München," Tradition, 5, 1960, 15-38.

1226. SALOMON, Elenor, "Die Anfänge der proletarischen Turn-
und Sportbewegung 1890 bis 1900," Wiss. Zs. d. Ernst-
Moritz-Arndt Universität (Gess. u. Sprachwiss.), 13,
1964, 351-62.

1227. SCHACHARDT, Jürgen, "Die Wirtschaftskrise vom Jahre
1866 in Deutschland," Jb. f. Wgesch., 1962 (2), 91-141.

1228. SCHÄFFLE, A. E. F., "Der 'grosse Börenkrach' des
Jahres 1873," ZgesStw., 30, 1874, 1-94.

1229. SCHEEL, H. V., "Die deutsche Handelsstatistik," Schmoll.
Jb., 6, 1882, 23-55.

1230. SCHMANDERER, Eberhard, "Die Entwicklung der Ultramarin-
Fabrikation im 19. Jahrhundert," Tradition, 14, 1969,
127-52.

1231. SCHMIDT, Benno, "Die deutschen Staatslotterien in den
letzten vier Jahrzehnten," ZgesStw., 68, 1912, 298-337.

1232. SCHMIDT, H. Th., "Belegsschaftsbildung im Ruhrgebiet im
Zeichen der Industrialisierung," Tradition, 2, 1957, 265-
73.

1233. _____, "Die Excelsior AG Hannovers älteste Gummiwaren-
fabrik," Tradition, 8, 1963, 29-43.

1234. SCHMIEDER, Eberhard, "Carl Bolle," Tradition, 5, 1960,
49-64.

1235. SCHMITT, Robert, "Die Geschichte der Rheinböller Hütte,"
Tradition, 6, 1961, 155-88.

1236. SCHNEIDER, Arthur von, "Die Erziehung und geistige Entwicklung Grossherzog Leopolds vor seinem Regierungsan-
tritt," ZGORh., 113, 1965, 197-211.

1237. _____, "Das Italienerlebnis Grossherzog Leopolds,"
ZGORh, 106, 1958, 396-436.

1238. _____, "Tagebuch der Italienreise des Grafen Leopold v.
Hochberg vom 30. Nov. 1816-18 April 1817," ZGORh.,
111, 1963, 241-93.

1239. SCHOEPS, Hans-Joachim, "Schriftstücke aus der Demago-
genverfolgung," ZRGG, 18, 1966, 349-69.

1240. SCHOMERUS, Friedrich, "Die Freien Interessenverbände
für Handel und Industrie und ihr Einfluss auf die Gesetzgebung und Verwaltung," Schmoll. Jb., 25, 1901, 439-
520.

1241. SCHORCHT, Karl W., "Neue Ergebnisse über den Ursprung
und den Werdegang der Jenaer Zeiss-Sippe," Tradition,
16, 1971, 236-47.

1242. SCHRAMM, Percy Ernst, "Kaufleute während Besatzung,
Krieg und Belagerung (1806-1815) Der Hamburger Handel
in der Franzosenzeit," Tradition, 4, 1959, 1-22, 88-114.

1243. SCHRÖTER, H., "Briefe von Friedr. Wilhelm Möller an seinen Sohn Theodor Adolf, späteren preussischen Handelsminister von Möller," Jahresber. f. Ravensberg, 65, 1968, 139-269.

1244. _____, "Handel, Gewerbe und Industrie im Landdrostei-bezirk Osnabrück 1815-1866," Osnabrücker Mitteilungen, 68, 1959, 309-58.

1245. SCHULZ, Gerhard, "Über Entstehung und Formen von Interessengruppen in Deutschland seit Beginn der Industrialisierung," Pol. Vjschr., 2, 1961, 124-54.

1246. SCHUMACHER, Hermann, "Die westdeutsche Eisenindustrie und die Moselkanalisierung," Schmoll. Jb., 34, 1910, 1281-1340.

1247. SCHUMACHER, Martin, "Die Bielefelder Leinenindustrie im Umbruch 1836-1839," Jahresber. Hist. Ver. Grafsch. Ravensberg, 65, 1966-67.

1248. _____, "Wirtschafts- und Sozialverhältnisse der Rheinischen Textilindustrie im frühen 19. Jahrhundert," Rhein. Vjsbll., 35, 1971, 301-34.

1249. _____, "Zweckbau und Industrieschloss: Fabrikbauten der rheinisch-westfälischen Textilindustrie vor der Gründerzeit," Tradition, 15, 1970, 1-48.

1250. SCHUSTER, Curt, "Heinrich Caro," Tradition, 6, 1961, 49-64.

1251. SCHUSTER, Ernst, "Bernhard Harms als Mensch und Lehrer," Weltwirtsch. Arch., 92, 1964, 23-30.

1252. SEELING, Hans, "Das Hochofenwerk 'Neusser Hütte' Eine frühe Eisenhütte an Düsseldorfs Peripherie," Tradition, 5, 1960, 271-81.

1253. SEIDEL, Bruno, "Zeitgeist und Wirtschaftsgesinnung im Deutschland der Jahrhundertwende," Schmoll. Jb., 83, 1963, 129-52.

1254. SEIDENZAHL, Fritz, "Eine Denkschrift David Hansemanns vom Jahre 1856," Tradition, 5, 1960, 83-94.

1255. _____, "Die Gründung der preussischen Central-Boden-Credit AG," Tradition, 9, 1964, 176-86.

1256. SEIFFERT, Herbert, "Die Entwicklung der Familie von Alvensleben zu Junkerindustriellen," Jb. f. Wgesch., 1963 (4), 209-43.

1257. SIEGENTHALER, Jürg K., "A scale analysis of nineteenth-century industrialization," EEH, 10, 1972-73, 75-107.

1258. SILBERMANN, Dr. Josef, "Die Frage der Kaufmännischen-schiedsgerichte in Deutschland," Arch. f. Sozialw. u. Sozialpol., 11, 1897, 658-87.

1259. SIMSON, Robert, "Entwickelung der Zinkindustrie Schlesiens nach Herstellung der Eisenbahnen, in den Jahren 1844 bis 1879," Schmoll. Jb., 5, 1881, 1251-57.

1260. SMITH, Clifford N., "Motivation and Ownership: history of the ownership of the Gelsenkirchener Bergwerks-A.G.," Bus. Hist., 12, 1970, 1-24.

1261. SPÅDING, Klaus, "Volksbewegungen in Städten Schwedisch-Pommerns um die Wende vom 18. zum 19. Jahrhundert," Jb. f. Regionalgesch., 2, 1967, 87-112.

1262.   STAROSTE, Wolfgang, "Daniel Staroste Tagebuch 1813/14,"
         Jb. d. Schles.-Fried.-Wilh. Univ. z. Breslau, 10, 1965,
         138-49.
1263.   STERN, Fritz, "Money, morals, and the pillars of Bis-
         marck's Society," Cen. Eur. Hist., 3, 1970, 49-72.
1264.   STIEDA, Dr. Wilhelm, "Deutschlands socialstatistische
         Erhebungen im Jahre 1876," Schmoll. Jb., 1, 1877, 205-
         37.
1265.   _____, "Franz Karl Achard und die Frühzeit der deutschen
         Zuckerindustrie," Schmoll. Jb., 52, 1928, 1055-74.
1266.   STOEHLE, H., "Remarques sur la politique économique et
         sociale de la Prusse," Rev. d'Econ. Pol., 60, 1950,
         141-56.
1267.   STOLBERG-WERNIGERODE, Otto Graf zu, "Deutschland am
         Vorabend des ersten Weltkrieges Eindrücke des schottis-
         chen Dichters Charles Sorley," WaG, 17, 1957, 113-18.
1268.   STROBEL, G., "Die Reise von Adam Mickiewicz durch Süd-
         deutschland im Sommer 1832," Jb. f. Gesch. Osteur.,
         17, 1969, 29-44.
1269.   STRÖSSNER, Georg, "Die Fusion der Aktiengesellschaft
         Maschinen Fabrik Augsburg und der Maschinenbau-Action-
         Gesellschaft Nürnberg im Jahre 1898," Tradition, 5,
         1960, 97-114.
1270.   STURM, Hanspeter, "Salamander," Tradition, 12, 1967,
         309-33.
1271.   THIEME, Horst, "Statistische Materialien zu Kongression-
         ierung von Aktiengesellschaften in Preussen bis 1867,"
         Jb. f. Wgesch., 1960 (2), 285-300.
1272.   THIESS, Dr. Karl, "Die Konsumvereine und die neueste
         deutsche Wirtschaftspolitik," Arch. f. Sozialw. u. Sozial-
         pol., 10, 1897, 49-82.
1273.   THUILLIER, Guy, "La Métallurgie rhénane de 1800 à 1830,"
         Annales, 16, 1961, 877-907.
1274.   _____, "Pour unde histoire de l'économie rhénane de
         1800 à 1830: les houillères de la Ruhr," Annales, 15,
         1960, 882-97.
1275.   THUN, Alphons, "Die Crefelder Seidenindustrie und die
         Krisis," Schmoll. Jb., 3, 1879, 113-43.
1276.   TIBURTIUS, Joachim, "Otto Hintzes Beitrag zur Volkswirt-
         schaftslehre," Schmoll. Jb., 86, 1966, 513-59.
1277.   TILLY, Richard, "Popular disorders in nineteenth-century
         Germany: a preliminary survey," J. Soc. Hist., 4,
         1970, 1-40.
1278.   TINTNER, Gerhard, "Die allgemeine Preisbildung 1890-
         1913," Schmoll. Jb., 57, 1933, 253-64.
1279.   TOEPFER, Helmuth, "Die Jahrmärkte in der preussischen
         Rheinprovinz um 1845," Rhein. Vjsbll., 35, 1971, 288-
         300.
1280.   TREUE, Wilhelm, "Caesar Wollheim und Eduard Arnold
         Die Geschichte einer Kohlen-Grosshandelsfirma von der
         Mitte des 19. Jahrhunderts bis zum Jahre 1925," Tradi-
         tion, 6, 1961, 65-83, 97-115.
1281.   _____, "Deutsche Wirtschaftsführer im 19. Jahrhundert,"

HZ, 167, 1943, 548-65.

1282.   _____, "Grundzüge einer Geschichte der wirtschaftlichen
         Entwicklung des Ruhrgebietes im Industriezeitalter,"
         Tradition, 13, 1968, 273-81.

1283.   _____, "Zur Geschichte einer hamburgischen Anwaltsso-
         zietät 1822-1972," Tradition, 17, 1972, 49-83.

1284.   _____, "Zur Gründungsgeschichte des Norddeutschen
         Lloyd," VSW, 33, 1940, 195-209.

1285.   VAGTS, Alfred, "Gustav Schwab 1822-1880 Ein deutsch-
         amerikanischer Unternehmer," Bremisches Jb., 50, 1965,
         337-60.

1286.   "VERGANGENHEIT und Gegenwart der deutschen Leinenin-
         dustrie," Jbb. f. Nationalökon. und Stat., 13, 1869, 215-
         51.

1287.   VIDALENC, Jean, "Les notables des départments hanséa-
         tiques," Rev. d'hist. mod., 17, 1970, 777-92.

1288.   VOGT, Martin, "Das vormärzliche Deutschland im en-
         glischen Urteil (1830-1847)," GiWuU, 16, 1965, 397-413.

1289.   WALKER, Mark, "Napoleonic Germany and the hometown
         communities," Cen. Eur. Hist., 2, 1969, 99-113.

1290.   WEINBERGER, Gerda, "Die deutschen Konsuln," Jb. f.
         Wgesch., 1969 (2), 203-23.

1291.   WEITZ, K. R., "Die Denkschrift des Niederrheinischen und
         westfälischen Adels von 26. Februar 1818 Eine Unter-
         suchung zur Verfassungs- und Sozialgeschichte des 19.
         Jahrhunderts," Rhein. Vjsbll., 35, 1971, 201-73.

1292.   WELCK, V., "Das Fabrikschulwesen im Königreich Sach-
         sen," Schmoll. Jb., 23, 1899, 53-108.

1293.   WEYDERT, Jean, "L'organisation commerciale de la Batel-
         lerie Allemande sur le Rhin (1900-1945)," Rev. d'hist.
         mod., 3, 1956, 120-37.

1294.   WILHELM, Irene, "Zur Gründung des Norddeutschen Lloyd,"
         VSW, 33, 1940, 195-209.

1295.   WILKEN, Folkert, "Gerhart von Schulze-Gaevernitz ein
         geistesgeschichtlicher Rückblick," Weltwirtsch. Arch.,
         59, 1944, 49-63.

1296.   WILLIAMS, Robert C., "Russians in Germany: 1900-1914,"
         J. Contemp. Hist., 1(4), 1966, 121-49.

1297.   WINKEL, Harald, "Kapitalquellen und Kapitalverwendung am
         Vorabend des industriellen Aufschwungs in Deutschlands,"
         Schmoll. Jb., 90, 1970, 275-301.

1298.   "Die WIRTHSCHAFTLICHE Reformbewegung in Deutschland,"
         Pr. Jbb., 6, 1860, 563-83.

1299.   "Die WIRTHSCHAFTLICHEN Ergebnisse der letzte Reichs-
         tags-Session," Pr. Jbb., 24, 1869, 351-66.

1300.   WOLF, Mechthild, "Hermann Heye und die Gründung des
         Europäischen Verbandes der Flaschenfabriken GMBH,"
         Tradition, 9, 1964, 219-34.

1301.   WOYTINSKY, Wladimir, "Die Preisbewegung der Jahre
         1901-1912 und 1925-1930," Weltwirtsch. Arch., 34, 1931,
         491-524.

1302.   WÜNDISCH, Fritz, "Zur Geschichte des rheinischen Braun-
         Kohlenbergbaus," Rhein. Vjsbll., 17, 1952, 197-221.

1303.   WURZBACHER, Gerhard, "Studien über den Wandel der
        sozialen und völkischen Struktur eines Landkreises im
        pommerschen-westpreussischen Grenzraum zwischen
        1773-1937," Zs. f. Ostforsch., 2, 1953, 190-207.
1304.   WYSOCKI, Josef, "Vor der Gründerzeit zu den zwanziger
        Jahren," Tradition, 14, 1967, 65-88.
1305.   ZAHN, Friedrich, "Deutschlands Volkswirtschaft beim Ein-
        tritt ins 20. Jahrhundert," Jbb. f. Nationalökon. u. Stat.,
        76, 1901, 1-53.
1306.   ZIEMER, Gerhard, "Nordhessen und die deutsche Jugendbe-
        wegung," Hess. Jahrb. Landesgesch., 19, 1969.
1307.   ZIMMERMANN, F. W. R., "Die deutsche Handelsstatistik
        in ihrer geschichtlichen Entwicklung und ihrem derzeiti-
        gen Stand," Jbb. f. Nationalökon. u. Stat., 90, 1908,
        289-324, 433-73.
1308.   ZIMMERMANN, Karl, "Die Strassenbaupolitik Preussens
        und seiner Nachbarn westlich der Elbe bis zum Zoll-
        verein," Rhein. Vjsbll., 2, 1932, 177-96.
1309.   ZORN, Wolfgang, "Das deutsche Unternehmerporträt in
        sozialgeschichtlicher Betrachtung," Tradition, 7, 1962,
        79-92.
1310.   _____, "Die historische Wirtschaftskarte der Rhein-
        provinz um 1820 vor der Fertigstellung," Rhein. Vjsbll.,
        32, 1968, 476-81.
1311.   _____, "Probleme der Industrialisierung Oberfrankens
        im 19. Jahrhundert," Jb. f. frank. Landesforsch., 29,
        1969, 295-310.
1312.   _____, "Die Struktur der rheinischen Wirtschaft in der
        Neuzeit," Rhein. Vjsbll., 28, 1963, 37-61.
1313.   _____, "Typen und Entwicklungskräfte deutschen Unterneh-
        mertums im 19. Jahrhundert," VSW, 44, 1957, 57-77.
1314.   _____, "Unternehmer und Aristokratie in Deutschland
        Ein Beitrag zur Geschichte des sozialen Stils und Selbst-
        bewusstseins in der Neuzeit," Tradition, 8, 1963, 241-54.
1315.   _____, "Die wirtschaftliche Struktur Altbayerns im Vor-
        märz (1815-1845)," Oberbayer. Arch., 93, 1971.
1316.   _____, "Die wirtschaftliche Struktur der Rheinprovinz
        um 1820," VSW, 54, 1967, 289-324, 477-80.
1317.   _____, "Eine Wirtschaftskarte Deutschlands um 1820 als
        Spiegel der gewerblichen Entwicklung," Jbb. f. National-
        ökon. u. Stat., 179, 1966, 344-55.
1318.   _____, "Wirtschafts- und Sozialgeschichtliche Zusammen-
        hänge der Deutschen Reichsgründungszeit (1850-1879),"
        HZ, 197, 1963, 318-42.
1319.   _____ (mitarbeit Rolf Warm), "Zur Betriebsstruktur der
        rheinischen Industrie um 1820," Tradition, 12, 1967,
        497-510.
1320.   ZUNKEL, Friedrich, "Beamtenschaft und Unternehmertum
        Beim Aufbau der Ruhrindustrie 1849-1880," Tradition,
        9, 1964, 261-77.

Franz von Baader (1765-1841)

1321. BENZ, Ernst, "Franz von Baaders Gedanken über den
        'Proletair' Zur Geschichte des vor-marxistischen Sozial-
        ismus," ZRGG, 1, 1948, 97-123.
1322. GRASSL, Hans, "Franz von Baader und München," Zs. f.
        bayer. LG., 16, 1951, 421-36.
1323. _____, ed., "Eine Philosophie der Liebe Aus den
        Schriften Franz von Baaders," Hochland, 43, 1950/51,
        374-85.
1324. KALTENBRUNNER, Gerd-Klaus, "Sozialrevolutionär, Poli-
        tiker und Laientheologe zum 200. Geburtstag Franz von
        Baaders," Zeitwende, 36, 1965, 151-60.
1325. REICHEL, Hans, "Die Sozietätsphilosophie Franz von Baa-
        ders," ZgesStw, 57, 1901, 193-264.
1326. SAUTER, Johannes, "Die Ästhetik Franz von Baaders,"
        Arch. f. Gesch. d. Phil., 38, 1927/28, 34-63.
1327. _____, "Die Grundlegung der deutschen Volkswirtschafts-
        lehre druch Franz von Baader (1765-1841)," Jbb. f. Na-
        tionalökon. u. Stat., 123, 1925, 433-87.
1328. SCHULZE, Wilhelm A., "Franz von Baader und der päpst-
        liche Primat," Theol. Zs., 16, 1960, 59-61.
1329. WINTER, Eduard, "Neues über Baader," Hochland, 26(2),
        1928/29, 433-36.

Karl Eugen Dühring (1833-1921)

1330. ALBRECHT, Gerhard, "Die Ausgestaltung des Listschen Na-
        tionalitätsprinzips durch Eugen Dühring," ZgesStw, 83,
        1927, 1-32.
1331. _____, "Dührings Stelling in der Dogmengeschichte der
        Volkswirtschaftslehre," Arch. f. Sozialw. u. Sozialpol.,
        54, 1925, 741-74.
1332. KALTENBRUNNER, Gerd-Klaus, "Eugen Dühring," ZRGG,
        22, 1970, 58-79.
1333. KÖPPE, H., "Das 'sozialitäre System' Eugen Dührings,"
        Arch. f. d. Gesch. d. Soz.; 4, 1913/14, 393-438.
1334. LASKINE, Edmond, "Les Doctrines économiques et sociales
        d'Eugène Dühring," Rev. d'hist. econ. soc., 5, 1912,
        228-76.

Friedrich Benedikt Wilhelm Hermann (1795-1868)

1335. HELFERICH, v., "Fr. B. W. v. Hermann als nationalö-
        konomischer schriftsteller," ZgesStw, 34, 1878, 638-51.
1336. WEINBERGER, Otto, "Friedrich Benedikt Wilhelm Hermann,"
        ZgesStw, 79, 1925, 464ff.

Victor Aimé Huber (1800-1869)

1337.   DROZ, Jacques, "Victor-Aimé Huber: un conservateur
        social du milieu du XIXe siècle," Arch. d. Soc. d. Rel.,
        10, 1960, 41-47.
1338.   HUBERNAGEL, G., "Der Universalismus in Sozialreform
        und Genossenschaftswesen bei V. A. Huber," Schmoll.
        Jb., 59, 1935, 423-45.

Friedrich and Alfred Krupp (1787-1826; 1812-1887)

1339.   McCREARY, Eugene C., "Social Welfare and Business: The
        Krupp Welfare Program, 1860-1914," Bus. Hist. Rev.,
        42, 1968, 24-49.
1340.   SCHRÖDER, Ernst, "Alfred Krupps Generalregulativ," Tra-
        dition, 1, 1956, 35-57.
1341.   SCHRÖTER, Hermann, "Die Firma Friedrich Krupp und die
        Stadt Essen," Tradition, 6, 1961, 260-270.

Friedrich List (1789-1846)

1342.   BAASCH, Ernst, "Die deutschen wirtschaftlichen Einheitsbe-
        strebungen, die Hansestädt und Friedrich List bis zum
        Jahre 1821," HZ, 122, 1920, 454-85.
1343.   BELL, John F., "Frederick List, Champion of Industrial
        Capitalism," Pennsyl. Mag. of Hist. & Biog., 66, 1942,
        56-83.
1344.   BELLOM, Maurice, "La Source des Théories de List,"
        Rev. d'hist. econ. soc., 2, 1909, 263-74.
1345.   BOUCHUT, Yves, "Frédérie List et le Marché commun,"
        Rev. d'hist. econ. soc., 45, 1967, 459-88.
1346.   BOUSQUET, G., "List et les Chemins de Fer," Rev. d'hist.
        econ. soc., 21, 1933, 269-79.
1347.   BROCK, P., "Friedrich List und die deutsche Verkehrwirt-
        schaft," Arch. f. Eisenbahnwesen, 1939, 1081-1218.
1348.   DAMASCHKE, Adolf, "Friedrich List," Soziale Zeitfragen,
        92, 1935, 1-24.
1349.   DIETZEL, Heinrich, "List's Nationales System und die 'na-
        tionale' Wirtschaftspolitik," Arch. f. Sozialw. u. Sozial-
        pol., 35, 1912, 366-417.
1350.   GOESER, Karl, "Der Anteil Friedrich Lists an der Grün-
        dung der staatswissenschaftlichen Fakultät in Tübingen,"
        Württemb. Vtljhefte. f. Landesgesch., 26, 1917, 436-41.
1351.   HÖLTZEL, Dr. M., "Ueber Friedrich List," Pr. Jbb., 113,
        1903, 420-42.
1352.   LENZ, Friedrich, "Friedrich List als politischer Publizist,"
        Zs. f. Pol., 3, 1956, 228-42.
1353.   _____, "Friedrich List und der Liberalismus," Schmoll.
        Jb., 48, 1924, 405-37.
1354.   _____, "Die politische Ökonomie und Friedrich List,"
        Weltwirtsch. Arch., 21, 1925, 184-98.

1355.   LEYEN, Alfred v. der, "Friedrich List der Vorkämpfer des
        Deutschen Eisenbahnwesens, " Archiv für Eisenbahnwesen,
        1931, 1067-1104.
1356.   MENSEL, Alfred, "Das Problem der äusseren Handelspolitik
        bei Friedrich List und Karl Marx, " Weltwirtsch. Arch.,
        27, 1928, 77-103.
1357.   NOTZ, William, "Friedrich List in Amerika, " Weltwirtsch.
        Arch., 21, 1925, 199-265; 22, 1925, 154-82.
1358.   SCHOENEBECK, Dr. v., "Friedrich List und die Lehre von
        den Zollwirkungen, " Schmoll. Jb., 51, 1927, 425-43.
1359.   SCHÖNINGH, Franz Josef, "Friedrich List, " Hochland, 28
        (2), 1930/31, 508-22.
1360.   SCHULZ, Erna, "Friedrich Lists Geschichtsauffassung Ihre
        Gestalt und ihre Bedeutung Für Lists Wirtschaftslehre, "
        ZgesStw, 97, 1936/37, 290-334.
1361.   SCHWARZ, Wilhelm, "Friedrich List--Lehrmeister Russ-
        lands, " Zs. F. Württbg. LG, 18, 1959, 143-49.
1362.   SEVIN, Ludwig, "Die Entwicklung von Friedrich Lists Ko-
        lonial- und weltpolitischen Ideen bis zum Plane einer
        englischen Allianz 1846, " Schmoll. Jb., 33, 1909, 1673-
        1715.
1363.   _____, "Die listische Idee einer deutsch-englischen Al-
        lianz in ihrem Ergebnis für Deutschland, " Schmoll. Jb.,
        34, 1910, 173-222.
1364.   SOMMER, Artur, "Friedrich List und Adam Müller, " Welt-
        wirtsch. Arch., 25, 1927, 345-76.
1365.   _____, "Mitteilung über ein bisher unbekanntes Werk
        Friedrich Lists, " Schmoll. Jb., 50, 1926, 687-718.
1366.   _____, "Der Wandel des Wissenschaftsbildes Friedrich
        Lists, " Schmoll. Jb., 59, 1935, 257-70.
1367.   SONNTAG, W. von, "Die Anschauung von Volk und Staat in
        Friedrich Lists Jugendschriften, " Schmoll. Jb., 56, 1932,
        393-414.

Wilhelm Heinrich Riehl (1823-1897)

1368.   BÜLOW, Friedrich, "Wilhelm Heinrich Riehl und die
        deutsche Volkswirtschaftslehre, " ZgesStw, 98, 1937/38,
        652-72.
1369.   EGNER, Erich, "Wirtschaftliche Volkskunde bei Wilhelm
        Heinrich Riehl, " Schmoll. Jb., 62, 1938, 1-28.
1370.   LOOSE, Gerhard, "The Peasant in Wilhelm Heinrich Riehl's
        Sociological and Novelistic Writings, " Ger. Rev., 15,
        1940, 263-72.

Christian von Rother (1778-1849)

1371.   HENDERSON, W. O., "Christian von Rother als Beamter
        und Unternehmer im Dienste des preussischen Staates
        1810-1848, " ZgesStw, 112, 1956, 523-50.
1372.   HENNING, Hansjoachim, "Preussiche Sozialpolitik im Vor-

märz Ein Beitrag zu den arbeiterfreundliche Bestrebungen
in unternehmen der Preussischen Seehandlung unter Christian von Rother," VSW, 52, 1965.

1373.   THIERFELDER, Hildegard, "Rother als Finanzpolitiker unter
Hardenberg 1778-1822," FBPG, 46, 1934, 70-111.

1374.   WEBERSINN, Gerhard, "Christian von Rother, ein Leben
für Preussen und Schlesien," Jb. d. Schles.-Fried.-Wilh.
Univ z. Breslau, 10, 1965, 150-187.

The Siemens Family
Werner von (1816-92); Karl (1829-1906);
Wilhelm (1823-83); Friedrich (1828-1904)

1375.   DANKE, Rudolf, "Das Siemens--Grundstück in Charlotten-
burg," Bär v. Ber., 6, 1956, 108-34.

1376.   KOCKA, Jürgen, "Family and Bureaucracy in German Industrial Management, 1850-1914: Siemens in Comparative Perspective," Bus. Hist. Rev., 45, 1971, 133-56.

1377.   _____, "Siemens und der Aufhaltsame Aufstieg der AEG,"
Tradition, 17, 1972, 125-42.

1378.   WEIHER, Sigfrid von, "Carl von Siemens 1829-1906 Ein
deutscher Unternehmer in Russland und England," Tradition, 1, 1956, 13-25.

Rudolf Sohm (1841-1917)

1379.   RUPPEL, Erich, "Kirche und Staat bei Rudolph Sohm,"
Zs. f. evan. KiR, 14, 1968/69, 225-38.

1380.   SOHM, Rudolf, "Ueber die Geschichte der Vereinsfreiheit,"
Schmoll. Jb., 6, 1882, 803-19.

Werner Sombart (1863-1941)

1381.   BELOW, Georg von, "Die wirtschaftsgeschichtliche Auffassung W. Sombarts," Schmoll. Jb., 45, 1921, 237-61.

1382.   BRINKMANN, Carl, "Werner Sombart," Weltwirtsch. Arch.,
54, 1941, 1-12.

1383.   CAROSSO, Vincent P., "Werner Sombart's Contribution to
Business History," Bus. Hist. Soc. Bull., 26, 1952, 27-
49.

1384.   DIEHL, Prof. Dr. Karl, "Sozialismus und soziale Bewegung
im 19. Jahrhundert," Pr. Jbb., 87, 1897, 319-347.

1385.   DOPSCH, Alfons, "Werner Sombart der moderne Kapitalismus," Arch. f. d. Gesch. d. Soz., 8, 1919, 330-82.

1386.   FECHNER, Erich, "Der Begriff des kapitalistischen Geistes
bei Werner Sombart und Max Weber," Weltwirtsch. Arch.,
30, 1929, 194-211.

1387.   _____, "Der Begriff des kapitalistischen Geistes und das
Schelersche Gesetz vom Zusammenhang der historischen
wirkfaktoren (Vergleich und Ausgleich zwischen Sombart

und Max Weber)," Arch. f. Sozialw. u. Sozialpol., 63, 1930, 93-120.

1388. HARMS, Bernhard, "Darstellung und Kritik der Wirtschafts- und Betrievssystematik im Sombartschen 'Kapitalismus'," Schmoll. Jb., 29, 1905, 1385-1431.

1389. KORSCH, Karl, "Sombarts 'verstehende Nationalökonomie'," Arch. f. d. Gesch. d. Soz., 15, 1930, 436-48.

1390. MÜLLER, August, "Sombarts proletarischer Sozialismus," Zs. f. Pol., 15, 1925/26, 348-57.

1391. PFISTER, Bernd, "Werner Sombarts 'Proletarischer Sozialismus'," ZgesStw, 83, 1927, 93-135.

1392. RIEKES, Hugo, "Sombarts Begriffsbestimmung des Sozialismus," Schmoll. Jb., 55, 1931, 655-84.

1393. SALIN, Edgar, "Hochkapitalismus Eine Studie über Werner Sombart, die deutsche Volkswirtschaftslehre und das Wirtschaftssystem der Gegenwart," Weltwirtsch. Arch., 25, 1927, 314-44.

1394. SAYOUS, André E., "'Der Moderne Kapitalismus' de W. Sombart, et Gênes aux XIIᵉ et XIIIᵉ Siècles," Rev. d'hist. econ. soc., 18, 1930, 427-45.

1395. SCHAMS, Ewald, "Die 'zweite' Nationalökonomie Bemerkungen zu Werner Sombarts Buch: 'Die drei Nationalökonomien'," Arch. f. Sozialw. u. Sozialpol., 64, 1930, 453-91.

1396. SCHUMPETER, Joseph, "Sombarts Dritter Band," Schmoll. Jb., 51, 1927, 349-69.

1397. SEIDENFUS, Helmuth St., "Werner Sombart und die reine Theorie," Jb. F. Sozialw. u. Sozialpol., 11, 1960, 257-69.

1398. SOMBART, Werner, "Die Arbeiterverhältnisse im Zeitalter des Frühkapitalismus," Arch. f. Sozialw. u. Sozialpol., 44, 1917/18, 19-51.

1399. _____, "Aus der Frühzeit der modernen Gesellschaftsformen," Arch. f. Sozialw. u. Sozialpol., 42, 1916/17, 462-504.

1400. _____, "Der Begriff der Gesetzmässigkeit bei Marx," Schmoll. Jb., 47, 1924, 11-31.

1401. _____, "Die deutsche Zigarrenindustrie und der Erlass des Bundesrats vom 9. Mai 1888," Archiv f. soziale Gesetzgebung u. Statistik, 2, 1889, 107-28.

1402. _____, "Die Elemente des Wirtschaftslebens," Arch. f. Sozialw. u. Sozialpol., 37, 1913, 1-45.

1403. _____, "Die Entstehung der Kapitalistischen Unternehmung," Arch. f. Sozialw. u. Sozialpol., 41, 1916, 299-334.

1404. _____, "Die gewerbliche Arbeit und ihre Organisation," Arch. f. Sozialw. u. Sozialpol., 14, 1899, 1-52, 310-405.

1405. _____, "Die Hausindustrie in Deutschland," Archiv f. soziale Gesetzgebung u. Statistik, 4, 1891, 103-56.

1406. _____, "Ideale der Sozialpolitik," Arch. f. Sozialw. u. Sozialpol., 10, 1897, 1-48.

1407. _____, "Die Idee des Klassenkampfes," Weltwirtsch.

Arch., 21, 1925, 22-36.

1408.   _____, "Die internationalen Wirtschaftsbeziehungen im
Zeitalter des Frühkapitalismus, Vornehmlich im 16. 17.
und 18. Jahrhundert," Weltwirtsch. Arch., 11, 1917, 1-22.

1409.   _____, "Der Kampf um die Edelmetalle im Zeitalter des
Frühkapitalismus, vornehmlich im 16., 17. und 18. Jahrhundert," Weltwirsch. Arch., 11, 1917, 147-70.

1410.   _____, "Karl Marx und die soziale Wissenschaft," Arch.
f. Sozialw. u. Sozialpol., 26, 1908, 429-50.

1411.   _____, "Objekt und Grundbegriffe der theoretischen Nationalökonomie," Arch. f. Sozialw. u. Sozialpol., 38,
1914, 647-61.

1412.   _____, "Der Stil des modernen Wirtschaftslebens," Arch.
f. Sozialw. u. Sozialpol., 17, 1902, 1-20.

1413.   _____, "Studien zur Entwicklungsgeschichte des nord-
amerikanischen Proletariats," Arch. f. Sozialw. u.
Sozialpol., 21, 1905, 210-36, 308-46.

1414.   _____, "Technik und Kultur," Arch. f. Sozialw. u.
Sozialpol., 33, 1911, 305-47.

1415.   _____, "Die Technik im Zeitalter des Frühkapitalismus,"
Arch. f. Sozialw. u. Sozialpol., 34, 1912, 721-60.

1416.   _____, "Die Vergeistung der Betriebe," Weltwirtsch.
Arch., 25, 1927, 149-78.

1417.   _____, "Versuch einer Systematik des Wirtschaftskrisen,"
Arch. f. Sozialw. u. Sozialpol., 19, 1904, 1-21.

1418.   _____, "Volk und Sprache," Schmoll. Jb., 63, 1939, 15-
42.

1419.   _____, "Zur Kritik des ökonomischen Systems von Karl
Marx," Arch. f. Sozialw. u. Sozialpol., 7, 1894, 555-94.

1420.   TIBURTIUS, Joachim, "Zum Gedenken Werner Sombarts,"
Schmoll. Jb., 84, 1964, 257-99.

1421.   ZIEGENFUSS, Werner, "Geist, Gesellschaft und Wirtschaft,"
Schmoll. Jb., 69, 1949, 257-82.

1422.   ZIMMERMANN, Waldemar, "Der proletarische Sozialismus
('Marxismus') von Werner Sombart," Schmoll. Jb., 56,
1932, 437-56.

Johann Heinrich von Thünen (1783-1850)

1423.   BRAEUER, Walter, "Falsche Deutungen Thünenscher Begriffe
und die sich daraus ergeben den Konsequenzen für die
Rekonstruktion der Lohn Formel," Jbb. f. Nationalökon.
u. Stat., 139, 1933, 315-25.

1424.   _____, "Thünen et la France," Rev. d'hist. econ. soc.,
28, 1950, 186-91.

1425.   BRINKMANN, Irmgard, "Die von Thünensche Rentenlehre
und die Entwicklung der neuzeitlichen Landwirtschaft,"
ZgesStw, 107, 1951, 307-56.

1426.   BÜLOW, Friedrich, "Johann Heinrich von Thünen als forst-
wirtschaftlicher Denker," Weltwirtsch. Arch., 80, 1958,
183-233.

1427.   _____, "Thünen als Raumdenker," Weltwirtsch. Arch.,

65, 1950, 1-24.
1428.   BUHR, Walter, "An Operational Generalized Version of von
        Thünen's Model," ZgesStw, 126, 1970, 427-32.
1429.   CARELL, Erich, "Johann Heinrich v. Thünen und die mo-
        derne Wirtschaftstheorie," ZgesStw, 106, 1950, 600-10.
1430.   ENGELHARDT, Werner, "Die Theorien der Produktion des
        Preises und der Verteilung bei J. H. von Thünen,"
        Schmoll. Jb., 73, 1953, 129-60.
1431.   HÄNTZSCHE, C. J. C., "Die handelspolitischen Anschauun-
        gen Heinrich von Thünen's," ZgesStw, 51, 1895, 95-115.
1432.   HOFFMANN, Friedrich, "J. H. v. Thünen im Blickfeld des
        deutschen Kameralismus," Weltwirtsch. Arch., 65, 1950,
        25-40.
1433.   KRZYMOWSKI, Richard (trans. by P. G. Minneman),
        "Graphical Presentation of Thuenen's Theory of Inten-
        sity," Journal of Farm Economics, 10, 1928, 461-82.
1434.   LIFSCHITZ, F., "Robert Thomas Malthus und Johann Hein-
        rich von Thünen als Bevölkerungstheoretiker," ZgesStw,
        59, 1903, 553-72.
1435.   PAET, Richard, "Von Thünen Theory and the Dynamics of
        Agricultural Expansion," EEH, 8, 1970/71, 181-201.
1436.   PASSOW, Richard, "Die Methode der nationalökonomischen
        Forschungen Johann Heinrichs von Thünen," ZgesStw, 58,
        1902, 1-38.
1437.   WERTH, August, "Albrecht Thaer und Johann Heinrich von
        Thünen," ZgesStw, 61, 1905, 56-70.

Thorstein Veblen (1857-1929)

1438.   DAVIS, Arthur K., "Thorstein Veblen Reconsidered," Sci-
        ence and Society, 21, 1957, 52-85.
1439.   HEINTZ, Peter, "Von der Ansätzen einer neuen Soziologie
        der Technik bei Thorstein Veblen," ZgesStw, 110, 1954,
        490-509.
1440.   LANDSMAN, Randolph H., "The Philosophy of Veblen's
        Economics," Science and Society, 21, 1957, 333-45.
1441.   SPENGLER, Joseph J., "Veblen und Mandeville Contrasted,"
        Weltwirtsch. Arch., 82, 1959, 35-67.
1442.   VISSER, Derk, "The German Captain of Enterprise: Veb-
        len's Imperial Germany Revisited," Explorations in Entre-
        preneurial History, 6, 1968/69, 309-28.
1443.   WALLACE, Henry A., "Veblen's 'Imperial Germany and the
        Industrial Revolution'," Political Science Quarterly, 55,
        1940, 435-45.

Adolph Wagner (1838-1917)

1444.   BARKIN, Kenneth, "Adolph Wagner and German Industrial
        Development," J. Mod. Hist., 41, 1969, 144-59.
1445.   CLARK, Evalyn A., "Adolph Wagner: From National Econo-
        mist to National Socialist," Pol. Sci. Q., 55, 1940, 378-

411.
1446.   HEUBNER, P. L., "Adolph Wagner," Schmoll. Jb., 66,
         1942, 641-56.
1447.   RADUCANU, Jon, "Von Leben und Werk Adolph Wagners,"
         Schmoll. Jb., 63, 1939, 171-76.
1448.   SCHMOLLER, Gustav and M. SERING, "Zum 70 Geburtstag
         von Adolph Wagner Zwei Ansprachen," Schmoll. Jb., 29,
         1905, 412-20.
1449.   VLEUGELS, Wilhelm, "Adolph Wagner," Schmoll. Jb., 59,
         1935, 129-41.
1450.   WAGNER, A., "Das Actiengesellschaftswesen," Jbb. f. Na-
         tionalökon. u. Stat., 21, 1873, 271-340.
1451.   _____, "Die Entwicklung des deutschen Staatsgebiets und
         das Nationalitätsprincip," Pr. Jbb., 21, 1868, I, 290-
         313; II, 379-402.
1452.   _____, "Die Entwicklung der europäischen Staatsterri-
         torien und das Nationalitätsprincip," Pr. Jbb., 19, 1867,
         540-79; 20, 1867, 1-42.
1453.   _____, "Finanzwissenschaft und Staatssozialismus mit
         einer Einleitung über [Lorenz] Stein's und Roscher's
         Finanzwissenschaft," ZgesStw, 43, 1887, 37-122, 675-746.
1454.   _____, "Die preussische Bankfrage, vom allgemein wirth-
         schaftlichen und politischen Standpunkte," Pr. Jbb., 15,
         1865, 390ff.
1455.   _____, "Der Staat und das Versicherungswesen," ZgesStw,
         37, 1881, 102-72.
1456.   _____, "Über Soziale Finanz- und Steuerpolitik," Archiv
         f. Soziale Gesetzgebung u. Statistik, 4, 1891, 1-81.

                     Carl Zeiss (1816-1888)

1457.   FRIESS, Herbert, "Carl Zeiss im Spiegel seiner mütter-
         lichen Verwandtschaft," Tradition, 16, 1971, 248-59.
1458.   WILLAM, Horst A., "Carl Zeiss Mensch und Werk," Tra-
         dition, 9, 1964, 58-69.

Agricultural History

1459.   BECKMANN, Fritz, "Der Bauer im Zeitalter des Kapitalis-
         mus," Schmoll. Jb., 50, 1926, 719-48.
1460.   BENTZIEN, Ulrich, "Landmaschinentechnik in Mecklenburg,"
         Jb. f. Wgesch., 1965 (3), 54-81.
1461.   BLEIBER, Helmut, "Zur Problematik des preussischen
         Wegen der Entwicklung des Kapitalismus in der Landwirt-
         schaft," Zs. f. Geschw., 13, 1965, 57-73.
1462.   BOG, Ingomar, "Die wirtschaftlichen Trends, der Staat und
         die Agrarverfassung in der Geschichte Hessens," Z.
         Agrargesch., Agrarsoziol., 1970.
1463.   BORCKE-STARGORDT, Henning v., "Die Bauernbefreiung
         1807," Der europäische Osten, 6, 1960, 331-35.
1464.   CETTO, Freiherr von, "Die Bayerische Landwirtschaftsbank,

ihre Entstehungsgeschichte Einrichtung und Geschäftsent-
wickelung," Schmoll. Jb., 30, 1906, 1595-1638.

1465. CONRAD, J., "Agrarstatistische Untersuchungen," Jbb. f.
Nationalökon. u. Stat., 17, 1871, 225-97; 18, 1872, 377-
416.

1466. CONZE, Werner, "Die Wirkungen der liberalen Agrarreform
auf die Volksordnung in Mitteleuropa im 19. Jahrhundert,"
VSW, 38, 1949, 2-43.

1467. DÄNDLIKER, Walter, "Adam Müller (1814-1879) von Ger-
hardsbrunn," Zs. f. Agrarg, 12, 1964, 193-99.

1468. DIEHL, Karl, "Der ältere Agrarsozialismus und die neuere
Bodenreformbewegung in Amerika, England und Deutschland," Arch. f. d. Gesch. d. Soz., 1, 1910/11, 225-84.

1469. DIETRICH, W. M., "Die Landwirthschaftlichen Creditanstal-
ten im Königreiche Sachsen," Jbb. f. Nationalökon. u.
Stat., 4, 1865, 219-48.

1470. DIETZE, Constantin, "Wege zur Agrarpolitik Ein Stück
Methodengeschichte der Nationalökonomie in Deutschland
von Moeser bis Roscher," H. Jb., 62/69, 1942/49, 491-
538.

1471. EHEBERG, K. Th., "Die Landwirtschaft in Bayern,"
Schmoll. Jb., 14, 1890, 1121-41.

1472. ENGLERT, Ferdinand, "Die landwirtschaftliche Verwaltung
in Bayern 1890-1897," Schmoll. Jb., 22, 1898, 411-39.

1473. ESSLEN, Joseph Bergfried, "Die Entwicklung von Fleischer-
zeugung und Fleischverbranch auf dem Gebiete des heutigen
Deutschen Reiches seit dem Anfang des 19. Jahrhunderts
und ihr gegenwärtiger Stand," Jbb. f. Nationalökon. u.
Stat., 98, 1912, 705-69.

1474. FLANINGAM, Miletus L., "The Rural Economy of North-
eastern France and the Bavarian Palatinate 1815 to 1830,"
Ag. Hist., 24, 1950, 166-70.

1475. FÖLDES, Déla, "Die Getreidepreise im 19. Jahrhundert,"
Jbb. f. Nationalökon. u. Stat., 84, 1905, 467-518.

1476. FRANZ, Günther, "Die Entstehung des Landwarenhandels,"
Tradition, 5, 1960, 65-82.

1477. GANGHOFER, Forstrath, "Der Wald im nationalen Wirth-
schaftsleben," Schmoll. Jb., 4, 1880, 455-90.

1478. GATES, Paul W., "Charles Lewis Fleischmann: German-
American Agricultural Authority," Ag. Hist., 35, 1961,
13-23.

1479. GOLTZ, Th. Freiherr von der, "Die Entwickelung der
ostpreussischen Landwirthschaft während der letzten 25
Jahre (1856-1881)," Schmoll. Jb., 7, 1883, 809-65.

1480. GROHMANN, H., "Betrachtungen über die Wirtschaften der
ländlichen Tagelöhner des deutschen Reichs," Schmoll.
Jb., 16, 1892, 855-910.

1481. GROSS, Reiner, "Die rechtlichen Verhältnisse der Bauern
in Sachsen zu Beginn des 19. Jahrhunderts," Letopis,
ser. B., 1970.

1482. HAUSER, Albert, "Wechselbeziehungen zwischen der
Schweizerischen und deutschen Landwirtschaft im 19.
Jahrhundert," Schw. Zs. f. Gesch., 13, 1963, 206-14.

1483. _____, "Die wirtschaftlichen Beziehungen der Schweiz zu
　　　　Deutschland in der ersten Hälfte des 19. Jahrhunderts,"
　　　　Schw. Zs. f. Gesch., 8, 1958, 355-82.
1484. HEISS, Cl., "Eine theoretische Würdigung des landwirt-
　　　　schaftlichen Genossenschaftswesens in Deutschland,"
　　　　Schmoll. Jb., 28, 1904, 723-42.
1485. HEITZ, Dr. E., "Die Anbauverhältnisse in Deutschland,
　　　　beschreibend und vergleichend dargestellt auf Grund der
　　　　Erhebung von 1878," Schmoll. Jb., 6, 1882, 859-943.
1486. HELD, A., "Die ländlichen Darlehenskassenvereine in der
　　　　Rheinprovinz und ihre Beziehungen zur Arbeiterfrage,"
　　　　Jbb. f. Nationalökon. u. Stat., 13, 1869, 1-84.
1487. HELLING, Gertrud, "Berechnung eines Index der Agrar-
　　　　produktion in Deutschland im 19. Jahrhundert," Jb. f.
　　　　Wgesch., 1965 (4), 125-43.
1488. _____, "Zur Entwicklung der Produktivität in der
　　　　deutschen Landwirtschaft im 19. Jahrhundert," Jb. f.
　　　　Wgesch., 1966 (1), 129-41.
1489. HEY, Karl, "Der mittlere und niedere Landwirtschaftliche
　　　　Unterricht in Deutschland," ZgesStw, 65, 1909, 224-87,
　　　　404-43.
1490. HÖTZSCH, Otto, "Der Bauernschutz in den deutschen Ter-
　　　　ritorien vom 16. vis ins 19. Jahrhundert," Schmoll. Jb.,
　　　　26, 1902, 1137-69.
1491. HORN, Hannelore, "Die Rolle des Bundes der Landwirte im
　　　　Kampf um den Bau des Mittellandkanals," Jb. f. Gesch.
　　　　M. O. Dtschl., 7, 1958, 273-358.
1492. KAYSER, Emanuel, "Weinbau und Winzer im Rheingau Ein
　　　　Beitrag zu den Agrarverhältnisse des Rheingaues,"
　　　　Schmoll. Jb., 31, 1907, 1147-87, 1625-66.
1493. KLEIN, Ernst, "Der Bauernaufstand in Schlesien im Feb-
　　　　ruar," Zs. f. Geschw., 3, 1955, 29-45.
1494. KNAPP, G. F., "Die Bauernbefreiung in Österreich und in
　　　　Preussen," Schmoll. Jb., 18, 1894, 409-31.
1495. _____, "Zur Geschichte der Bauernbefreiung in den
　　　　älteren Teilen Preussens," FBPG, 1, 1888, 573-85.
1496. KULISCHER, Josef, "Das Aufkommen der landwirtschaft-
　　　　lichen Maschinen um die Wende des 18. und in der ersten
　　　　Hälfte des 19. Jahrhunderts," Jbb. f. Nationalökon. u.
　　　　Stat., 139, 1933, 321-68.
1497. LANDGRAF, J., "Der Anteil der deutschen Handels- und
　　　　Gewerbekammern an der Landwirtschaftlichen Entwicklung
　　　　Deutschlands im letzten Decennium (1864-1873)," Jbb. f.
　　　　Nationalökon. u. Stat., 21, 1873, 341-59.
1498. LAUBERT, Manfred, "Die Genesis der Kabinettsordre vom
　　　　6. Mai 1819 über den Bauernschutz in der Provinz
　　　　Posen," VSW, 18, 1925, 348-68.
1499. LEBOVICS, Herman, "'Agrarians' versus 'Industrializers'
　　　　Social Conservative Resistance to Industrialism in late
　　　　Nineteenth Century Germany," Int. Rev. Soc. Hist., 12,
　　　　1967, 31-65.
1500. LÜTGE, Friedrich, "Über die Auswirkungen der Bauernbe-
　　　　freiung in Deutschland," Jbb. f. Nationalökon. u. Stat.,

157, 1943, 353-404.

1501. MAUER, Hermann, "Die Verschuldungsgesetze für Bauerngü-
      ter in Preussen (1811-1843)," Arch. f. Sozialw. u.
      Sozialpol., 24, 1907, 547-57.

1502. MÜLLER-WILLE, Wilhelm, "Der Feldbau in Westfalen im
      19. Jahrhundert," Westfäl. Forschg., 1, 1939, 302-25.

1503. _____, "Feldsysteme in Westfalen um 1860," Dt. geogr.
      Bl., 42, 1939, 119-45.

1504. MUTH, Heinrich, "Zur Geschichte des Hunsrücker Bauern-
      vereins," Jb. f. Gesch. Kunst d. MRh, 20/21, 1968/69,
      178-219.

1505. NOBBE, Moritz, "Agrarpolitische Probleme," Pr. Jbb.,
      92, 1898, 220-46.

1506. RAUCHBERG, H., "Die Landwirtschaft im Deutschen Reich
      Nach der Landwirtschaftlichen Betriebszählung im Deutsch-
      en Reich vom 14. Juni 1895," Arch. f. Sozialw. u.
      Sozialpol., 15, 1900, 554-97.

1507. ROTHKEGEL, Walter, "Die Bewegung die Kaufpreise für
      ländliche Besitzungen und die Entwicklung der Getreide-
      preise im Königreich Preussen von 1895 bis 1909,"
      Schmoll. Jb., 34, 1910, 1689-1747.

1508. RUDLOFF, Hans L., "Wirtschaftsergebnisse eines mittleren
      bäuerlichen Betrieber im hessischen Bergland (1888-
      1909)," Schmoll. Jb., 35, 1911, 251-83.

1509. SCHMOLLER, Gustav, "Der Kampf des preussischen König-
      thums um die Erhaltung des Bauernstandes," Schmoll.
      Jb., 12, 1888, 645-55.

1510. SCHNORBUS, Axel, "Die ländlichen Unterschichten in der
      bayerischen Gesellschaft am Ausgang des 19. Jahrhun-
      derts," Zs. f. bayer. LG., 30, 1967, 824-52.

1511. SCHREMMER, Eckart, "Agrareinkommen und Kapitalbildung
      im 19. Jahrhundert in Süddeutschland," Jbb. f. Na-
      tionalökon. u. Stat., 176, 1964, 196-240.

1512. STÖLZ, Otto, "Die Bauernbefreiung in Süddeutschland im
      Zusammenhang der Geschichte," VSW, 33, 1940, 1-68.

1513. STRAUSS, Rudolph, "Löhne und Preise in Deutschland 1750
      bis 1850," Jb. f. Wgesch., 1963 (1), 189-219; 1963 (2),
      212-29; 1963 (2), 230-36; 1963 (3), 257-75; 1963 (4), 263-80;
      1964 (1), 270-80; 1964 (4), 307-17; 1965 (1), 233-49; 1965
      (2), 185-92; 1965 (3), 211-19; 1965 (4), 266-80.

1514. TREUE, Wolfgang, "Die preussische Agrarreform zwischen
      Romantik und Rationalismus," Rhein. Vjsbll., 20, 1955,
      337-57.

1515. WALD, Annmarie, "Die Bauernbefreiung und die Ablösung
      des Obereigentums--eine Befreiung der Herren?," Hist.
      Vjschr., 28, 1933/34, 795-811.

1516. WALTEMATH, Kuno, "Der Bund der Landwirte in Han-
      nover," Pr. Jbb., 141, 1910, 61-77.

1517. _____, "Der deutsche Bauer," Pr. Jbb., 145, 1911, 193-
      222.

1518. _____, "Der Stand der mitteldeutschen Kleinbauern,"
      Pr. Jbb., 150, 1912, 269-91.

1519. WEBER-KELLERMANN, Ingeborg, "Betrachtungen zu Wilhelm

Mannhardts Umfrage von 1865 über Arbeitsgerät und bäuerliche Arbeit," Zs. f. Agrarg, 14, 1966, 45-53.

1520. WIEDENFELD, Kurt, "Die Organisation des deutschen Getreidehandels und die Getreidepreisbildung im 19. Jahrhundert," Schmoll. Jb., 24, 1900, 623-61.

1521. ZAKRZEWSKI, C. A., "Zur ländlichen Arbeiterfrage im Osten Deutschlands," Schmoll. Jb., 14, 1890, 891-911.

Alcoholism

1522. ALBERG, Moritz, "Die Trunksucht und ihre Bekämpfung," Pr. Jbb., 53, 1884, 248-63.

1523. BAER, Dr. A., "Gesetzliche Massregeln zur Bekämpfung der Trunksucht," Pr. Jbb., 46, 1880, 603-11.

1524. BERNDT, Wolfgang and Gotthard MÜNCH, "Der Abstinentenbund von Strausseney," Jb. d. Schles.-Fried.-Wilh. Univ z. Breslau, 13, 1968, 122-40.

1525. SEIDEL, Dr., "Der Alkoholismus in Deutschland," ZgesStw, 63, 1907, 454-89.

1526. WEYMANN, Konrat, "Die Bedeutung des Alkoholmissbrauchs für unser Volksleben," Pr. Jbb., 125, 1906, 493-530.

Banking

See also entries 968, 1454, 4658.

1527. BÖHME, Helmut, "Gründung und Anfänge des Schaaffhausenschen Bankvereins, der Bank des Berliner Kassenvereins, der Direktion der Disconto-Gesellschaft und der Darmstädter Bank für Handel und Industrie Ein Beitrag zur preussischen Bankpolitik von 1848-1853," Tradition, 10, 1965, 189-212; 11, 1966, 34-56.

1528. BOPP, K. R., "Die Tätigkeit der Reichsbank von 1876 bis 1914," Weltwirtsch. Arch., 72, 1954, 34-59, 179-224.

1529. CAMERON, Rondo E., ed., "Dokumente zur Gründung der Darmstädter Bank," Tradition, 2, 1957, 125-31.

1530. _____, "Founding the Bank of Darmstadt," Explorations in Entrepreneurial History, 8, 1955/56, 113-30.

1531. _____, "Die Gründung der Darmstädter Bank," Tradition, 2, 1957, 104-24.

1532. DANIELS, Emil, "Zur Genesis der 'Deutschen Bank'," Pr. Jbb., 188, 1922, 129-45.

1533. ELSAS, Fritz, "Der Kampf um die Gründung einer Notenbank in Württemberg (1847-1871)," Schmoll. Jb., 40, 1916, 1737-1819.

1534. HELFFERICH, Karl, "Die Entwicklung der deutschen Notenwesens unter dem Bankgesetz von 1875," Schmoll. Jb., 22, 1898, 995-1035.

1535. HOFFMANN, Walter, "Deutsche Banken in der Türkei," Weltwirtsch. Arch., 6, 1915, 410-21.

1536. _____, "Die Entwicklung der Sparkassen im Rahmen des

Wachstums der deutschen Wirtschaft (1850-1967), "
ZgesStw, 125, 1969, 561-605.

1537. KLEIN, Ernst, "Die Königlich Württembergische Hofbank
und ihre Bedeutung für die Industrialisierung in der ersten
Hälfte des 19. Jahrhundert, " Jbb. f. Nationökon. u. Stat.,
179, 1966, 324-43.

1538. KÜMMEL, H., "Die Aufgaben der Sparkassen in Deutschland
als Lebensversicherungsinstitute für die unteren Volksklas-
sen, " Schmoll. Jb., 27, 1903, 99-140.

1539. LEXIS, W., "The German Bank Commission 1908-09, "
Econ. J., 20, 1910, 211-21.

1540. NASSE, E., "Die deutschen Zettelbanken während der Krisis
von 1866, " Jbb. f. Nationalökon. u. Stat., 11, 1868, 1-
23.

1541. OBERMANN, Karl, "Die Rolle der ersten deutschen Aktien-
banken in den Jahren 1848 bis 1856, " Jb. f. Wgesch.,
1960 (2), 47-75.

1542. POSCHINGER, Heinrich von, "Die Bankentwicklung im
Königreich Sachsen Nach amtlichen Quellen dargestellt, "
Jbb. f. Nationalökon. u. Stat., 26, 1876, 296-356; 28,
1877, 73-129.

1543. RADANT, Hans, "'100 Jahre Deutsche Bank' Eine typische
Konzerngeschichte, " Jb. f. Wgesch., 1972 (3), 37-62.

1544. ROSENDORFF, Richard, "Die deutschen Banken im über-
seeischen Verkehr, " Schmoll. Jb., 29, 1904, 1245-86.

1545. SCHNEE, Heinrich, "Hofbankier Salomon von Haber als
badischer Finanzier, " ZGORh., 109, 1961, 341-59.

1546. _____, "175 Jahre Bankhaus Salomon Oppenheim jr. Bonn/
Köln, " Bonner Geschichtsblätter, 18, 1964, 66-79.

1547. SCHUMACHER, H. A., "The Concentration of German Bank-
ing, " Pol. Sci. Q., 22, 1907, 83-104.

1548. _____, "Die Ursachen und Wirkungen der Konzentration
im deutschen Bankwesen, " Schmoll. Jb., 30, 1906, 883-
925.

1549. SEIDENZAHL, Fritz, "Das Spannungsfeld zwischen Staat und
Bankier im Wilhelminischen Zeitalter, " Tradition, 13,
1968, 142-50.

1550. STEINBACH, Rudolph, "Die Verwaltungsunkosten der Berliner Grossbanken, " Schmoll. Jb., 29, 1905, 481-511,
957-95.

1551. THORWART, F., "Die Entwicklung des Banknotenumlaufs
in Deutschland von 1851-1880, " Jbb. Nationalökon. u.
Stat., 41, 1883, 193-250.

1552. TRENDE, Adolf, "Beiträge zur Geschichte der deutschen
Sparkassen, " Tradition, 3, 1958, 120-27.

1553. TREUE, Wilhelm, "Dagobert Oppenheim Zeitungsherausgeber,
Bankier und Unternehmer in der Zeit des Liberalismus
und Neumerkantilismus, " Tradition, 9, 1964, 145-75.

1554. _____, "Der Privatbankier auf der Wende vom 19. zum
20. Jahrhundert, " Tradition, 15, 1970, 225-38.

1555. VAGTS, Alfred, "M. M. Warburg & Co. Ein Bankhaus in
der deutschen Weltpolitik 1905-1933, " VSW, 45, 1958,
289-388.

1556.   WEBERSINN, Gerhard, "Gustav Heinrich Ruffer Breslauer
         Bankherr--Pionier des Eisenbahngedankens-Förderer
         schlesischer Wirtschaft," Jb. d. Schles.-Fried.-Wilh.
         Univ z. Breslau, 11, 1966, 154-96.
1557.   WISSKIRCHEN, Wilhelm, "Burkhardt & Co. Privatbankiers
         im Herzen des Ruhrgebiets," Tradition, 2, 1957, 229-46.
1558.   ZORN, Wolfgang, "Neuerscheinungen zur deutschen Bank-
         geschichte 1956-1959," Tradition, 5, 1960, 231-35.

Cities

1559.   BLASCHKE, Kerlheinz, "Qualität, Quantität und Raumfunk-
         tion als Wesensmerkmale der Stadt vom Mittelalter bis
         zur Gegenwart," Jb. f. Regionalgesch., 3, 1968, 34-50.
1560.   BLAUM, Dr., "Die Wohnlage der Armenbevölkerung einer
         Grosstadt," Zs. f. d. Armenwesen, 15, 1914, 265-78.
1561.   BÖHME, Helmut, "Stadtregiment, Repräsentativverfassung
         und Wirtschaftskonjunktur in Frankfurt am Main und Ham-
         burg im 19. Jahrhundert," Esslinger Stud., 15, 1969.
1562.   BOSL, Karl, "München Deutschlands heimische Hauptstadt
         Historische Bemerkungen zur Strukturanalyse des moder-
         nen Hauptstadt- und Grossstadttypus in Deutschland," Zs.
         f. bayer. LG., 30, 1967, 298-313.
1563.   BUCHNER, Max, "Ebbe und Flut des nationalen Gedankens
         in Münchens Vergangenheit," Gelbe Hefte, 4, 1927/28,
         673-726.
1564.   BÜSCH, Otto, "Festungsstadt und Industrie Zur Geschichte
         von Spandau und Siemensstadt im Zeitalter der Industrial-
         isierung," Jb. f. Gesch. M. O. Dtschl., 20, 1971, 161-
         82.
1565.   CROON, Helmuth, "Forschungsprobleme der neueren Städte-
         geschichte," Bl. deutsch. Landesgesch., 105, 1969.
1566.   _____, "Die Versorgung der Grosstädte des Ruhrgebietes
         im 19. und 20. Jahrhundert," Jbb. f. Nationalökon. u.
         Stat., 179, 1966, 356-68.
1567.   CZOK, Karl, "Zur Stellung der Stadt in der deutschen
         Geschichte," Jb. f. Regionalgesch., 3, 1968, 9-33.
1568.   DIX, Arthur, "Die deutschen Ostseestädte und die Grund-
         lagen ihrer wirthschaftlichen Entwicklung," Pr. Jbb.,
         101, 1900, 460-512.
1569.   DREYFUS, François G., "Révolution industrielle et villes
         Allemandes," Annales, 17, 1962, 773-79.
1570.   FREYHAN, Wilhelm, "Breslaus Stadtbild im 19. Jahrhundert
         Eine Verkehrgeographische Studie," Jb. d. Schles.-Fried.-
         Wilh. Univ z. Breslau, 10, 1965, 262-74.
1571.   HECKE, W., "Die Bevölkerungszuwanderung in die Gros-
         städte Wien und Berlin," Deutsches Archiv für Landes-
         und Volksforschung, 1941, 81-87.
1572.   HEUBNER, P., "100 Jahre Wandel und Wachstum der Leip-
         ziger Messen," Schmoll. Jb., 61, 1937, 589-606.
1573.   HÜFFER, Hermann, "Peter Joseph Boosfeld und die Stadt
         Bonn unter Französischer Herrschaft," Ann. Niederrhein,

13/14, 1863, 118-47.

1574.   KÖLLMANN, Wolfgang, "Industrialisierung, Binnenwanderung
        und 'soziale Frage' (Zur Entstehungsgeschichte der deut-
        schen Industriegrossstadt im 19. Jahrhundert)," VSW, 46,
        1959, 45-70.

1575.   _____, "The process of urbanization in Germany at the
        height of the industrialization period," J. Contemp. Hist.,
        4(3), 1969, 59-76.

1576.   LACROIX, Emil, "Zur Baugeschichte des Karlsruher Markt-
        platzes Ein Beitrag zur Geschichte des Städtebaus im 19.
        Jahrhundert," ZGORh., 86, 1933/34, 24-57.

1577.   MEINHARDT, Günther, "Göttingen in der napoleonischen
        Zeit," Göttinger Jb., 18, 1970.

1578.   MONZ, Heinz, "Die Bevölkerungsstruktur einer mitteleuro-
        päischen Stadt und ihrer Region im Jahre 1802 im Ver-
        gleich zu den Jahren 1961/64," Arch. f. Sozialgesch., 5,
        1965, 147-91.

1579.   "NOTSTANDSARBEITEN der Stadt Düsseldorf im Winter
        1907/08," Zs. f. d. Armenwesen, 9, 1908, 339-46.

1580.   SCHWEMMER, Wilhelm, "Die Stadtmauer von Nürnberg ...
        im 19. und 20. Jahrhundert," Mitteil. d. Vereins f.
        Gesch. der Stadt Nürnberg, 56, 1969.

1581.   SEUTEMANN, Karl, "Die selbständige Organisation der
        amtlichen Statistik der deutschen Städte," Schmoll. Jb.,
        30, 1906, 1345-65.

1582.   SHEEHAN, James J., "Liberalism and the City in Nine-
        teenth Century Germany," Past and Present, 42, 1971,
        116-37.

1583.   STIEDA, Wilhelm, "Grossstädtische Berufsverhältnisse,"
        Schmoll. Jb., 9, 1885, 127-54.

1584.   WEISS, Konrad, "Johann Georg v. Schuh, Oberbürgermeister
        von Nürnberg," Zs. f. bayer. LG., 3, 1930, 407-80.

1585.   "WOHNUNGSVERHÄLTNISSE in grossen Städten," Zs. f. d.
        Armenwesen, 7, 1906, 207-15; 8, 1907, 98-103.

1586.   ZAHN, Friedrich, "Die Volkszählung 1900 und die Gross-
        stadtfrage," Jbb. f. Nationalökon. u. Stat., 81, 1903,
        191-215.

1587.   ZORN, Wolfgang, "Zu den Anfängen der Industrialisierung
        Augsburgs im 19. Jahrhundert," VSW, 38, 1949, 155-68.

                              Berlin

1588.   BALLOD, Carl, "Richard Böckh und das Statistische Jahr-
        buch der Stadt Berlin 1876-1900," Schmoll. Jb., 26, 1902,
        341-56.

1589.   BLEIBER, Helmut, "Die Moabiter Unruhen 1910 Bemerkun-
        gen zu sozialen Lage der Arbeiter in Berlin und zu ihren
        wirtschaftlichen und politischen Kampf vor dem Herbst
        1910," Zs. f. Geschw., 3, 1955, 171-211.

1590.   BORKENHAGEN, Erich, "Das Bier im alten Berlin," Bär v.
        Ber., 17, 1968, 77-104.

1591.   DELLE, Eberhard, "Dramatisches Mädchen für Alles Das

Viktoria-Theater in Berlin," Jahrbuch Ver f. d. Gesch.
Berlins, 2, 1952, 161-82.

1592.   DIETRICH, Richard, "Probleme Stadtgeschichtlicher Untersuchungen im Zeitalter der Industrialisierung am Beispiel
Berlins," Jb. f. Gesch. M. O. Dtschl., 16/17, 1968,
169-209.

1593.   _____, "Von der Residenzstadt zur Weltstadt," J. f.
Gesch. des d. Ostens, 1, 1952, 111-39.

1594.   FRICKE, Hermann, "Berlin als Lebensraum im Werke
Friedrich Hebbels," Jahrbuch Ver. f. d. Gesch. Berlins, 3, 1953, 70-96.

1595.   GOOCH, G. P., "Berlin in the Nineties," Ger. Life Letters, 9, 1955/56, 56-63.

1596.   GRANDKE, H., "Die Entstehung der Berliner Wäsche-In-
dustrie im 19. Jahrhundert," Schmoll. Jb., 20, 1896,
587-607.

1597.   GRIEWANK, Karl, "Vulgärer Radikalismus und demokratische Bewegung in Berlin 1842-48," FBPG, 36, 1924,
14-37.

1598.   GRUNER, J. V., "Der Anfang des königlichen Polizeipräsi-
diums in Berlin unter dem ersten Polizeipräsidenten
Justus Gruner," Mitt. d. Ver. f. Gesch., 6, 1889, 75-
78.

1599.   _____, "Das Feuerlöschwesen in Berlin in den Jahren
1809-1811," Mitt. d. Ver. f. Gesch., 8, 1891, 111-14,
140-42, 148-49, 153-55.

1600.   _____, "Die Strassenbeleuchtung der Stadt Berlin in den
Jahren 1809 bis 1810," Mitt. d. Ver. f. Gesch., 7,
1890, 19-23, 42-44, 56-58, 62-64.

1601.   _____, "Der Zustand der öffentlichen Sicherheit in der
Mark im Jahre 1810," Mitt. d. Ver. f. Gesch., 10,
1893, 5-12.

1602.   HAENCHEN, Karl, "Zur revolutionären Unterwühlung Berlins vor den Märztagen des Jahres 1848," FBPG, 55,
1943, 83-114.

1603.   HAUBNER, Fritz, "Aus den Anfängen der öffentlichen Elek-
trizitätsversorgung in Berlin (1882-1899)," Tradition, 7,
1962, 1-11.

1604.   HENGSBACH, Arne, "Die Berliner Heerstrasse Ein Kapitel
Planungsgeschichte," Bär v. Ber., 9, 1960, 87-112.

1605.   _____, "Berliner Verkehrsplanung vor hundert Jahren
Anfänge einer Städtischen Verkehrspolitik," Bär v. Ber.,
18, 1969, 36-59.

1606.   _____, "Im Stromkreis der Havel Spandau im 19. Jahrhundert," Jahrbuch Ver. f. d. Gesch. Berlins, 2, 1952,
183-99.

1607.   _____, "Die Kirche und die Schnellbahn Ein Kapitel Berliner Verkehrsgeschichte," Bär v. Ber., 14, 1965, 243-
60.

1608.   _____, "Zwischen Spandau und Berlin Aus der Geschichte
des Berliners Nahverkehrs," Bär v. Ber., 5, 1955, 95-
125.

1609.   HERZFELD, Hans, "Berlin als Kaiserstadt und Reichshauptstadt 1871-1945," J. f. Gesch. des d. Ostens, 1, 1952, 141-70.

1610.   HESSEN, Robert, "Die Berliner Wohnungsnoth," Pr. Jbb., 67, 1891, 635-62.

1611.   HIRSCH, Helmut, "Die Berliner Welcker-Kundgebung Zur frühgeschichte der Volksdemonstrationen," Arch. f. Sozialgesch., 1, 1961, 27-42.

1612.   HIRSCHMANN, Lothar, "Pariser 'Trux' und literarisches Experiment über das Berliner Residenz-Theater," Bär v. Ber., 5, 1955, 74-94.

1613.   JARCHOW, Walter, "Hundert Jahre Baukunst in Berlin," Bär v. Ber., 14, 1965, 87-121.

1614.   KAEBER, Ernst, "Die Oberbürgermeister Berlins seit der Steinschen Städteordnung," Jahrbuch Ver f. d. Gesch. Berlins, 2, 1952, 53-114.

1615.   _____, "Die Stadt Berlin u. der Staat Eine historisch-politische Betrachtung," Zs. f. Pol., 9, 1916, 426-70.

1616.   KANTOROWIEZ, Moritz, "Die Wirksamkeit der Spekulation im Berliner Kornhandel 1850-1890," Schmoll. Jb., 15, 1891, 1183-97.

1617.   KETTIG, Konrad, "Gemeinsinn und Mitverantwortung Beiträge zur Geschichte der Berliner Stadtverordnetenvertreters Heinrich Kochhann," Bär v. Ber., 12, 1963, 7-27.

1618.   _____, "Wilhelm Wackernagel Schicksal eines Berlin Demagogen von 1819," Bär v. Ber., 9, 1960, 7-27.

1619.   KNUDSEN, Knud, "Hundert Jahre Berliner Litfass-Säulen Ernst Litfass in seiner Zeit," Bär v. Ber., 4, 1954, 7-44.

1620.   KUTZSCH, Gerhard, "Hinter den Fassaden Das Volk Berlins im 19. Jahrhundert," Bär v. Ber., 20, 1971, 7-26.

1621.   _____, "Der Staat und die Stadt Berlin Skizzierung ihres Verhältnisses zueinander im 19. Jahrhundert," Bär v. Ber., 17, 1968, 7-21.

1622.   _____, "Vom 'Sozialen Defizit' Berlins 1875-1915 Zur Geschichte der Prostitution der Reichshauptstadt," Bär v. Ber., 13, 1964, 108-16.

1623.   LAFORGUE, Jules, "Unter den Linden in the 'Eighties'," Yale Review, 1956, 410-16.

1624.   LIANG, Hsi-Huey, "Lower-Class Immigrants in Wilhelmine Berlin," Cen. Eur. Hist., 3, 1970, 94-111.

1625.   MIECK, Ilja, "Das Berliner Fabriken-Gericht 1815-1875," Jb. f. Gesch. M. O. Dtschl., 6, 1958, 249-71.

1626.   _____, "Die werdende Grosstadt Berliner Verkehrsprobleme in der Biedermeierzeit," Bär v. Ber., 9, 1960, 49-68.

1627.   MIELKE, Friedrich, "Studie über den Berliner Wohnungsbau Zwischen den Kriegen 1870/71 und 1914-1918," Jb. f. Gesch. M. O. Dtschl., 20, 1971, 202-38.

1628.   MORITZ, Lilli, "Die Dorfschule von Wilmersdorf 1785-1855," Bär v. Ber., 7, 1957/58, 124-46; 13, 1964, 68-88.

1629.   NAGEL, Carl, "Zeit zwischen den Zeiten Bilder aus dem

Berliner Vormärz," Bär v. Ber., 11, 1962, 7-26.

1630. PIERSON, Kurt, "Als die 'S-Bahn'noch dampfte Erinnerungen zu ihrem 100 Geburtstag," Bär v. Ber., 20, 1971, 64-72.

1631. RAVE, Paul O., "Aus der Frühzeit Berliner Sammlertums 1670-1870 Ein Beitrag zur Kulturgeschichte," Bär v. Ber., 8, 1959, 7-32.

1632. REDSLOB, Erwin, "Berlin in Gründungsjahr seines Geschichtsvereins," Bär v. Ber., 15, 1966, 147-62.

1633. SCHATTEN, Lore, "Louis Schneider Porträt eines Berliners," Bär v. Ber., 8, 1959, 116-41.

1634. SCHMIDT, Wilhelm and Helmut WINZ, "Von Rixdorf zu Neukölln Die Entwicklung der Stadtlandschaft eines Berliner Ortsteils," Jb. f. Gesch. M. O. Dtschl., 15, 1966, 175-202.

1635. STEPHAN, Walther, "Johann Friedrich Dannenberger Ein Bahnbrecher der Berliner Grossindustrie," Bär v. Ber., 7, 1957/58, 19-37.

1636. T., "Berlin und Sein Verkehr," Pr. Jbb., 57, 1886, 355-97.

1637. WARNECKE, Heinz, "Berliner Studenten-Lützower, Burschenschaftler, Mitinitiatoren des Wartburgfestes 1817," Wiss. Zs. d. Univ. Jena, 15, 1966, 213-21.

1638. WEICHERT, Friedrich, "Die Planung des letzten Berliner Domes Ein Beitrag zu seiner Geschichte," Bär v. Ber., 20, 1971, 73-96.

1639. WERTHEIMER, Eduard von, "Ein K. und K. Militärattaché über das politische Leben in Berlin (1880-1895)," Pr. Jbb., 201, 1925, 264-82.

1640. WIRTH, Irmgard, "Menzel und Berlin," Bär v. Ber., 14, 1965, 161-78.

Carl Ludwig von Hinckeldey (1805-1856)

1641. SCHULZE, Berthold, "Polizeipräsident Carl v. Hinckeldey," Jb. f. Gesch. M. O. Dtschl., 4, 1955, 81-108.

1642. SYBEL, Heinrich Von, "Carl Ludwig Von Hinckeldey 1852 bis 1856," HZ, 189, 1959, 108-23.

Bremen

1643. ENGELSING, Rolf, "Die bremische Dampfschiffahrt mit England im 19. Jahrhundert," Bremisches Jb., 46, 1959, 279-303.

1644. _____, "Ein Reisebericht von 1842 Bremen im Urteil eines Anhängers des Jungen Deutschlands," Bremisches Jb., 48, 1962, 375-401.

1645. ENTHOLT, E., "Bürgermeister Smidt und seine Korrespondenten," Bremisches Jb., 42, 1947, 11ff.

1646. ENTHOLT, Hermann, "Ansicht der Geschichte Bremens im dritten Viertel des 19. Jahrhunderts," Bremisches Jb.,

42, 1947, 52-81.

1647. _____, "Ungedrucktes aus dem Nachlass von Bürgermeister Arnold Duckwitz," Bremisches Jb., 37, 1937, 258-322.

1648. HELM, Karl, "Bremens Holzschiffbau vom Mittelalter bis zum Ausgang des 19. Jahrhunderts," Bremisches Jb., 44, 1955, 175-243.

1649. HEYDERHOFF, Julius, "Johann Friedrich Benzenberg und das Fockesche Haus in Bremen," Bremisches Jb., 31, 1928, 305-34.

1650. JACOBS, Alfred, "Bremen im Wandel der Weltwirtschaft," Bremisches Jb., 50, 1965, 361-73.

1651. KELLENBENZ, Hermann, "Der Bremer Kaufmann Versuch einer sozialgeschichtlichen Deutung," Bremisches Jb., 51, 1969, 19-49.

1652. KIESSELBACH, Arnold, "Der Bremer Dr. Phil. Wilhelm Kiesselbach als Vorkämpfer für den deutschen Einheitsgedanken 1848-1864," Bremisches Jb., 39, 1940, 11-62.

1653. KOSSOK, Manfred, "Preussen, Bremen und die 'Texasfrage' 1835-1845," Bremisches Jb., 49, 1964, 73-104.

1654. LAMMERS, A., "Bürgermeister Smidt," Pr. Jbb., 32, 1873, 625-41.

1655. LEMELSON, Fritz, "Die bremische Bürgerwehr 1813-1853," Bremisches Jb., 33, 1931, 205-304.

1656. PAETOW, Dr., "Das bremische Gesetz betr. den armenpolizeilichen Arbeitszwang," Zs. f. d. Armenwesen, 12, 1912, 67-76.

1657. PATEMANN, Reinhard, "Johann Hermann Holler 1818-1868," Bremisches Jb., 51, 1969, 237-46.

1658. PETERS, Fritz, "Über bremische Firmengründungen in der ersten Hälfte des 19. Jahrhunderts (1814-1847)," Bremisches Jb., 36, 1936, 306-61.

1659. PRÜSER, Friedrich, "Bremische Firmengeschichte," Bremisches Jb., 46, 1959, 319-35.

1660. SCHWARZ, K., "Der Bremer Wohnungsmarkt während der Handelskonjunktur um 1800," Niedersächs. Jb. für LG, 43, 1971, 122-40.

1661. STUCKENSCHMIDT, Hans, "Das Bremische Feldbataillon 1813-1867," Bremisches Jb., 35, 1935, 325-57; 36, 1936, 259-305.

1662. TAUBE, Arved Freiherr von, "Johann Georg Kohl und die Baltischen Lande Die 'Wiederaufseglung' Livlands durch eines Bremer zur Biedermeierzeit," Bremisches Jb., 48, 1962, 261-318.

1663. TIDEMANN, Heinrich, "Die Gesellschaft 'Euphrosyne' Ein Beitrag zur politischen und zur Geistesgeschichte Bremens im 19. Jahrhundert," Bremisches Jb., 29, 1924, 82-113.

1664. WÄTJEN, Hermann, "Dr. Rudolf Schleiden als Diplomat in Bremischen Diensten 1853-1866," Bremisches Jb., 34, 1933, 262-76.

Frankfurt a. M.

1665. BÖHME, H., "Stadtregiment Repräsentativverfassung und
Wirtschaftskonjunktur in Frankfurt am Main und Hamburg
im 19. Jahrhundert," Jb. f. Gesch. d. Reichsstädte, 15,
1969, 75-146.

1666. COCHENHAUSEN, F., "Aus dem Frankfurter Reichskriegs-
ministerium," Arch. f. Frankfurts Gesch., 5, 1938, 82ff.

1667. KANTZENBACH, Friedrich W., "Die Anfänge der ökumen-
ischen Bewegung im Frankfurt der Romantik," ZRGG, 7,
1955, 304-22.

1668. MUTIUS, Albert v., "Aus einem Frankfurter Patrizierhause
Nach der Autobiographie Moritz August v. Bethmann-
Hollwegs," Pr. Jbb., 229, 1932, 254-63.

1669. STERNE, Margaret, "The End of the Free City of Frankfort," J. Mod. Hist., 30, 1958, 203-214.

1670. _____, "Die Frankfurter Berichte des letzten nieder-
ländischen Gesandten am Bundestag Friedrich Heinrich
Wilhelm von Scherff 1863-1866," Arch. f. Frankfurts
Gesch., 51, 1968, 65-83.

Hamburg

1671. BÖHME, H., "Wirtschaftskrise, Merchant Bankers und Ver-
fassungsreform. Zur Bedeutung der Weltwirtschaftskrise
von 1857 in Hamburg," Zs. d. Ver f. hamburg. Gesch.,
54, 1968, 77-127.

1672. ENGELSING, Rolf, "Lebenshaltungen und Lebenshaltungskos-
ten im 18. und 19. Jahrhundert in den Hansestädten Bremen und Hamburg," Int. Rev. Soc. Hist., 11, 1966, 73-
107.

1673. FRANCKE, E., "Die Arbeitsverhältnisse im Hafen zu Hamburg," Schmoll. Jb., 22, 1898, 943-65.

1674. "HAMBURG und die Handelskrisis," Pr. Jbb., 1, 1858,
275-92.

1675. HANSCHILD-THIESSEN, R., "Hamburg im Kriege 1870/71,"
Zs. d. Ver f. Hamburg Gesch., 57, 1971, 1-45.

1676. NAHRSTEDT, Wolfgang, "Freizeit und Aufklärung zum Funk-
tionswandel der Feiertage seit dem 18. Jahrhundert in
Hamburg (1743-1860)," VSW, 57, 1970, 46-92.

1677. SCHRAMM, Percy Ernst, "Zur Bildungsgeschichte Hamburger
Kaufleute um 1860-1870," Tradition, 8, 1963, 1-14.

1678. SIEVEKING, Heinr., "Hamburger Kolonisationspläne 1840-
42," Pr. Jbb., 86, 1896, 149-70.

1679. _____, "Die Hamburgische Firma Kunst & Albers in
Wladiwostok 1864-1914," VSW, 34, 1941, 268-99.

1680. THOMSEN, Helmuth, "C. Boysen 1867-1957 Eine Hamburger
Buchhandlung im Wandel der letzten neunzig Jahre," Tradition, 2, 1957, 293-306.

1681. TÖNNIES, Ferdinand, "Der Hamburger Strike von 1896/97,"
Arch. f. Sozialw. u. Sozialpol., 10, 1897, 673-720.

1682. TUCH, Gustav, "Sonderstellung und Zollanschluss Hamburgs

Ein Bruchstück deutschen Geschichte," Schmoll. Jb., 6,
1882, 113-232.

1683. TVEITE, Stein, "Hamburg og norsk naeringsliv 1814-1860,"
Hist. Tidsskr., 42, 1963, 197-229.

1684. "Die WAHRHEIT im Streik der Hafenarbeiter und Seeleute
in Hamburg im Jahre 1896/97," Schmoll. Jb., 21, 1897,
681-714.

Koblenz

1685. FABER, Karl-Georg, "Graf Karl August von Reisach Ein
Beitrag zur Geschichte des Staatsarchivs Koblenz und
der politischen Polizei am Rhein," Jb. f. Gesch. Kunst.
d. MRh, 8/9, 1956/57, 111-26.

1686. MARTIN, Hortense, "Soziale Bestrebungen im Koblenzer
Katholizismus in der ersten Hälfte des 19. Jahrhunderts,"
Jb. f. Gesch. Kunst d. MRh, 4/5, 1952/53, 74-88.

1687. PRÖSSLER, Helmut, "Hubert Joseph Codenbach (1800-1867)
Oberbürgermeister von Koblenz 1858-1867," Jb. f. Gesch.
Kunst d. MRh, 20/21, 1968/69, 159-77.

Demography

1688. COHN, Gustav, "The Increase in Population in Germany,"
Econ. J., 22, 1912, 34-45.

1689. EBERHARDT, Hans, "Bevölkerungs- und Wirtschaftsgeschichte des Amtes Königsee in der ersten Hälfte des 19.
Jhs.," Rudolstädter Heimathefte, 10, 1964, 18-31, 61-
73.

1690. KÖLLMANN, W., "Die Bevölkerung Rheinland-Westfalens in
der Hochindustrialisierungsperiode," VSW, 58, 1071, 350-
88.

1691. _____, "Die Bevölkerung der westdeutschen Industrie-
grossstadt Barmen vor und während der Industrialisierungs-
periode," Zs. d. berg. gesch. Ver., 81, 1965, 152-74.

1692. KOLLMANN, Paul, "Neue Forschungen zur deutschen Be-
völkerungs Geschichte," Schmoll. Jb., 8, 1884, 523-40.

1693. _____, "Das statistische Amt für das Grossherzogtum
Oldenburg in der ersten fünfzig Jahren seines Bestehens,"
Jbb. f. Nationalökon. u. Stat., 83, 1904, 723-55.

1694. QUANTE, Peter, "Die Bevölkerungsentwicklung der preussischen ostprovinzen im 19. und 20. Jahrhundert," Zs. f.
Ostforsch., 8, 1959, 481-99.

1695. RAUCHBERG, Prof. Dr. H., "Die Berufs- und Gewerbe-
bezählung im deutschen Reich vom 14. Juni 1895," Arch.
f. Sozialw. u. Sozialpol., 14, 1899, 227-309, 603-57.

1696. REICHEL, Carl, "Die Statistik des deutschen Reiches und
der grösseren Staaten desselben," Schmoll. Jb., 1, 1877,
339-62, 537-75; 2, 1878, 143-215.

1697. SCHAAB, Meinrad, "Die Herausbildung einer Bevölkerungs-
statistik in Württemberg und in Baden während der ersten

Hälfte des 19. Jahrhunderts," Zs. f. Württbg. LG, 30, 1971, 164-200.

1698.   SCHLAER, Friedrich-Wilhelm, "Die Mitwirkung der na-
        tionalökonomischen Disziplin bei der Neuorganisation des
        Preussischen Statistischen Büros im Jahre 1860," VSW,
        56, 1969, 233-44.
1699.   SCHÜTT, Horst, "Bevölkerungsentwicklung im nordwest-
        lichen Vorpommer von 1767 bis 1952," Zs. f. Ostforsch.,
        8, 1959, 215-31.
1700.   ZAHN, Friedrich, "Hans von Scheel und die Reichsstatistik,"
        Schmoll. Jb., 26, 1902, 325-39.
1701.   ZIMMERMANN, F. W. R., "Einflüsse des Lebensraums auf
        die Gestaltung der Bevölkerungsverhältnisse im Herzogtum
        Braunschweig," Schmoll. Jb., 21, 1897, 489-562.

Education

1702.   AGAHD, Konrad, "Die Erwerbsthätigkeit schulpflichtiger
        Kinder im deutschen Reich," Arch. f. Sozialw. u. Sozial-
        pol., 12, 1898, 373-428.
1703.   ASBACH, Dr. J., "Der Zustand des bergischen Schulwesens
        im Jahre 1809 und die Napoleonische Universität in Düs-
        seldorf," Ann. Niederrhein, 69, 1900, 128-37.
1704.   BONITZ, H., "Die gegenwärtigen Reformfragen in unserem
        höheren Schulwesen," Pr. Jbb., 35, 1875, 143-64.
1705.   BÜNGER, Dr. Richard, "Die Lage des höheren Lehrer-
        standes in Preussen," Pr. Jbb., 100, 1900, 452-80.
1706.   BUSSHOFF, Heinrich, "Die preussische Volksschule als
        soziales Gebilde und politischer Bildungsfaktor in der
        ersten Hälfte des 19. Jahrhunderts," GiWuU, 22, 1971.
1707.   DÜWELL, K., "Die Gründung des Kgl. Polytechnischen
        Schule in Aachen," Zs. des Aachener Gesch. ver., 81,
        1971, 173-212.
1708.   ECKERT, Christian, "Staatsbürgerliche Erziehung,"
        Schmoll. Jb., 36, 1912, 1321-63.
1709.   GEHRING, Paul, "Pläne eines Stuttgarter Polytechnikums
        von 1817 Ein Beitrag zur württembergischen Bildungs-
        politik zu Anfang des 19. Jahrhunderts," Zs. f. Württbg.
        LG, 27, 1968, 397-416.
1710.   HARTLIEB von Wallthor, Alfred, "Höhere Schulen in West-
        falen vom Ende des 15. bis zur Mitte des 19. Jahrhun-
        derts," Westf. Zs., 107, 1957, 1-105.
1711.   HERZIG, A., "Alexander Haindorfs Bedeutung für die Päda-
        gogik in Westfalen," Westf. Forsch., 23, 1972, 57-74.
1712.   HICKS, W. C. R., "German Education: A Retrospect and
        Re-Assessment," Ger. Life Letters, 2, 1937/38, 50-61.
1713.   HIRZEL, Gymasialrektor, "Die verwaltungsrechtliche Stel-
        lung des mittelschulwesens in seinem Verhältnis zu Staat,
        Gemeinde und Kirche in Württemberg," ZgesStw., 58,
        1902, 577-633.
1714.   JEISMANN, Karl-Ernst, "Die Eingabe eines Schwelmer
        Lehrers an das preussische Innenministerium ... aus

dem Jahre 1814," Westf. Zs., 118, 1968, 115-33.

1715. _____, "Gymnasium Staat und Gesellschaft in Preussen. Vorbemerkungen zur Untersuchung der politischen und sozialen Bedeutung der 'höheren Bildung' im 19. Jahrhundert," GiWuU, 21, 1970, 453-70.

1716. _____, "Tendenzen zur Verbesserung des Schulwesens in Grafschaft Mark 1798-1848," Westf. Forsch., 22, 1969/70.

1717. KIEFERT, Hans-Joachim, "Wilhelm Friedrich Hesse und sein Kommunalschulplan," Arch. f. hessische Gesch., 25, 1955/57, 199-284.

1718. KLÖTZER, Wolfgang, ed., "Erinnerungen des Lehrers Georg Wilhelm Pietzsch (1844-1920) Ein Beitrag zur Geschichte des Schulwesens im 19. Jahrhundert," Arch. f. Frankfurts Gesch., 49, 1965, 5-78.

1719. KUSKE, Erich, "Die Beteiligung der höheren Schulen Preussens an der Erhebung im Jahre 1813," Pr. Jbb., 154, 1913, 437-50.

1720. LAMMERS, A., "Das preussische Gesetz über öffentliche Erziehung verwahrloster Kinder," Schmoll. Jb., 2, 1878, 315-23.

1721. LOTZ, Albert, "Die Kosten der Volksschule in Preussen," Schmoll. Jb., 22, 1898, 1339-57.

1722. LUNDGREEN, Peter, "Analyse preussischer Schulbücher als Zugang zum Thema 'Schulbildung und Industrialisierung'," Int. Rev. Soc. Hist., 15, 1970, 85-121.

1723. MOMMSEN, Tycho, "Sechszehn Thesen zur Frage über die Gymnasialreform," Pr. Jbb., 34, 1874, 149-84.

1724. NEUBACH, Helmut, "Karl Friedrich Wilhelm Wander (1803-1879) Ein Beitrag Schlesiens zur deutschen Pädagogik," Jb. d. Schles.-Fried.-Wilh. Univ. z. Breslau, 16, 1971, 324-40.

1725. O'BOYLE, Lenore, "Klassische Bildung und Soziale Struktur In Deutschland zwischen 1800 und 1848," HZ, 207, 1968, 584-608.

1726. PETERSILIE, Prof. Dr. A., "Das öffentliche Volksschulwesen Preussens in statistischer Beleuchtung," Pr. Jbb., 74, 1893, 49-104.

1727. RADTKE, M., "Charakteristik der schulpolitischen Entwicklung 1889-1919 in Deutschland Dargestellt am Beispiel Preussen," Wiss. Zs. d. Ernst-Moritz-Arndt. Univ. Greifswald, (Ges.-u. sprach.-wiss.), 7, 1957/58, 39-57.

1728. RICHTER, Wilhelm, "Beiträge zur Geschichte des Paderborner Volksschulwesens im 19. Jahrhundert," Westf. Zs., 70(2), 1912, 347-429; 73(2), 1915, 215-65; 74(2), 1916, 133-68; 75(2), 1917, 1-62; 76(2), 1918, 1-58; 77(2), 1919, 3-75; 83(2), 1925, 77-141.

1729. RITTERSHAUSEN, Dietrich, "Beiträge zur Geschichte des Berliner Elementar-Schulwesens Von der Reformation bis 1836," Märkische Forschungen, 9, 1865, 178-317.

1730. ROTHKRANZ, Edmund, "Die Kirchen- und Schulpolitik der Düsseldorfer Regierung in den Jahren 1820-1840 Johann Vinzenz Josef Bracht (1771-1840)," Düsseldorfer Jb., 52,

1966, 1-76.
1731.   SCHAAF, E., "Gutachten der Trierer Regierung zu dem
        preussischen Schulgesetzentwurf von 1819 (Ein Dokument
        liberaler Gesinnung in den Anfangsjahren der Restaura-
        tion)," L. kundl. Vjbll., 16, 1970, 8-20.
1732.   SCHMID, Eugen, "Theodor Eisenlohr (1805-1869)," Zs. f.
        Württbg. LG, 5, 1941, 390-429.
1733.   SPRANGER, Eduard, "Philosophie und Pädagogik der preus-
        sischen Reformzeit," HZ, 104, 1910, 278-321.
1734.   STAHLECKER, R., "Beiträge zur Geschichte des höhern
        Schulwesens in Tübingen," Württemberg. Vtljh F. Landes-
        geschichte, 15, 1906, 1-102.
1735.   STÜPPERICH, Dorothea, "Ferdinand Hasenklever und die
        Schulreform in Schwelm (1804-1814)," Jb. Ver. Westfäl.
        Kirchengesch., 63, 1970.
1736.   TREITSCHKE, Heinrich v., "Einige Bemerkungen über unser
        Gymnasialwesen," Pr. Jbb., 51, 1883, 158-90.
1737.   W., "Zur Literatur über die Schulfrage," Pr. Jbb., 24,
        1869, 367-77, 481-96.

Emigration, Immigration

1738.   BLENDINGER, Friedrich, "Die Auswanderung nach Nord-
        amerika aus dem Regierungs Bezirk Oberbayern in den
        Jahren 1846-52," Zs. f. bayer. LG., 27, 1964, 431-487.
1739.   BREITENBACH, Wilhelm, "Die deutsche Auswanderung und
        die Frage der deutschen Kolonisation in Süd-Brasilien,"
        Schmoll. Jb., 11, 1887, 233-99.
1740.   "Die DEUTSCHE Auswanderung," Pr. Jbb., 2, 1858, 389-
        412, 483-521, 639-63.
1741.   DIENER, Walter, "Die Auswanderung aus dem Amte Gemün-
        den (Hunsrück) im 19. Jahrhundert," Rhein. Vjsbll., 5,
        1935, 199-222.
1742.   _____, "Die Auswanderung aus dem Kreise Simmern
        (Hunsrück) im 19. Jahrhundert," Rhein. Vjsbll., 8, 1938,
        91-148.
1743.   GLEASON, Philip, "An Immigrant Group's Interest in Pro-
        gressive Reform: The Case of the German-American
        Catholics," AHR, 73, 1967/68, 367-79.
1744.   GRANDJONG, Jacques, "La presse de l'émigration allemande
        en France (1795-1848) et en Europe (1830-1848)," Arch.
        f. Sozialgesch., 10, 1970, 95-152.
1745.   GÜNTHER, Kurt, "Beiträge zum Problem der kurhessischen
        Auswanderung im 18. und 19. Jh., insbesondere nach
        Nordamerika (1830-1866)," Zs. d. Vereins f. Hess. Gesch.
        u. Landeskunde, 75/76, 1964/65, 489-538.
1746.   HAM, Hermann Van, "Quellen zur rheinischen Auswanderer-
        forschung in den Staatsarchiven Koblenz und Düsseldorf,"
        Rhein. Vjsbll., 6, 1936, 295-326; 8, 1938, 315-32.
1747.   HEYNE, Bodo, "Schlesische Auswanderung nach Südaustralien
        aus den Anfangszeiten der deutschen Auswanderung," Jb.
        d. Schles.-Fried.-Wilh. Univ z. Breslau, 10, 1965, 188-

202.
1748.   REISSNER, H. G., "The German-American Jews (1800-
        1850)," Leo Baeck Inst. Yrbk., 10, 1965, 57-116.
1749.   SEEGER, Irmgard, "Zur Geschichte der deutschen Auswan-
        derungsbewegung um die Mitte des 19. Jahrhunderts,"
        Württemberg. Jb. f. Statistik u. Landeskunde, 1938/39,
        1940, 23-38.
1750.   STRUCK, Wolf-Heino, "Zur Geschichte der nassauischen
        Auswanderung nach Texas 1844-1847," Nass. Ann., 82,
        1971.
1751.   SUDHAUS, Fritz, "Deutschland und die Auswanderung nach
        Brasilien im 19. Jahrhundert," Dt. Arch. f. Landes-
        und Volksforschg., 4, 1940, 594-601.
1752.   "UEBER Auswanderung und Kolonisation," Schmoll. Jb., 5,
        1881, 225-45.
1753.   WÄTJEN, Hermann, "Die deutsche Auswanderung nach
        Brasilien in den Jahren 1820-1870," Weltwirtsch. Arch.,
        19, 1923, 595-609.
1754.   WINKEL, Harald, "Der Texasverein--ein Beitrag zur
        Geschichte der deutschen Auswanderung im 19. Jahr-
        hundert," VSW, 55, 1968, 348-372.
1755.   WITTKE, Carl, "The German Forty-Eighters in America.
        A Centennial Appraisal," AHR, 53, 1947/48, 711-25.
1756.   YOUNG, G. F. W., "Bernardo Philippi, Initiator of Ger-
        man Colonization in Chile," Hisp. AHR, 51, 1971, 478-
        96.

The Frauenfrage (The Women's Movement)

1757.   ALTMANN-GOTTHEINER, Dr. Elisabeth, "Die deutschen
        politischen Parteien und ihre Stellung zur Frauenfrage,"
        Zs. f. Pol., 3, 1909/10, 581-98.
1758.   ARNDT, H. J., "Der erste Reichskongress werktätiger
        Frauen Deutschlands," Zs. f. Geschw., 20, 1972, 467-
        79.
1759.   BÄUMER, Gertrud, "Persönlichkeit, Familie, Gesellschaft
        in der Frauenfrage," Pr. Jbb., 151, 1913, 509-28.
1760.   BEERENSSON, Adele, "Soziale Frauenbildung in Deutsch-
        land," Zs. f. d. Armenwesen, 16, 1915, 78-87.
1761.   BOEHM, Laetitia, "Von den Anfängen des akademischen
        Frauenstudiums in Deutschland," H. Jb., 77, 1957, 298-
        327.
1762.   BRAUN, Lily, "Die Anfänge der Frauenbewegung," Arch. f.
        Sozialw. u. Sozialpol., 13, 1899, 314-81.
1763.   _____, "Der Kampf um Arbeit in der bürgerlichen Frauen-
        welt," Arch. f. Sozialw. u. Sozialpol., 16, 1901, 40-141.
1764.   DELBRÜCK, Hans, "Ein Nachwort zum Frauenkongress,"
        Pr. Jbb., 148, 1912, 125-41.
1765.   KEMPIN, Frau E., "Grenzlinien der Frauenbewegung,"
        Schmoll. Jb., 21, 1897, 1195-1221.
1766.   KREYENBERG, Dr. Gotthold, "Ein Kapitel aus der Deutschen
        Frauenfrage," Pr. Jbb., 84, 1896, 158-65.

1767.   NELL, Bernarda von, "Frauenstimmrecht und weibliche
        Gutachten in öffentlichen Angelegenheiten," Pr. Jbb.,
        150, 1912, 414-38.
1768.   PAULSEN, Friedrich, "Die Frau im Recht der Vergangen-
        heit und der Zukunft," Pr. Jbb., 132, 1908, 396-413.
1769.   RÖSSLER, Constantin, "Hingeworfene Gedanken zur Frauen-
        frage," Pr. Jbb., 74, 1893, 19-48.
1770.   SCHEEL, H. v., "Frauenfrage und Frauenstudium," Jbb. f.
        Nationalökon. u. Stat., 22, 1874, 1-16.
1771.   SCHELLENBERG, Anna, "'Die wirtschaftlichen Tatsachen'
        und die Ziele der Frauenbewegung," Pr. Jbb., 150, 1912,
        292-319.
1772.   SILBERMANN, J., "Die Frauenarbeit nach den beiden letzten
        Berufszählungen," Schmoll. Jb., 35, 1911, 721-59.

Foreign Trade

1773.   BECKMANN, Friedrich, "Die Entwicklung des deutsch--rus-
        sischen Getreideverkehrs unter den Handels--Verträgen
        von 1894 und 1904," Jbb. f. Nationalökon. u. Stat., 101,
        1913, 145-71.
1774.   BLAICH, Fritz, "Der 'Standard-Oil-Fall' vor dem Reichstag
        Ein Beitrag zur deutschen Monopolpolitik vor 1914,"
        ZgesStw, 126, 1970, 663-82.
1775.   BOYSEN, L., "Die Verkehrwege zwischen Deutschland und
        Skandinavien," Weltwirtsch. Arch., 1, 1913, 377-88.
1776.   "Der DEUTSCH-FRANZÖSISCHE Handelsvertrag," Pr. Jbb.,
        9, 1862, 557-79.
1777.   DIETSCHI, Erich, "Die Handelsverträge der Schweiz mit
        dem süddeutschen Staaten 1824-1828," ZGORh., 83, 1930/
        31, 55-100.
1778.   _____, "Die Schweiz und die handelpolitischen Bewegungen
        in Deutschland nach dem Fall der Kontinentalsperre 1815-
        1824," ZGORh., 82, 1929/30, 507-63.
1779.   DUNAN, Marcel, "Eine württembergische Handelssperre
        gegen die Schweiz vor hundert Jahren 1810-1811," Zs. f.
        Württbg. LG, 22, 1913, 445-54.
1780.   ENGELSING, Rolf, "Schlesische Leinenindustrie und Han-
        seatischer Überseehandel im 19. Jahrhundert," Jb. d.
        Schles.-Fried.-Wilh. Univ z. Breslau, 4, 1959, 207-27.
1781.   _____, "Zur Geschichte der deutschen Handelsschiffahrt,"
        Tradition, 5, 1960, 39-48.
1782.   EUDE, Michel, "Les Relations Économiques et Financiéres
        entre la France et l'Allemagne de 1898 a 1914," Rev.
        d'hist. econ. soc., 49, 1971, 129-34.
1783.   FEIG, Johannes, "Der Schiffbau Deutschlands und seiner
        Konkurrenzländer," Schmoll. Jb., 26, 1902, 1691-1700.
1784.   FLANINGAM, M. L., "German Eastward Expansion, Fact
        and Fiction: A Study in German-Ottoman Trade Relations
        1890-1914," J. Cen. Eur. Aff., 14, 1955, 319-33.
1785.   FLUX, A. W., "British Trade and German Competition,"
        Econ. J., 7, 1897, 34-45.

1786.   FRANZ, Eugen, "Die Entstehungsgeschichte des preus-
        sisch-französischen Handelsvertrags vom 29. März
        1862," VSW, 25, 1932, 1-37, 105-29.

1787.   _____, "Ludwig Freiherrn von der Pfordtens Kampf gegen
        den preussisch-französischen Handelsvertrag vom 29.
        März 1862," FBPG, 44, 1932, 130-55.

1788.   _____, "Preussens Kampf mit Hannover um die Anerken-
        nung des preussisch-französischen Handelsvertrags von
        1862," Hist. Vjschr., 26, 1931, 787-839.

1789.   FUCHS, Konrad, "Neue Beiträge zur Bedeutung der König-
        lichen Seehandlung für die Schlesische Spinnstoff- und
        Metallindustrie," Tradition, 11, 1966, 57-69.

1790.   GIGNILLIAT, John L., "Pigs, Politics, and Protection:
        The European Boycott of American Pork 1879-1891,"
        Ag. Hist., 35, 1961, 3-12.

1791.   HALLE, E. von, "The Rise and Tendencies of German
        Transatlantic Enterprise," Econ. J., 17, 1907, 490-503.

1792.   HARDACH, Karl W., "Anglomanie und Anglophobie während
        der Industriellen Revolution in Deutschland," Schmoll. Jb.,
        91, 1971, 153-81.

1793.   _____, "Beschäftigungspolitische Aspekte in der deutschen
        Aussenhandelspolitik ausgangs der 1870er Jahre," Schmoll.
        Jb., 86, 1966, 641-54.

1794.   HENDERSON, W. O., "German Economic Penetration in The
        Middle East 1870-1914," Econ. Hist. Rev., 18, 1948,
        54-64.

1795.   HIEKE, Ernst, "Aud der Frühzeit des deutschen Handels
        mit China," Ostasiat. Rs., 20, 1939, 93-97.

1796.   _____, "Der Beginn des Hauses C. Woermann in Afrika,"
        VSW, 30, 1937, 261-65.

1797.   _____, "Gründung, Kapital und Kapitalgeber der Deutsch-
        Amerikanischen Petroleum-Gesellschaft (DAPG) 1890-
        1904," Tradition, 16, 1971, 16-48.

1798.   _____, "Das hamburgische Handelshaus Wm. O'swald &
        Co. und der Bcginn des deutschen Afrikahandels 1848-
        1853," VSW, 30, 1937, 346-78.

1799.   HUBERTI, Franz H., "Maritime Aspekte der Weltgeschichte
        im 19. Jahrhundert," Saec., 22, 1971, 274-304.

1800.   JERUSSALIMSKI, A. S., "Das Eindringen der deutschen
        Monopole in China an der Wende vom 19. zum 20. Jahr-
        hundert," Zs. f. Geschw., 8, 1960, 1832-61.

1801.   KELLENBENZ, Hermann, "Bremer Kaufleute im Norden
        Brasiliens," Bremisches Jb., 50, 1965, 325-36.

1802.   KERST, Georg, "Die Bedeutung Bremens für die frühen
        deutsch-japanischen Beziehungen," Bremisches Jb., 50,
        1965, 303-23.

1803.   KÖRNER, Karl W., "Johann Christian Zimmermann Ein
        deutscher Unternehmer in Übersee," Tradition, 15, 1970,
        282-95.

1804.   KUMPF-KORFES, Sigrid, "Die ökonomische Expansion des
        deutschen Finanzkapitals in Bulgarien...," Zs. f. Geschw.,
        17, 1969, 1427-41.

1805.   KUTZ, Martin, "Die deutsch-britischen Handelsbeziehungen von 1790 bis zur Gründung des Zollvereins," VSW, 56, 1969, 178-214.

1806. LAVES, W. H. C., "German Governmental Influence on Foreign Investments 1871-1915," Pol. Sci. Q., 43, 1928, 498-519.

1807. LENZ, Friedrich, "Wesen und Struktur des deutschen Kapitalexports vor 1914," Weltwirtsch. Arch., 18, 1922, 42-54.

1808. MAI, Joachim, "Das deutsche Kapital in Industrie und Handel Russlands von 1850 bis 1876," Jb. f. Wgesch., 1968 (2), 205-36.

1809. _____, "Das deutsche Kapital im russischen Eisenbahnwesen 1857 bis 1876," Jahrb. f. Gesch. d. UdSSR u.d. volksdemokratischen Länder Europas, 12, 1968.

1810. MEHLAN, Arno, "Historischen Überblick über die deutschbulgarischen Wirtschaftsbeziehungen," Schmoll. Jb., 61, 1937, 425-44.

1811. MEISTER, Aloys, "Die Wirkung des wirtschaftlichen Kampfes zwischen Frankreich und England von 1791 bis 1813 auf Westfalen," Westf. Zs., 71, 1913, 219-89.

1812. MEYER, Henry Cord, "German Economic Relations with Southeastern Europe, 1870-1914," AHR, 57, 1951/52, 77-90.

1813. MÜHLMANN, C., "Die deutschen Bahnunternehmungen in der asiatischen Türkei, 1888-1914," Weltwirtsch. Arch., 24, 1926, 365-99.

1814. O'FARRELL, H. H., "British and German Export Trade Before the War," Econ. J., 26, 1916, 161-67.

1815. OPPEL, A., "Hamburgs und Bremens Stellung im internationalen Warenhandel," Weltwirtsch. Arch., 1, 1913, 361-76.

1816. POIDEVIN, Raymond, "Les intérêts Financiers Français et allemands en Serbie de 1895 à 1914," RH, 232, 1964, 49-66.

1817. RATHGEN, Karl, "Der deutsche Handel in Ostasien," Schmoll. Jb., 9, 1885, 583-604.

1818. _____, "Deutschland und England auf dem Weltmarkt," Schmoll. Jb., 37, 1913, 1-14.

1819. SCHAEFER, Arnold, "Verhandlungen der Hansestädte mit dem Sultan von Marocco," HZ, 22, 1869, 66-79.

1820. SCHOENE, Elmar, "Der Stettiner Seehandel nach 1813," Balt. Stud., 55, 1969.

1821. SCHRAMM, Percy Ernst, "Die deutschen Überseekaufleute im Rahmen der Sozialgeschichte," Bremisches Jb., 49, 1964, 31-54.

1822. _____, "Hamburg-Brasilien Die Forderung einer Dampferverbindung, 1854 verwirklicht," VSW, 52, 1965, 86-90.

1823. _____, "Überseekaufleute im 19. Jahrhundert," Tradition, 7, 1962, 93-107.

1824. SCHWARTZE, E., "Der Gang nach Ceylon Die Gründung des Hauses Freudenberg & Co. in Colombo und ihre geschichtlichen Voraussetzungen," Bremisches Jb., 42, 1947, 82-96.

1825. SIEVEKING, Heinrich, "Die Anfänge des Hauses Behn-Meyer & Co. in Singaport, 1840-1856," VSW, 35, 1942, 179-211.

1826. _____, "Die Hamburgische Firma Knust und Albers in
        Wladiwostock, 1864-1914," VSW, 34, 1941, 268-99.

1827. SNYDER, Louis L., "The American-German Pork Dispute,
        1879-1891," J. Mod. Hist., 17, 1945, 16-28.

1828. STRÖLL, Moriz, "Über die wirtschaftspolitischen Beziehun-
        gen Deutschlands zu Rumänien," Schmoll. Jb., 19, 1895,
        1143-63.

1829. TREUE, Wilhelm, "Das österreichisch-mitteldeutsche und
        das norddeutsche staats- und privatwirtschaftliche In-
        teresse am Bau des Suez-Kanals," VSW, 58, 1971, 534-
        55.

1830. _____, "Russland und die Eisenbahnen im fernen Osten,"
        HZ, 158, 1938, 504-40.

1831. _____, "Wirtschaft und Aussenpolitik Zu dem Problem
        der deutschen Weltmachtstellung, 1900-1914," Tradition,
        9, 1964, 193-218.

1832. WÄTJEN, Hermann, "Die Hansestädte und Brasilien 1820
        bis 1870," Weltwirtsch. Arch., 22, 1925, 33-56, 221-50.

1833. _____, "Das wirtschaftliche Emporkommen der Hawaii-
        Inseln im 19. Jahrhundert," Bremisches Jb., 41, 1944,
        278-304.

1834. WEINBERGER, Gerda, "Das Victoria-Falls-Power Projekt
        der AEG und die deutsche Kapitaloffensive in Südafrika
        vor den ersten Weltkrieg," Jb. f. Wgesch., 1971 (4),
        57-82.

1835. ZANE, G., "Die österreichischen und die deutschen Wirt-
        schaftsbeziehungen zu den rumänischen Fürstentümern,
        1774-1874," Weltwirtsch. Arch., 26, 1927, 30-47, 262-
        81.

1836. ZIMMERMANN, Alfred, "Die russisch-preussischen Han-
        delsbeziehungen, 1814-1833," Schmoll. Jb., 16, 1892,
        333-79.

The Labor Movement

1837. ADELMANN, Gerhard, "Die Beziehungen zwischen Arbeit-
        geber und Arbeitnehmer in der Ruhrindustrie vor 1914,"
        Jbb. f. Nationalökon. u. Stat., 175, 1963, 412-27.

1838. ALBRECHT, Gerhard, "Das Einnahmebudget des Arbeiter-
        haltes," ZgesStw., 70, 1914, 371-424.

1839. ANDREAS, Bert and Georges HAUPT, "Bibliographie der
        Arbeiterbewegung Heute und Morgen," Int. Rev. Soc.
        Hist., 12, 1967, 1-30.

1840. ANDREAS, Bert, "Zur Agitation und Propaganda des Allge-
        meinen Deutschen Arbeitervereins 1863/64," Arch. f.
        Sozialgesch., 3, 1963, 297-423.

1841. BAAR, Lothar, "Der Kampf der Berliner Arbeiter während
        der industriellen Revolution," Jb. f. Regionalgesch., 2,
        1967, 27-49.

1842. BARTEL, Horst, "Die Durchsetzung des Marxismus in der
        deutschen Arbeiterbewegung in letzten Drittel des 19.
        Jahrhunderts. Probleme der zweitem Hauptperiode der

Geschichte der deutschen Arbeiterbewegung, " Zs. f. Geschw., 14, 1966, 1334-71.

1843. _____, "Die Haltung der revolutionären deutschen Arbeiterbewegung zur Reichsgründung von 1871, " Zs. f. Geschw., 16, 1968, 430-42.

1844. BEHM, Erika and Jürgen KUCZYNSKI, "Die Reflexion der Arbeiterbewegung in der Regierungspresse vor dem ersten Weltkrieg Eine vornehmlich quantitative Analyse (Deutschland), " Jb. f. Wgesch., 1971 (3), 123-30.

1845. BERTHOLD, G., "Die deutschen Arbeiterkolonien ihre Entstehung, Organisation, Bedeutung und Frequenz auf Grund offizieller Materialien, " Schmoll. Jb., 10, 1886, 453-76.

1846. BEVERIDGE, W. H., "Public Labour Exchanges in Germany, " Econ. J., 17, 1907, 1-18.

1847. BÖDIKER, Dr. T., "Arbeiterlohnstatistik, " Pr. Jbb., 71, 1893, 239-49.

1848. BRAUER, Theodor, "Zur Entwicklung der Christlichen Gewerkschaften, " Zs. f. Pol., 8, 1915, 532-45.

1849. BRUST, August, "Der Bergarbeiterstreik im Ruhrrevier, " Arch. f. Sozialw. u. Sozialpol., 20, 1905, 480-506.

1850. BUNZEL, Julius, "Die Landarbeiterfrage, " Arch. f. Sozialw. u. Sozialpol., 24, 1907, 433-50, 680-709.

1851. COHEN, Arthur, "Die Lohn- und Arbeitsverhältnisse der Münchener Kellnerinnen, " Arch. f. Sozialw. u. Sozialpol., 5, 1892, 97-131.

1852. COHN, Gustav, "Die gesetzliche Regelung der Arbeitszeit im deutschen Reich, " Jbb. f. Nationalökon. u. Stat., 40, 1883, 39-71.

1853. _____, "Ideen und Thatsachen in Genossenschaftswesen, " Schmoll. Jb., 7, 1883, 1-52.

1854. CRÜGER, Hans, "Die Schulze-Delitzschen Genossenschaften in Posen als ein Bollwerk des Deutschtums, " Schmoll. Jb., 37, 1913, 813-24.

1855. DELBRÜCK, Hans, "Die Arbeitslosigkeit und das Recht auf Arbeit, " Pr. Jbb., 85, 1896, 80-96.

1856. DLUBEK, Rolf and Walter SCHMIDT, "Die Herausbildung der marxistischen Partei der deutschen Arbeiterklasse Konzeptionelle Fragen der ersten Hauptperiode der Geschichte der deutschen Arbeiterbewegung, " Zs. f. Geschw., 14, 1966, 1282-1333.

1857. "Ein DOKUMENT aus den Anfängen der Gewerkschaftsbewegung in der Kaliindustrie (1897/98), " Beitr. z. Gesch. d. dt. Arbeiterbeweg., 2, 1960, 366-72.

1858. DRAHN, Ernst, ed., "Ein Aufruf Julius Vahlteichs aus dem Jahre 1863, " Arch. f. d. Gesch. d. Soz., 10, 1921/22, 392-97.

1859. ECKERT, Georg, "Das 'Deutsche Wochenblatt' und die Internationale Arbeiter-Assoziation Ein früher Abdruck der Inauguraladresse, " Arch f. Sozialgesch., 4, 1964, 579-98.

1860. _____, "Samuel Spier und die Internationale Arbeiter-Assoziation, " Arch f. Sozialgesch., 4, 1964, 599-615.

1861. _____, "Zur Geschichte der 'sektionen' Wiesbaden und

Mainz der Internationen Arbeiter-Assoziation, " Arch f.
Sozialgesch., 8, 1968, 365-523.

1862. ENDEMANN, W., "Das Genossenschaftswesen nach dem
Bundesgesetz vom 4. Juli 1868," Pr. Jbb., 25, 1870,
1-32.

1863. ENGEL, Gerhard, "Johann Knief," Beitr. z. Gesch. d. dt.
Arbeiterbeweg., 12, 1970.

1864. ETTELT, Werner and Hans-Dieter KRAUSE, "Die Durchsetzung der marxistischen Gewerkschaftspolitik in der deutschen Arbeiterbewegung, 1869-1878," Zs. f. Geschw.,
18, 1970, 1023-1046.

1865. FREESE, Heinrich, "Zehn Jahre in einem Arbeiterparla-
ment," Pr. Jbb., 80, 1895, 110-25.

1866. FRICKE, Dieter, "Der Aufschwung der Massenkämpfe der
deutschen Arbeiterklasse unter dem Einfluss der russischen Revolution von 1905," Zs. f. Geschw., 5, 1957,
770-90.

1867. _____, "Eine wichtige Quelle zur Geschichte der deutschen Arbeiterbewegung," Beitr. z. Gesch. d. dt. Arbeiterbeweg., 3, 1961, 94-103.

1868. FRIEDERICI, Hans Jürgen and Jutta SEIDEL, "Der Wieder-
hall der Pariser Kommune in der deutschen Arbeiterbewegung," Beitr. z. Gesch. d. dt. Arbeiterbeweg., 3,
1961, 280-98.

1869. GEBAUER, C., "Deutsche Geselligkeit gegen Ende des 18.
und zu Anfang des 19. Jahrhunderts," Pr. Jbb., 147,
1912, 487-502.

1870. GNAUCK-KÜHNE, Elisabeth, "Die Lage der Arbeiterinnen
in der Berliner Papierwaren-Industrie," Schmoll. Jb.,
20, 1896, 373-440.

1871. GRIEP, Günter, "Hermann Duncker," Beitr. z. Gesch. d.
dt. Arbeiterbeweg., 13, 1971, 96-105.

1872. GROH, Dieter, "Hundert Jahre Deutsche Arbeiterbewegung, "
Staat, 2, 1963, 351-66.

1873. GRÜNBERG, Carl, "Bruno Hildebrand über den Kommunistischen Arbeiterbildungsverein in London," Arch. f. d.
Gesch. d. Soz., 11, 1923, 445-59.

1874. _____, "Die Londoner Kommunistische Zeitschrift und
andere Urkunden aus den Jahren 1847-1848," Arch. f. d.
Gesch. d. Soz., 9, 1920-21, 249-341.

1875. HACKETHAL, Eberhard, "Der Allgemeine Deutsche Arbeiterverein unter dem Einfluss der Pariser Kommune, "
Zs. f. Geschw., 16, 1968, 443-461.

1876. _____, "Der historische Platz der Pariser Kommune im
praktischen Wirken und theoretischen Denken der zeitgenössischen deutschen Arbeiterbewegung (1871-1878), "
Jb. f. Gesch., 2, 1967, 75-122.

1877. HAMPKE, Thilo, "Die deutsche Handwerkerorganisation
Eine statistische Studie," Jbb. f. Nationalökon. u. Stat.,
80, 1903, 577-637.

1878. _____, "Die Innungsentwickelung in Preussen eine statistische Studie," Schmoll. Jb., 18, 1894, 195-228.

1879. _____, "Der Verband Deutscher Gewerbevereine, Seine

Entstehung, Organisation und bisherige Wirksamkeit,"
Schmoll. Jb., 17, 1893, 1141-73.

1880. HEISS, Clemens, "Die deutsche Strikestatistik," Arch. f.
Sozialw. u. Sozialpol., 17, 1902, 150-68.

1881. _____, "Die gelbe Arbeiterbewegung," Schmoll. Jb., 35,
1911, 1905-46.

1882. HERRFAHRDT, Heinrich, "Das Problem der berufsständ-
ischen Vertretung im Zeitalter Bismarcks," Schmoll. Jb.,
44, 1920, 369-97.

1883. HESS, Ulrich, "Louis Viereck und siene Münchner Blätter
für Arbeiter 1882-1889," Dortmunder Beiträge zur Zeit-
ungsforchung, 6, 1-50.

1884. HEXELSCHNEIDER, Erhard and Michael WEGNER, "Deutsche
Arbeiterbewegung und russische Literatur," Zs. für Sla-
wistik, 10, 1965, 1-34.

1885. HUNDT, Martin, "Zur Kontinuität der deutschen Arbeiterbewegung vom Bund der Kommunisten zur Eisenacher Partei: Die Taktikdiskussion von 1856," Beitr. z. Gesch.
d. dt. Arbeiterbeweg., 11, 1969.

1886. JACOBI, Dr. jur Johannes, "Die Innungsbewegung in Deutschland und die Novelle zur Reichs-Gewerbeordnung vom 18.
Juli 1881," Schmoll. Jb., 7, 1883, 1197-1233.

1887. JAHROW, Franz, "Die revolutionäre Arbeiterbewegung und
die Entwicklung des deutschen Nationalcharakters," Dt.
Zs. f. Phil., 11, 1963, 708-27.

1888. KESSLER, Gerhard, "Die Geschichtliche Entwicklung der
deutschen Arbeitgeberorganisation," ZgesStw., 63, 1907,
223-63.

1889. KLEIN, F., A. LASCHITZA, B. RADLAK and F. TYCK,
"Die Stellung der internationalen Arbeiterbewegung zu
Militarismus und Imperialismus zwischen den Kongressen
in Stuttgart und Basel (1907-1912)," Beitr. z. Gesch. d.
dt. Arbeiterbeweg., 15, 1973, 42-63.

1890. KOSZYK, Kurt, "Der schlesische Weberaufstand von 1844
nach Berichten der 'Mannheimer Abendzeitung'," Jb. d.
Schles.-Fried.-Wilh. Univ z. Breslau, 7, 1962, 224-32.

1891. KOTOWSKI, Georg, "Zur Geschichte der Arbeiterbewegung
im Mittel- und Ostdeutschland," Ein Literaturbericht, Jb.
f. Gesch. M. O. Dtschl., 8, 1959, 409-70.

1892. KRAUSE, Hans-Dieter, "Gewerkschaften und politischer
Kampf in Dtsl. i. d. Jh. 1873/74," Beitr. z. Gesch. d.
dt. Arbeiterbeweg., 14, 1972, 83-98.

1893. KRIENKE, Gerhard, "Der schulische Aspekt der Kinderar-
beit in Berlin 1825-1848 Zur Sozial- und Schulgeschichte
der preussischen Hauptstadt," Bär v. Ber., 18, 1969,
94-121.

1894. LANGE, Dr. E., "Die ortsüblichen Tagelöhne Gewöhnlicher
Tagearbeiter im deutschen Reiche," Arch. f. Sozialw. u.
Sozialpol., 6, 1893, 1-13.

1895. LANGERHANS, Heinz, "Richtungsgewirkschaft und gewerk-
schaftliche Autonomie 1890-1914," Int. Rev. Soc. Hist.,
2, 1957, 22-51, 187-208.

1896. LASCHITZA, Annelies, "Der Imperialismus und die neuen

Aufgaben der Partei der Arbeiterklasse Grundprobleme,
neue Fragestellung und Forschungsergebnisse der Geschichte der deutschen Arbeiterbewegung in der dritten
Hauptperiode, " Zs. f. Geschw., 14, 1966, 1372-99.

1897.   LOCH (Leipzig), Werner, "Le mouvement ouvrier allemand
devant la commune, " Rev. d'hist. mod., 19, 1972, 156-
72.

1898.   LÖSCHE, Peter, "Arbeiterbewegung und Wilhelminismus, "
GiWuU, 20, 1969, 519-33.

1899.   LOEWENFELD, Dr. Theodor, "Kontraktbruch und Koali-
tionsrecht im Hinblick auf die Reform der deutschen
Gewerbegesetzgebung, " Archiv f. soziale Gesetzgeburg
u. Statistik, 3, 1890, 383-488.

1900.   LUDWIG, Karl-Heinz, "Die Fabrikarbeit von Kindern im
19. Jahrhundert, " VSW, 52, 1965, 63-85.

1901.   MANGOLDT, Dr. Karl von, "Die gewerblichen Fortbildungs-
bestrebungen der Dresdner Arbeiterschaft, " Arch. f.
Sozialw. u. Sozialpol., 6, 1893, 290-302.

1902.   MATULL, Wilhelm, "Arbeiterpresse in Ost- und Westpreussen, " Jahrb. Albrechts-Univ. Königsberg, 20, 1970.

1903.   MAYER, Gustav, "Der Allgemeine Deutsche Arbeiterverein
und die Krisis 1866, " Arch. f. Sozialw. u. Sozialpol.,
57, 1927, 167-75.

1904.   MEHNER, H., "Der Haushalt und die Lebenshaltung einer
leipziger Arbeiterfamilie, " Schmoll. Jb., 11, 1887, 301-
34.

1905.   MÖLLERS, Paul, "Die Essener Arbeiterbewegung in ihren
Anfängen, " Rhein. Vjsbll., 25, 1960, 42-65.

1906.   MOMBERT, P., "Aus der Literatur über die soziale Frage
und über die Arbeiterbewegung in Deutschland in der
ersten Hälfte des 19. Jahrhunderts, " Arch. f. d. Gesch.
d. Soz., 9, 1920/21, 169-236.

1907.   MÜLLER, Harald, "Die deutsche Arbeiterklasse und die
Sedanfeier, " Zs. f. Geschw., 17, 1969, 1554-64.

1908.   _____, "Der Rathenower Bauarbeiterstreik von 1885 und
die Berliner politische Polizei, " Jb. f. Wgesch., 1972
(3), 63-76.

1909.   NA'AMAN, Shlomo, "Der Fall Eichler Zur Frühgeschichte
der deutschen Arbeiterbewegung, " Int. Rev. Soc. Hist.,
15, 1970, 347-74.

1910.   NEUMANN, J., "Ueber die Ausführung einer Enquête, betreffend die bisherige Durchführung die Wirkungen und die
Reformbedürftigkeit deutscher Fabrikgesetzgebung, " Jbb.
f. Nationalökon. u. Stat., 21, 1873, 1-109.

1911.   OBERMANN, Karl, "Zur Geschichte der deutschen Arbeiterbewegung nach der Revolution von 1848/49 zu Beginn der
Fünfziger Jahre, " Beitr. z. Gesch. d. dt. Arbeiterbeweg., 3, 1960, 842-73.

1912.   OLDENBERG, Karl, "Studien über die rheinisch-westfälische
Bergarbeiterbewegung, " Schmoll. Jb., 14, 1890, 603-73,
913-66.

1913.   OLISCHEWSKY, W. G., "An der Wiege der deutschen Arbeiterbewegung St. Born in Berlin, " Jb. d. Ver. f. d.

Gesch. Berlins, 1953, 143ff.

1914.   ONEKEN, Hermann, "Der Nationalverein und die Auflänge der deutschen Arbeiterbewegung 1862/63 Aus den Papieren des Nationalvereins," Arch. f. d. Gesch. d. Soz., 2, 1911/12, 120-27.

1915.   OSCHILEWSKI, Walther G., "An der Wiege der deutschen Arbeiterbewegung Stephan Born in Berlin," Jb. d. Ver. f. d. Gesch. Berlins, 2, 1952, 143-60.

1916.   PELGER, Hans, "Das Verbot eines rheinischwestfälischen Arbeitertages zu Duisburg im Januar 1866," Arch f. Sozialgesch., 4, 1964, 617-31.

1917.   PETER, Heinrich, "Zur Lage der Kellnerinnen im Grossherzogtum Baden," Arch. f. Sozialw. u. Sozialpol., 24, 1907, 558-612.

1918.   QUARCK, Max, "Die erste Frankfurter Arbeiterzeitung," Arch. f. d. Gesch. d. Soz., 11, 1923, 122-41.

1919.   RAUBAUM, Jörg, "Die deutsche Arbeiterklasse und die Konsumgenossenschaften bis zum Ersten Weltkrieg," Zs. f. Geschw., 16, 1968, 54-67.

1920.   REICHARD, Richard W., "The German Working Class and the Russian Revolution of 1905," J. Cen. Eur. Aff., 13, 1953, 136-53.

1921.   RJASANOFF, N., ed., "Zur Biographie von Johann Philipp Becker," Arch. f. d. Gesch. d. Soz., 4, 1914/14, 313-29.

1922.   RÖSEN, Heinrich, "Der Aufstand der Krefelder 'Seidenfabrikarbeiter' 1828 und die Bildung einer 'Sicherheitswache'," Das Heimat Krefeld, 36, 1965, 32-61.

1923.   ROESICKE, Richard (Mtgd. d. Reichstags), "Über das Verhältnis der Arbeitgeber zu ihren Arbeitnehmern," Schmoll. Jb., 17, 1893, 1-22.

1924.   ROTHFELS, Hans, "Die erste diplomatische Aktion zugunstem des internationalen Arbeiterschutzes," VSW, 16, 1922, 70-87.

1925.   SCHÄFER, H. P., "Die 'Gelben Gewerkschaften' am Beispiel des Unterstützungsvereins der Siemens-Werke Berlin," VSW, 59, 1972, 41-76.

1926.   SCHMIDT, Walter, "Die Kommunisten im Brüsseler Deutschen Arbeiterverein und in der Association démocratique Zur Biographie Wilhelm Wolffs an Vorabend der Revolution von 1848/49," Zs. f. Geschw., 18, 1970 (1), 23-45.

1927.   SCHRAEPLER, Ernst, "Der Bund der Gerichten Seine Tätigkeit in London 1840-1847," Arch f. Sozialgesch., 2, 1962, 5-29.

1928.   SCHRAEPLER, Ernst, Henryk SKRZYPCZAK, Siegfried BAHNE, and Georg KOTOWSKI, "'Grundriss der Geschichte der deutschen Arbeiterbewegung' Kritik einer Legende," Jb. f. Gesch. M. O. Dtschl., 13/14, 1965, 268-347.

1929.   _____, "Der Zwölfer-Ausschuss des Vereinstages Deutscher Arbeitervereine und die Ereignisse von 1866," Jb. f. Gesch. M. O. Dtschl., 16/17, 1968, 210-53.

1930.   SCHRÖDER, Wolfgang and Gustav SEEBER, "Zu einigen

Problemen des revolutionären Kampfes der deutschen Arbeiterklasse in den neunziger Jahren und ihrer Darstellung in der westdeutschen Historiographie," Beitr. z. Gesch. d. dt. Arbeiterbeweg., 3, 1961, 593-620.

1931. SEEBER, Gustav and Heinz WOLTER, "1870/71 Die Gründung des Deutschen Reiches und die Arbeiterbewegung," Beitr. z. Gesch. d. dt. Arbeiterbeweg., 13, 1971, 3-22.

1932. SEIDEL, Jutta (Leipzig), "Le mouvement ouvrier allemand et les événements de 1870-1871," Rev. d'hist. mod., 19, 1972, 283-88.

1933. SEIDER-HÖPPNER, Waltraud, "Frühproletarisches Denken oder erwachendes Klassenbewusstsein: Die Anfänge der Arbeiterbewegung im Blickwinkel formierter Heidelberger Historiographie," Jb. f. Gesch., 3, 1969, 95-136.

1934. SEIDL, Helmut, "Der Arbeitsplatzwechsel als eine frühe Form des Klassenkampfes der mittel- und ostdeutschen Braunkohlenbergarbeiter in der Zeit von 1870 bis 1900," Jb. f. Wgesch., 1965 (4), 102-24.

1935. SIEGER, Walter, "Zur Geschichte des Verbandes junger Arbeiter und Arbeiterinnen Deutschlands (Sitz Mannheim)," Zs. f. Geschw., 4, 1956, 12-38.

1936. SIKLOS-VINCZE, Edit, "Die Solidarität der Sozialisten Ungarns mit den deutschen Arbeitern im Kampf gegen das Sozialistengesetz (1878-1881)," Beitr. z. Gesch. d. dt. Arbeiterbeweg., 13, 1971, 799-811.

1937. STEARNS, Peter N., "Adaptation to Industrialization: German Workers as a Test Case," Cen. Eur. Hist., 3, 1970, 303-31.

1938. STEGLICH, Walter, "Eine Streiktabelle für Deutschland 1864 bis 1880," Jb. f. Wgesch., 1960 (2), 235-83.

1939. STEINHAUSEN, Prof. Dr. Georg, "Fachmenschentum und Arbeitsmenschentum als geistige Typen des letzten Menschenalters," Pr. Jbb., 204, 1926, 288-304.

1940. STRUCK, Wolf-Heino, "Die Anfänge der Arbeiterbewegung in Wiesbaden 1848-1851," Gesch. Landesk., 5, 1969.

1941. TROELTSCH, W., "Die soziale Lage der Pforzheimer Bijonteriearbeiter," Jbb. f. Nationalökon u. Stat., 77, 1901, 305-42, 449-72.

1942. ULBRICHT, Walter, "Referat zum 'Grundriss der Geschichte der deutsche Arbeiterbewegung'," Zs. f. Geschw., 10, 1962, Heft 6 (all).

1943. VARAIN, Heinz Joseph, "Die deutschen Gewerkschaften in ihrem politisch-sozialen Wirken zu Ausgang des 19. Jahrhunderts," GiWuU, 5, 1954, 544-58.

1944. VOIGT, Paul, "Die deutschen Innungen eine statistische Studie," Schmoll. Jb., 22, 1898, 695-723.

1945. WAGNER, M., "Die Arbeiterverhältnisse in den preussischen Staatsforsten," Schmoll. Jb., 15, 1891, 759-815.

1946. WAGNER, Woldemar, "Zu einigen Fragen des Crimmitschauer Textilarbeiterstreiks von 1903/04," Zs. f. Geschw., 1, 1953, 566-92.

1947. WEBER, Alfred, "Die Bureaukratisierung und die gelbe Arbeiterbewegung," Arch. f. Sozialw. u. Sozialpol., 37,

1913, 361-79.
1948.   WHITMAN, Sidney, "Der deutsche und der englische Ar-
        beiter," Pr. Jbb., 66, 1890, 386-404.
1949.   WYGODZINSKI, W., "Raiffeisen Notizen zur Geschichte des
        Landwirtschaftlichen Genossenschaftswesen in Deutsch-
        land," Schmoll. Jb., 23, 1899, 1071-86.
1950.   ZIESE, Gerhard, "Über die Anfänge der Arbeiterbewegung in
        Berlin," Beitr. z. Gesch. d. dt. Arbeiterbeweg., Supp.,
        1965, 140-56.
1951.   ZMARZLY, Manfred, "Einer der Führer des Bundes der
        Gerechten: Hermann Ewerbeck," Beitr. z. Gesch. d. dt.
        Arbeiterbeweg., 12, 1970.

The Post, Telegraph

1952.   ASCHE, Kurt, "Buchdrucker- und Buchbinderornamente auf
        Postwertzeichen des neunzehnten Jahrhunderts," Arch. f.
        dt. Postgesch., 1972 (1), 49-59.
1953.   BERGEMANN, Ulrich, "Die letzte Konferenz des Deutschen
        Postvereins: 13. November 1865 bis 2. März 1866,"
        Arch. f. dt. Postgesch., 1970 (1), 9-28.
1954.   BOES, Julius, "Das Postwesen in den Fürstentümern Waldeck
        und Pyrmont," Arch. f. dt. Postgesch., 1961 (2), 28-51.
1955.   FOERMER, Richard, "Die Post in Koblenz," Arch. f. dt.
        Postgesch., 1960 (2), 17-32.
1956.   FRANCKE, Richard, "Das Lübecker Boten- und Postwesen,"
        Arch. f. dt. Postgesch., 1959 (1), 18-34.
1957.   GALLITSCH, Albert, "Carl Ferdinand Friedrich von Nagler
        Diplomat und Generalpostmeister," Arch. f. dt. Post-
        gesch., 1956 (1), 3-8; 1956 (2), 3-12; 1957 (1), 3-16;
        1957 (2), 3-12; 1958 (1), 3-14; 1958 (2), 3-14.
1958.   GREINER, Karl, "Die Post in Württemberg unter Herzog,
        Kurfürst und König Friedrich," Arch. f. dt. Postgesch.,
        1962 (2), 17-51.
1959.   GRÜNEWALD, Hans, "Die Postverbindungen Stettin-Bordeaux
        in der 1. Hälfte des 19. Jahrhunderts," Arch. f. dt.
        Postgesch., 1968 (2), 22-28.
1960.   HEINSEN, Alfred, "Die Postscheine der Stadt Goslar von
        1733 bis 1832," Arch. f. dt. Postgesch., 1957 (1), 18-26.
1961.   HENNIG, Martin, "Carl Pistor Geheimer Postrat und Meister
        der Mechanik," Arch. f. dt. Postgesch., 1959 (2), 3-12.
1962.   KOCH, Alfred, "Die deutschen Postverwaltungen um 1850 und
        die deutsche Posteinheit," Arch. f. dt. Postgesch., 1972
        (2), 153-59.
1963.   _____, "Deutsche Schiffs- und Seeposten," Arch. f. dt.
        Postgesch., 1964 (1), 1-46; 1964 (2), 21-52; 1965 (1), 40-
        71.
1964.   _____, "Die deutschen Postverwaltungen im Zeitalter Na-
        poleons I Der Kampf um das Postregal in Deutschland und
        die Politik Napoleons I (1798-1815)," Arch. f. dt. Post-
        gesch., 1967 (2), 1-38.
1965.   _____, "Die Oberpostdirektionen in den Ostgebieten des

deutschen Reiches ein historischer Rückblick, " Arch. f.
dt. Postgesch., 1958 (2), 15-46.

1966.　KORELLA, Gottfried, "Die Leiter der Preussischen und
deutschen Telegraphie bis zum Jahre 1876, " Arch. f. dt.
Postgesch., 1969 (2), 18-27.

1967.　_____, "Die preussische Feldtelegrafie insbesondere ihre
Zusammenarbeit mit der Staatstelegrafie, " Arch. f. dt.
Postgesch., 1971 (2), 47-58.

1968.　KÜHNDELT, O., "Vor 50 Jahren:　Erste Postluftfahrt, "
Arch. f. dt. Postgesch., 1962 (1), 3-12.

1969.　LAPP, Günter, "Die Kaiserliche Reichspost und die Ortsna-
men im Herzogtum Schleswig, " Arch. f. dt. Postgesch.,
1972 (1), 60-73.

1970.　NEUMANN, Heinz, "Die Oberpostdirektion Minden (Westf.)
1850-1869 und 1876-1934, " Arch. f. dt. Postgesch.,
1966 (1), 17ff.

1971.　_____, "Zur Geschichte des Telegrafen- und Fernsprech-
wesens im Bereich der ehemaligen Oberpostdirektion, "
Mitteil. Mindener Gesch. u. Museumsver., 41, 1969.

1972.　PIENDL, Max, "Das bayerische Projekt der Thurn und
Taxis-Post 1831-1842, " Zs. f. bayer. LG., 33, 1970,
272-306.

1973.　_____, "Thurn und Taxis 1517-1867, " Arch. f. dt. Postgesch., 1967 (1).

1974.　SCHARFF, Alexander, "Von der schleswig-holsteinischen
zur deutschen Post, " Arch. f. dt. Postgesch., 1969 (2),
1-9.

1975.　SCHMID, K. A. H., "Zur Geschichte der BriefportoReform
in Deutschland, " Jbb. f. Nationalökon. u. Stat., 3, 1864,
1-52.

1976.　SCHRAUTZER, Friedrich, "Aus Leben und Laufbahn eines
Sächsischen Postschriftstellers (1837-1921), " Arch. f. dt.
Postgesch., 1956 (2), 23-31.

1977.　SIEBEN, Peter, "Der Kampf um die Einführung der Post-
sparkasse im Deutschen Reich, " Arch. f. dt. Postgesch.,
1970 (2).

1978.　STÄBLER, Fritz, "Erinnerungen an den Alten Postplatz und
die Post in Stuttgart, " Arch. f. dt. Postgesch., 1960 (2),
47-53.

1979.　TAPPER, W., "Das Privatpostwesen von 1885 bis 1900, "
Arch. f. dt. Postgesch., 1963 (2), 10-26.

1980.　WINTERSCHEID, Theo, "Das Postamt Neuwied im Cholera-
jahr 1831, " Arch. f. dt. Postgesch., 1968 (2), 28-29.

Poverty, Public and Private Welfare

1981.　"18 Jahresbericht der Gesellschaft der Armenfreunde in Leipzig 1865, " Zs. f. Armenwesen, 2, 1865, 159-65.

1982.　ADICKES, F., (Bürgermeister in Altona), "Der erste deutsche
Armenpfleger-Kongress und die brennenden Fragen des
Armenwesens, " Schmoll. Jb., 6, 1882, 605-661.

1983.　_____, "Der Verhandlungen von 1882 und die ferneren

        Aufgaben des deutschen Vereins für Armenpflege und
        Wohlthätigkeit," Schmoll. Jb., 7, 1883, 513-59.

1984.   "Der ALLGEMEINE Wohlthätigkeits-Verein im Königreich
        Württemberg," Zs. f. Armenwesen, 1, 1864, 10-17, 41-
        51, 66-74, 119-28, 129-33, 173-87.

1985.   "ARMENWESEN der stadt Barmen," Zs. f. Armenwesen,
        2, 1865, 223-29, 272-80.

1986.   ASCHROTT, Dr. Felix, "Das Oldenburgische Armenwesen,"
        Schmoll. Jb., 6, 1882, 285-301.

1987.   "Das BAYRISCHE Armenwesen," Zs. f. d. Armenwesen, 4,
        1903, 138-45.

1988.   "BERICHT der Armen-Commission zu Treysa (1865)," Zs.
        f. Armenwesen, 2, 1865, 151-58.

1989.   "BERICHT über den Zustand des Armenwesens in der Stadt
        Hildesheim in den Jahren 1860 bis 1864," Zs. f. Armen-
        wesen, 2, 1865, 91-117.

1990.   BERTHOLD, G., "Die Verhandlungen des deutschen Vereins
        für Armenpflege und Wohlthätigkeit am 5. und 6. Oktober
        1883 zu Dresden," Schmoll. Jb., 8, 1884, 497-522.

1991.   "Die BEZIRKS-Armen-Arbeitshäuser im Königreich Sach-
        sen," Zs. f. Armenwesen, 1, 1864, 201-09, 221-29.

1992.   BITTER, C. H., "Bericht über den Nothstand in der Senne
        zw. Bielefeld und Paderborn," J. ber. f. d. Gft. Ravens-
        berg, 64, 1966, 1-108.

1993.   BUEHL, Dr., "Die Reorganisation des hamburgischen Armen-
        wesens und ihre Erfolge," Zs. f. d. Armenwesen, 4,
        1903, 264-74.

1994.   , "Über Armenstatistik," Zs. f. d. Armenwesen,
        4, 1903, 19-28, 42-48.

1995.   DECKER, Rudolf, "Die Reform der bayerischen Heimat- und
        Armengesetzgebung," Zs. f. d. Armenwesen, 13, 1912,
        2-18, 44-57.

1996.   "Der DEUTSCHE Verein Für Armenpflege und Wohltätigkeit,"
        Zs. f. Armenwesen, 6, 1906, 289-98.

1997.   "DEUTSCHER Verein für Armenpflege und Wohltätigkeit
        Bericht über die 27. Jahresversammlung," Zs. f. d.
        Armenwesen, 8, 1907, 289-94.

1998.   DRECHSLER, Dr., "Die Stellung der Gemeinden zur öffent-
        lichen und privaten Armenpflege in Deutschland und dem
        Auslande," Zs. f. d. Armenwesen, 16, 1915, 37-54.

1999.   "Die 23. Jahresversammlung des deutschen Vereins für
        Armenpflege und Wohltätigkeit," Zs. f. d. Armenwesen,
        4, 1903, 289-301.

2000.   "Der EINFLUSS der wirtschaftlichen Lage der Jahre 1901
        und 1902 auf die Armenlast," Zs. f. d. Armenwesen, 5,
        1904, 143-47.

2001.   "FRAUEN in öffentlichen Armenpflege," Zs. f. d. Armen-
        wesen, 8, 1907, 104-10.

2002.   "FRAUENTÄTIGKEIT in der Armen- und Wohlfahrtspflege,"
        Zs. f. d. Armenwesen, 5, 1904, 129-38.

2003.   FRICKE, Alfred, "Die Ausgaben für die offene Armenpflege
        in den deutschen Grossstädten (1900-1910)," Zs. f. d.
        Armenwesen, 14, 1913, 97-112.

2004.   "FÜRSORGE für Arbeitslose Die Arbeitslosen Fürsorge
        deutscher Städte durch Notstandsarbeiten während der
        Winter 1908/09 und 1909/10," Zs. f. d. Armenwesen,
        11, 1910, 303-10.
2005.   "GEDANKEN zur Geschichte und Theorie des Armenwesens,"
        Zs. f. d. Armenwesen, 9, 1908, 163-86.
2006.   "GESCHICHTE des Badischen Frauenvereins," Zs. f. d.
        Armenwesen, 8, 1907, 365-73.
2007.   "Die GESELLSCHAFT der Armenfreunde in Leipzig," Zs.
        f. Armenwesen, 1, 1864, 133-43.
2008.   "Der GOTHAER Congress und die Genossenschaftsbewegung
        in Deutschland," Pr. Jbb., 2, 1858, 413-38.
2009.   KLUGE, R., "Statistik der Hamburgischen Armenpflege,"
        Zs. f. d. Armenwesen, 9, 1908, 42-50.
2010.   KLUMKER, Professor, "Armenpflege und Kinder Fürsorge
        im letzten Jahrhundert in Deutschland," Zs. f. d. Armen-
        wesen, 14, 1913, 2-14.
2011.   _____, "Die Mängel des deutschen Armenwesens," Pr.
        Jbb., 123, 1906, 463-77.
2012.   KOCH, C. F., "Ueber die Verbreitung der wichtigsten
        Social-Krankheiten im Regierungsbezirk Merseburg, näm-
        lich: des Armen-, Verbrecher-, Vagabunden- und Zieh-
        kinderwesens," Jbb. f. Nationalökon. u. Stat., 15, 1870,
        324-88.
2013.   KRAUS-FESSEL, Meta, "Die Leistungen der öffentlichen
        Armenpflege für Kinder und Jugendliche im Königreich
        Bayern von 1881-1909," Zs. f. d. Armenwesen, 17,
        1916, 43-61.
2014.   KULLEN, Siegfried, "Die Notstandsgemeinden des König-
        reichs Württemberg um 1850 und ihre Entwicklung bis
        zur Gegenwart," Alemann. Jb., 1968/69.
2015.   LAMMERS, A., "Armenpflege in Deutschland," Pr. Jbb.,
        24, 1869, 679-705.
2016.   _____, "Fortschritte in praktischer Armenpflege," Pr.
        Jbb., 43, 1879, 521-33.
2017.   LAVOS, Theodor, "Die bayerische Armenpflege von 1847
        bis 1880," Schmoll. Jb., 8, 1884, 541-94.
2018.   MARQUARDT, Frederick D., "Pauperismus in Germany
        during the Vormärz," Cen. Eur. Hist., 2, 1969, 77-88.
2019.   MUENSTERBERG, Dr., "Zur Geschichte des Armenwesens,"
        Zs. f. d. Armenwesen, 8, 1907, 257-77.
2020.   RICHTER, Pastor, "Die Bezirksarmenverein zu Mühltroff,"
        Zs. f. Armenwesen, 1, 1864, 187-95.
2021.   SCHMIDT, Dr., (Bürgermeister-Mainz), "Das öffentliche
        Armenwesen der Stadt Mainz," Zs. f. d. Armenwesen,
        9, 1908, 202-14.
2022.   "Die 26. Jahresversammlung des Deutschen Verein für
        Armenpflege und Wohltätigkeit," Zs. f. d. Armenwesen,
        7, 1906, 65-72.
2023.   "STÄDTISCHE Armenverwaltung Barmen," Zs. f. Armen-
        wesen, 2, 1865, 36-72.
2024.   STERN, Julius, "Die Entwicklung und der gegenwärtige
        Stand des Rettungswesens," Zs. f. d. Armenwesen, 8,

112 German History and Civilization

1907, 33-57.
2025. TENNEY, Alvan A., "Die öffentliche Kinder Fürsorge der Stadt Berlin," Schmoll. Jb., 26, 1902, 41-65.
2026. "UEBER die Besuche der Armen," Zs. f. Armenwesen, 1, 1864, 272-84.
2027. "UEBER eine zeitgemässe Umgestaltung der Armenpflege," Zs. f. Armenwesen, 2, 1865, 25-35.
2028. "Die VERHÄLTNISSE des Armenwesens in Bayern 1858-59," Zs. f. Armenwesen, 1, 1864, 197-200.
2029. "Die 24. Jahresversammlung des deutschen Vereins für Armenpflege und Wohltätigkeit," Zs. f. d. Armenwesen, 5, 1904, 257-71.
2030. WANDERER, A., "Die Armenkinderpflege im Grossherzogtum Baden," Zs. f. d. Armenwesen, 17, 1916, 162-82.
2031. _____, "Statistik der Armenkinder im Grossherzogtum Oldenburg," Zs. f. d. Armenwesen, 18, 1917, 51-60.
2032. "Die WOHLTHÄTIGKEITS-Anstalten zu Treysa in Kurhessen," Zs. f. Armenwesen, 1, 1864, 74-85.
2033. "ZWEITER Bericht über die Anstalt und Erziehung blödsinniger Kinder in der Kückenmühle bei Stettin vom Jahre 1864," Zs. f. Armenwesen, 2, 1865, 73-90.

The Press, Censorship

See also entries 169, 943, 1844, 1883, 1890, 1902, 1918, 4508, 4546, 4589, 4591, 5105, 5285

2034. DAMMANN, Oswald, "Richard Roepell und die deutsche Zeitung Mit einem ungedruckten Brief Roepells an G. G. Gervinus," ZGORh., 98, 1950, 307-16.
2035. DORNEICH, Julius, "Matthias Josef Scheiben und Benjamin Herder (Aus ihren Briefwechsel 1861-1888)," Theol. Qu.-Schr., 117, 1936, 27ff.
2036. DROZ, Jacques, "Une revue conservatrice allemande peu connue: Concordia (1849)," H. Jb., 74, 1954, 485-89.
2037. ECKEL, M., "Die politische Presse Hessens 1830-50," Zeitung und Leben, 62, 1938.
2038. EISENHARDT, U., "Die Garantie der Pressefreiheit in der Bundesakte von 1815," Staat, 10, 1971, 339-56.
2039. FORSTREUTER, Kurt, "Zur Geschichte der Presse in Königsberg," Hamb. Mittel- u. ostdt. Forsch., 4, 1963, 30-47.
2040. FRANZ, Eckhart G., "Jakob Grimm in der Kasseler Zensurkommission (1816-1829)," Zs. d. Vereins f. Hess. Gesch. u. Landeskunde, 75/76, 1964/65, 455-75.
2041. GRISAR, Joseph, "Ein bayerischer Polizeibericht über Ernst Zander aus dem Jahre 1842," H. Jb., 76, 1956, 161-81.
2042. HAACKE, Wilmont, "Geistesgeschichte der politischen Zeitschrift," ZRGG, 21, 1969, 115-51.
2043. HÖLZLE, Erwin, "Cotta, der Verleger und die Politik," Hist. Vjschr., 29, 1934/35, 576-96.
2044. HOLTZMANN, Walther, "Demosthenes an die Deutschen Ein

Beitrag zur Geschichte der Zensur in Baden während der Befreiungskriege, " ZGORh., 75, 1921, 295-302.

2045.   KREBS, Engelbert, "Hermann Herder Ein katholischer und deutscher Verleger, " Gelbe Hefte, 14, 1937/38, 575-612.

2046.   KROEGER, Gert, "Julius Eckhardts Artikelreihe 'Für und Wider das Elsass-Projekt' August 1870, " Zs. f. Ostforsch., 10, 1961, 201-25.

2047.   KROPAT, Wolf-Arno, "Obrigkeitsstaat und Pressefreiheit. Methoden staatlicher Propaganda und Pressegesetzgebung im 19. Jh. am Beispiel der preussischen Pressepolitik in Hessen-Nassau (1866-1870), " Nass. Ann, 77, 1966, 233-88.

2048.   KUNTZEMÜLLER, Dr. Otto, "Das Hannoversche Zeitungswesen vor dem Jahre 1848 Ein Beitrag zur Geschichte der deutschen Presse, " Pr. Jbb., 94, 1898, 425-53.

2049.   O'BOYLE, Lenore, "The Image of the Journalist in France, Germany, and England, 1815-1848, " Comp. Stud. Soc. Hist., 10, 1967/68, 290-317.

2050.   OBSER, Karl, "Zur Geschichte der badischen Presse in der Rheinbundszeit, " ZGORh., 53, 1899, 111-35.

2051.   RICHTER, Gregor, "Der Staat und die Presse in Württemberg bis zur Mitte des 19. Jahrhunderts, " Zs. f. Wurttbg. LG, 25, 1966, 394-425.

2052.   SCHOEPS, Hans-Joachim, "Neue Briefe zur Gründung des 'Berliner Politischen Wochenblatts', " ZRGG, 13, 1961, 114-27.

2053.   STERNE, Margaret, "German Liberalism and Austrian Censorship in 1865, " J. Cen. Eur. Aff., 21, 1961, 153-64.

2054.   STOKLOSSA, Paul, "Die periodischen Druckschriften Deutschlands Eine statistische Untersuchung, " Schmoll. Jb., 37, 1913, 757-90.

2055.   TIDEMANN, Heinrich, "Die Zensur in Bremen von den Karlsbader Beschlüssen 1819 bis zu ihren Aufhebung 1848, " Bremisches Jb., 31, 1928, 370-414; 32, 1929, 1-110.

2056.   TREITSCHKE, H. v., "Baiern und die Karlsbader Beschlüsse, " Pr. Jbb., 52, 1883, 373-82.

2057.   "ZUR Pressgesetzgebung in Preussen, " Pr. Jbb., 3, 1859, 408-19.

Maximilian Harden (1861-1927)

2058.   BERGLAR, Peter, "Harden und Rathenau, " HZ, 209, 1969, 75-94.

2059.   GOTTGETREU, Erich, "Maximilian Harden: Ways and Errors of a Publicist, " Leo Baeck Inst. Yrbk., 7, 1962, 215-46.

2060.   WELLER, B. Uwe, "'Imperialismus und Resignation' Maximilian Hardens politische Publizistik, " Publizistik, 1970.

2061.   WERNER, Carl M., "Maximilian Harden, " Pol. Stud., 12, 1961, 654-58.

Prisons

2062.   ASCHROTT, P. F., "Betrachtungen über die Bewegung der
        Kriminalität in Preussen während der Jahre 1872 bis
        1881," Schmoll. Jb., 8, 1884, 185-223.
2063.   DUBOE, J., "Zur Gafängnissreform in Preussen," Pr. Jbb.,
        16, 1865, 448-61.
2064.   FUCHS, Finanzrat, "Die Vereinsfürsorge für entlassene
        Gefangene in Deutschen Reiche," Schmoll. Jb., 14, 1890,
        873-89.
2065.   MITTELSTÄDT, O., "Die Reform des deutschen Gefängniss-
        wesens," Pr. Jbb., 40, 1877, 425-35, 487-99.
2066.   REICHARDT, Dr., "Der Verband der deutschen Schutz-
        vereine für entlassene Gefangen," Zs. f. d. Armenwesen,
        11, 1910, 234-39.
2067.   REUSS, Heinrich, "Die Reform der Gefängnisarbeit," Pr.
        Jbb., 85, 1896, 295-313.
2068.   SCHEEL, H. v., "Die Ergebnisse der deutschen Kriminal-
        statistik 1882-1899," Jbb. f. Nationalökon. u. Stat., 77,
        1901, 123-36.
2069.   SCHEFFER, (Herr Gefängnissprediger), "Die verschiedenen
        Systeme der Gefängisshaft und ihre Beurtheilung vom
        christlichen Standpunkte aus," Zs. f. Armenwesen, 1,
        1864, 100-19.

Public Finance

2070.   BENNATHAN, Esra, "German National Income, 1850-1960,"
        Bus. Hist., 5, 1962, 45-53.
2071.   BLAICH, F., "Zinsfreiheit als Problem der deutschen Wirt-
        schaftspolitik zwischen 1857 und 1871," Schmoll. Jb., 91,
        1971, 269-306.
2072.   BÖHMERT, Wilhelm, "Die mittleren Klassen der Einkom-
        mensteuer in einigen deutschen Grossstädten in den Jah-
        ren 1880-1895," Schmoll. Jb., 20, 1896, 1227-53.
2073.   BORNHAK, Conrad, "Die preussische Finanzreform von
        1810," FBPG, 3, 1890, 555-608.
2074.   BRÜNING (Oberbürgermeister in Osnabrück), "Die Heranzie-
        hung der Beamten und Offiziere zu den Gemeindesteuern,"
        Schmoll. Jb., 7, 1883, 995-1002.
2075.   BUSCHE, Manfred, "Zur Gründungsgeschichte der preus-
        sischen Zentralgenossenschaftskasse," Tradition, 13,
        1969, 81-89.
2076.   COHN, Gustav, "German Experiments in Fiscal Legislation,"
        Econ. J., 23, 1913, 537-46.
2077.   _____, "Taxation of Unearned Increment in Germany,"
        Econ. J., 21, 1911, 211-22.
2078.   DAWSON, W. H., "The Genesis of the German Tariff,"
        Econ. J., 14, 1904, 11-23.
2079.   GOLDSCHEID, Rudolf, "The Political Economy of Public
        Finance and the Industrialization of Prussia, 1815-1866,"
        J. Econ. Hist., 26, 1966, 484-97.

2080. JASTROW, Dr. J., "Die preussische Steuerreform Ihre
Stellung in der allgemeinen Verwaltungs- und Sozialpolitik," Arch. f. Sozialw. u. Sozialpol., 7, 1894, 103-65.

2081. KALLE, Fr., "Zur Staats- und Communalsteuerreform in
Preussen," Pr. Jbb., 50, 1882, 439-63.

2082. LEHMANN, Max, "Der Ursprung der preussischen Einkommensteuer," Pr. Jbb., 103, 1901, 1-37.

2083. LOTZ, Prof. Dr. Walther, "Die Reform der direkten
Steuern in Bayern," Arch. f. Sozialw. u. Sozialpol., 11,
1897, 549-634.

2084. MAMROTH, Karl, "Die Luxussteuer in Preussen von 1810-
1814," FBPG, 1, 1888, 281-99.

2085. PIERSTORFF, Julius, "Entwicklung der Tabacksteuer-
Gesetzgebung in Deutschland seit Anfang dieses Jahrhunderts," Jbb. f. Nationalökon. u. Stat., 33, 1879, 232-88.

2086. SCHÖNBECK, Dr. Otto, "Die Einkommensteuer unter den
Nachfolgern Steins Ein Beitrag zur Geschichte des Minis-
teriums Altenstein-Dohna," FBPG, 25, 1913, 117-77.

2087. SIEBERT, A., "Die Entwicklung der direkten Besteuerung
in den Süddeutschen Bundesstaaten im letzten Jahrhundert," ZgesStw., 68, 1912, 1-52.

2088. SOETBEER, Ad., "Volkseinkommen im preussischen Staate
1876 und 1888," Jbb. f. Nationalökon. u. Stat., 52, 1889,
414-27.

2089. TILLY, Richard, "The Political Economy of Public Finance
and the Industrialization of Prussia, 1815-1866," J. Econ.
Hist., 26, 1966, 484-97.

2090. WIELANDT, Friedrich, "Die Frankfurter Bundesversammlung
und die Frage der deutschen Münzeinheit," Blätter für
Münzfreunde und Münzforschung, 80, 1956, 483-501.

2091. WINKEL, Harald, "Die Ablösung der Grundlasten im Herzogtum Nassau im 19. Jahrhundert," VSW, 52, 1965, 42-62.

2092. WINTZINGERODE, Graf von, "Ein Beitrag zur Grundsteuer-
frage in Preussen," Pr. Jbb., 30, 1872, 572-90.

2093. ZEDLITZ, von, "Die directen Steuern in Preussen," Pr.
Jbb., 44, 1879, 115-51.

Railroads

2094. COHN, Gustav, "Die Anfänge des deutschen Eisenbahnwesens,"
ZgesStw., 47, 1891, 655-79.

2095. ECKERT, Georg, "Der Arbeitertag in Bad Harzburg und der
Kampf gegen die Privatisierung der Braunschweiger Staats-
bahn," Arch. f. Sozialgesch., 3, 1963, 465-95.

2096. FRAENKEL, Eugen, "Die Lage der Arbeiter in den werkstät-
ten der Bayerischen Staatsbahnen," Arch. f. Sozialw. u.
Sozialpol., 37, 1913, 808-72.

2097. FREYHAN, Wilhelm, "Breslau und der Eisenbahnverkehr im
19. Jahrhundert," Jb. d. Schles.-Fried.-Wilh. Univ z.
Breslau, 11, 1966, 344-55.

2098. FUCHS, Konrad, "Der Übergang zum Staatsbahnsystem am
Mittelrhein," Arch. f. hessische Gesch., 26, 1958/61,

151-60.
2099. GEYER, Ph., "Kosten und Leistungen der staatlichen und der privaten Eisenbahnverwaltung in Preussen," Schmoll. Jb., 2, 1878, 347-92.
2100. KITTEL, Theodor, "Der Plan eines 'Bundes der deutschen Staatseisenbahnen'," Arch. f. Eisenbahnwesen, 1941, 537-50.
2101. KOLLMANN, Dr. Paul, "Statistischer Ueberblick über die Eisenbahnen Deutschlands, insbesondere während der Betriebsperiode 1880-1881," Schmoll. Jb., 7, 1883, 1271-1345.
2102. LÖSER, Wolfgang, "Die Rolle des preussischen Staates bei der Ausrüstung der Eisenbahnen mit elektrischen Telegraphen in der Mitte des 19. Jahrhunderts," Jb. f. Wgesch., 1963 (4), 193-208.
2103. MAUEL, K., "Joseph von Baaders Vorschläge zum Bau von Eisenbahnen in Bayern 1800 bis 1835," Technikgeschichte, 38, 1971, 48-56.
2104. METZELTIN, Erich, "Von Lichterfelde zur AEG Aus dem Jugendjahren eines deutschen Lokomotivbauers," Bär v. Ber., 9, 1960, 28-48.
2105. MORK, Gordon R., "The Prussian Railway Scandal of 1873: Economics and Politics in the German Empire," Eur. Stud. Rev., 1, 1971, 35-48.
2106. OBERMANN, Karl, "Zur Rolle der Eisenbahnarbeiter im Progress der Formierung der Arbeiterklasse in Deutschland," Jb. f. Wgesch., 1970 (2), 129-40.
2107. PAUL, Helmut, "Die preussische Eisenbahnpolitik von 1835-1838," FBPG, 50, 1938, 250-303.
2108. QUAATZ, R., "Der nationale Gedanke und die Eisenbahnen," Pr. Jbb., 145, 1911, 237-76.
2109. SCHÄFER, Otto, "Die badische Eisenbahnbetriebs- und Tarifpolitik von ihren Anfängen bis zum Ende des 19. Jahrhunderts," ZGORh., 93, 1940/41, 251-75.
2110. _____, "Die Entwicklung des Staatsbahngedankens in Baden," ZGORh., 89, 1936/37, 716-27.
2111. WIEDENFELD, Kurt, "Deutsche Eisenbahngestalter aus Staatsverwaltung Wirtschaftsleben im 19. Jahrhundert," Arch. f. Eisenbahnwesen, 1940, 733-824.

Social Insurance

2112. BÄHR, O., "Das Unfallversicherungsgesetz," Pr. Jbb., 49, 1882, 227-42.
2113. BARFELS, Friedrich, "Invalidenversicherung und Armenpflege in Schleswig-Holstein," Schmoll. Jb., 38, 1914, 2009-28.
2114. BÖDIKER, T., "Die Fortschritte der deutschen Arbeiterversicherung in den letzten 15 Jahren," Schmoll. Jb., 28, 1904, 529-58.
2115. BORGHT, Dr. R. van der, "Die Aufgaben und die Organisation des Reichs-Versicherungsamtes," Archiv f. soziale

Gesetzgeburg u. Statistik, 3, 1890, 1-56.

2116. _____, "Statistik der Entschädigungspflichtigen Unfälle im Deutschen Reich für 1887," Archiv f. soziale Gesetzgeburg u. Statistik, 3, 1890, 539-66.

2117. BRANDT, J. W., "Die Organisation der gewerblichen Unfallversicherung (Berufsgenossenschaften) und ihre Bedeutung für das Gewerbe," Schmoll. Jb., 35, 1911, 761-806, 1281-1338.

2118. BRIGGS, Asa, "The Welfare State in historical Perspective," Eur. J. Soc., 2, 1961, 221-58.

2119. BROOKS, John G., "A Weakness in the German 'Imperial Socialism'," Econ. J., 2, 1892, 302-15.

2120. COHN, Gustav, "Ueber Internationale Arbeiterschutzgebung," Pr. Jbb., 65, 1890, 315-40.

2121. FAY, S. B., "German Unemployment Insurance," Current History, 18, 1950, 65-70.

2122. FRANKENBERG, H. von, "Die Gemeinden und die Arbeiterversicherung," Schmoll. Jb., 21, 1897, 871-98.

2123. _____, "Der tote Punkt der deutschen Arbeiterversicherung," Arch. f. Sozialw. u. Sozialpol., 12, 1898, 75-96.

2124. FRIEDENSBURG, Dr. Ferdinand, "Die Praxis der deutschen Arbeiterversicherung," Zs. f. Pol., 4, 1910/11, 329-69.

2125. GIBBON, I. G., "Insurance Against Sickness and Invalidity and Old Age in Germany," Econ. J., 21, 1911, 185-201.

2126. GREISSL, Fabrikdirektor, "Wirtschaftliche Untersuchungen über die Belastung der deutschen Industrie durch die Arbeiter-Versicherungs- und Schutzgesetzgebung," Schmoll. Jb., 23, 1899, 855-912.

2127. LANGE, Dr. Ernst, "Erweiterung und Reform der deutschen Unfallversicherungsgesetzgebung," Arch. f. Sozialw. u. Sozialpol., 7, 1894, 410-29.

2128. PETERSEN, Julius, "Das Gesetz vom 15. Juni 1883 betr. die Krankenversicherung der Arbeiter," Schmoll. Jb., 8, 1004, 63-134.

2129. PLATTER, Dr. J., "Die geplante Alters- und Invalidenversicherung im deutschen Reich," Archiv f. soziale Gesetzgebung und Statistik, 1, 1888, 7-42.

2130. RUMPE, Dr. med R., "Das deutsche Kranken-Versicherungs-Gesetz nach zwanzigjährigem Bestande zur Erinnerung an den Einführung 1. Dezember 1884," Pr. Jbb., 119, 1905, 97-120.

2131. WELLS, B. W., "Compulsory Insurance in Germany," Pol. Sci. Q., 6, 1891, 43-65.

2132. ZAHN, Friedrich, "Arbeiterversicherung und Armenwesen in Deutschland," Arch. f. Sozialw. u. Sozialpol., 35, 1912, 418-86.

Socialism

2133. BARTEL, Horst, "Dokumente zur Vorgeschichte der II Internationale," Beitr. z. Gesch. d. dt. Arbeiterbeweg., 1, 1959, 549-67.

2134. BECKER, Gerhard and Karl OBERMANN, "Zur Genesis der
       'Neuen Rheinischen Zeitung', " Beitr. z. Gesch. d. dt.
       Arbeiterbeweg., 12, 1970.
2135. BERG, Hermann von, "Die deutsche Fassung des 'Kathe-
       chismus der Proletariers' von Tedesco, " Zs. f. Geschw.,
       18, 1970, 76-87.
2136. BIERMAN, Dr. W. Ed., "Die neuere Entwicklung des So-
       zialismus, " Zs. f. Pol., 1, 1907/08, 488-95.
2137. BRAUNTHAL, Julius, "Die Stärke der ersten internationale
       --Legende und Wirklichkeit, " Int. Rev. Soc. Hist., 5,
       1960, 249-64.
2138. BRIDENTHAL, Renate, "The 'Greening of Germany,' 1848:
       Karl Grün's 'True' Socialism, " Sci. Soc., 35, 1971,
       439-62.
2139. CONZE, Werner, "Vom 'Pöbel' zum 'Proletariat': Sozial-
       geschichtliche Voraussetzungen für den Sozialismus in
       Deutschland, " VSW, 41, 1954, 333-64.
2140. CORNU, Auguste, "German Utopianism: 'True' Socialism, "
       Sci. Soc., 12, 1948, 97-112.
2141. CZOBEL, Ernst, "Zur Verbreitung der Worte 'Sozialist'
       und 'Sozialismus' in Deutschland und Ungarn, " Arch. f.
       d. Gesch. d. Soz., 3, 1912/13, 481-85.
2142. DLUBEK, Rolf and Ernst ENGELBERG, "Die I. Interna-
       tionale und die deutsche Arbeiterbewegung, " Zs. f.
       Geschw., 12, 1964, 968-93.
2143. DLUBEK, Rolf and Ursula HERRMANN, "Die Magdeburger
       Sektion der I. Internationale und der Kampf um die Schaf-
       fung einer revolutionären Massenpartei der deutschen Ar-
       beiterklasse, " Beitr. z. Gesch. d. dt. Arbeiterbeweg.,
       Supp., 1962, 189-218.
2144. ECKERT, Georg, "Eine Denkschrift der Braunschweiger
       Lassaleaner zur Reform des Kommunalwahlrechts, "
       Arch. f. Sozialgesch., 3, 1963, 435-63.
2145. GEMKOW, Heinrich, "Aus dem Kampf deutscher und Franzö-
       sischer Sozialisten gegen Militarismus und Kriegsprovoka-
       tionen in den Jahren 1886/1887, " Beitr. z. Gesch. d. dt.
       Arbeiterbeweg., 3, 1961, 34-49.
2146. _____, "Zur Tätigkeit der Berliner Sektion der I. Interna-
       tionale, " Beitr. z. Gesch. d. dt. Arbeiterbeweg., 1,
       1959, 515-31.
2147. GRÜNBERG, Carl, "L'Origine des Mots 'Socialisme' et
       'Socialiste', " Rev. d'hist. econ. soc., 2, 1909, 289-308.
2148. _____, "Der Ursprung der Worte 'Sozialismus' und
       'Sozialist', " Arch. f. d. Gesch. d. Soz., 2, 1911/12,
       372-79.
2149. HAMMACHER, Emil, "Zur Würdigung des 'wahren' Sozialis-
       mus, " Arch. f. d. Gesch. d. Soz., 1, 1910/11, 41-100.
2150. HAMMEN, Oscar J., "The Spectre of Communism in the
       1840's, " J. Hist. Ideas, 14, 1953, 404-20.
2151. HAYES, Carlton J. H., "German Socialism Reconsidered, "
       AHR, 23, 1917/18, 62-101.
2152. HEIMENDAHL, Herbert, "Die Stellung des Sozialismus zum
       Bankwesen, " Schmoll. Jb., 44, 1920, 1117-75.

2153.   KÖPPE, H., "Der Sozialismus und die soziale Bewegung in der neuesten Lehrbücherliteratur," Arch. f. d. Gesch. d. Soz., 5, 1914, 423-58.

2154.   KURENBACH, W., "Studie über Ernst Dronke," Arch. f. d. Gesch. d. Soz., 15, 1930, 221-37.

2155.   LASKINE, Edmond, "Die Entwicklung des juristischen Sozialismus," Arch. f. d. Gesch. d. Soz., 3, 1912/13, 17-70.

2156.   MAYER, Gustav, "Der Untergang der 'Deutsch-Französischen Jahrbücher' und des Pariser 'Vorwärts'," Arch. f. d. Gesch. d. Soz., 3, 1912/13, 415-37.

2157.   MICHELS, Robert, "Zur Geschichte des Sozialismus," Arch. f. Sozialw. u. Sozialpol., 23, 1906, 786-843.

2158.   MOLNAR, Miklós, "Die Londoner Konferenz der Internationale 1871," Arch. f. Sozialgesch., 4, 1964, 283-445.

2159.   NERRLICH, Paul, "Der Sozialismus und die deutsche Philosophie," Pr. Jbb., 82, 1895, 385-401.

2160.   NETTLAU, Max, "Londoner deutsche Kommunistische Diskussionen 1845," Arch. f. d. Gesch. d. Soz., 10, 1921/22, 362-91.

2161.   NEUMANN, Annemarie, "Die Entwicklung der sozialistischen Frauenbewegung," Schmoll. Jb., 45, 1921, 815-77.

2162.   OBERMANN, Karl, "Zur Geschichte des Kommunistischen Korrespondenzkomitees im Jahre 1846, insbesondere im Rheinland und in Westfalen," Beitr. z. Gesch. d. dt. Arbeiterbeweg., Supp., 1962, 116-43.

2163.   OECKEL, Heinz, "Zum Volkswehrproblem im proletarischen Militärprogramm vom Ausgang des 19. Jahrhunderts bis zum Vorabend der Grossen Sozialistischen Oktoberrevolution," Zs. f. MilitarG., 6, 1967, 554-67.

2164.   OSTERROTH, Franz, "Die Lassaleaner von Neumünster," Arch. f. Sozialgesch., 3, 1963, 425-33.

2165.   POULAT, Emile, "Socialisme et Anticléricalisme Une enquête socialiste internationale (1902-1903)," Arch. d. Soc. d. Rel., 10, 1960, 109-31.

2166.   SALOMON-DELATOUR, Gottfried, "Neue Mosaiksteine zur Geschichte des Frühsozialismus," Schmoll. Jb., 84, 1964, 129-73.

2167.   SCHRAEPLER, Ernst, "Der Zerfall der Ersten Internationale im Spiegel des 'Neuen Social-Demokrat'," Arch. f. Sozialgesch., 3, 1963, 509-59.

2168.   SCHULZE, Winfred, "'Sozialistische Bestrebungen in Deutschland': Bemerkungen zu einer Aufsatzfolge Karl Biedermanns (1846)," VSW, 58, 1970, 93-104.

2169.   SNELL, John L., "Some German Socialist Newspapers in European Archives," J. Mod. Hist., 24, 1952, 380-82.

2170.   STEINBERG, Hans-Josef, "Sozialismus, Internationalismus und Reichsgründung," Das Parlament, 1970.

2171.   TREITSCHKE, H. v., "Der Socialismus und der Meuehelmord," Pr. Jbb., 41, 1878, 637-47.

2172.   _____, "Der Socialismus und seine Gönner," Pr. Jbb., 34, 1874, 67-110, 248-301.

2173.   WARTH, Hermann, "Der Frühsozialismus," Pol. Stud.,

22, 1971, 402-14.

The Communist League

2174.   BECKER, Gerhard, "Der 'Neue Arbeiter-Verein in London'
        1852 Ein Beitrag zur Geschichte des Bundes der Kom-
        munisten," Zs. f. Geschw., 14, 1966, 74-97.
2175.   BERG, Hermann von, "Die 'Deutsche Arbeiterhalle' von
        1851 Zum theoretisch-ideologischen Wirksamkeit des
        Bundes der Kommunisten in Norddeutschland nach der
        Niederschlagung der Revolution von 1848-49," Zs. f.
        Geschw., 19, 1971, 352-68.
2176.   BLUMENBERG, Werner, "Zur Geschichte des Bundes der
        Kommunisten Die Aussagen des Peter Gerhardt Röser,"
        Int. Rev. Soc. Hist., 9, 1964, 81-122.
2177.   CZOBEL, Ernst, "Zur Geschichte des Kommunistenbundes
        Die Kölner Bundesgemeinde vor der Revolution," Arch.
        f. d. Gesch. d. Soz., 11, 1923, 299-335.
2178.   DLUBEK, Rolf, "Ein unbekanntes Dokument über den Kampf
        des Bundes der Kommunisten für die selbständige Or-
        ganisation des Proletariats nach der Revolution von 1848/
        49," Beitr. z. Gesch. d. dt. Arbeiterbeweg., 4, 1962,
        87-101.
2179.   DOWE, Dieter, "Der Bund der Kommunisten in der Rhein-
        provinz nach der Revolution von 1848/49," Rhein. Vjsbll.,
        34, 1970, 267-97.
2180.   ECKERT, Georg, "Aus der Korrespondenz des Kommunisten-
        bundes (Fraktion Willich-schapper)," Arch. f. Sozialgesch.,
        5, 1965, 273-318.
2181.   FÖRDER, Herwig, "Die Nürnberger Gemeinde des Bundes
        der Kommunisten und die Verbreitung des Manifestes der
        Kommunistischen Partei im Frühjahr 1851," Beitr. z.
        Gesch. d. dt. Arbeiterbeweg., Supp., 1962, 165-88.
2182.   LEIDIGKEIT, Karl-Heinz, "Zur Tradition des Bundes der
        Kommunisten nach dem Kölner Kommunistenprozess,"
        Beitr. z. Gesch. d. dt. Arbeiterbeweg., 4, 1962, 858-71.
2183.   NA'AMAN, Shlomo, "Zur Geschichte des Bundes der Kom-
        munisten in Deutschland in der zweiten Phase seines
        Bestehens," Arch. f. Sozialgesch., 5, 1965, 5-82.
2184.   NICOLAEVSKY, B., "Toward a History of 'The Communist
        League' 1847-1852," Int. Rev. Soc. Hist., 1, 1956, 234-
        52.
2185.   OBERMANN, Karl, "The Communist League: A Forerunner
        of the American Labor Movement," Sci. Soc., 30, 1966,
        433-46.
2186.   _____, "Zu den Propaganda- und Flugblattaktionen des
        Bundes der Kommunisten in Deutschland 1850/51," Beitr.
        z. Gesch. d. dt. Arbeiterbeweg., 13, 1971, 785-98.
2187.   _____, "Zum Anteil des deutschen Proletariats und des
        Bundes der Kommunisten an der Vorbereitung der Revolu-
        tion von 1848," Zs. f. Geschw., 16, 1968, 1023-30.
2188.   _____, "Zur Geschichte des 'Bundes der Kommunisten'

1849 bis 1852," Zs. f. Geschw., 1, 1953, 409-44.

2189.   SCHIEDER, Wolfgang, "Der Bund der Kommunisten im
Sommer 1850 Drei Dokumente aus dem Marx-Engels-
Nachlass," Int. Rev. Soc. Hist., 13, 1968, 29-57.

2190.   SCHMIDT, Walter, "Der Bund der Kommunisten und die
Versuche einer Zentralisierung der deutschen Arbeitervereine im April und Mai 1848," Zs. f. Geschw., 9,
1961, 577-614.

2191.   WINKLER, Gerhard, "Über die historische Stellung des
'Bundes der Kommunisten' in der deutschen Arbeiterbewegung," Zs. f. Geschw., 2, 1954, 538-50.

Friedrich Engels (1820-1895)

2192.   ALEXANDER, Dietrich and Erhard LANGE, "Grundfragen
der materialistischen Geschichtsauffassung in Friedrich
Engels' Altersbriefen," Dt. Zs. f. Phil., 18, 1970,
1193-1212.

2193.   BARTEL, Horst and Erich KUNDEL, "Die Bedeutung der
Aufsätze von Friedrich Engels im 'Volkstaat' für den
Kampf der deutschen Arbeiterklasse gegen den preus-
sisch-deutschen Militarismus in den Jahren 1874/75,"
Beitr. z. Gesch. d. dt. Arbeiterbeweg., Supp., 1962,
219-41.

2194.   BARTEL, Horst and Walter SCHMIDT, "Friedrich Engels
zu einigen Grundproblem der Geschichte des deutschen
Volkes im 19. Jahrhundert," Jb. f. Gesch., 6, 1972,
147-90.

2195.   BECKER, Gerhard, "Briefe von Elise Engels an ihren Sohn
1848/49," Zs. f. Geschw., 18, 1970, 1335-47.

2196.   BITSCHKO, I. W., "Friedrich Engels und die Begründung
des Marxistischen Humanismus," Dt. Zs. f. Phil., 18,
1970, 1184-92.

2197.   BLOCH, Ernst, "Friedrich Engels als Polyhistor," Dt.
Zs. f. Phil., 3, 1955, 669-77.

2198.   CADOGAN, Peter, "Harney and Engels," Int. Rev. Soc.
Hist., 10, 1965, 66-104.

2199.   DLUBEK, Rolf, "Friedrich Engels als publizistischer An-
walt des Willichschen Freikorps," Beitr. z. Gesch. d.
dt. Arbeiterbeweg., 9, 1967, 235-47.

2200.   _____, "Zur politischen Tätigkeit von Friedrich Engels
in der Schweiz Ende 1848- Anfange 1849," Beitr. z.
Gesch. d. dt. Arbeiterbeweg., 2, 1960, 742-86.

2201.   ESCHKE, Hans-Günter, "Friedrich Engels über das Verhältnis von Gesamtwillen und Einzelwillen in der Gesellschaft," Dt. Zs. f. Phil., 18, 1970, 1213-31.

2202.   FÖRDER, Herwig and Martin HUNDT, "Zur Vorgeschichte
von Engels' Arbeit 'Grundsätze des Kommunismus',"
Beitr. z. Gesch. d. Arbeiterbeweg., 12, 1970.

2203.   FORSTREUTER, Kurt, "Eine Stimme zu der Schrift von
Friedrich Engels über 'Die Lage der arbeitenden Klasse
in England'," VSW, 53, 1966, 366-69.

2204. GEMKOW, Heinrich, "Friedrich Engels' Reise auf den Kontinent im Jahre 1893," Beitr. z. Gesch. d. dt. Arbeiterbeweg., Supp., 1962, 242-56.

2205. GOEBEL, Klaus and Helmut HIRSCH, "Engels: Forschungsmaterialien im Bergischen Land," Arch. f. Sozialgesch., 9, 1969, 429-50.

2206. GRUNWALD, Manfred, "Wissenschaft und Wissenschaftstheorie bei Friedrich Engels," Dt. Zs. f. Phil., 18, 1970, 1232-49.

2207. GUSTAFSSON, Bo, "Friedrich Engels and the Historical Role of Ideologies," Sci. Soc., 30, 1966, 257-74.

2208. HELMERT, Heinz and Rudolf KOSCHULLA, "Friedrich Engels--Soldat der Revolution und Militärtheoretiker der Arbeiterklasse," Zs. f. MilitärG., 9, 1970, 389-405.

2209. HELMERT, Heinz and Ernst ROLOFF, "Die militär-politische Tätigkeit von Friedrich Engels in der Periode nach der Pariser Kommune," Zs. f. MilitärG., 9, 1970, 645-58.

2210. HERKNER, H., "Ueber Engels und Lassalle," Pr. Jbb., 181, 1920, 1-21.

2211. KAUTSKY, Karl, "Gustav Mayers Engels-Biographie," Arch. f. d. Gesch. d. Soz., 9, 1920/21, 342-55.

2212. KOSING, Alfred, "Friedrich Engel's Beitrag zur revolutionären Weltanschauung des Marxismus," Dt. Zs. f. Phil., 18, 1970, 1149-68.

2213. MALORNY, Heinz, "Friedrich Engels und die Fragen der Philosophiegeschichte," Dt. Zs. f. Phil., 18, 1970, 1270-90.

2214. MAYER, Gustav, ed., "Ein Brief von Friedrich Engels an Johann Jacoby," Arch. f. d. Gesch. d. Soz., 1, 1910/11, 354-57.

2215. _____, "Ein Pseudonym von Friedrich Engels," Arch. f. d. Gesch. d. Soz., 4, 1913/14, 86-89.

2216. MERKEL, Renate, "Friedrich Engels' Beitrag zur Entwicklung der wissenschaftlichen Sozialismusauffassung in der Periode des Übergangs vom revolutionären Demokratismus zum Kommunismus (1842-1844)," Jb. f. Gesch., 5, 1971, 71-117.

2217. _____, "Materialistische Geschichtsauffassung und Sozialismusbild in der Schrift 'Die Lage der arbeitenden Klasse in England'," Zs. f. Geschw., 17, 1970, 1310-24.

2218. OBERMANN, Karl, "Über die Bedeutung der Tätigkeit von Friedrich Engels im Frühjahr und Sommer 1848," Zs. f. Geschw., 9, 1961, 28-47.

2219. ONCKEN, Hermann, "Friedrich Engels und die Anfänge des deutschen Kommunismus," HZ, 123, 1920, 239-66.

2220. OPITZ, Waldtraut, "Friedrich Engels und die deutsche Sozialdemokratie in den Jahren 1890/91," Zs. f. Geschw., 17, 1969, 1403-15.

2221. _____, "Die Hilfe von Friedrich Engels für die deutsche Sozialdemokratie im Kampf gegen den preussisch-deutschen Militarismus und die Militärvorlage 1893," Zs. f. Geschw., 18, 1970, 1292-1309.

2222. OSCHILEWSKI, Walther G., "Im Banne Hegels Friedrich

Engels' Berliner Militär- und Studienjahr, " Bär v. Ber.,
4, 1954, 144-59.

2223. PASTORE, Annibale, "Der kritische Kommunismus bei
Friedrich Engels, " Arch. f. d. Gesch. d. Soz., 5, 1914,
163-68.

2224. RICHTER, Friedrich, et al., "Zum 150. Geburtstag von
Friedrich Engels, " Beitr. z. Gesch. d. dt. Arbeiterbeweg., 12, 1970.

2225. ROSDOLSKY, Roman, "Friedrich Engels und das Problem
der 'Geschichtslosen' Völker (Die Nationalitätenfrage in
der Revolution 1848-1849 im Lichte der 'Neuen Rheinischen Zeitung', " Arch. f. Sozialgesch., 4, 1964, 87-282.

2226. SCHULZE, W. A., "Friedrich Engels und Marheinecke, "
Zs. f. KiG, 67, 1955/56, 141-44.

2227. SELESNJOW, K. L., "Die Erforschung des Lebens und
Werkes von Friedrich Engels durch die sowjetischen Wis-
senschaftler, " Beitr. z. Gesch. d. dt. Arbeiterbeweg.,
13, 1971, 74.

2228. SIEBER, Rolf, "Friedrich Engels und die marxistische politische Ökonomie, " Dt. Zs. f. Phil., 18, 1970, 1169-
83.

2229. SILBERNER, Edmund, "Friedrich Engels and the Jews, "
Jew. Soc. Stud., 11, 1949, 323ff.

2230. STEINBERG, Hans-Josef, "Revolution und Legalität Ein
unveröffentlicher Brief Friedrich Engels' an Richard
Fischer, " Int. Rev. Soc. Hist., 12, 1967, 177-89.

2231. STERN, Berhard J., "Engels on the Family, " Sci. Soc.,
12, 1948, 42-64.

2232. STOLZ, Ruth, "Friedrich Engels über die politische Aktion
der Arbeiterklasse, " Beitr. z. Gesch. d. dt. Arbeiterbeweg., 3, 1961, 874-77.

2233. ULLRICH, Horst, "Friedrich Engels' 'Anti-Schelling', " Dt.
Zs. f. Phil., 20, 1972, 1227-49.

2234. "Eine UNBEKANNTE Jugendarbeit von Friedrich Engels, "
Beitr. z. Gesch. d. dt. Arbeiterbeweg., 2, 1960, 99-122.

2235. WOROBJEWA, A. K., "Friedrich Engels und die revolutionäre Bewegung in Russland in den letzten Jahren seines
Lebens, " Beitr. z. Gesch. d. dt. Arbeiterbeweg., 14,
1972, 621-37.

Ferdinand Lassalle (1825-1864)

See also entries, 4594, 4595

2236. COMPAGNON, Marcel E., "Le duel et la mort de Ferdinand Lassalle (Genève, août 1864), " Zs. f. Schw. Gesch.,
21, 1941, 79-115.

2237. DREES, Willem, "Lassalle en de oprichting van de algemene
Duitse arbeidersvereiniging in 1863, " Socialisme en demo-
cratie, 7/8, 1963, 546-71.

2238. FRIEDERICI, Hans Jürgen, "Zur Einschätzung Lassalles und
des Lassalleanismus in der bürgerlichen und rechtsozial-

demokratischen Geschichtsschreibung," Beitr. z. Gesch.
d. dt. Arbeiterbeweg., 2, 1960, 294-313.

2239. HENTSCHEL, Cedric, "Disraeli and Lassalle," Ger. Life
Letters, 2, 1937/38, 93-106.

2240. HEWETT-THAYER, Harvey W., "Ferdinand Lassalle in the
Novels of Spielhagen and Meredith," Ger. Rev., 19,
1943, 186-96.

2241. HOLL, Karl, "Unbekannte Briefe Ferdinand Lassalles," Zs.
f. d. Gesch. d. Juden, 6, 1969, 169-74.

2242. KNIEF, Johann, "Lassalle," Arch. f. d. Gesch. d. Soz.,
10, 1921/22, 1-21.

2243. KOSZYK, Kurt, "Die Organisator Ferdinand Lassalle im
Jahre 1863," Jb. d. Schles.-Fried.-Wilh. Univ z. Breslau, 8, 1963, 154-71.

2244. LUKACS, Georg, "Die neue Ausgabe von Lassalles Briefen,"
Arch. f. d. Gesch. d. Soz., 11, 1923, 401-23.

2245. MAYER, Gustav, ed., "Briefe Ferdinand Lassalles an Ferdinand Freiligrath," Arch. f. d. Gesch. d. Soz., 7,
1916, 431-45.

2246. _____, "Lassalleana Unbekannte Briefe Lassalles," Arch.
f. d. Gesch. d. Soz., 1, 1910/11, 176ff.

2247. _____, ed., "Ein Spitzelbericht Lassalles über sich
selbst," Arch. f. d. Gesch. d. Soz., 10, 1921/22, 398-
410.

2248. NA'AMAN, Shlomo, "Heine und Lassalle Ihre Beziehungen
im Zeichen der Dämonie des Geldes," Arch. f. Sozialgesch., 4, 1964, 45-86.

2249. _____, "Lassalle--Demokratie und Sozialdemokratie,"
Arch. f. Sozialgesch., 3, 1963, 21-80.

2250. _____, "Lassalles Beziehungen zu Bismarck: Ihr Sinn
und Zweck," Arch. f. Sozialgesch., 2, 1962, 55-85.

2251. _____, "Die theoretischen Grundlagen der Aktion Lassalles im Briefwechsel mit Rodbertus," Int. Rev. Soc.
Hist., 6, 1961, 431-55.

2252. ONCKEN, Hermann, ed., "Briefe Lassalles an Dr. Otto
Dammer in Leipzig Vizepräsidenten des Allgemeinen
deutschen Arbeitervereins," Arch. f. d. Gesch. d. Soz.,
2, 1911/12, 380-422.

2253. _____, ed., "Neue Lassalle Briefe," Arch. f. d. Gesch.
d. Soz., 4, 1913/14, 439-65.

2254. RIASANOFF, N., ed., "Briefe Lassalles an Dr. Moses
Hess," Arch. f. Gesch. d. Soz., 3, 1912/13, 129-42.

2255. ROSENBAUM, Eduard, "Ferdinand Lassalle--A Historio-
graphical Meditation," Leo Baeck Inst. Yrbk., 9, 1964,
122-30.

2256. ROTHFELS, Hans, "Lassalle und die Gräfin Hatzfeldt,"
Pr. Jbb., 198, 1924, 185-92.

2257. SCHILLMANN, Fritz, ed., "Zum Streit um das Erbe Lassalles Briefe aus dem Nachlasse von Gustav Schoenberg,"
Arch. f. d. Gesch. d. Soz., 5, 1914, 464-70.

2258. SCHMID., Carlo, "Ferdinand Lassalle und die politisierung
der deutschen Arbeiterbewegung," Arch. f. Sozialgesch.,
3, 1963, 5-20.

2259. SICLÓS-VINCZE, Edit, "Der Kampf in der ungarischen Arbeiterbewegung gegen den lassaleanischen Einfluss (1867-
1872), " Beitr. z. Gesch. d. dt. Arbeiterbeweg., 2, 1960,
314-31.
2260. SPEIER, Hans, "Die Geschichtsphilosophie Lassalles, "
Arch. f. Sozialw. u. Sozialpol., 61, 1929, 103-27, 360-
88.

Karl Marx (1818-1883)

See also entries 572, 1356, 1400, 1410, 1419, 3441, 3482,
3544, 3554, 3581, 3746

2261. ACHMINOW, Herman, "Mythos und Wahrheit in der Geschichtslehre von Marx, " Saec., 11, 1960, 266-94.
2262. ACTON, H. B., "The Marxist Outlook, " Philosophy, 22,
1947, 208-30.
2263. ADLER, Max, "Der Kommunismus bei Marx, " Arch. f. d.
Gesch. d. Soz., 6, 1915, 229-68.
2264. _____, "Mach und Marx Ein Beitrag zur Kritik des
modernen Postivismus, " Arch. f. Sozialw. u. Sozialpol.,
33, 1911, 348-400.
2265. _____, "Marxismus und Kantischer Kritizismus, " Arch.
f. d. Gesch. d. Soz., 11, 1923, 336-67.
2266. _____, "Der soziale Sinn der Lehre von Karl Marx, "
Arch. f. d. Gesch. d. Soz., 4, 1913/14, 1-29.
2267. ALBRECHT, Gerhard, "Die Marxsche Grundrententheorie, "
Jbb. f. Nationalökon. u. Stat., 101, 1913, 1-38.
2268. ALTSCHUL, S. E., "Die logisische Struktur des historischen
Materialismus, " Arch. f. Sozialw. u. Sozialpol., 37,
1913, 46-87.
2269. ANDRÉAS, Bert, "Briefe und Dokumente der Familie Marx
aus den Jahren 1862-1873 nebst zwei unbekannten Aufsät-
zen von Friedrich Engels, " Arch. f. Sozialgesch., 2,
1962, 167-293.
2270. _____, "Marx über die SPD, Bismarck und das Sozialistengesetz, " Arch. f. Sozialgesch., 5, 1965, 363-76.
2271. _____ and Wolfgang MÖNKE, "Neue Daten zur 'Deutschen
Ideologie' Mit einem unbekannten Brief von Karl Marx und
anderen Dokumenten, " Arch. f. Sozialgesch., 8, 1968, 5-
159.
2272. ASHCRAFT, R., "Marx and Max Weber on Liberalism as
Bourgeois Ideology, " Comp. Stud. Soc. Hist., 14, 1972,
130-68.
2273. AVINERI, Shlomo, "The Hegelian Origins of Marx's Political
Thought, " Rev. Metaphysics, 21, 1967/68, 33-56.
2274. _____, "Marx and the Intellectuals, " J. Hist. Ideas, 28,
1967, 269-78.
2275. _____, "Marx and Jewish Emancipation, " J. Hist. Ideas,
25, 1964, 445-50.
2276. _____, "Marx and Modernization, " Rev. Pol., 31, 1969,
172-88.

2277.   BAJT, Alexander, "Labor as Scarcity in Marx's Value
        Theory: An Alternative Interpretation," Hist. Pol. Econ.,
        3, 1971, 152-69.

2278.   BALASSA, Bela A., "Karl Marx and John Stuart Mill,"
        Weltwirtsch. Arch., 83, 1959, 147-65.

2279.   BALBUS, Isaac D., "The Concept of Interest in Pluralist
        and Marxian Analysis," Pol. Soc., 1, 1970/71, 151-77.

2280.   BARTEL, Horst, "Um die Durchsetzung des Marxismus in
        der deutschen Arbeiterbewegung," Beitr. z. Gesch. d.
        dt. Arbeiterbeweg., 6, 1964, 859-70.

2281.   _____ and Walter SCHMIDT, "Zur Entwicklung des Par-
        teibegriffs bei Marx und Engels," Beitr. z. Gesch. d.
        dt. Arbeiterbeweg., 11, 1969.

2282.   BARTLETT, Francis H., "Marxism and the Psychoanalytic
        Theory of the Unconscious," Sci. Soc., 16, 1951/52, 44-
        52.

2283.   BAUER, Stephan, "Neue Marxstudien D. Rjasanows," Arch.
        f. d. Gesch. d. Soz., 14, 1929, 149-54.

2284.   BECKER, Gerhard, "Die Rolle von Marx und Engels und des
        Kölner Arbeitervereins bei der Vorbreitung einer revolu-
        tionären Massenpartei des deutschen Proletariats im Früh-
        jahr 1849," Beitr. z. Gesch. d. dt. Arbeiterbeweg.,
        Supp., 1962, 144-64.

2285.   _____, "Zwei neuentdeckte Briefe von Karl Marx Ergän-
        zende Tatsachen zu seiner Biographie für das Jahr 1848,"
        Zs. f. Geschw., 16, 1968, 306-26.

2286.   BELOW, G. v., "Die deutsche wirtschaftsgeschichtliche
        Literatur und der Ursprung des Marxismus," Jbb. f. Na-
        tionalökon. u. Stat., 98, 1912, 561-92.

2287.   BENSE, Max, "Die 'Pariser Manuskripte' des jungen Marx,"
        Aussenpol., 2, 1951, 556-60.

2288.   BERNSTEIN, Eduard, "Karl Marx und Michael Bakunin,"
        Arch. f. Sozialw. u. Sozialpol., 30, 1910, 1-29.

2289.   BERNSTEIN, Samuel, "The first International on the eve of
        the Paris Commune," Sci. Soc., 5, 1941, 24-42.

2290.   _____, "From Utopianism to Marxism," Sci. Soc., 14,
        1949/50, 59-67.

2291.   _____, "Marx in Paris, 1848: A neglected chapter,"
        Sci. Soc., 3, 1939, 323-55; 4, 1944, 211-17.

2292.   BLASIUS, Dirk, "Carl von Clausewitz und die Hauptdenker
        des Marxismus," Wehrw. Rs., 16, 1966, 278-94, 335-54.

2293.   BLOCH, Ernst, "Keim und Grundlinie Zu den Elf Thesen
        von Marx über Feuerbach," Dt. Zs. f. Phil., 1, 1953,
        237-61.

2294.   BLOOM, Solomon F., "Karl Marx and the Jews," Jew. Soc.
        Stud., 4, 1942, 3-16.

2295.   BLUM, Oskar, "Max Adlers Neugestaltung der Marxismus,"
        Arch. f. d. Gesch. d. Soz., 8, 1919, 177-247.

2296.   BLUMENBERG, Werner, "Marx' und Engels' Briefwechsel
        mit Franz Duncker," Int. Rev. Soc. Hist., 10, 1965,
        105-19.

2297.   _____, "Ein unbekanntes Kapitel aus Marx' Leben Briefe
        an die holländischen Verwandten," Int. Rev. Soc. Hist.,

1, 1956, 54-111.

2298. BORTKIEWICZ, L. v., "Wertrechnung und Preisrechnung im Marxschen System," Arch. f. Sozialw. u. Sozialpol., 23, 1906, 1-50; 25, 1907, 10-51, 445-88.

2299. _____, "Zur Berichtigung der Grundlegenden theoretischen Konstruktion von Marx im dritten Band des 'Kapital'," Jbb. f. Nationalökon. u. Stat., 89, 1907, 319-35.

2300. BOTTOMORE, T. B., "Karl Marx: Sociologist or Marxist?," Sci. Soc., 30, 1966, 11-24.

2301. BRIEFS, Goetz A., "The rise and fall of the proletarian utopias," Rev. Pol., 1, 1939, 31-50.

2302. BRONFENBRENNER, Martin, "Das Kapital for the Modern Man," Sci. Soc., 29, 1965, 419-38.

2303. BÜCKLING, G., "Der Einzelne und der Staat bei Stirner und Marx," Schmoll. Jb., 44, 1920, 1071-1115.

2304. BURCHARDT, Fritz, "Die Schemata des stationären Kreislaufs bei Böhm-Bawerk und Marx," Weltwirtsch. Arch., 34, 1931, 525-64; 35, 1932, 116-76.

2305. CATON, Hiram, "Marx's Sublation of Philosophy into Praxis," Rev. Metaphysics, 26, 1972/73, 233-59.

2306. CHAMBERLAIN, Gary L., "The man Marx made," Sci. Soc., 27, 1963, 302-20.

2307. COHEN, Gerald A., "Bourgeois and proletarians," J. Hist. Ideas, 29, 1968, 211-30.

2308. COLLINS, Henry, "Karl Marx, the International and the British Trade Union movement," Sci. Soc., 26, 1962, 400-21.

2309. COLLINS, Kins, "Marx on the English agricultural revolution: theory and evidence," Hist. Theor., 6, 1967, 351-81.

2310. COMMONS, J. R., "Karl Marx and Samuel Gompers," Pol. Sci. Q., 41, 1926, 281-86.

2311. CROSS, Truman B., "Young Marx, Marxism: Viktor Chernov's use of 'The Theses on Feuerbach'," J. Hist. Ideas, 32, 1971, 600-06.

2312. DANIELS, Robert V., "Fate and Will in the Marxian philosophy of history," J. Hist. Ideas, 21, 1960, 538-52.

2313. DAVIS, Horace B., "Imperialism and Labor: An analysis of Marxian views," Sci. Soc., 26, 1962, 26-45.

2314. _____, "Nations, colonies and social classes: the position of Marx and Engels," Sci. Soc., 29, 1965, 26-43.

2315. DELBRÜCK, Hans, "Die marxsche Geschichtsphilosophie," Pr. Jbb., 182, 1920, 157-80.

2316. DEMETZ, Peter, "Early beginnings of Marxist literary theory," Ger. Rev., 29, 1954, 201-13.

2317. DESROCHE, Henri, "Athéisme et socialisme dans le Marxisme classique K. Marx - F. Engels," Arch. d. Soc. d. Rel., 10, 1960, 71-108.

2318. DIEHL, Karl, "Die Grundrententheorie im ökonomischen System von Karl Marx," Jbb. f. Nationalökon. u. Stat., 72, 1899, 433-80.

2319. DLUBEK, Rolf and Hannes SKAMBRAKS, "Der Einfluss der 'Kapitels' von Karl Marx auf die deutsche Arbeitsbewe-

gung 1867-1878," Beitr. z. Gesch. d. dt. Arbeiterbeweg.,
9, 1967, 216-34, 414-40.

2320.   DOBB, Maurice, "Marx's Capital and its place in economic
thought," Sci. Soc., 31, 1967, 527-40.

2321.   _____, "A note on some aspects of the economic theory
of Marx," Sci. Soc., 2, 1937/38, 322-31.

2322.   DOLLÉANS, Édouard, "La Rencontre de Proudhon et de
Marx (1843-1847)," Rev. d'hist. mod., 11, 1936, 5-30.

2323.   DRUCKER, H. M., "Marx's concept of ideology," Philosophy, 47, 1972, 152-61.

2324.   DUFFIELD, J., "The value concept in Capital in light of
recent criticism," Sci. Soc., 34, 1970, 293-302.

2325.   DUNAN, Jack, "The Marxist and Christian concept of man,"
Sci. Soc., 32, 1968, 278-87.

2326.   ECKERT, Georg, "Wilhelm Bracke und die Propaganda für
den 1. Band des 'Kapital' von Karl Marx (1867-68),"
Braunschweig. Jb., 48, 1967, 102-37.

2327.   EICKELSCHULTE, Dietmar, "Aspekte der Freiheit in der
Frühschriften von Karl Marx," Freiburger Zs. f. Phil.,
13/14, 1966/67, 47-92.

2328.   EIFLER, Rudolf, "Vorkapitalistische Klassengesellschaft und
aufsteigende Folge von Gesellschaftsinformationen im
Werk von Karl Marx," Zs. f. Gesch., 20, 1972, 577-96.

2329.   ELLIOTT, Charles F., "Quis custodiet Sacra? Problems
of Marxist Revisionism," J. Hist. Ideas, 28, 1967, 71-
86.

2330.   ENGELBERG, Ernst, "Die Rolle von Marx und Engels bei
der Herausbildung einer selbständigen deutschen Arbeiter-
partei (1864-1869)," Zs. f. Geschw., 2, 1954, 509-37,
637-66.

2331.   EPPSTEIN, Paul, "Die Fragestellung nach der Wirklichkeit
im historischen Materialismus," Arch. f. Sozialw. u.
Sozialpol., 60, 1928, 449-507.

2332.   EVENITSKY, Alfred, "Marx's model of expanded reproduction," Sci. Soc., 27, 1963, 159-75.

2333.   _____, "Monopoly Capitalism and Marx's economic doctrines," Sci. Soc., 24, 1960, 134-49.

2334.   FABBRI, Luigi, "Die historischen und sachlichen Zusam-
menhänge zwischen Marxismus und Anarchismus," Arch.
f. Sozialw. u. Sozialpol., 26, 1908, 559-605.

2335.   FALK, Werner, "Hegels Freiheitsidee in der Marx'schen
Dialektik," Arch. f. Sozialw. u. Sozialpol., 68, 1932/33,
165-93.

2336.   FAYE, Jean-Pierre, "Marx et la théorie du developpement,"
Rev. d'hist. econ. soc., 38, 1960, 320-38.

2337.   FETSCHER, Iring, "Marxismus und Bürokratie," Int. Rev.
Soc. Hist., 5, 1960, 378-99.

2338.   FIREMAN, P., "Kritik der Marx'schen Werttheorie," Jbb.
f. Nationalökon. u. Stat., 58, 1892, 793-808.

2339.   FÖRDER, Herwig, "Die politischen und taktischen Richt-
linien von Marx und Engels für den allgemein-demokrat-
ischen Kampf der Kölner Kommunisten im Jahre 1846,"
Zs. f. Geschw., 4, 1956, 291-306.

2340. FONER, Philip S., "Two neglected interviews with Karl Marx," Sci. Soc., 36, 1972, 3-28.

2341. FORRESTER, Duncan B., "The attack on Christendom in Marx and Kierkegaard," Scott. J. Theol., 25, 1972, 181-96.

2342. GABLENTZ, Otto Heinrich v. d., "Der Marx'sche Begriff der gesellschaftlichen Produktionsverhältnisse und die gesellschaftliche Wirklichkeit," Schmoll. Jb., 70, 1950, 129-46.

2343. GEYER, Karlheinz, "Die Marxsche Kritik der ethisch-idealistischen Geschichtskonzeption Karl Höchbergs," Dt. Zs. f. Phil., 16, 1968, 452-67.

2344. GLASS, James M., "Marx, Kafka, and Jung: The appearance of Species-being," Pol. Soc., 2, 1971/72, 255-71.

2345. GOLDWAY, David, "Appearance and reality in Marx's Capital," Sci. Soc., 31, 1967, 428-447.

2346. GOTTSCHLING, Gerhard, "Die weltanschaulichen Grundlagen und der historische Charakter des marxistischen Atheismusbegriff," Dt. Zs. f. Phil., 18, 1970, 534-44.

2347. GREGOR, James, "Giovanni Gentile and the philosophy of the young Karl Marx," J. Hist. Ideas., 24, 1963, 213-30.

2348. GREGOR, A. James, "Marx, Feuerbach and the reform of the Hegelian dialectic," Sci. Soc., 29, 1965, 66-80.

2349. GROH, Dieter, "Marx, Engels und Darwin: Naturgesetzliche Entwicklung oder Revolution zum Problem der Einheit von Theorie und Praxis," Pol. Vjschr., 8, 1967, 544-59.

2350. GROPP, Rugard O., "Die marxistische dialektische Methode und ihr Gegensatz zur idealistischen Dialektik Hegels," Dt. Zs. f. Phil., 2, 1954, 69-112, 344-83.

2351. GROSSMANN, Henryk, "Die Änderung der ursprünglichen Aufbauplans des Marxschen 'Kapital' und ihre Ursachen," Arch. f. d. Gesch. d. Soz., 14, 1929, 305-38.

2352. _____, "Die Wert-Preis Transformation bei Marx und das Krisenproblem," Zs. f. Sozialforschung, 1, 1932, 55-84.

2353. GRUBER, Utta, "Wachstums theoretische Beziehungen in der Akkumulationstheorie von Karl Marx," Jbb. f. Nationalökon. u. Stat., 172, 1960, 392-99.

2354. _____, "Zur Frage der Gesamtgrössenbetrachtung bei Marx und Keynes," Jbb. f. Nationalökon. u. Stat., 173, 1961, 313-42.

2355. GRÜNBERG, Carl, "Marx als Abiturient," Arch. f. d. Gesch. d. Soz., 11, 1923, 424-44.

2356. _____, ed., "Urkundliches aus den Universitätsjahren von Karl Marx," Arch. f. Gesch. d. Soz., 12, 1926, 232-40.

2357. GÜSTEN, Rolf, "Bemerkungen zur Marxschen Theorie des technischen Fortschritts," Jbb. f. Nationalökon. u. Stat., 178, 1965, 109-21.

2358. GUSTAFSSON, Bo. G., "Rostow, Marx und the theory of economic growth," Sci. Soc., 25, 1961, 229-44.

2359.   HAENISCH, Walter, "Karl Marx and the Democratic Associ-
         ation of 1847," Sci. Soc., 2, 1937/38, 83-102.
2360.   HAMMEN, Oscar J., "Alienation, communism, and revolu-
         tion in the Marx-Engel Briefwechsel," J. Hist. Ideas, 33,
         1972, 77-100.
2361.   _____, "Marx and the agrarian question," AHR, 77, 1972,
         679-704.
2362.   _____, "The young Marx, reconsidered," J. Hist. Ideas.,
         31, 1970, 109-20.
2363.   HARICH, Wolfgang, "Die Lehre von Marx und die philoso-
         phische Bildung der deutschen Intelligenz," Dt. Zs. f.
         Phil., 1, 1953, 261-85.
2364.   HARRIS, Abram L., "Utopian Elements in Marx's thought,"
         Ethics, 60, 1949/50, 79-99.
2365.   HASHAGEN, J., "Marxismus und Imperialismus," Jbb. f.
         Nationalökon. u. Stat., 114, 1920, 193-216.
2366.   HAUPT, Heinz-Gerhard and Stephan LEIBFRIED, "Marxian
         analysis of politics or theory of social change? Towards
         a Marxian theory of the political domain," Pol. Soc., 3,
         1972/73, 33-47.
2367.   HEIMANN, Eduard, "Marxism: 1848 and 1948," J. Pol.,
         11, 1949, 523-31.
2368.   HEISE, Wolfgang, "Zu einigen Grundfragen der Marxistischen
         Ästhetik," Dt. Zs. f. Phil., 5, 1957, 50-81.
2369.   HERKNER, H., "Marxismus und Sozialdemokratie," Pr.
         Jbb., 142, 1910, 406-32.
2370.   HERTZ-EICHENRODE, Dieter, "Karl Marx über das Bauern-
         tum und die Bündnisfrage," Int. Rev. Soc. Hist., 11,
         1966, 382-402.
2371.   HERZBERG, Guntolf, "Die Bedeutung der Kritik von Marx
         und Engels an Max Stirner," Dt. Zs. f. Phil., 16, 1968,
         1454-71.
2372.   HILL, Christopler, "The English Civil War interpreted by
         Marx and Engels," Sci. Soc., 12, 1948, 130-56.
2373.   HIRSCH, Helmut, "Karl Marx und die Bittschriften für die
         Gleichberechtigung der Juden," Arch. f. Sozialgesch.,
         8, 1968, 229-45.
2374.   _____, "Marxens Milieu Zu dem Werk von Heinz Monz,
         Karl Marx und Trier," Cahiers de l'Inst. Sc. Econ., 164,
         1965, 214-30.
2375.   HIRSCH, Rudolf, "Der erste Kritiker Marxens," ZRGG, 9,
         1957, 246-57.
2376.   HODGES, Donald Clark, "Marx's contribution to humanism,"
         Sci. Soc., 29, 1965, 173-91.
2377.   _____, "The role of classes in historical materialism,"
         Sci. Soc., 23, 1959, 16-26.
2378.   _____, "The value judgment in Capital," Sci. Soc., 29,
         1965, 296-311.
2379.   HÖFER, Manfred, "Zur philosophischen Auswertung der
         Erfahrungen der bürgerlich-demokratischen Revolutionen
         von 1848 durch Marx und Engels," Wiss. Zs. d. Fr.-Sch.-
         Univ. Jena, 17, 1968, 207-22.
2380.   HÖPPNER, Joachim, "Aspekte der marxistischen Freiheits-

begriffs und ihre Ausprägung beim jungen Marx, " Dt. Zs.
f. Phil., 11, 1963, 728-56.

2381. HOFFMAN, Robert, "Marx and Proudhon: A Reappraisal
of their Relationship, " Historian, 29, 1966/67, 409-30.

2382. HOHOFF, Curt, "Die Literaturdoctrin des Marxismus, "
Hochland, 52, 1959/60, 122-29.

2383. HOOK, Sidney, "The Enlightenment and Marxism, " J. Hist.
Ideas, 29, 1968, 93-108.

2384. _____, "Myth and Fact in the Marxist Theory of Revolution and Violence, " J. Hist. Ideas, 34, 1973, 271-80.

2385. HORN, Adam, "Materielles und Formelles Kapitalverhältnis
bei Karl Marx, " Schmoll. Jb., 71, 1951, 319-39.

2386. HOSELITZ, Bert F., "Karl Marx on Secular Economic and
Social Development, " Comp. Stud. Soc. Hist., 6, 1963/
64, 142-63.

2387. HUNDT, Martin, "Eine Notiz von Karl Marx als Präsident
des Kölner Arbeitervereins, " Beitr. z. Gesch. d. dt.
Arbeiterbeweg., 8, 1966, 75-81.

2388. HYMAN, Stanley E., "The Marxist Criticism of Orthodoxy, "
Antioch Review, 7, 1947/48, 487-501.

2389. IRRLITZ, Gerd, "Geschichte der marxistischen Philosophie
und Geschichte der deutschen Arbeiterbewegung, " Dt. Zs.
f. Phil., 13, 1965, 1417-34.

2390. JACOBSON, N. P., "Marxism and religious Naturalism, "
J. Rel., 29, 1949, 95-113.

2391. JÄGER, Georg, "Marxismus, klassische Nationalökonomie
und materialistische Geschichtsphilosophie, " Pr. Jbb.,
124, 1906, 277-320, 451-84.

2392. _____, "Der marxistische Neukritizismus, " Schmoll. Jb.,
39, 1915, 375-422.

2393. _____, "Sinn und Wert des Marxismus, " Schmoll. Jb.,
34, 1910, 1135-89, 1547-80.

2394. JOPKE, Walter, "Karl Marx und die deutsche bürgerliche
Philosophie im 20. Jahrhundert, " Dt. Zs. f. Phil., 16,
1969, 427-51.

2395. KABERMANN, Heinz, "Volk und Staat bei Karl Marx, " Zs.
f. Pol., 28, 1938, 219-37.

2396. KAGAN, Georges, "Durkheim et Marx, " Rev. d'hist. econ.
soc., 24, 1938, 233-44.

2397. "KARL Marx 1818-1883, " Zs. f. Geschw., 1, 1953,
172-364.

2398. KAUTSKY, Karl, ed., "Drei Kleine Schriften über Marx, "
Arch. f. d. Gesch. d. Soz., 8, 1919, 314-29.

2399. KELSEN, Hans, "Marx oder Lassalle Wandlungen in der
politischen Theorie des Marxismus, " Arch. f. d. Gesch.
d. Soz., 11, 1923, 261-98.

2400. _____, "Sozialismus und Staat Eine Untersuchung der
politischen Theorie des Marxismus, " Arch. f. d. Gesch.
d. Soz., 9, 1920/21, 1-129.

2401. KERSCHAGL, Richard, "Was kann Marx uns heute noch
sagen, " Schmoll. Jb., 80, 1960, 189-208.

2402. KIMMERLE, Heinz, "Der Marxistische Atheismus zur Religionskritik bei Marx, Engels und Lenin, " Ev. Theol.,

26, 1966, 434-47.
2403. KIRKENFELD, Thomas, "The Paradox of Profit," Sci. Soc.,
12, 1948, 33-41.
2404. KLATT, Sigurd, "Wachstumstheoretische Beziehungen in der
Akkumulationstheorie von Karl Marx," Jbb. f. Nationalökon. u. Stat., 172, 1960, 240-48.
2405. KLEHR, Harvey, "Marxism in Search of America," J. Pol.,
35, 1972, 311-37.
2406. KLEIN, Matthäus, "Karl Marx als Humanist, Denker und
Revolutionär," Dt. Zs. f. Phil., 6, 1958, 175-98.
2407. KOCH, Gerhard, "Philosophische Aspekte der Marxschen
Analyze der ökonomischen Gesetz im 'Kapital' und ihre
Bedeutung für Sozialismus," Dt. Zs. f. Phil., 15, 1967,
922-33.
2408. KOCH, Traugott, "Revolutionsprogramm und Religionskritik
bei Karl Marx," Zs. f. Theol. u. K., 68, 1971, 53-81.
2409. KOCKA, H. Jürgen, "Karl Marx und Marx Weber ein
methodologischer Vergleich," ZgesStw., 122, 1966, 328-
57.
2410. KÖLLNER, Lutz, "Wissens- und geldsozialogische Bemerkungen zu Karl Marx und Josef Schumpeter," Jb. F.
Sozialw., 15, 1964, 365-76.
2411. KOFLER, Leo, "Das Prinzip der Arbeit in der Marxschen
und in der Gehlenschen Anthropologie," Schmoll. Jb., 78,
1958, 71-86.
2412. KOPF, Eike, "Bibliographie zur Wirkungsgeschichte von
Karl Marx' 'Das Kapital' bis 1872," Wiss. Zs. d. Fr.-
Sch.-Univ. Jena, 17, 1968, 223-31.
2413. _____, "Die Ideen des 'Kapitals' von Karl Marx werden
zur materiellen Gewalt. Zur Wirkungsgeschichte des
'Kapitals' in Deutschland bis 1872," Wiss. Zs. d. Fr.-
Sch.-Univ. Jena, 17, 1968, 145-53.
2414. KORSCH, Karl, "Marxismus und Philosophie," Arch. f. d.
Gesch. d. Soz., 11, 1923, 52-121.
2415. KOWALZIK, Heinz, "Die materialistische Widerspruchsdialek-
tik in Marx' 'Kapital', Bd. I," Wiss. Zs. d. Fr.-Sch.-
Univ. Jena, 17, 1968, 155-65.
2416. KRAHL, Franz, "Karl Marx über Th. R. Malthus," Dt. Zs.
f. Phil., 2, 1954, 384-417.
2417. KRAUSS, Werner, "Karl Marx im Vormärz," Dt. Zs. f.
Phil., 1, 1953, 429-60.
2418. _____, "Marx und Engels in ihrer Stellungnahme zur nationalen Frage," Dt. Zs. f. Phil., 2, 1954, 601-12.
2419. KRELLE, Wilhelm, "Marx as a Growth Theorist," Ger.
Econ. Rev., 9, 1971, 122-33.
2420. KRIEGER, Leonard, "Marx and Engels as Historians," J.
Hist. Ideas, 14, 1953, 381-403.
2421. _____, "The Uses of Marx for History," Pol. Sci. Q.,
75, 1960, 355-78.
2422. KROMPHARDT, Wilhelm, "Der Logische Emanatismus und
die Systematisierungsform bei Marx," Arch. f. Sozialw.
u. Sozialpol., 55, 1926, 407-52.
2423. KUNDEL, E., "Aus dem Briefwechsel der 'Volksstaat'--

Redaktion mit Karl Marx und Friedrich Engels. Unveröffentlichte Briefe von Wilhelm Liebknecht, Adolf Hep-
ner, Wilhelm Blos und Hermann Ramm, " Beitr. z.
Gesch. d. dt. Arbeiterbeweg., 11, 1969, 639-63.

2424. LAM, Elizabeth P., "Does MacMurray understand Marx?, "
J. Rel., 20, 1940, 47-65.

2425. LANGE, Ernst, "Karl Marx als volkswirtschaftlichen Theoretiker, " Jbb. f. Nationalökon. u. Stat., 69, 1897, 540-
78.

2426. LAWRENCE, Clifford, "Roots of the Marxist Concept of
Practice, " Sci. Soc., 13, 1948/49, 229-42.

2427. LENK, Kurt, "Marx, Bernstein und die Wissenssoziologie, "
Pol. Vjschr., 6, 1965, 132-44.

2428. LENZ, Georg, "Karl Marx über die epikureische Philosophie, " Arch. f. d. Gesch. d. Soz., 13, 1928, 218-31.

2429. LEPIN, Nikolai I., "Vergleichende Analyse der drei Quellen
des Einkommens in den 'Ökonomischphilosophischen Manu-
skripten' von Marx, " Dt. Zs. f. Phil., 17, 1969, 196-212.

2430. LEQUIEN, Edmond, "Bakounine et le Marxisme, " Rev.
d'hist. econ. soc., 32, 1954, 389-412.

2431. LESSING, Arthur, "Marxist Existentialism, " Rev. Metaphysics, 20, 1966/67, 461-82.

2432. LEWALTER, Ernst, "Zur Systematik der Marxschen Staats-
und Gesellschaftslehre, " Arch. f. Sozialw. u. Sozialpol.,
68, 1932/33, 641-75.

2433. LEWIS, John D., "The Individual and the Group in Marxist
Theory, " Ethics, 47, 1936/37, 45-56.

2434. LEY, Hermann, "Karl Marx' Einleitung in die Grundrisse
der Kritik der politischen Ökonomie, " Dt. Zs. f. Phil.,
2, 1954, 574-600.

2435. LICHTHEIM, George, "The Origins of Marxism, " J. Hist.
Phil., 3, 1965, 96-105.

2436. LOBKOWICZ, N., "Karl Marx's Attitude Toward Religion, "
Rev. Pol., 26, 1964, 319-52.

2437. LÖWITH, Karl, "Max Weber und Karl Marx, " Arch. f.
Sozialw. u. Sozialpol., 67, 1932, 53-99, 175-214.

2438. LORIA, Achille, "Bemerkungen zum dritten Bande von Marx'
Theorien über den Mehrwert, " Arch. f. d. Gesch. d.
Soz., 2, 1911/12, 134-43.

2439. LUCAS, Erhard, "Marx' und Engels' Auseinandersetzung mit
Darwin Zur Differenz Zwischen Marx und Engels, " Int.
Rev. Soc. Hist., 9, 1964, 433-69.

2440. _____, "Marx' Studien zur Frühgeschichte und Ethnologie
1880-1882 Nach unveröffentlichen Exzerpten, " Saec., 15,
1964, 327-43.

2441. LUKACS, Georg, "Das Besondere im Lichte des dialektischen
Materialismus, " Dt. Zs. f. Phil., 3, 1955, 157-89.

2442. _____, "Karl Marx und Friedrich Theodor Vischer, " Dt.
Zs. f. Phil., 1, 1953, 471-513.

2443. _____, "Zur philosophischen Entwicklung des jungen Marx
(1840-1844), " Dt. Zs. f. Phil., 2, 1954, 288-343.

2444. LUKAS, Eduard, "Die physiokratische Wirtschaftstheorie und
die Marxsche Arbeitswertlehre, " Jbb. f. Nationalökon. u.

Stat., 133, 1930, 1-21.

2445.   MARCUSE, Ludwig, "Heine and Marx: A History and a Legend," Ger. Rev., 30, 1955, 110-24.

2446.   MARKOVIC, Mihailo, "Marxist Humanism and Ethics," Sci. Soc., 27, 1963, 1-22.

2447.   MARKUS, György, "Marxist Humanism," Sci. Soc., 30, 1966, 274-87.

2448.   MARTIN, Neil A., "Marxism, Nationalism, and Russia," J. Hist. Ideas, 29, 1968, 231-52.

2449.   MAUTNER, Wilhelm, "Zur Geschichte des Begriffes 'Diktatur des Proletariats'," Arch. f. d. Gesch. d. Soz., 12, 1926, 280-83.

2450.   MAYER, Gustav, "Karl Marx und der zweite Teil der 'Posaune'," Arch. f. d. Gesch. d. Soz., 7, 1916, 332-63.

2451.   _____, "Marx und Engels in ihren Briefwechsel," Zs. f. Pol., 7, 1914, 428-44.

2452.   _____, "Neue Beiträge zur Biographie von Karl Marx," Arch. f. d. Gesch. d. Soz., 10, 1921/22, 54-66.

2453.   MAYER, Ingrid, "Marxistische Philosophie und sozialistisches Menschenbild," Dt. Zs. f. Phil., 17, 1969, 645-64.

2454.   MAYER, Jacob P., "Alexis de Tocqueville und Karl Marx: Affinitäten und Gegensätze," Zs. f. Pol., 13, 1966, 1-13.

2455.   MAZLISH, Bruce, "The Tragic Farce of Marx, Hegel, and Engels: A Note," Hist. Theor., 11, 1972, 335-37.

2456.   McGOVERN, Arthur F., "The Young Marx on the State," Sci. Soc., 34, 1970, 430-66.

2457.   McINNES, Neil, "The Young Marx and the New Left," J. Contemp. Hist., 6, 1971, 141-59.

2458.   McLELLAN, David, "Marx's View of the Unalienated Society," Rev. Pol., 31, 1969, 459-65.

2459.   MEEK, Ronald L., "Marx's 'Doctrine of Increasing Misery'," Sci. Soc., 26, 1962, 422-41.

2460.   MEHRING, Franz, "Engels und Marx," Arch. f. d. Gesch. d. Soz., 5, 1914, 1-38.

2461.   _____, "Eine Episode des Marxismus," Arch. f. d. Gesch. d. Soz., 8, 1919, 308-14.

2462.   _____, "Marx im Brüsseler Exil," Arch. f. d. Gesch. d. Soz., 7, 1916, 281-331.

2463.   MENDE, Georg, "Die Doktordissertation von Karl Marx und der Entfremdungsbegriff," Wiss. Zs. d. Fr.-Sch.-Univ. Jena (Ges.- und Sprachwiss Reihe), 13, 1964, 344-51.

2464.   _____, "Karl Marx - Schöpfer der Kommunistischen Weltanschauung," Dt. Zs. f. Phil., 6, 1958, 337-54.

2465.   _____, "Der Marxsche Entfremdungsbegriff," Wiss. Zs. Fr.-Sch.-Univ. Jena (Ges. u. Sprachwiss.), 13, 1964, 307-16.

2466.   MERKEL, Renate; Karl REISSIG and Walter SCHMIDT, "Karl Marx und der Sozialismus Die Entwicklung des Sozialismusbildes durch Marx und Engels," Zs. f. Geschw., 16, 1968.

2467.   MEYER, Hermann, "Karl Marx und die deutsche Revolution

1848, " HZ, 172, 1951, 517-34.

2468.   MIELCKE, K., "Der Humanismus des jungen Marx,"
        GiWuU, 10, 1959, 201-14.

2469.   _____, "Wissenschaft & Utopie in der Geschichtslehre
        von Karl Marx," GiWuU, 10, 1959, 146-62.

2470.   MINS, Henry F., "Marx' Doctoral Dissertation," Sci. Soc.,
        12, 1948, 157-69.

2471.   MINS, Leonard E., ed., "Unpublished Letters of Karl Marx
        and Friedrich Engels to Americans," Sci. Soc., 2, 1937/
        38, 218-31, 348-75.

2472.   MONZ, Heinz, "Die rechtsethischen und rechtspolitischen
        Anschauungen des Heinrich Marx," Arch. f. Sozialgesch.,
        8, 1968, 261-83.

2473.   _____, "Unbekannte Kapitel aus dem Leben der Familie
        Johann Ludwig v. Westphalen," Arch. f. Sozialgesch., 8,
        1968, 247-60.

2474.   MOORE, Stanley, "Marx and the State of Nature," J. Hist.
        Phil., 5, 1967, 133-48.

2475.   MORAIS, Herbert M., "Marx and Engels on America," Sci.
        Soc., 12, 1948, 3-21.

2476.   MORIDE, Pierre, "Karl Marx et l'idée de Justice," Rev.
        d'hist. econ. soc., 2, 1909, 169-94.

2477.   MORRIS, Jacob, "Marx as a Monetary Theorist," Sci. Soc.,
        31, 1967, 404-27.

2478.   MÜHLESTEIN, Hans, "Marx and the Utopian Wilhelm Weit-
        ling," Sci. Soc., 12, 1948, 113-29.

2479.   MÜLLER, Kurt, "Karl Marx' Schrift 'Zur Judenfrage',"
        Judaica, 25, 1969, 185-98.

2480.   NEEDLEMAN, Martin and Carolyn NEEDLEMAN, "Marx and
        the Problem of Causation," Sci. Soc., 33, 1969, 322-39.

2481.   NETTLAU, Max, "Marxanalekten," Arch. f. d. Gesch. d.
        Soz., 8, 1919, 389-401.

2482.   OBERMANN, Karl, "Über den Anteil von Marx und Engels
        an der politischen Bewegung zur Vorbereitung der Revolu-
        tion von 1848," Zs. f. Geschw., 7, 1959, 1028-64.

2483.   OETZEL, Egon, "Zu den Reaktionsweisen der bürgerlichen
        Philosophie auf das Vordringen des Marxismus in der
        Periode des 'Sozialistengesetzes'," Wiss. Zs. Fr.-Sch.-
        Univ. Jena (Ges. u. Sprachwiss.), 13, 1964, 359-66.

2484.   OKISIO, Nobuo, "A Mathematical Note on Marxian Theorems,"
        Weltwirtsch. Arch., 91, 1963, 287-99.

2485.   OLLMAN, Bertell, "Is There a Marxian Ethic?," Sci. Soc.,
        35, 1971, 156-68.

2486.   _____, "Toward Class Consciousness Next Time: Marx
        and the Working Class," Pol. Soc., 3, 1972/73, 1-24.

2487.   OLSSEN, E. A., "Marx and the Resurrection," J. Hist.
        Ideas, 29, 1968, 131-40.

2488.   O'MALLEY, Joseph J., "History and Man's 'Nature' in
        Marx," Rev. Pol., 28, 1966, 508-27.

2489.   _____, "Methodology in Karl Marx," Rev. Pol., 32, 1970,
        219-30.

2490.   ONCKEN, Hermann, "Marx und Engels," Pr. Jbb., 155,
        1914, 209-56.

2491. _____, "Marx und Engels in der Epoche des Krim-
       krieges," Pr. Jbb., 173, 1918, 364-85.
2492. O'NEILL, John, "Marxism and Mythology," Ethics, 77,
       1966/67, 38-49.
2493. OSCHILEWSKI, Walther G., "Karl Marx als Student in
       Berlin," H. Jb., 73, 1953, 97-124.
2494. OTT, Alfred E., "Marx and Modern Growth Theory," Ger.
       Econ. Rev., 5, 1967, 189-95.
2495. OWEN, D. R. G., "Marxism and the Scientific Tradition,"
       Univ. of Toronto Quarterly, 16, 1947, 239-45.
2496. PANNEKOEK, Antonie, "Society and Mind in Marxian Philos-
       ophy," Sci. Soc., 1, 1936/37, 445-53.
2497. PAPPE, H. O., "Wakefield and Marx," Econ. Hist. Rev.,
       4, 1951/52, 88-97.
2498. PARSONS, Howard L., "The Prophetic Mission of Karl
       Marx," J. Rel., 44, 1964, 52-72.
2499. PATEL, Surendra J., "Marxism and Recent Economic
       Thought," Sci. Soc., 11, 1947, 52-65.
2500. PETER, Hans, "Dynamische Theorie bei Marx und bei
       Keynes," Jbb. f. Nationalökon. u. Stat., 162, 1950,
       260-77.
2501. PETRUS, Joseph, "Marx and Engels on the National Ques-
       tion," J. Pol., 33, 1971, 797-824.
2502. PLATTER, J., "Carl Marx und Malthus," Jbb. f. National-
       ökon. u. Stat., 29, 1877, 321-41.
2503. PLENGE, Johann, "Marx oder Kant?," ZgesStw., 66, 1910,
       213-39.
2504. POLLOCK, Friedrich, "Zur Marxschen Geldtheorie," Arch.
       f. d. Gesch. d. Soz., 13, 1928, 193-209.
2505. PRANGER, Robert J., "Marx and Political Theory," Rev.
       Pol., 30, 1968, 191-208.
2506. PRINZ, Arthur, "New Perspectives on Marx as a Jew,"
       Leo Baeck Inst. Yrbk., 15, 1970, 107-24.
2507. RAUH, Hans-Christoph, "Zur Herkunft, Vorgeschichte und
       ersten Verwendungsweise des Ideologiebegriffs bei Marx
       und Engels bis 1844," Dt. Zs. f. Phil., 18, 1970, 689-
       715.
2508. REID, John Patrick, "Marx on the Unity of Man," Thomist,
       28, 1964, 259-301.
2509. RIEKES, Hugo, "Die philosophische Wurzel des Marxismus,"
       ZgesStw., 62, 1906, 407-32.
2510. RJASANOFF, D., "Neueste Mitteilungen über den liter-
       arischen Nachlass von Karl Marx und Friedrich Engels,"
       Arch. f. d. Gesch. d. Soz., 11, 1923, 385-400.
2511. RJASANOFF, N., "Karl Marx und Friedrich Engels über
       die Polenfrage," Arch. f. d. Gesch. d. Soz., 6, 1915,
       175-221.
2512. ROBINSON, Joan, "Marx on Unemployment," Econ. J., 51,
       1941, 234-48.
2513. RÖNSCH, Dieter, "Karl Marx über die ökonomische Basis
       der Gesellschaft," Dt. Zs. f. Phil., 2, 1954, 556-73.
2514. ROTHMAN, Stanley, "Marxism and the Paradox of Contem-
       porary Political Thought," Rev. Pol., 24, 1962, 212-32.

2515.   RUBEL, Maximilien, "Les Cahiers d'Etude de Karl Marx, "
        Int. Rev. Soc. Hist., 2, 1957, 392-420; 5, 1960, 39-76.
2516.   _____, "La premiére édition du Capital. Note sur sa
        diffusion, " RH, 239, 1968, 101-110.
2517.   RUNKLE, Gerald, "Karl Marx and the American Civil War, "
        Comp. Stud. Soc. Hist., 6, 1963/64, 117-41.
2518.   _____, "Marxism and Charles Darwin, " J. Pol., 23,
        1961, 109-26.
2519.   SASS, Andreas, "Marx' Beziehungen zu Bartholomäus von
        Szemere, " Arch. f. d. Gesch. d. Soz., 10, 1921/22,
        38-48.
2520.   SASS, Hans-Martin, "Feuerbach staat Marx Zur Verfas-
        serschaft des Aufsatzes 'Luther als Schiedsrichter
        zwischen Strauss und Feuerbach', " Int. Rev. Soc. Hist.,
        12, 1967, 108-19.
2521.   SCHACK, Herbert, "Die Chancen des Marxismus, " Schmoll.
        Jb., 84, 1964, 641-74.
2522.   _____, "Notwendigkeit und Freiheit im Marxismus Die
        marxistische Theorie der Lebenspraxis, " Schmoll. Jb.,
        74, 1954, 385-420.
2523.   SCHAEFER, Alfred, "Praxis Zur Religionskritik von Karl
        Marx, " ZRGG, 19, 1967, 127-39.
2524.   _____, "Reichtum und Gewalt Industrielle und politische
        Revolution in den schriften des jungen Marx, " Zs. f.
        Pol., 14, 1967, 130-49.
2525.   SCHAFF, Adam, "Marxist Theory on Revolution and Vio-
        lence, " J. Hist. Ideas, 34, 1973, 263-70.
2526.   _____, "Die marxistische Auffassung vom Menschen, "
        Dt. Zs. f. Phil., 13, 1965, 578-89.
2527.   SCHIEDER, Theodor, "Karl Marx und seine Stellung in der
        europäischen Geschichte, " GiWuU, 15, 1964, 16-32.
2528.   SCHLAUCH, Margaret, "The Neue Rheinische Zeitung,
        1848-49, " Sci. Soc., 12, 1948, 170-80.
2529.   SCHMIDT, Walter, "Karl Marx und die deutsche Arbeiter-
        bewegung in der Revolution von 1848/49, " Beitr. z.
        Gesch. d. dt. Arbeiterbeweg., 10, 1968, 195-202.
2530.   _____, "Proletarischer Internationalismus in der bürger-
        lich-demokratischen Revolution, " Jb. f. Gesch., 4, 1969,
        109-48.
2531.   _____, "Wilhelm Wolff als Redakteur der 'Neuen Rhein-
        ischen Zeitung' 1848/49, " Zs. f. Geschw., 12, 1964,
        603-28.
2532.   SCHMIDT, Wolff A. von, "Heine und Marx, " Arch. f. KuG.,
        54, 1972, 143-52.
2533.   SCHMITT-RINK, Gerhard, "Kapitalintensität und Kapital-
        rentabilität im Marxschen Modell, " Schmoll. Jb., 87,
        1967, 129-53.
2534.   SCHMOLLER, Gustav, "Friedrich Engels und Karl Marx
        Ihr Briefwechsel von 1844 bis 1883, " Schmoll. Jb., 39,
        1915, 423-32.
2535.   SCHNERB, Robert, "Marx Contre Proudhon, " Annales, 5,
        1950, 484-90.
2536.   SCHOLZ, Dietmar, "Politische und menschliche Emanzipa-

tion Karl Marx' Schrift 'zur Judenfrage' aus dem Jahre
1844, " GiWuU, 18, 1967, 1-16.

2537. SCHRAEPLER, Ernst, "Die Entwicklung des Karl-Marx
Bildes in der biographischen Literatur, " GiWuU, 6, 1955,
719-37.

2538. SCHREY, H. H., "Literatur zum Marxismus Die neueste
Phase der Begegnung von Marxismus und Christentum, "
Theol. Rs., 32, 1967, 322-43; 33, 1968, 77-91.

2539. SCHRÖDER, Wolfgang, "Marxismus und Opportunismus in
der Gewerkschaftsfrage 1891-1893, " Jb. f. Gesch., 6,
1972, 191-262.

2540. SCHULZE, Hans, "Marxismus und Geschichtsprognose, "
Dt. Zs. f. Phil., 16, 1968, 397-414.

2541. SCHWANN, Stanislaw, "Die neue Oder-Zeitung und Karl
Marx als ihr Korrespondent, " Int. Rev. Soc. Hist., 4,
1959, 59-90.

2542. SEIDEL-HÖPPNER, Waltraud, "Aufklärung und revolutionäre
Aktion--ein Grundproblem im Arbeiterkommunismus und
bei Marx, " Jb. f. Gesch., 5, 1971, 7-69.

2543. SELSAM, Howard, "The Ethics of the Communist Mani-
festo, " Sci. Soc., 12, 1948, 22-32.

2544. SHERMAN, Howard J., "Marx and the Business Cycle, "
Sci. Soc., 31, 1967, 486-504.

2545. _____, "Marxist Models of Cyclical Growth, " Hist. Pol.
Econ., 3, 1971, 28-55.

2546. _____, "The Marxist Theory of Value Revisited, " Sci.
Soc., 34, 1970, 257-92.

2547. SHOUL, Bernice, "Karl Marx's Solutions to some The-
oretical Problems of Classical Economics, " Sci. Soc.,
31, 1967, 448-60.

2548. _____, "Similarities in the Work of John Stuart Mill and
Karl Marx, " Sci. Soc., 29, 1965, 270-95.

2549. SIEGMUND, Georg, "Die Glaubensentscheidung von Karl
Marx, " Hochland, 56, 1963/64, 322-31.

2550. SIEMENS, Johannes, "Karl Marx im Urteil des sozialen
Rechts, " Staat, 11, 1972, 376-88.

2551. SIEVEKING, Heinrich, "Der Gebrauchswert bei Marx, "
Schmoll. Jb., 46, 1922, 1-34.

2552. SILBERNER, Edmund, "Was Marx an anti-Semite?, " Hist.
Judaica, 11, 1949, 3-52.

2553. SMITH, Golwin, "Karl Marx and St. George, " J. Hist.
Ideas, 2, 1941, 401-19.

2554. SMITH, Henry, "Marx and the Trade Cycle, " Review of
Economic Studies, 4, 1937, 192-265.

2555. SPANN, Othmar, "Kantische und marxische Sozialphiloso-
phie, " Arch. f. d. Gesch. d. Soz., 2, 1911/12, 128-34.

2556. SPITZ, Philipp, "Das Problem der allgemeinen Grundrente
bei Ricardo, Rodbertus und Marx, " Jbb. f. Nationalökon.
u. Stat., 106, 1916, 492-524, 593-629.

2557. STÄDLER, Peter, "Wirtschaftskrise und Revolution Bei
Marx und Engels Zur Entwicklung ihres Denkens in den
1850er Jahren, " HZ, 199, 1964, 113-44.

2558. STEGEMANN, Dr. R., "Die ökonomische Grundanschauung

von Karl Marx," Pr. Jbb., 57, 1886, 213-34.

2559.   STERN, Bernhard J., "Some Aspects of Historical Materialism," Sci. Soc., 21, 1957, 10-27.

2560.   STERN, Victor, "Karl Marx über den Französischen Materialismus," Dt. Zs. f. Phil., 1, 1953, 461-70.

2561.   STIEHLER, G., "Die Marxsche Analyse der Widersprüche
des Kapitalismus und im 'Kapital' und der staatsmonopo-
listische Kapitalismus," Dt. Zs. f. Phil., 15, 1967, 952-
67.

2562.   STOLJAROW, Vitali, "Zu Marx Auffassung vom System-
character der Gesellschaft," Dt. Zs. f. Phil., 16, 1968,
415-26.

2563.   STRASBURGER, K., "Zur Kritik der Lehre Marx' vom
Kapital," Jbb. f. Nationalökon. u. Stat., 16, 1871, 93-
103.

2564.   STREY, Joachim, "Die Haltung der 'Neuen Rheinischen
Zeitung' zu den preussischen Kammerwahlen im Januar/
Februar 1849," Zs. f. Geschw., 16, 1968, 165-81.

2565.   STREY, Joachim and Gerhard WINKLER, "Die Politik und
Taktik der 'Neuen Rheinischen Zeitung' in der September-
krise 1848," Zs. f. Geschw., 16, 1968, 999-1022.

2566.   _____, "Die politische Konzeption der 'Neuen Rheinischen
Zeitung' in der Reichsverfassungskampagne 1849," Zs. f.
Geschw., 17, 1969, 573-91.

2567.   _____, "Zu Karl Marx' Verallgemeinerung der revolutionären Erfahrungen," Beitr. z. Gesch. d. dt. Arbeiterbeweg., 10, 1968, 237-62.

2568.   STRUIK, Dirk J., "Marx and Mathematics," Sci. Soc., 12,
1948, 181-96.

2569.   _____, "Marx's Economic-Philosophical Manuscripts,"
Sci. Soc., 27, 1963, 283-301.

2570.   STRUVE, Peter von, "Die Marxsche Theorie der sozialen
Entwicklung Ein kritischer Versuch," Arch. f. Sozialw.
u. Sozialpol., 14, 1899, 658-704.

2571.   SWEEZY, Paul M., "Marxian and Orthodox Economics,"
Sci. Soc., 11, 1947, 225-233.

2572.   TILLICH, Paul, "Christentum und Marxismus," Zeitwende,
32, 1961, 24-29.

2573.   TOGLIATTI, Palmiro, "Von Hegel zum Marxismus," Dt. Zs.
f. Phil., 4, 1956, 627-41.

2574.   TOPOLSKI, Jerzy, "Levi-Strauss and Marx on History,"
Hist. Theor., 12, 1973, 192-207.

2575.   ULLRICH, Horst, "Die geistigen Väter der modernen imperialistischen Marxkritik Zur Reaktion der bürgerlichen
Ideologie auf die Entwicklung der marxistischen Weltanschauung im letzten Drittel des 19. Jahrhunderts," Zs.
f. Geschw., 16, 1968, 327-46.

2576.   _____, "Zur Reaktion der bürgerlichen Ideologie auf die
'Heilige Familie' im Jahre 1845," Dt. Zs. f. Phil., 17,
1969, 817-39.

2577.   "UNBEKANNTE Artikel von Karl Marx über den Bürgerkrieg
in den U.S.A.," Beitr. z. Gesch. d. dt. Arbeiterbeweg.,
1, 1959, 231-42.

2578. VALARCHÉ, Jean, "Karl Marx au dela des Utopistes,"
       Rev. d'hist. econ. soc., 28, 1950, 348-63.
2579. VARAIN, Heinz J., "Die Entwicklung der Revolutions
       Theorie bei Karl Marx bis zum Jahre 1844," GiWuU, 14,
       1963, 342-59.
2580. VIGOUROUX, Camille, "Karl Marx et la législation fores-
       tière rhénane de 1842," Rev. d'hist. econ. soc., 43,
       1965, 222-33.
2581. VILLEY, Daniel, "Karl Marx (A propos du centenaire du
       'Manifeste communiste')," Rev. d'hist. econ. soc., 35,
       1957, 198-226.
2582. VOEGLIN, Eric, "The Formation of the Marxian Revolu-
       tionary Idea," Rev. Pol., 12, 1950, 275-302.
2583. VOLPE, Galvano Della, "Methodologische Fragen in Karl
       Marx' Schriften von 1843 bis 1859," Dt. Zs. f. Phil.,
       6, 1958, 777-804.
2584. VORLÄNDER, Karl, "Marx oder Kant? Ein Beitrag zur
       neuesten Diskussion über dieses Thema," Arch. f. So-
       zialw. u. Sozialpol., 28, 1909, 693-705.
2585. WEINBERGER, Otto, "Das 'Kapital' von Karl Marx und
       seine Beurteilung durch Vilfredo Pareto," Schmoll. Jb.,
       76, 1956, 565-80.
2586. WEISS, Hilde, "Die 'Enquête Ouvrière' von Karl Marx,"
       Zs. f. Sozialforschung, 5, 1936, 76-98.
2587. WENCKSTERN, Adolph v., "Die Marx eigentümliche ma-
       terialistische Geschichtsauffassung und Deutschland am
       Ende des neunzehnten Jahrhunderts," Schmoll. Jb., 22,
       1898, 247-310.
2588. WENDT, Siegfried, "Grundsätzliches zur Marxschen Kritik
       an der Quantitätstheorie," Schmoll. Jb., 54, 1930, 881-
       920.
2589. WILCZEK, Gerhard, "Die Geschichtsbetrachtung im marxist-
       ischen Denkbereich," Pol. Stud., 16, 1965, 692-700.
2590. _____, "Psyche und Materie nach der marxistisch-
       Leninistischen Lehre," Pol. Stud., 21, 1970, 426-34.
2591. WILSON, John C., "A Note on Marx and the Trade Cycle,"
       Review of Economic Studies, 5, 1938, 107-13.
2592. WINKLER, G., "Die Erfahrungen der Pariser Juni-Insurrek-
       tion 1848 im Spiegel der 'Neuen Rheinischen Zeitung',"
       Zs. f. Geschw., 17, 1970, 1310-24.
2593. WINTERNITZ, J., "The Marxist Theory of Crises," Modern
       Quarterly, 4, 1949, 310-27.
2594. WIZNITZER, A., "Marx und die irische Frage," Arch. f. d.
       Gesch. d. Soz., 10, 1921/22, 49-53.
2595. WOLF, Heidi, "Wilhelm Eichhoff und Karl Marx," Zs. f.
       Geschw., 18, 1970, 197-208.
2596. WOLF, Julius, "Das Rätsel der Durchschnittsprofitrate bei
       Marx," Jbb. f. Nationalökon. u. Stat., 57, 1891, 352-67.
2597. WOOD, Allen W., "Marx's Critical Anthropology: Three
       Recent Interpretations," Rev. Metaphysics, 26, 1972/73,
       118-39.

Johann Karl Rodbertus-Jagetzow (1805-1875)

See also entries 2251, 2556

2598.   ADICKES, F., "Die Bestrebungen zur Förderung des Ar-
        beiterversicherung in den Jahren 1848 und 1849 und K.
        Rodbertus-Jagetzow," ZgesStw., 39, 1883, 561-92.
2599.   BORTKIEWICZ, L. von, "Die Rodbertus'sche Grundrenten-
        theorie und die Marx'sche Lehre von der absoluten
        Grundrente," Arch. f. d. Gesch. d. Soz., 1, 1910/11,
        1-40, 391-434.
2600.   _____, "Zu den Grundrententheorien von Rodbertus und
        Marx," Arch. f. d. Gesch. d. Soz., 8, 1919, 248-57.
2601.   BRADKE, Elisabeth von, "Die Gesellschaftslehre von Karl
        Rodbertus-Jagetzow," Arch. f. Sozialw. u. Sozialpol.,
        50, 1923, 34-86.
2602.   CONRAD, J., "Das Rentenprincip nach Rodbertus' Vorschlag
        und seine Bedeutung für die Landwirtschaft," Jbb. f. Na-
        tionalökon. u. Stat., 14, 1870, 149-82.
2603.   DEHIO, Ludwig, "Die preussische Demokratie und der Krieg
        von 1866 Aus dem Briefwechsel von Karl Rodbertus mit
        Franz Ziegler," FBPG, 39, 1927, 229-59.
2604.   DIETZEL, H., "K. Rodbertus," Pr. Jbb., 55, 1885, 1-27.
2605.   "ERINNERUNGEN an Rodbertus," Schmoll. Jb., 15, 1891,
        585-607.
2606.   RODBERTUS-JAGETZOW, "Was waren Mediastini? Und
        woher der Name?," Jbb. f. Nationalökon. u. Stat., 20,
        1873, 241-73.
2607.   _____, "Zur Frage der Sachwerths des Geldes im Alter-
        thum," Jbb. f. Nationalökon. u. Stat., 15, 1870, 341-
        420; 16, 1870, 182-234.
2608.   SULTAN, Herbert, "Rodbertus und der agrarische Sozial-
        konservativismus," ZgesStw., 82, 1927, 71-113.
2609.   WAGNER, Adolph, ed., "Einiges von und über Rodbertus-
        Jagetzow," ZgesStw., 34, 1878, 199-237.
2610.   WANSTRAT, Renate, "Johann Karl Rodbertus," Schmoll. Jb.,
        70, 1950, 385-408.

Wilhelm Weitling (1808-1871)

2611.   BRETTSCHNEIDER, Werner, "Weitling und Born, der Prophet
        und der Organisator des deutschen Frühsozialismus,"
        GiWuU, 6, 1955, 568-79.
2612.   REICHENAU, Charlotte von, "Wilhelm Weitling," Schmoll.
        Jb., 49, 1925, 293-328.
2613.   SCHIEDER, Wolfgang, "Wilhelm Weitling und die deutsche
        politische Handwerkerlyrik im Vormärz," Int. Rev. Soc.
        Hist., 5, 1960, 265-90.
2614.   VUILLEUMIER, Marc, "Frankreich und die Tätigkeit Weit-
        lings und seiner Schüler in der Schweiz (1841-1845),"
        Arch. f. Sozialgesch., 5, 1965, 247-71.

Sozialpolitik

2615.   ASCHER, Abraham, "Professors as Propagandists: The
        Politics of the Kathedersozialisten," J. Cen. Eur. Aff.,
        23, 1963, 282-302.
2616.   BÖHMERT, Viktor, "Die soziale Frage und das Wahlrecht,"
        Pr. Jbb., 85, 1896, 1-16.
2617.   BORN, K. E., "Sozialpolitische Probleme und Bestrebungen
        von 1848 bis zur Bismarckschen Sozialgesetzgebung,"
        VSW, 46, 1959, 29-44.
2618.   COHEN, Dr. Hermann, "Friedrich Albert Lange," Pr. Jbb.,
        37, 1876, 353-81.
2619.   DEMETER, Karl, "Der Geist der deutschen Sozialpolitik vor
        dem Kriege," Pr. Jbb., 198, 1924, 67-79.
2620.   HEINE, Wolfgang, "Die Sozialpolitik des Handelsstandes und
        das deutsche Handelsgesetzbuch," Arch. f. Sozialw. u.
        Sozialpol., 11, 1897, 279-322.
2621.   HELD, Dr. A., "Die fünfte Generalversammlung des Vereins
        für Socialpolitik," Schmoll. Jb., 1, 1877, 791-825.
2622.   _____, "Der volkswirthschaftliche Kongress und der
        Verein für Socialpolitik," Schmoll. Jb., 1, 1877, 159-77.
2623.   KÖLLMANN, Wolfgang, "Die Anfänge der staatlichen Sozial-
        politik in Preussen bis 1869," VSW, 53, 1966, 28-52.
2624.   MEYER, A., "Zum Begriffe der Socialpolitik," Pr. Jbb.,
        14, 1864, 315-30.
2625.   MOST, Otto, "Zur Wirtschafts- und Sozialpolitik der höheren
        Beamten in Preussen," Schmoll. Jb., 39, 1915, 181-218.
2626.   RAUMER, Kurt von, "Ein Halbjahrhundert deutscher Sozial-
        politik," Zeitwende, 8(1), 1932, 369-81.
2627.   STELLER, Paul, "Unsere 'Uebersozialisten' auf dem Kathe-
        der," Pr. Jbb., 149, 1912, 276-87.

Lujo Brentano (1844-1931)

2628.   BRENTANO, Lujo, "Agrarian Reform in Prussia," Econ. J.,
        7, 1897, 1-20, 165-84.
2629.   _____, "Die Arbeiter und die Produktionskrisen," Schmoll.
        Jb., 2, 1878, 565-632.
2630.   _____, "Die beabsichtige Alters- und Invalid-versicherung
        für Arbeiter und ihre Bedeutung," Jbb. f. Nationalökon.
        u. Stat., 50, 1888, 1-46.
2631.   _____, "Die christlich-soziale Bewegung in England,"
        Schmoll. Jb., 7, 1883, 737-807.
2632.   _____, "Entwicklung und Geist der englischen Arbeiteror-
        ganisationen," Arch. f. Sozialw. u. Sozialpol., 8, 1895,
        75-139.
2633.   _____, "Geschichte und Wirken eines deutschen Gewerkver-
        eins," Schmoll. Jb., 6, 1882, 993-1001.
2634.   _____, "Die Gewerkvereine im Verhältnis zur Arbeits-
        gesetzgebung," Pr. Jbb., 29, 1872, 586-600.
2635.   _____, "Die Hirsch-Dunckerischen Gewerkvereine,"
        Schmoll. Jb., 3, 1879, 487-503.

2636. _____, "Der Krieg und die Verhütung seiner Wiederkehr, "
Arch. f. Sozialw. u. Sozialpol., 40, 1914/15, 30-42.
2637. _____, "Die liberale Partei und die Arbeiter, " Pr. Jbb.,
40, 1877, 112-23.
2638. _____, "Ueber einige in der Natur des Beobachtungs-
objektes liegende Schwierigkeiten des volkswirtschaftlichen
Forschens, " Arch. f. Sozialw. u. Sozialpol., 38, 1914,
58-82.
2639. _____, "Ueber Werturteile in der Volkswirtschaftslehre, "
Arch. f. Sozialw. u. Sozialpol., 33, 1911, 695-714.
2640. _____, "Ueber eine zukünftige Handelspolitik des deutschen
Reichs, " Schmoll. Jb., 9, 1885, 1-29.
2641. _____, "Zur Lehre von den Lohnsteigerungen, " ZgesStw.,
32, 1876, 466-78.
2642. _____, "Zur Reform der deutschen Fabrikgesetzgebung, "
Jbb. f. Nationalökon. u. Stat., 19, 1872, 168-212; 20,
1873, 359-62.
2643. GOETZ, Walter, ed., "Der Briefwechsel Gustav Schmollers
mit Lujo Brentano, " Arch. f. KuG., 28, 1938, 316-54;
29, 1939, 147-83; 30, 1940/41, 142-207.
2644. LOTZ, Walther, "Erinnerungen an Lujo Brentano, " Schmoll.
Jb., 56, 1932, 1-6.
2645. MENZE, Ernst A., "Historismus, Economic Theory and
Social Harmony: Lujo Brentano and the Methodenstreit
in historical Perspective, " Can. J. Hist., 7, 1972, 257-
83.

Heinrich Herkner (1863-1932)

See also entries 2210 and 2369

2646. HERKNER, H., "Das Frauenstudium der Nationalökonomie, "
Arch. f. Sozialw. u. Sozialpol., 13, 1899, 227-54.
2647. _____, "Gustav Schmoller als Soziologe, " Jbb. f. Nationalökon. u. Stat., 118, 1922, 1-8.
2648. _____, "Zur Kritik und Reform der deutschen Arbeiter-
schutzgesetzgebung, " Arch. f. soziale Gesetzgebung u.
Statistik, 3, 1890, 209-61.
2649. _____, "Zur Stellung G. Schmollers in der Geschichte
der Nationalökonomie, " Schmoll. Jb., 47, 1924, 3-10.
2650. _____, "Seelenleben und Lebenslauf in der Arbeiterklasse, " Pr. Jbb., 140, 1910, 393-412.
2651. LEUBUSCHER, Charlotte, "Heinrich Herkner als Sozialpolitiker, " Schmoll. Jb., 57, 1933, 13-25.

Gustav von Schmoller (1838-1917)

See also entries 1448, 1509, 2534, 2643, 2647, 2649, 2674,
2690, 2973, 3090, 3347, 3758, 4640, 4641, 5404

2652. ALBRECHT, Gerhard, "Gustav von Schmollers Beitrag zur

allgemeinen Steuerlehre," Schmoll. Jb., 62, 1938, 615-37.
2653. BECKERATH, Erwin von, "Gustav von Schmollers Finanz-geschichtliche Studien und seine Finanztheoretische Be-trachtung," Schmoll. Jb., 62, 1938, 596-614.
2654. BELOW, Georg v., "Zur Stellung G. Schmollers in der Geschichte der Nationalökonomie," Schmoll. Jb., 48, 1924, 315-19.
2655. BOESE, Franz, "Aus Gustav von Schmollers letztem Lebens-jahrzehnt," Schmoll. Jb., 62, 1938, 749-57.
2656. BRINKMANN, Carl, "Schmollers Gerechtigkeit," Schmoll. Jb., 62, 1938, 437-47.
2657. CLAUSING, Gustav, "Gustav von Schmollers Handelspolitik," Schmoll. Jb., 62, 1938, 548-72.
2658. EUCKEN, Walter, "Wissenschaft im Stile Schmollers," Weltwirtsch. Arch., 52, 1940, 468-506.
2659. HARTUNG, Fritz, "Gustav von Schmoller und die preus-sische Geschichtschreibung," Schmoll. Jb., 62, 1938, 661-86.
2660. KROMPHARDT, Wilhelm, "Die Überwindung der Klassen-kämpfe nach Gustav von Schmoller," Schmoll. Jb., 62, 1938, 717-32.
2661. LÜTGE, Friedrich, "Gustav von Schmoller als Sozialpoliti-ker," Schmoll. Jb., 62, 1938, 573-95.
2662. MENZER, Paul, "Gustav von Schmollers Lehre von der Entwicklung," Schmoll. Jb., 62, 1938, 466-73.
2663. MÖNCH, Hermann, "Über einige Ordnungsgedanken im Werke Gustav von Schmollers," Schmoll. Jb., 62, 1938, 474-96.
2664. RITSCHL, Hans, "Die Lehren der Geschichte im Werke Gustav von Schmollers," Schmoll. Jb., 62, 1938, 638-60.
2665. RÖSSLE, Karl, "Gustav von Schmoller und der Mittelstand," Schmoll. Jb., 62, 1938, 536-47.
2666. SALIN, Edgar, "Zur Stellung G. Schmollers in der Ges-chichte der Nationalökonomie," Schmoll. Jb., 48, 1924, 307-14.
2667. SCHMOLLER, Gustav, "Allerlei über Polens Vergangenheit und Gegenwart," Schmoll. Jb., 40, 1916, 991-1002.
2668. _____, "Analekten und Randglossen zur Debatte über Erhöhung der Getreidezölle," Schmoll. Jb., 9, 1885, 559-82.
2669. _____, "Die Arbeiterfrage," Pr. Jbb., 14, 1864, 393-424, 523-47; 15, 1865, 32-63.
2670. _____, "Arbeitseinstellungen und Gewerkvereine Referat auf der Eisenacher Versammlung vom 6. und 7. October 1872 über die sociale Frage," Jbb. f. Nationalökon. u. Stat., 19, 1872, 293-320.
2671. _____, "Die beabsichtigte Neuorganisation der deutschen Volkswirtschaft," Süddeutsche Monatshefte, 1, 1904, 254-82.
2672. _____, "Die Demokratie auf der Anklagebank," Schmoll. Jb., 37, 1913, 2049-78.
2673. _____, "Der deutsche Beamtenstaat vom 16. - 18. Jahr-hundert," Schmoll. Jb., 18, 1894, 695-714.
2674. _____, "Der deutsche Verein gegen den Missbrauch geisti-

ger Getränke und die Frage der Schrankkonzessionen, "
Schmoll. Jb., 7, 1883, 1347-66.

2675. _____, "Die Einkommenverteilung in alter und neuer Zeit," Schmoll. Jb., 19, 1895, 1067-94.

2676. _____, "Die englische Gewerkvereinsentwickelung im Licht der Webbschen Darstellung," Schmoll. Jb., 25, 1901, 291-314.

2677. _____, "Die englische Handelspolitik des 17. und 18. Jahrhunderts," Schmoll. Jb., 23, 1899, 1211-41.

2678. _____, "Die Entstehung der deutschen Volkswirtschaft und der deutschen Sozialreform," Schmoll. Jb., 39, 1915, 1609-39.

2679. _____, "Die Epochen der Getreidehandelsverfassung und -politik," Schmoll. Jb., 20, 1896, 695-744.

2680. _____, "Die Epochen der preussischen Finanzpolitik," Schmoll. Jb., 1, 1877, 33-114.

2681. _____, "Ernst Abbes sozialpolitische Schriften," Schmoll. Jb., 31, 1907, 1-29.

2682. _____, "Frau Sidney Webb und die britische Genossenschaftsbewegung," Schmoll. Jb., 17, 1893, 575-95.

2683. _____, "Freihändlerischer Sozialismus," Schmoll. Jb., 10, 1886, 855-64.

2684. _____, "Fünfhundert Jahre Hohenzollern Herrschaft," Schmoll. Jb., 40, 1916, 1-19.

2685. _____, "Die Gerechtigkeit in der Volkswirthschaft," Schmoll. Jb., 5, 1881, 19-54.

2686. _____, "Die geschichtliche Entwicklung der Unternehmung," Schmoll. Jb., 14, 1890, 735-83, 1035-76; 17, 1893, 359-91, 959-1018.

2687. _____, "Gewerbeordnung und Unterstützungswesen," Schmoll. Jb., 1, 1877, 471-501.

2688. _____, "Die Handels- und Zollannäherung Mitteleuropas," Schmoll. Jb., 40, 1916, 529-50.

2689. _____, "Hermann Schulze-Delitzsch und Eduard Lasker," Schmoll. Jb., 8, 1884, 595-620.

2690. _____, "Die Hetze von Alexander Tille und Konsorten gegen Lujo Brentano," Schmoll. Jb., 37, 1913, 1085-1101.

2691. _____, "Historische Betrachtungen über Staatenbildung und Finanzentwicklung," Schmoll. Jb., 33, 1909, 1-64.

2692. _____, "Der Jahresversammlung des volkswirthschaftlichen Kongresses und des Vereins für Sozialpolitik im Spätherbst 1882." Schmoll. Jb., 7, 1883, 285-301.

2693. SCHMOLLER, Gustav and Hermann Frhrn. von der HEYDEN-RYNSCH, "Materialien zum Arbeiterversicherungswesen," Schmoll. Jb., 5, 1881, 259-318.

2694. SCHMOLLER, Gustav, "Die Lohntheorie," Schmoll. Jb., 38, 1914, 1705-36.

2695. _____, "Neue Arbeiten über Geldwertveränderung und neuere Preissteigerung," Schmoll. Jb., 37, 1913, 373-82.

2696. _____, "Neue Litteratur über unsere handelspolitische Zukunft," Schmoll. Jb., 15, 1891, 275-82.

2697. _____, "Neues über das britische und das deutsche Genossenschaftswesen," Pr. Jbb., 76, 1894, 1-31.

2698. _____, "Die neuesten Publikationen über die Lage des preussischen und deutschen Bauerstandes," Schmoll. Jb., 7, 1887, 613-30.

2699. _____, "Obrigkeitsstaat und Volksstaat, ein missverstandlicher Gegensatz," Schmoll. Jb., 40, 1916, 2031-42.

2700. _____, "Die preussische Wahlrechtsreform von 1910," Schmoll. Jb., 34, 1910, 1261-79.

2701. _____, "Die soziale Bewegung Englands von 1770-1912 Im Lichte der marxistischen Klassenkampfidee," Schmoll. Jb., 38, 1914, 1-42.

2702. _____, "Die soziale Frage und der preussische Staat," Pr. Jbb., 33, 1874, 323-42.

2703. _____, "Sozialpolitik und Umsturzvorlage," Die Zukunft, 10, 1895, 397-407.

2704. _____, "Studien über die wirthschaftliche Politik Friedrich des Grossens und Preussens überhaupt von 1680-1786," Schmoll. Jb., 8, 1884, 1-61, 345-421, 999-1091.

2705. _____, "Studien über die wirthschaftliche Politik Friedrich des Grossen und Preussens überhaupt von 1680 bis 1786," Schmoll. Jb., 10, 1886, 1-45; 11, 1887, 327-73, 675-727, 789-883.

2706. _____, "Die Tatsachen der Lohnbewegung in Geschichte und Gegenwart," Schmoll. Jb., 38, 1914, 525-56.

2707. _____, "Die Thatsachsen der Arbeitsteilung," Schmoll. Jb., 13, 1889, 1003-74.

2708. _____, "Theorie und Praxis der deutschen Steuerreform," Schmoll. Jb., 5, 1881, 859-925.

2709. _____, "Über die Ausbildung einer richtigen Scheidemünzpolitik vom 14. bis 19. Jahrhundert," Schmoll. Jb., 24, 1900, 1247-74.

2710. _____, "Ueber den Einfluss der heutigen Verkehrsmittel," Pr. Jbb., 31, 1873, 413-30.

2711. _____, "Das untere und mittlere gewerbliche Schulwesen in Preussen," Schmoll. Jb., 5, 1881, 1259-81.

2712. _____, "Die Urgeschichte der Familie: Mutterrecht und Untilverfassung," Schmoll. Jb., 23, 1899, 1-21.

2713. _____, "Das Verhältnis der Kartelle zum Staate," Schmoll. Jb., 29, 1905, 1559-97.

2714. _____, "Die Verwaltung des Mass- und Gewichtswesens im Mittelalter," Schmoll. Jb., 17, 1893, 289-309.

2715. _____, "Die Wandlungen in der europäischen Handelspolitik des 19. Jahrhunderts Eine Säkularbetrachtung," Schmoll. Jb., 24, 1900, 373-82.

2716. _____, "Wechselnde Theorien und feststehende Wahrheiten im Gebiete der Staats- und Socialwissenschaften und die heutige deutsche Volkswirtschaftslehre," Schmoll. Jb., 21, 1897, 1387-1408.

2717. _____, "Das Wesen der Arbeitsteilung und der socialen Klassenbildung," Schmoll. Jb., 14, 1890, 45-105.

2718. _____, "Zur Methodolgie der Staats- und Sozialwissenschaften," Schmoll. Jb., 7, 1883, 975-94.

2719. SCHUMPETER, Joseph, "Gustav v. Schmoller und die Probleme von heute," Schmoll. Jb., 50, 1926, 337-88.

2720. SKALWEIT, August, "Gustav von Schmoller und der Mer-
kantilismus," Schmoll. Jb., 62, 1938, 687-703.

2721. SPIETHOFF, Arthur, "Gustav von Schmoller und die
anschauliche Theorie der Volkswirtschaft," Schmoll. Jb.,
62, 1938, 400-19.

2722. STIEDA, Wilhelm, "Zur Erinnerung an Gustav Schmoller
und seine Strassburger Zeit," Schmoll. Jb., 45, 1921,
1155-93.

2723. TREITSCHKE, H. v., "Die gerechte Vertheilung der Güter
Offener Brief an Gustav Schmoller," Pr. Jbb., 35, 1875,
409-44.

2724. VLEUGELS, Wilhelm, "Gustav von Schmoller und die ethisch-
politische Theorie der Volkswirtschaft," Schmoll. Jb., 62,
1938, 420-36.

2725. WEIPPERT, Georg, "Gustav von Schmoller im Urteil Wilhelm Diltheys und Yorck von Wartenburgs," Schmoll. Jb.,
62, 1938, 448-65.

2726. _____, "Die wirtschaftstheoretische und wirtschaftspoli-
tische Bedeutung der Kartelldebatte auf der Tagung des
Vereins für Socialpolitik im Jahre 1905 Ein Beitrag zur
Schmollerbild," Jb. F. Sozialw., 11, 1960, 125-83.

2727. WESSELS, Theodor, "Gustav von Schmollers Stellung zur
Agrarfrage," Schmoll. Jb., 62, 1938, 497-512.

2728. WIESE, Leopold v., "Aristokratie und Demokratie bei Gustav v. Schmoller," Schmoll. Jb., 62, 1938, 704-16.

2729. ZIMMERMANN, Waldemar, "Gustav von Schmoller und der
nationalökonomische Nachwuchs," Schmoll. Jb., 62, 1938,
733-48.

2730. ZWIEDINECK-SÜDENHORST, Otto von, "Gustav von Schmollers Gewerbepolitik," Schmoll. Jb., 62, 1938, 513-35.

Syndicatcs

See also entries 2713, 2726

2731. [Von EINEM rheinischen Industriellen,] "Die Aera der
wirthschaftlichen Kartelle," Pr. Jbb., 89, 1897, 309-25.

2732. BLAICH, Fritz, "Die Anfänge der deutschen Antikartellpoli-
tik zwischen 1897 und 1914," Jb. F. Sozialw., 21, 1970.

2733. FISCHER, Curt Eduard, "Die Geschichte der deutschen Versuche zur Lösung des Kartell- und Monopol- Problems,"
ZgesStw., 110, 1954, 425-56.

2734. GROSSMANN, Friedrich, "Über industrielle Kartelle,"
Schmoll. Jb., 15, 1891, 237-74.

2735. MACGREGOR, D. H., "The Development and Control of
German Syndicates," Econ. J., 24, 1914, 24-32.

2736. PAPE, Ernst, "Der deutsche Braunkohlenhandel unter dem
Einfluss der Kartelle," ZgesStw., 62, 1906, 234-71.

2737. SCHOENLANK, Dr. Bruno, "Die Kartelle Beiträge zu einer
Morphologie der Unternehmer Verbände," Archiv f. soziale Gesetzgebung u. Statistik, 3, 1890, 489-538.

2738.   SCHULZE-GÄVERNITZ, v., "Dr. Fritz Kestner als Kartell-
        politiker," Schmoll. Jb., 42, 1918, 651-68.
2739.   STIEDA, Wilhelm, "Ältere deutsche Kartelle," Schmoll. Jb.,
        37, 1913, 725-55.
2740.   WIEDENFELD, Kurt, "Der Handel und die Industriekartelle,"
        Schmoll. Jb., 33, 1909, 1727-43.

The Zollverein

2741.   BISSING, W. M. Frhr. v., "Der deutsche Zollverein und die
        monetären Probleme," Schmoll. Jb., 79, 1959, 199-214.
2742.   DIETSCHI, Erich, "Die Schweiz und der entstehende deutsche
        Zollverein 1828-35," ZGORh., 83, 1930/31, 287-344.
2743.   ECKERT, Christian, "Zur Vorgeschichte des deutschen Zoll-
        vereins," Schmoll. Jb., 26, 1902, 505-56.
2744.   FISCHER, G., "Ueber das Wesen und die Bedingungen eines
        Zollvereins," Jbb. f. Nationalökon. u. Stat., 7, 1866,
        225-304; 8, 1867, 252-350.
2745.   FRANZ, Eugen, "Ein Weg zum Reich Die Entstehung des
        Deutschen Zollvereins," VSW, 27, 1934, 105-36.
2746.   FUCHS, Konrad, "Die Bedeutung des Deutschen Zollvereins
        als Institution zur Austragung des preussisch-österreich-
        ischen Gegensatzes 1834-1866," Nass. Ann., 78, 1967,
        208-15.
2747.   GORDON, Nancy M., "Britain and the Zollverein Iron Duties,
        1842-5," Econ. Hist. Rev., 22, 1969, 75-87.
2748.   HENDERSON, W. O., "Mitteleuropäische Zollvereinspläne
        1840-1940," ZgesStw., 122, 1966, 130-62.
2749.   _____, "The Zollverein," History, 19, 1934, 1-19.
2750.   HERMES, Gertrud, "Statistische Studien zur wirtschaftlichen
        und gesellschaftlichen Struktur des zollvereinten Deutsch-
        lands," Arch. f. Sozialw. u. Sozialpol., 63, 1930, 121-
        62.
2751.   LAMMERS, A., "Die Stellung der Hansestädte zum Zoll-
        verein," Pr. Jbb., 19, 1867, 652-75.
2752.   PATZE, Hans, "Die Zollpolitik der thüringischen Staaten von
        1815 bis 1833," VSW, 40, 1953, 28-58.
2753.   PONTEIL, Felix, "Le Zollverein et les debuts de la Grande
        Industrie allemande," Rev. d'hist. mod., 9, 1934, 48-54.
2754.   RICHTER, S., "Die preussische Zollpolitik vom Wiener
        Kongress bis zur Gründung des deutschen Zollvereins
        (1814/15-1834)," Wiss. Zs. d. Martin-Luther-Univ. Halle-
        Wittenberg (Ges.-u. sprachwiss Reihe), 7, 1957/58, 561-
        70.
2755.   ROLOFF, Barbara, "Die Zollvereinskrise von 1850-1853,"
        Arch. f. hessische Gesch., 20, 1938, 293-363; 21, 1940,
        1-61.
2756.   SCOTT, Franklin D., "An 1813 Proposal for a Zollverein,"
        J. Mod. Hist., 22, 1950, 359-61.
2757.   TREITSCHKE, Heinrich von, "Die Anfänge des deutschen
        Zollvereins," Pr. Jbb., 30, 1872, 397-466, 479-571,
        648-97.

HISTORIOGRAPHY, HISTORICISM

General Studies

2758. ACTON, Lord, "German Schools of History," EHR, 1, 1886, 7-42.

2759. ALAND, Kurt, "Aus der Blütezeit der Kirchenhistorie in Berlin," Saec., 21, 1970, 235-63.

2760. ANDERSON, Eugene N., "Recent Works on German Unification," J. Mod. Hist., 7, 1935, 183-98.

2761. ANDREAS, Willy, "Zur Geschichtsschreibung von Erich Marcks," ZGORh., 102, 1954, 811-21.

2762. AUBIN, Hermann, "Georg von Below als Sozial- und Wirtschaftshistoriker," VSW, 21, 1928, 1-32.

2763. "Die AUFGABE deutscher Staats- und Rechtsgeschichte," Pr. Jbb., 1, 1858, 31-45.

2764. BAUER, Clemens, "Ludwig von Pastor/Ein Profil," Hochland, 26(1), 1928/29, 578-88.

2765. BECK, Robert N., and Dwight E. LEE, "The Meaning of 'Historicism'," AHR, 59, 1953/54, 568-77.

2766. BELOW, G. v., "Romantik und realistische Geschichtsforschung," VSW, 15, 1919, 82-91.

2767. BERNBAUM, John A., "The Captured German Records: A Bibliographical Survey," Historian, 32, 1969/70, 564-75.

2768. BEUTE, Hermann, "Weltwirtschaft Weltwirtschaftlicheslehre, Weltwirtschaftliches Archiv Betrachtungen zum 50. Bande der Zeitschrift des Instituts für Weltwirtschaft," Weltwirtsch. Arch., 50, 1939, 3-32.

2769. BOCK, Helmut, "1789 und 1813 Das Zeitalter der französischen Revolution in der reaktionären deutschen Geschichtsschreibung," Zs. f. Geschw., 12, 1964, 1359-83.

2770. BÖMER, Aloys, "Die deutsche landgeschichtliche Gesichtsschreibung seit dem Ausgang des Weltkrieges," Bl. f. dtsch. Landesgesch., 85, 1939, 91-116.

2771. BORN, Lester K., "The Archives and Libraries of Postwar Germany," AHR, 56, 1950/51, 34-57.

2772. BRUCHMANN, Karl G., "Das Bundesarchiv in Koblenz," GiWuU, 15, 1964, 83-98.

2773. BRUCKNER, Rolf-Robert, "Laufende Bibliographien zur deutschen Geschichte und ihre Stellung im einheitlichen System der Information," Jb. f. Gesch., 2, 1967, 378-419.

2774. BRUNNER, Otto, "Der Historiker und die Geschichte von Verfassung und Recht," HZ, 209, 1969, 1-16.

2775. BRUNSCHWIG, Henri, "Die historischen Generationen in Frankreich und Deutschland," VjHZG, 2, 1954, 373-83.

2776. CURSCHMANN, Fritz, "Die Entwicklung der historisch-geographischen Forschung in Deutschland durch zwei Jahrhunderte," Arch. f. KuG., 12, 1916, 129-63, 285-325.

2777. CZOK, Karl, "Der Methodenstreit und die Gründung des Seminars für Landesgeschichte und Siedlungskunde 1906 an der Universität Leipzig," Jb. f. Regionalgesch., 2, 1967, 11-26.

2778. DAMMANN, Oswald, "Alfred Dove and Heidelberg," ZGORh., 89, 1936/37, 161-69.

2779. DANKE, Rudolf, "100 Jahre Verein für die Geschichte Berlins," Bär v. Ber., 14, 1965, 325-405.

2780. DORNER, Dr., "Die Aufgabe der Philosophie der Geschichte," Pr. Jbb., 177, 1919, 313-44.

2781. DORPALEN, Andreas, "The German Struggle Against Napoleon: The East German View," J. Mod. Hist., 41, 1969, 485-516.

2782. _____, "Post-Mortem on Prussia: The East German Position," Cen. Eur. Hist., 4, 1971, 322-45.

2783. _____, "The Unification of Germany in East German Perspective," AHR, 73, 1965/66, 826-45.

2784. DROYSEN, Joh. G., "Die Erhebung der Geschichte zum Rang einer Wissenschaft," HZ, 9, 1863, 1-22.

2785. DROZ, Jacques, "Les Tendances actuelles de L'historiographie Allemande," RH, 215, 1956, 1-24.

2786. ENGEL, Josef, "Die deutschen Universitäten und die Geschichtswissenschaft," HZ, 189, 1959, 223-378.

2787. ENGEL-JANOSI, Friedrich, "Krise und Überwindung des Historismus," Wissenschaft und Weltbild, 1953, 8-18.

2788. ERBEN, Wilhelm, "Theodor Sickel," Hist. Vjschr., 11, 1908, 333-59.

2789. ERDMANN, Karl D., "Nationale und übernationale Ordnung in der deutschen Geschichte," GiWuU, 7, 1956, 1-14.

2790. ESSELBORN, Karl, "Hundert Jahre Historischer Verein für Hessen," Arch. f. hessische Gesch., 18, 1933/34, 1-183.

2791. EUCKEN, Walter, "Die Überwindung des Historismus," Schmoll. Jb., 62, 1938, 191-214.

2792. FABER, Karl-Georg, "Christian von Strambergs 'Rheinischer Antiquarius' als Geschichtswerk der rheinischen Restauration," Jb. f. Gesch. Kunst d. MRh, 4/5, 1952/53, 7-51.

2793. FINKE, Heinrich, "Die Anfänge des Historischen Jahrbuches Ein Gedenkblatt für Georg Hüffer," H. Jb., 45, 1925, 477-94.

2794. _____, "Geschichtswissenschaft an der Universität Freiburg zu Anfang des 19. Jahrhunderts und die Berufung August Friedrich Gfrörers," H. Jb., 50, 1930, 70-96.

2795. FIRDA, Richard A., "German Philosophy of History and Literature in the North American Review: 1815-1860," J. Hist. Ideas, 32, 1971, 133-42.

2796. FISCHEL, Walter J., "Der Historismus in der Wirtschafts-

wissenschaft Dargestellt an der Entwicklung von Adam
Müller bis Bruno Hildebrand," VSW, 47, 1960, 1-31.
2797.   FISCHER, Hermann, "Die beiden Heyd," Zs. F. Württbg.
LG, 28, 1919, 265-323.
2798.   "FRIEDRICH Christoph Schlosser," Pr. Jbb., 9, 1862,
373-433.
2799.   FÜLLING, Erich, "Der Historismus in christlicher Sicht,"
Z. f. systematische Theol., 22, 1953, 274-99.
2800.   GILBERT, Felix, "German Historiography during the Second
World War: A Bibliography Survey," AHR, 53, 1947/48,
50-58.
2801.   GOETZ, Walter, "Die Bairische Geschichtsforschung im 19.
Jahrhundert," HZ, 138, 1928, 255-314.
2802.   GOLLWITZER, Heinz, "Karl Alexander von Müller 1882-
1964 Ein Nachruf," HZ, 205, 1967, 295-322.
2803.   GUILLAND, Antoine, "German Historical Publications 1914-
1920," AHR, 25, 1919/20, 640-59.
2804.   HÄNSEL, Ludwig, "Herman Hefele," Hochland, 26(2), 1928/
29, 358-74, 516-33, 631-45.
2805.   HAERING, Hermann, "Gegenwartsnöte der Bibliographie der
Deutschen Geschichte," WaG, 12, 1952, 54-60.
2806.   HAUCK, Dorothea, "Verzeichnis der Schriften von Prof. Dr.
Willy Andreas 1905-1955," ZGORh., 105, 1957, 295-324.
2807.   HEFELE, Herman, "Über Methodik und Methodologie der
Geschichtswissenschaft," Arch. f. KuG., 13, 1917, 1-8.
2808.   HEIMPEL, Hermann, "Rudolf Stadelmann und die Deutsche
Geschichts-Wissenschaft," HZ, 172, 1951, 285-307.
2809.   _____, "Über Organisationsformen: Historischer Forschung in Deutschland," HZ, 189, 1959, 139-222.
2810.   HERRMANN, Alfred, "Hermann Hüffer Nach seinen hinter-
lassenen Aufzeichnungen," Ann. Niederrhein, 80, 1906,
1-78.
2811.   HEYNEN, Walter, "Die Blauen Blätter Erinnerungen an die
Preussischen Jahrbücher," Bär v. Ber., 8, 1959, 84-115.
2812.   HIRSCH, Felix E., "Hermann Oncken and the End of An
Era," J. Mod. Hist., 18, 1946, 148-59.
2813.   "HISTORISCHE Forschungen in der DDR Analysen und Berichte," Zs. f. Geschw., 8, 1960 (Sonderheft), 188-324.
2814.   IGGERS, George G., "The Decline of the National Tradition
of German Historiography," Hist. Theor., 6, 1967, 382-
412.
2815.   IRMSCHER, Johannes, "August Boeckh und seine Bedeutung
für die Entwicklung der Altertumswissenschaft," Jb. f.
Wgesch., 1971 (2), 107-18.
2816.   JEDIN, Hubert, "Briefe Constantin Höflers an Augustin
Theiner 1841 bis 1845," H. Jb., 91, 1971, 118-27.
2817.   _____, "Kirchenhistorikerbriefe an Augustin Theiner,"
Röm. Qu.-Schr., 66, 1971, 187-224.
2818.   _____, "Die Vertretung der Kirchengeschichte in der
katholisch-theologischen Fakultät Bonn 1823-1929," Ann.
Niederrhein, 155/56, 1954, 411-53.
2819.   JORDAN, Karl, "Von Dahlmann zu Treitschke Die Kieler
Historiker im Zeitalter der schleswig-holsteinischen Bewe-

gung, " Arch. f. KuG., 49, 1967, 262-96.

2820. KAHL, Hans-Dietrich, "Zum Stande der Einbeziehung von Städten und historischen Stätten in das allgemeine Geschichtsbild, " H. Jb., 82, 1962, 300-44.

2821. KAHN, S. B., "Der Befreiungskrieg von 1813 in der deutschen historischen Literatur, " Zs. f. Geschw., 3, 1955, 358-73.

2822. KANTOROWICZ, Hermann U., "Volksgeist und historische Rechtsschule, " HZ, 108, 1912, 295-325.

2823. KLINKENBORG, Melle, "Reinhold Koser Ein Nachruf, " FBPG, 28, 1915, 285-310.

2824. KNOLL, Joachim H., "Werk und Methode des Historikers Erich Eyck, " GiWuU, 16, 1965, 277-85.

2825. KOHLS, E. W., "Das Bild der Reformation bei Wilhelm Dilthey, Adolf von Harnach und Ernst Troeltsch, " Neue Zs. f. system. Theol. u. RP, 11, 1969, 269-91.

2826. _____, "Das Bild der Reformation in der Geisteswissenschaft des 19. Jahrhunderts, " Neue Zs. f. system. Theol. u. RP, 9, 1967, 229-46.

2827. KOHN, Hans, "Re-thinking Recent German History, " Rev. Pol., 14, 1952, 325-45.

2828. KOSER, R., "Zur preussischen Geschichte im neunzehnten Jahrhundert, " FBPG, 3, 1890, 221-38.

2829. KRAMMER, Mario, "Grosse Geschichtsschreiber im Lebens Berlins, " Jahrbuch Ver. f. d. Gesch. Berlins, 2, 1952, 9-52; 3, 1953, 19-69.

2830. KRASUSKI, J., "The Problem of Prussia in Germany's Modern History in the Light of Modern German Historiography, " Pol. West. Aff., 2, 1961, 103-18.

2831. KRAUSE, Hermann, "Der Historiker und sein Verhältnis zur Geschichte von Verfassung und Recht, " HZ, 209, 1969, 17-26.

2832. KRIECK, Ernst, "Germanische Grundzüge im deutschen Geschichtsbild, " HZ, 159, 1938/39, 524-37.

2833. KRIEGER, Albert, "Fünfundsiebzig Jahre Zeitschrift für die Geschichte des Oberrheins, " ZGORh., 79, 1927, 4-33.

2834. KROHN, Margot, "Zwei Jahrzehnte Schlesischen Geschichte in dem Spalten der 'Times' von 1848 bis 1870, " Jb. d. Schles.-Fried.-Wilh. Univ z. Breslau, 9, 1964, 207-60.

2835. LIEBEL, Helen P., "Philosophical Idealism in the 'Historische Zeitschrift', 1859-1914, " Hist. Theor., 3, 1963/64, 316-30.

2836. LINNEBORN, J. and L. SCHMIDT-KALLENBERG, "Rückblick auf die Geschichte des Vereins für Geschichte und Altertumskunde Westfalesn während der ersten hundert Jahre seines Bestehens, " Westf. Zs., 82, 1924, IX-XXXXVI.

2837. LIPGENS, W., "Zum geschichtlichen Standort der Reichsgründung 1870/71, " GiWuU, 22, 1971, 513-28.

2838. LOVEJOY, Arthur O., "The Meaning of Romanticism for the Historian of Ideas, " J. Hist. Ideas, 2, 1941, 257-78.

2839. LÜCKERATH, Carl August, "Prologomena zur elektronischen Datenverarbeitung im Bereich der Geschichtswissenschaft, "

HZ, 207, 1968, 265-96.

2840.   LUKACS, Georg, "Der Verfall des historischen Bewusst-
         seins," Dt. Zs. f. Phil., 3, 1955, 451-64.

2841.   MANNHEIM, Karl, "Historismus," Arch. f. Sozialw. u.
         Sozialpol., 52, 1924, 1-60.

2842.   MAYR, Josef K., "Hormayrs Verhaftung 1813," Zs. f.
         bayer. LG., 13, 1940, 330ff.

2843.   MEIER, P. J., "The Work of the Hamburg Research Center
         in Entrepreneurial History," J. Econ. Hist., 21, 1961,
         364-71.

2844.   MEINECKE, Friedrich, "Germanischer und romanischer
         Geist im Wandel der deutschen Geschichtsauffassung,"
         HZ, 115, 1916, 516-36.

2845.   MEINERT, Hermann, "Der Frankfurter Verein für Ge-
         schichte und Altertumskunde (Landeskunde) 1857-1957,"
         Arch. f. Frankfurts Gesch., 45, 1957, 19-48.

2846.   MEISNER, Heinrich O., "Preussen und der 'Revisionismus',"
         FBPG, 43, 1930, 252-89.

2847.   METSCHIES, K., "Bestandsinformation für dem Wirtschafts-
         historiker aus dem Deutschen Zentralarchiv Potsdam,"
         Jb. f. Wgesch., 1968 (3), 385-91; 1969 (4), 213-25;
         1970 (3), 256-80.

2848.   MEYER, Ernst, "Schliemann und Virchow Zwei grosse
         Männer der deutschen Vorgeschichtsforschung," Bär v.
         Ber., 16, 1967, 48-67.

2849.   MITCHELL, Allan, "German History in France after 1870,"
         J. Contemp. Hist., 2, 1967, 81-100.

2850.   MORK, Gordon R., "The Archives of the German Democratic
         Republic," Cen. Eur. Hist., 2, 1969, 273-84.

2851.   MÜLLER, Gert, "Oswald Spenglers Bedeutung für die Ge-
         schichtswissenschaft," Saec., 13, 1962, 380-93.

2852.   MÜLLER, Karl A. v., "Probleme der neuesten bayerischen
         Geschichte (1799-1871)," HZ, 118, 1917, 222-49.

2853.   MULTHOFF, Robert F., "Das Amerikanische Bild der
         deutschen Geschichte," Aussenpol., 10, 1959, 570-76.

2854.   NETTLESHEIM, Josefine, "Carl Adolf Cornelius in seinem
         Briefen an Wilhelm Junkmann," H. Jb., 82, 1962, 277-99.

2855.   NEUMÜLLER, M., "Zur deutschliberalen Geschichtsschrei-
         bung des 19. Jahrhundert in Böhmen," Zs. f. Ostforsch.,
         20, 1971, 441-65.

2856.   NEUSS, Erich, "Werkgeschichte und Unternehmerbiographie
         in Mitteldeutschland," Tradition, 5, 1960, 217-30.

2857.   NIKOLAEV, P. A., "Versuche zur Rehabilitierung des
         deutschen Militarismus in der modernen bürgerlichen
         Historiographie," Zs. f. Geschw., 10, 1962, 50-71.

2858.   OBERMANN, Karl, "Über die Entwicklung der deutschen
         Geschichtsschreibung in der ersten Hälfte des 19. Jahr-
         hunderts," Zs. f. Geschw., 5, 1957, 713-48.

2859.   OESTREICH, Gerhard, "Die Fachhistorie und die Anfänge
         der sozialgeschichtlichen Forschung in Deutschland," HZ,
         208, 1969, 320-63.

2860.   OHNSORGE, Werner, "Georg Heinrich Pertz und die Landes-
         geschichte," H. Jb., 74, 1954, 447-61.

2861. ONCKEN, Hermann, "Wandlungen des Geschichtsbildes in Revolutionären Epochen," HZ, 189, 1959, 124-38.

2862. _____, "Zur Quellenanalyse modernster deutscher Geschichtschreibung," Pr. Jbb., 89, 1897, 83-125.

2863. PETSCH, Robert, "Zur deutschen Geistesgeschichte im Zeitalter des Idealismus," Pr. Jbb., 171, 1918, 226-41.

2864. PREDÖHL, Andreas, "Bernhard Harms und das Institut für Weltwirtschaft," Weltwirtsch. Arch., 92, 1964, 2-22.

2865. PRÜSER, Friedrich, "Die Hundertjahrfeier," Bremisches Jb., 49, 1964, 1-30.

2866. RAND, Calvin G., "Two Meanings of Historicism in the Writings of Dilthey, Troeltsch, and Meinecke," J. Hist. Ideas, 25, 1964, 503-18.

2867. RANKE, L. von, "Johann Friedrich Böhmer," HZ, 20, 1868, 393-404.

2868. REDLICH, Fritz, "Recent Developments in German Economic History," J. Econ. Hist., 18, 1958, 516-30.

2869. REXIUS, Gunnar, "Studien zur Staatslehre der historischen Schule," HZ, 107, 1911, 496-539.

2870. RICHTER, Wilhelm, "Rückblick auf die fünfundsiebzigjährige Geschichte und Thätigkeit des Vereins," Westf. Zs., 57 (2), 1899, 153-71.

2871. RIEDEL, Manfred, "Der Staatsbegriff der deutschen Geschichtsschreibung des 19. Jahrhunderts in seinem Verhältnis zur klassisch-politischen Philosophie," Staat, 2, 1963, 41-63.

2872. RIESE, A., "Rückblick auf die Entstehung und Entwickelung des Vereins für Geschichte und Altertumskunde in Frankfurt a. M. 1857-1907," Arch. f. Frankfurts Gesch., 1907, 1-34.

2873. RITTER, Gerhard, "Gegenwärtige Lage und Zukunftsaufgaben deutscher Geschichtswissenschaft," HZ, 170, 1950, 1-22.

2874. _____, "Scientific History, Contemporary History, and Political Science," Hist. Theor., 1, 1961, 261-79.

2875. _____, "Wissenschaftliche Historie Einst und Jetzt, Betrachtungen und Erinnerungen," HZ, 202, 1966, 574-602.

2876. ROSS, Ronald J., "Heinrich Ritter von Srbik and 'Gesamtdeutsch' History," Rev. Pol., 31, 1969, 88-107.

2877. ROTHACKER, Erich, "Historismus," Schmoll. Jb., 62, 1938, 388-99.

2878. _____, "Savigny, Grimm, Ranke Ein Beitrag zur Frage nach dem Zusammenhang der Hist. Schule," HZ, 128, 1923, 415-45.

2879. RÜSEN, Jörn, "Technik und Geschichte in der Tradition der Geisteswissenschaften- Geistesgeschichtliche Anmerkungen zu einem theoretischen Problem," HZ, 211, 1970, 529-55.

2880. SAGAVE, Pierre-Paul, "Les historiens allemands et la Réhabilitation de la Prusse," Annales, 15, 1960, 130-50.

2881. _____, "Die Reichsgründung 1871 aus französischer Sicht," ZRGG, 22, 1970, 45-57.

2882. SCHÄFER, Karl Heinz, "1813 - Die Freiheitskriege in der Sicht der marxistischen Geschichtsschreibung der DDR," GiWuU, 21, 1970, 2-21.

2883. SCHEEL, Heinrich, "Die Mainzer Republik im Spiegel der
       deutschen Geschichtsschreibung," Jb. f. Gesch., 4, 1969,
       9-92.
2884. SCHIEDER, Theodor, "Die deutsche Geschichtswissenschaft
       im Spiegel der historischen Zeitschrift," HZ, 189, 1959,
       1-104.
2885. _____, "Möglichkeiten und Grenzen vergleichender Metho-
       den in der Geschichtswissenschaft," HZ, 200, 1965, 529-
       51.
2886. _____, "Nation und Nationalstaat in der deutschen Ge-
       schichte. Zum Gedenktag der Reichsgründung," Aus Pol.
       u. Zeitgesch., 12, 1971, 3-15.
2887. SCHLAICH, Heinz Wolf, "Die Gründung des deutschen Na-
       tionalstaats als historisches und politisches Problem,"
       Pol. Stud., 22, 1971, 3-19.
2888. SCHLEIER, Hans, "Johannes Zierkursch," Jb. f. Gesch.,
       3, 1969, 137-96.
2889. SCHLETTE, Friedrich, "Friedrich Kruse und der Beginn
       einer Urgeschichtsforschung in Halle," Wiss. Z. Univ.
       Halle, Ges.-und Sprachwiss. Reihe, 16, 1967, 161-72.
2890. SCHNÜTGEN, Alexander, "Fünfundsiebzig Jahre Historischer
       Verein für den Niederrhein," Ann. Niederrhein, 115, 1929,
       5-37.
2891. _____, "Zur Vereinsgeschichte Persönliche Erinnerun-
       gen," Ann. Niederrhein, 102, 1918, 146-61.
2892. SCHOCHOW, Werner, "Bibliographie Fritz Hartung," Jb. f.
       Gesch. M. O. Dtschl., 3, 1954, 211-41.
2893. SCHÖNBACH, Armin, "Zur älteren Schule der politischen
       Ökonomie und ihrer historischen Methode," Zs. f. Geschw.,
       18, 1970, 1053-60.
2894. SCHOEPS, Hans Joachim, "Realistische Geschichtsprophetien
       um 1850," ZRGG, 3, 1951, 97-107.
2895. SCHRAEPLER, E., "Die Forschung über den Ausbruch des
       Ersten Weltkrieges im Wandel des Geschichtsbildes 1919-
       1969," GiWuU, 23, 1972, 321-38.
2896. SCHRÖRS, Heinrich, "Der historische Verein für den Nieder-
       rhein in seiner Entstehung und Entwickelung," Ann. Nie-
       derrhein, 79, 1905, 1-27.
2897. _____, "Johann Heinrich Floss (1819-1881)," Ann. Nieder-
       rhein, 117, 1930, 3-150.
2898. _____, "Nochmals zur Entstehungsgeschichte des His-
       torische Vereins für den Niederrhein," Ann. Niederrhein,
       92, 1912, 133-38.
2899. _____, "Zur Entstehungsgeschichte des historischen
       Vereins für den Niederrhein," Ann. Niederrhein, 88,
       1910, 180-86.
2900. SCHÜDDEKOPF, Otto-Ernst, "Bürgerliche Geschichtsschrei-
       bung und materialistische Geschichtsauffassung um 1850
       Ein Beitrag zur Entwicklung der Wirtschafts- und Sozial-
       geschichtsschreibung in Preussen," Arch. f. Sozialgesch.,
       1, 1961, 61-68.
2901. SCHULTZE, Johannes, "Der Verein für Geschichte der Mark
       Brandenburg," FBPG, 35, 1923, 1-20.

2902.   SEEBER, Gustav and Heinz WOLTER, "Neue Tendenzen im
        bürgerlichen Geschichtsbild der BRD über die Reichs-
        gründung von 1871," Zs. f. Geschw., 20, 1972, 1069-
        1101.
2903.   SEIBT, Ferdinand, "Die bayerische 'Reichshistoriographie'
        und die Ideologie des deutschen Nationalstaates 1806-
        1918," Zs. f. bayer. LG., 28, 1965, 521-54.
2904.   SHEEHAN, James J., "Germany 1890-1918: A Survey of
        Recent Research," Cen. Eur. Hist., 1, 1968, 345-72.
2905.   _____, "The Primacy of Domestic Politics: Eckart
        Kehr's Essays on Modern German History," Cen. Eur.
        Hist., 1, 1968, 166-74.
2906.   SKALWEIT, Stephan, "Preussen als historisches Problem,"
        Jb. f. Gesch. M. O. Dtschl., 3, 1954, 189-211.
2907.   SKIDMORE, Thomas E., "Survey of Unpublished Sources on
        the Central Government and the Politics of the German
        Empire, 1871-1918," AHR, 65, 1959/60, 848-59.
2908.   SRBIK, Heinrich Ritter von, "Gesamtdeutsche Geschichtsauf-
        fassung," Vjschr. f. Litw., 8, 1930, 1-12.
2909.   _____, "Zur Gesamtdeutschen Geschichtsauffassung Ein
        Versuch und sein Schicksal," HZ, 156, 1937, 229-62.
2910.   STÄHLIN, Karl, "Erich Marcks zum Gedächtnis," HZ, 160,
        1939, 496-533.
2911.   STRACK, Paul, "Ferdinand Stein der Geschichtsschreiber
        von Lahr (1791-1835)," ZGORh., 98, 1950, 443-69.
2912.   STUPPERICH, Robert, "Karl Holls Oststudien und ihr Ein-
        fluss auf sein politisches Denken," HZ, 215, 1972, 345-
        67.
2913.   SUTTER, Walter, "Fünfundsiebzig Jahre Verein für Ge-
        schichte und Kunst des Mittelrheins," Jb. f. Gesch. Kunst
        d. MRh, 10, 1958, 5-17.
2914.   SYRBE, Horst, "Revanchismus unter dem Banner der Euro-
        paideologie Hans Rothfels und die 'abendländische Neuord-
        ung Osteuropas'," Zs. f. Geschw., 11, 1963, 679-703.
2915.   TAUBE, Arved Freiherr von, "Von ständischer Libertät zu
        Nationaler Selbstbehauptung Johann Reinhold von Patkul
        im baltisch-deutschen Geschichtsbild (1707-1957)," Zs. f.
        Ostforsch., 6, 1957, 481-510.
2916.   THIEME, Hans, "Der Historiker und die Geschichte von
        Verfassung und Recht," HZ, 209, 1969, 27-36.
2917.   TILLY, Richard Hugh, "Los von England Probleme des Na-
        tionalismus in der deutschen Wirtschaftsgeschichte,"
        ZgesStw., 124, 1968, 179-96.
2918.   _____, "Soll und Haben: Recent German Economic His-
        tory and the Problem of Economic Development," J. Econ.
        Hist., 19, 1969, 298-319.
2919.   TRAUT, Hermann, "Die Archiv des vormaligen Deutschen
        Bundes und der deutschen konstituierenden Nationalversam-
        mlung und ihre Uebergabe an die Stadt Frankfurt a.M. im
        Jahre 1867," Arch. f. Frankfurts Gesch., 1929, 204-19.
2920.   TREUE, Wilhelm, "Die Bedeutung der Unternehmerbiographie
        für die wirtschaftsgeschichtliche Forschung," Tradition, 10,
        1965, 254-65.

2921.   _____, "A Journal for Company Histories and Entre-
        preneurial Biography," Bus. Hist. Rev., 31, 1957, 323-
        36.

2922.   _____, "Zur jüngeren Wirtschaftsgeschichtsschreibung in
        der DDR über den deutschen Imperialismus," Aus. Pol.
        u. Zeitgesch., 33, 1971, 1-31.

2923.   USCZEK, Hansjürgen, "Zur Darstellung der Völkerschlacht
        in der imperialistischen deutschen Militärgeschichts-
        schreibung vor dem ersten Weltkrieg," Zs. f. MilitärG.,
        2, 1963, 347-54.

2924.   VALENTIN, Veit, "Graf Reventlow als Geschichtsschreiber,"
        Pr. Jbb., 165, 1916, 243-52.

2925.   VOGEL, Emanuel H., "Der Anteil der deutschen historischen
        Schule an der Entwicklung der 'politischen Ökonomie' zu
        einer 'nationalen Volkswirtschaftslehre'," VSW, 30, 1937,
        209-28.

2926.   VOLKERT, Wilhelm, "Marginalien zur bayerischen Ge-
        schichte 1800-1810," Zs. f. bayer. LG., 25, 1962, 414-
        69.

2927.   WACH, Joachim, "Die Geschichtsphilosophie des 19. Jahr-
        hunderts und die Theologie der Geschichte," HZ, 142,
        1930, 1-15.

2928.   WEECH, Friedrich von, ed., "Briefe Heidelberger Gelehrten
        an Franz Joseph Mone," ZGORh., 57, 1903, 458-92.

2929.   _____, "Briefwechsel Johann Friedrich Böhmers mit
        Franz Joseph Mone und Fridegar Mone," ZGORh., 55,
        1901, 422-63, 650-90.

2930.   WEHLER, Hans-Ulrich, "Zum Verhältnis von Geschichtswis-
        senschaft und Psychoanalyse," HZ, 208, 1969, 529-54.

2931.   WELCH, Claude, "The Problem of a History of Nineteenth-
        Century Theology," J. Rel., 52, 1972, 1-21.

2932.   WENDORF, Hermann, "Dialektik und materialistische Ge-
        schichtsauffassung," Hist. Vjschr., 21, 1922/23, 139-75.

2933.   WILBRANDT, Robert, "Das Ende der historisch-ethischen
        Schule," Weltwirtsch. Arch., 24, 1926, 73-108, 228-74.

2934.   WITTRAM, Reinhard, "Historismus und Geschichtsbewusst-
        sein," HZ, 157, 1937/38, 229-40.

2935.   WRIGHT, J. R. C., "Libraries and Archives for Historians:
        1. Germany," History, 53, 1968, 385-88.

2936.   ZITELMANN, Ernst, "Der Materialismus in der Geschichts-
        schreibung," Pr. Jbb., 37, 1876, 177-96, 217-41; 38,
        1876, 513-31, 650-63.

2937.   ZUHORN, Karl, "Heinrich Finke," Westf. Zs., 105, 1955,
        83-96.

Friedrich Christoph Dahlmann (1785-1860)

2938.   BERTHEAU, v., ed., "Briefe von Dahlmann, Ernst Moritz
        Arndt und Falck an der Oberappellationsgerichtsrat Bur-
        chardi in Kiel," Zeitschrift d. Gesellschaft f. Schlesw.-
        holstein. Geschichte, 42, 1912, 231ff.

2939.   "DAHLMANN," Pr. Jbb., 7, 1861, 185-203.

2940.   CHRISTERN, H., "Dahlmanns polit. Entwicklung bis 1848,"
        Zeitschrift d. Gesellschaft f. Schlesw.-holstein. Ge-
        schichte, 50, 1921.
2941.   HÖLZLE, Erwin, "Dahlmann und der Staat," VSW, 17, 1924,
        350-58.
2942.   SCHARFF, Alexander, "Friedrich Christoph Dahlmann Leis-
        tung und Bedeutung für Universität und Land," Zeitschrift
        d. Gesellschaft f. Schlesw.-holstein. Geschichte, 90,
        1965, 83-100.
2943.   VARRENTRAPP, Conrad, "Zur Erinnerung an Friedrich
        Christoph Dahlmann," Pr. Jbb., 55, 1885, 485-510.
2944.   WESTPHAL, Otto, "Zur Beurteilung Hegels und Dahlmanns,"
        HZ, 129, 1924, 252-80.

Hans Delbrück (1848-1929)

See also entries 774, 1764, 1855, 2315, 4271, 4501, 4502,
4723, 4863, 4889, 4952, 5030, 5412, 5413

2945.   MOLINSKI, Konrad, "Hans Delbrück Geschichtswissenschaft
        und Politik," Hochland, 27(2), 1929/30, 158-65.
2946.   SCHLEIER, Hans, "Treitschke, Delbrück und die 'Preus-
        sischen Jahrbücher' in den 80er Jahren des 19. Jahrhun-
        derts," Jb. f. Gesch., 1, 1967, 134-79.

Johann Gustav Droysen (1808-1884)

See also entry 2784

2947.   ANDREAS, Willy, "Briefe Erdmannsdörffers an Johann Gus-
        tav Droysen," ZGORh., 81, 1928/29, 557-87.
2948.   DIETHER, Otto, "Leopold von Ranke und Johann Gustav
        Droysen Eine Parallele," Pr. Jbb., 142, 1910, 1-20.
2949.   DUNCKER, Max, "Johann Gustav Droysen," Pr. Jbb., 54,
        1884, 134-67.
2950.   HERRMANN, Erwin, "Staat und Politik in der 'Historik'
        J. G. Droysens," Zs. f. Pol., 15, 1968, 99-106.
2951.   HINTZE, Otto, "Johann Gustav Droysen und der deutsche
        Staatsgedanke im 19. Jahrhundert," ZgesStw., 88, 1930,
        1-21.
2952.   HÜBNER, Rudolf, "Joh. Gust. Droysens Vorlesungen über
        Politik," Zs. f. Pol., 10, 1917, 325-76.
2953.   KAERST, J., "Die Geschichtsauffassung Rankes und Droy-
        sens in ihrer nationalen Bedeutung," VSW, 20, 1928, 219-
        33.
2954.   MEINECKE, F., "Johann Gustav Droysen, Briefwechsel und
        seine Geschichtsschreibung," HZ, 141, 1929/30, 249-87.
2955.   MEISTER, Ernst, "Die geschichtsphilosophischen Voraus-
        setzungen von J. G. Droysens 'Historik'," Hist. Vjschr.,
        23, 1926/27, 25-63, 199-221.
2956.   MOMIGLIANO, Arnaldo, "J. G. Droysen Between Greeks and

Jews," Hist. Theor., 9, 1970, 139-53.
2957.   ROTHACKER, Erich, "J. G. Droysens Historik," HZ, 161,
         1939/40, 84-92.
2958.   STEINHÄUSER, Martin, "Karl Francke und Johann Gustav
         Droysen Ein schleswig- holsteinischer Briefwechsel
         (1850-1860)," Hist. Vjschr., 27, 1932/33, 795-826.
2959.   ULMANN, Heinrich, "Johann Gustav Droysen als Abgeord-
         neter zur Paulskirche im Jahre 1848," FBPG, 42, 1929,
         263-73.

Max Duncker (1811-1886)

2960.   BRODE, Reinhold, "Max Dunckers Anteil an der deutschen
         Geschichtsschreibung," FBPG, 6, 1893, 501-27.
2961.   GRUBE, Walter, "Aus der Geschichte der Einheitsbewegung
         in Württemberg Max Duncker im Briefwechsel mit Karl
         Klüpsel, A. L. Reyscher Hermann Reuchlin und W. L.
         Holland 1859-1871," Zs. F. Wurttbg. LG, 42, 1936,
         323-56.
2962.   RÖSSLER, Constantin, "Das Leben Max Dunckers," Pr. Jbb.,
         68, 1891, 404-25.
2963.   TREITSCHKE, H. v., "Max Duncker," Pr. Jbb., 58, 1886,
         489-508.

Georg Gottfried Gervinus (1805-1871)

2964.   HILDEBRAND, Karl, "G. G. Gervinus," Pr. Jbb., 32,
         1873, 379-428.
2965.   McCLELLAND, Charles E., "History in the Service of
         Politics: A Reassessment of G. G. Gervinus," Cen. Eur.
         Hist., 4, 1971, 371-89
2966.   RANKE, Leopold von, "Georg G. Gervinus," HZ, 27, 1872,
         134-46.
2967.   WAGNER, Jonathan F., "Georg Gottfried Gervinus: The
         Tribulations of a Liberal Federalist," Cen. Eur. Hist.,
         4, 1971, 354-70.

Otto Hintze (1861-1940)

See also entries 308, 566, 660, 661, 1123, 1124, 1276,
2951, 3714, 3812, 5041

2968.   GERHARD, Dietrich, "Otto Hintze: His Work and His Sig-
         nificance in Historiography," Cen. Eur. Hist., 3, 1970,
         17-48.
2969.   MEISNER, Heinrich Otto, "Otto Hintzes Lebenswerk," HZ,
         164, 1941, 66-90.
2970.   OESTREICH, G., "Otto Hintze und die vergleichende Ver-
         waltungsgeschichte," Annali della Fondazione italiana per
         la storia amministrativa, 3, 1966, 59-80.

Karl Lamprecht (1856-1915)

2971.   JAHN, Georg, "Karl Lamprecht als Wirtschafts- und Kultur-
        historiker," Schmoll. Jb., 76, 1956, 129-42.
2972.   LEWALD, Ursula, "Karl Lamprecht und die rheinische Ge-
        schichtsforschung," Rhein. Vjsbll., 21, 1956, 279-304.
2973.   SCHMOLLER, Gustav, "Zur Würdigung von Karl Lamprecht,"
        Schmoll. Jb., 40, 1916, 1113-40.
2974.   SCHÖNEBAUM, Herbert, "Gustav Mevissen und Karl Lam-
        precht Zur rheinischen Kulturpolitik von 1880-1890,"
        Rhein. Vjsbll., 17, 1952, 180-96.
2975.   _____, "Karl Lamprechts wissenschaftlicher Anruf an
        Rheinland und Sachsen und an die gesamte Deutsche Na-
        tion," Hamb. Mittel- u. ostdt. Forsch., 1, 1957, 139-
        65.
2976.   _____, "Vom Werden der deutschen Geschichte Karl Lam-
        prechts," Vjschr. f. Litw., 25, 1951, 94-111.

Friedrich Meinecke (1862-1954)

See also 691, 2844, 2866, 2954, 3025, 3521, 3875, 4176,
4246, 4419, 4567, 4568, 4569, 4733, 4773, 4774, 4917, 5167

2977.   GOETZ, W., "Friedrich Meinecke Leben und Persönlich-
        keit," HZ, 174, 1952, 231-50.
2978.   HERKLESS, J. L., "Meinecke and the Ranke-Burckhardt
        Problem," Hist. Theor., 9, 1970, 290-321.
2979.   HOFER, Walther, "Friedrich Meinecke zum 90. Geburtstag,"
        Schweizer Monatshefte, 1952, 503-07.
2980.   HOLLDACK, Heinz, "Friedrich Meinecke Das Machtproblem
        in der neuesten deutschen Geschichte," Hochland, 46,
        1953/54, 437-51.
2981.   LATOUR, C. F., "Portrait of a German Historian, Fried-
        rich Meinecke 1862-1954," Historian, 17, 1955, 157-71.
2982.   LIEBESCHÜTZ, Hans, "Friedrich Meinecke and the Revival
        of German Idealism," Ger. Life Letters, 10, 1956/57,
        285-88.
2983.   LOZEK, Gerhard, "Friedrich Meinecke--ein Stammvater der
        NATO--Historiker in Westdeutschland," Zs. f. Geschw.,
        10, 1962, 1538-74, 1786-1807.
2984.   POIS, Robert A., "Two Poles within Historicism: Croce
        and Meinecke," J. Hist. Ideas, 31, 1970, 253-72.
2985.   SCHNABEL, Franz, "Friedrich Meinecke und die deutsche
        Geschichtsschreibung," Hochland, 34(2), 1936/37, 157-62.
2986.   SCHULIN, Ernst, "Das problem der Individualität Eine kri-
        tische Betrachtung des Historismus-Werkes von Friedrich
        Meinecke," HZ, 197, 1963, 102-33.
2987.   SEEBERG, Erich, "Zur Entstehung der Historismus Gedan-
        ken zu Friedrich Meineckes jüngstem Werk," HZ, 157,
        1937/38, 241-66.
2988.   WOLFSON, Philip J., "Friedrich Meinecke (1862-1954),"
        J. Hist. Ideas, 17, 1956, 511-25.

Theodor Mommsen (1817-1903)

See also entry 4958

2989.   BAMMEL, Ernst, "Judentum, Christentum und Heidentum:
        Julius Welhausens Briefe an Theodor Mommsen 1881-
        1902," Zs. f. KiG, 80, 1909, 221-54.
2990.   BENGTSON, Hermann, "Theodor Mommsen," WaG, 15,
        1955, 87-99.
2991.   KAERST, Julius, "Theodor Mommsen," Hist. Vjschr., 7,
        1904, 313-42.
2992.   LIEBESCHÜTZ, Hans, "Treitschke and Mommsen on Jewry
        and Judaism," Leo Baeck Inst. Yrbk., 7, 1962, 153-82.
2993.   MOMMSEN, Dr. Th., "Die Promotionsreform," Pr. Jbb.,
        37, 1876, 335-52.
2994.   PAULS, V., "Mommsen und die schleswig-holsteinische
        Erhebung," Z. d. Ges. f. schleswig-holsteinische Gesch.,
        58, 1929, 594ff.
2995.   WICKERT, Lothar, "Theodor Mommsen und Jacob Bernays
        Ein Beitrag zur Geschichte des deutschen Judentums zu
        Mommsens 150. Geburtstag, 30.11. 1967," HZ, 205,
        1967, 265-94.
2996.   WUCHER, Albert, "Theodor Mommsen als Kritiker der
        deutschen Nation," Saec., 2, 1951, 256-70.

Johannes von Müller (1752-1809)

2997.   ANDREAS, Willy, "Johannes von Müller Berufung nach
        Tübingen," Zs. F. Württbg. LG, 14, 1955, 445-65.
2998.   BONJOUR, Edgar, "Johannes von Müller als beschirmer
        deutscher Universitäten," HZ, 180, 1955, 245-63.
2000.   CRAIG, Gordon A., "Johannes von Müller: The Historian
        in Search of a Hero," AHR, 74, 1968/69, 1487-1502.
3000.   SCHIB, Karl, "Die Gründung der Universität Berlin und
        Johannes von Müllers unfreiwillige Rücktritt aus dem
        Dienste Preussens," Schw. Zs. f. Gesch., 13, 1963,
        161-76.

Barthold Georg Niebuhr (1776-1831)

3001.   BRIDENTHAL, Renate, "Was There a Roman Homer?
        Niebuhr's Thesis and its Critics," Hist. Theor., 11,
        1972, 193-213.
3002.   CHRIST, Karl, "Römische Geschichte und Universalge-
        schichte bei Barthold Georg Niebuhr," Saec., 19, 1968,
        172-96.
3003.   DREYHAUS, Hermann, "Niebuhr auf der Flucht der preus-
        sischen Behörden 1806/07," HZ, 110, 1913, 91-103.
3004.   _____, "Niebuhr und Goethe," Pr. Jbb., 142, 1910,
        433-44.
3005.   _____, "Der Preussische Correspondent von 1813/14 und

der Anteil seiner Gründer Niebuhr und Schleiermacher, "
FBPG, 22, 1909, 375-446.

3006.   JACOBSON, N. P., "Niebuhr's Philosophy of History, "
Har. Theol. Rev., 37, 1944, 238-68.

3007.   KORNEMANN, Ernst, "Niebuhr und der Aufbau der altrö-
mischen Geschichte, " HZ, 145, 1931, 277-300.

3008.   LENEL, Edith, "Barthold Georg Niebuhr und Wilhelm Von
Humboldt: Briefe im Nachlass Von Franz Lieber, " HZ,
200, 1965, 316-31.

3009.   MEIER, "Schön und Niebuhr, " Pr. Jbb., 31, 1873, 503-22.

3010.   VISCHER, Eduard, "Barthold Georg Niebuhr und die
Schweiz, " WaG, 16, 1956, 1-40.

Karl Wilhelm Nitzsch (1818-1880)

3011.   JASTROW, J., "Karl Wilhelm Nitzsch und die deutsche
Wirtschaftsgeschichte, " Schmoll. Jb., 8, 1884, 873-97.

3012.   JORDAN, K., "Karl Wilhelm Nitzsch und seine Stellung in
der schlesw.-holstein. Geschichtswissenschaft des 19.
Jahrhunderts, " Zs. Schlesw.-Holst., 94, 1969, 267-84.

Leopold von Ranke (1795-1886)

See also entries 2867, 2878, 2948, 2953, 2966

3013.   DEHIO, Ludwig, "Ranke und der deutsche Imperialismus, "
HZ, 170, 1950, 307-28.

3014.   DUCH, Arno, "Zu Rankes Erneuerung, " Zeitwende, 2(2),
1926, 41-51.

3015.   FUCHS, W., "Der Nachlass Leopold v. Rankes, " HZ, 195,
1962, 63-90.

3016.   _____, "Heinrich Ranke, " Jb. f. Fränk. Ldforsch., 25,
1965, 115-207.

3017.   HENZ, Günter Johannes, "Zu Leopold von Rankes Briefwechsel, " Arch. f. KuG., 54, 1972, 285-324.

3018.   HÜFFER, H., "Alfred von Reumont und Leopold von Ranke, "
Ann. Niederrhein, 77, 1904, 191-209.

3019.   IGGERS, Georg G., "The Image of Ranke in American and
German Historical Thought, " Hist. Theor., 2, 1962/63,
17-40.

3020.   KAUFMANN, Georg, "Ranke und die Beurteilung Friedrich
Wilhelms IV, " HZ, 88, 1902, 436-73.

3021.   KESSEL, Eberhard, "Ranke und Burckhardt, " Arch. f. KuG.,
33, 1951, 351-79.

3022.   _____, "Rankes Idee der Universalhistorie, " HZ, 178,
1954, 269-308.

3023.   LUPAS, Johann, "Leopold von Ranke und Mihail Kogăl-
niceanu, " Jbb. f. Gesch. Osteur., 4, 1939, 322-30.

3024.   MAYER-KULENKAMPFF, Ilse, "Rankes Lutherverhältnis
dargestellt nach dem Lutherfragment von 1817, " HZ, 172,
1951, 65-99.

3025. MEINECKE, Friedrich, "Zur Beurteilung Rankes," HZ, 111, 1913, 582-99.

3026. MÜLLER, Karl A. von, "Ein unbekannter Vortrag Rankes aus dem Jahr 1862," HZ, 151, 1934/35, 311-31.

3027. NEUMANN, Carl, "Ranke und Burckhardt und die Begriffes 'Renaissance' insbesondere für Deutschland," HZ, 150, 1934, 485-96.

3028. NOACK, Ulrich, "Das Werden unseres neuen Geschichtsbildes im Geiste Rankes," H. Jb., 74, 1954, 506-19.

3029. NOORDEN, C. v., "Ranke und Macaulay," HZ, 16, 1867, 87-138.

3030. PAHLMANN, F., "Ein Predigtentwurf Leopold von Rankes," HZ, 180, 1955, 489-506.

3031. RANKE, Ermentrude von, "Leopold von Rankes Elternhaus," Arch. f. KuG., 48, 1966, 114-32.

3032. RANTZAU, Johann A. v., "Das deutsche Geschichtsdenken der Gegenwart und die Nachwirkung Rankes," GiWuU, 1, 1950, 514-25.

3033. RAUMER, Kurt von, "Ranke als Spiegel deutscher Geschichtsschreibung im 19. Jahrhundert," WaG, 12, 1952, 242-58.

3034. SCHEVILL, Ferdinand, "Ranke: Rise, Decline, and Persistence of a Reputation," J. Mod. Hist., 24, 1952, 219-34.

3035. SCHIEDER, Theodor, "Die Entstehung von Rankes 'Epochen Der Neueren Geschichte'," HZ, 199, 1964, 1-30.

3036. SCHMEIDLER, B., "Zur Entwicklung der Geschichtsschreibung Rankes," Schmoll. Jb., 27, 1903, 465-510.

3037. SCHULIN, Ernst, "Rankes Erstes Buch," HZ, 203, 1966, 581-609.

3038. SKALWEIT, Stephan, "Ranke und Bismarck," HZ, 176, 1953, 277-90.

3039. STENGEL, Edmund E., "Jugendbriefe von Georg Waitz aus der Frühzeit Rankes und der Monumenta Germaniae," HZ, 121, 1920, 234-55.

3040. SYBEL, Heinrich v., "Gedächtnisrede auf Leopold v. Ranke," HZ, 56, 1886, 463.

3041. SZCZEPANSKI, Max v., "Rankes Anschauungen über den Zusammenhang zwischen der auswärtigen und der inneren Politik der Staaten," Zs. f. Pol., 7, 1914, 489-623.

3042. VARRENTRAPP, C., ed., "Briefe an Ranke von älteren und gleichalterigen deutschen und französischen Historikern," HZ, 105, 1910, 105-31.

3043. _____, "Briefe an Ranke von einigen Schüler: Sybel, Carlson, Hermann, Pauli und Noorden," HZ, 107, 1911, 44-69.

3044. _____, "Rankes Historisch-politische Zeitschrift und das Berliner Politische Wochenblatt," HZ, 1907, 99, 35-119.

3045. VIERHAUS, Rudolf, "Rankes Verhältnis zur Presse," HZ, 183, 1957, 543-67.

3046. _____, "Rankes Verständnis der 'neuesten Geschichte'," Arch. f. KuG., 39, 1957, 81-102.

3047. VISCHER, Eduard, "Leopold von Rankes 'Neuere Geschichte' von 1833," Schw. Zs. f. Gesch., 3, 1953, 385-425.

3048. _____, "Zu Leopold von Rankes Briefen," Schw. Zs. f.
Gesch., 1, 1951, 275-91.

3049. WAGNER, Fritz, "Rankes Geschichtsbild und die moderne
Universalhistorie," Arch. f. KuG., 44, 1968, 1-26.

Alfred von Reumont (1808-1887)

See also entry 3018

3050. HÜFFER, H., "Alfred von Reumont im Dienste des Staates
und der Wissenschaft," Ann. Niederrhein, 77, 1904, 124-
73.

3051. _____, "Alfred von Reumont und Hermann von Thile,"
Ann. Niederrhein, 77, 1904, 174-90.

3052. _____, "Reumont und seiner Beziehungen zum Kaiser-
hause," Ann. Niederrhein, 77, 1904, 210-39.

3053. JUST, Leo, "Alfred von Reumont," Ann. Niederrhein, 131,
1937, 133-48.

3054. REUMONT, Alfred v., "Jugenderinnerungen," Ann. Niederrhein, 77, 1904, 17-123.

3055. "VERZEICHNIS der auf den vorhergehenden Blättern genann-
ten Schriften Reumonts," Ann. Niederrhein, 77, 1904,
240-41.

Gerhard Ritter (1888-1967)

See also entries 2873, 2874, 2875, 4196, 4197, 4198, 4294,
4435, 4614, 4615, 5055, 5313

3056. BERTHOLD, Werner, "Der politisch-ideologische Weg Gerhard Ritters, eines führenden Ideologen der deutschen
Bourgeoisie," Zs. f. Geschw., 6, 1958, 959-89.

3057. DORPALEN, Andreas, "Historiography as History: The
Work of Gerhard Ritter," J. Mod. Hist., 34, 1962, 1-18.

Franz Schnabel (1887-1966)

See also entries 157, 717, 2985, 3203, 4642, 4643, 5320,
5430

3058. SCHUBERT, Friedrich Hermann, "Franz Schnabel und die
Geschichtswissenschaft des 20. Jahrhunderts," HZ, 205,
1967, 323-57.

3059. ZEEDEN, Ernst W., "Das Jahrhundert des Bürgertums,
Franz Schnabels 'Deutsche Geschichte im 19. Jahrhundert'," Saec., 3, 1952, 509-21.

Heinrich von Sybel (1817-1895)

See also entries 735, 3040, 3043, 4224, 4873, 5213

3060. BUCHHEIM, Karl, "Heinrich von Sybel und der Staatsge-
       danke," Hist. Vjschr., 26, 1931, 96-116.
3061. HÜBINGER, Paul Egon, "Heinrich von Sybel und der Bonner
       Philologenkrieg," H. Jb., 83, 1963, 162-216.
3062. SEIER, Hellmut, "Sybels Vorlesung über Politik und die
       Kontinuität des 'Staatsbildenden' Liberalismus," HZ, 187,
       1959, 90-112.

Aloys Schulte (1857-1941)

3063. BRAUBACH, Max, "Aloys Schulte," H. Jb., 61, 1941, 193-
       207.
3064. _____, "Aloys Schulte und die rheinische Geschichte,"
       Rhein. Vjsbll., 22, 1957, 1-30.
3065. _____, "Zwei deutsche Historiker aus Westfalen: Briefe
       Heinrich Finkes an Aloys Schulte," Westf. Zs., 118,
       1968, 9-113.
3066. METZ, Friedrich, "Aloys Schulte und die deutsche Landes-
       und Volksforschung," Rhein. Vjsbll., 7, 1937, 107-10.
3067. SPÖRL, J., "Aloys Schulte," H. Jb., 61, 1941.

Heinrich von Treitschke (1834-1896)

See also entries 533, 739, 740, 741, 838, 839, 933, 1007,
1736, 2056, 2171, 2172, 2723, 2757, 2946, 2963, 2992,
3893, 4052, 4053, 4227, 4355, 4356, 4460, 4461, 4462,
4822, 4958

3068. ANDREAS, Willy, "Briefe Treitschkes an Historiker und
       Politiker vom Oberrhein," Pr. Jbb., 237, 1934, 207-26;
       238, 1934, 1-17, 97-105.
3069. BEYERHAUS, Gisbert, "Das Recht des nationalen Historikers
       Heinrich von Treitschke zum Gedächtnis," Vjschr. f.
       Litw., 13, 1935, 207-27.
3070. BUSSMANN, W., "Treitschke als Politiker," HZ, 177, 1954,
       249-79.
3071. CRAEMER, Rudolf, "Über die völkische Haltung Treitschkes,"
       HZ, 158, 1938, 77-105.
3072. DANIELS, Emil, "Die politischen Korrespondenzen Treitsch-
       kes in den Preussischen Jahrbüchern," Pr. Jbb., 237,
       1934, 250-76.
3073. DORPALEN, Andreas, "Heinrich von Treitschke," J. Con-
       temp. Hist., 7, 1972, 21-35.
3074. EBBINGHAUS, Th., "Heinrich von Treitschke und die
       deutsche Literatur," Pr. Jbb., 165, 1916, 67-87.
3075. GASS, Elisabeth, "Erinnerungen an Heinrich von Treitschke
       Seine Freundschaft mit Wilhelm Gass," Zeitwende, 4(1),

1928, 453-61.

3076. GOLDSCHMIDT, Hans, "Treitschke, Bismarck und die 'Deutsche Geschichte im 19. Jahrhundert'," Pr. Jbb., 237, 1934, 226-49.

3077. GRAU, Wilhelm, "Heinrich von Treitschke und die Judenfrage," Zeitwende, 11(1), 1934/35, 82-90.

3078. GUNDEL, Hans Georg, "Treitschke und Oncken um 1870," Nachrichten d. Giessener Hochschulges., 35, 1966, 169-81.

3079. HALLGARTEN, George W. F., "Heinrich von Treitschke, The Role of the 'Outsider' in German Political Thought," History, 36, 1951, 227-43.

3080. HERZFELD, Dr. Hans, "Staat und Persönlichkeit bei Heinrich von Treitschke," Pr. Jbb., 194, 1923, 267-94.

3081. HOLZHEY, H., "Zwei Briefe Hermann Cohens an Heinrich von Treitschke (1879)," Leo Baeck Inst. Yrbk., 12, 1969, 183-204.

3082. KAUFMANN, Georg, "Treitschkes Urteil über Johannes Ronge," HZ, 99, 1907, 515-30.

3083. KRETZSCHMAR, Hellmut, "Heinrich von Treitschkes Verhältnis zu Sachsen," Pr. Jbb., 239, 1935, 251-63.

3084. MAGDEFRAU, Werner, "Heinrich von Treitschke und die imperialistische 'Ostforschung'," Zs. f. Geschw., 11, 1963, 1444-65.

3085. MARCKS, Erich, "Heinrich von Treitschke Eine Erinnerung," Pr. Jbb., 237, 1934, 193-206.

3086. MORDSTEIN, Friedrich, "Heinrich von Treitschkes Etatismus," Zs. f. Pol., 8, 1961, 30-53.

3087. MÜLLER, Karl A. v., "Treitschke als Journalist," HZ, 135, 1927, 382-412.

3088. NEUMANN, Carl, "Die Vorgeschichte der Berufung Heinrich von Treitschkes nach Heidelberg (1867)," HZ, 139, 1928/29, 534ff.

3089. PFEIL, S. G. v., "Heinrich v. Treitschke und das Judentum," WaG, 21, 1961, 49-62.

3090. SCHMOLLER, G., "Offenes Sendschreiben an Herrn Professor Dr. Heinrich von Treitschke über einige Grundfragen des Rechts und der Volkswirthschaft," Jbb. f. Nationalökon. u. Stat., 23, 1874, 225-349; 24, 1875, 81-119.

3091. WORTHMANN, Ferd., "Heinrich von Treitschke und die 'Kathedersozialisten'," Jbb. f. Nationalökon. u. Stat., 30, 1878, 1-34.

Friedrich Otto von Weech (1837-1905)

See also entries 744, 2928, 2929

3092. BAIER, Hermann, "Aus der geistigen Umwelt eines jungen deutschen Historikers von 1856 bis 1870 Zu Friedrich von Weechs 100. Geburtstag," ZGORh., 90, 1937/38, 385-442.

3093. _____, "Heidelberger Professorenbriefe," ZGORh., 89,

1936/37, 170-206.
3094. WEECH, Friedrich von, ed., "Beiträge zur Geschichte der badischen Landtage von 1819-1845," ZGORh., 48, 1894, 581-628.

Paul Wigand (1786-1866)

3095. RICHTER, W., "Paul Wigand Ein Juristen-Publizisten, Poeten- und Historikerleben," Westf. Zs., 72(2), 1914, 90-146.
3096. STEFFENS, Wilhelm, "Paul Wigand und die Anfänge planmässiger landesgeschichtlicher Forschung in Westfalen," Westf. Zs., 94, 1938, 143-237.

INTELLECTUAL AND CULTURAL HISTORY

General Studies

3097. ANDERSON, Eugene N., "German Romanticism as an Ideology of Cultural Crisis," J. Hist. Ideas, 2, 1941, 301-17.

3098. ANDREAS, Willy, "Ludwig Häusser und Karl Hillebrand Eine geistesgeschichtliche Studie," ZGORh., 104, 1956, 489-507.

3099. ARENDT, Dieter, "Der Nihilismus-Ursprung und Geschichte im Spiegel der Forschungs-Literatur seit 1945," Vjschr. f. Litw., 43, 1969, 346-69, 544-66.

3100. ARVON, Henri, "Proudhon et le radicalisme Allemand," Annales, 6, 1951, 194-201.

3101. BAADER, Berndt P., "Caspar David Friedrich Der Neuschöpfer der deutschen Landschaftsmalerei," Gelbe Hefte, 14, 1937/38, 430-42.

3102. BABINGER, Franz, "Othmar Frank (1770-1840) Ein Beitrag zur Geschichte der morgenländischen Studien in Bayern," Zs. f. bayer. LG., 22, 1959, 77-123.

3103. BADER, Karl Siegfried, "Zur Charakteristik des Reichsfreiherrn Joseph von Lassberg," Zs. F. Württbg. LG, 5, 1941, 124-40.

3104. BEATON, K. B., "Der konservative Roman in Deutschland nach der Revolution von 1848," ZRGG, 19, 1967, 215-34.

3105. BECKER, Albert, "Zur Kultur- und Geistesgeschichte der Südwestdeutschen Grenzmark 1760-1848," Arch. f. KuG., 26, 1936, 296-323.

3106. BEENKEN, Hermann, "Der Historismus in der Baukunst," HZ, 157, 1937/38, 27-68.

3107. BENZ, Ernst, "Die Reinkarnationslehre in Dichtung und Philosophie der deutschen Klassik und Romantik," ZRGG, 9, 1957, 150-75.

3108. BERINGER, Jos. Aug., "Jakob Friedrich Dyckerhoff 1774-1845 Ingenieur, Architekt, Maler und Daguerreotypeur in Mannheim," ZGORh., 86, 1933/34, 259-352.

3109. _____, "Moritz von Schwinds Karlsruher Zeit Ein Beitrag zur badischen Kunstgeschichte des 19. Jahrhunderts," ZGORh., 69, 1915, 137-200.

3110. BERTRAM, Ernst, "Norden und deutsche Romantik," Zeitwende, 2(1), 1926, 47-61.

3111. BETTERIDGE, H. T., "The Romantic Spirit in Germany," Ger. Life Letters, 3, 1938/39, 12-24.

3112. BIETAK, Wilhelm, "Zwischen Romantik, Jungen Deutsch-
       land und Realismus," Vjschr. f. Litw., 13, 1935, 163-
       206.

3113. BOLLE, Fritz, "Darwinismus und Zeitgeist," ZRGG, 14,
       1962, 143-78.

3114. BROWN, Clifford W., "Adolph Zeising and the Formalist
       Tradition in Aesthetics," Arch. f. Gesch. d. Phil., 45,
       1963, 23-32.

3115. BRÜCK, Anton Ph., "Friedrich Schneider (1836-1907) Ein
       Beitrag zur deutschen Geistesgeschichte des 19. Jahr-
       hunderts," Arch. f. mrh. KiG., 9, 1957, 166-92.

3116. BRUNSCHWIG, Henri, "Jena, la Crise de l'état Prussien
       et la Genèse du Romantisme," Annales, 1, 1946, 306-13.

3117. BUSKE, Thomas, "Revelatio Dei Die Paralipomena des
       deutschen Idealismus," Arch. f. Gesch. d. Phil., 52,
       1970, 269-86.

3118. CARR, C. T., "Julius Langbehn--A Forerunner of National
       Socialism," Ger. Life Letters, 3, 1938/39, 45-54.

3119. CARTER, T. E., "Comments on German Book Production
       in the Nineteenth Century," Ger. Life Letters, 23, 1969/
       70, 112-18.

3120. CASSER, Paul, "Die Westfälischen Musenalmanache und
       poetischen Taschenbücher Ein Beitrag zur Geschichte
       der literarischen Kultur in der ersten Hälfte des 19. Jahr-
       hunderts," Westf. Zs., 85, 1928, 97-282.

3121. COPLESTON, F. C., "Pantheism in Spinoza and the German
       Idealists," Philosophy, 21, 1946, 42-56.

3122. CRAIG, Gordon A., "German Intellectuals and Politics,
       1789-1815: The Case of Heinrich von Kleist," Cen. Eur.
       Hist., 2, 1969, 3-21.

3123. DAMMANN, Oswald, "Zur Charakteristik Friedrich Christoph
       Schlossers," ZGORh., 84, 1931/32, 135-45.

3124. DIEFFENBACHER, Julius, "Hofmaler Wilhelm Dürrs Briefc
       im Rosenberger Altarbildstreit (1858/59)," ZGORh., 70,
       1916, 94-115.

3125. DUNNING, W. A., "The German Idealists," Pol. Sci. Q.,
       28, 1913, 193-206, 480-95.

3126. DYRSSEN, Dr., "Ueber die religiöse Grundstimmung der
       Romantik und ihre Gefahren," Zs. f. Theol. u. K., 30,
       1922, 129-47.

3127. ENGELSING, Rolf, "Romantische Buchhandelsutopien,"
       Archiv f. Gesch. d. Buchwesens, 8, 1966, 323-31.

3128. ESSELBORN, Karl, "Der Verein für Wissenschaft, Literatur
       und Kunst in Darmstadt (1835-1838)," Arch. f. hessische
       Gesch., 14, 1923/25, 72-92.

3129. EWALD, Oscar, "Contemporary Philosophy in Germany
       (1906)," Phil. Rev., 16, 1907, 237-65.

3130. _____, "German Philosophy in 1907," Phil. Rev., 17,
       1908, 400-26.

3131. _____, "Germany Philosophy in 1908," Phil. Rev., 18,
       1909, 514-35.

3132. _____, "German Philosophy in 1909," Phil. Rev., 19,
       1910, 481-504.

3133.   _____, "German Philosophy in 1910," Phil. Rev., 20,
         1911, 589-609.
3134.   _____, "Philosophy in Germany in 1911," Phil. Rev.,
         21, 1912, 499-526.
3135.   _____, "German Philosophy in 1912," Phil. Rev., 22,
         1913, 484-501.
3136.   _____, "German Philosophy in 1913," Phil. Rev., 23,
         1914, 615-33.
3137.   FABER, Karl-Georg, "Rheinisches Geistesleben zwischen
         Restauration und Romantik," Rhein. Vjsbll., 21, 1956,
         245-78.
3138.   FISCHER, Hermann, "Die Hallischen Jahrbücher und die
         Schwaben," Zs. F. Württbg. LG, 25, 1916, 558-71.
3139.   FLEIG, Edgar, "Zur Geschichte des Einströmens franzö-
         sischen Restaurationsdenkens nach Deutschlands," H. Jb.,
         55, 1935, 500-20.
3140.   FLEISSNER, E. M., "In Defense of German Idealism,"
         Ger. Rev., 22, 1947, 270-86.
3141.   FLORING, K., "Julius Königer das Leben eines Idealisten
         in den Jahren vor der Reichsgründung," Arch. f. hes-
         sische Gesch., 30, 1967/68, 88-140.
3142.   GERHARTZ, Heinrich, "Christian Hohe Ein Beitrag zur
         Geschichte der rheinischen Malerei im 19. Jahrhundert,"
         Ann. Niederrhein, 128, 1936, 90-120.
3143.   GERSCHENKRON, Alexander, "The Concept of Continuity in
         German Anthropology," Comp. Stud. Soc. Hist., 13,
         1971, 351-57.
3144.   GETZENY, Heinrich, "Die Gemeinschaftsauffassung der
         Romantik in der frühen Tübinger Schule," H. Jb., 74,
         1954, 405-15.
3145.   _____, "Kierkegaards Eindeutschung Ein Beitrag zur
         deutschen Geistesgeschichte der letzten hundert Jahre,"
         H. Jb., 76, 1956, 181-92.
3146.   GRANDJONC, Jacques, "Die Stimme des Volkes 1839 oder
         Blätter der Zukunft 1846: Zur 'Deutschen Ideologie',"
         Arch. f. Sozialgesch., 9, 1969, 499-507.
3147.   GRASSL, Hans, "Bayerns Beitrag zur Frühromantik," Zs.
         f. Pol., 14, 1967, 175-86.
3148.   _____, "Die Münchner Romantik zur Frage ihrer Grund-
         lagen," Zs. f. bayer. LG., 21, 1958, 110-29.
3149.   GREVEN, Helio A., "Leben und Werke des Hofbaumeisters
         Christian Heinrich Tramm (1819-1861)," Hannoversche
         Geschichtsbl., 1969.
3150.   GRUNDMANN, Günther, "Schlesiens Beitrag zur Geschichte
         des deutschen Theaterbaus im 18. und 19. Jahrhundert,"
         Jb. d. Schles.-Fried.-Wilh. Univ z. Breslau, 15, 1970,
         242-55.
3151.   HARTMANN, Abbert, "Der Spätidealismus in seinen Anfängen
         Über die Philosophie Karl Christian Friedrich Krauses,"
         Theol. Qu.-Schr., 125, 1944, 37-56.
3152.   HASELIER, Günther, "Der junge Wilhelm Furtwängler und
         das Karlsruher Hoftheater," ZGORh., 107, 1959, 183-204.
3153.   HAVENSTEIN, Martin, "Der Kampf des neunzehnten Jahr-

hunderts mit dem Geiste der Romantik," Pr. Jbb., 162, 1915, 217-35.

3154. HENGESBACH, J., "Friedrich Althoff," Gelbe Hefte, 5, 1928/29, 491-99.

3155. HOLBORN, Hajo, "Der deutsche Idealismus in Sozialgeschichtlicher Beleuchtung," HZ, 174, 1952, 359-84.

3156. HOLL, Karl, "Der Wandel des deutschen Lebensgefühls im Spiegel der deutschen Kunst seit der Reichsgründung," Vjschr. f. Litw., 4, 1926, 548-63.

3157. HUETER, C., "Zur Frage der Promotionsreform," Pr. Jbb., 38, 1876, 499-512.

3158. JACOBY, Günther, "Philosophie und Geistesleben im neunzehnten Jahrhundert," Arch. f. KuG., 9, 1911, 483-512; 10, 1912, 154-239.

3159. KALTENBRUNNER, Gerd-Klaus, "Houston Stewart Chamberlains germanischer Mythos," Pol. Stud., 18, 1967, 568-83.

3160. _____, "Von Dostojewski zum Dritten Reich Arthur Moeller van den Bruch und die 'Konservative Revolution'," Pol. Stud., 20, 1969, 184-200.

3161. KAUFMANN, Paul, "An der Wiege der deutschen Malkunst des neunzehnten Jahrhunderts Niebuhr und Cornelius," Pr. Jbb., 212, 1928, 290-309.

3162. KINDERMANN, Heinz, "Romantik und Realismus," Vjschr. f. Litw., 4, 1926, 651-75.

3163. KIRCHEISEN, Frédéric M., "Napoléon Ier et les poètes allemands," Rev. d'hist. dipl., 46, 1932, 487-96.

3164. KLAGES, Helmut, "Zum Standort der deutschen Soziologie im ersten Jahrhundertdrittel," Jb. F. Sozialw., 15, 1964, 256-80.

3165. KLUCKHOHN, Paul, "Neueste Literatur zur deutschen Romantik," Vjschr. f. Litw., 7, 1929, 705-44.

3166. KNEBEL, Karl, "Das Mindener Sonntagsblatt (1817-53) Ein Beitrag zur Geschichte des westfälischen Geistesleben in der ersten Hälfte des 19. Jahrhunderts," Westf. Zs., 66, 1908, 91-162.

3167. KRAUSE, Werner, "Ludwig Gall--ein deutscher Utopist," Zs. f. Geschw., 4, 1956, 307-25.

3168. KREFT, Jürgen, "Die Entstehung der dialektischen Geschichtsmetaphysik aus den Gestalten des utopischen Bewusstseins bei Novalis," Vjschr. f. Litw., 39, 1965, 213-45.

3169. KUEHNEMUND, Richard, "German Prophets of Doom and Hope," J. Hist. Ideas, 3, 1942, 443-57.

3170. KUPISCH, Karl, "Der Deutsche zwischen 1850 und 1865," ZRGG, 18, 1966, 108-42.

3171. LANGENBUCHER, Wolfgang R., "Der Roman als Quelle geistesgeschichtlicher Forschung," ZRGG, 20, 1968, 259-72.

3172. LENEL, Edith, "Das Americabild von vier Deutschen im frühen 19. Jahrhundert," GiWuU, 20, 1969, 409-22.

3173. LEWALD, Ursula and Rudolf SCHENDA, "Leben und Briefe des Bonner Germanisten Anton Birlinger," Rhein. Vjsbll.,

32, 1968, 419-29.

3174.   LIEPE, Wolfgang, "Hebel zwischen G. H. Schubert u. L.
         Feuerbach Studien zur Entstehung seines Weltbildes,"
         Vjschr. f. Litw., 26, 1952, 447-77.

3175.   LIPPERT, Werner, "Brücken zu den Geschichtsromanen von
         Willibald Alexis (1798-1871)," Bär v. Ber., 16, 1967,
         17-47.

3176.   LÖHNEYSEN, Wolfgang von, "Der Einfluss der Reichsgründ-
         ung von 1871 auf Kunst und Kunstgeschmach in Deutsch-
         land," ZRGG, 12, 1960, 17-44.

3177.   MAYER-MONTFORT, Elvira, "Dorothea Schlegel im Ideen-
         kreis ihrer zeit und in ihrer religiösen, philosophischen
         und ethischen Entwicklung," Gelbe Hefte, 2, 1925/26,
         414-33, 489-517.

3178.   MEAKIN, David, "Decadence and the Devaluation of Work:
         The Revolt of Sorel, Péguy and the German Expression-
         ists," Eur. Stud. Rev., 1, 1971, 49-60.

3179.   MERLO, J. J., "Zur Geschichte des Kölner Theaters im
         18. und 19. Jahrhundert," Ann. Niederrhein, 50, 1890,
         145-219.

3180.   MÜLLER, Iso, "Das Wirken des Bamberger Romantikers
         Ignaz Christian Schwarz in der Schweiz," Zs. f. Schw.
         Gesch., 25, 1945, 66-99.

3181.   MÜLLER, Joachim, "Das Weltbild Wilhelm Raabes,"
         Vjschr. f. Litw., 21, 1943, 196-227.

3182.   NETTESHEIM, Josefine, "Wissen und Dichtung in der ers-
         ten Hälfte des 19. Jahrhunderts am Beispiel der geistigen
         Welt Annettes von Droste-hülshoff," Vjschr. f. Litw., 32,
         1958, 516-53.

3183.   NEUBAUER, John, "Dr. John Brown (1735-88) and Early
         German Romanticism," J. Hist. Ideas, 27, 1967, 367-82.

3184.   O'BOYLE, Lenore, "The Problem of an Excess of Educated
         Men in Western Europe, 1800-1850," J. Mod. Hist., 42,
         1970, 471-95.

3185.   PAULUS, Rudolf, "Zur Philosophie und Religion des deutschen
         Idealismus," Zs. f. Theol. u. K., 32, 1924, 121-50, 342-
         81; 35, 1927, 396-402; 36, 1928, 67-80; 38, 1930, 299-
         321; 40, 1932, 244-68.

3186.   PFANNKUCH, Karl, "Zeitgeist um die Jahrhundertwende
         Methodisches - Philosophisches - Literarisches," ZRGG,
         14, 1962, 98-123.

3187.   PLENGE, Johann, "Realistische Glossen zu einer Geschichte
         des deutschen Idealismus," Arch. f. Sozialw. u. Sozial-
         pol., 32, 1911, 1-35.

3188.   PÖLNITZ, Winfrid von, "Friedrich Overbeck Ein Lebenslauf
         im Dienste der christlichen Kunst," Gelbe Hefte, 4, 1927/
         28, 407-38.

3189.   RAECK, Kurt, "Das 'Deutsche Theater zu Berlin' unter der
         Direktion Adolph l'Arrange," Mitt. d. Ver. f. Gesch.,
         45, 1928, 1-39.

3190.   REIN, Wilhelm, "Hermann Wislicenus Ein Künstlerleben
         aus der Gegenwart," Pr. Jbb., 44, 1879, 246-67.

3191.   REQUADT, Paul, "Deutsche Romantik," Arch. f. KuG., 24,

1934, 257-71.
3192. RICHTER, Fritz, "Willibald Alexis (1798-1871), " Jb. d. Schles.-Fried.-Wilh. Univ z. Breslau, 16, 1971, 275-85.
3193. RINTELEN, Fritz-Joachim von, "Entwicklung des Idealismus in Deutschland nach Hegel, " J. Hist. Phil., 5, 1967, 237-44.
3194. ROHDE, Ursula, "Wilhelm Titel Studie über einen pommerschen Maler aus der ersten Hälfte des 19. Jahrhunderts, " Hamb. Mittel-u. ostdt. Forsch., 4, 1963, 94-156.
3195. ROHRMOSER, G., "Metaphysik und das Ende der Emanzipation (Nietzsche-Marx), " Neue Zs. f. system. Theol. u. RP, 12, 1970, 229-66.
3196. RÜSCH, Ernst G., "Christliche Motive in der Dichtung Eduard Mörikes, " Theol. Zs., 11, 1955, 206-23.
3197. SASS, Hans-Martin, "Daseinsbedeutende Funktionen von Wissen und Glauben in Jahrzehnt 1860-70, " ZRGG, 20, 1968, 113-38.
3198. SCHARFE, Wolfgang, "Topographische Aufnahmen in Brandenburg 1816-1821 Das Deckersche Kartenwerk, " Jb. f. Gesch. M. O. Dtschl., 18, 1969, 180-215.
3199. SCHASLER, Dr. Max, "Die staatlichen Einrichtungen für den Kunstunterricht in Deutschland, " Schmoll. Jb., 3, 1879, 297-351.
3200. SCHATZKY, Brigitte, "The German Stage in the Nineteenth Century, " Ger. Life Letters, 13, 1950/60, 207-13.
3201. SCHIRMER, Walter F., "German Literature, Historiography and Theology in Nineteenth Century England, " Ger. Life Letters, 1, 1947/48, 165-74.
3202. SCHMITT, Carl, "Romantik, " Hochland, 22(1), 1924/25, 157-71.
3203. SCHNABEL, Franz, "Böhmen, das Reich und die deutsche Romantik, " Hochland, 36(2), 1938/39, 89-103.
3204. SCHNEIDER, Arthur, "Johann Christian Lotsch (1790-1873) Ein badischer Bildhauer und Zeichner des Klassizismus, " ZGORh., 109, 1961, 323-40.
3205. _____, "Künstler und Landesherr Briefwechsel zwischen Hans Thomas und Grossherzog Friedrich I, " ZGORh., 105, 1957, 512-26.
3206. SCHOEPS, Hans-Joachim, "Geistesgeschichte im Spiegel der Grossen Brockhaus II, " ZRGG, 7, 1955, 343-50.
3207. _____, "Neues zur preussischen Geistesgeschichte des 19. Jahrhunderts, " Zs. f. KiG, 76, 1965, 282-306.
3208. SCHRÖTER, Klaus, "Chauvinism and its tradition: German Writers and the Outbreak of the First World War, " Ger. Rev., 43, 1968, 120-35.
3209. SCHULTZ, Franz, "'Romantik' und 'Romantisch' als Literarhistorische Terminologien und Begriffsbildungen, " Vjschr. f. Litw., 2, 1924, 349-66.
3210. SCHULTZE, Ernst, "Die deutschen Volksbibliotheken, " Arch. f. Sozialw. u. Sozialpol., 25, 1907, 250-70.
3211. SEDLMAYR, Hans, "Die Grenzen der Stilgeschichte und die Kunst des 19. Jahrhunderts, " H. Jb., 74, 1954, 394-404.

3212.   SEIBERTH, Philipp, "Romanticism," Ger. Rev., 1, 1926,
        336-43.
3213.   SEIDLIN, Oskar, "Georg Brandes (1842-1927)," J. Hist.
        Ideas, 3, 1942, 415-42.
3214.   SELL, Friedrich Carl, "Thomas Mann and the Problem of
        Anti-Intellectualism," Ger. Rev., 15, 1940, 281-91.
3215.   SENGLE, Friedrich, "Voraussetzungen und Erscheinungs-
        formen der deutschen Restaurationsliteratur," Vjschr. f.
        Litw., 30, 1956, 268-94.
3216.   SIETZ, Reinhold, "Heinrich Giehme Ein Beitrag zur Ge-
        schichte des Karlsruher Musiklebens vor 100 Jahren,"
        ZGORh., 104, 1956, 291-302.
3217.   SIMON, Karl, "Romantik und bildende Kunst in Deutsch-
        land," Pr. Jbb., 171, 1918, 165-79.
3218.   STANGE, Carl, "Novalis Weltanschauung," Neue Zs. f.
        system. Theol. u. RP, 1, 1923, 609-36.
3219.   STEINHAUSEN, Georg, "Beiträge zur Geistesgeschichte der
        letzten Jahrzehnte," Arch. f. KuG., 16, 1926, 222-58.
3220.   TAMPIER-METZKER, G., "Anton Johann Gross-Hoffinger
        Leben und Werk eines Publizisten des Vormärz," MIÖG,
        75, 1967, 403-30.
3221.   THIELE, Joachim, "Paul Carus und Ernst Mach: Wechsel-
        beziehungen zwischen deutscher und amerikanischer Phi-
        losophie um 1900," Isis, 62, 1971, 208-19.
3222.   THILLY, Frank, "Romanticism and Rationalism," Phil. Rev.,
        22, 1913, 107-32.
3223.   THOMAS, R. Hinton, "German Intellectuals on the Eve of
        1848," Ger. Life Letters, 2, 1948/49, 13-21.
3224.   TYMMS, Ralph, "Cultural Affinities between Berlin and
        Vienna in the Vormärz," Ger. Life Letters, 4, 1950/51,
        153-61.
3225.   _____, "Romanticism in Germany," Ger. Life Letters,
        2, 1937/38, 140-49.
3226.   VALDENAIRE, Arthur, "Heinrich Hübsch Eine Studie zur
        Baukunst der Romantik," ZGORh., 78, 1926, 421-44,
        527-56; 79, 1927, 181-206.
3227.   WALTER, Paula, "Hyacinth Holland Ein Münchener Samm-
        ler, Lehrer und Gelehrter des 19. Jahrhunderts,"
        Gelbe Hefte, 4, 1927/28, 50-70.
3228.   WEHRUNG, Georg, "Über Grösse und Problematik des
        deutschen Idealismus," Z. f. systematische Theol., 7,
        1930, 284-311.
3229.   WEINHOLD, Karl, "Friedrich Heinrich Jacobi," Pr. Jbb.,
        24, 1869, 645-78.
3230.   WENBERG, Gotthart, "Utopie und fin de siècle Zur deut-
        schen Literaturkritik vor der Jahrhundertwende," Vjschr.
        f. Litw., 43, 1969, 685-706.
3231.   WENDEHORST, A., "Frankens Barockkultur im Urteil des
        19. Jahrhunderts," Jb. f. fränk. Ldforsch., 27, 1967,
        383-98.
3232.   WEYDT, Günther, "Biedermeier und junges Deutschland
        Eine Literatur- und Problemschau," Vjschr. f. Litw.,
        25, 1951, 506-21.

3233.   , "Literarisches Biedermeier," Vjschr. f. Litw.,
          9, 1931, 628-51.
3234.   WHYTE, John, "Economic Influences on the Literature of
          the Nineteenth Century," Ger. Rev., 2, 1927, 287-97.
3235.   WILLOUGHBY, L. A., "Classic and Romantic--A Re-
          Examination," Ger. Life Letters, 6, 1952/53, 1-11.
3236.   WINTTERLIN, A., "Der Stuttgarter Kaufmann Gottlob Hein-
          rich Rapp. 1761-1832 Ein Beitrag zur württembergischen
          Kunst- und Kulturgeschichte," Zs. F. Württbg. LG, 1,
          1892, 141-74.
3237.   WUNDT, Max, "Die Philosophie in der Zeit des Bieder-
          meiers," Vjschr. f. Litw., 13, 1935, 118-48.
3238.   ZEYDEL, Edwin H., "The Concepts 'Classic and Romantic',"
          Ger. Rev., 19, 1944, 161-69.

Ernst Mortiz Arndt (1769-1860)

3239.   BRANDIS, Carl G., "Briefe v. Ernst Moritz Arndt aus dem
          Frankfurter Parlament," Deutsche Rundschau, 81, 117-28.
3240.   "BRIEFE von Dahlmann, Ernst Moritz Arndt und Falck an
          den Oberappellationsgerichtsrat Burchardi in Kiel," Zs.
          d. Gesellschaft f. Schlesw.-holstein. Gesch., 42, 1912,
          231ff.
3241.   DOEBNER, R., "E. M. Arndt zur schleswig-holsteinischen
          Frage," HZ, 68, 1892, 444-49.
3242.   DÜHR, Albrecht, "Probleme der Arndt-Biographie," HZ,
          115, 1916, 537-69.
3243.   "ERNST Moritz Arndt," Pr. Jbb., 5, 1860, 470-512.
3244.   GRUNER, Justus von, "Die Glaubwürdigkeit der autobio-
          graphischen Schriften E. M. Arndt's," FBPG, 25, 1913,
          461-74.
3245.   HANOW, v. Wilhelm, ed., "Briefe E. M. Arndts," Pr.
          Jbb., 151, 1913, 461-92.
3246.   HASHAGEN, Justus, "Freiheit und Gebundenheit bei Ernst
          Moritz Arndt," Hist. Vjschr., 26, 1931, 312-19.
3247.   KOESTER, W., "E. M. Arndt über die Erbkaiserpartei und
          über die deutsche Einigung Ungedruckte Briefe Arndts,"
          Deutsche Revue, 40, 1915, 267-82.
3248.   KOHN, Hans, "Arndt and the Character of German Nation-
          alism," AHR, 54, 1948/49, 787-803.
3249.   LOH, Gerhard, "Unbekannte Arndtbriefe in Autographenkatalo-
          gen," Wiss. Zs. Univ. Greifswald Ges.-u. Sprachwiss.
          Reihe, 14, 1965, 325-43.
3250.   MEISNER, H., "E. M. Arndt im Parlament," Deutsche Re-
          vue, 21, 1896, 345-51.
3251.   , "Ernst Moritz Arndt im Parlamente," Berliner
          Bär, 38, 1897, 448-50; 39, 1897, 459-61.
3252.   MEUSEL, Friedrich, "E. M. Arndt und Friedrich Wilhelm
          IV über die Kaiserfrage," Hohenzollernjahrbuch, 12, 1908,
          231-39.
3253.   MÜSEBECK, Ernst, "Die Einleitung des Verfahrens gegen
          E. M. Arndt Eine Untersuchung zur Geschichte der

Reaktion in Preussen nach 1815," HZ, 105, 1910, 515-63.
3254. _____, "Ernst Moritz Arndts Stellung zum Friedericianischen Preussen und zur französischen Revolution," Pr. Jbb., 117, 1904, 255-91.
3255. _____, "Eine neu aufgefunde Schrift E. M. Arndts aus dem Jahre 1810," Pr. Jbb., 141, 1910, 78-105.
3256. PRAHL, Dr. Karl, "Die Soldatenkatschismen von E. M. Arndt," Pr. Jbb., 153, 1913, 450-64.
3257. SCHILDHAUER, Johannes, et al., "Ernst Moritz Arndt 1769-1969," Wiss. Z. Univ. Greifswald. Ges.-u. Sprach-wiss. Reihe, 18, 1969.
3258. SCHNEIDER, Martha, "Ernst Moritz Arndt und der 'Rheinische Merkur'," FBPG, 34, 1922, 25-48.
3259. SCHREINER, Helmuth, "Zur Wiederentdeckung Arndts," Zeitwende, 11(2), 1934/35, 281-90.

Bettina von Arnim (1785-1859)

3260. KAYSER, Rudolf, "Bettina von Arnim and the Jews," Hist. Judaica, 20, 1958, 47-60.
3261. MALLON, Otto, "Zu Bettina von Arnims Berliner politischen Schriften," FBPG, 45, 1933, 150-60.
3262. MOLTMANN-WENDEL, Elisabeth, "Bettina von Arnim und Schleiermacher," Ev. Theol., 31, 1971, 395-414.

Bruno Bauer (1809-1882)

3263. BARNIKOL, Ernst, "Bruno Bauers Kampf gegen Religion und Christentum und die Spaltung der vormärzlichen preussischen Opposition," Zs. f. KiG, 46, 1928, 1-34.
3264. MEHLHAUSEN, Joachim, "Die religionsphilosophische Begründung der spekulativen Theologie Bruno Bauers," Zs. f. KiG, 78, 1967, 102-29.
3265. ROSEN, Z., "The Radicalism of a Young Hegelian: Bruno Bauer," Rev. Pol., 33, 1971, 377-404.
3266. SASS, Hans-Martin, "Bruno Bauers Idee der 'Rheinischen Zeitung'," ZRGG, 19, 1967, 321-32.

Georg Büchner (1813-1837)

3267. IMMELT, K., "Der 'Hessische Landbote' und seine Bedeutung für die revolutionäre Bewegung des Vormärz im Grossherzogtum Hessen-Darmstadt," Mitt. Oberhess. Gesch. vereins, 52, 1967, 13-77.
3268. WERNER, Fritz, "Georg Büchners Drama 'Dantons Tod' und das Problem der Revolution," WaG, 12, 1952, 167-76.

Wilhelm Dilthey (1833-1911)

See also entries 448, 465, 2866

3269.   BERGSTRAESSER, Arnold, "Wilhelm Dilthey and Max
        Weber: An Empirical Approach to Historical Synthesis,"
        Ethics, 57, 1946/47, 92-110.

3270.   DILTHEY, Wilhelm, "Auffassung und Analyse des Menschen
        im 15. und 16. Jahrhundert," Arch. f. Gesch. d. Phil.,
        4, 1891, 604-51.

3271.   _____, "Das natürliche System des Geisteswissenschaften
        im siebzehnten Jahrhundert," Arch. f. Gesch. d. Phil.,
        5, 1892, 480-502; 6, 1893, 60-127, 225-56, 347-79, 509-
        45.

3272.   _____, "Der Streit Kants mit der Censur über das Recht
        freier Religionsforschung," Arch. f. Gesch. d. Phil., 3,
        1890, 418-50.

3273.   _____, "Thomas Carlyle," Arch. f. Gesch. d. Phil., 4,
        1891, 260-85.

3274.   FLACH, Werner, "Die wissenschaftstheoretische Einschat-
        zung der Selbstbiographie bei Dilthey," Arch. f. Gesch.
        d. Phil., 52, 1970, 172-86.

3275.   FRISCHEISEN-KÖHLER, M., "Wilhelm Dilthey," Kant Stu-
        dien, 17, 161ff.

3276.   GROETHUYSEN, B., "Wilhelm Dilthey," Deutsche Rundschau,
        154, 69ff.

3277.   HÄNSEL, Ludwig, "Die Philosophie Wilhelm Diltheys,"
        Hochland, 35(2), 1937/38, 277-94.

3278.   HÖFER, Jos., "Das Lebenswerk W. Diltheys in theologischer
        Sicht," Theol. Qu.-Schr., 115, 1934, 319-60, 471-90;
        116, 1935, 189-202.

3279.   HOLBORN, Hajo, "Wilhelm Dilthey and the Critique of His-
        torical Reason," J. Hist. Ideas, 11, 1950, 93-118.

3280.   HORKHEIMER, Max, "The Relation between Psychology and
        Sociology in the Work of Wilhelm Dilthey," Zs. f. Sozial-
        forschung, 8, 1939, 430-43.

3281.   KORNBERG, Jacques, "Wilhelm Dilthey on the Self and His-
        tory: Some Theoretical Roots of Geistesgeschichte,"
        Cen. Eur. Hist., 5, 1972, 295-317.

3282.   KRAUSSER, Peter, "Dilthey's philosophische Anthropologie,"
        J. Hist. Phil., 1, 1963, 211-21.

3283.   _____, "Dilthey's Revolution in the Theory of the Struc-
        ture of Scientific Inquiry and Rational Behavior," Rev.
        Metaphysics, 22, 1968/69, 262-80.

3284.   KUPISCH, Karl, "Wilhelm Dilthey," ZRGG, 14, 1962, 1-19.

3285.   LORENZ, Heinz, "Das Bewusstsein der Krise und der Ver-
        such ihrer Überwindung bei Dilthey und Graf Yorck von
        Wartenburg," ZRGG, 11, 1959, 59-68.

3286.   MAKKREEL, Rudolf A., "Wilhelm Dilthey and the Neo-
        Kantians: The Distinction of the Geisteswissenschaften
        and the Kulturwissenschaften," J. Hist. Phil., 7, 1969,
        423-40.

3287.   MASUR, Gerhard, "Wilhelm Dilthey und die europäische

Geistesgeschichte, " Vjschr. f. Litw., 12, 1934, 479-503.
3288. _____, "Wilhelm Dilthey and the History of Ideas, " J.
Hist. Ideas, 13, 1952, 94-107.
3289. MORGAN, George A., "Wilhelm Dilthey, " Phil. Rev., 42,
1933, 351-80.
3290. MÜLLER, Joachim, "Dilthey und das Problem der historischen Biographie, " Arch. f. KuG., 23, 1933, 89-108.
3291. SCHLEGEL, Wolfgang, "Der Standort Diltheys und Yorcks
von Wartenburg, " ZRGG, 12, 1960, 45-59.
3292. SCHRAMM, Erich, "Erinnerungen an Wilhelm Dilthey, ZRGG,
7, 1955, 355-58.
3293. SCHREY, Heinz-Horst, "Leben, Geschichte, Existenz Die
Philosophie Wilhelm Diltheys und ihre Nachfolge, " Theol.
Rs., 16, 1944, 20-37.
3294. SCHULTZ, "Wesen und Begründung der Religion bei Wilhelm
Dilthey, " Zs. f. Theol. u. K., 29, 1921, 21-45.
3295. SPANN, Othmar, "Zur soziologischen Auseinandersetzung
mit Wilhelm Dilthey, " ZgesStw., 59, 1903, 193-222.
3296. STANGE, Carl, "Dilthey und Graf York von Wartenburg, "
Zs. f. systematische Theol., 2, 1924/25, 235-45.
3297. STEIN, Ludwig, "Historical Optimism: Wilhelm Dilthey, "
Phil. Rev., 33, 1924, 329-44.
3298. TAPPER, Bonno, "Dilthey's Methodology of the Geisteswissenschaften, " Phil. Rev., 34, 1925, 333-49.
3299. TUMARKIN, Anna, "Wilhelm Dilthey, " Arch. f. Gesch. d.
Phil., 25, 1911, 143-53.
3300. WANSTRAT, Renate, "Das sozialwissenschaftliche Verstehen
bei Dilthey und Max Weber, " Schmoll. Jb., 70, 1950, 19-
44.
3301. ZEECK, Hans, "Im Druck erschienene Schriften von Wilhelm
Dilthey, " Arch. f. Gesch. d. Phil., 25, 1911, 156-61.

Ludwig Feuerbach (1804-1872)

See also entries 2293, 2348

3302. BANKS, Robert, "Ludwig Feuerbach: Still 'A Thorn in the
Flesh of Modern Theology'?, " Evan. Q., 44, 1972, 30-
46.
3303. BAYER, Oswald, "Gegen Gott für den Menschen Zu Feuerbach Lutherrezeption, " Zs. f. Theol. u. K., 69, 1972,
34-71.
3304. CORNEHL, Peter, "Feuerbach und die Naturphilosophie Zur
Genese der Anthropologie und Religionskritik des jungen
Feuerbach, " Neue Zs. f. system. Theol. u. RP, 11,
1969, 37-93.
3305. EBBINGHAUS, Julius, "Ludwig Feuerbach, " Vjschr. f.
Litw., 8, 1930, 283-305.
3306. FINGER, Otto, "Von der anthropologisch-materialistischen
Religionskritik zur historisch-materialistischen Ideologien-
analyze, " Dt. Zs. f. Phil., 20, 1972, 1110-35.
3307. GAGERN, Michael, "Ludwig Feuerbachs 'dritter und letzter

Gedanke'," Freiburger Zs. f. Phil., 17, 1970, 139-60.

3308.   GLASSE, John, "Barth on Feuerbach," Har. Theol. Rev.,
57, 1964, 69-96.

3309.   HARICH, Wolfgang, "Über Ludwig Feuerbach," Dt. Zs. f.
Phil., 2, 1954, 279-87.

3310.   HUMMEL, Gert, "Die Sinnlichkeit der Gottesfahrung. Ludwig Feuerbachs Philosophie als Anfrage an die Theologie
der Gegenwart," Neue Zs. f. system. Theol. u. RP, 12,
1970, 44-62.

3311.   KANTZENBACH, Friedrich W., "Im Schatten der Grösseren:
Friedrich Feuerbach, Bruder und Gesinnungsgefährte Ludwigs Feuerbachs," Mitteil. Ver. Gesch. Stadt Nürnberg,
57, 1970.

3312.   KOSING, Alfred, "Ludwig Feuerbachs materialistische Er-
kenntnistheorie," Dt. Zs. f. Phil., 20, 1972, 1090-1109.

3313.   LEHMANN, Gerhard, "Feuerbach Zwei Notizen aus der
unveröffentlichten Selbstphilosophie," Arch. f. Gesch. d.
Phil., 37, 1926, 40-48.

3314.   ORSINI, G. N. G., "Feuerbach's Supposed Objection to
Hegel," J. Hist. Ideas, 30, 1969, 85-90.

3315.   RICHTER, Friedrich, "Ludwig Feuerbach, der wissenschaftliche Sozialismus und die Arbeiterklasse," Dt. Zs. f.
Phil., 20, 1972, 1077-89.

3316.   SCHMIDT, Erik, "Ludwig Feuerbach Lehre von der Religion," Neue Zs. f. system. Theol. u. RP, 8, 1966, 1-
35.

3317.   SCHUFFENHAUER, Werner, "Materialismus und Naturbe-
trachtung bei Ludwig Feuerbach," Dt. Zs. f. Phil., 20,
1972, 1461-73.

3318.   STIEHLER, Gottfried, "Ludwig Feuerbachs Kritik der Religion," Dt. Zs. f. Phil., 20, 1972, 1136-45.

3319.   VOGEL, Manfred H., "The Barth-Feuerbach Confrontation,"
Har. Theol. Rev., 59, 1966, 27-52.

3320.   WALLMANN, Johannes, "Ludwig Feuerbach und die theologische Tradition," Zs. f. Theol. u. K., 67, 1970,
56-86.

3321.   WEBER, Joseph C., "Feuerbach, Barth and Theological
Methodology," J. Rel., 46, 1966, 24-36.

3322.   WINTZER, Wilhelm, "Die ethischen Untersuchungen Ludwig
Feuerbachs," Arch. f. Gesch. d. Phil., 12, 1899, 187-
201.

Johann Gottlieb Fichte (1762-1814)

3323.   ARENS, Franz, "J. G. Fichte im Spiegel eigenen und
Freunden Briefwechsels," Hochland, 22(2), 1924/25, 240-
45.

3324.   BARNOUW, Jeffrey, "'Der Trieb, bestimmt zu werden'
Hölderlin, Schiller und Schelling als Antwort auf Fichte,"
Vjschr. f. Litw., 46, 1972, 248-93.

3325.   BAUMGARTNER, Hans Michael, "Transzendentales Denken
und Atheismus der Atheismusstreit um Fichte," Hochland,

56, 1963/64, 40-48.

3326.   BETTERIDGE, H. T., "Fichte's Political Ideas: A Retro-
        spect," Ger. Life Letters, 1, 1936/37, 293-304.

3327.   BUHR, Manfred, "Das Verhältnis von Handeln und Denken
        in der Philosophie Johann Gottlieb Fichtes," Dt. Zs. f.
        Phil., 10, 1962, 429-42.

3328.   ERBEN, Wilhelm, "Fichte-Studien," Hist. Vjschr., 21,
        1922/23, 282-304.

3329.   "Eine ERINNERUNG an Johann G. Fichte," Pr. Jbb., 7,
        1861, 244-60.

3330.   GOLDAMMER, Peter, "Der Gelehrte als Erzieher der
        Menschheit Ein Beitrag zur Gesellschaftslehre J. G.
        Fichtes," Dt. Zs. f. Phil., 4, 1956, 35-59.

3331.   HASHAGEN, Justus, "Fichte und Sozialismus," Jbb. f. Na-
        tionalökon. u. Stat., 136, 1932, 495-98.

3332.   HAUCK, Dr. P., "Das Problem der Erziehung bei Joh.
        Gottlieb Fichte," Pr. Jbb., 156, 1914, 193-213.

3333.   HIELSCHER, Hans, "Die Aussöhnung von 'Glauben' und
        'Denken' in Fichtes Religionslehre," Zs. f. Theol. u.
        K., 20, 1910, 141-53.

3334.   HINTZE, Hedwig, "Fichte und Frankreich," Hist. Vjschr.,
        28, 1933/34, 535-59.

3335.   HOLZ, Harald, "Die Struktur der Dialektik in den Früh-
        schriften von Fichte und Schelling," Arch. f. Gesch. d.
        Phil., 52, 1970, 71-90.

3336.   KAUFMANN, F. W., "Fichte and National Socialism,"
        Amer. Pol. Sc. Rev., 36, 1942, 460-70.

3337.   KÖRNER, Rudolf, "Die Wirkung der Reden Fichtes," FBPG,
        40, 1927, 65-87.

3338.   KOHN, Hans, "The Paradox of Fichte's Nationalism," J.
        Hist. Ideas, 10, 1949, 319-43.

3339.   LANZ, Dr., "Fichte und der transzendentale Wahrheitsbe-
        griff," Arch. f. Gesch. d. Phil., 26, 1912/13, 1-25.

3340.   LEHMANN, Max, "Fichtes Reden an die deutsche Nation vor
        der preussischen Zensur," Pr. Jbb., 82, 1895, 501-15.

3341.   LEIGHTON, J. A., "Fichte's Conception of God," Phil. Rev.,
        4, 1895, 143-53.

3342.   LINDNER, Herbert, "Fichtes Humanismus der Tat," Dt. Zs.
        f. Phil., 10, 1962, 443-55.

3343.   LUCKA, Emil, "Spinoza und Fichte," Pr. Jbb., 153, 1913,
        193-216.

3344.   MÜSEBECK, Ernst, "Das Verhalten der preussischen Re-
        gierung im Fichteschen Atheismusstreit," HZ, 115, 1916,
        278-310.

3345.   SCHAUB, Edward L., "J. G. Fichte and Anti-Semitism,"
        Phil. Rev., 49, 1940, 37-52.

3346.   ————, "J. G. Fichte as a Christian Preacher," J. Rel.,
        19, 1939, 134-65.

3347.   SCHMOLLER, G., "Johann Gottlieb Fichte Eine Studie aus
        dem Gebiete der Ethik und der Nationalökonomie," Jbb. f.
        Nationalökon. u. Stat., 5, 1865, 1-62.

3348.   SCHOLZ, Heinrich, "Fichte und Napoleon," Pr. Jbb., 152,
        1913, 1-12.

3349. SCHUFFENHAUER, Heinz, "Das Problem Erziehung und Gesellschaft in J. G. Fichtes 'Reden an die deutsche Nation'," Dt. Zs. f. Phil., 10, 1962, 1359-70.
3350. TALBOT, Ellen B., "The Philosophy of Fichte in its Relation to Pragmatism," Phil. Rev., 16, 1907, 488-505.
3351. WELLNHOFER, Dr. Matthias, "Unveröffentlichte Briefe Johann Gottlieb Fichtes an Fr. Ph. Im. Niethammer," H. Jb., 48, 1928, 461-71.
3352. ZELLER, E., "Johann Gottlieb Fichte als Politiker," HZ, 4, 1860, 1-35.

Theodor Fontane (1819-1898)

See also entry 451

3353. BARLOW, D., "Fontane and the Aristocracy," Ger. Life Letters, 8, 1954/55, 182-91.
3354. DANKE, Rudolf, "Unser Ehrenmitglied Theodor Fontane," Bär v. Ber., 14, 1965, 281-311.
3355. DAVIS, Arthur L., "Fontane and the German Empire," Ger. Rev., 11, 1936, 258-73.
3356. _____, "Fontane as a Political Thinker," Ger. Rev., 8, 1933, 183-94.
3357. FRICKE, Hermann, ed., "Theodor Fontane Privat," Bär v. Ber., 8, 1959, 69-83.
3358. _____, "Theodor Fontanes 'Der Deutsche Krieg 1866' und seine militärgeschichtlichen Helfer," Jb. f. Gesch. M. O. Dtschl., 15, 1966, 203-24.
3359. _____, "Theodor Fontanes Kriegsgefangenschaft 1870," Bär v. Ber., 5, 1955, 53-73.
3360. _____, "Theodor Fontanes letzter Wille und seine Vollstreckung," Bär v. Ber., 11, 1962, 86-101.
3361. _____, "Theodor Fontanes Parole d'honneur von 1870," Bär v. Ber., 14, 1965, 49-70.
3362. _____, "Über Fontane Verehrung," Bär v. Ber., 19, 1970, 74-83.
3363. HAGEN, Maximilian von, "Theodor Fontanes politische Wandlung," WaG, 17, 1957, 106-12.
3364. HEYNEN, Walter, "Fontane im Gespräch," Bär v. Ber., 19, 1970, 7-50.
3365. _____, "'Was sollen mir da noch die Itzenplitze' Variationen über ein Fontane-Thema," Bär v. Ber., 15, 1966, 71-98.
3366. HÖFELE, Karl H., "Theodor Fontanes Kritik am Bismarckreich," GiWuU, 14, 1963, 337-42.
3367. HOLTZE, Friedrich, "Erinnerungen an Theodor Fontane," Mitt. d. Ver. f. Gesch., 43, 1926, 29-38, 67-78.
3368. JOLLES, Charlotte, "Theodor Fontane und die Ära Manteuffel," FBPG, 49, 1937, 57-114; 50, 1938, 60-85.
3369. KÜHN, Joachim, "Die schöne Frau von Crayen und die Ihren Ein Nachwort zu Fontanes 'Schach von Wuthenow'," Bär v. Ber., 21, 1972, 89-108.

3370.   LUDWIG, Renate, "Theodor Fontanes ethische Sendung,"
        Ev. Theol., 9, 1949/50, 37-43.
3371.   MEY, Hans J., "Fontane in seinen Briefen," Bär v. Ber.,
        19, 1970, 51-73.
3372.   SCHERING, Ernst, "Von der Revolution zur preussischen
        Idee: Fontanes Tätigkeit im Mutterhaus Bethanien und
        der Wandel seiner politischen Einstellung," ZRGG, 22,
        1970, 289-323.
3373.   STURZBECHER, Manfred, "Die Apothekenschwestern im
        Krankenhaus Bethanien und Theodor Fontane," Bär v.
        Ber., 19, 1970, 84-105.
3374.   VOGT, Wilhelm, "Fontane Vater und Sohn," Zeitwende, 11
        (2), 1934/35, 26-35.
3375.   _____, "Die Lebensweisheit des alten Fontane," Zeit-
        wende, 7(2), 1931, 498-515.
3376.   ZWOCH, Gerhard, "Theodor Fontane als Zeit- und Gesell-
        schaftskritiker," Das Parlament, 1969.

                    Ferdinand Freiligrath (1810-1876)

3377.   SCHOOF, Wilhelm, ed., "Briefe aus dem Freundeskreis
        Dingelstedt-Freiligrath-Levin Schücking," Westf. Zs.,
        115, 1965, 219-54.
3378.   _____, "Freiligrath und Andersen," Westf. Zs., 111,
        1961, 119-29.
3379.   _____, "Hoffmann von Fallersleben und Freiligrath,"
        Westf. Zs., 120, 1970, 231-38.
3380.   SCHÜLLER, Andreas, "Hoffmann von Fallersleben und
        Freiligrath als Demokraten vor der rheinischen Polizei,"
        Rhein. Vjsbll., 13, 1948, 193-99.

                      Gustav Freytag (1816-1895)

3381.   BUSSMANN, Walter, "Gustav Freytag Massstäbe seiner Zeit-
        kritik," Arch. f. KuG., 34, 1952, 261-87.
3382.   CARTER, T. E., "Freytag's Soll und Haben: A Liberal
        National Manifesto as a Bestseller," Ger. Life Letters,
        21, 1967/68, 320-29.

                    Joseph von Görres (1776-1848)

3383.   BAUM, W., "Josef Görres und Südtirol," Schlern, 45, 1971,
        354-59.
3384.   BERGSTRÄSSER, Ludwig, "Der Görres-Kreis im bayrischen
        Landtag von 1837," Oberbayrisches Archiv für vaterländ.
        Geschichte, 56, 1912, 248-66.
3385.   BRAUBACH, Max, "Ein neuer Görresfund?," H. Jb., 55,
        1935, 81-90.
3386.   D'ESTER, Karl, "Joseph Görres und die Journalistik,"
        Gelbe Hefte, 3, 1927, 173-86.

3387. DOEBERL, Anton, "Der alte Görres als Ahnherr der katholischen Bewegung in Bayern und Deutschland, " Gelbe Hefte, 3, 1927, 163-72.

3388. FABER, K., "Görres. Weitzel u. d. Revolution (1819), " HZ, 194, 1962, 37-62.

3389. FOLLERT, Pfarrer, "Ein Sonntagabend im Görreshause zu München, " Gelbe Hefte, 3, 1927, 219-40.

3390. GRÜNBECK, Max, "Der Kampf gegen den 'Rheinischen Merkur' in Württemberg, " Gelbe Hefte, 3, 1927, 187-209.

3391. HAGMANN, Reinhard, "Joseph Görres und sein Rheinischer Merkur im zeitgenössischen Urteil 1814 bis 1816, " Jb. f. Gesch. Kunst. d. MRh, 14, 1962, 59-97.

3392. _____, "Die politischen Schriften von Josef Görres im zeitgenössischen Urteil 1817-1822, " Jb. f. Gesch. Kunst d. MRh, 20/21, 1968/69, 109-50.

3393. HERMANNS, Will, "Josef Görres--Cisrhenanbriefe, " Rhein. Vjsbll., 19, 1954, 466-98.

3394. JAPPE, Hajo-Fritz, "Görres' Staatsbild, " Gelbe Hefte, 6, 1929/30, 279-304.

3395. _____, "Die Vorstellungen von Volk und Nation, Staat und Reich im Rheinischen Merkur, " FBPG, 46, 1934, 112-46.

3396. JUST, Leo, "Görres in Heidelberg, " H. Jb., 74, 1954, 416-31.

3397. KAUFMANN, Dr. Paul, "Görres im Kampfe gegen die preussische Reaktion, " H. Jb., 48, 1928, 31-41.

3398. KLINKENBERG, Heinrich, "Besinnung auf Görres, " Gelbe Hefte, 3, 1927, 153-62.

3399. MÜLLER, Karl A. von, "Briefe von und an Josef von Görres, " Arch. f. KuG., 9, 1911, 438-74.

3400. MÜLLER, Karl Alexander von, "Drei Unbekannte Görresbriefe, " Gelbe Hefte, 1, 1924/25, 181-89.

3401. _____, "Der junge Görres, " Arch. f. KuG., 10, 1912, 414-54.

3402. NADLER, Josef, "Görres und Heidelberg, " Pr. Jbb., 198, 1924, 279-91.

3403. OSWALD, Josef, "Goethe, Stein und Görres/Gegensätze und Beziehungen, " Hochland, 26(1), 1928/29, 476-501.

3404. RAAB, Heribert, "Joseph von Görres und die Schweiz, " H. Jb., 89, 1969, 81-115.

3405. SCHMITT, Robert, "Zur Biographie von Josef Görres für die Jahre 1802-1808, " Jb. f. Gesch. Kunst d. MRh, 10, 1958, 67-95.

3406. SCHOOF, Wilhelm, "Josef Görres und die Brüder Grimm, " Jb. f. Gesch. Kunst d. MRh, 8/9, 1956/57, 94-103.

3407. STEIN, Guido, "Die Beziehungen von Joseph von Görres zu Wien nebst zwei Briefe von Görres an Anton Günther, " H. Jb., 73, 1953, 142-52.

3408. STEIN, Robert, "Die Ernte des Görresjahres, " Gelbe Hefte, 3, 1927, 241-57.

3409. TSCHIRCH, Otto, "Joseph Görres, der Rheinische Merkur und der preussische Staat, " Pr. Jbb., 157, 1914, 225-47.

3410. WENTZCKE, Paul, "Josef Görres und das Elsass, " ZGORh.,

68, 1914, 304-19.

Johann von Goethe (1749-1832)

See also entries 466, 3403, 3560, 3561

3411.   BAXA, Jakob, "Goethes volkswirtschaftliche Anschauungen, "
        Jbb. f. Nationalökon. u. Stat., 136, 1932, 365-81.
3412.   BORNHAUSEN, Karl, "Goethe über Schöpfung, Prädestina-
        tion, Gnade," Zs. f. Theol. u. K., 40, 1932, 97-110.
3413.   BRUCK, W. F., "Goethe und die Botanik," Pr. Jbb., 131,
        1908, 29-36.
3414.   COLLARD, A., "Goethe et Quetelet Leurs relations de 1829
        à 1832," Isis, 20, 1933/34, 426-35.
3415.   EKOWSKI, Adalbert, "Goethe als Philosoph," Vjschr. f.
        Litw., 22, 1944, 300-26.
3416.   GOGARTEN, Friedrich, "Goethes Frömmigkeit," Zeitwende,
        8(1), 1932, 161-73.
3417.   HALLER, Rudolf, "Goethe und die Welt des Biedermeiers, "
        Vjschr. f. Litw., 14, 1936, 442-61.
3418.   HEINEMANN, Fritz, "Goethe's Phenomenological Method, "
        Philosophy, 9, 1934, 67-81.
3419.   HENNIG, John, "Zu Goethes Philosophiebegriff," Vjschr. f.
        Litw., 29, 1955, 509-22.
3420.   IHME, Gerhard, "Schiller, Reinhard und Goethe," Zs. F.
        Württbg. LG, 18, 1959, 255-316.
3421.   KURSANOW, G. A., "Die Weltanschauung Goethes," Dt. Zs.
        f. Phil., 7, 1959, 759-78.
3422.   MUTH, Karl, "Goethes Persönlichkeit," Hochland, 29(1),
        1931/32, 518-39.
3423.   PRYS, Joseph, "Das württembergische Nachdruck-privileg
        für Goethe," Zs. F. Württbg. LG, 39, 1933, 136-60.
3424.   RÖCK, Hubert, "Glossen zu Goethes Glossen über das 'Sys-
        tem der Natur'," Arch. f. Gesch. d. Phil., 37, 1926,
        75-99.
3425.   SCHMIDT, Franz, "Goethes Kantianismus und Pragmatismus, "
        ZRGG, 23, 1971, 50-59.
3426.   SCHULTZ, Werner, "Goethes Urfaust und Faust II in ihrer
        religiösen Problematik," Zs. f. Theol. u. K., 35, 1927,
        274-300.
3427.   _____, "Zeit und Ewigkeit in der Weltanschauung Goethes, "
        Zs. f. Theol. u. K., 36, 1928, 288-309.
3428.   SEEBERG, Erich, "Goethes Stellung zur Religion," Zs. f.
        KiG, 51, 1932, 202-27.
3429.   SICKEL, Paul, "Leibnitz und Goethe," Arch. f. Gesch. d.
        Phil., 32, 1920, 1-26.
3430.   TÜMMLER, Hans, "Der Minister Goethe und die Hochschul-
        reform," Arch. f. KuG., 54, 1972, 113-42.
3431.   VÖLKER, Walther, "Goethes religiöse Entwicklung," Theol.
        Zs., 5, 1949, 241-63.
3432.   YOURGRAU, Wolfgang, "Reflections on the Natural Philosophy
        of Goethe," Philosophy, 26, 1951, 69-84.

3433.   ZIEGLER, Klaus, "Zu Goethes Deutung der Geschichte,"
        Vjschr. f. Litw., 30, 1956, 232-67.

        ## Georg Wilhelm Friedrich Hegel (1770-1831)

3434.   AKAMATSU, K., "Wie ist das vernünftige Sollen und die
        Wissenschaft des Sollens bei Hegel möglich," Arch. f.
        Gesch. d. Phil., 38, 1927/28, 1-17.
3435.   ALBRECHT, Erhard, "Hegel und das Problem von Sprache
        und Bewusstsein," Dt. Zs. f. Phil., 18, 1970, 843-60.
3436.   AVINERI, Shlomo, "Hegel and Nationalism," Rev. Pol., 24,
        1962, 461-84.
3437.   _____, "Hegel revisited," J. Contemp. Hist., 3, 1968,
        133-47.
3438.   _____, "A Note on Hegel's Views on Jewish Emancipa-
        tion," Jew. Soc. Stud., 25, 1963, 145-51.
3439.   _____, "The Problem of War in Hegel's Thought," J.
        Hist. Ideas, 22, 1961, 463-74.
3440.   BAEUMLER, Alfred, "Hegel und Kierkegaard," Vjschr. f.
        Litw., 2, 1924, 116-30.
3441.   BARTH, Paul, "Zu Hegel's und Marx Geschichtsphilosophie,"
        Arch. f. Gesch. d. Phil., 8, 1895, 240-55, 315-35.
3442.   BEHN, Siegfried, "Das Schicksal der Hegelschen Philoso-
        phie," Hochland, 29(1), 1931/32, 115-22.
3443.   BÉNARD, M. Ch., "Analytical and Critical Essay upon the
        Aesthetics of Hegel," Journal of Speculative Philosophy,
        1, 1867, 36-52, 92-116, 169-76, 220-24; 2, 1868, 39-46,
        157-64; 3, 1869, 31-46, 147-66, 281-87, 317-36.
3444.   BENZ, Ernst, "Hegels Religionsphilosophie und die Linkshe-
        gelianer," ZRGG, 7, 1955, 247-70.
3445.   BERGMANN, Frithjof H., "The Purpose of Hegel's System,"
        J. Hist. Phil., 2, 1964, 189-204.
3446.   BEYER, Wilhelm R., "Der Begriff der Praxis bei Hegel,"
        Dt. Zs. f. Phil., 6, 1958, 749-76.
3447.   _____, "Hegel als praktischer Verwaltungsbeamter (Lo-
        kal-Schulrat in Nürnberg)," Dt. Zs. f. Phil., 9, 1961,
        747-66.
3448.   _____, "Hegels Mitarbeit am 'Würtembergischen Volks-
        freund," Dt. Zs. f. Phil., 14, 1966, 709-24.
3449.   _____, "Der Stellenwert der französischen Juli-Revolution
        von 1830 im Denken Hegels," Dt. Zs. f. Phil., 19, 1971,
        628-43.
3450.   BORNHAUSEN, Karl, "Theologische Erinnerung an Hegel,"
        Zs. f. Theol. u. K., 39, 1931, 400-06.
3451.   BRACKETT, Anna C., "Analysis of an Article on Hegel,"
        Journal of Speculative Philosophy, 5, 1871, 38-48.
3452.   BRAND, Friedrich, "Über Hegels Anschauungen zur geo-
        graphischen Grundlage der Geschichte in seiner Philoso-
        phie der Weltgeschichte," GiWuU, 16, 1965, 611-23.
3453.   BRANN, Hellmut W., "Rousseaus Einfluss auf die hegelsche
        Staatsphilosophie in ihrer Entwicklung und Vollendung,"
        Schmoll. Jb., 50, 1926, 807-32.

3454.   BROCK, Erich, "Hegel in Berlin," Hochland, 50, 1957/58,
        47-54.
3455.   BÜLOW, Friedrich, "Hegel, der Historismus und die Dialek-
        tik," Schmoll. Jb., 69, 1949, 283-318; 70, 1950, 513-46.
3456.   _____, "Hegels Staats- und Geschichtsphilosophie als
        Gärstoff der Abendländischen Geistesentwicklung,"
        ZgesStw., 100, 1939/40, 457-76.
3457.   CHRISTENSEN, Darrel E., "Nelson and Hegel on the
        Philosophy of History," J. Hist. Ideas, 25, 1964, 439-44.
3458.   COHEN, Morris R., "Hegel's Rationalism," Phil. Rev., 37,
        1928, 283-301.
3459.   COOK, Daniel J., "Language and Consciousness in Hegel's
        Jena Writings," J. Hist. Phil., 10, 1972, 197-211.
3460.   CRITES, Stephen D., "A Critique of Kaufmann's Hegel,"
        J. Hist. Ideas, 27, 1966, 296-307.
3461.   _____, "The Gospel According to Hegel," J. Rel., 46,
        1966, 246-63.
3462.   CUNNINGHAM, G. W., "The Significance of the Hegelian
        Conception of Absolute Knowledge," Phil. Rev., 17, 1908,
        619-42.
3463.   DIETERICH, K., "Buckle und Hegel," Pr. Jbb., 32, 1873,
        257-302, 463-81.
3464.   DÖDERLEIN, Johann L., "Neue Hegel-Dokumente," ZRGG,
        1, 1948, 2-18.
3465.   DOVE, Kenley R., "Hegel's Phenomenological Method,"
        Rev. Metaphysics, 23, 1969/70, 615-41.
3466.   DYDE, S. W., "Hegel's Conception of Crime and Punish-
        ment," Phil. Rev., 7, 1898, 62-71.
3467.   _____, "Hegel's Conception of Freedom," Phil. Rev., 3,
        1894, 655-71.
3468.   DYKE, C., "Collective Decision Making in Rousseau, Kant,
        Hegel, and Mill," Ethics, 80, 1969/70, 21-37.
3469.   EUCHNER, Walter, "Freiheit, Eigentum und Herrschaft bei
        Hegel," Pol. Vjschr., 11, 1970, 531-55.
3470.   FACKENHEIM, Emil L., "On the Actuality of the Rational
        and the Rationality of the Actual," Rev. Metaphysics, 23,
        1969/70, 690-98.
3471.   FALKENHEIM, Hugo, "Eine unbekannte politische Druck-
        schrift Hegels," Pr. Jbb., 138, 1909, 193-210.
3472.   FEUERLEIN, Emil, "Ueber die culturgeschichtliche Bedeu-
        tung Hegel's," HZ, 24, 1870, 314-68.
3473.   FITZER, Joseph, "Hegel and the Incarnation: A Response to
        Hans Küng," J. Rel., 52, 1972, 240-67.
3474.   FLAY, Joseph C., "Hegel's 'Inverted World'," Rev. Meta-
        physics, 23, 1969/70, 662-78.
3475.   FLECHTHEIM, Ossip K., "Hegel and the Problem of Punish-
        ment," J. Hist. Ideas, 8, 1947, 293-308.
3476.   FOSS, Laurence, "Hegel, Spinoza, and a Theory of Experi-
        ence as Closed," Thomist, 35, 1971, 435-46.
3477.   FRANK, Erich, "Das Problem des Lebens bei Hegel und
        Aristoteles," Vjschr. f. Litw., 5, 1927, 609-43.
3478.   GADAMER, Hans-Georg, "Hegel und der geschichtliche
        Geist," ZgesStw., 100, 1939/40, 25-37.

3479. GEDÖ, András, "Die Einheit von Geschichtlichkeit und Objektivität der Erkenntnis," Dt. Zs. f. Phil., 18, 1970, 825-42.

3480. GLOCKNER, Hermann, "Hegel und Schleiermacher im Kampf um Religionsphilosophie und Glaubenslehre," Vjschr. f. Litw., 8, 1930, 233-59.

3481. GROH, Dieter, "Junghegelianer und noch kein Ende," Staat, 3, 1964, 346-57.

3482. GROPP, Rugard Otto, "Geschichte und System der Philosophie--bei Hegel und im Marxismus," Dt. Zs. f. Phil., 4, 1956, 650-71.

3483. _____, "Über Hegels 'Geschichte der Philosophie'," Dt. Zs. f. Phil., 5, 1957, 457-75.

3484. HAINES, Nicolas, "Politics and Protest: Hegel and Social Criticism," Pol. Sci. Q., 86, 1971, 406-28.

3485. HALDANE, Elizabeth S., "Jacob Böhme and his Relation to Hegel," Phil. Rev., 6, 1897, 146-61.

3486. HALDAR, H., "Some Aspects of Hegel's Philosophy," Phil. Rev., 5, 1896, 263-77.

3487. HARRIS, Errol E., "The Philosophy of Nature in Hegel's System," Rev. Metaphysics, 3, 1949/50, 213-28.

3488. HARRIS, Wm. T., "Analysis of Hegel's Phenomenology," Journal of Speculative Philosophy, 2, 1868, 99-102, 181-87.

3489. _____, "Paul Janet and Hegel," Journal of Speculative Philosophy, 1, 1867, 250-56.

3490. HELLER, Hermann, "Hegel und die deutsche Politik," Zs. f. Pol., 13, 1923/24, 132-43.

3491. HERTZ-EICHENRODE, Dieter, " 'Massenpsychologie' bei den Junghegelianern," Int. Rev. Soc. Hist., 7, 1962, 231-59.

3492. HESS, M. Whitcomb, "Hegelianism and the Making of the Modern Mind," Thomist, 14, 1951, 335-50.

3493. HIRSCH, Emanuel, "Die Beisetzung der Romantiker in Hegels Phänomenologie," Vjschr. f. Litw., 2, 1924, 510-32.

3494. _____, "Die Romantik und der Christentum, insbesondere bei Novalis und dem jungen Hegel," Z. f. Systematische Theol., 1, 1923, 28-43.

3495. HOČEVAR, R. K., "Hegel und das Allgemeine Landrecht für die Preussischen Staaten von 1794," Staat, 11, 1972, 189-208.

3496. _____, " 'Staatsbürger' und 'potische Freiheit' im Gesamtwerk Hegels," Pol. Stud., 22, 1971, 131-48.

3497. HÖNIGSWALD, Richard, "Gedanken zur Philosophie Hegels," Pr. Jbb., 226, 1931, 148-68.

3498. HOFFMEISTER, Johannes, "Hegel und Creuzer," Vjschr. f. Litw., 8, 1930, 266-82.

3499. _____, "Zum Geistbegriff des deutschen Idealismus bei Hölderin und Hegel," Vjschr. f. Litw., 10, 1932, 1-44.

3500. HOOK, Sidney, "The Contemporary Significance of Hegel's Philosophy," Phil. Rev., 37, 1928, 237-60.

3501. KAUFMANN, Walter A., "The Hegel Myth and its Method,"

Phil. Rev., 60, 1951, 459-86.

3502.   , "Hegel's Early Antitheological Phase, " Phil. Rev.,
               63, 1954, 3-18.
3503.   KELLY, George Armstrong, "Notes on Hegel's 'Lordship
        and Bondage'," Rev. Metaphysics, 19, 1965/66, 780-802.
3504.   KELM, Hans-Joachim, "Zur Frage der Parteilichkeit in der
        Staatsphilosophischen Theorie Hegels," Dt. Zs. f. Phil.,
        5, 1957, 196-215.
3505.   KLAUS, Georg, "Hegel und die Dialektik in der Formalen
        Logik," Dt. Zs. f. Phil., 11, 1963, 1489-1503.
3506.   KLENNER, Hermann, "Hegel und der Klassencharakter des
        Staates," Dt. Zs. f. Phil., 4, 1956, 642-49.
3507.   KLINE, George L., "Dialectic of Action and Passion in
        Hegel's Phenomenology of Spirit," Rev. Metaphysics,"
        23, 1969/70, 679-89.
3508.   KNOX, T. M., "Hegel and Prussianism," Philosophy, 15,
        1940, 51-63.
3509.   KROEGER, A. E., "The Difference Between the Dialectic
        Method of Hegel and the Synthetic Method of Kant and
        Fichte," Journal of Speculative Philosophy, 6, 1872, 184-
        87.
3510.   KRÜGER, Gerhard, "Die Aufgabe der Hegelforschung,"
        Theol. Rs., 7, 1935, 86-130, 294-318.
3511.   KUHN, Helmut, "Hegels Ästhetik als System des Klassizis-
        mus," Arch. f. Gesch. d. Phil., 40, 1931, 90-105.
3512.   LARENZ, Karl, "Die Bedeutung der völkischen Sitte in
        Hegels Staatsphilosophie," ZgesStw., 98, 1937/38, 109-
        50.
3513.   LEE, Otis, "Method and System in Hegel," Phil. Rev., 48,
        1939, 355-80.
3514.   LEIGHTON, J. A., "Hegel's Conception of God," Phil. Rev.,
        5, 1896, 601-18.
3515.   LUCAS, R. L., "Hegel und die Abstraktion Ein Beitrag
        zur Problematik der modernen Kunst," Vjschr. f. Litw.,
        38, 1964, 361-87.
3516.   MAIER, Hans, "Hegels Schrift über die Reichsverfassung,"
        Pol. Vjschr., 4, 1963, 334-49.
3517.   MARCUSE, Herbert, "An Introduction to Hegel's Philosophy,"
        Zs. f. Sozialforschung, 8, 1939, 394-412.
3518.   MAURER, Reinhart, "Hegels politischer Protestantismus,"
        Staat, 10, 1971, 455-79.
3519.   MAYER, Gustav, "Die Jungheglianer und der preussische
        Staat," HZ, 121, 1920, 413-40.
3520.   McGILVARY, E. B., "The Presupposition Question in
        Hegel's Logic," Phil. Rev., 6, 1897, 497-520.
3521.   MEINECKE, Friedrich, "Hegel und die Anfänge des deutschen
        Machtstaatsgedankens im 19. Jahrhundert," Zs. f. Pol.,
        13, 1923/24, 197-211.
3522.   MERLAN, Philip, "Ist die 'These-Antithese-Synthese-'
        Formel unhegelisch?," Arch. f. Gesch. d. Phil., 53,
        1971, 35-40.
3523.   MÖLLER, Joseph, "Thomistische Analogie und hegelsche
        Dialektik," Theol. Qu.-Schr., 137, 1957, 129-59.

3524. MÜLLER, Friedrich, "Der Denkansatz der Staatsphilosophie bei Rousseau und Hegel," Staat, 10, 1971, 215-27.

3525. MUELLER, Gustav E., "The Hegel Legend of 'Thesis-Antithesis-Synthesis'," J. Hist. Ideas, 19, 1958, 411-14.

3526. _____, "Hegel on the Relation of Church and State," J. Church State, 5, 1963, 95-104.

3527. MÜNCH, Fritz, "Die Problemstellung von Hegels 'Phänomenologie des Geistes'," Arch. f. Gesch. d. Phil., 26, 1912/13, 149-73.

3528. MUIRHEAD, J. H., "How Hegel came to America," Phil. Rev., 37, 1928, 226-40.

3529. MUNSON, Thomas N., "Hegel as Philosopher of Religion," J. Rel., 46, 1966, 9-23.

3530. MURE, G. R. G., "Hegel, Luther, and the Owl of Minerva," Philosophy, 41, 1966, 127-39.

3531. NADLER, Käte, "Die Idee des Tragischen bei Hegel," Vjschr. f. Litw., 19, 1941, 354-68.

3532. _____, "Volksreligion und Christentum in Hegels theologischen Jugendschriften," Zs. f. Theol. u. K., 43, 1935, 254-72.

3533. NANIWADA, Haruo, "Smith-Hegel-Marx (Über den inneren Zusammenhang der drei Sozialphilosophien)," ZgesStw., 111, 1955, 397-417.

3534. NOACK, Hermann, "Zur Problematik der philosophischen und Theologischen Hegel-Interpretation und -Kritik," Neue Zs. f. system. Theol. u. RP, 7, 1965, 161-73.

3535. O'BRIEN, George Denis, "Does Hegel have a Philosophy of History?," Hist. Theor., 10, 1971, 295-317.

3536. PRÉVOST, René, "L'Evolution Economique vue par Hegel," Rev. d'hist. écon. soc., 42, 1964, 74-88.

3537. RAFF, Emil, "Hegels Lehre im Lichte wissenschaftlicher Kritik," Arch. f. Gesch. d. Phil., 38, 1927/28, 180-204.

3538. RAJU, P. T., "The Hegelian Absolute and the Individual," Philosophy, 9, 1934, 336-42.

3539. RAMSEY, Paul, "Existenz and the Existence of God: A Study of Kierkegaard and Hegel," J. Rel., 28, 1948, 157-76.

3540. RIEDEL, Manfred, "Wissen, Glauben und moderne Wissenschaft im Denken Hegels," Zs. f. Theol. u. K., 66, 1969, 171-91.

3541. ROGERS, A. K., "The Hegelian Conception of Thought," Phil. Rev., 9, 1900, 152-66, 293-310.

3542. _____, "The Neo-Hegelian 'Self' and Subjective Idealism," Phil. Rev., 10, 1901, 139-61.

3543. ROHRMOSER, Günter, "Hegels Lehre vom Staat und das Problem der Freiheit in der Modernen Gesellschaft," Staat, 3, 1964, 391-403.

3544. _____, "Die Religionskritik von Karl Marx im Blickpunkt der Hegelschen Religionsphilosophie," Neue Zs. f. system. Theol. u. RP, 2, 1960, 44-64.

3545. _____, "Die theologische Bedeutung von Hegels Auseinandersetzung mit der Philosophie Kants und dem Prinzip der

Subjektivität, " Neue Zs. f. system. Theol. u. RP, 4,
1962, 89-111.

3546. _____, "Die Virulenz der Theologie im Denken Hegels, "
Zeitwende, 41, 1970, 311-22.

3547. ROSENBLOOM, Noah H., "Hegelian Juridical Dialectics as
a Matrix for Jewish Law, " Rev. d. Étud. Juives, 122,
1963, 75-122.

3548. ROSENTHAL, Abigail L., "A Hegelian Key to Hegel's
Method, " J. Hist. Phil., 9, 1971, 205-212.

3549. ROTENSTREICH, Nathan, "Hegel's Image of Judaism, "
Jew. Soc. Stud., 15, 1953, 33-52.

3550. SABINE, George H., "Hegel's Political Philosophy, " Phil.
Rev., 37, 1928, 261-82.

3551. SCHAUB, Edward L., "Hegel's Criticisms of Fichte's Sub-
jectivism, " Phil. Rev., 21, 1912, 566-84; 22, 1913, 17-
37.

3552. SCHLAWE, Fritz, "Die Berliner Jahrbücher für Wissenschaftliche Kritik Ein Beitrag zur Geschichte des He-
gelianismus, " ZRGG, 11, 1959, 240-58, 343-56.

3553. _____, "Die junghegelische Publizistik, " WaG, 20, 1960,
30-50.

3554. SCHMIDT, Ferdinand J., "Hegel und Marx, " Pr. Jbb., 151,
1913, 415-36.

3555. SCHMITZ, Kenneth L., "Hegel's Philosophy of Religion:
Typology and Strategy, " Rev. Metaphysics, 23, 1969/70,
717-36.

3556. SCHOEPS, Hans-Joachim, "Die Ausserchristlichen Religionen
bei Hegel, " ZRGG, 7, 1955, 1-34.

3557. SCHOLZ, Dr. Heinrich, "Hegels erstes System, " Pr. Jbb.,
166, 1916, 1-14.

3558. SCHUBERT, Dr. Johannes, "Der junge Hegel, " Pr. Jbb.,
130, 1907, 389-409.

3559. SCHÜSSLER, Ingrid, "Böhme und Hegel, " Jb. d. Schles.-
Fried.-Wilh. Univ z. Breslau, 10, 1965, 46-58.

3560. SCHULTZ, Werner, "Die Bedeutung des Tragischen für das
Verstehen der Geschichte bei Hegel und Goethe, " Arch. f.
KuG., 38, 1956, 92-115.

3561. _____, "Der Sinn der Geschichte bei Hegel und Goethe, "
Arch. f. KuG., 39, 1957, 209-27.

3562. _____, "Die Transformierung der Theoligia Crucis bei
Hegel und Schleiermacher, " Neue Zs. f. system. Theol.
u. RP, 6, 1964, 290-317.

3563. SCHWARZ, Justus, "Die Bedeutung des Gefühls für Hegels
Erfahrung des Geistes, " Vjschr. f. Litw., 11, 1933, 340-
63.

3564. SCHWEITZER, Carl G., "Geist bei Hegel und heiliger Geist, "
Neue Zs. f. system. Theol. u. RP, 6, 1964, 318-28.

3565. _____, "Zur Methode der Hegel-Interpretation Eine Ent-
gegnung auf Karl Löwiths 'Hegels Aufhebung der christlichen Religion', " Neue Zs. f. system. Theol. u. RP, 5,
1963, 248-62.

3566. SEIDEL, George J., O.S.B., "Hegel and Monasticism, "
Thomist, 35, 1971, 423-34.

3567.   SHEPHERD, William C., "Hegel as a Theologian," Har.
         Theol. Rev., 61, 1968, 583-602.
3568.   SHMUELI, Efraim, "Some Similarities between Spinoza and
         Hegel on Substance," Thomist, 36, 1972, 645-57.
3569.   SIEGMUND, Georg, "Hegels religiöse Urentscheidung,"
         Hochland, 51, 1958/59, 508-20.
3570.   SMITH, Constance I., "Hegel on War," J. Hist. Ideas, 26,
         1965, 282-90.
3571.   SMITH, John E., "Hegel's Critique of Kant," Rev. Meta-
         physics, 26, 1972/73, 438-60.
3572.   SOLOMON, R. C., "Hegel's Concept of 'Geist'," Rev. Meta-
         physics, 23, 1969/70, 642-61.
3573.   STEIGER, Hugo, "Hegel als Rektor des Melanchtlongymnasi-
         ums in Nürnberg," Zeitwende, 7(2), 1931, 533-46.
3574.   STOLTENBERG, H. L., "Hegels Lehre vom Geist und die
         Soziologie," ZgesStw., 89, 1930, 496-513.
3575.   STRAHM, Hans, "Aus Hegels Berner Zeit Nach bisher un-
         bekannten Dokumenten," Arch. f. Gesch. d. Phil., 41,
         1932, 514-33.
3576.   THULSTRUP, Niels, "Kierkegaards Verhältnis zu Hegel,"
         Theol. Zs., 13, 1957, 200-26.
3577.   TÖNNIES, Ferdinand, "Hegels Naturrecht," Schmoll. Jb.,
         56, 1932, 71-85.
3578.   TOWNSEND, H. G., "The Pragmatism of Peirce and
         Hegel," Phil. Rev., 37, 1928, 297-303.
3579.   TRENDELENBURG, "The Logical Question in Hegel's Sys-
         tem," Journal of Speculative Philosophy, 5, 1871, 349-
         59; 6, 1872, 82-93, 163-75, 350-60.
3580.   TRESCHER, Hildegard, "Montesquieus Einfluss auf die
         philosophischen Grundlagen der Staatslehre Hegels,"
         Schmoll. Jb., 42, 1918, 471-501, 907-44.
3581.   TUCKER, Robert C., "The Cunning of Reason in Hegel and
         Marx," Rev. Pol., 18, 1956, 269-95.
3582.   ULRICH, Ferdinand, "Begriff und Glaube Über Hegels Denk-
         weg ins 'absolute Wissen'," Freiburger Zs. f. Phil., 17,
         1970, 344-99.
3583.   VERENE, Donald P., "Kant, Hegel and Cassirer: The Ori-
         gins of the Philosophy of Symbolic Forms," J. Hist.
         Ideas, 30, 1969, 33-46.
3584.   WAHL, Jean, "Das unglückliche Bewusstsein Seine Bedeutung
         für Hegels Philosophie," Arch. f. Gesch. d. Phil., 40,
         1931, 383-95.
3585.   WALSH, W. H., "On the Philosophy of Hegel," Philosophy,
         28, 1953, 207-28.
3586.   WATSON, John, "The Problem of Hegel," Phil. Rev., 3,
         1894, 546-67.
3587.   WESTPHAL, Merold, "Hegel, Tillich, and the Secular," J.
         Rel., 52, 1972, 223-39.
3588.   WHITTEMORE, Robert C., "Hegel's 'Science' and White-
         head's 'Modern World'," Philosophy, 31, 1956, 36-54.
3589.   WILKINS, Burleigh Taylor, "James, Dewey, and Hegelian
         Idealism," J. Hist. Ideas, 17, 1956, 332-46.
3590.   WISDOM, J. O., "Hegel's Dialectic in historical Philosophy,"

Philosophy, 15, 1940, 243-68.
3591.   ZIEGENGEIST, Gerhard, "Wissarion Belinskis Kritik des
          hegelschen Philosophie (1840-1843)," Dt. Zs. f. Phil.,
          3, 1955, 413-50.

Heinrich Heine (1797-1856)

See also entries 2248, 2445, 2532

3592.   BAYERDÖRFER, Hans-Peter, "'Politische Ballade' Zu den
          'Historien' in Heins 'Romanzero'," Vjschr. f. Litw., 46,
          1972, 435-68.
3593.   BIEBER, Hugo, "Recent Literatur on Heine's Attitude to-
          ward Judaism," Hist. Judaica, 10, 1948, 175-83.
3594.   BRILLING, Bernhard, "Heinrich Heines Berliner Verwandte
          und deren Vorfahren Ein Beitrag zur Heineforschung,"
          Bär v. Ber., 5, 1955, 33-52.
3595.   GALLEY, Eberhard, "Heine und der Kölner Dom," Vjschr.
          f. Litw., 32, 1958, 99-110.
3596.   HARNACK, Otto, "Heinrich Heine Eine Säkularbetrachtung,"
          Pr. Jbb., 97, 1899, 24-31.
3597.   KOCH, Hans-Gerhard, "Heinrich Heine und die Religion,"
          Zeitwende, 32, 1961, 742-53.
3598.   LANDSBERG, Abraham, "Last Traces of Heinrich Heine in
          Hamburg," Leo Baeck Inst. Yrbk., 1, 1956, 360-69.
3599.   LIMPER, Wilhelm, "Ein verschollener Heinebrief," Ann.
          Niederrhein, 105, 1921, 143-47.
3600.   MEINHOLD, Peter, "Heinrich Heine als kritiker seiner
          Zeit," ZRGG, 8, 1956, 319-45.
3601.   PROX, Lothar, "Wagner und Heine," Vjschr. f. Litw., 46,
          1972, 684-98.
3602.   ROS, Guido, "Heinrich Heine und die 'Pariser Zeitung' von
          1838," Publizistik, 1970.
3603.   SLOCHOWER, Harry, "Attitudes Towards Heine in German
          Literary Criticism," Jew. Soc. Stud., 3, 1941, 355-74.
3604.   WIELAND, Wolfgang, "Heinrich Heine und die Philosophie,"
          Vjschr. f. Litw., 37, 1963, 232-48.

Gottfried Kinkel (1815-1882)

3605.   BOLLERT, Martin, "Gottfried Kinkel im Zuchthause," Pr.
          Jbb., 158, 1914, 405-30.
3606.   _____, "Kinkel vor dem Kriegsgericht," Pr. Jbb., 155,
          1914, 488-512.
3607.   GOSLICH, Marie, ed., "Briefe von Johanna Kinkel," Pr.
          Jbb., 97, 1899, 185-222, 398-433.
3608.   HEYNEN, Walter, "Kinkels Flucht," Pr. Jbb., 236, 1934,
          162-76.
3609.   KAUFMANN, Paul, "Johanna Kinkel," Pr. Jbb., 221, 1930,
          290-304, 222, 1930, 48-67.
3610.   _____, "Johanna und Gottfried Kinkel Nach Kaufmannschen

Familienpapieren, " Ann. Niederrhein, 118, 1931, 105-31.
3611.   , "Noch einmal auf Johanna Kinkels Spuren, " Pr.
Jbb., 229, 1932, 263-68.
3612.   SCHULTHEISS, Oskar, "Gottfried Kinkels Jugendentwicklung
und der Maikäferbund, " Ann. Niederrhein, 113, 1928,
97-128.

Paul de Lagarde (1827-1891)

3613.   BREITLING, Richard, "Die Einflüsse der Aufklärung und
Romantik auf Lagarde, " Arch. f. KuG., 18, 1928, 97-
103.
3614.   EISENHUTH, Heinz Erich, "Die Idee der nationalen Kirche
bei Paul de Lagarde, " Zs. f. Theol. u. K., 42, 1934,
145-66.
3615.   KANTZENBACH, Friedrich W., "Friedrich Wilhelm Bötticher, Wilhelm Löhe und Paul de Lagarde   Beobachtungen
zu ihren gegenseitigen Beziehungen, " Jb. f. Ber.-Bran-
denburg. KiG, 41, 1966, 112-21.
3616.   KARPP, Heinrich, "Lagardes Kritik an Kirche und Theologie, " Zs. f. Theol. u. K., 49, 1952, 367-85.
3617.   KOSELLECK, Arno, "Die Entfaltung des völkischen Bewusstseins bei Paul de Lagarde, " Hist. Vjschr., 30, 1935,
316-60.
3618.   LOUGEE, Robert W., "Paul de Lagarde as Critic--A Romantic Protest in an Age of Realism, " J. Cen. Eur.
Aff., 13, 1953, 232-45.
3619.   ROLFFS, E., "Kierkegaard und de Lagarde zwei religiöse
Kritiker der Volkskirche, " Zs. f. systematische Theol.,
18, 1941, 384-403.
3620.   ROTT, Wilhelm, "Nationale Religion und Entstaatlichung der
Kirche bei Paul de Lagarde, " Ev. Theol., 5, 1938, 58-
67.
3621.   SCHÜTTE, Hans-Water, "Theologie als Religionsgeschichte
Das Reformprogram Paul de Lagardes, " Neue Zs. f.
system. Theol. u. RP, 8, 1966, 111-20.

Heinrich Leo (1799-1878)

3622.   BELOW, Georg v., "Heinrich Leo, " Vjschr. f. Litw., 2,
1924, 533-55.
3623.   "BRIEFE Heinrich Leos aus dem Vormärz, " ZRGG, 4,
1952, 68-77, 172-79, 261-67.
3624.   LEO, Heinrich, "Der Heglianismus in Preussen, " ZRGG,
10, 1958, 51-60.
3625.   MAUTZ, Kurt, "Leo und Ranke, " Vjschr. f. Litw., 27,
1953, 207-35.

Conrad Ferdinand Meyer (1825-1898)

3626. ERMATINGER, Emil, "Conrad Ferdinand Meyer und der
        Protestantismus," Zeitwende, 3(1), 1927, 142-59.
3627. HOEHNE, Gerhard, "Conrad Ferdinand Meyer als Dichter
        des Protestantismus," Z. f. systematische Theol., 21,
        1950/52, 399-418.
3628. LÖWENTHAL, Leo, "Conrad Ferdinand Meyers heroische
        Geschichtsauffassung," Zs. f. Sozialforschung, 2, 1933,
        34-62.

Friedrich Nietzsche (1844-1900)

3629. BANNERJEA, Devendra Nath, "The Indian Origin of
        Nietzsche's Theory of the Eternal Return," Ger. Life
        Letters, 7, 1953/54, 161-69.
3630. BENZ, Ernst, "Nietzsches Ideen zur Geschichte des
        Christentums," Zs. f. KiG, 56, 1937, 169-223.
3631. BESSELL, Georg, "Nietzsche und das deutsche Schicksal,"
        Pr. Jbb., 201, 1925, 158-77.
3632. BLUHM, Heinz, "Nietzsche's Early Religious Development,"
        Ger. Rev., 11, 1936, 164-83.
3633. BLUMENTHAL, Albrecht von, "Nietzsche und die klassische
        Altertumswissenschaft in Deutschland," WaG, 5, 1939,
        156-67.
3634. BÖCKMANN, Paul, "Die Bedeutung Nietzsches für die Situ-
        ation der modernen Literatur," Vjschr. f. Litw., 27,
        1953, 77-101.
3635. BREYSIG, Kurt, "Nietzsches ethische und sociologische
        Anschauungen," Schmoll. Jb., 20, 1896, 349-71.
3636. BROMILEY, G. W., "The Message of Friedrich Nietzsche,"
        Evan. Q., 11, 1939, 30-43.
3637. CAMPBELL, Thomas M., "Aspects of Nietzsche's Struggle
        with Philology to 1871," Ger. Rev., 12, 1937, 251-66.
3638. CLEGG, Jerry S., "Nietzsche's Gods in The Birth of
        Tragedy," J. Hist. Phil., 10, 1972, 431-38.
3639. COLMAN, S. J., "Nietzsche as Politique et Moraliste,"
        J. Hist. Ideas, 27, 1966, 548-74.
3640. COPLESTON, F. C., "Friedrich Nietzsche," Philosophy,
        17, 1942, 231-44.
3641. CUNNINGHAM, G. Watts, "Nietzsche on the Philosopher,"
        Phil. Rev., 54, 1945, 155-72.
3642. CYSARZ, Herbert, "Friedrich Nietzsche in dem Wandlungen
        der Mit- und Nachwelt," Vjschr. f. Litw., 4, 1926, 676-
        95.
3643. DOLSON, Grace N., "The Influence of Schopenhauer upon
        Friedrich Nietzsche," Phil. Rev., 10, 1901, 241-50.
3644. DREWS, Arthur, "Nietzsche als Antipode Wagners," Pr.
        Jbb., 175, 1919, 1-27.
3645. ECKSTEIN, Walter, "Friedrich Nietzsche in the Judgment
        of Posterity," J. Hist. Ideas, 6, 1945, 310-24.
3646. ECKSTEIN, Walter; Kurt RIEZLER and James GUTTMANN,

"Nietzsche--Discussion," J. Hist. Ideas, 6, 1945, 294-306.

3647.   EGGENSCHUYLER, W., "War Nietzsche Pragmatist," Arch. f. Gesch. d. Phil., 26, 1912/13, 35-47.

3648.   ENGEL, Morris, "An Early Nietzsche Fragment on Language," J. Hist. Ideas, 24, 1963, 279-86.

3649.   ERNST, Joachim, "Quellen zu Nietzsches Christentumspolemik," ZRGG, 4, 1952, 241-51.

3650.   FURNESS, Raymond, "Nietzsche's Views on the English and His Concept of a European Community," Ger. Life Letters, 17, 1963/64, 319-25.

3651.   GALLWITZ, Hans, "Friedrich Nietzsche als Erzieher zum Christentum," Pr. Jbb., 83, 1896, 324-47.

3652.   GRAY, J. Glenn, "Heidegger 'Evaluates' Nietzsche," J. Hist. Ideas, 14, 1953, 304-09.

3653.   GROTH, J. H., "Wilamowitz--Möllendorf on Nietzsche's Birth of Tragedy," J. Hist. Ideas, 11, 1950, 179-90.

3654.   GRÜTZMACHER, R. H., "Spengler und Nietzsche," Pr. Jbb., 224, 1931, 29-52.

3655.   HAMMACHER, Emil, "Nietzsche und die soziale Frage," Arch. f. Sozialw. u. Sozialpol., 31, 1910, 779-809.

3656.   HARTMANN, Eduard von, "Nietzsche's 'neue Moral'," Pr. Jbb., 67, 1891, 504-21.

3657.   HAZELTON, Roger, "Nietzsche's Contribution to the Theory of Language," Phil. Rev., 52, 1943, 47-60.

3658.   _____, "Was Nietzsche an Anti-christian?," J. Rel., 22, 1942, 63-88.

3659.   HEIDEGGER, Martin, "Who is Nietzsche's Zarathustra?," Rev. Metaphysics, 20, 1966/67, 411-31.

3660.   HOFMANN, Hasso, "Jacob Burckhardt und Friedrich Nietzsche als Kritiker des Bismarcksreiches," Staat, 10, 1971, 433-53.

3661.   HUMBLE, M. E., "Early British Interest in Nietzsche," Ger. Life Letters, 24, 1970/71, 327-35.

3662.   HUMMEL, Hermann, "Emerson and Nietzsche," New England Quarterly, 1946, 63-84.

3663.   HUSZAR, George de, "Nietzsche's Theory of Decadence and the Transvaluation of all values," J. Hist. Ideas, 6, 1945, 259-72.

3664.   JERSILD, Paul T., "Nietzsche's Attack on Christendom," Luth. Q., 16, 1964, 231-38.

3665.   KAUFMANN, Walter, "Nietzsche in the Light of his Suppressed Manuscripts," J. Hist. Phil., 2, 1964, 205-25.

3666.   _____, "Nietzsche's Admiration for Socrates," J. Hist. Ideas, 9, 1948, 472-91.

3667.   KIEFER, Robert, "Nietzsche und Overbeck--eine Arbeitsgemeinschaft," Zs. f. KiG, 57, 1938, 523-53.

3668.   KINDT, Karl, "Nietzsche und die Deutschen," Zeitwende, 12(1), 1935/36, 1-11.

3669.   _____, "Nietzsches Heidentum," Zeitwende, 12, 1935/36, 41-49.

3670.   KNIGHT, A. H. J., "Nietzsche and Epicurean Philosophy," Philosophy, 8, 1933, 431-45.

3671. _____, "Nietzsche's Views on Culture and the Problems of Culture," Ger. Life Letters, 1, 1936/37, 161-70.

3672. KÜNNETH, Walter, "Friedrich Nietzsche, ein Künder der deutschen Katastrophe," Zeitwende, 19, 1947/48, 692-705.

3673. LAING, Bertram M., "The Metaphysics of Nietzsche's Immoralism," Phil. Rev., 24, 1915, 386-418.

3674. LANDMANN, Michael, "Nietzsches Lehre vom Bösen," ZRGG, 1, 1948, 59-71.

3675. LANDOR, A. C., "Nietzsche, An Artist-Philosopher," Ger. Life Letters, 1, 1947/48, 204-08.

3676. _____, "The Philosophy of Friedrich Nietzsche," Ger. Life Letters, 3, 1949/50, 134-38.

3677. LEHMANN, Rudolf, "Friedrich Nietzsche und das Deutschtum," Zs. f. Pol., 10, 1917, 377-97.

3678. LESTER, John A., Jr., Friedrich Nietzsche and John Davidson: A Study in Influence," J. Hist. Ideas, 18, 1957, 411-29.

3679. LINDEMANN, Reinhold, "Friedrich Nietzsche in unserer Zeit," Hochland, 22(2), 1924/25, 645-60.

3680. LÖWITH, Karl, "Friedrich Nietzsche (1844-1900)," Church Hist., 13, 1944, 163-81.

3681. _____, "Kierkegaard und Nietzsche," Vjschr. f. Litw., 11, 1933, 43-66.

3682. _____, "Nietzsche's Doctrine of Eternal Recurrence," J. Hist. Ideas, 6, 1945, 273-84.

3683. _____, "Zur neusten Nietzsche-Forschung," Theol. Rs., 10, 1938, 187-99.

3684. MÖLLER, Joseph, "Nietzsche und die Metaphysik," Theol. Qu.-Schr., 142, 1962, 283-309.

3685. MORRIS, Charles, "Nietzsche--an Evaluation," J. Hist. Ideas, 6, 1945, 285-93.

3686. MÜLLER-FREIENFELS, Richard, "Nietzsche und der Pragmatismus," Arch. f. Gesch. d. Phil., 26, 1912/13, 339-58.

3687. NITZSCH, Fr., "Die Weltanschauung Friedrich Nietzsche's," Zs. f. Theol. u. K., 5, 1895, 344-60.

3688. ODENWALD, Theodor, "Die Verkündigung Nietzsches und die religiöse Krisis der Gegenwart," Zs. f. Theol. u. K., 31, 1923/24, 449-66.

3689. PLATZ, Hermann, "Nietzsche und Pascal," Hochland, 37, 1939/40, 264-73.

3690. RIE, Robert, "Nietzsche and After," J. Hist. Ideas, 13, 1952, 349-69.

3691. ROGERS, A. K., "Nietzsche and Democracy," Phil. Rev., 21, 1912, 32-50.

3692. ROHRMOSER, Günther, "Anlässlich Heideggers Nietzsche," Neue Zs. f. system. Theol. u. RP, 6, 1964, 35-50.

3693. RUNESTAM, Arvid, "Nietzsches Übermensch und Luthers freier Christenmensch," Z. f. systematische Theol., 1, 1923, 520-32.

3694. SALTER, William M., "An Introductory Word on Nietzsche," Har. Theol. Rev., 6, 1913, 461-77.

3695. SANDVOSS, Ernst, "Nietzsches Kritik an den Angelsachsen,"
ZRGG, 17, 1965, 147-61.

3696. SCHIEDER, Theodor, "Nietzsche und Bismarck," HZ, 196,
1963, 320-42.

3697. _____, "Nietzsche and Bismarck," Historian, 29, 1966/
67, 584-604.

3698. SCHREY, H. H., "Die Überwindung des Nihilismus bei Kierkegaard und Nietzsche," Z. f. systematische Theol., 21,
1950/52, 50-68.

3699. SCHWARTZKOPFF, Paul, "Nietzsche und die Entstehung der
sittlichen Vorstellungen," Arch. f. Gesch. d. Phil., 17,
1903, 94-125.

3700. SCHWEITZER, Carl, "Nietzsche und die reformatorische Botschaft," Zeitwende, 12 (1), 1935/36, 25-41.

3701. SIEGMUND, Georg, "Die Wurzeln von Nietzsches Anti-
christentum," Zeitwende, 35, 1964, 379-88.

3702. TILLICH, Paul, "Nietzsche and the Bourgeois Spirit," J.
Hist. Ideas, 6, 1945, 307-09.

3703. TRILLHAAS, Wolfgang, "Psychologie und Christentum bei
Friedrich Nietzsche," Zeitwende, 6(1), 1930, 531-44.

3704. TUSKA, Jon, "Thomas Mann and Nietzsche: A Study in
Ideas," Ger. Rev., 39, 1964, 281-99.

3705. VIRTANEN, Reino, "Nietzsche and the Action Française,"
J. Hist. Ideas, 11, 1950, 191-214.

3706. VOEGELIN, Eric, "Nietzsche, The Crisis and the War,"
J. Pol., 6, 1944, 177-212.

3707. WARBEKE, John M., "Friedrich Nietzsche, Antichrist,
Superman, and Pragmatist," Har. Theol. Rev., 2, 1909,
366-85.

3708. WENZEL, Fritz, "Sören Kiekegaard und Friedrich Nietzsche
Ihr Verhältnis zu Christentum und Kirche," Zeitwende,
14, 1937/38, 526-36.

3709. WESENDONK, O. G. von, "Nietzsche und seine iranischen
Quellen," Pr. Jbb., 233, 1933, 56-62.

3710. WILHELM, Julius, "Nietzsches Wirkung auf das zeitgenössische Frankreich," Theol. Qu.-Schr., 134, 1954, 19-38.

3711. WISSER, Richard, "Friedrich Nietzsche Missverständnisse
eines Denkerlebens," ZRGG, 17, 1965, 307-39.

Max Scheler (1874-1928)

3712. HAECKER, Theodor, "Geist und Leben zum Problem Max
Scheler," Hochland, 23 (2), 1925/26, 129-55.

3713. HILDEBRAND, Dietrich von, "Max Scheler als Persönlichkeit," Hochland, 26(1), 1928/29, 70-80.

3714. HINTZE, Otto, "Max Schelers Ansichten über Geist und
Gesellschaft," ZgesStw., 81, 1926, 40-79.

3715. KUHN, Helmut, "Max Scheler im Rückblick," Hochland, 51,
1958/59, 324-38.

3716. LÜTZELER, Heinrich, "Zu Max Schelers Persönlichkeit,"
Hochland, 26(1), 1928/29, 413-18.

3717. RÜSSEL, Herbert, "Max Scheler und die Probleme der

deutschen Politik," Hochland, 27(2), 1929/30, 518-29.
3718.   SYBEL, Alfred v., "Zu Schelers Ethik," Zs. f. Theol. u.
K., 33, 1925, 216-32.

Friedrich Wilhelm von Schelling (1775-1854)

See also entries 489, 3324, 3335

3719.   BROWARZIK, U., "Die dogmatische Frage nach der Gött-
lichkeit Jesu Dargestellt an Schellings Interpretation von
Phil. 2, 5-11 im Zusammenhang der neueren Exegese,"
Neue Zs. f. system. Theol. u. RP, 13, 1971, 166-75.
3720.   DEWING, Arthur S., "The Significance of Schelling's Theory
of Knowledge," Phil. Rev., 19, 1910, 154-67.
3721.   FACKENHEIM, Emil L., "Schelling's Conception of Positive
Philosophy," Rev. Metaphysics, 3, 1949/50, 563-82.
3722.   FORD, Lewis S., "The Controversy Between Schelling and
Jacobi," J. Hist. Phil., 3, 1965, 75-89.
3723.   KANTZENBACH, F. W., "Die Rezeption der Philosophie
Schellings in Bayern," Zs. f. bayer. LG., 35, 1972,
691-727.
3724.   KUPISCH, Karl, "Schelling in Berlin," Zs. f. KiG, 76,
1965, 258-81.
3725.   _____, "Schelling in Berlin," Jb. f. Ber.-Brandenburg.
KiG, 42, 1967, 77-108.
3726.   LINDSAY, James, "The Philosophy of Schelling," Phil. Rev.,
19, 1910, 259-75.
3727.   LUKACS, Georg, "Schellings Irrationalismus," Dt. Zs. f.
Phil., 1, 1953, 53-102.
3728.   MAUGÉ, Francis, "La liberté dans l'idéalisme transcendantal
de Schelling," Arch. f. Gesch. d. Phil., 14, 1901, 361-
83, 517-35.
3729.   PENZEL, Klaus, "A Nineteenth Century Ecumenical Vision:
F. W. J. Schelling," Luth. Q., 18, 1968, 362-78.
3730.   SASS, Hans Martin, "Schelling und die Junghegelianer Ein
unbekannter Brief Schellings," ZRGG, 14, 1962, 282-85.
3731.   SCHULZE, Wilhelm A., "Schelling und die Kabbala," Judaica, 13, 1957, 65-99, 143-70, 210-32.
3732.   THEUNISSEN, Michael, "Schellings anthropologischer An-
satz," Arch. f. Gesch. d. Phil., 47, 1965, 174-89.

August Wilhelm Schlegel (1767-1845)

3733.   DEMPF, Alois, "Vom Schlegelnachlass der Görresgesell-
schaft," H. Jb., 74, 1954, 432-38.
3734.   KÖRNER, Josef, "August Wilhelm Schlegel und der Katholizismus," HZ, 139, 1928/29, 62-83.
3735.   _____, ed., "Friedrich Tieck und August Wilhelm Schlegel über Gottlieb Schick," Zs. F. Württbg. LG, 41, 1935,
118-27.

Friedrich Schlegel (1772-1829)

See also entry 488

3736. BEHLER, Ernst, "Zur Theologie der Romantik Das
        Gottesproblem in der Spätphilosophie Friedrich Schlegels,"
        Hochland, 52, 1959/60, 339-53.
3737. BROMILEY, G. W., "The Jacobi Essays of Friedrich
        Schlegel," Evan. Q., 16, 1944, 110-24.
3738. KÖRNER, Josef, "Friedrich Schlegel und Madame de Staël,"
        Pr. Jbb., 236, 1934, 221-35.
3739. LORENZ, Reinhold, "Friedrich Schlegels Wiener Vorlesun-
        gen über die Neuere Geschichte," Vjschr. f. Litw., 4,
        1926, 696-717.
3740. SCHMIDT, Wolff A. von, "Die persönlichen Beziehungen
        zwischen Herder und Friedrich Schlegel," Arch. f. KuG.,
        51, 1969.
3741. SCHRÖRS, Heinrich, "Zu Friedrich Schlegels Konversion in
        Köln," Ann. Niederrhein, 107, 1923, 163-65.

Lorenz von Stein (1815-1890)

See also entry 1453

3742. BAASCH, Ernst, "Lorenz v. Stein und die Frage der deut-
        schen wirthschaftlichen Einigung," Schmoll. Jb., 45,
        1921, 1031-50.
3743. BLAUSIUS, D., "Gesellschaftsgeschichte und Gesellschafts-
        wissenschaft bei Lorenz von Stein," Arch. f. Rechts-
        und Sozialphilosophie, 57, 1971, 261-85.
3744. _____, "Lorenz von Stein und Preussen," HZ, 212, 1971,
        339-62.
3745. _____, "Lorenz von Steins Lehre von Königtum der so-
        zialen Reform und ihre verfassungspolitischen Grundlagen,"
        Staat, 10, 1971, 33-51.
3746. FÖLDES, Bela, "Bemerkungen zu dem Problem Lorenz
        Stein--Karl Marx," Jbb. f. Nationalökon. u. Stat., 102,
        1914, 289-99.
3747. GROLLE, Joist, "Lorenz von Stein als preussischer Ge-
        heimagent," Arch. f. KuG., 50, 1968, 82-96.
3748. KANELLOPOULOS, Panajotis, "Die Grundrichtungen der
        Gesellschaftlehre Lorenz von Steins," Arch. f. Gesch. d.
        Phil., 39, 1929/30, 246-62.
3749. KOSELLECK, Reinhart, "Geschichtliche Prognose in Lorenz
        v. Steins Schrift zur preussischen Verfassung," Staat, 4,
        1965, 469-81.
3750. MENGELBERG, Kaethe, "Lorenz von Stein and his contribu-
        tion to Historical Sociology," J. Hist. Ideas, 22, 1961,
        267-74.
3751. MENGER, Carl, "Lorenz von Stein," Jbb. f. Nationalökon.
        u. Stat., 56, 1881, 193-209.
3752. MÖNCH, Hermann, "Der Gedanke der Arbeits Verwaltung bei

Lorenz von Stein," Schmoll. Jb., 61, 1937, 551-69.

3753. MÜLLER, Eberhard, "Lorenz von Stein und Jurij Samarins
Vision des absoluten Sozialstaates," Jbb. f. Gesch. Osteur., 15, 1967, 575-96.

3754. RICHTER, B., "Lorenz von Stein über die deutsche Einheit
und die internationalen Aspekte des Schleswig-Holstein-
Problems (1843-1890)," Zs. Schlesw.-Holst., 95, 1970,
9-92.

3755. RIHS, Charles, "Lorenz von Stein un jeune hégélien Liberal
Observateur du mouvement social dans la France contemporaine à Paris (1840-1842)," Rev. d'hist. écon. soc.,
47, 1969, 404-46.

3756. RONNEBERGER, Franz, "Lorenz von Stein Wiederkehr
seines Geburtstages am 15. 11. 1965," Staat, 4, 1965,
395-408.

3757. SCHMITT, Carl, "Die Stellung Lorenz von Steins in der
Geschichte des 19. Jahrhunderts," Schmoll. Jb., 64,
1940, 641-46.

3758. SCHMOLLER, Gustav, "Lorenz Stein," Pr. Jbb., 19, 1867,
245-70.

3759. WEISS, John, "Dialectical Idealism and the Work of Lorenz
von Stein," Int. Rev. Soc. Hist., 8, 1963, 75-93.

3760. WINKLER, Heinrich August, "Gesellschaftsform und Aussenpolitik Eine Theorie Lorenz von Steins in zeitgeschicht-
licher Perspektive," HZ, 214, 1972, 335-62.

Max Stirner (1806-1856)

See also entries 2303, 2371

3761. BOUSQUET, G. H., "Max Stirner (1806-1856) L'Unique et
sa Propriété," Rev. d'hist. econ. soc., 34, 1956, 60-74.

3762. ROMUNDT, Heinrich, "Max Stirner und die nachkantische
Philosophie," Pr. Jbb., 133, 1908, 33-47.

3763. SCHULZE, Wilh. A., "Zur Religionskritik Max Stirners,"
Zs. f. KiG, 69, 1958, 98-110.

Ferdinand Tönnies (1855-1936)

See also entries 583, 1681, 3577

3764. FREYER, Hans, "Ferdinand Tönnies und seine Stellung in
der deutschen Soziologie," Weltwirtsch. Arch., 44, 1936,
1-9.

3765. HEBERLE, Rudolf, "Das soziologische system von Ferdinand Tönnies," Schmoll. Jb., 75, 1965, 385-402.

3766. MITZMAN, Arthur, "Tönnies and German Society, 1887-
1914: from cultural Pessimism to the Celebration of
the Volksgemeinschaft," J. Hist. Ideas, 32, 1971, 507-24.

3767. ROSENBAUM, Eduard, "Ferdinand Tönnies Werk," Schmoll.
Jb., 38, 1914, 2149-96.

3768. TÖNNIES, Ferdinand, "Begriff und Gesetz des menschlichen
       Fortschrittes," Arch. f. Sozialw. u. Sozialpol., 53,
       1924/25, 1-10.
3769. _____, "Demokratie und Parlamentarismus," Schmoll. Jb.,
       51, 1927, 173-216.
3770. _____, "Die Enquête über Zustände der Arbeit im Ham-
       burger Hafen," Arch. f. Sozialw. u. Sozialpol., 12,
       1898, 303-48.
3771. _____, "Ethik und Sozialismus," Arch. f. Sozialw. u.
       Sozialpol., 25, 1907, 573-612.
3772. _____, "Die Gesetzmässigkeit in der Bewegung der Be-
       völkerung," Arch. f. Sozialw. u. Sozialpol., 39, 1915,
       150-73, 767-94.
3773. _____, "Hafenarbeiter und Seeleuten in Hamburg vor dem
       Strike 1896/97," Arch. f. Sozialw. u. Sozialpol., 10,
       1897, 173-238.
3774. _____, "Individuum und Welt in der Neuzeit," Weltwirsch.
       Arch., 1, 1913, 37-66.
3775. _____, "Neuere Philosophie der Geschichte Hegel, Marx,
       Comte," Arch. f. Gesch. d. Phil., 7, 1894, 486-515.
3776. _____, "Soziologie und Hochschulreform," Weltwirtsch.
       Arch., 16, 1920/21, 212-45.
3777. _____, "Studie zur Schleswig-holsteinischen Agrarstatis-
       tik," Arch. f. Sozialw. u. Sozialpol., 30, 1910, 285-332.
3778. _____, "Das Verbrechen als soziale Erscheinung," Arch.
       f. Sozialw. u. Sozialpol., 8, 1895, 329-44.
3779. _____, "Zur Soziologie des demokratischen Staates,"
       Weltwirtsch. Arch., 19, 1923, 540-84.
3780. _____, "Volkswirtschaft und Privatwirtschaft," Schmoll.
       Jb., 27, 1903, 1425-42.
3781. _____, "Zur Theorie der öffentlichen Meinung," Schmoll.
       Jb., 40, 1916, 2001-30.

Friedrich Theodor Vischer (1807-1887)

3782. EGELHAAF, Gottlob, "Briefe Friedrich Theodor Vischers
       aus der Paulskirche," Deutsche Rundschau, 132, 1907,
       203-26.
3783. GLOCKNER, Hermann, "Friedrich Theodor Vischer als
       ethisch-politischer Persönlichkeit," HZ, 128, 1923, 26-91.
3784. HELLER, Ruth, "Auch Einer: The Epitome of F. TH.
       Vischer's Philosophy of Life," Ger. Life Letters, 8,
       1954/55, 9-18.
3785. MÜLLER, Karl A. v., "Fr. Th. Vischer als Politiker,"
       Deutsche Rundschau, 1912, 238-60.
3786. RÜRUP, Reinhard, "Friedrich Theodor Vischer und die An-
       fänge der Kunstgeschichte an der Technischen Hochschule
       Karlsruhe," ZGORh., 113, 1965, 415-27.

Richard Wilhelm Wagner (1813-1883)

3787.   ADORNO, T. W., "Fragmente über Wagner," Zs. f. Sozial-
        forschung, 8, 1939, 1-49.
3788.   BROD, Max, "Some Comments on the Relationship between
        Wagner and Meyerbeer," Leo Baeck Inst. Yrbk., 9, 1964,
        202-05.
3789.   HARASZTI, Emile, "Deux agents secrets de deux causes
        ennemies: Wagner et Liszt," Rev. d'hist. dipl., 66,
        1952, 223ff.
3790.   HERZSTEIN, Robert E., "Richard Wagner at the Cross-
        roads of German Anti-Semitism 1848-1933 A Re-Inter-
        pretation," Zs. f. d. Gesch. d. Juden, 4, 1967, 119-40.
3791.   RAPP, Adolf, "Die Erscheinung Richard Wagners im Geis-
        tesleben," Arch. f. KuG., 11, 1914, 70-112.
3792.   SCHMIDT, Julian, "Richard Wagner," Pr. Jbb., 38, 1876,
        414-35.

Max Weber (1864-1920)

See also entries 1386, 1387, 2272, 2409, 2437, 3269, 3300

3793.   ALATAS, Syed Hussein, "The Weber Thesis and South East
        Asia," Arch. d. Soc. d. Rel., 15, 1963, 21-34.
3794.   ARON, Raymond, "Max Weber und die Machtpolitik," Zs. f.
        Pol., 11, 1964, 100-13.
3795.   ASSEL, Hans-Günther, "Normen in der Politik Eine
        kritische Betrachtung zum Wertfreiheitsprinzip Max
        Webers," Zs. f. Pol., 16, 1969, 198-222.
3796.   BAUMGARTEN, Edward, "Max Weber--The Man and His
        Influence," Ger. Econ. Rev., 2, 1964, 256-61.
3797.   BERGSTRAESSER, Arnold, "Max Webers Antrittsvorlesung
        in Zeitgeschichtlicher Perspektive," VjHZG, 5, 1957, 209-
        19.
3798.   BLUM, Fred H., "Max Weber: The Man of Politics and
        the Man Dedicated to Objectivity and Rationality,"
        Ethics, 70, 1959/60, 1-20.
3799.   BOURDIEU, Pierre, "Une interprétation de la théorie de
        la religion selon Max Weber," Eur. J. Soc., 12, 1971,
        3-21.
3800.   BRINKMANN, Carl, "Die Bedeutung Max Webers für die
        heutigen Sozialwissenschaften," Schmoll. Jb., 67, 1943,
        129-35.
3801.   DIBBLE, Vernon K., "Social Science and Political Commit-
        ments in the Young Max Weber," Eur. J. Soc., 9, 1968,
        92-110.
3802.   EISENSTADT, J. N., "Some Reflections on the Significance
        of Max Weber's Sociology of Religions for the Analysis of
        non-European Modernity," Arch. d. Soc. d. Rel., 32,
        1971, 29-52.
3803.   EISERMANN, Gottfried, "Der lebendige Max Weber,"
        Schmoll. Jb., 85, 1965, 303-11.

3804.   FISCHER, H. Karl, "Kritische Beiträge zu Prof. M.
        Webers Abhandlung: 'Die protestantische Ethik und der
        Geist des Kapitalismus'," Arch. f. Sozialw. u. Sozialpol.,
        25, 1907, 232-42.

3805.   FREUND, Julien, "L'Éthique Économique et les Religions
        mondiales selon Max Weber," Arch. d. Soc. d. Rel.,
        26, 1968, 3-25.

3806.   FRYE, Bruce B., "Max Weber: The German Professor in
        Politics," Rocky Mt. Soc. Sci. J., 1971.

3807.   GERHARDT, Johannes, "Max Weber," Zeitwende, 4(1),
        1928, 139-52.

3808.   GODDARD, David, "Max Weber and the Objectivity of Social
        Science," Hist. Theor., 12, 1973, 1-22.

3809.   GOLLIN, Gillian Lindt, "The Religious Factor in Social
        Change: Max Weber and the Moravian Paradox," Arch.
        d. Soc. d. Rel., 23, 1967, 91-97.

3810.   HÄTTICH, Manfred, "Der Begriff des politischen bei Max
        Weber," Pol. Vjschr., 8, 1967, 40-50.

3811.   HERTZ, Karl H., "Max Weber and American Puritanism,"
        J. Sci. Stud. Rel., 1, 1961, 189-97.

3812.   HINTZE, Otto, "Max Webers Soziologie," Schmoll Jb., 50,
        1926, 83-95.

3813.   HONIGSHEIM, Paul, "Max Weber as Historian of Agriculture
        and Rural Life," Ag. Hist., 23, 1949, 179-213.

3814.   _____, "Max Weber: his religious and ethical background
        and development," Church Hist., 19, 1950, 219-39.

3815.   KOELLREUTLER, Otto, "Die staatspolitischen Anschauungen
        Max Webers und Oswald Spenglers," Zs. f. Pol., 14,
        1924/25, 481-500.

3816.   KOLKO, Gabriel, "A Critique of Max Weber's Philosophy of
        History," Ethics, 70, 1959/60, 21-36.

3817.   KORF, Gertraud, "Der Idealtypus Max Webers und die his-
        torisch-gesellschaftlichen Gesetzmässigkeiten," Dt. Zs. f.
        Phil., 12, 1964, 1328-43.

3818.   LENK, Kurt, "Das Werturteilsproblem bei Max Weber,"
        ZgcsStw., 120, 1964, 56-64.

3819.   LIEBERT, Arthur, "Max Weber," Pr. Jbb., 210, 1927,
        304-20.

3820.   LIEBESCHÜTZ, Hans, "Max Weber's Historical Interpreta-
        tion of Judaism," Leo Baeck Inst. Yrbk., 9, 1964, 41-68.

3821.   LIPP, Wolfgang, "Handlung und Herrschaft-Systemkategorien
        bei V. Pareto, M. Weber und T. Parsons," Jb. F. So-
        zialw., 19, 1968, 332-62.

3822.   LITTLE, David, "Max Weber Revisited The 'Protestant
        Ethic' and the Puritan Experience of Order," Har. Theol.
        Rev., 59, 1966, 415-28.

3823.   LUHMANN, Niklas, "Zweck-Herrschaft-System Grundbegriffe
        und Prämissen Max Webers," Staat, 3, 1963, 129-58.

3824.   MEANS, Richard L., "Weber's Thesis of the Protestant
        Ethic: The Ambiguities of Resolved doctrine," J. Rel.,
        45, 1965, 1-11.

3825.   MOMMSEN, Wolfgang J., "Neue Max-Weber-Literatur,"
        HZ, 211, 1970, 616-30.

3826. _____, "Die Vereinigten Staaten von Amerika im politischen Denken Max Webers," HZ, 213, 1971, 358-81.
3827. NAFZIGER, Estel Wayne, "The Mennonite Ethic in the
Weberian Framework," Explorations in Entrepreneurial
History, 2, 1964/65, 187-204.
3828. NOLTE, Ernst, "Max Weber vor dem Faschismus," Staat,
2, 1963, 1-24.
3829. PARSONS, Talcott, "Max Weber and the Contemporary Political Crisis," Rev. Pol., 4, 1942, 61-76, 155-72.
3830. PFISTER, Bernhard, "Max Weber," Hochland, 50, 1957/58,
128-38.
3831. RAPHAËL, Freddy, "Max Weber et le judaisme antique,"
Eur. J. Soc., 11, 1970, 297-336.
3832. RIEMERSMA, Jelle C., "Max Weber's 'Protestant Ethic',"
Explorations in Entrepreneurial History, 1, 1949, 11-19.
3833. ROTH, Guenther, "Max Weber's Empirical Sociology in
Germany and the United States: Tensions between Par-
tisanship and Scholarship," Cen. Eur. Hist., 2, 1969,
196-215.
3834. SCHELTING, Alexander von, "Die Logische Theorie der historischen Kulturwissenschaft von Max Weber und im be-
sonderen sein Begriff des Idealtypus," Arch. f. Sozialw.
u. Sozialpol., 49, 1922, 623-752.
3835. SCHULZ, Gerhard, "Geschichtliche Theorie und politisches
Denken bei Max Weber," VjHZG, 12, 1964, 325-50.
3836. SÉGUY, Jean, "Max Weber et la Sociologie historique des
Religions," Arch. d. Soc. d. Rel., 33, 1972, 71-103.
3837. SPRENKEL, Otto B. van der, "Max Weber on China,"
Hist. Theor., 3, 1963/64, 348-70.
3838. SPRINZAK, Ehud, "Weber's Thesis as an historical Ex-
planation," Hist. Theor., 11, 1972, 294-320.
3839. VOEGELIN, Erich, "Über Max Weber," Vjschr. f. Litw.,
3, 1925, 177-93.
3840. WEBER, Max, "Entwickelungstendenzen in der Lage der
Ostelbischen Landarbeiter," Arch. f. Sozialw. u. Sozialpol., 7, 1894, 1-41.
3841. _____, "Die protestantische Ethik und der 'Geist' des
Kapitalismus," Arch. f. Sozialw. u. Sozialpol., 20, 1905,
1-54; 21, 1905, 1-110.
3842. _____, "Roscher und Knies," Schmoll. Jb., 27, 1903,
1181ff; 29, 1905, 1323-84.
3843. _____, "R. Stammler 'Ueberwindung' der materialistischen
Geschichtsauffassung'," Arch. f. Sozialw. u. Sozialpol.,
24, 1907, 94-151.
3844. _____, "Russlands Übergang zum Scheinkonstitutionalis-
mus," Arch. f. Sozialw. u. Sozialpol., 23, 1906, 165-
401.
3845. _____, "Die Stadt Eine soziologische Untersuchung,"
Arch. f. Sozialw. u. Sozialpol., 47, 1920/21, 621-772.
3846. _____, "Die Wirtschaftsethik der Weltreligionen," Arch.
f. Sozialw. u. Sozialpol., 41, 1916, 1-87, 335-421, 613-
744; 42, 1916/17, 345-461, 687-814; 44, 1917/18, 52-
138, 349-443, 601-26; 46, 1918/19, 40-113, 311-66,

541-604.
3847.   _____, "Zur Lage der bürgerlichen Demokratie in Russ-
         land," Arch. f. Sozialw. u. Sozialpol., 22, 1906, 234-
         353.
3848.   WILBRANDT, Robert, "Max Weber als Erkenntniskritiker
         der Sozialwissenschaften," ZgesStw., 79, 1925, 583-674.

Wilhelm Wundt (1832-1920)

3849.   HARTMANN, Eduard von, "Wundt's System der Philosophie,"
         Pr. Jbb., 66, 1890, 1-31, 123-52.
3850.   JUDD, Chas. H., "Wundt's System of Philosophy," Phil.
         Rev., 6, 1897, 370-85.
3851.   SOMMER, Hugo, "Der ethische Evolutionismus Wilhelm
         Wundt's," Pr. Jbb., 59, 1887, 189-208.
3852.   THIEME, Karl, "Wilhelm Wundts Bedeutung für die The-
         ologie," Zs. f. Theol. u. K., 29, 1921, 213-38.
3853.   WASHBURN, Margaret F., "Wundtian Feeling Analysis and
         the Genetic Significance of Feeling," Phil. Rev., 14,
         1905, 21-29.

Universities

See also entries 704, 1637, 1703

3854.   ACHELIS, Thomas D., "Die Studenten aus dem Schleswiger
         Herzogtum von 1814 bis 1864 Vom gesamtstaatlichen zum
         nationalen Denken," Arch. f. KuG., 35, 1953, 334-41.
3855.   BARYCZ, H., "L'université de Koenigsberg au service de
         l'idée prussienne," Cahiers Pologne-Allemagne, 8, 1961,
         8-23.
3856.   BERGSTRÄSSER, Ludwig, "Der Weg zur Burschenschaft,"
         Arch. f. KuG., 26, 1936, 199-226.
3857.   BEYERLE, Konrad and Karl OBSER, ed., "Verzeichnis
         badischer Studierender an der Universität Göttingen aus
         den Jahren 1734-1870," ZGORh., 68, 1914, 612-45.
3858.   DAMMANN, Oswald, "Die geplante Berufung Ludwig Häussers
         nach Jena (1859)," ZGORh., 104, 1956, 524-30.
3859.   "Die DEUTSCHEN Universitäten im neunzehnten Jahrhundert,"
         Pr. Jbb., 2, 1858, 107-41.
3860.   DÖRRER, Anton, "Karl Domanig, der katholische deutsche
         Burschenschafter," Gelbe Hefte, 1, 1924/25, 947-74.
3861.   EYCK, F. G., "The Political Theories and Activities of the
         German Academic Youth between 1815 and 1819," J. Mod.
         Hist., 27, 1955, 27-38.
3862.   FABER, K. G., "Student und Politik in der ersten deutschen
         Burschenschaft," GiWuU, 21, 1970, 68-80.
3863.   GEHRING, Paul, "Professor Wucherer und seine Freiburger
         Polytechnische Schule von 1818 Ein Beitrag zur Grün-
         dungsgeschichte der Technischen Hochschule in Karlsruhe,"
         ZGORh., 116, 1968, 369-81.

3864.   GRAUERT, Hermann von, "Schwarz-rot-goldene und Schwarz-
        weiss-rote Gedanken an deutschen Universitäten," H. Jb.,
        38, 1917, 1-40.
3865.   GRÖNING, Albert von, "Über die Göttinger 'Sieben',"
        Bremisches Jb., 39, 1940, 157-68.
3866.   HAGEN, Hermann, "Zur Entstehung und geschichtlichen Ent-
        wicklung der katholischen Studentenkorporationen," Gelbe
        Hefte, 1, 1924/25, 877-90.
3867.   HELLFÁIER, Karl-Alexander, "Die politische Funktion der
        Burschenschaft von ihren Anfängen 1814 bis zum Revolu-
        tionsjahr 1848 an der Universität Halle-Wittenberg," Jb.
        f. Gesch. M. O. Dtschl., 12, 1963, 103-49.
3868.   HOFMEISTER, Adolph, "Rostocker Studentenleben von 15.
        bis ins 19. Jahrhundert," Arch. f. KuG., 4, 1906, 1-50,
        171-96, 310-48.
3869.   HÜBNER, Hans, "Robert Prutz als Student und Professor an
        der Universität Halle-Wittenberg," Wiss. Z Univ Halle
        (Ges. und Sprachwiss Reihe), 16, 1967, 197-205.
3870.   JOLLY, Ludwig, "Geschichte der Staatswissenschaftlichen
        Fakultät in Tübingen," Schmoll. Jb., 13, 1889, 159-81.
3871.   KEMPE, Hans-Joachim, "Die Burschenschaften an der Uni-
        versität Breslau," Jb. d. Schles.-Fried.-Wilh. Univ z.
        Breslau, 6, 1961, 138-49.
3872.   KRÜGER, Paul, "'Hochverräterische Unternehmungen' in
        Studentenschaft und Bürgertum des Vormärz in Oberhessen
        (bis 1838)," Mitt. d. Oberhessischen Geschichtsvereins,
        49/50, 1965, 73-136.
3873.   LAUTENSCHLAGER, Friedrich, "Die Universität Heidelberg
        und der Fall Martin," ZGORh., 85, 1932/33, 636-63.
3874.   LENZ, Max, "Freiheit und Macht im Lichte der Entwicklung
        der Universität Berlin," HZ, 108, 1912, 77-96.
3875.   MEINECKE, Friedrich, "Drei Generationen deutscher Gelehr-
        tenpolitik," HZ, 125, 1922, 248-83.
3876.   MEISSNER, Rudolf, "Der germanistische Unterricht an der
        Universität Bonn 1818-1911," Ann. Niederrhein, 104,
        1920, 86-120.
3877.   NIEBLING, Georg, "Zu Jacob Philipp Fallmerayer Leben
        und Werk," ZRGG, 23, 1971, 351-68.
3878.   OEHME, Ruthardt, "Die Geschichte der Bibliothek der
        Technischen Hochschule Fridericiana in Karlsruhe 1825-
        1906," ZGORh., 112, 1964, 1-62.
3879.   RINGER, Fritz K., "Higher Education in Germany in the
        Nineteenth Century," J. Contemp. Hist., 2, 1967, 123-38.
3880.   ROSENBERG, Hans, "Geistige und politische Strömungen an
        der Universität Halle in der ersten Hälfte des 19. Jahr-
        hunderts," Vjschr. f. Litw., 7, 1929, 560-86.
3881.   SCHOLZ, Heinrich, "Wandlungen im Wesen der Universität
        seit 100 Jahren," Pr. Jbb., 153, 1913, 316-28.
3882.   SCHOOF, Wilhelm, "Der Protest der Göttinger Sieben,"
        GiWuU, 13, 1962, 333-44.
3883.   SCHRÖDER, Willi, "Über 'Politische Ansichten und Aktionen'
        der 'Unbedingten' in der Burschenschaft," Wiss. Zs. d.
        Univ. Jena (ges. u. sprachwiss Reihe), 15, 1966, 223-46.

3884.   SCHULTE, Joh. Friedrich von, "Die Besoldungsverhältnisse
        der Universitäts-Professoren in Preussen, " Jbb. f. Na-
        tionalökon. u. Stat., 48, 1887, 1-36.
3885.   SCHWABE, Klaus, "Zur Politischen haltung der deutschen
        Professoren im ersten weltkrieg, " HZ, 193, 1961, 601-
        34.
3886.   SCHWARZ, Jürgen, "Deutsche Studenten und Politik im 19.
        Jahrhundert, " GiWuU, 20, 1969, 72-94.
3887.   SRBIK, Heinrich Ritter von, "Grossdeutsch und Kleindeutsch
        an der Universität Heidelberg, " ZGORh., 82, 1929/30,
        202-33.
3888.   STEIGER, Günter, "Literatur zur Geschichte des Wartburg-
        festes von 1817 und der 'Urburschenschaft' (1815-1819), "
        Der Bibliothekar, 22, 1968, 738-44.
3889.   _____, "Das 'Phantom der Wartburgverschwörung' 1817
        im Spiegel neuer Quellen aus den Akten der preussischen
        politischen Polizei, " Wiss. Zs. d. Univ. Jena (Ges. u.
        sprachwiss Reihe), 15, 1966, 183-212.
3890.   STIEHLER, Gottfried, "Die Gesellschaftswissenschaften an
        der Berliner Universität 1810-1945, " Dt. Zs. f. Phil.,
        8, 1960, 987-1002.
3891.   "STUDENTENBRIEFE aus der Zeit der Romantik, " ZRGG,
        3, 1951, 12-23.
3892.   STUMPFE, O., "Professoren, Reaktion u. Männerbünde
        zwischen 1870 u. 1933, " Pol. Stud., 13, 1962, 145, 551-
        63.
3893.   TREITSCHKE, Heinrich v., "Zur Reform der Universitäten, "
        Pr. Jbb., 23, 1869, 406-22.
3894.   TÜMMLER, Hans, "Wartburg, Weimar und Wien der Staat
        Carl Augusts in der Auseinandersetzung mit den Folgen
        des Studentenfestes von 1817, " HZ, 215, 1972, 49-106.
3895.   UBBELOHDE, A., "Ein Frommer Wunsch für die preus-
        sischen Universitäten," Pr. Jbb., 25, 1870, 455-74.
3896.   WEISS, Josef, "Aus dem ersten Jahrzehnt der ältesten
        Münchener Verbindung des Cartellverbandes der katholis-
        chen deutschen Studentenverbindungen, " Gelbe Hefte, 1,
        1924/25, 975-90.
3897.   WIEGAND, Friedrich, "Eduard Zellers Berufung nach Mar-
        burg und August Vilmar, " HZ, 105, 1910, 285-95.

JUDAISM, ANTISEMITISM

General Studies

See also entries 1748, 3345, 3438, 3547, 3549, 3593, 4476, 5698

3898. ADLER-RUDEL, S., "Moritz Baron Hirsch Profile of a Great Philanthropist," Leo Baeck Inst. Yrbk., 8, 1963, 29-69.

3899. ALEXANDER, Kurt, "Die soziale Unruhe der modernen Juden," Pr. Jbb., 127, 1907, 35-57.

3900. ANGRESS, Werner T., "Prussia's Army and the Jewish Reserve Officer Controversy before World War I," Leo Baeck Inst. Yrbk., 17, 1972, 19-42.

3901. ARONSFELD, C. C., "German Jews in Victorian England," Leo Baeck Inst. Yrbk., 7, 1962, 312-29.

3902. ASCH, Adolph and Johanna PHILIPPSON, "Self-Defense at the Turn of the Century: The Emergence of the K.C.," Leo Baeck Inst. Yrbk., 3, 1958, 122-39.

3903. ASCHKEWITZ, M., "Der Anteil der Juden am wirtschaftlichen Leben Westpreussens um die Mitte des 19. Jahrhunderts," Zs. f. Ostforsch., 11, 1962, 482-91.

3904. AUERBACH, Rabb. H. B., "Der Brand in der Synagoge zu Halberstadt im Jahre 1845," Zs. f. d. Gesch. d. Juden, 6, 1969, 151-54.

3905. _____, "Halberstadt als sitz und Tagungsort jüdischer Verbände," Zs. f. d. Gesch. d. Juden, 6, 1969, 155-58.

3906. BARON, Salo W., "Aspects of the Jewish Communal Crisis in 1848," Jew. Soc. Stud., 14, 1952, 99-144.

3907. _____, "The Impact of the Revolution of 1848 on Jewish Emancipation," Jew. Soc. Stud., 11, 1949, 195-248.

3908. _____, "The Jewish Question in the Nineteenth Century," J. Mod. Hist., 10, 1938, 51-65.

3909. _____, "Zur ostjüdischen Einwanderung in Preussen," Zs. f. d. Gesch. d. Juden in Dtsch., 3, 1931, 193-203.

3910. BARTYS, Julian, "Grand Duchy of Poznań under Prussian Rule Changes in the Economic Position of the Jewish Population 1815-1848," Leo Baeck Inst. Yrbk., 17, 1972, 191-204.

3911. BARZILAY, Isaac E., "National and Antinational Trends in the Berlin Haskalah," Jew. Soc. Stud., 21, 1959, 165-92.

3912. BAUMGARDT, David, "The Ethics of Lazarus and Steinthal," Leo Baeck Inst. Yrbk., 2, 1957, 205-17.

3913. BAUMGART, Peter, "Absoluter Staat und Judenemanzipation in Brandenburg-Preussen," Jb. f. Gesch. M.O. Dtschl., 13/14, 1965, 60-87.

3914. BEIN, Alexander, "Die moderne Antisemitismus und seine Bedeutung für die Judenfrage," VjHZG, 6, 1958, 340-60.

3915. BERGMAN, Hugo, "Eduard von Hartmann und die Judenfrage in Deutschland," Leo Baeck Inst. Yrbk., 5, 1960, 177-97.

3916. BERGMAN, Shlomo, "Some Methodological Errors in the Study of Antisemitism," Jew. Soc. Stud., 5, 1943, 43-60.

3917. BODENHEIMER, Rosy, "Beitrag zur Geschichte der Juden in Oberhessen von ihrer frühesten Erwähnung bis zur Emanzipation," Zs. f. d. Gesch. d. Juden in Dtsch., 3, 1931, 251-62; 4, 1932, 11-30.

3918. BRAATZ, Werner E., "Antisemitismus, Antimodernismus und Antiliberalismus im ausgehenden 19. Jahrhundert," Pol. Stud., 22, 1971, 20-33.

3919. BRAUBACH, Max, "Jüdischer Anteil an der Bonner Gelehrsamkeit," Rhein. Vjsbll., 32, 1968, 402-18.

3920. BREINES, Paul, "The Jew as Revolutionary The Case of Gustav Landauer," Leo Baeck Inst. Yrbk., 12, 1967, 75-84.

3921. BRESLAUER, Walter, "Jews of the City of Posen One Hundred Years Ago," Leo Baeck Inst. Yrbk., 8, 1963, 229-37.

3922. BRILLING, B., "Geschichte des jüdischen Goldschmiedegewerbes in Schlesien," Hamb. Mittel- u. ostdt. Forsch., 6, 1967, 163-221.

3923. _____, "Das jüdische Goldschmiedegewerbe in Berlin 1700-1900," Bär v. Ber., 19, 1970, 106-38.

3924. BURKHARDT, C. A. H. and M. STERN, "Aus der Zeitschriften-Literatur zur Geschichte der Juden in Deutschland," Zs. f. d. Gesch. d. Juden in Dtsch., 2, 1888, 1-46, 109-49.

3925. CAHNMANN, Werner, "Die Münchener Judenbeschreibung von 1904," Zs. f. d. Gesch. d. Juden in Dtsch., 7, 1937, 180-88.

3926. _____, "Munich and the First Zionist Congress," Hist. Judaica, 3, 1941, 7-23.

3927. COHEN, Arthur, "Die Münchener Judenschaft 1750-1861 Eine bevölkerungs- und wirtschaftsgeschichtliche Studie," Zs. f. d. Gesch. d. Juden in Dtsch., 3, 1931, 262-83.

3928. COHEN, Carl, "The Road to Conversion," Leo Baeck Inst. Yrbk., 6, 1961, 259-79.

3929. COHN, Emil, "Probleme im modernen Judentum," Pr. Jbb., 129, 1907, 302-24.

3930. _____, "Die religiöse Judenfrage," Pr. Jbb., 143, 1911, 432-40.

3931. DÁN, Robert, "Zeitschrift für die Geschichte der Juden in Deutschland," Zs. f. d. Gesch. d. Juden, 5, 1968, 27-39.

3932. DAVIDSOHN, Georg, "Die Juden im preussischen Staate von 1837," Zs. f. d. Gesch. d. Juden in Dtsch., 7, 1937, 114-16.

3933.   DIENEMANN, Max, "Die jüdischen Gemeinden in Elsass-
        Lothringen 1871-1918," Zs. f. d. Gesch. d. Juden in
        Dtsch., 7, 1937, 77-85.

3934.   "DOKUMENTE aus den Anfängen der Emanzipationszeit in
        Preussen," Zs. f. d. Gesch. d. Juden in Dtsch., 6,
        1935, 174-75.

3935.   DUGGAN, Paul R., "German-Jewish Relations in the Wil-
        helminian Period," Leo Baeck Inst. Yrbk., 17, 1972,
        43-54.

3936.   ECKSTEIN, Adolf, "Die Stellungsnahme der bayerischen
        Staatsregierung zu den Reformrabbinerversammlungen, "
        Zs. f. d. Gesch. d. Juden in Dtsch., 6, 1935, 51-54.

3937.   EISNER, Isi Jacob, "Reminiscences of the Berlin Rabbinical
        Seminary," Leo Baeck Inst. Yrbk., 12, 1967, 32-52.

3938.   ENGELMAN, Uriah Zevi, "Intermarriage among Jews in
        Germany, U.S.S.R., and Switzerland," Jew. Soc. Stud.,
        2, 1940, 157-78.

3939.   FEDER, Ernst, "Paul Nathan, the Man and his Work," Leo
        Baeck Inst. Yrbk., 3, 1958, 60-80.

3940.   FEIST, Siegmund, "Zur Geschichte des 'Rassenantisemitis-
        mus' in Deutschland," Zs. f. d. Gesch. d. Juden in
        Dtsch., 2, 1930, 40-67.

3941.   FEUCHTWANGER, Ludwig, "Die Juden und das Wirtschafts-
        leben," Schmoll. Jb., 35, 1911, 1433-66.

3942.   FREUND, Ismar, "Die deutsche Judenfrage vor 100 Jahren, "
        Zs. f. d. Gesch. d. Juden in Dtsch., 5, 1935, 34-42.

3943.   FRIEDLANDER, Albert H., "The Wohlwill-Moser Corres-
        pondence, " Leo Baeck Inst. Yrbk., 11, 1966, 262-99.

3944.   GALLINER, Arthur, "The Philanthropin in Frankfurt. Its
        educational and cultural significance for German Jewry, "
        Leo Baeck Inst. Yrbk., 3, 1958, 169-86.

3945.   GEIGER, Ludwig, "Die Ertheilung des Bürgerrechts an die
        Juden in Frankfurt 1811," Zs. f. d. Gesch. d. Juden in
        Dtsch., 5, 1890/92, 54-74.

3946.   GELBER, N. M., "The Intervention of German Jews at the
        Berlin Congress 1878," Leo Baeck Inst. Yrbk., 5, 1960,
        221-48.

3947.   GOLDSCHMIDT, E. D., "Studies on Jewish Liturgy by Ger-
        man-Jewish Scholars," Leo Baeck Inst. Yrbk., 2, 1957,
        119-35.

3948.   GOLDSTÜCKER, Eduard, "Jews between Czechs and Ger-
        mans around 1848," Leo Baeck Inst. Yrbk., 17, 1972,
        61-71.

3949.   GRAUPE, Heinz M., "Steinheim und Kant Eine Unter-
        suchung zum Verhältnis von Theologie und Religions-
        philosophie," Leo Baeck Inst. Yrbk., 5, 1960, 140-75.

3950.   GROSS, Walter, "The Zionist Students' Movement," Leo
        Baeck Inst. Yrbk., 4, 1959, 143-64.

3951.   GRUBE, Walter, "Quellen zur Geschichte der Judenfrage in
        Württemberg," Zs. F. Württbg. LG, 2, 1938, 117-54.

3952.   GRUNWALD, Kurt, "Europe's Railways and Jewish Enter-
        prise German Jews as Pioneers of Railway Promotion, "
        Leo Baeck Inst. Yrbk., 12, 1967, 163-209.

3953. HAMBURGER, Ernest, "Jews in Public Service under the German Monarchy," Leo Baeck Inst. Yrbk., 9, 1964, 206-38.

3954. _____, "One Hundred Years of Emancipation Four Legal Texts," Leo Baeck Inst. Yrbk., 14, 1969, 3-66.

3955. HARMELIN, Wilhelm, "Jews in the Leipzig Fur Industry," Leo Baeck Inst. Yrbk., 9, 1964, 239-66.

3956. _____, "Juden in der Leipziger Rauchwarenwirtschaft," Tradition, 11, 1966, 249-82.

3957. HEINEMANN, F. H., "Jewish Contributions to German Philosophy (1755-1933)," Leo Baeck Inst. Yrbk., 9, 1964, 161-77.

3958. HERLITZ, Georg, "Three Jewish Historians Isaak Markus Jost - Heinrich Graetz - Eugen Taeubler," Leo Baeck Inst. Yrbk., 9, 1964, 69-90.

3959. HESSEN, Robert, "Unsere Aufgaben gegenüber dem Judenthum Ein Rückblick auf den Antisemitismus," Pr. Jbb., 64, 1889, 560-79.

3960. HIRSCH, Felix, "Eduard von Simson Das Problem der deutsch-jüdische Symbiose im Schatten Goethes und Bismarcks," GiWuU, 16, 1965, 261-77.

3961. JACOBSON, Jacob, "Das Naturalisationsverzeichnis der jüdischen Gemeinde in Posen 1834-1848," Zs. f. Ostforsch., 17, 1968, 481-533.

3962. _____, "Some Observations on the Jewish Citizens' Books of the City of Berlin," Leo Baeck Inst. Yrbk., 1, 1956, 317-30.

3963. _____, "Von Mendelssohn zu Mendelssohn-Bartholdy," Leo Baeck Inst. Yrbk., 5, 1960, 251-61.

3964. "JAMES Simon Industrialist, Art Collector, Philanthropist," Leo Baeck Inst. Yrbk., 10, 1965, 3-23.

3965. "Die JUDENFRAGE noch einmal vor beiden Häussern des Landtags," Pr. Jbb., 7, 1861, 11-50.

3966. KAHN, Lothar, "Michael Beer (1800-1833)," Leo Baeck Inst. Yrbk., 12, 1967, 149-60.

3967. KAHN, Siegbert, "Dokumente des Kampfes der revolutionären deutschen Arbeiterbewegung gegen Antisemitismus und Judenverfolgung," Beitr. z. Gesch. d. dt. Arbeiterbeweg., 2, 1960, 552-64.

3968. KANN, Robert A., "Assimilation and Antisemitism in the German-French Orbit in the Nineteenth and Early Twentieth Century," Leo Baeck Inst. Yrbk., 14, 1969, 92-115.

3969. KARBACH, Dr. Oskar, "Die politischen Grundlagen des deutsch-österreichischen Antisemitismus," Zs. f. d. Gesch. d. Juden, 1, 1964, 1-8, 103-16, 169-78.

3970. KATSH, Abraham I., "Nachman Krochmal and the German Idealists," Jew. Soc. Stud., 8, 1946, 87-102.

3971. KATZ, Jacob, "The Fight for Admission to Masonic Lodges," Leo Baeck Inst. Yrbk., 11, 1966, 171-209.

3972. KISCH, Guido, "Die deutsch-jüdische Bibliographie seit dem 19. Jahrhundert," ZRGG, 22, 1970, 143-52.

3973. _____, "Jewry-Law in Central Europe--Past and Present," J. Cen. Eur. Aff., 2, 1943, 396-422.

3974.   KLIBANSKY, Erich, "Zur Statistik des jüdischen Schul-
        wesens in Breslau von 1834-1844, " Zs. f. d. Gesch. d.
        Juden in Dtsch., 3, 1931, 280.
3975.   KNAUSS, Erwin, "Der politische Antisemitismus im Kaiser-
        reich (1871-1900), " Mitteil d. Oberhessischen Gesch.,
        53/54, 1969, 43-68.
3976.   KOBER, Adolf, "Emancipation's Impact on the Education
        and Vocational Training of German Jewry, " Jew. Soc.
        Stud., 16, 1954, 3-32.
3977.   _____, "Jewish Communities in Germany from the Age of
        Enlightenment to their Destruction by the Nazis, " Jew.
        Soc. Stud., 9, 1947, 195-238.
3978.   _____, "Jewish Preaching and Preachers A Contribution
        to the History of the Jewish Sermon in Germany and
        America, " Hist. Judaica, 7, 1946, 103ff.
3979.   _____, "The Jewish Theological Seminary of Breslau and
        'Wissenschaft des Judentums', " Hist. Judaica, 16, 1954,
        85-122.
3980.   _____, "Jews in the Revolution of 1848 in Germany, " Jew.
        Soc. Stud., 10, 1948, 135-64.
3981.   _____, "150 Years of Religious Instruction, " Leo Baeck
        Inst. Yrbk., 2, 1957, 98-118.
3982.   KÖRNER, Josef, "Mendelssohns Töchter, " Pr. Jbb., 214,
        1928, 167-82.
3983.   LAMBERTI, Marjorie, "The Attempt to Form a Jewish
        Bloc: Jewish Notables and Politics in Wilhelmian Ger-
        many, " Cen. Eur. Hist., 3, 1970, 73-93.
3984.   _____, "The Prussian Government and the Jews Official
        Behavior and Policymaking in the Wilhelminian Era, "
        Leo Baeck Inst. Yrbk., 17, 1972, 5-17.
3985.   LAMM, Dr., "Organisationsentwicklung der jüdischen
        Wohlfahrtspflege in Berlin, " Zs. f. d. Armenwesen, 15,
        1914, 165-73.
3986.   LAQUEUR, Walter, "The German Youth Movement and the
        'Jewish Question', " Leo Baeck Inst. Yrbk., 6, 1961,
        193-205.
3987.   _____, "Zionism and its Liberal Critics 1896-1958, " J.
        Contemp. Hist., 6, 1971, 161-82.
3988.   LAUBERT, Manfred, "Die Judenfrage auf den Posener Pro-
        vinziallandtagen von 1827 und 1845, " Zs. f. d. Gesch. d.
        Juden in Dtsch., 4, 1932, 30-46.
3989.   LEHNHARDT, Erich, "Judenthum und Antisemitismus, " Pr.
        Jbb., 55, 1885, 667-80.
3990.   LESTSCHINSKY, Jakob, "Die Umsiedlung und Umschichtung
        des jüdischen Volkes im Laufe des letzten Jahrhunderts, "
        Weltwirtsch. Arch., 30, 1929, 123-56; 32, 1930, 563-99.
3991.   LIEBESCHÜTZ, Hans, "Hermann Cohen and his Historical
        Background, " Leo Baeck Inst. Yrbk., 13, 1968, 3-33.
3992.   _____, "Problems of Diaspora History in 19th Century
        Germany, " J. Jew. Stud., 8, 1957, 103-11.
3993.   LIEBESCHÜTZ, Rahel, "The Wind of Change Letters of
        Two Generations from the Biedermeier Period, " Leo
        Baeck Inst. Yrbk., 12, 1967, 227-56.

3994. LITTMANN, Ellen, "Saul Ascher First Theorist of Pro-
       gressive Judaism," Leo Baeck Inst. Yrbk., 5, 1960,
       107-21.
3995. LOEVINSON, Ermanno, "Ausländische Juden im Kirchen-
       staat während der Revolution 1848-1849," Zs. f. d.
       Gesch. d. Juden in Dtsch., 2, 1930, 247-48.
3996. LOWENTHAL, Ernst G., "The Ahlem Experiment: A
       Brief Survey of the 'Jüdische Gartenbauschule'," Leo
       Baeck Inst. Yrbk., 14, 1969, 165-81.
3997. MACK, Rüdiger, "Otto Böckel und die antisemitische Bauern-
       bewegung in Hessen (1887-1894)," Wetterauer Geschichts-
       bl., 16, 1967, 113-47.
3998. MAYER, Gustav, "Early German Socialism and Jewish
       Emancipation," Jew. Soc. Stud., 1, 1939, 409-22.
3999. MENES, A., "Zur Statistik des jüdischen Schulwesens in
       Preussen um die Mitte des vorigen Jahrhunderts," Zs. f.
       d. Gesch. d. Juden in Dtsch., 3, 1931, 203-06.
4000. MEYER, Michael A., "Great Debate on Antisemitism Jewish
       Reaction to New Hostility in Germany 1879-1881," Leo
       Baeck Inst. Yrbk., 11, 1966, 137-70.
4001. _____, "Jewish Religious Reform and Wissenschaft des
       Judentums The Positions of Zunz, Geiger and Frankel,"
       Leo Baeck Inst. Yrbk., 16, 1971, 19-41.
4002. MILLER, Max, "Zur neueren Geschichte der Juden in Würt-
       temberg," Zs. F. Württbg. LG, 26, 1967, 121-31.
4003. MOLDENHAUER, R., "Jewish Petitions to the German Na-
       tional Assembly in Frankfurt 1848/49," Leo Baeck Inst.
       Yrbk., 16, 1971, 185-223.
4004. MORGENSTERN, Friedrich, "Hardenberg and the Emancipa-
       tion of Franconian Jewry," Jew. Soc. Stud., 15, 1953,
       253-74.
4005. MOSSE, George L., "The Image of the Jew in German
       Popular Culture: Felix Dahn and Gustav Froytag," Leo
       Baeck Inst. Yrbk., 2, 1957, 218-27.
4006. MOSSE, Werner E., "The Conflict of Liberalism and Na-
       tionalism and its Effect on German Jewry," Leo Baeck
       Inst. Yrbk., 15, 1970, 125-39.
4007. _____, "Rudolf Mosse and the House of Mosse 1867-
       1920," Leo Baeck Inst. Yrbk., 4, 1959, 237-59.
4008. MUELLER, Ernst, "Wandlungen des jüdischen Bewusst-
       seins in den letzten zwei Jahrhunderten," Judaica, 10,
       1954, 129-54.
4009. OELSNER, Toni, "The Place of the Jews in Economic His-
       tory as Viewed by German Scholars," Leo Baeck Inst.
       Yrbk., 7, 1962, 183-212.
4010. _____, "Three Jewish Families in Modern Germany,"
       Jew. Soc. Stud., 4, 1942, 241-68, 349-98.
4011. OESTMANN, Erika, "Antisemitischer Nationalismus und na-
       tionales Judentum," Pol. Stud., 12, 1961, 575-90.
4012. PEGORARO-CHIARLONI, Anna, "Antisemitismo in Germania
       1848-1871," Stud. Stor., 11, 1970, 97-112.
4013. PELI, Moshe, "Intimations of Religious Reform in the Ger-
       man Hebrew Haskalah Literature," Jew. Soc. Stud., 32,

1970, 3-13.

4014. PHILIPPSON, Johanna, "The Philippsons, A German-Jewish
       Family 1775-1933," Leo Baeck Inst. Yrbk., 7, 1962, 95-
       118.
4015. PHILIPSBORN, Alexander, "The Jewish Hospitals in Ger-
       many," Leo Baeck Inst. Yrbk., 4, 1959, 220-34.
4016. PINKUSS, Fritz, "Saul Ascher, ein Theoretiker der Juden-
       emanzipation aus der Generation nach Moses Mendels-
       sohn," Zs. f. d. Gesch. d. Juden in Dtsch., 6, 1935.
4017. POIS, Robert A., "Walther Rathenau's Jewish Quandary,"
       Leo Baeck Inst. Yrbk., 13, 1968, 120-31.
4018. PRYS, Joseph, "Zum Anteil der Familie von Hirsch auf
       Gereuth am Kampfe um die bayerische Judenemanzipa-
       tion," Zs. f. d. Gesch. d. Juden in Dtsch., 5, 1935,
       69-72.
4019. "Die RECHTE der Juden in Preussen," Pr. Jbb., 5, 1860,
       105-42.
4020. REISSNER, H. G., "Feliz Mendelssohn-Bartholdy and Eduard
       Gans," Leo Baeck Inst. Yrbk., 4, 1959, 92-110.
4021. _____, "Rebellious Dilemma: The Case Histories of
       Eduard Gans and Some of his Partisans," Leo Baeck Inst.
       Yrbk., 2, 1957, 179-93.
4022. RINOTT, Moshe, "Gabriel Riesser Fighter for Jewish
       Emanzipation," Leo Baeck Inst. Yrbk., 7, 1962, 11-38.
4023. ROSENAU, Helen, "German Synagogues in the Early Period
       of Emancipation," Leo Baeck Inst. Yrbk., 8, 1963, 214-
       25.
4024. ROSENBAUM, Eduard, "M. M. Warburg & Co. Merchant
       Bankers of Hamburg," Leo Baeck Inst. Yrbk., 7, 1962,
       121-49.
4025. ROSENBLOOM, Noah H., "The 'Nineteen Letters of Ben
       Uziel' - A Hegelian Exposition," Hist. Judaica, 22, 1960,
       23-60.
4026. ROSENTHAL, Erich, "Trends of Jewish Population in Ger-
       many, 1910-39," Jew. Soc. Stud., 6, 1944, 233-74.
4027. ROSENTHAL, Heinz, "Jews in the Solingen Steel Industry,"
       Leo Baeck Inst. Yrbk., 17, 1972, 205-23.
4028. ROTENSTREICH, Nathan, "For and against Emancipation
       The Bruno Bauer Controversy," Leo Baeck Inst. Yrbk.,
       4, 1959, 3-36.
4029. RÜRUP, Reinhard, "Jewish Emancipation and Bourgeois So-
       ciety," Leo Baeck Inst. Yrbk., 14, 1969, 67-91.
4030. _____, "Die Judenemanzipation in Baden," ZGORh., 114,
       1966, 241-300.
4031. SCHLEIER, Hans, "Gustav Seeber, Zur Entwicklung und
       Rolle des Antisemitismus in Deutschland von 1871-1914,"
       Zs. f. Geschw., 7, 1961, 1592-97.
4032. SCHMIDT, Ferdinand Jakob, "Das modernistische Judentum
       und die christliche Weltkultur," Pr. Jbb., 143, 1911, 193-
       216.
4033. SCHMIDT, H. D., "Anti-Western and Anti-Jewish Tradition
       in German Historical Thought," Leo Baeck Inst. Yrbk., 4,
       1959, 37-60.

4034.   , "Chief Rabbi Nathan Marcus Adler (1803-1890),"
           Leo Baeck Inst. Yrbk., 7, 1962, 289-311.
4035.   , "The Terms of Emancipation 1781-1812   The
           public debate in Germany and its effect on the mentality
           and ideas of German-Jewry," Leo Baeck Inst. Yrbk., 1,
           1956, 28-47.
4036.   SCHWARZ, Walter, "A Jewish Banker in the Nineteenth
           Century," Leo Baeck Inst. Yrbk., 3, 1958, 300-10.
4037.   SEELIGER, Herbert, "Origin and Growth of the Berlin
           Jewish Community," Leo Baeck Inst. Yrbk., 3, 1958,
           159-68.
4038.   SILBERNER, Edmund, "German Social Democracy and the
           Jewish Problem Prior to World War I," Hist. Judaica,
           15, 1953, 3-48.
4039.   STEINBERG, S., "Bekanntmachungen des Konsistoriums
           der Israeliten zu Kassel aus den Jahren 1808-1813,"
           Zs. f. d. Gesch. d. Juden in Dtsch., 2, 1930, 242-46.
4040.   STEINTHAL, H., "Die jüdische Volksschule in Anhalt von
           1830-1840," Zs. f. d. Gesch. d. Juden in Dtsch., 4,
           1890, 66-74.
4041.   STERLING, Eleonore O., "Anti-jewish Riots in Germany in
           1819: A Displacement of Social Protest," Hist. Judaica,
           12, 1950, 105ff.
4042.   , "Jewish Reaction to Jew-Hatred in the First Half
           of the Nineteenth Century," Leo Baeck Inst. Yrbk., 3,
           1958, 103-21.
4043.   STERN, Wilhelm, "Die Juden in Unterfranken während der
           ersten Hälfte des 19. Jahrhunderts," Zs. f. d. Gesch. d.
           Juden in Dtsch., 6, 1936, 229-38.
4044.   STERN-TAEUBLER, Selma, "The First Generation of
           Emancipated Jews," Leo Baeck Inst. Yrbk., 15, 1970,
           3-40.
4045.   , "The Jew in the Transition from Ghetto to Eman-
           cipation," Hist. Judaica, 2, 1940, 102-19.
4046.   STRAUSS, Herbert, "The Jugendverband   A Social and In-
           tellectual History," Leo Baeck Inst. Yrbk., 6, 1961, 206-
           35.
4047.   , "Pre-Emancipation Prussian Policies towards the
           Jews 1815-1847," Leo Baeck Inst. Yrbk., 11, 1966, 107-
           36.
4048.   TAL, Uriel, "Liberal Protestantism and the Jews in the
           Second Reich 1870-1914," Jew. Soc. Stud., 26, 1964, 23-
           41.
4049.   TOURY, Jacob, "Jewish Manual Labour and Emigration
           Records from some Bavarian Districts," Leo Baeck Inst.
           Yrbk., 16, 1971, 45-62.
4050.   , "'The Jewish Question' A Semantic Approach,"
           Leo Baeck Inst. Yrbk., 11, 1966, 85-106.
4051.   , "Organizational Problems of German Jewry:
           Steps towards the Establishment of a Central Organiza-
           tion (1893-1920)," Leo Baeck Inst. Yrbk., 13, 1968, 57-
           90.
4052.   TREITSCHKE, H. v., "Der jüdische Einwanderung in Preus-

sen," Pr. Jbb., 52, 1882, 534-38.
4053.   _____, "Noch einige Bemerkungen zur Judenfrage," Pr.
         Jbb., 45, 1880, 85ff.
4054.   WALLACH, Luitpold, "The Beginnings of the Science of
         Judaism in the Nineteenth Century," Hist. Judaica, 8,
         1946, 33-60.
4055.   WASSERMANN, Rudolf, "Die Juden und das deutsche Wirt-
         schaftsleben der Gegenwart," Pr. Jbb., 149, 1912, 267-
         75.
4056.   WEICHERT, Friedrich, "Die Anfänge der Berliner Judenmis-
         sion," Jb. f. Ber.-Brandenburg. KiG, 38, 1963, 106-41.
4057.   _____, "Der Berliner Judenmissionar Professor D.
         Paulus Cassel (1821-1892)," Jb. f. Ber.-Brandenburg.
         KiG, 42, 1967, 109-32.
4058.   WEILER, Gershon, "Fritz Mauthner: A Study in Jewish
         Self-Rejection," Leo Baeck Inst. Yrbk., 8, 1963, 136-48.
4059.   WEINRYB, Bernard D., "Prolegomena to an Economic His-
         tory of the Jew in Germany in Modern Times," Leo
         Baeck Inst. Yrbk., 1, 1956, 279-306.
4060.   WILHELM, Kurt, "The Jewish Community in the Post-
         Emancipation Period," Leo Baeck Inst. Yrbk., 2, 1957,
         47-75.
4061.   WOLF, Immanuel, "On the Concept of a Science of Judaism
         (1822)," Leo Baeck Inst. Yrbk., 2, 1957, 194-204.
4062.   ZMARZLIK, H. G., "Der Antisemitismus im Zweiten Reich,"
         GiWuU, 14, 1963, 273-87.

Ludwig Börne (1786-1837)

4063.   BOCK, Helmut, "Ludwig Börne und das Julikönigtum in
         Frankreich," Zs. f. Geschw., 9, 1961, 1278-97.
4064.   DANIELS, Emil, "Ludwig Börne und E. Th. Amadeus Hoff-
         mann," Pr. Jbb., 153, 1913, 217-44.

David Friedländer (1750-1834)

4065.   FRAENKEL, Ernst, "David Friedländer und seine Zeit,"
         Zs. f. d. Gesch. d. Juden in Dtsch., 6, 1935, 65-77.
4066.   FREUND, Ismar, "David Friedländer und die politische
         Emanzipation der Juden in Preussen," Zs. f. d. Gesch.
         d. Juden in Dtsch., 6, 1935, 77-92.
4067.   GRUNWALD, Max, "Briefe von David Friedländer," Zs. f.
         d. Gesch. d. Juden in Dtsch., 6, 1935, 171.
4068.   JACOBSON, Jacob, "Aus David Friedländers Mussestunden,"
         Zs. f. d. Gesch. d. Juden in Dtsch., 6, 1935, 134-40.
4069.   STERN, Moritz, "Gutachten und Briefe David Friedländers,"
         Zs. f. d. Gesch. d. Juden in Dtsch., 6, 1935, 113-30.

Moses Hess (1812-1875)

4070. BUBER, Martin, "Moses Hess," Jew. Soc. Stud., 7, 1945, 137-48.
4071. LADEMACHER, Horst, "Die politische und soziale Theorie bei Moses Hess," Arch. f. KuG., 42, 1960, 194-230.
4072. LUKÁCS, Georg, "Moses Hess und die Probleme der idealistischen Dialektik," Arch. f. d. Gesch. d. Soz., 12, 1926, 105-55.
4073. MICHAEL, Reuwen, "Graetz and Hess," Leo Baeck Inst. Yrbk., 9, 1964, 91-121.
4074. ROTENSTREICH, Nathan, "Moses Hess and Karl Ludwig Michelet," Leo Baeck Inst. Yrbk., 7, 283-86.
4075. SILBERNER, Edmund, "Einige Manuskripte von Moses Hess," Int. Rev. Soc. Hist., 11, 1966, 113-19.
4076. _____, "Der junge Moses Hess im Lichte bisher uner-schlossener Quellen," Int. Rev. Soc. Hist., 3, 1958, 43-70, 239-68.
4077. _____, "Der 'Kommunistenrabbi' und der 'Gesellschafts-spiegel'," Arch. f. Sozialgesch., 3, 1963, 87-102.
4078. _____, "Moses Hess," Hist. Judaica, 13, 1951, 3-28.
4079. _____, "Moses Hess als Begründer und Redakteur der Rheinischen Zeitung," Arch. f. Sozialgesch., 4, 1969, 5-44.
4080. _____, "Moses Hess und die Internationale Arbeiteras-soziation," Arch. f. Sozialgesch., 5, 1965, 83-146.
4081. _____, "Ein unveröffentlicher Dialog von Moses Hess," Int. Rev. Soc. Hist., 10, 1965, 455-70.
4082. _____, "Zur Hess-Bibliographie Mit zwei bisher un-veröffentlichten Manuskription über Marx," Arch. f. Sozialgesch., 6/7, 1966/67, 241-314.

Samson Raphael Hirsch (1808-1888)

4083. HEINEMANN, Isaac, "Samson Raphael Hirsch The Forma-tive Years of the Leader of Modern Orthodoxy," Hist. Judaica, 13, 1951, 29ff.
4084. "The SECESSION from the Frankfurt Jewish Community under Samson Raphael Hirsch," Hist. Judaica, 10, 1948, 99-122.

Samuel Hirsch (1809-1889)

4085. GREENBERG, Gershon, "Samuel Hirsch: Jewish Hegelian," Rev. d. Étud. Juives, 129, 1970, 205-16.
4086. KATZ, Jacob, "Samuel Hirsch - Rabbi, Philosopher and Freemason," Rev. d. Étud. Juives, 125, 1966, 112-25.

Leopold Zunz (1794-1886)

4087.   ALTMANN, Alexander, "Zur Frühgeschichte der jüdischen
        Predigt in Deutschland Leopold Zunz als Prediger, "
        Leo Baeck Inst. Yrbk., 6, 1961, 3-59.
4088.   GLATZER, Nahum N., "Leopold Zunz and the Revolution of
        1848, " Leo Baeck Inst. Yrbk., 5, 1960, 122-39.
4089.   KISCH, Guido, "Zunz' Briefwechsel mit Meir Wiener, "
        Hebrew Union College Ann., 38, 1967, 237-58.

MILITARY HISTORY

General Studies

4090.   ARNDT, Ad., "Der Rechtscharakter des deutschen Heeres,"
        Pr. Jbb., 110, 1902, 250-85.
4091.   BACH, Hugo, "Heer und Staat in Kurhessen," Wehrw. Rs.,
        19, 1969, 632-39.
4092.   BADER, Karl, "Zur Geschichte des Grossherzoglich hes-
        sischen Freiwilligen Jägercorps 1813-1814," Arch. f.
        hessische Gesch., 2, 1895/99, 483-520.
4093.   BAECKER, Th., "Blau gegen Schwarz. Der amerikanische
        Kriegsplan von 1913 für einen deutsch-amerikanischen
        Krieg," Marine Rs., 69, 1972, 347-60.
4094.   BAHREMANN, Jörg, "Der Begriff der Strategie bei Clause-
        witz, Moltke und Liddel Hart," Wehrw. Rs., 18, 1968,
        33-57.
4095.   BENJAMIN, Hazel C., "Official Propaganda and the French
        Press during the Franco-Prussian War," J. Mod. Hist.,
        4, 1932, 214-30.
4096.   BERGHAHN, Volker R. and W. DEIST, "Kaiserliche Marine
        und Kriegsausbruch 1914 Neue Dokumente zur Juli-krise,"
        Militärgesch. Mitt., 2, 1970(1), 37-58.
4097.   BERNER, Ernst, ed., "Eine Denkschrift von Motz aus dem
        Jahre 1817 über den Abschluss von Militärkonventionen
        zwischen Preussen und den kleineren norddeutschen Staa-
        ten," FBPG, 6, 1893, 483-99.
4098.   BERNHARDI, Theodor v., "Die neuere Literatur der Be-
        freiungskriege 1812-14 und ihre Ergebnisse," HZ, 1,
        1859, 269-326.
4099.   BESELER, G., "Das Reichs-Militärgesetz und das Budget-
        recht," Pr. Jbb., 33, 1874, 589.
4100.   BETHCKE, Dr., "Yorck," Gelbe Hefte, 11, 1934/35, 476-
        93.
4101.   BLUME, v., "Landwirthschaft, Industrie und Handel in
        ihrer Bedeutung für die deutsche Wehrkraft," Pr. Jbb.,
        101, 1900, 1-28.
4102.   BOCK, Helmut, "Konservatives Rebellentum im antinapoleon-
        ischen Unabhängigkeits Kampf Zur Beurteilung des
        Freicharzuges unter Ferdinand von Schill 1809," Jb. f.
        Gesch., 6, 1972, 107-45.
4103.   BUCHNER, Rudolf, "Die deutsche patriotische Dichtung vom
        Kriegsbeginn 1870 über Frankreich und die elsässische
        Frage," HZ, 206, 1968, 327-36.

4104.   BUSCH, W., "Der Kampf um den Frieden in dem preus-
        sischen Hauptquartier zu Nikolsburg im Juli 1866," HZ,
        92, 1904, 418-55.
4105.   CARROLL, E. Malcolm, "French Public Opinion on War
        with Prussia in 1870," AHR, 31, 1925/26, 679-700.
4106.   CECIL, Lamar J. R., "Coal for the Fleet that had to Die,"
        AHR, 69, 1963/64, 990-1005.
4107.   COLER, Christfried, "Palastrevolte in der Marine 1878/79
        Zur Geschichte der 'Ära Stosch'," Wehrw. Rs., 17,
        1967, 638-56.
4108.   CRAIG, Gordon A., "Military Diplomats in the Prussian and
        German Service: The Attachés, 1816-1914," Pol. Sci.
        Q., 64, 1949, 65-94.
4109.   DEHIO, Ludwig, "Um den deutschen Militarismus," HZ, 180,
        1955, 43-64.
4110.   DEUERLEIN, Ernst, "Wehrordnung und Föderalismus in
        Deutschland," Wehrw. Rs., 6, 1956, 223-40.
4111.   "Der DEUTSCHE Bund und die deutsche Flotte," Pr. Jbb.,
        6, 1860, 146-78.
4112.   DIETRICH, Richard, "Preussen als Besatzungsmacht in
        Königreich Sachsen 1866-1868," Jb. f. Gesch. M. O.
        Dtschl., 5, 1956, 273-93.
4113.   "DOCUMENTS relatifs à la bataille de Sédan (1870)," RH,
        26, 1884, 303-17.
4114.   DÖNHOFF, Fritz, "Wilhelm Krüger und die preussische
        Kriegswirtschaft 1806-1813," FBPG, 48, 1936, 48-70.
4115.   EMERY, Harold W., Jr., "Les manoeuvres allemandes a
        Metz en 1893 et leurs conséquences sur les rapports
        Franco-italiens," Rev. d'hist. dipl., 72, 1958, 193-209.
4116.   ENDRES, Franz Carl, "Soziologische Struktur und ihr
        entsprechende Ideologien des deutschen Offizierkorps vor
        dem Weltkriege," Arch. f. Sozialw. u. Sozialpol., 58,
        1927, 282-319.
4117.   ENGEL, Josef, "Der Wandel in der Bedeutung des Krieges
        im 19. und 20. Jh.," GiWuU, 19, 1968, 468-86.
4118.   ENGELBERG, Ernst, "Der preussische Militarismus und die
        Reichsgründung 1870/71," Zs. f. MilitärG., 10, 1971.
4119.   "Die ERZIEHUNG der Jugend zur Wehrhaftigkeit," Pr. Jbb.,
        6, 1860, 543-59.
4120.   FISCHER, Otto, "Dr. Laurenz Hannibal Fischer und die
        Auflösung der deutschen Flotte 1852-53," HZ, 85, 1900,
        250-89.
4121.   FORSTMEIER, Friedrich, "Deutsche Invasionspläne gegen
        die USA um 1900," Marine-Rs., 68, 1971.
4122.   FRANKE, Immo, "Die Schlesier im Feldzug gegen Frank-
        reich 1870/71," Jb. d. Schles.-Fried-Wilh. Univ z.
        Breslau, 14, 1969, 164-233.
4123.   FRANZ, Werner, "Zu einigen Fragen des Entstehens und
        des Charakters der preussischen Landwehr im Frühjahr
        1813," Zs. f. MilitärG., 3, 1964, 477-82.
4124.   FRAUENHOLZ, Eugen v., "Die Grundzüge der geschicht-
        lichen Entwicklung des deutschen Heeres," Gelbe Hefte,
        2, 1925/26, 621-40.

4125. _____, "Sigmund Freiherr von Pranckh, der bayerische
Reformkriegsminister (1821-1888), " Gelbe Hefte, 6,
1929/30, 581-94.

4126. FRICKE, Dieter, "Militarismus und Volksschule. Zum
Bildungsniveau preussischer Rekruten am Beginn der
imperialistischen Epoche, " Militärgesch. Mitt., 11,
1972, 155-67.

4127. _____, "Zur Militarisierung des deutschen Geiteslebens
im Wilhelminischen Kaiserreich Der Fall Leo Arons, "
Zs. f. Geschw., 8, 1960, 1069-1107.

4128. FRIED, Hans Ernest, "'German Militarism' Substitute for
Revolution, " Pol. Sci. Q., 58, 1943, 481-513.

4129. GALL, Lothar, "Zur Frage der Annexion von Elsass und
Lothringen 1870, " HZ, 206, 1968, 265-326.

4130. GEBSATTEL, Ludwig von, "Generalfeldmarschall Walter
Freiherr von Loë, " Gelbe Hefte, 3, 1927, 367-92, 426-
60.

4131. GRANIER, Herman, "Aktenstücke zur Geschichte des Krieges
von 1806/07, " FBPG, 13, 1900, 514-41.

4132. GRUNER, Wolf D., "Die bayerischen Kriegsminister 1805-
1885. Eine Skizze zum sozialen Herkommen der Minister, " Zs. f. bayer. LG., 34, 1971, 238-315.

4133. GÜNTHER, Norbert, "Zur Vorgeschichte der Fertigung
Militäroptischer Geräte im Jenaer Zeisswerk, " Tradition,
3, 1958, 1-16.

4134. GÜTH, R., "Hundert Jahre Marine-Akademie, " Marine Rs.,
69, 1972, 296-302.

4135. GULAT-WELLENBURG, Max v., "Die Belagerung von Neu-
breisach im Jahre 1815, " ZGORh., 60, 1906, 441-62.

4136. _____, "Bericht des Oberstleutnants von Porbeck über das
Gefecht bei Ulderup am 6. April 1849, " ZGORh., 64,
1910, 652-59.

4137. HAERING, Hermann, "Die Organisierung von Landwehr und
Landsturm in Baden in den Jahren 1813 und 1814, "
ZGORh., 68, 1914, 266-303, 464-516.

4138. HÄUSSLER, Hans-Joachim, "Küstenschutz und deutsche Flotte
1859-64 Zur Geschichte der Neuen Ära und der preussisch-deutschen Reichseinigung, " FBPG, 51, 1939, 311-43.

4139. "HEER und Volksvertretung, " Pr. Jbb., 51, 1883, 503-25.

4140. HELD, A., "Bemerkungen über die Freiwillige Krankenpflege
im Kriege von 1870, " Pr. Jbb., 27, 1871, 121-44, 251-
73.

4141. HELFER, Christian, "Über militärische Einflüsse auf die
industrielle Entwicklung in Deutschland, " Schmoll. Jb.,
83, 1963, 597-609.

4142. HELMERT, Heinz, "Zu den Ursachen der militärischen
Siege Preussens in den Kriegen von 1864, 1866, und
1870/71, " Zs. f. MilitärG., 6, 1967, 5-22.

4143. _____ and Hermann RAHNE, "Zur Kriegsführung des
preussischen Generalstabes 1870/71, " Zs. f. MilitärG.,
9, 1970, 532-46.

4144. HELMREICH, E. C., "An Unpublished Report on Austro-
German Military Conversations of November 1912, " J.

Mod. Hist., 5, 1933, 197-207.

4145.   HERWIG, Holger H. and David F. TRASK, "Naval Opera-
         tions Plans between Germany and the United States of
         America 1898-1913. A Study of Strategic Planning in the
         Age of Imperialism," Militärgesch. Mitt., 2, 1970(2),
         5-32.

4146.   HERZFELD, Hans, "Zur neueren Literatur über das Herres-
         problem in der deutschen Geschichte," VjHZG, 4, 1956,
         361-86.

4147.   HÖROLDT, Dietrich, "Maximilian von Spee (1861-1914),"
         Wehrw. Rs., 13, 1963, 707-28.

4148.   HOFFMANN, Joachim, "Wandlungen im Kriegsbild der
         preussischen Armee zur Zeit der nationalen Einigungs-
         kriege," Militärgesch. Mitt., 1, 1969, 5-33.

4149.   HUBATSCH, Walther, "Der Kukminationspunkt der deutschen
         Marinepolitik im Jahre 1912," HZ, 176, 1953, 291-322.

4150.   HUBER, Ernst Rudolf, "Volksheer und Verfassung Ein Bei-
         trag zu der Kernfrage der Scharnhorst-Boyenschen Re-
         form," ZgesStw., 97, 1936/37, 213-57.

4151.   JÄHNS, Max, "Zur Geschichte der Kriegsverfassung des
         Deutschen Reiches," Pr. Jbb., 39, 1877, 1-28, 113-40,
         443-90; 40, 1877, 500-28.

4152.   KEINEMANN, Friedrich, "Auswirkungen des preussisch-
         österreichischen Krieges 1866 auf die Haltung des
         katholischen Adels in der Provinz Westfalen," Westf. Zs.,
         119, 1969, 411-22.

4153.   KIRCHEISEN, Fr. M., "Pourquoi la Guerre Éclata en 1806
         entre la France et la Prusse?," Rev. d'hist. dipl., 43,
         1929, 237-50.

4154.   KLEMZ, Bernhard, "Die Feldzeitung der preussischen
         Armee im Freiheitskrieg 1813-1814," Wehrw. Rs., 20,
         1970.

4155.   KLENNER, Jochen, "Die Geschichte des Bundeskriegswesens
         des norddeutschen Bundes," Wehrw. Rs., 19, 1969, 388-
         410.

4156.   KNAPP, Rudolf, ed., "Feldpostbriefe eines württemberg-
         ischen Freiwilligen im Kriege 1870/71," Zs. F. Württbg.
         LG, 29, 1970, 294-314.

4157.   KOLB, Eberhard, "Der Pariser Commune-Aufstand und die
         Beendigung des deutsch-französischen Krieges," HZ, 215,
         1972, 265-98.

4158.   KRAUS, Karl, "Der preussisches Generalstab und der Geist
         der Reformzeit," Wehrw. Rs., 7, 1957, 203-16.

4159.   _____, "Vom Werden, Wesen und Wirken des Preussischen
         Generalstabes," GiWuU, 9, 1958, 199-217, 257-76.

4160.   KREKER, Hans-Justus, "Die französischen Festungen 1870/
         71," Wehrw. Rs., 20, 1970.

4161.   KYTE, George W., "The Vanquished must Surrender: Jules
         Favre and the Franco-German Armistice of 1871," His-
         torian, 9, 1946/47, 19-36.

4162.   LACHMANN, Manfred, "Probleme der Bewaffnung des kaiser-
         lichen deutschen Heeres," Zs. f. MilitärG., 6, 1967, 23-
         37.

4163.   LAMMERS, A., "Die wirthschaftlichen Vorgänge im deutsch-
        französischen Kriege," Pr. Jbb., 26, 1870, 419-40.
4164.   LANCELLE, F., "Die alte Armee und der monarchische
        Gedanke," Gelbe Hefte, 2, 1925/26, 652-74.
4165.   LEHMANN, Max, "Der Feldzug von Sedan nach französ-
        ischen Quellen," HZ, 30, 1873, 72-146.
4166.   _____, "General Borstell und der Ausbruch des Krieges
        von 1813," HZ, 37, 1877, 55-76.
4167.   _____, "Der Krieg von 1870 bis zur Einschliessung von
        Metz nach Französischen Quellen," HZ, 29, 1873, 111-55.
4168.   _____, "Die Schlacht von Vionville und Mars la Tour,"
        Pr. Jbb., 29, 1872, 709-46; 30, 1872, 1-50.
4169.   _____, "Zur Geschichte der preussische Heeresreform
        von 1808," HZ, 126, 1922, 436-57.
4170.   LENZ, Rudolf, "Kosten und Finanzierung der Deutsch-
        Französischen Krieges 1870-1871 Dargestellt am Württem-
        bergs und Badens," Zs. F. Württbg. LG, 28, 1969, 118-
        71.
4171.   LINDEINER-WILDAU, Christoph, "Burg Hohenzollern als
        preussisch-deutsche Garnison und befestigter Platz," Z.
        hohenzoll. Gesch., 3, 1967.
4172.   MARX, Ernst, "Einige Randglossen zum 12. u. 13. Juli
        1870," HZ, 109, 1912, 508-25.
4173.   MAYER, A. J., "Internal Causes and Purposes of War in
        Europe 1870-1956," J. Mod. Hist., 41, 1969, 291-303.
4174.   MEHNER, Heinz, "Militärkaste, Sozialdemokratie und
        Armee in den 70er und 80er Jahren des 19. Jahrhun-
        derts," Zs. f. MilitärG., 2, 1963, 223-30.
4175.   MEIER-WELCKER, Hans, "Militär und Militärverwaltung in
        ihrem Verhältnis in der deutschen Heeresgeschichte,"
        Wehrw. Rs., 17, 1967, 241-65.
4176.   MEINECKE, Friedrich, "Landwehr und Landsturm seit
        1814," Schmoll. Jb., 40, 1916, 1087-1112.
4177.   MEINHARDT, Günther, "Die preussische Flotte im Feldzuge
        von 1807," Jb. der Albertus-Universität zu Königsberg/
        Pr., 19, 1969, 92-114.
4178.   MORRIS, William O'Connor, "The Campaign of Sedan," EHR,
        3, 1888, 209-32.
4179.   _____, "The War of 1870-1: After Sedan," EHR, 4,
        1889, 417-40.
4180.   MÜLLER, Harald, "Zu den Anfängen der militärischen
        Absprachen zwischen Deutschland und Österreich-Ungarn
        im Jahre 1882," Zs. f. MilitärG., 7, 1968, 206-15.
4181.   MÜNCH, Gotthard, "Detlev von Liliencron in Schlesien,"
        Jb. d. Schles.-Fried.-Wilh. Univ z. Breslau, 12, 1967,
        231-45.
4182.   NIETHAMMER, Hermann, "Ludwig Friedrich von Stockmayer
        1779-1837," Zs. F. Württbg. LG, 3, 1939, 449-74.
4183.   OTTO, Helmut, "Entstehung und Wesen der Blitzkriegsstrat-
        egie des deutschen Imperialismus vor dem ersten Welt-
        krieg," Zs. f. MilitärG., 6, 1967, 400-14.
4184.   _____, "Zum Strategisch-operativen Zusammenwirken
        des deutschen und österreichisch-ungarischen General-

stabes bei der Vorbereitung des ersten Weltkrieges," <u>Zs.</u>
<u>f. MilitärG.</u>, 2, 1963, 423-40.

4185.   PETERS, Herbert, "Patriotische Offiziere in der anti-feudal-
en Vormärzbewegung in Deutschland," <u>Zs. f. MilitärG.</u>,
9, 1970, 192-202.

4186.   PETSCHKE, G., "Die Bekleidung und Ausrüstung der preussischen Kürassiere in der Zeit von 1809-1918," <u>Zs. f.</u>
<u>Heeres-u. Uniformkunde</u>, 22, 1958, 5-10, 86-94; 23,
1959, 62-69, 110-14.

4187.   PFLUGK-HARTTUNG, Julius von, "Aus dem bayerischen
Hauptquartier 1814-1815," <u>H. Jb.</u>, 35, 1914, 356-74.

4188.   _____, "Aus dem bayerischen Hauptquartier, 1815,"
<u>H. Jb.</u>, 32, 1911, 825-32.

4189.   _____, "Aus den Tagen des 17. und 18. Juni 1815,"
<u>Hist. Vjschr.</u>, 8, 1905, 181-200.

4190.   _____, "Das Gefecht bei Limale (18. Juni 1815)," <u>H. Jb.</u>,
27, 1906, 34-66.

4191.   _____, "General von Kleist als Befehlshaber 1815,"
<u>FBPG</u>, 23, 1910, 469-92.

4192.   _____, "Der Oberbefehl 1813," <u>H. Jb.</u>, 35, 1914, 836-47.

4193.   _____, "Die preussische Berichterstattung an Wellington
vor der Schlacht bei Ligny," <u>H. Jb.</u>, 24, 1903, 41-61.

4194.   PRERADOVICH, Nikolaus v., "Die Führer der deutschen
Heere 1866 in sozialer Sicht," <u>VSW</u>, 53, 1966, 370-76.

4195.   RADBRUCH, Eberhard, "Offiziere im Konflikt um Eid und
Gehorsam Die Haltung des kurhessischen Offizierkorps
im Verfassungskonflikt von 1850," <u>GiWuU</u>, 19, 1968, 137-
45.

4196.   RITTER, Gerhard, "Der Anteil der Militärs an der Kriegs-
katastrophe von 1914," <u>HZ</u>, 193, 1961, 72-91.

4197.   _____, "The Military and Politics in Germany," <u>J. Cen.</u>
<u>Eur. Aff.</u>, 17, 1958, 259-71.

4198.   _____, "Das Problem des Militarismus in Deutschland,"
<u>HZ</u>, 177, 1954, 21-48.

4199.   RÖDER, Reinhold, "Zur Entwicklung der deutsch-russischen
Waffenbrüderschaft am Beginn des Jahres 1813," <u>Zs. f.</u>
<u>MilitärG.</u>, 2, 1963, 94-100.

4200.   RÖHL, J. C. G., "Admiral von Müller and the Approach of
War, 1911-1914," <u>Hist. J.</u>, 12, 1969, 651-73.

4201.   ROLOFF, Gustav, "Abrüstung und Kaiserplan vor dem Kriege
von 1870," <u>Pr. Jbb.</u>, 214, 1928, 183-98.

4202.   ROSE, J. Holland, "A Report of the Battles of Jena-Auer-
städt and the Surrender at Prenzlau," <u>EHR</u>, 19, 1904,
550-53.

4203.   RUMSCHÖTTEL, Hermann, "Bildung und Herkunft der bayerischen Offiziere 1866 bis 1914 Zur Geschichte von Mentalität und Ideologie des bayerischen Offizierkorps," <u>Mili-</u>
<u>tärgesch. Mitt.</u>, 2, 1970(2), 81-131.

4204.   SALEWSKI, M., "Selbstverständnis und historischens Bewusstsein der deutschen Kriegsmarine," <u>Marine Rs.</u>, 67,
1970, 65-88.

4205.   SAMUEL, Dr., "Die Sanitätspflege der Armee im Feldzuge
von 1866," <u>Pr. Jbb.</u>, 19, 1867, 379-412.

4206. SAUL, K., "Der 'Deutsche Kriegerbund'. Zur innenpoliti-
       schen Funktion eines 'nationalen Verbandes im kaiser-
       lichen Deutschland'," Militärgesch. Mitt., 1, 1969(2),
       95-160.

4207. _____, "Der Kampf um die Jugend zwischen Volksschule
       und Kaserne ... 1890-1914," Militärgesch. Mitt., 1(1),
       1971.

4208. SCHEEL, Heinrich, "Zur Problematik des deutschen Be-
       freiungskrieges 1813," Zs. f. Geschw., 11, 1963, 1277-
       98.

4209. SCHILL, Wilhelm F., "Militärische Beziehungen zwischen
       Preussen und Baden in den Jahren 1849-1850," FBPG, 43,
       1930, 290-333.

4210. "Die SCHLACHT von Königgrätz," Pr. Jbb., 22, 1868, 186-
       244, 655-97; 23, 1869. 1-18, 158-90, 522-615; 24, 1870,
       505-72.

4211. SCHOEPS, Hans-Joachim, "Vom Yorckschen Korps zum
       Zarenhof Aus den Briefen des Johann Paul Franz von
       Lucadou," ZRGG, 15, 1963, 347-60.

4212. "SCHRIFTTUM zur deutschen Wehr- und Kriegsgeschichte
       des 19. u. 20. Jahrhunderts," Pol. Stud., 5, 1954/55,
       55-60.

4213. SCHÜCKING, Lothar, "Die Franzosen im Münsterlande,"
       Westf. Zs., 58, 1900, 153-85.

4214. SHOWALTER, Dennis E., "Diplomacy and the Military in
       France and Prussia, 1870," Cen. Eur. Hist., 4, 1971,
       346-53.

4215. _____, "Manifestation of Reform: The Rearmament of
       the Prussian Infantry, 1806-13," J. Mod. Hist., 44,
       1972, 364-80.

4216. _____, "The Prussian 'Landwehr' and Its Critics, 1813-
       1819," Cen. Eur. Hist., 4, 1971, 3-33.

4217. STEHLIN, Stewart A., "Guelph Plans for the Franco-
       Prussian War," Hist. J., 13, 1970, 789-98.

4218. STEINBERG, Jonathan, "A German Plan for the Invasion of
       Holland and Belgium, 1897," Hist. J., 6, 1963, 107-19.

4219. _____, "The Kaiser's Navy and German Society," Past
       and Present, 28, 1964, 102-10.

4220. STEINBERG-v. Pape, Chr. and J. BRACKER, "Briefe des
       sächsischen Oberleutnants Ernst Freiherr von Friesen aus
       der Zeit der Bundesexekution 1863/64," Zs. Schlesw.-
       Holst., 95, 1970, 91-157.

4221. STONE, Norman, "Moltke-Conrad: Relations Between the
       Austro-Hungarian and German General Staffs, 1909-14,"
       Hist. J., 9, 1966, 201-28.

4222. STRAUBE, Fritz, "Über den Anteil der russischen Truppen
       am deutschen Befreiungskrieg im Frühjahr 1813," Zs. f.
       MilitärG., 2, 1963, 196-208.

4223. STROHBUSCH, Erwin, "Geh. Rat Hüllmann Eine Biographie
       mit Ausblicken auf den deutschen Kriegsschriffbau um
       1910," Tradition, 10, 1965, 33-45.

4224. SYBEL, Heinrich v., "Graf Brandenburg in Warschau
       (1850)," HZ, 58, 1887, 245-78.

4225.   TERVEEN, Frity, "Die Ballonfahrt in den Heeren des 18.
        und 19. Jahrhunderts," Wehrw. Rs., 7, 1957, 447-59.
4226.   THIMME, Friedrich, ed., "Zu den Erhebungsplänen der
        preussischen Patrioten im Sommer 1808 Ungedruckte
        Denkschriften Gneisenau's und Scharnhorst's," HZ, 86,
        1901, 78-110.
4227.   TREITSCHKE, Heinrich v., "Das Reichs-Militärgesetz,"
        Pr. Jbb., 33, 1874, 302-14.
4228.   "UEBER Reformen in der preussischen Kriegsverfassung,"
        Pr. Jbb., 5, 1860, 143-74.
4229.   ULMANN, H., "Die Detachements der freiwilligen Jäger in
        den Befreiungskriegen," Hist. Vjschr., 10, 1907, 483-505.
4230.   _____, "Wie es zur Schlacht bei Leipzig gekommen ist,"
        Hist. Vjschr., 16, 1913, 210-42.
4231.   VERNOIS, J. von Verdy du, "Heer und Flotte," Pr. Jbb.,
        99, 1900, 377-409.
4232.   "VOR der Militärdebatte im preussischen Abgeordneten-
        hause," Pr. Jbb., 11, 1863, 387-413.
4233.   WEGENER, Edward, "Nochmals: Selbstverständnis und his-
        torisches Bewusstsein der deutschen Kriegsmarine,"
        Marine Rs., 67, 1970.
4234.   WEHLER, Hans-Ulrich, "'Absoluter' und 'totaler' Krieg:
        Von Clausewitz zu Ludendorff," Pol. Vjschr., 10, 1969,
        220-48.
4235.   WIENHÖFER, Elmar, "Die Aachener Militärkonferenz über
        die deutsche Bundesarmee im Jahre 1818," Wehrw. Rs.,
        19, 1969, 552-56.
4236.   WILKE, Johannes, "Die preussische Heerorganisation von
        1859/60," Zs. f. Heeres- und Uniformkunde, 24, 1960,
        89-93.
4237.   WOLTER, H., "Das lothringische Erzgebiet als Kriegsziel
        der deutschen Grossbourgeoisie im deutsch-französischen
        Krieg 1870/71," Zs. f. Geschw., 19, 1971, 34-64.
4238.   ZURBONSEN, Dr., "Der ehemalige Freischarenführer v.
        Lützow in Münster und sein Kreis, 1817-1830," Westf.
        Zs., 58, 1900, 186-217.

                Gerhard Leberecht von Blücher (1742-1819)

4239.   BLASENDORFF, C., "Fünfzig Briefe Blücher's," HZ, 54,
        1885, 193-224.
4240.   DREETZ, Dieter, "Zur Rolle des Feldmarschalls Gebhardt
        Leberecht von Blücher bei der Organisierung des mili-
        tärischen Widerstandskampfes gegen die napoleonische
        Fremdherrschaft in den Jahren 1807-08," Zs. f. MilitärG.,
        1, 1962, 236-44.
4241.   GRANIER, Hermann, ed., "Aus Blüchers Korrespondenz,"
        FBPG, 26, 1913, 149-85.
4242.   PFLUGK-HARTTUNG, Julius von, "Die Ernennung Blüchers
        zum Oberfeldherrn 1815," H. Jb., 33, 1912, 580-85.
4243.   _____, "Die Verhandlungen Wellingtons und Blüchers auf
        der Windmühle bei Brye (16 Juni 1815)," H. Jb., 23, 1902,

80-97.

Hermann von Boyen (1771-1848)

4244. FORD, Guy S., "Boyen's Military Law," AHR, 20, 1915,
528-38.
4245. KESSEL, E., "Zu Boyens Entlassung," HZ, 175, 1953, 41-
54.
4246. MEINECKE, Friedrich, "Boyen und Roon," HZ, 77, 1896,
207-33.

Karl von Clausewitz (1780-1831)

4247. "AUS Gneisenaus Hauptquartier Briefe von Clausewitz,
Groeben und Gneisenau," ZRGG, 2, 1949/50, 241-46.
4248. BEYERHAUS, Gisbert, "Der ursprüngliche Clausewitz,"
Wehr. Rs., 3, 1953, 102-10.
4249. GEMBRUCH, Werner, "Zu Clausewitz' Gedanken über das
Verhältnis von Krieg und Politik," Wehrw. Rs., 9, 1959,
619-33.
4250. HAHLWEG, W., "Clausewitz und die preussische Heeresreform," Zs. f. Heeres- und Uniformkunde, 23, 1959,
27-33.
4251. KESSEL, Eberhard, "Zur Genesis der modernen Kriegslehre
Die Entstehungsgeschichte von Clausewitz Buch 'Vom
Kriege'," Wehrw. Rs., 3, 1953, 405-23.
4252. NOHN, E. A., "Clausewitz contra Bülow," Wehrw. Rs., 5,
1955, 323-30.
4253. _____, "Jomini und Clausewitz," Pol. Stud., 10, 1959,
175-81.
4254. PARET, Peter, "An Anonymous Letter by Clausewitz on the
Polish Insurrection of 1830-31," J. Mod. Hist., 42,
1970, 184-90.
4255. _____, "Education, Politics, and War in the Life of
Clausewitz," J. Hist. Ideas, 29, 1968, 394-408.
4256. ROSINSKI, Herbert, "Die Entwicklung vom Clausewitz' Werk
'Vom Kriege' im Lichte seiner 'Vorreden' und Nachrichten'," HZ, 151, 1934/35, 278-93.
4257. ROTHFELS, Hans, ed., "Eine Denkschrift Carls v. Clausewitz aus den Jahren 1807-08," Pr. Jbb., 178, 1919, 223-
45.
4258. SCHMITT, Carl, "Clausewitz als politischer Denker," Staat,
6, 1967, 479-502.
4259. SCHRAMM, Wilhelm von, "Clausewitz und die politische
Philosophie," Aussenpol., 9, 1958, 708-16.
4260. _____, "Der wiederentdeckte Clausewitz," Pol. Stud., 8,
1956/57, 1-10.

August Wilhelm Anton Neidhardt von Gneisenau (1760-1831)

4261. BETHCKE, Dr., "Gneisenau," Gelbe Hefte, 12, 1935/36, 606-30.
4262. LEHMANN, Max, "Gneisenau's Sendung nach Schweden und England im Jahre 1812," HZ, 62, 1889, 466-517.
4263. STERN, Alfred, "Gneisenau's Reise nach London im Jahre 1809 und ihre Vorgeschichte," HZ, 85, 1900, 1-44.
4264. TESKE, Hermann, "Gneisenau--Staatsbürger und Mensch," Wehrw. Rs., 10, 1960, 521-47.
4265. USINGER, Rudolf, "Gneisenau," HZ, 14, 1865, 351-96.
4266. WILL, Günter, "Neithardt Graf von Gneisenau," Wehrw. Rs., 12, 1962, 437-51.

Helmuth von Moltke (1800-1891)

4267. ANDREAS, Willy, "Helmut von Moltke," Zeitwende, 1(1), 1927, 594-610.
4268. BLUME, W. v., "Politik und Strategie, Bismarck und Moltke 1866 und 1870/71," Pr. Jbb., 111, 1903, 223-54.
4269. BUCHFINK, Ernst, "Moltke und Schlieffen," HZ, 158, 1938, 308-22.
4270. DANIELS, Emil, "Roon und Moltke vor Paris," Pr. Jbb., 121, 1905, 1-25, 220-41.
4271. DELBRÜCK, Hans, "Moltke," Pr. Jbb., 102, 1900, 108-30.
4272. HAEFTEN, Oberst von, "Bismarck und Moltke," Pr. Jbb., 177, 1919, 85-105.
4273. HELMERT, Heinz, "Helmuth v. Moltke und der preussische Generalstab in der Vorgeschichte des Krieges von 1866," Jb. f. Gesch., 1, 1967, 24-64.
4274. HOLBORN, Hajo, "Moltke's Strategical Concepts," Military Affairs, 6, 1942, 153-68.
4275. HUGO, Conrad von, "Carl von Brandenstein, Chef des Feldeisenbahnwesens und engster Mitarbeiter Moltkes 1870-71," Wehrw. Rs., 14, 1964, 676-84.
4276. PESCHKE, Rudolf, "Moltke als Politiker," Pr. Jbb., 158, 1914, 16-35.
4277. SCHIFF, Otto, "Moltke als politischer Denker," Pr. Jbb., 181, 1920, 318-36.
4278. STONE, Norman, "Moltke-Conrad: Relations Between the Austro-Hungarian and the German General Staffs, 1909-14," Hist. J., 9, 1966, 201-28.

Karl Ludwig von Prittwitz (1790-1871)

4279. HAENCHEN, Karl, "Aus dem Nachlass des Generals v. Prittwitz," FBPG, 45, 1933, 99-125.
4280. HAENCHEN, Karl, ed., "Aus den Briefen Nobilings an Prittwitz," FBPG, 53, 1941, 129-54.
4281. RACHFAHL, Felix, "Die Opposition des Generals v. Prittwitz," FBPG, 18, 1905, 252ff.

4282.   THIMME, Friedrich, "General von Prittwitz und der 18./19.
        März 1848," FBPG, 17, 1904, 588-601.
4283.   _____, "König Friedrich Wilhelm IV, General v. Pritt-
        witz und die Berliner Märzrevolution," FBPG, 16, 1903,
        545-82; 17, 1904, 588ff.
4284.   _____, "Der 'Ungehorsam' des Generals v. Prittwitz,"
        FBPG, 18, 1905, 360ff.

Albrecht von Roon (1803-1879)

See also entries 4246, 4270

4285.   "AUS dem badischen Feldzuge 1849   Erinnerungen aus
        nachgelassenen Briefen des Generalfeldmarschalls von
        Roon," Deutsche Revue, 6, 1881, 1-12.

Gerhard Johann David von Scharnhorst (1755-1813)

4286.   GEMBRUCH, W., "Das Reformwerk Scharnhorsts," Wehrw.
        Rs., 8, 1958, 627-42.
4287.   LEHMANN, Max, "Scharnhorst's Kampf für die stehenden
        Heere," HZ, 53, 1885, 276-99.
4288.   ROHR, Wilhelm, "Scharnhorsts Sendung nach Wien Ende
        1811 und Metternichs Politik," FBPG, 43, 1930, 76-128.
4289.   STADELMANN, Rudolf, "Das Duell zwischen Scharnhorst
        und Borstell im Dezember 1807," HZ, 161, 1939/40,
        263-76.
4290.   TESKE, Hermann, "Scharnhorst," Wehrw. Rs., 5, 1955,
        518-27.

Alfred Schlieffen (1833-1913)

See also entries 949, 4269

4291.   BETHCKE, Dr., "Schlieffen eine biographische Skizze,"
        Gelbe Hefte, 9, 1932/33, 719-39.
4292.   GROENER, General Wilhelm, "Rückzug   Eine operative
        Studie zum hundertsten Geburtstag des Grafen Schlieffen,"
        Pr. Jbb., 231, 1933, 219-26.
4293.   OERTZEN, K. L. von, "Alfred Graf Schlieffen Zum 100.
        Geburtstage des Generalfeldmarschals," Pr. Jbb., 231,
        1933, 252-59.
4294.   RITTER, Gerhard, "Le 'Plan Schlieffen' de l'état-major
        Allemand de 1914   Considérations sur sa critique mili-
        taire et politique," Rev. d'hist. mod., 7, 1960, 215-31.

Alfred von Tirpitz (1849-1930)

4295.   BECKER, Willy, "Bülow kontra Tirpitz   Ein Beitrag zu den

Kontroversen über die deutsche Flottenpolitik, " Zs. f.
Pol., 16, 1926/27, 297-330.

4296.   HUBATSCH, Walther, "Zur Beurteilung von Tirpitz," WaG,
11, 1951, 174-84.

4297.   KENNEDY, Paul M., "Tirpitz, England and the Second Navy
Law of 1900: A Strategical Critique, " Militärgesch.
Mitt., 2, 1970(2), 33-57.

4298.   STÖLTENBERG, G., "Tirpitz und seine Flottenpolitik, "
GiWuU, 13, 1962, 549-58.

Alfred von Waldersee (1832-1904)

4299.   KESSEL, Eberhard, "Die Tätigkeit des Grafen Waldersee
als Generalquartiermeister und Chef des Generalstabs
der Armee, " WaG, 14, 1954, 181-211.

4300.   MEISNER, Heinrich O., "Graf Waldersees Pariser Informa-
tionen 1887, " Pr. Jbb., 224, 1931, 125-48.

Friedrich von Wrangel (1784-1877)

4301.   LEHMANN, Max, "Major v. Wrangel, der angebliche Urheber
der Konvention von Tauroggen, " Pr. Jbb., 131, 1908,
428-42.

4302.   THIMME, Friedrich, "Freiherr Ludwig v. Wrangel und die
Konvention von Tauroggen, " HZ, 100, 1908, 112-29.

4303.   ZURBONSEN, Dr., "General von Wrangel und die Mün-
sterschen Dezember-Unruhen 1837, " Westf. Zs., 63,
1905, 257-68.

NATIONALISM, NATIONALITIES, MINORITIES

General Studies

See also entry 3248

4304. BERDAHL, Robert M., "New Thoughts on German Nationalism," AHR, 77, 1972, 65-80.

4305. BESSELL, Dr. Georg, "Preussentum und Hanseatentum und ihre Bedeutung für die Entstehung des Deutschen Reiches," Pr. Jbb., 216, 1929, 129-51.

4306. BEYER, Hans Joachim, "Hauptlinien einer Geschichte der ostdeutschen Volksgruppen im 19. Jahrhundert," HZ, 162, 1940, 509-39.

4307. BÖHNING, P., "Westpreussisches Polentum und polnische Nation. Zur Aussenorientierung der nationalpolnischen Bewegung in Westpreussen vor der Reichsgründung," Zs. f. Ostforsch., 20, 1971, 78-94.

4308. BRUNSCHWIG, Henri, "Propos sur les nationalismes Allemands," Annales, 5, 1950, 9-14.

4309. _____, "Propos sur le Prussianisme," Annales, 3, 1948, 16-20.

4310. BUCHNER, Max, "Schwarz-Rot-Gold und Schwarz-Weiss-Rot im Vergangenheit und Gegenwart Betrachtungen über den Werdegang und Stand der 'deutschen Frage'," Gelbe Hefte, 1, 1924/25, 153-80, 197-238.

4311. CALLESEN, Gerd, "Die Auseinandersetzungen um die deutsche Nationalitätenpolitik in Nordschleswig," Zs. Schlesw.-Holst., 92, 1967, 129-54.

4312. DIX, Arthur, "Das Slaventum in Preussen Seine Bedeutung für die Bevölkerungsbewegung und Volkswirtschaft in den letzten Jahrzehnten," Jbb. f. Nationalökon. u. Stat., 70, 1898, 561-602.

4313. "ELSASS-Lothringen unter deutscher Verwaltung," Pr. Jbb., 33, 1874, 269-301, 388-413, 551-88; 34, 1874, 404-30, 473-504.

4314. GÜNTHER, Adolf, "Karl Friedrich Vollgraff Kämpfer im Vormärz für Rasse, Volk u. Staat," Schmoll. Jb., 59, 1935, 59-82.

4315. HAGEN, William W., "National Solidarity and Organic Work in Prussian Poland, 1815-1914," J. Mod. Hist., 44, 1972, 38-64.

4316. HAGENAH, H., "Lebenserinnerungen von F. Reventlow," Zs. d. Ges. f. Schlesw.-Holst. Gesch., 61, 1933, 493ff.

4317.   HARTWIG, Edgar, "Der Alldeutsche Verband und Polen,"
         Wiss. Z. Univ. Jena (Ges.-u. sprachwiss. Reihe), 1970.
4318.   HAUSER, O. v., "Obrigkeitstaat u. demokratisches Prinzip
         im Nationalitätenkampf Preussen in Nordschleswig," HZ,
         192, 1961, 318-61.
4319.   _____, "Zum Problem der Nationalisierung Preussens,"
         HZ, 202, 1966, 529-41.
4320.   HAYES, Carlton J. H., "Contributions of Herder to the
         Doctrine of Nationalism," AHR, 32, 1926/27, 719-36.
4321.   HENDERSON, W. O., "Germany and Mitteleuropa," Ger.
         Life Letters, 2, 1937/38, 161-74.
4322.   _____, "The Pan-German Movement," History, 26, 1941,
         188-98.
4323.   HERRE, Franz, "Modelle für deutschen Nationalismus,"
         Pol. Mein., 12, 1967, 107-18.
4324.   HIRSCH, Helmut, "Bibliographical Article--Some Recent Ma-
         ..terial on the Saar," J. Mod. Hist., 23, 1951, 366-76.
4325.   HÖFELE, Karl H., "Sendungsglaube und Epochenbewusstsein
         in Deutschland 1870/71," ZRGG, 15, 1963, 266-76.
4326.   HUBATSCH, Walther, "Masuren und Preussisch-Litauen in
         der Nationalitätenpolitik Preussens 1870-1912," Zs. f.
         Ostforsch., 14, 1965, 641-70; 15, 1966, 1-55.
4327.   JAFFE, Fritz, "Gedanken über Preussen," Zeitwende, 21,
         1949/50, 481-500.
4328.   JOACHIMSEN, Paul, "Epochen des deutschen Nationalbewusst-
         seins," Zeitwende, 6(1), 1930, 97-109.
4329.   KANN, Robert A., "Wolfgang Menzel: Pioneer of Integral
         Nationalism," J. Hist. Ideas, 6, 1945, 213-30.
4330.   KOEHL, R. L., "Colonialism inside Germany: 1886-1918,"
         J. Mod. Hist., 25, 1953, 255-72.
4331.   KOHN, Hans, "The Eve of German Nationalism (1789-1812),"
         J. Hist. Ideas, 12, 1951, 256-84.
4332.   _____, "Romanticism and the Rise of German Nationalism,"
         Rev. Pol., 12, 1950, 443-72.
4333.   LAUBERT, Manfred, "Eine Denkschrift des Legationsrats
         Heinrich Küpfer über der Germanisierung der Provinz Po-
         sen (1837)," FBPG, 19, 1906, 187-221.
4334.   LUNDIN, C. Leonard, "The Road from Tsar to Kaiser:
         Changing Loyalties of the Baltic Germans, 1905-1914,"
         J. Cen. Eur. Aff., 20, 1950, 223-55.
4335.   MEYER, Henry Cord, "Der 'Drang nach Osten' in den Jahren
         1860-1914," WaG, 17, 1957, 1-8.
4336.   MITSCHERLICH, Waldemar, "Der Nationalismus und seine
         Wurzeln," Schmoll. Jb., 36, 1912, 1285-1320.
4337.   MOMMSEN, Hans, "Nationalitätenfrage und Arbeiterbewegung,"
         Schriften aus dem Karl-Marx Haus, 6, 1971, 465.
4338.   NEVEUX, Jean-B., "Une province polonaise de l'Etat des
         Hohenzollern La Wielkopolska et Poznán (1815-1840),"
         RH, 230, 1963, 347-90.
4339.   NIPPERDEY, Thomas, "Nationalidee und Nationaldenkmal in
         Deutschland im 19. Jahrhundert," HZ, 206, 1968, 529-85.
4340.   ONCKEN, Hermann, "Deutsche geistige Einflüsse in der
         europäischen Nationalitätenbewegung des 19. Jahrhunderts,"

Vjschr. f. Litw., 7, 1929, 607-27.

4341. OPPEN, Dietrich von, "Deutsche, Polen und Kaschuben in
       Westpreussen 1871-1914," Jb. f. Gesch. M. O. Dtschl.,
       4, 1955, 157-223.

4342. PASSON, Helga, "Der Nationalismus in der deutschen jugend-
       bildenden Literatur des 19. Jahrhunderts," Int'l Jahrb.
       Geschichtsunter., 12, 1968/69.

4343. PAULS, V., "U. J. Lornsen und die schleswig-holsteinische
       Bewegung," Z. d. Ges. f. schleswig-holsteinische Gesch.,
       60, 1930, 436ff.

4344. PFLANZE, Otto, "Nationalism in Europe, 1848-1871," Rev.
       Pol., 28, 1966, 129-43.

4345. ROSENTHAL, H. K., "Germans and Poles in 1890. Pos-
       sibilities for a New Course," East Europ. Quart., 5,
       1971, 302-12.

4346. ROTHFELS, Hans, "Nationalität und Grenze im späten 19.
       und frühen 20. Jahrhundert," VjHZG, 9, 1961, 225-34.

4347. RUNGE, Johann, "Uwe Jens Lornsen in Flensburg," Zs.
       Schlesw.-Holst., 93, 1968, 107-46.

4348. SCHARFF, A., "Warum scheiterte die schleswig-holstein-
       ische Erhebung," Der Schleswig-Holsteiner, 23, 1942,
       99ff.

4349. "Die SCHLESWIG-holsteinische und die 'deutsch-dänische'
       Frage," Pr. Jbb., 1, 1858, 166-85.

4350. SCHULTHEISS, Fr. Guntram, "Der Einfluss der Romantik
       auf die Vertiefung des Nationalgefühls," Arch. f. KuG.,
       5, 1907, 55-82.

4351. SIMON, W. M., "Variations in Nationalism during the Great
       Reform Period in Prussia," AHR, 59, 1953/54, 305-21.

4352. SOMMER, Erich Franz, "Die Russlanddeutschen im Wandel
       des Gesamtdeutschen Schichsals," HZ, 163, 1940/41, 503-
       18.

4353. SWART, F., "Zwanzig Jahre deutscher Kulturarbeit Tätig-
       keit und Aufgaben neupreussischer Kolonisation in West-
       preussen und Posen 1886-1906," Schmoll. Jb., 31, 1907,
       1817-31.

4354. SWEET, Paul, "Recent German Literature on Mitteleuropa,"
       J. Cen. Eur. Aff., 3, 1943, 1-24.

4355. TREITSCHKE, Heinrich von, "Die Lösung der schleswig-
       holsteinischen Frage," Pr. Jbb., 15, 1865, 169-87.

4356. _____, "Die Parteien und die Herzogthümer," Pr. Jbb.,
       16, 1865, 375-401.

4357. WEHLER, Hans-Ulrich, "Elsass-Lothringen von 1870 bis
       1918 das 'Reichland' als politisch-staatsrechtliches Prob-
       lem des zweiten deutschen Kaiserreichs," ZGORh., 109,
       1961, 133-99.

4358. WITTRAM, Reinhard, "Der Nationalismus als Forschungsauf-
       gabe," HZ, 174, 1952, 1-16.

4359. ZWAHR, Hartmut, "Zur antisorbischen Staatspolitik im
       preussisch-deutschen Reich," Jb. f. Regionalgesch., 1,
       1965, 89-135.

Friedrich Ludwig Jahn (1778-1852)

4360.   HERMANN, Otto, "Der Turnvater Jahn," Pr. Jbb., 118,
         1904, 19-37.
4361.   KÖRNER, Rudolf, "Friedrich Ludwig Jahn und sein Turn-
         wesen," FBPG, 41, 1928, 38-82, 480.
4362.   KOHN, Hans, "Father Jahn's Nationalism," Rev. Pol., 11,
         1949, 419-32.
4363.   MEYER, Dr. W., "Der Prozess F. L. Jahns," Pr. Jbb.,
         138, 1909, 245-80.

POLITICAL HISTORY, POLITICAL THOUGHT, POLITICAL PARTIES

<u>General Studies</u>

4364. "Der ALTE und der neue preussische Landtag," Pr. Jbb.,
       2, 1858, 555-79.
4365. BAUMGARTEN, H., "Der deutsche Liberalismus Eine
       Selbstkritik," Pr. Jbb., 18, 1866, 455-515, 575-628.
4366. BEHREND-ROSENFELD, E., "Die politischen Ideen O. V.
       Wydenbrugks," Z. d. Ver. f. Thur. Gesch., 25, 1924,
       105ff; 26, 1925, 140ff; 27, 1926, 185ff.
4367. BERDAHL, Robert M., "Conservative Politics and Aristo-
       cratic Landholders in Bismarckian Germany," J. Mod.
       Hist., 44, 1972, 1-20.
4368. BLUM, Hans, "Robert Blum im Tagebuch des Grafen von
       Hübner," Nord und Süd, 58, 1891, 35-56.
4369. BOSL, Karl, "Heinrich Held Journalist - Parteipolitiker -
       Staatsman," Zs. f. bayer. LG., 31, 1968, 747-67.
4370. _____, "La société allemande moderne: ses origines
       médiévales," Annales, 17, 1962, 839-56.
4371. BRANDENBURG, Erich, "Fünfzig Jahre Nationalliberale
       Partei 1867-1917," HZ, 119, 1918/19, 62ff.
4372. BRAUBACH, Max, "Deutsche Geschichte von Untergang des
       ersten Reiches bis zur Reichsgründung Bismarcks," H.
       Jb., 58, 1938, 463-509; 59, 1939, 171-201.
4373. _____, "Deutschland und Europa im 19. Jahrhundert
       Ein Sammelbericht," H. Jb., 56, 1936, 525-80.
4374. BRUNSCHWIG, Henri, "L'Allemagne au XIXe Siècle Thèses
       et Synthèses," RH, 207, 1952, 49-59.
4375. BUCHHEIM, Karl, "Von der Paulskirche zur Bundesrepublik
       Gestaltwandel der demokratischen Kräfte in Deutschland,"
       Zeitwende, 29, 1958, 658-70.
4376. BUCHNER, Max, "Geschichte und Politik Gedanken eines
       Konservativen der napoleonischen Zeit," Gelbe Hefte, 15,
       1938/39, 353-67.
4377. BUSSMANN, W., "Zur Geschichte des deutschen Liberalis-
       mus im 19. Jahrhundert," HZ, 186, 1958, 527-57.
4378. DEHIO, Ludwig, "Benedict Waldeck," HZ, 136, 1927, 25-57.
4379. DEMETER, Karl, "Die soziale Schichtung des deutschen
       Parlaments seit 1848," VSW, 39, 1952, 1-29.
4380. DICKINSON, Z. Clark, "The Library and Works of Karl
       Heinrich Rau," ZgesStw., 114, 1958, 577-93.
4381. DROZ, Jacques, "Histoire de L'Allemagne (1789-1914)," RH,

242, 1969, 141-72.
4382. _____, "Préoccupations religieuses et préoccupations sociales aux origines du parti conservateur prussien, " Rev.
d'hist. mod., 2, 1955, 280-300.
4383. ELSENER, F., "Das 'Staats-Lexikon' von Rotteck und Welck-
er als liberale Bibel in der Innerschweiz, " Alem. Jb.,
1970, 280-86.
4384. ENGELSING, Rolf, "Zur politischen Bildung der deutschen
Unterschichten 1789-1863, " HZ, 206, 1968, 337-69.
4385. EYCK, F. Gunther, "English and French Influences on German Liberalism before 1848, " J. Hist. Ideas, 18, 1957,
313-41.
4386. FABER, Karl-Georg, "Konservatorischer Liberalismus, "
Umstürzender Liberalismus, 'Konservatorischer Obsku-
rantismus', " Nass. Ann., 78, 1967, 177-207.
4387. FEHRENBACH, Elisabeth, "Über die Bedeutung der politischen Symbole im Nationalstaat, " HZ, 213, 1971, 296-
357.
4388. FLEIG, Edgar, "Aus der konservativen Gedankenwelt eines
Restaurationspolitikers, " H. Jb., 56, 1936, 331-50.
4389. FRAENKEL, Ernst, "Historische Vorbelastungen des deutschen Parlamentarismus, " VjHZG, 8, 1960, 323-40.
4390. FRANZ, Eugen, "Persönlichkeiten um Ludwig Frh. v. d.
Pfordten, " Zs. f. bayer. LG., 12, 1939, 137ff.
4391. FRICKE, Dieter, "Die bürgerlichen Parteien und die Le-
bensfragen der deutschen Nation zur Erforschung und
Darstellung der Geschichte der bürgerlichen Parteien in
Deutschland, " Zs. f. Geschw., 11, 1963, 29-77.
4392. _____, "Methodologische Probleme der Erforschung der
Geschichte der bürgerlichen Parteien, " Zs. f. Geschw.,
13, 1965, 189-208.
4393. FRIEDRICH, Fritz, "Aus den Frühlingstagen des deutschen
Liberalismus, " Pr. Jbb., 127, 1907, 80-100.
4394. GOLLWITZER, Heinz, "Die politische Landschaft in der
deutschen Geschichte des 19/20. Jahrhunderts, " Zs. f.
bayer. LG., 27, 1964, 523-52.
4395. GRAF, O., "Der monarchische Gedanke in Deutschland, "
Pol. Stud., 9, 1958, 833-41.
4396. GREBING, Helga, "Die Konservativen von 1848-1918, " Pol.
Stud., 9, 1958, 403-12.
4397. HARNACK, von, "Ernst Bassermann, " HZ, 133, 1926, 465-
67.
4398. HARRIS, David, "European Liberalism in the Nineteenth
Century, " AHR, 60, 1954/55, 501-26.
4399. HASELIER, G., "Adolf Geck als Politiker und Mensch im
Spiegel seines schriftlichen Nachlasses, " ZGORh., 115,
1967, 331-430.
4400. HENNIS, Wilhelm, "Zum Problem der deutschen Staatsanschauung, " VjHZG, 7, 1959, 1-23.
4401. HUBRICH, Eduard, "Das monarchische Prinzip in Preussen, "
Zs. f. Pol., 1, 1907/08, 193-218.
4402. _____, "Zur Entstehung der preussischen Staatseinheit, "
FBPG, 20, 1907, 347-427.

4403.   HÜSER, Karl, ed., "Die Lebenserinnerungen des Johann
        Matthias Gierse (1807-1881)," Westf. Zs., 121, 1971,
        71-95.
4404.   KALTHEUNER, Herbert, "Der Freiherr Georg von Vincke
        und die Liberalen in der preussischen zweiten Kammer
        1849-1855," Westf. Zs., 85, 1928, 1-96.
4405.   KANTOROWICZ, Hermann, "Zur Theorie des Sozialiberalis-
        mus," Schmoll. Jb., 28, 1904, 673-82, 1520-23.
4406.   KÖHLER, Jul. Paul, "Politische Romantik, Nation und
        Weltwirtschaft," VSW, 18, 1925, 368-80.
4407.   KOHNEN, "Zur Vorgeschichte des ersten Oldenburgischen
        Landtags," Old. Jb., 31, 1927, 199ff.
4408.   KOSZYK, Kurt, "Der Schlesische Revolutionär Friedrich
        Wilhelm Wolff (1809-1864)," Jb. d. Schles.-Fried.-Wilh.
        Univ z. Breslau, 9, 1964, 187-206.
4409.   KRETZSCHMAR, Helmut, "Das sächsische Königtum im 19.
        Jahrhundert Ein Beitrag zur Typologie der Monarchies in
        D.," HZ, 170, 1950, 457-93.
4410.   KROEGER, Gert, "Die politische Denkweise des livländischen
        Hegelianers Johann Eduard Erdmann (1805-1892)," Zs. f.
        Ostforsch., 7, 1958, 338-73.
4411.   LAMBERTI, Marjorie, "Lutheran Orthodoxy and the Begin-
        ning of Conservative Party Organization in Prussia,"
        Church Hist., 37, 1968, 439-53.
4412.   LANG, Wilhelm, "Julius Hölder Vier Jahrzehnte württem-
        bergischer Politik," Pr. Jbb., 61, 1888, 213-43.
4413.   LINSE, Ulrich, "Der deutsche Anarchismus 1870-1918 Eine
        politischen Bewegung zwischen Utopie und Wirklichkeit,"
        GiWuU, 20, 1969, 513-19.
4414.   LOUGEE, Robert W., "German Romanticism and Political
        Thought," Rev. Pol., 21, 1959, 631-45.
4415.   MAGILL, C. P., "An English Liberal in Germany 1840-42,"
        Ger. Life Letters, 1, 1936/37, 218-28.
4416.   MAIER, Hans, "Probleme einer demokratischen Tradition in
        Deutschland," GiWuU, 18, 1967, 394-415.
4417.   MANNHEIM, Karl, "Soziologische Beiträge zum Werden des
        politisch-historischen Denkens in Deutschland," Arch. f.
        Sozialw. u. Sozialpol., 57, 1927, 68-142, 470-95.
4418.   MARTIN, Alfred von, "Der preussische Altkonservativismus
        und der politische Katholizismus in ihren gegenseitigen
        Beziehungen," Vjschr. f. Litw., 7, 1929, 489-514.
4419.   MEINECKE, Friedrich, "Preussen und Deutschland im 19.
        Jahrhundert," HZ, 97, 1906, 119-36.
4420.   MENKE, P. Benitius, "Friedrich Wilhelm Weber und sein
        Freund Alfred Hüffer," Gelbe Hefte, 3, 1927, 461-71.
4421.   MOMMSEN, Wilhelm, "Julius Fröbel Wirrnis und Weitsicht,"
        HZ, 181, 1956, 497-532.
4422.   ———, "Zur Bedeutung des Reichsgedankens," HZ, 174,
        1952, 385-415.
4423.   MULERT, Hermann, "Religiöser und politischer Liberalis-
        mus," Zs. f. Pol., 4, 1910/11, 374-90.
4424.   NAROCNICKIJ, A. L., "Völker und Regierungen zu Beginn
        des Befreiungskrieges 1813," Zs. f. Geschw., 12, 1964,

                46-61.
4425.   NEU, Heinrich, "Die preussische Regierung und der Na-
         poleonkult im Rheinland," Jb. f. Gesch. Kunst d. MRh,
         18/19, 1966/67, 167-71.
4426.   NIPPERDEY, Thomas, "Die Funktion der Utopie im poli-
         tischen Denken der Neuzeit," Arch. f. KuG., 44, 1962,
         357-78.
4427.   NITZSCH, "Deutsch Stände und deutsche Parteien einst und
         jetzt," Pr. Jbb., 27, 1871, 627-64.
4428.   ONCKEN, Hermann, "Albert Schäffles Lebenserinnerungen,"
         HZ, 96, 1906, 243-58.
4429.   _____, "Bennigsen und die Epochen des Parlamentarischen
         Liberalismus in Deutschland und Preussen," HZ, 104,
         1910, 53-79.
4430.   PETERSDORFF, Herman von, "Graf Albrecht von Alvensle-
         ben-Erxleben," HZ, 100, 1908, 263-316.
4431.   PIECHOCKI, Werner, "Die kommunalpolitische Wirksamkeit
         Arnold Ruges in Halle während der Jahre 1831 bis 1841,"
         Wiss. Z. Univ Halle (Ges. und Sprachwiss Reihe), 16,
         1967, 173-96.
4432.   REIS, H. S., "The Political Ideas of the German Romantic
         Movement," Ger. Life Letters, 8, 1954/55, 1-8.
4433.   RIEBER, H., "Liberaler Gedanke und Französische Revolu-
         tion im Spiegel der Publizistik der Reichsstadt Ulm,"
         Ulm und Oberschwaben, 39, 1970, 121-48.
4434.   RINGEL, Martin and Gerhard SCHMIDT, "Die Kartei der
         politisch Verfolgten 1830-1867 im Staatsarchiv Dresden,"
         Beitr. z. Gesch. d. dt. Arbeiterbeweg., 12, 1970.
4435.   RITTER, Gerhard, "Geschichtliche Wandlungen des Monarch-
         ischen Staatsgedankens in Preussen-Deutschland," Pr.
         Jbb., 184, 1921, 234-52.
4436.   ROSENBERG, Hans, "Theologischer Rationalismus und
         Vormärzlicher Vulgärliberalismus," HZ, 141, 1929/30,
         497-541.
4437.   SAUER, Wolfgang, "Das Problem des deutschen National-
         staates," Pol. Vjschr., 3, 1962, 159-86.
4438.   SCHEIDT, Friedrich J., "Die Entfremdung von Philosophie
         und Politik Politische Theorien des neunzehnten Jahr-
         hunderts," Hochland, 57, 1964/65, 276-83.
4439.   SCHIEDER, Theodor, "Das Problem der Revolution im 19.
         Jahrhundert," HZ, 170, 1950, 233-71.
4440.   SCHMID, Eugen, "Friedrich Albert Hamber (1806-1883) in
         seiner Tätigkeit auf dem Gebiet der Politik," Zs. F.
         Württbg. LG, 5, 1941, 141-53.
4441.   SCHMIDT, Richard, "Volksstaat und Obrigkeitsstaat Ein
         Rückblick und ein Ausblick," Zs. f. Pol., 15, 1925/26,
         193-222.
4442.   SCHMIDT, Siegfried, "Zur Frühgeschichte der bürgerlichen
         Parteien in Deutschland," Zs. f. Geschw., 13, 1965, 972-
         91.
4443.   SCHOEPS, Hans Joachim, "CDU vor 75 Jahren Die sozial-
         politischen Bestrebungen des Reichsfreiherrn Friedrich
         Carl von Fechenbach (1836-1907)," ZRGG, 9, 1957, 266-

77.

4444. _____, "Hermann Wagener - Ein konservativer Sozialist,"
ZRGG, 8, 1956, 193-217.

4445. SCHRAEPLER, Ernst, "Die politische Haltung des liberalen
Bürgertums im Bismarckreich," GiWuU, 5, 1954, 529-44.

4446. SCHREUER, H., "Das deutsche Königtum Eine germanistische Studie," Schmoll. Jb., 42, 1918, 883-906.

4447. SCHRÖDER, Wolfgang, et al., "Die Pariser Kommune und
die herrschenden Klassen in Deutschland," Zs. f.
Geschw., 19, 1971, 309-38.

4448. SCHUBERT, Friedrich Hermann, "Wilhelm von Kügelgen und
das konservative Preussen," H. Jb., 82, 1962, 187-218.

4449. SCHULZ, Ursula, "Wilhelm Levysohn (1815-1871) Ein
Schlesischer Verleger und Politiker," Jb. d. Schles.-
Fried.-Wilh. Univ z. Breslau, 14, 1969, 75-137.

4450. SCHWAB, Herbert, "Von Düppel bis Königgrätz Die politische Haltung der deutschen Bourgeoisie zur nationalen
Frage 1864-1866," Zs. f. Geschw., 14, 1966, 588-610.

4451. SELL, Friedrich Carl, "Intellectual Liberalism in Germany
about 1900," J. Mod. Hist., 15, 1943, 227-36.

4452. SHANAHAN, William O., "The Social Outlook of Prussian
Conservatism," Rev. Pol., 15, 1953, 209-53.

4453. SICKEL, Paul, "Friedrich Hebbel als Politiker und Patriot,"
Pr. Jbb., 163, 1916, 281-304.

4454. SILBERNAGL, Dr., "Die geheimen politischen Verbindungen
der Deutschen in der ersten Hälfte des neunzehnten Jahrhunderts," H. Jb., 14, 1893, 775-813.

4455. SNELL, John L., "The World of German Democracy 1789-
1914," Historian, 31, 1968/69, 521-38.

4456. SPAHN, Martin, "Zur Entstehung der nationalliberalen
Partei," Zs. f. Pol., 1, 1907/08, 346-470.

4457. SRBIK, Heinrich Ritter von, "Die Reichsidee und das Werden
deutscher Einheit," HZ, 164, 1941, 457-71.

4458. STERN, Alfred, "Georg Klindworth Ein politischer Geheim-
agent des neunzehnten Jahrhunderts," Hist. Vjschr., 25,
1929/31, 430-58, 695-96.

4459. STRUCK, W. H., "Zur ideenpolitischen Vorbereitung des
Bundeslandes Hessen seit dem 19. Jahrhundert," Hess.
Jb. f. LG, 20, 1970, 282-324.

4460. TREITSCHKE, Heinrich von, "Bund und Reich," Pr. Jbb.,
34, 1874, 513-49.

4461. _____, "Der Krieg und die Bundesreform," Pr. Jbb., 17,
1866, 677-96.

4462. _____, "Parteien und Fractionen," Pr. Jbb., 27, 1871,
175-208, 347-67.

4463. UNRUH, G.-Chr. von, "Ursachen, Massstäbe und Erfolg
staatlicher Reformmassnahmen in 19. und 20. Jahrhundert," Westf. Forsch., 23, 1972, 20-43.

4464. VALENTIN, Veit, "Why Parliamentarism in Germany was
a Failure," Ger. Life Letters, 1, 1936/37, 197-203.

4465. VIERHAUS, Rudolf, "Preussen und die Rheinlande 1815-
1915," Rhein. Vjsbll., 30, 1965, 152-75.

4466. _____, "Wahlen und Wählerverhalten in Ostwestfalen und

Lippe untersucht an den Reichstags- und Landtagswahlen
von 1867 bis 1912/13," Westf. Forsch., 21, 1968.

4467.   WAGNER, Fritz, "Zur politischen Geschichte des 19. Jahr-
        hunderts," Vjschr. f. Litw., 31, 1957, 443-55.
4468.   WAHL, Adalbert, "Beiträge zur deutschen Parteigeschichte
        im 19. Jahrhundert," HZ, 104, 1910, 537-94.
4469.   WEBERSINN, Gerhard, "Dr. Felix Porsch Vizepräsident
        des Preussischen Landtags," Jb. d. Schles.-Fried.-Wilh.
        Univ z. Breslau, 13, 1968, 232-83.
4470.   WEINACHT, P. L., "'Staatsbürger'. Zur Geschichte und
        Kritik eines politischen Begriffs," Staat, 8, 1969, 41-63.
4471.   WENKE, Hans, "Der deutsche und sein Staat in Vergangen-
        heit und Gegenwart," GiWuU, 2, 1951, 449-65.
4472.   WINKLER-SERAPHIM, Brigitte, "Die Verhältnis der preus-
        sischen Ostprovinzen insbesondere Ostpreussens zum
        Deutschen Bund im 19. Jahrhundert," Zs. f. Ostforsch.,
        4, 1955, 321-50; 5, 1956, 1-33.

Ludwig Bamberger (1823-1899)

4473.   ONCKEN, Hermann, "Ludwig Bamberger," Pr. Jbb., 100,
        1900, 63-94.
4474.   WOLFFSOHN, Lily, "Traits in the Life of a great German
        liberal," Gentleman's Magazine, 296, 1904, 296-308,
        397-414.
4475.   ZUCKER, Stanley, "Ludwig Bamberger and the Politics of
        the Cold Shoulder: German Liberalism's Response to
        Working Class Legislation in the 1870's," Eur. Stud. Rev.,
        2, 1972, 201-26.
4476.   _____, "Ludwig Bamberger and the Rise of Anti-Semitism
        in Germany, 1848-1893," Cen. Eur. Hist., 3, 1970, 332-
        52.

Otto von Bismarck (1815-1898)

See also entries 371, 947, 2250, 3038, 3076, 3696, 3697,
4268, 4272, 4763

4477.   ADAM, Reinhard, "Bismarcks Reichsgründung und der nahe
        Osten," HZ, 161, 1939/40, 62-83.
4478.   ANDREAS, Willy, ed., "Gespräche Bismarcks mit dem
        badischen Finanzminister Moritz Ellstätter," ZGORh., 82,
        1929/30, 440-51.
4479.   ANDREWS, Herbert D., "Bismarck's Foreign Policy and
        German Historiography," J. Mod. Hist., 37, 1965, 345-
        56.
4480.   AULNEAU, M. J., "Mide Bismarck a la Diète de Francfort
        et la Politique de la Prusse pendant la Guerre de Crimée,"
        Rev. d'hist. dipl., 23, 1909, 403-38.
4481.   BAARE, Th., "Die Anfänge der deutschen Sozialgesetzgebung
        Ein archivalischer Beitrag zu den Beziehungen Bismarcks

zu L. Baare," Gelbe Hefte, 10, 1933/34, 549-61.
4482. BAUMGARTEN, Otto, "Bismarck als religiöser Charakter,"
Pr. Jbb., 160, 1915, 1-16.
4483. BECKER, Josef, "Baden, Bismarck und die Annexion von
Elsass und Lothringen," ZGORh., 115, 1967, 167-204.
4484. _____, "Zum Problem der bismarckschen Politik in der
Spanischen Thronfrage 1870," HZ, 212, 1971, 529-607.
4485. BECKER, O., "Der Sinn der dualistischen Verständigungs-
versuche Bismarcks für dem Kriege 1866," HZ, 169,
1949, 264-99.
4486. BETHCKE, Dr., "Bismarck und Caprivi vor dem Jahre
1890," Gelbe Hefte, 13, 1936/37, 384-91.
4487. BLANKE, Richard, "Bismarck and the Prussian Polish Policies of 1886," J. Mod. Hist., 45, 1973, 211-39.
4488. BÖHME, Helmut, "Big-Business Pressure Groups and Bismarck's Turn to Protectionism, 1873-79," Hist. J., 10,
1967, 218-36.
4489. _____, "Guid Graf Henckel von Donnersmarck, Bismarck
und der Krieg von 1866," Tradition, 12, 1967, 378-87.
4490. BOURGIN, Georges, "Une Entente Franco-Allemande Bismarck, Thiers, Jules Favre et la Répression de la
Commune de Paris (Mai, 1871)," Int. Rev. Soc. Hist., 1,
1956, 41-53.
4491. BROWN, Marvin L., Jr., "The Monarchical Principle in
Bismarckian Diplomacy After 1870," Historian, 15, 1952,
41-56.
4492. BUCHNER, Max, "Bismarck und die Religion," Gelbe Hefte,
11, 1934/35, 541-61.
4493. BUSCH, Wilhelm, "Bismarck und die Entstehung des Norddeutschen Bundes," HZ, 103, 1909, 52-78.
4494. BUSSMANN, Walter, "Wandel und Kontinuität der Bismarck-
wertung," WaG, 15, 1955, 126-36.
4495. COLER, Christfried, "Bismarck und die See," Wehrw. Rs.,
19, 1969, 584-94, 640-54.
4496. _____, "Der Konflikt Bismarck-Stosch März/April 1877,"
Wehrw. Rs., 17, 1967, 578-93.
4497. CORTI, E. Conte, "Bismarck und Italien am Berliner Kongress 1878," Hist. Vjschr., 23, 1926/27, 456-71.
4498. DANIELS, Emil, "Die englischen Liberalen und Fürst Bismarck," Pr. Jbb., 123, 1906, 220-60.
4499. DEHIO, Ludwig, "Beiträge zu Bismarcks Politik im Sommer
1866 unter Benutzung der Papiere Robert von Keudells,"
FBPG, 46, 1934, 147-65.
4500. _____, "Bismarck und die Herresvorlagen der Konflikts-
zeit," HZ, 144, 1931, 31-47.
4501. DELBRÜCK, Hans, "Bismarck - Historiographie," Pr. Jbb.,
96, 1899, 461-80.
4502. _____, "Bismarcks letzte politische Idee," Pr. Jbb., 147,
1912, 1-12.
4503. DITTRICH, Jochen, "Bismarck, Frankreich und die Hohenzollernkandidatur," WaG, 13, 1953, 42-57.
4504. DORPALEN, Andreas, "The German Historians and Bismarck," Rev. Pol., 15, 1953, 53-67.

4505. ERDMANN, Sylvia, "Ausfahrten des alten Bismarcks Aus
       den Tagebüchern seines Kutschers," GiWuU, 23, 1972,
       28-35.

4506. FAY, S. B., "Bismarck's Welfare State," Current History,
       18, 1950, 1-7.

4507. FELDMANN, Joseph, "Bismarck et la Question polonaise,"
       RH, 173, 1934, 540-58.

4508. FORSTREUTER, Kurt, "Zu Bismarcks Journalistik," Jb. f.
       Gesch. M. O. Dtschl., 2, 1953, 191-210.

4509. FRAHM, Friedrich, "Bismarcks Briefwechsel mit General
       Prim," Hist. Vjschr., 23, 1926/27, 64-86.

4510. _____, "Bismarck vor der Option zwischen Russland und
       Österreich im Herbst 1876," HZ, 149, 1933/34, 522-43.

4511. FRAUENDIENST, Werner, "Bismarck und das Herrenhaus,"
       FBPG, 45, 1933, 286-314.

4512. GACKENHOLZ, Hermann, "Der Kriegsrat von Czernahora
       von 12. Juli 1866 Ein Beitrag zur Kritik der 'Gedanken
       und Erinnerungen'," Hist. Vjschr., 26, 1931, 332-48.

4513. "Der GEWERBLICHE Unterricht unter dem Handelsminister
       Fürsten Bismarck," Schmoll. Jb., 14, 1890, 855-71.

4514. GITTERMANN, Valentin, "Die geschichtsphilosophischen
       Anschauungen Bismarcks," Arch. f. Sozialw. u. Sozial-
       pol., 51, 1923/24, 382-440.

4515. GOLDSCHMIDT, Hans, "Mitarbeiter Bismarcks im aussen-
       politischen Kampf," Pr. Jbb., 235, 1934, 29-48, 126-56;
       236, 1934, 27-51, 236-61.

4516. GOOCH, G. P., "Bismarck's Legacy," Foreign Affairs,
       1952, 517-30.

4517. GOTHEIN, Eberhard, "Bismarcks Jugend," HZ, 104, 1904,
       322-40.

4518. GRABOWSKY, Adolf, "Bismarck und der Staat," Zs. f. Pol.,
       2, 1955, 75-84.

4519. GREBE, Paul, "Bismarcks Sturz und der Bergarbeiterstreik
       von Mai 1889," HZ, 157, 1937/38, 84-97.

4520. GRIEWANK, Karl, "Wissenschaft und Kunst in der Politik
       Kaiser Wilhelms I und Bismarcks," Arch. f. KuG., 34,
       1952, 288-307.

4521. GRUBE, Hans B., "Erinnerungen an Otto von Bismarck,"
       Gelbe Hefte, 9, 1932/33, 129-43, 193-219.

4522. HAGEN, Maximilian von, "Das Bismarckbild der Gegen-
       wart," Zs. f. Pol., 22, 1932/33, 369-94, 465-81.

4523. _____, "Das Bismarckbild der Gegenwart," Zs. f. Pol.,
       28, 1938, 196-202, 241-52, 404-12.

4524. _____, "Das Bismarckbild der Gegenwart Bismarck in
       der Literatur 1915-1927," Zs. f. Pol., 18, 1928/29, 240-
       65, 299-320, 396-412, 472-84.

4525. _____, "Neuste Bismarckliteratur," Zs. f. Pol., 19,
       1929/30, 539-75.

4526. HALLGARTEN, George W. F., "War Bismarck ein Im-
       perialist?," GiWuU, 22, 1971.

4527. HALLMANN, Hans, "Bismarck und Marokko," Schmoll. Jb.,
       60, 1936, 195-208.

4528. HALPERIN, S. W., "Bismarck and the Italian Envoy in Ber-

lin on the Eve of the Franco-Prussian War," J. Mod.
Hist., 33, 1961, 33-39.

4529. HARRIS, David, "Bismarck's Advance to England, 1876,"
J. Mod. Hist., 3, 1931, 441-56.

4530. HARTUNG, Fritz, "Bismarck und die deutsche Revolution
1848-1851," WaG, 6, 1940, 167-78.

4531. _____, "Bismarck und Graf Harry Arnim," HZ, 171,
1951, 47-77.

4532. HEFFTER, Heinrich, "Bismarcks Sozialpolitik," Arch. f.
Sozialgesch., 3, 1963, 141-56.

4533. HERRE, Franz, "Der bayerische Gesandte in Berlin Freiherr Pergler von Perglas, und die Bismarckishe Regierung," H. Jb., 74, 1954, 532-45.

4534. HERTZER, E., "Bismarcks liberales Jahrzehnt," Gelbe
Hefte, 10, 1933/34, 400-22.

4535. HERZFELD, Hans, "Bismarck und die Skobelew-episode,"
HZ, 142, 1930, 279-302.

4536. HOLBORN, Hajo, "Bismarck's Realpolitik," J. Hist. Ideas,
21, 1960, 84-98.

4537. _____, "Über die Staatskunst Bismarcks," Zeitwende,
3(1), 1927, 321-34.

4538. HOLLYDAY, Frederic, "'Love Your Enemies! Otherwise
Bite Them!' Bismarck, Herbert, and the Morier Affair,
1888-1889," Cen. Eur. Hist., 1, 1968, 56-79.

4539. JAFFÉ, Fritz, "War Bismarcks Politik prorussisch?,"
Aussenpol., 2, 1951, 613-22.

4540. JELAVICH, Charles and Barbara, "Bismarck's Proposal for
the Revival of the Dreikaiserbund in October 1878," J.
Mod. Hist., 29, 1957, 249-60.

4541. KALKSCHMIDT, Eugen, "Bismarcks Bekehrung," Zeitwende,
12, 1935/36, 268-77.

4542. _____, "Bismarck und die öffentliche Meinung," Zeitwende, 11(1), 1934/35, 288-97.

4543. KALTENSTADLER, W., "König Ludwig II. von Bayern und
Bismarck," Zs. f. bayer. LG., 34, 1971, 715-28.

4544. KENT, George O., "The Bismarck Problem in our Time,"
Maryland Hist., 1970.

4545. KESSEL, E., "Bismarck und die 'Halbgötter' Zu dem Tagebuch von Paul Braunsart von Schellendorf," HZ, 181, 1956,
249-86.

4546. KEYSERLINGK, Robert H., "Bismarck and the Press: the
Example of the National Liberals," Can. Hist. Assoc.
Report, 1967, 198-215.

4547. KLEEFISCH, Dr., "Dostojewski, Bismarck und Deutschland,"
Gelbe Hefte, 3, 1927, 721-34.

4548. KLUKE, Paul, "Bismarck und Salisbury Ein diplomatisches
Duell," HZ, 175, 1953, 285-306.

4549. _____, "Frankfurt in Bismarcks Entscheidung 1866,"
Arch. f. Frankfurts Gesch., 51, 1968, 85-100.

4550. KOLB, Eberhard, "Bismarck und das Aufkommen der An-
nexionsforderung 1870," HZ, 209, 1969, 318-56.

4551. KRAEHE, Enno, "Practical Politics in the German Confederation Bismarck and the Commercial Code," J. Mod. Hist.,

25, 1953, 13-25.

4552. KRAUSNICK, Helmut, "Das Bismarckbild der französischen Schulgeschichtsbücher," GiWuU., 3, 1952, 513-30.

4553. _____, "Botschafter Graf Hatzfeldt und die Aussenpolitik Bismarcks," HZ, 167, 1943, 566-83.

4554. KROPAT, Wolf-Arno, "Die nassauischen Liberalen und Bismarcks Politik in den Jahren 1866-1867," Hess. Jb. f. LG., 16, 1966, 215-96.

4555. KÜHN, Joachim, "Bismarck und der Bonapartismus im Winter 1870/71," Pr. Jbb., 163, 1916, 49-100.

4556. LENZ, Max, "Bismarck," Pr. Jbb., 95, 1899, 191-207.

4557. LINDENBERG, Paul, "Bismarcks Abschied von Schönhausen," Gelbe Hefte, 14, 1937/38, 1-25.

4558. LIPGENS, Walter, "Bismarck und die Frage der Annexion 1870," HZ, 206, 1968, 586-617.

4559. _____, "Bismarcks Österreich-Politik vor 1866," WaG, 10, 1950, 240-62.

4560. _____, "Zwei unbekannte Bismarck-Briefe 1863 und 1869 Gedanken zum Problem der deutschen Innenpolitik," HZ, 173, 1952, 315-24.

4561. LORENZ, Ottokar, "Der Kronprinz, Fürst Bismarck und die Kaiserfrage," Pr. Jbb., 109, 1902, 286-304.

4562. LÜTGE, Friedrich, "Die Grundprinzipien der Bismarckschen Sozialpolitik," Jbb. f. Nationalökon. u. Stat., 134, 1931, 580-96.

4563. LULVÈS, Jean, "Bismarck und die römische Frage," Hochland, 26(2), 1928/29, 263-84.

4564. MARCKS, Erich, "Zwei Studien an neuen Bismarck-Quellen," HZ, 144, 1931, 472-508.

4565. MASUR, Gerhard, "Bismarcks Sprache," HZ, 147, 1933, 70-88.

4566. MEIBOOM, Siegmund, "Bismarck und Bayern am Bundestag (1851-1859)," Hist. Vjschr., 26, 1931, 320-31.

4567. MEINECKE, Friedrich, "Die Gedanken und Erinnerungen Bismarck's," HZ, 82, 1899, 282-95.

4568. _____, "Zur Geschichte Bismarcks," HZ, 87, 1901, 22-55.

4569. _____, "Zur Geschichte Bismarcks Bismarcks Eintritt in den Christlich-germanischen Kreis," HZ, 90, 1903, 56-92.

4570. MEISNER, Heinrich O., "Bismarcks Bündnispolitik 1871-1890," Pr. Jbb., 190, 1922, 265-397.

4571. MERKATZ, Hans-Joachim von, "Gedanken um Bismarck," Pol. Mein., 10, 1965, 34-42.

4572. MEYER, Arnold O., "Bismarcks Friedenspolitik," Zeitwende, 6(1), 1930, 289-305.

4573. _____, "Bismarcks Glaube im Spiegel der Loosungen und Lehrtexte," Zeitwende, 9(1), 1933, 9-26, 92-103.

4574. MICHAELIS, Herbert, "Ein italienisches Heiratsprojekt Bismarcks," Hist. Vjschr., 31, 1936/37, 705-33.

4575. MITCHELL, Allan, "Unfinished Business: Otto Pflanze's Biography of Bismarck," Cen. Eur. Hist., 2, 1969, 89-94.

4576. MOELLER, Richard, "Bismarcks Friedenspolitik und der Machtverfall Deutschlands," Hist. Vjschr., 25, 1929/31, 564-601; 26, 1931, 117-77.

4577. _____, "Noch Einmal Bismarcks Bündnisangebot an England vom Januar 1889," HZ, 163, 1940/41, 100-13.

4578. MOMMSEN, Wilhelm, "Bismarck," GiWuU, 16, 1965, 197-207.

4579. _____, "Bismarck und Lassalle," Arch f. Sozialgesch., 3, 1963, 81-6.

4580. MORK, Gordon R., "Bismarck and the 'Capitulation' of German Liberalism," J. Mod. Hist., 43, 1971, 59-75.

4581. MORSEY, Rudolf, "Bismarck als Reichskriegsminister," Wehrw. Rs., 6, 1956, 629-39.

4582. _____, "Bismarck und der Kulturkampf Ein Forschungs- und Literaturbericht 1945-1957 Unter Verwendung neuen Aktenmaterials," Arch. f. KuG., 39, 1957, 232-70.

4583. MÜLLER, Karl A. v., "Bismarck und Ludwig II im September 1870," HZ, 111, 1913, 89-132.

4584. _____, ed., "Bismarck und Ludwig II im September 1870 Aktenstücke aus den Papieren des Grafen Karl von Tauffkirchen," FBPG, 27, 1914, 572-92.

4585. MÜSEBECK, Ernst, "Zur religiösen Entwicklung Bismarcks," Pr. Jbb., 107, 1902, 397-425.

4586. MULLEN, Thomas E. and Helmuth ROGGE, "Zwei unbekannte Briefe Bismarcks," HZ, 202, 1966, 352-62.

4587. MURALT, Leonhard von, "Bismarck-Forschung und Bismarck-Problem," Schweizer Monatshefte, 1954, 148-62.

4588. _____, "Über Bismarcks Glauben," HZ, 176, 1953, 45-92.

4589. NAUJOKS, Eberhard, "Bismarck und die Organization der Regierungspresse," HZ, 205, 1967, 46-80.

4590. _____, "Bismarck und das Wolffsche Telegraphenbüro," GiWuU., 15, 1963, 605-16.

4591. _____, "Rudolf Lindau und die Neuorientierung der Auswärtigen Pressepolitik Bismarcks (1871/78)," HZ, 215, 1972, 299-344.

4592. NEU, Heinrich, "Bismarcks Versuch einer Einflussnahme auf die Kölnische Zeitung," Rhein. Vjsbll., 30, 1965, 221-33.

4593. ONCKEN, Hermann, "Die Baden-Badener Denkschrift Bismarcks über die deutsche Bundesreform (Juli, 1861)," HZ, 145, 1931, 106-30.

4594. _____, "Bismarck, Lassalle und die Oktroyierung des gleichen und direkten Wahlrechts in Preussen während des Verfassungskonflikts," Pr. Jbb., 146, 1911, 107-40.

4595. _____, ed., "Publizistische Quellen zu den Beziehungen zwischen Bismarck und Lassalle," Arch. f. d. Gesch. d. Soz., 4, 1913/14, 90-94.

4596. OTTO, Helmut, "Militärische Aspekte der Aussenpolitik Bismarcks (1871-1890)," Zs. f. MilitärG., 6, 1967, 150-66.

4597. PAHLMANN, Franz, "Der Stand des Gesprächs über Bismarcks Glauben," GiWuU, 7, 1956, 207-22.

4598. PFLANZE, Otto, "Bismarck and German Nationalism," AHR, 60, 1955, 548-66.

4599. _____, "Bismarck's Realpolitik," Rev. Pol., 20, 1958, 492-514.

4600. _____, "Toward a Psychoanalytic Interpretation of Bismarck," AHR, 77, 1972, 419-44.

4601. PHILIPPI, Hans, "Preussisch-sächsische Verstimmungen im Jahrzehnt nach der Reichsgründung Ein Beitrag zu Bismarcks Verhältnis zu den Bundesstaaten," Jb. f. Gesch. M. O. Dtschl., 15, 1966, 225-68.

4602. PÖLS, Werner, "Bismarckverehrung und Bismarcklegende als innenpolitisches Problem der wilhelminischen Zeit," Jb. f. Gesch. M. O. Dtschl., 20, 1971, 183-201.

4603. POHL, Heinrich, "Die Note Bismarcks an Antonelli vom 12. Februar 1873," ZRG, 16, 1927, 353-60.

4604. POSCHINGER, Heinrich von, "Fürst Bismarck und das Bankwesen," Schmoll. Jb., 34, 1910, 541-51.

4605. _____, "Fürst Bismarck und das Tabakmonopol," Schmoll. Jb., 35, 1911, 213-25.

4606. RACHFAHL, Felix, "Der Rückversicherungsvertrag der 'Balkandreibund' und das angebliche Bündnisangebot Bismarcks an England vom Jahre 1887," Weltwirtsch. Arch., 16, 1920/21, 23-81.

4607. _____, "Zur auswärtigen Politik Bismarcks," Weltwirtsch. Arch., 21, 1925, 76-134.

4608. RALL, Hans, "Bismarcks Reichsgründung und die Geldwünsche aus Bayern," Zs. f. bayer. LG., 22, 1959, 396-497.

4609. RATHMANN, Lothar, "Bismarck und der Übergang Deutschlands zur Schutzzollpolitik (1873/75-1879)," Zs. f. Geschw., 4, 1956, 899-949.

4610. REIN, Adolf, "Bismarcks Afrika-Politik," HZ, 160, 1939, 79-89.

4611. _____, "Bismarcks gegenrevolutionäre Aktion in den Märztagen 1848," WaG., 13, 1953, 246-62.

4612. _____, "Bismarcks Royalismus," GiWuU., 5, 1954, 331-49.

4613. RIEDEL, Dr., "Geschichte des Schlossgesessenen adligen Geschlechtes von Bismarck bis zur Erwerbung von Crevese und Schönhausen," Märkische Forschungen (FBPG), 11, 1867, all.

4614. RITTER, Gerhardt, "Bismarck et la Politique Rhénane de Napoléon III," Rev. d'hist. dipl., 78, 1964, 291-329.

4615. _____, "Bismarck und die Rhein-Politik Napoleons III," Rhein. Vjsbll., 15/16, 1950/51, 339-70.

4616. RÖHL, John C. G., "The Disintegration of the KARTELL and the Politics of Bismarck's Fall from Power 1887-90," Hist. J., 9, 1966, 60-89.

4617. _____, "Staatsstreichplan oder Staatsstreichbereitschaft," HZ, 203, 1966, 610-24.

4618. RÖSSLER, Constantin, "Fürst Bismarck," Pr. Jbb., 65, 1890, 443-60.

4619. ROGGE, Helmuth, "Bismarcks Kolonialpolitik als aussenpolitisches Problem," Hist. Vjschr., 21, 1922/23, 305-33, 423-43.

4620. _____, "Die Entlassung eines Kanzlers," Pol. Mein., 8, 1963, 43-60.
4621. ROLOFF, Gustav, "Bismarcks Friedensschlüsse mit den Süddeutschen im Jahre 1866," HZ, 146, 1932, 1-70.
4622. _____, "Frankreich, Preussen und der Kirchenstaat im Jahre 1866; eine Episode aus dem Kampfe zwischen Bismarck und Napoleon," FBPG, 51, 1939, 103-33.
4623. ROSENBERG, Hans, "Die Maximen von Bismarcks innerer Politik," Pr. Jbb., 202, 1925, 193-218.
4624. ROSENDAHL, Erich, "Bismarck und Braunschweig im Jahre 1866," Hist. Vjschr., 25, 1929/31, 547-61.
4625. ROTHFELS, Hans, "Bismarck und die Nationalitätenfrage des Ostens," HZ, 147, 1933, 89-105.
4626. _____, "Bismarck's Social Policy and the Problem of State Socialism," Sociological Rev., 20, 1938, 81-94, 288-302.
4627. _____, "Bismarcks Staatsanschauung," GiWuU., 4, 1953, 676-703.
4628. _____, "Bismarcks Sturz als Forschungsproblem," Pr. Jbb., 191, 1923, 1-29.
4629. _____, "Problems of a Bismarck Biography," Rev. Pol., 9, 1947, 362-80.
4630. _____, "Zum 150. Geburtstag Bismarcks," VjHZG, 13, 1965, 225-35.
4631. _____, "Zur Bismarck-Krise von 1890," HZ, 123, 1920, 267-96.
4632. _____, "Zur Stellung Bismarcks im deutschen Geschichtsbild," GiWuU., 12, 1961, 209-19.
4633. RUVILLE, Albert von, "Bismarck und der grossdeutsche Gedanke," FBPG, 16, 1903, 403-44.
4634. SALEWSKI, M., "Bismarcks Weg zum Frieden 1870/71," Mov.-Nachrichten, 4, 1971, 95-98.
4635. SASS, Johann, "Hermann von Thile und Bismarck," Pr. Jbb., 217, 1929, 257-79.
4636. SATTLER, Paul, "Bismarcks Entschluss zum Kulturkampf," FBPG, 52, 1940, 66-101.
4637. SCHARFF, Alexander, "Bismarck, Andrássy und die Haltung Österreichs zum Nordschleschleswigschen Vorbehalt," Zs. Schlesw.-Holst., 87, 1962, 181-256.
4638. _____, "Zur Problematik der Bismarckschen Nordschleswigpolitik," WaG., 16, 1956, 211-17.
4639. SCHLABRENDORFF, Fabian von, "Hundert Jahre nach Bismarcks Berufung," Aussenpol., 13, 1962, 692-700.
4640. SCHMOLLER, Gustav, "Gedanken und Erinnerungen von Otto Fürst von Bismarck," FBPG, 12, 1899, 55-70.
4641. _____, "Vier Briefe über Bismarcks volkswirtschaftliche und socialpolitische Stellung und Bedeutung," FBPG, 12, 1899, 1-55.
4642. SCHNABEL, Franz, "Bismarck und die klassische Diplomatie," Aussenpol., 3, 1952, 635-42.
4643. _____, "Das Problem Bismarck," Hochland, 42, 1949/50, 1-27.
4644. SCHNEE, Heinrich, "Bismarck und der deutsche Nationalis-

mus in Österreich," H. Jb., 81, 1961, 123-51.

4645. SCHNEIDER, Oswald, "Bismarck und die preussisch-deutsche Freihandelspolitik (1862-1876)," Schmoll. Jb., 34, 1910, 1047-1108.

4646. SCHOCH, Gustav von, "Bismarck und die orientalische Frage im Jahre 1870," Pr. Jbb., 192, 1923, 326-42.

4647. SCHOEPS, Hans J., "Bismarck und Beckerath," ZRGG, 3, 1951, 366-67.

4648. _____, "Der junge Bismarck als Journalist," ZRGG, 3, 1951, 1-12.

4649. _____, "Neue Bismarckiana 1851-54," ZRGG, 4, 1952, 166-72.

4650. _____, "Unbekannte Bismarckbriefe," ZRGG, 18, 1966, 1-15.

4651. _____, "Unveröffentliche Bismarcksbriefe," ZRGG, 2, 1949/50, 2-20.

4652. SCHOOP, Albert W., "Minister Kern und Bismarck," Schw. Zs. f. Gesch., 3, 1953, 190-239.

4653. SCHÜSSLER, Wilhelm, "Bismarck zwischen England und Russland in der Krise von 1879/80," Hist. Vjschr., 27, 1932/33, 328-73.

4654. _____, "Bismarcks Bündnisangebot an Russland 'Durch Dick und Dünn' im Herbst 1876," HZ, 147, 1933, 106-14.

4655. _____, "Noch Einmal Bismarck zwischen England und Russland 1889," HZ, 163, 1940/41, 547-54.

4656. SCHWEITZER, Carl, "Bismarck's äussere Politik und sein Christentum," Pr. Jbb., 187, 1922, 305-31.

4657. SEEBERG, Bengt, "Bismarck und die soziale Frage," Zs. f. KiG., 59, 1940, 388-409.

4658. SEIDENZAHL, Fritz, "Bismarck und die Gründung der Darmstädter Bank," Tradition, 6, 1961, 252-59.

4659. SELL, Friedrich, "Motive, Methoden und Ideen des Bismarckschen Kulturkampfes," Theol. Rs., 9, 1937, 228-72.

4660. SEMPELL, Charlotte, "Briefe der Eltern Bismarcks an seinen Bruder Bernhard," HZ, 214, 1972, 557-79.

4661. _____, "The Rastaat Dispute 1857-58, New Light on Bismarck's Policy at the Federal Diet," J. Cen. Eur. Aff., 2, 1952, 397-406.

4662. _____, "Unbekannte Briefstellen Bismarcks," HZ, 207, 1968, 609-27.

4663. SLOANE, W. M., "Bismarck as a Maker of Empire," Pol. Sci. Q., 15, 1900, 647-66.

4664. _____, "Bismarck's Apprenticeship," Pol. Sci. Q., 14, 1899, 18-43.

4665. SMEDOVSKY, Assen, "La Diplomatie de Bismarck et la Crise Bulgare de 1886-1887," Rev. d'hist. dipl., 49, 1935, 101-6.

4666. SMITH, Munroe, "Bismarck Reconsidered," Pol. Sci. Q., 35, 1919, 476-85.

4667. SNYDER, Louis L., "Bismarck and the Lasker Resolution, 1884," Rev. Pol., 29, 1967, 41-64.

4668. _____, "Political Implications of Herbert von Bismarck's

Marital Affairs, 1881, 1892, " J. Mod. Hist., 35, 1964, 155-69.

4669.   SPENCER, Frank, "Bismarck and the Franco-Prussian War, " History, 40, 1955, 319-25.

4670.   STEEFEL, Lawrence D., "Bismarck, " J. Mod. Hist., 2, 1930, 74-95.

4671.   STEHLIN, Stewart, "Bismarck and the New Province of Hanover, " Can. J. Hist., 4, 1969, 67-94.

4672.   _____, "Bismarck and the Secret Use of the Guelph Fund, " Historian, 33, 1970/71, 21-39.

4673.   STEIMLE, Theodor, "Bismarck als Sozialpolitiker, " Schmoll. Jb., 64, 1940, 737-47.

4674.   STEINMETZ, Hans-Otto, "Noch einmal: Bismarck-Stosch, " Wehrw. Rs., 19, 1969, 703-13.

4675.   STERN, Alfred, "Bismarck und die Schweiz, " Zs. f. Schw. Gesch., 4, 1924, 188-92.

4676.   STERN, Fritz, et al., "Big Business in German Politics: Four Studies, " "Gold and Iron: The Collaboration and Friendship of Gerson Bleichröder and Otto von Bismarck, " AHR, 75, 1969, 37-46.

4677.   STOECKER, Helmut, "Zur Politik Bismarcks in der english-russischen Krise von 1885, " Zs. f. Geschw., 4, 1956, 1187-1202.

4678.   STREISAND, Joachim, "Bismarck und die deutsche Einigungs-bewegung des 19. Jahrhunderts in der westdeutschen Geschichtsschreibung, " Zs. f. Geschw., 2, 1954, 349-69.

4679.   STRIBRNY, Wolfgang, "Glaube und Politik Bismarcks, " Zeitwende, 37, 1966, 226-36.

4680.   STÜRMER, Michael, "Bismarck in Perspective, " Cen. Eur. Hist., 4, 1971, 291-331.

4681.   _____, "Bismarck-Mythos und Historie, " Aus. Pol. u. Zeitgesch., 12, 1971, 3-30.

4682.   _____, "Staatsstreichgedanken im Bismarckreich, " HZ, 209, 1969, 566-615.

4683.   THADDEN, Rudolf von, "Bismarcks Weg zur deutschen Reichsgründung, " Tradition, 16, 1971, 228-35.

4684.   THIEME, Karl, "Bismarcks Sozialpolitik, " Arch. f. Pol. u. Gesch., 9, 1927, 382-407.

4685.   THIMME, Friedrich, "Wilhelm I, Bismarck und der Ursprung des Annexionsgedankens 1866, " HZ, 89, 1902, 401-56.

4686.   ULMANN, Heinrich, "Kritische Streifzüge in Bismarcks Memoiren, " Hist. Vjschr., 5, 1902, 48-78.

4687.   _____, "Störungen im Vertragssystem Bismarcks Ende 1887, " HZ, 128, 1923, 92-104.

4688.   VAGTS, Alfred, "Bismarck's Fortune, " Cen. Eur. Hist., 1, 1968, 203-32.

4689.   VALENTIN, Veit, "Bismarck and Lasker, " J. Cen. Eur. Aff., 3, 1944, 400-15.

4690.   _____, "Y a-t-il des Lois dans la Politique extérieure de Bismarck?, " RH, 178, 1936, 1-16.

4691.   VIERHAUS, Rudolf, "Otto von Bismarck, " Bär v. Ber., 15, 1966, 166-89.

4692.   VOELEKER, Heinrich, "Das gesellschaftliche und geistige

Leben in Frankfurt a. M. zur Zeit der Bundesgesandtschaft
Otto von Bismarcks 1851-59," Arch. f. Frankfurts Gesch.,
1929, 182-203.

4693. VOGT, Wilhelm, "Otto Kaemmel und Bismarck," Gelbe
Hefte, 14, 1937/38, 569-75.

4694. VOSSLER, Otto, "Bismarcks Ethos," HZ, 171, 1951, 263-
92.

4695. _____, "Bismarcks Sozialpolitik," HZ, 167, 1943, 336-57.

4696. WACHHOLZ, Johannes, "Bismarck und die Kirche," Zeitwende, 35, 1964, 441-52.

4697. _____, "Reich, Bund, und Bismarck," Hochland, 54,
1961/62, 523-38.

4698. WAHL, Adalbert, "Neue Bismarckliteratur," Pr. Jbb., 183,
1921, 41-56.

4699. _____, "Die Unterredung Bismarcks mit dem Herzog
Friedrich von Augustenburg am 1. Juni 1864," HZ, 95,
1905, 58-70.

4700. WALTER, Johannes von, "Luther und Bismarck über das
politische Können," Zeitwende, 8(1), 1932, 197-210.

4701. WARD, J. E., "Leo XIII and Bismarck: The Kaiser's
Vatican Visit of 1888," Rev. Pol., 24, 1962, 392-415.

4702. WERTHEIMER, Eduard von, "Bismarcks Sturz Nach neuen
Quellen," Pr. Jbb., 184, 1921, 300-36.

4703. _____, "Neues zur Geschichte der letzten Jahre Bismarcks (1890-1898)," HZ, 133, 1926, 220ff.

4704. WINCKLER, Martin B., "Die Aufhebung des Artikels V des
Prager Friedens und Bismarcks Weg zum Zweibund," HZ,
179, 1955, 471-509.

4705. _____, "Bismarcks Rumänienpolitik und die europäischen
Grossmächte 1878/79," Jbb. f. Gesch. Osteur., 2, 1954,
53-88.

4706. _____, "Noch einmal: Zur Zielsetzung in Bismarcks
Nordschleswig-Politik," WaG., 17, 1957, 203-10.

4707. _____, "Die Zielsetzung in Bismarcks Nordschleswig-
Politik und die schleswigsche Grenzfrage," WaG., 16,
1956, 41-63.

4708. _____, "Zur Entstehung und vom Sinn des Bismarckschen
Bündnissystems," WaG., 13, 1963, 137-48.

4709. WINDELL, George G., "The Bismarckian Empire as a
Federal State, 1866-1880: A Chronicle of Failure," Cen.
Eur. Hist., 2, 1969, 291-311.

4710. WITTRAM, Reinhard, "Bismarcks Russlandpolitik nach der
Reichsgründung," HZ, 186, 1958, 261-84.

4711. WITZIG, Carole, "Bismarck et la Commune," Int. Rev.
Soc. Hist., 17, 1972, 191-221.

Gerson von Bleichröder (1822-1893)

See also entry 4676

4712. LANDES, David S., "The Bleichröder Bank: An Interim
Report," Leo Baeck Inst. Yrbk., 5, 1960, 201-20.

4713.   LUWEL, Marcel, "Gerson von Bleichröder, L'Ami Commun
        de Leopold II et de Bismarck, " Africa-Tervuren, 8,
        1965, 93-110.
4714.   PÖLS, Werner, "Bleichröder und die Arnim-Affäre, " HZ,
        211, 1970, 65-76.

                    Ludolf Camphausen (1803-1890)

4715.   ANGERMANN, Erich, "Ludolf Camphausen (1803-1890), "
        Rheinische Lebensbilder, 2, 1966, 195-219.
4716.   BEYERHAUS, Gisbert, "Ludolf Camphausen Staat und
        Wirtschaft 1848, " Deutsche Rundschau, 52, 1925, 24ff.
4717.   EYLL, Klara van, "Camphausen und Hansemann - Zwei
        Rheinische Eisenbahnunternehmer 1833-1844, " Tradition,
        11, 1966, 218-31.
4718.   HANSEN, Joseph, "König Friedrich Wilhelm IV und das
        liberale Märzministerium der Rheinländer Camphausen
        und Hansemann in Jahr 1848, " Westdeutsche Zeitschrift
        für Geschichte und Kunst, 32, 1913, 133-204.
4719.   OBERMANN, Karl, "Ludolf Camphausen und die bourgeoise
        Konterrevolution: Zur Rolle der liberalen Bourgeoisie in
        der Revolution von 1848/49, " Zs. f. Geschw., 18, 1970,
        1448-69.

           Friedrich Wilhelm IV (Prussia) (1795-1861)

        See also entries 3020, 3252, 4283, 4718

4720.   ANDREAS, W., "Der Briefwechsel König Friedrich Wilhelms
        IV von Preussen und des Zaren Nikolaus I. von Russland
        1848-50, " FBPG, 43, 1930, 129-66.
4721.   BAILLEU, Paul, "Kronprinz Friedrich Wilhelm im Stände-
        kampf 1820, " HZ, 87, 1901, 67-73.
4722.   BELOW, Georg von, "Aus der Zeit Friedrich Wilhelms IV
        Briefwechsel des Generals Gustav v. Below, " Deutsche
        Rundschau, 109, 1901, 101-33.
4723.   DELBRÜCK, Hans, "Die Regierung Friedrich Wilhelm's IV, "
        Pr. Jbb., 65, 1890, 73-88.
4724.   GEYER, Albert, "König Friedrich Wilhelm IV und seine
        Bauten, " Mitt. d. Ver. f. Gesch., 42, 1925, 81-88.
4725.   HASENCLEVER, Adolf, "König Friedrich Wilhelm IV und die
        Londoner Konvention vom 15. Juli 1840, " FBPG, 25, 1913,
        475-90.
4726.   _____, ed., "Eine österreichische Denkschrift über Fried-
        rich Wilhelm IV. und seine Kirchenpolitik (Juni 1840), "
        Zs. f. KiG, 34, 1913, 111-20.
4727.   HASSELBERG, Felix, "Willibald Alexis und Friedrich Wil-
        helm IV, " Mitt. d. Ver. f. Gesch., 48, 1931, 9-15.
4728.   HECKEL, Johannes, "Ein Kirchenverfassungsentwurf Fried-
        rich Wilhelms IV von 1847, " ZRG, 11, 1921, 444-59.
4729.   KOSER, Reinhold, "Friedrich Wilhelm IV am Vorabend der

Märzrevolution, " HZ, 83, 1899, 43-84.

4730. KRETZSCHMAR, Hellmut, "König Friedrich Wilhelms IV
Briefe an König Friedrich August II von Sachsen, " Pr.
Jbb., 227, 1932; 28-50, 142-53, 245-63.

4731. KRUSCH, Bruno, "Letters of Queen Victoria to Frederich
William IV, 1848-49, " EHR, 40, 1925, 106-10.

4732. KUTZSCH, Gerhard, "Friedrich Wilhelm IV und Carl Wilhelm Saegert, " Jb. f. Gesch. M. O. Dtschl., 6, 1957,
133-72.

4733. MEINECKE, Friedrich, "Friedrich Wilhelm IV und Deutschland, " HZ, 89, 1902, 17-53.

4734. METZEL, Dr., "Erinnerungen an König Friedrich Wilhelm
IV von Preussen, " Mitt. d. Ver. f. Gesch., 15, 1898,
88-90; 16, 1899, 30-33, 57-59.

4735. NITHACK-STAHN, Walther, "Die preussische Landeskirche
unter Friedrich Wilhelm IV, " Pr. Jbb., 128, 1907, 191-
208.

4736. POSCHINGER, Heinrich von, "Aus der unveröffentlichten
Korrespondenz des Königs von Preussen, Friedrich Wilhelm IV, " Deutsche Revue, 31, 1906, 1-7.

4737. _____, "Friedrich Wilhelm IV und Wilhelm I Charak-
terzüge aus unveröffentlichten Briefen beider Könige, "
Konservative Monatsschrift, 64, 1907, 820-32.

4738. RACHFAHL, F., "König Friedrich Wilhelm IV. und die Berliner Märzrevolution im Lichte neuer Quellen, " Pr. Jbb.,
110, 1902, 264-309, 413-62.

4739. _____, "Zur Beurteilung König Friedrich Wilhelm IV und
der Berliner Märzrevolution, " Hist. Vjschr., 5, 1902,
196-229.

4740. SCHARFF, Alexander, "General Carl Graf von der Groeben
und die deutsche Politik König Friedrich Wilhelms IV, "
FBPG, 48, 1936, 1-47.

4741. SCHNEIDER, Arthur von, "Aus dem Briefwechsel Grossherzog Leopolds von Baden und König Friedrich Wilhelm IV
von Preussen, " ZGORh., 108, 1960, 256-65.

4742. SCHNEIDER, Eugen, "Berichte des Agenten Klindworth und
Schreiben des Königs Friedrich Wilhelm IV an König Wilhelm I von Württemberg, " Zs. F. Württbg. LG, 32, 1925/
26, 260-76.

4743. SCHNEIDER, Reinhold, "Das Schicksal König Friedrich Wilhelms IV von Preussen, " Gelbe Hefte, 11, 1934/35, 18-
25.

4744. SIMONS, Eduard, "Die rheinisch-westfälische Kirchenordnung
und das Kirchenideal Friedrich Wilhelms IV, " Theolog.
Arbeiten d. rhein. wissenschaftlichen Predigervereins, 15,
1914, 62-74.

4745. STERN, Alfred, ed., "Der Briefwechsel Friedrich Wilhelms
IV und Napoleons III über die Neuenburger Angelegenheit, "
Z. f. Schweiz. Gesch., 1, 1921, 18-34.

4746. _____, "A Letter of Sir Robert Peel relative to King
Frederich William IV's Proposal to Summon the Combined
Diets, 1847, " EHR, 28, 1913, 542-46.

4747. "UNVERÖFFENTLICHTE Handbillette des Königs Friedrich

Wilhelm IV," Deutsche Revue, 32, 1907, 154-58.
4748.   ZINKEISEN, J. W., "König Friedrich Wilhelm IV und seine
Verdienste um die Entwicklung unseres Verfassungslebens
und die Förderung der deutschen Einheitsbestrebungen, "
Pr. Jbb., 2, 1861, 169ff.

Constantin Frantz (1817-1891)

4749.   COUTINHO, Arno Carl, "The Federalism of Karl Marlo and
Konstantin Frantz," Pol. Sci. Q., 53, 1938, 400-22.
4750.   PHILIPPSON, Johanna, "Constantin Frantz, " Leo Baeck Inst.
Yrbk., 13, 1968, 102-19.
4751.   SAUTTER, Udo, "Constantin Frantz und die Zweite Republik, " HZ, 210, 1970, 560-82.

The von Gagern Family

Heinrich (1799-1880); Max (1810-89);
Friedrich (1794-1848); Hans (1766-1852)

4752.   BAMMEL, Ernst, "Gagerns Plan und die Frankfurter Nationalversammlung, " Arch. f. Frankfurts Gesch., 1948,
5-33.
4753.   BERGSTRAESSER, Ludwig, "Heinrich von Gagern und der
vormärzliche Liberalismus," Zs. f. Pol., 7, 1960, 139-
50.
4754.   DROZ, J. and Lothar W. SILBERHORN, "Une conversation
politique entre M. Guizot et le Baron Max von Gagern en
1846 a Paris, " Rev. d'hist. mod., 4, 1957, 229-38.
4755.   HALE, Douglas, "The Making of a Liberal Leader: Heinrich
von Gagern, 1799-1848," Historian, 32, 1969/70, 34-51.
4756.   "HANS von Gagern, " Pr. Jbb., 8, 1861, 444-78.
4757.   "HEINRICH von Gagerns 'Bureaukratie'," Pol. Vjschr., 1,
1960, 83-90.
4758.   KLÖTZER, Wolfgang, "Heinrich von Gagerns Pariser Briefe
(Februar bis April 1832), " Arch. f. hessische Gesch.,
28, 1963, 383-415.
4759.   SCHMIDT, Julian, "Heinrich von Gagern," Pr. Jbb., 45,
1880, 616-25.
4760.   WENTZCKE, Paul, "Ideale und Irrtümer deutschen Ein-
heitsstrebens in Lebensläufen der Brüder Fritz, Heinrich
und Max von Gagern, " H. Jb., 71, 1951, 212-45.
4761.   _____, ed., "Ludwig von Edelsheim und Franz von Roggenbach Aufzeichnungen und Briefe aus dem Nachlass
Heinrichs von Gagern, " ZGORh., 99, 1951, 568-612; 100,
1952, 342-82.
4762.   _____, "Max von Gagern und die Bonner Hochschule
(1837-1840 sowie 1854), " Ann. Niederrhein, 153/54,
1953, 236-62.
4763.   _____, "Wege zur Politik im Vormärz Heinrich von
Gagern und Otto von Bismarck, " ZgesStw., 109, 1953,

460-82.

Ernst Ludwig von Gerlach (1795-1877)

4764. GERLACH, Ludwig von, "Napoleon III im Juli 1859," ZRGG, 2, 1949/50, 136-58.
4765. KANTZENBACH, Friedrich W., "Ernst Ludwig von Gerlach und August von Bethmann-Hollweg," ZRGG, 9, 1957, 257-66.
4766. _____, "Heinrich W. Josias Thiersch und Ernst Ludwig von Gerlach," ZRGG, 8, 1956, 56-60.
4767. MARTIN, Alfred v., "Autorität und Freiheit in der Gedankenwelt Ludwig v. Gerlachs Ein Beitrag zur Geschichte der religiöskirchlichen und politischen Ansichten des Altkonservativismus," Arch. f. KuG., 20, 1930, 154-82.
4768. SCHOEPS, Hans-Joachim, ed., "Eine Denkschrift für Friedrich Wilhelm IV. als Kronprinz aus der Feder des Gerichtspräsidenten Ernst Ludwig von Gerlach vom Jahre 1839," Jb. Stift. pr. Kulturbesitz, 3, 1964/65, 298-305.
4769. _____, "Friedrich Julius Stahl und Friedrich Wilhelm IV Zwei Briefe E. L. v. Gerlachs," ZRGG, 1, 1948, 207-09.
4770. _____, "Ungedrucktes aus dem Gerlachschen Familienarchiv," ZRGG, 17, 1965, 250-59.
4771. _____, "Ungedrucktes aus den Tagebüchern Ludwig von Gerlachs," ZRGG, 16, 1964, 69-76.
4772. WACHHOLZ, Johannes, "Die christlich-konservative Opposition der Brüder von Gerlach," Zeitwende, 34, 1963, 294-309.

Leopold von Gerlach (1790-1861)

4773. MEINECKE, Friedrich, "Die Tagebücher des Generals v. Gerlach," HZ, 70, 1893, 52-80.
4774. _____, "Gerlach und Bismarck," HZ, 72, 1894, 44-70.
4775. NÄF, Werner, "Die Idee der heiligen Allianz bei Leopold von Gerlach," Z. f. Schweiz Gesch., 11, 1931, 459-72.

Karl Ludwig von Haller (1768-1854)

4776. GUGGISBERG, Kurt, "Das Christentum in Hallers 'Restauration der Staatswissenschaft'," Zs. f. KiG, 55, 1936, 193-226.
4777. RAAB, H., "Friedrich Leopold zu Stolberg und Karl Ludwig von Haller," Zs. f. Schweiz. KiG., 62, 1968, 333-60.
4778. REINHARD, Ewald, "Karl Ludwig von Haller und Heinrich Zschokke Ungedruckte Briefe Hallers," Gelbe Hefte, 4, 1927/28, 829-47.
4779. _____, "Präludien zu einer Biographie Karl Ludwigs von Haller," H. Jb., 35, 1914, 591-605.

4780. _____, "Der Streit um K. L. von Hallers 'Restauration
der Staatswissenschaft'," ZgesStw., 111, 1955, 115-30.
4781. _____, "Zwei Denkschriften Karl Ludwigs von Haller,"
H. Jb., 37, 1916, 411-24.

Friedrich Wilhelm Harkort (1793-1880)

4782. KÖLLMANN, Wolfgang, "Gesellschaftsanschauungen und
sozialpolitisches Wollen Friedrich Harkorts," Rhein.
Vjsbll., 25, 1960, 81-99.
4783. KRATZSCH, Gerhard, "Friedrich Harkort, ein märkischer
Liberaler: Bemerkungen zur regionalen Bedingtheit und
sozialen Funktion seiner politisch-sozialen Gedankenwelt," Westf. Forsch., 22, 1969/70.
4784. WOLTER, Gustav, "Friedrich Harkort als Politiker," Jahrbuch des Vereins für Orts- und Heimatkunde in der
Grafschaft Mark, 39, 1926, 1-156.

Rudolf Haym (1821-1901)

See also entry 465

4785. HAYM, Rudolf, "Arthur Schopenhauer," Pr. Jbb., 14, 1864,
45-91, 179-243.
4786. _____, "Varnhagen von Ense," Pr. Jbb., 11, 1863, 445-
515.
4787. HEYDERHOFF, Jul., "Rudolf Haym und Karl Twesten: Ein
Briefwechsel über positive Philosophie und Fortschritts-
politik 1859-63," Pr. Jbb., 161, 1915, 232-56.
4788. KROHN, Margot, "Rudolf Haym, der Politiker und Herausge-
ber der Preussischen Jahrbücher," Jb. d. Schles.-Fried.-
Wilh. Univ z. Breslau, 15, 1970, 92-145.
4789. WENTZCKE, Paul, ed., "Aus den Letzten Tagen der Paulskirche Briefe Rudolf Hayms," Arch. f. Frankfurts
Gesch., 1, 1925, 46-80.

George Herwegh (1817-1875)

4790. BRAZILL, William J., "Georg Herwegh and the Aesthetics
of German Unification," Cen. Eur. Hist., 5, 1972, 99-
126.
4791. BÜTTNER, Wolfgang, "Georg Herwegh und die deutsche Arbeiterbewegung," Zs. f. Geschw., 15, 1967, 801-21.
4792. TADDEY, G., "Georg Herwegh und Württemberg. Ide-
ologisches Wunschbild und Wirklichkeit," Zs. F. Württbg.
LG, 29, 1970, 189-212.

Johann Jacoby (1805-1877)

4793.   ADAM, R., "Johann Jacobys politischer Werdegang 1805-
         1840," HZ, 143, 1930, 48-76.
4794.   LEBE, Reinhard, "Der streitbare Demokrat aus Königsberg
         Ein Bericht über Johann Jacoby," Hamb. Mittel- u. ostdt.
         Forsch., 6, 1967, 269-74.
4795.   MATULL, Wilhelm, "Johann Jacoby und Eduard von Simson
         Ein Vergleich," Jb. Albertus- u. Königsberg, 21, 1971.
4796.   MEHRING, Franz, "Johann Jacoby und die wissenschaftlichen
         Sozialisten," Arch. f. d. Gesch. d. Soz., 1, 1910/11,
         449-57.
4797.   SCHOELL, Theodor, "Johann Georg Jacobi's Briefe an
         Pfeffel," ZGORh., 50, 1896, 36-80.
4798.   SCHUPPAN, Peter, "Aus dem Briefwechsel Johann Jacobys
         in den Jahren 1848/1849," Jb. f. Gesch., 5, 1971, 343-
         77.
4799.   SILBERNER, Edmund, "Johann Jacoby 1843-1846 Beitrag
         zur Geschichte des Vormärz," Int. Rev. Soc. Hist., 14,
         1969, 353-411.
4800.   _____, "Johann Jacoby in der Revolution von 1848/49,"
         Arch. f. Sozialgesch., 10, 1970, 153-260.
4801.   _____, "Zur Jugendbiographie von Johannes Jacoby,"
         Arch. f. Sozialgesch., 9, 1969, 5-112.

Eduard Lasker (1829-1884)

See also entries 2689, 4667, 4689

4802.   HARRIS, James F., "Eduard Lasker and Compromise
         Liberalism," J. Mod. Hist., 42, 1970, 342-60.
4803.   MORK, Gordon R., "Eduard Lasker (1829-1884): Thoughts
         on the Relevance of Studying Obscure, Dead Politicians,"
         The Cententennial Review, 1971, 273-87.
4804.   _____, "The Making of a German Nationalist: Eduard
         Lasker's Early Years, 1829-1847," Sociètas, 1, 1971, 23-
         32.

Ludwig I (Bavaria) (1825-1848)

4805.   ARETIN, Erwein von, "Der Staatgedanke Ludwigs I," Gelbe
         Hefte, 4, 1927/28, 652-57.
4806.   BASTGEN, Hubert, "Ludwigs I von Bayern 'Liberalismus'
         und 'Jesuitenfurcht' Nuntiaturberichte aus dem Jahre
         1829," H. Jb., 49, 1929, 646-51.
4807.   CHROUST, Anton, "Ein Kritiker König Ludwigs I von Bayern
         (zugleich ein Beitrag zur Geschichte der inneren Ver-
         waltung Bayerns)," Zs. f. bayer. LG., 13, 1940, 53ff.
4808.   DICKOPF, Karl, "König Ludwig I und Staatsrat Georg Lud-
         wig von Maurer Ein Beitrag zur Geschichte des Vormärz
         in Bayern," Zs. f. bayer. LG., 29, 1966, 157-98.

4809.   HEIGEL, K. Th., "Ludwig I von Bayern und Martin von
        Wagner," Arch. f. KuG., 10, 1912, 295-316.
4810.   MATHÄFER, P. Willibald, "König Ludwig I von Bayern als
        Förderer des Deutschtums und des Katholizismus in
        Nordamerika," Gelbe Hefte, 1, 1924/25, 616-49.
4811.   RALL, Hans, "König Ludwig I und Schelling," Zs. f. bayer.
        LG., 17, 1953/55, 419-34.
4812.   SCHWAIGER, Georg, "König Ludwig I von Bayern," Zs. f.
        KiG, 79, 1968, 180-97.
4813.   WINKLER, Wilhelm, "Der schriftliche Nachlass König Lud-
        wigs I von Bayern," Archivalische Zeitschrift, 3, 1926,
        226ff.

Ludwig II (Bavaria) (1845-1886)

See also entries 4543, 4583, 4584

4814.   PHILIPPI, Hans, "König Ludwig II von Bayern und der Wel-
        fenfonds," Zs. f. bayer. LG., 23, 1960, 66-111.
4815.   RALL, Hans, "Ausblicke auf Weltentwicklung und Religion
        im Kreise Max' II und Ludwigs II," Zs. f. bayer. LG.,
        27, 1964, 488-522.

Edwin von Manteuffel (1809-1885)

4816.   CRAIG, Gordon A., "Portrait of a Political General: Edwin
        von Manteuffel and the Constitutional Conflict in Prussia,"
        Pol. Sci. Q., 66, 1951, 1-36.
4817.   DEHIO, Ludwig, "Edwin von Manteuffels politische Ideen,"
        HZ, 131, 1925, 41-71.
4818.   LERCHE, Otto, "Generalfeldmarschall Edwin Freiherr von
        Manteuffel als Domherr von Merseberg 1864-1885," Zs.
        f. KiG, 58, 1939, 167-240.
4819.   SACHSE, Arnold, "Die Schulpolitik des Statthalters Freiherrn
        von Manteuffel," ZGORh., 78, 1926, 557-70.

Karl Mathy (1806-1868)

4820.   ANGERMANN, Erich, "Karl Mathy als Sozial- und Wirt-
        schaftspolitiker (1842-1848)," ZGORh., 103, 1955, 499-
        622.
4821.   STERN, Alfred, ed., "Zwei Briefe Karl Mathys aus seiner
        Flüchtlingszeit," ZGORh., 58, 1904, 138-45.
4822.   TREITSCHKE, Heinrich von, "Karl Mathy," Pr. Jbb., 21,
        1868, 325-38.

Johannes von Miquel (1828-1901)

4823.   MIQUEL, Johannes von, "Einige Mitteilungen aus meinen

Erinnerungen zur deutschen Einheitsbewegung, " Dt. Revue, 40, 1915, 171ff.

4824. MOMMSEN, Wilhelm, "Zur Biographie Johannes von Miquels, " HZ, 164, 1941, 529-52.

4825. SCHWARZ, Otto, "Johannes von Miquel, " Schmoll. Jb., 64, 1940, 257-70.

4826. WIESE, Leopold von, "Johannes von Miquel, " Berliner Mh., 17, 1939, 695-710.

Robert von Mohl (1799-1875)

4827. ANGERMANN, Erich, "Eine Rede Robert Mohls über den Saint-Simonismus aus dem Jahr 1832, " VSW, 49, 1962, 195-214.

4828. _____, "Republikanismus, amerikanisches Vorbild und soziale Frage 1848 Eine unveröffentlichte Flugschrift Robert Mohls, " WaG, 21, 1961, 185-93.

4829. _____, "Die Verbindung des 'polizeistaatlichen' Wohlfahrtsideas mit dem Rechtsstaatsgedanken im deutschen Frühliberalismus Eine Studie über die Verwaltungslehre Robert von Mohls, " H. Jb., 74, 1954, 462-72.

4830. BECKER, Josef, "Ein Promemoria Robert von Mohls für die badische Regierung zum I. Vatikanischen Konzil, " Arch. f. KuG., 45, 1963, 334-51.

4831. MEIER, Ernst, "Robert von Mohl, " ZgesStw., 34, 1878, 431-528.

Adam Müller (1779-1829)

See also entries 1364, 2796

4832. BAXA, Jacob, "Adam Müller, " ZgesStw., 86, 1929, 1-34.

4833. _____, "Adam Muller über die Revolutionen in Südeuropa, " ZgesStw., 111, 1955, 100-14.

4834. _____, "Justus Möser und Adam Müller, " Jbb. f. Nationalökon. u. Stat., 123, 1925, 14-30.

4835. _____, "Die Wirtschaftspolitik Adam Müllers, " Jbb. f. Nationalökon. u. Stat., 130, 1929, 1-30.

4836. DOMBROWSKY, Alexander, "Adam Müller, die historische Weltanschauung und die politische Romantik, " ZgesStw., 65, 1909, 377-403.

4837. LENZ, Friedrich, "Ueber Adam Müllers Staats- und Gesellschaftslehre, " Jbb. f. Nationalökon. u. Stat., 118, 1922, 214-20.

4838. REINHARD, Ewald, "Adam von Müller und Franz Bernhard von Bucholtz Neue Briefe Müllers, " ZgesStw., 107, 1951, 488-509.

4839. WEINBERGER, Otto, "Die wissenschafts- und Gesellschaftslehre Adam Müllers, " ZgesStw., 77, 1922/23, 89-114; 78, 1924, 394-434.

4840. WOLFF, Karl, "Staat und Individuum bei Adam Müller, "

Hist. Vjschr., 30, 1935, 59-107.

Eugen Richter (1838-1906)

4841.   RACHFAHL, Felix, "Eugen Richter und der Linksliberalis-
         mus im Neuen Reiche," Zs. f. Pol., 5, 1911/12, 261-
         374.
4842.   RICHTER, Eugen, "Die Vorbildung der höheren Verwaltungs-
         beamten in Preussen," Pr. Jbb., 17, 1866, 1-19.

Franz von Roggenbach (1825-1907)

See also entry 4761

4843.   BAUMHAUER, A., "Der badische Staatsmann und letze
         badische Aussenminister Franz Freiherr von Roggen-
         bach," GiWuU, 10, 1959, 461-78.
4844.   FUCHS, W. P., "Zur Bismarckkritik Franz von Roggen-
         bachs," WaG, 10, 1950, 39-55.
4845.   HEYDERHOFF, Julius, ed., "Franz von Roggenbach und
         Julius Jolly Politischer Briefwechsel 1848-1882," ZGORh.,
         86, 1933/34, 77-116; 87, 1934/35, 189-244.
4846.   ROSEN, Edgar R., "Zwei Briefe zum Regierungseintritt
         Franz von Roggenbachs im Mai 1861," HZ, 213, 1971,
         69-90.

Friedrich Julius Stahl (1802-1861)

See also entry 4769

4847.   EXNER, Fritz, "Zur Staatsauffassung Friedrich Julius
         Stahls," Gelbe Hefte, 6, 1929/30, 443-51.
4848.   HECKEL, Johannes, "Der Einbruch des jüdischen Geistes
         in das deutsche Staats- und Kirchenrecht durch Friedrich
         Julius Stahl," HZ, 155, 1936/37, 506-41.
4849.   KANN, Robert A., "Friedrich Julius Stahl A Re-examina-
         tion of his Conservatism," Leo Baeck Inst. Yrbk., 12,
         1967, 55-74.
4850.   SALZER, Ernst, "Stahl und Rotenhan Briefe des ersten an
         den Zweiten," Hist. Vjschr., 14, 1911, 199-247, 514-51.
4851.   SCHMIDT, Martin, "Der Streit zwischen Karl Josias von
         Bunsen und Friedrich Julius Stahl in den Jahren 1855
         und 1856 in seiner kirchengeschichtlichen und grundsätz-
         lichen Bedeutung," Jb. f. Ber.-Brandenburg. KiG, 44,
         1969, 113-66.

Johann Bertram Stüve (1798-1872)

4852.   FRENSDORFF, F., "Carl Bertram Stüve," Pr. Jbb., 20,

.1872, 266-301; 31, 1873, 589-643; 32, 1873, 176-211.

4853.   MÜLHAN, B., "Hannover und sein Ministerium; Stüve im
preussisch-österreichischen Spiel um das Dritte Deutschland," Niedersächs. Jb., 22, 1950, 87ff.

Ludwig Uhland (1787-1862)

4854.   RAPP, Adolf, "Uhland in der Politik," HZ, 108, 1912,
593-610.
4855.   _____, "Uhland im politischen Leben," Zs. F. Württbg.
LG, 33, 1927, 44-67.
4856.   WOHLHAUPTER, Eugen, "Recht und Rechtwissenschaft im
Leben und literarischen Werk Ludwig Uhlands," Schmoll.
Jb., 68, 1944, 49-98, 237-78.

Karl August Varnhagen von Ense (1785-1858)

See also entry 4786

4857.   HAERING, Hermann, "Varnhagen und seine diplomatischen
Berichte Karlsruhe 1816-1819," ZGORh., 75, 1921, 52-86,
129-58.
4858.   KUHN, Joachim, "Zwei Briefe Varnhagens an Carlyle Aus
dem Berliner Kulturleben der Biedermeierzeit," Bär v.
Ber., 20, 1971, 97-106.
4859.   LAUBERT, Manfred, ed., "Varnhagen von Enses Briefe an
Legationssekretär Heinrich Küpfer 1817/18," ZGORh.,
92, 1940, 338-82.

Wilhelm I (Germany) (1797-1888)

See also entry 4520

4860.   BAILLEU, P., "Der Prinzregent und die Reform der
deutschen Kriegsverfassung," HZ, 78, 1897, 385-402.
4861.   BINDER, Hilde, "Queen Victoria und König Wilhelm im
Jahre 1866," FBPG, 47, 1935, 104-21.
4862.   BRONSART, Friedrich v., "Der alte Kaiser und sein Kriegsminister v. Bronsart," Hist. Vjschr., 30, 1935, 293-
306.
4863.   DELBRÜCK, Hans, "Kaiser Wilhelm I in seiner Bedeutung
für Handel und Industrie," Pr. Jbb., 88, 1897, 125-46.
4864.   FRIEDRICH, Fritz, "Die Prinzessin von Preussen Auf
Grund ihres historischen Nachlasses," Pr. Jbb., 156,
1914, 285-307.
4865.   HÜBNER, Reinhard, "Kaiser Wilhelm I als Christ," Zeitwende, 13, 1936/37, 257-62.
4866.   MARCKS, Erich, "Ein Brief Kaiser Wilhelms I vom 14.
Mai 1849," HZ, 102, 1909, 374-77.
4867.   MEISNER, Heinrich O., "Militärkabinett, Kriegsminister

und Reichskanzler zur Zeit Wilhelms I, " FBPG, 50, 1938, 86-103.

4868. PETERSDORFF, Herman von, "Kaiser Wilhelm I in seinen Briefen, " Pr. Jbb., 213, 1928, 160-75.
4869. RIESS, Ludwig, "Eine noch unveröffentlichte Emser Depesche König Wilhelms I vom 11. Juli 1870, " FBPG, 26, 1913, 187-212.
4870. SCHULTZE, Johannes, "Prinz Wilhelm im Sommer 1848 Briefe an dem Ministerpräsidenten Rudolf v. Auerswald, " FBPG, 39, 1927, 123-33.
4871. SRBIK, Heinrich Ritter v., "Der Prinz von Preussen und Metternich 1835-1848, " Hist. Vjschr., 23, 1926, 188-98.
4872. STERN, Alfred, "Ein apokrypher Brief des Prinzen von Preussen, " HZ, 87, 1901, 73-75.
4873. SYBEL, Heinrich von, "Denkschrift des Prinzen von Preussen (Kaiser Wilhelm I.) über die deutsche Frage, " HZ, 70, 1893, 90-95.
4874. TREUE, Wilhelm, "Wollte König Wilhelm I 1862 zurücktreten?, " FBPG, 51, 1939, 275-310.
4875. VALENTIN, Veit, "Die Prinzessin von Preussen (Kaiserin u. Königin August) über die deutsche Frage, " Deutsche Revue, 34, 1909, 20-24.
4876. WERTHEIMER, Eduard von, "Kronprinz Friedrich Wilhelm und die spanischen Hohenzollern-Thronkandidatur (1868-1870), " Pr. Jbb., 205, 1926, 273-307.

Wilhelm I (Württemberg) (1816-1864)

See also entry 4742

4877. GEHRING, Paul, "Das Wirtschaftsleben in Württemberg unter König Wilhelm I (1816-1864), " Zs. F. Württbg. LG, 9, 1949/50, 196-257.
4878. GRAUER, Karl-Johannes, "König Wilhelm I von Württemberg und die europäischen Dynastien, " Zs. F. Württbg. LG, 15, 1956, 253-78.
4879. HERMELINK, Heinrich, "Kirche und Schule unter der Regierung König Wilhelms I von Württemberg, " Zs. F. Württbg. LG, 9, 1949/50, 175-95.
4880. _____, ed., "König Wilhelm I von Württemberg und der Krimkrieg, " Zs. F. Württbg. LG, 41, 1935, 332-40.
4881. SCHNEIDER, Eugen, "König Wilhelm I und die Entstehung der württembergischen Verfassung, " Zs. F. Württbg. LG, 25, 1916, 532-47.
4882. STOCKMAYER, Karl von, "Des Dichters Franz Dingelstedt Stuttgarter Jahre im Dienste König Wilhelm I 1843-1850, " Zs. F. Württbg. LG, 5, 1941, 154-69.

1806-1848

See also entries 3094, 3388, 4376, 4388, 4424, 4425, 4436

4883.   BECKER, Albert, "Die Pfalz vor 100 Jahren zur Geschichte
        des Hambacher Festes," Zs. f. bayer. LG., 2, 1929,
        65-88.

4884.   BERNEY, A., "Reichstradition und Nationalstaatsgedanke
        1789-1815," HZ, 140, 1929, 57-86.

4885.   BITTERAUF, Theodor, "Der Prozess gegen Johann Philipp
        Palm und Konsorten 1806," Hist. Vjschr., 12, 1909,
        366-94.

4886.   _____, "Zur Geschichte der öffentlichen Meinung im
        Königreich Bayern im Jahre 1813 Bis zum Abschluss
        des Vertrages von Ried," Arch. f. KuG., 11, 1914, 31-
        69.

4887.   BRINKMANN, Carl, "Eine neue Quelle zur Preussischen
        Geschichte nach dem Tilsiter Frieden," FBPG, 24, 1911,
        371-445.

4888.   DEHIO, Ludwig, "Eine Reform-Denkschrift Beymes aus dem
        Sommer 1806," FBPG, 38, 1926, 321-38.

4889.   DELBRÜCK, Hans, "Neues über 1813," Pr. Jbb., 157, 1914,
        34-69.

4890.   DUNAN, Marcel, "Nouveaux Documents sur L'Allemagne Na-
        poléonienne Lettres du Roi de Bavière au Maréchal Ber-
        thier (1806-1813)," RH, 186, 1939, 112-43.

4891.   EBLING, Hanswerner, "Die hessische Politik in der Rhein-
        bundzeit 1806-13," Arch. f. hessische Gesch., 24, 1951/
        53, 195-261.

4892.   GAUER, Wilhelm, "Badische Staatsräson und Frühliberalis-
        mus um die Juliwende Regierung, Presse und öffentliche
        Meinung in Baden 1830-32," ZGORh., 84, 1931/32, 341-
        406.

4893.   GLASER, Maria, "Die badische Politik und die deutsche
        Frage zur Zeit der Befreiungskriege und des Wiener Kon-
        gresses," ZGORh., 80, 1928, 268-317.

4894.   GRIEWANK, Karl, "Das Jahr 1813," GiWuU, 6, 1955, 556-
        67.

4895.   _____, "Preussen und die Neuordnung Deutschlands 1813-
        1815," FBPG, 52, 1940, 234-79.

4896.   HASHAGEN, Justus, "Der Rhythmus im Wandel von Reaktion
        und Revolution 1815-1852," Hist. Vjschr., 30, 1935, 108-
        14.

4897.   HAUSER, O., "Die Eingliederung der Rheinlande in Preus-
        sen," Zs. des berg. Gesch. ver., 84, 1969, 16-28.

4898.   HEIGEL, Karl T., "Das Hambacher Fest vom 27 Mai 1832,"
        HZ, 111, 1913, 54-88.

4899.   HERRMANN, Alfred, "Die Stimmung der Rheinländer gegen-
        über Preussen 1814/16," Ann. Niederrhein, 115, 1929,
        366-94.

4900.   HÖLZLE, E., "Das napoleonische Staatensystem in Deutsch-
        land," HZ, 148, 1933, 277-93.

4901.   HOUBEN, H. H., "Karl Gutzkow als württembergischer
        Politiker," Zs. F. Württbg. LG, 20, 1911, 249-63.

4902.   JEISMANN, Karl-Ernst, "'Nationalerziehung' Bemerkungen
        zum Verhältnis von Politik und Pädagogik in der Zeit der
        preussischen Reform 1806-1815," GiWuU, 19, 1968, 201-

18.

4903.   JUST, Leo, "Der Mittelrhein im Zeitalter der Französischen
Revolution und Napoleons, " Jb. f. Gesch. Kunst. d. MRh,
10, 1948, 52-66.

4904.   KALLENBERG, Fritz, "Die Fürstentümer Hohenzollern im
Zeitalter der Französischen Revolution und Napoleons, "
ZGORh., 111, 1963, 357-472.

4905.   "KARL August von Wangenheim Ein Capitel aus der
Geschichte des deutschen Bundes, " Pr. Jbb., 11, 1863,
15-64.

4906.   KAYSER, Emil, "Die Neuenburger Revolution vor 100 Jahren
(September und Dezember 1831), " Hist. Vjschr., 26,
1931, 589-604.

4907.   KEINEMANN, F., "Zu den Auswirkungen der Julirevolution
in Westfalen, " Westf. Zs., 121, 1971, 351-64.

4908.   KETTIG, Konrad, "Der Professor als Parlamentarier
Clemens August Karl Klenze als Mitglied der Berliner
Stadtverordnetenversammlung in den Jahren 1833-38, "
Bär v. Ber., 14, 1965, 122-36.

4909.   KOSER, Reinhold, "Die preussische Reformgesetzgebung in
ihrem Verhältnis zur Französischen Revolution, " HZ, 73,
1894, 193-210.

4910.   KOSZYK, Kurt, "Carl D'ester als Gemeinderat und Parlamentarier (1846-1849), " Arch. f. Sozialgesch., 1, 1961,
43-60.

4911.   LEHMANN, Max, "Die Erhebung von 1813, " Pr. Jbb., 151,
1913, 397-414.

4912.   _____, "Die preussische Reform von 1808 und die französische Revolution, " Pr. Jbb., 132, 1908, 211-29.

4913.   LEMPFRID, Wilhelm, "Der Bayerische Landtag 1831 und die
öffentliche Meinung, " Zs. f. bayer. LG., 24, 1961, 1-
101.

4914.   LUTZ, Rolland Ray, Jr., "The 'New Left' of Restoration
Germany, " J. Hist. Ideas, 31, 1970, 235-52.

4915.   MAENNER, Ludwig, "Ein Querkopf des vormärzlichen
Liberalismus: Wilhelm Schulz (-Bodmer), " Arch. f.
hessische Gesch., 13, 1921/22, 288-321.

4916.   MAYER, Gustav, "Die Anfänge des politischen Radikalismus
im vormärzlichen Preussen, " Zs. f. Pol., 6, 1913, 1-
113.

4917.   MEINECKE, Friedrich, "Zur Geschichte des älteren deutschen Parteiwesens, " HZ, 118, 1917, 46-63.

4918.   MIHM, Karl, "Alex. Friedrich Ludwig Weidig Ein Beitrag
zur Geschichte des vormärzlichen Liberalismus, " Arch.
f. hessische Gesch., 15, 1928, 348-84, 574-608.

4919.   MILLER, Max, "Salomo Michaelis Schützling, Mitarbeiter
und Freund des Frhrn. v. Wangenheim Ein Beitrag zur
Geschichte des politischen Schriftums während der Verfassungskämpfe (1815/19) und zum List-Prozess (1821), "
Zs. F. Württbg. LG, 3, 1939, 158-211.

4920.   OBERMANN, Karl, "Die Volksbewegung in Deutschland von
1844 bis 1846, " Zs. f. Geschw., 5, 1957, 503-25.

4921.   RAACK, R. C., "When Plans Fail: Small group behavior and decision-making in the conspiracy of 1808 in Germany," J. of Conflict Resolution, 14, 1970, 3-19.

4922. RAUMER, Kurt von, "Hügels Gutachten zur Frage der Niederlegung der deutschen Kaiserkrone (17 Mai 1806)," Zs. f. bayer. LG., 27, 1964, 390-408.

4923. _____, "Zur Beurteilung der preussischen Reform," GiWuU, 18, 1967, 333-48.

4924. REINFRIED, Hermann, "Karl Ludwig Sand nach badischen Akten," ZGORh., 86, 1933/34, 509-33.

4925. RICHTERING, H., "Friedrich Alexander von Hövel (1766-1826)," Dortm. Beitr., 66, 1970, 5-43.

4926. RIEMERTS, K., "Die Oldenburgische Bundespolitik 1815-48," Niedersächs. Jb., 9, 1932, 52ff.

4927. SAUER, W., "Nassau unter dem Minister v. Marschall," Ann. d. Ver. f. Nass. Alt. Kunde u. Gesch. Forsch., 22, 1890, 79ff.

4928. SCHMIDT, Walter, "Zur Rolle der Bourgeoisie in den bürgerlichen Revolutionen von 1789 und 1848," Zs. f. Geschw., 21, 1973, 301-20.

4929. SCHÖNBECK, Otto, "Der kurmärkische Landtag vom Frühjahr 1809," FBPG, 20, 1907, 1-103.

4930. SCHWAIGER, Georg, "Das dalbergische Fürstentum Regensburg (1803-1810)," Zs. f. bayer. LG, 23, 1960, 42-65.

4931. SNELDERS, H. A. M., "The Influence of the Dualistic System of Jakob Joseph Winterl (1732-1809) on the German Romantic Era," Isis, 60, 1970, 231-40.

4932. ULMANN, H., "Die Anklage des Jakobinismus in Preussen im Jahre 1815," HZ, 95, 1905, 435-46.

4933. _____, "Hessen-Darmstadt am Scheideweg im Herbst 1813," Arch. f. hessische Gesch., 9, 1913, 281-97.

4934. _____, "Minister du Thil im Kampf um das monarchische Prinzip 1832-1835 nach seinen Briefen," Arch. f. hessische Gesch., 14, 1923/25, 52-71.

4935. _____, "Zur Entstehung der Kaisernote der 29 Kleinstaaten vom 16. November 1814," HZ, 116, 1916, 459.

4936. VIVIER, Robert, "L'esprit d'opposition à Strasbourg de 1830 à 1848," La révolution francaise, 77, 1924, 230-46, 313-32; 78, 1925, 48-57.

4937. VOLPERS, Dr. Richard, "Der Staat nach Friedr. v. Hardenberg (Novalis)," Pr. Jbb., 148, 1912, 98-108.

4938. WACHTLER, Hans, "Die Ursachen des jähen Zusammenbruchs Preussens im Jahre 1806," Wehrw. Rs., 8, 1958, 571-79.

4939. WINDELBAND, Wolfgang, "Badens Austritt aus dem Rheinbund 1813," ZGORh., 64, 1910, 102-50.

4940. WINTER, Georg, "Zur Entstehungsgeschichte des Oktoberedikts und der Verordnung vom 14. Februar 1808," FBPG, 40, 1927, 1-33.

4941. ZIEHEN, Eduard, "Winkopps 'Rheinischer Bund' (1806-13) und der Reichsgedanke," Arch. f. hessische Gesch., 18, 1933/34, 292-326.

4942. ZIEKURSCH, Johannes, "Friedrich von Cölln und der Tugendbund," Hist. Vjschr., 12, 1909, 38-76.

Karl Theodor von Dalberg (1744-1817)

4943. DARD, Emile, "Lettres inédites de Dalberg à Talleyrand,"
        Rev. d'hist. dipl., 51, 1937, 164-83.
4944. DYROFF, Adolf, "Dalbergs und Napoleons Kirchenpolitik in
        Deutschland," H. Jb., 40, 1920, 222-30.
4945. HERTLING, Karl von, "Beitrag zur Geschichte des Fürsten-
        Primas Karl Freihr. von Dalberg," H. Jb., 16, 1895,
        575-85.
4946. RAAB, H., "Karl Theodor von Dalberg Das Ende der
        Reichskirche und das Ringen um den Wiederaufbau des
        kirchlichen Lebens 1803-1815," Arch. f. mrh. KiG., 18,
        1966, 27-39.
4947. REINHARDT, Rudolf, "Fürstprimas Karl Theodor von Dal-
        berg (1744-1817) im Lichte der neueren Forschung,"
        Tübinger Theolog. Quartalschrift, 144, 1964, 257-75.
4948. WOHLFEIL, Rainer, "Untersuchungen zur Geschichte des
        Rheinbundes 1806-1813 Das Verhältnis Dalbergs zu Na-
        poleon," ZGORh., 108, 1960, 85-108.

Friedrich I (Württemberg) (1754-1816)

4949. HÖLZLE, Erwin, "König Friedrich von Württemberg," Zs.
        F. Württbg. LG, 36, 1930, 269-98.
4950. SAUER, Paul, "Die Neuorganisation des württembergischen
        Heerwesens unter Herzog, Kürfurst und König Friedrich
        (1797-1816)," Zs. F. Württbg. LG, 26, 1967, 395-420.

Friedrich Wilhelm III (Prussia) (1770-1840)

4951. BENRATH, Adolf, ed., "Ein Schreiben Schleiermachers v.
        J. 1802 aus Stolp, das Friedrich Wilhelm III im Interesse
        der Unionentgegentritt," Zs. f. KiG, 40, 1922, 172-77.
4952. DELBRÜCK, Hans, "Friedrich Wilhelm III und Hardenberg
        auf dem Wiener Kongress," HZ, 63, 1889, 242-65.
4953. DUNCKER, Max, "Friedrich Wilhelm III im Jahre 1809,"
        Pr. Jbb., 41, 1878, 136-59.
4954. HAAKE, Paul, "König Friedrich Wilhelm III, Hardenberg und
        die preussische Verfassungsfrage," FBPG, 26, 1913,
        523-73; 28, 1915, 175-200, 305-69; 30, 1918, 317-65; 32,
        1919, 109-80.
4955. HERRMANN, Alfred, "Friedrich Wilhelm III und sein Anteil
        an der Heeresreform bis 1813," Hist. Vjschr., 11, 1908,
        484-516.
4956. KAEBER, Ernst, "Friedrich Wilhelm III bei seinem Re-
        gierungsantritt," Konservative Monatsschrift, 1911, 1100-
        11.
4957. LEHMANN, Max, "Ein Regierungsprogramm Friedrich Wil-
        helm's III," HZ, 61, 1889, 441-60.
4958. MOMMSEN, Theodor and Heinrich v. TREITSCHKE, "Königin
        Luise," Pr. Jbb., 37, 1876, 417-37.

4959.   "RÜCHEL unter der Regierung Friedrich Wilhelm III 1798-
         1823," Pr. Jbb., 47, 1881, 111-32.
4960.   SCHNÜTGEN, Alexander, "Vom preussischen Königshaus und
         dem Rheinland unter Friedrich Wilhelm III Rheinische
         Briefe des Kronprinzen an die Kronprinzess 1833-39,"
         Ann. Niederrhein, 140, 1942, 60-111.
4961.   THIMME, Friedrich, "König Friedrich Wilhelm III, sein An-
         teil an der Konvention von Tauroggen und an der Reform
         von 1807-1812," FBPG, 18, 1905, 1-59.

Karl August von Hardenberg (1750-1822)

See also entries 4004, 4952, 4954

4962.   BORN, Karl E., "Hardenbergs Pläne und Versuche zur
         Neuordnung Europas und Deutschlands 1813/1815,"
         GiWuU, 8, 1957, 550-64.
4963.   DUNCKER, Max, "Die Denkwürdigkeiten des Staatkanzlers
         Fürsten von Hardenberg," Pr. Jbb., 39, 1877, 606-43.
4964.   _____, "Graf Haugwitz und Freiherr von Hardenberg,"
         Pr. Jbb., 42, 1878, 571-625.
4965.   GRIEWANK, Karl, "Hardenberg und die preussische Politik
         1804-1806," FBPG, 47, 1935, 227-308.
4966.   HAUSSHERR, Hans, "Hardenberg und der Friede von Basel,"
         HZ, 184, 1957, 292-335.
4967.   _____, "Hardenbergs Reformdenkschrift Riga 1807," HZ,
         157, 1937/38, 267-308.
4968.   KÜHN, Joachim, "Hardenberg und die Frauen," Bär v. Ber.,
         20, 1971, 27-63.
4969.   LEHMANN, Max, "Hardenberg's Memoiren," HZ, 39, 1878,
         77-110.
4970.   NASSE, Erwin, "Die preussische Finanz- und Ministerkrisis
         im Jahre 1810 und Hardenberg's Finanzplan," HZ, 26,
         1871, 282-342.
4971.   SIMON, Walter M., "Prince Hardenberg," Rev. Pol., 18,
         1956, 88-99.
4972.   ZIMMERMANN, Gerhard, "Hardenbergs Versuch einer Re-
         form der preussischen Archivverwaltung und deren
         weitere Entwicklung bis 1933," Jb. der Stiftung Preus-
         sischer Kulturbesitz, 4, 1966, 69-87.

Wilhelm von Humboldt (1767-1835)

See also entries 382, 3008

4973.   EHLEN, Leo, "Die Entwicklung der Geschichtsphilosophie
         W. von Humboldts," Arch. f. Gesch. d. Phil., 24, 1910/
         11, 22-60.
4974.   ERDMANN, Karl Dietrich, "Wilhelm von Humboldt," GiWuU,
         20, 1969, 670-83.
4975.   ERHARDT, L., "W. v. Humboldt's Abhandlung über die

Aufgabe des Geschichtschreibers', " HZ, 55, 1886, 385-424.

4976. GEBHARDT, Bruno, "Wilhelm v. Humboldt und die Anfänge der preussischen Gesandtschaft in Rom, " FBPG, 7, 1894, 363-76.

4977. _____, "Wilhelm v. Humboldt's Ausscheiden aus dem Ministerium 1810, " HZ, 74, 1895, 44-68.

4978. GOLDSMITH, Robert E., "The Early Development of Wilhelm von Humboldt, " Ger. Rev., 42, 1967, 30-48.

4979. GRÜTZMACHER, Richard H., "Wilhelm von Humboldt und die geistige Situation der Gegenwart, " Pr. Jbb., 240, 1935, 31-44.

4980. HUMBOLDT, Wilhelm von, "On the Historian's Task, " Hist. Theor., 6, 1967, 57-71.

4981. KAEHLER, Siegfried, "Das Wahlrecht in Wilhelm von Humboldts Entwurf einer Ständischen Verfassung für Preussen vom Jahre 1819, " Zs. f. Pol., 10, 1917, 195-240.

4982. _____, "Wilhelm und Alexander v. Humboldt in den Jahren der Napoleonischen Krise, " HZ, 116, 1916, 231-70.

4983. _____, "Wilhelm von Humboldts Anfänge im diplomatischen Dienst, " Arch. f. KuG., 13, 1917, 98-121.

4984. KESSEL, Eberhard, "Wilhelm von Humboldt und Preussen, " Jb. Preussischen Kulturbesitz, 1967, 25-54.

4985. LEITZMANN, Albert, ed., "Briefe Wilhelm von Humboldts an Schiller, " Pr. Jbb., 239, 1935, 201-22.

4986. _____, "Jugendbriefe Wilhelm von Humboldts, " Pr. Jbb., 240, 1935, 10-31.

4987. _____, "Politische Jugendbriefe Wilhelm von Humboldts an Gentz, " HZ, 152, 1935, 48-89.

4988. MAUER, Hermann, "Wilhelm von Humboldt und die Entschuldung des ländlichen Grundbesitzes, " Schmoll. Jb., 36, 1914, 297-302.

4989. REISS, Hans, "Justus Möser und Wilhelm von Humboldt Konservative und liberale politischen Ideen im Deutschland des 18. Jahrhunderts, " Pol. Vjschr., 8, 1967, 23-39.

4990. SCHAUMKELL, Ernst, "Wilhelm von Humboldt und der preussische Staatsgedanke, " FBPG, 47, 1935, 309-35.

4991. SCHULTZ, Werner, "Das Erlebnis der Individualität bei Wilhelm von Humboldt, " Vjschr. f. Litw., 7, 1929, 654-81.

4992. _____, "Das Problem der historischen Zeit bei Wilhelm v. Humboldt, " Vjschr. f. Litw., 6, 1928, 293-316.

4993. _____, "Die religiösen Motive in der Sonettdichtung Wilhelm v. Humboldts, " Zs. f. Theol. u. K., 34, 1926, 219-39.

4994. _____, "Wilhelm von Humboldts Erleben der Natur als Ausdruck seiner Seele, " Vjschr. f. Litw., 12, 1934, 572-99.

4995. SHEPPARD, R., "Two Liberals: A Comparison of the Humanism of Mathew Arnold and Wilhelm von Humboldt, " Ger. Life Letters, 24, 1970/71, 219-33.

4996. SPRANGER, Eduard, "Wilhelm v. Humboldts Rede 'Über die

Aufgabe des Geschichtschreibers' und die Schellingsche
Philosophie, " HZ, 100, 1908, 540-63.

4997. SWEET, Paul R., "Wilhelm von Humboldt (1767-1835): His
legacy to the Historian, " Centennial R., 1971.

4998. TROFIMOWA, R. P., "Wilhelm von Humboldt und seine
Lehre von der ästhetischen Wirkung der Sprache, " Dt.
Zs. f. Phil., 20, 1972, 1044-54.

4999. ULMANN, Heinrich, "Aus amtlichen Berichten Wilhelms von
Humboldt im Jahre 1816, " FBPG, 7, 1894, 113-25.

Friedrich August Ludwig von der Marwitz (1777-1837)

5000. BETHCKE, Dr., "Ludwig von Marwitz Ein preussischer
General und märkischer Edelmann, " Gelbe Hefte, 14,
1937/38, 151-65.

5001. GEMBRUCH, Werner, "Gedanken von Stein und Marwitz zur
Agrar-Gewerbe- und Steuer-politik, " Nass. An., 82, 1971.

5002. HÜBNER, Reinhard, "'Preussisches Christentum' Zur Le-
bensgeschichte des Fr. A. Ludwig v. d. Marwitz, " Zeitwende, 15, 1938/39, 549-55.

5003. LÜTGE, Friedrich, "Friedrich August Ludwig von der Marwitz der grosse Gegner Stein-Hardenbergs, " Jbb. f. Nationalökon. u. Stat., 139, 1933, 481-99.

5004. MEUSEL, Friedrich, "Marwitz' Schilderung der altpreus-
sischen Armee, " Pr. Jbb., 131, 1908, 460-84.

Maximilian I (Bavaria) (1756-1825)

5005. MAYER, Fritz, "König Max I von Bayern als Grossgrund-
besitzer in Schlesien Posen und Polen, " Zs. f. bayer.
LG, 26, 1963, 378-91.

5006. ZOEPFL, Friedrich, "Die Begegnung zwischen König Maximilian I Joseph von Bayern und Napoleon I in Dillingen
am 17. April 1809, " Zs. f. bayer. LG., 18, 1955, 435-
41.

Clemens Lothar Wenzel von Metternich (1773-1859)

See also entry 4288

5007. ARETIN, Karl Otmar von, "Metternichs Verfassungspläne
1817/18, " H. Jb., 74, 1954, 718-27.

5008. BASTGEN, Hubert, "Vatikanische Aktenstücke zu Metternichs Anwesenheit beim ersten Kölner Dombaufest (4 September 1842), " Röm. Qu.-Schr., 36, 1928, 299-320.

5009. KRAEHE, Enno E., "Raison d'Etat et idéologie dans la politique allemande de Metternich (1808-1820), " Rev. d'hist.
mod., 13, 1966, 181-94.

5010. KÜHN, Joachim, "Gentz, Metternich und Herzog Karl II.
nach dessen Vertreibung, " Braunschweig. Jb., 48, 1967,

78-101.
5011. LAUBERT, Manfred, "Metternich und die Kritik der deutschen Presse an der Revolution in Krakau und Galizien 1846," Hist. Vjschr., 17, 1914/15, 34-53.
5012. SRBIK, Heinrich Ritter von, "Der Prinz von Preussen und Metternich 1835-1848," Hist. Vjschr., 23, 1926/27, 188-98.

Maximilian Joseph von Montgelas (1759-1838)

5013. ARETIN, Erwein von, "Christoph Freiherr von Aretin Ein Lebensbild aus der Zeit des Ministers Montgelas," Gelbe Hefte, 3, 1927, 15-34, 100-33, 317-29.
5014. ARETIN, Karl O. von, "Der Sturz des Grafen Montgelas," Zs. f. bayer. LG., 20, 1957, 83-135.
5015. VEDELER, Harold C., "The Genesis of the Toleration Reforms in Bavaria under Montgelas," J. Mod. Hist., 10, 1938, 473-95.
5016. WEIS, Eberhard, "Montgelas' innenpolitisches Reformprogramm: Das Ansbacher Memoire für den Herzog von 30. 9. 1796," Zs. f. bayer. LG., 33, 1970, 219-56.

Karl von Rotteck (1775-1840)

5017. JOBST, Hans, "Die Staatslehre Karl von Rottecks Ihr Wesen und ihr Zusammenhang mit der Staatsphilosophie des 18. Jahrhunderts," ZGORh., 103, 1955, 468-98.
5018. SCHMELZEISEN, G. Kl., "Karl von Rotteck und die Zehntfrage," Zs. f. Agrarg., 16, 1968, 55-71.

Theodor Heinrich von Schön (1773-1856)

5019. BAUMANN, Margarete, "Schöns Urteil über Stein als Finanzmann," Hist. Vjschr., 16, 1913, 337-65.
5020. ESAU, Lotte, "Eine Landtagsrede Theodor von Schöns," Zs. f. Ostforsch., 13, 1964, 516-25.
5021. GRAY, Marion W., "Schroetter, Schön, and Society: Aristocratic Liberalism versus Middle-Class Liberalism in Prussia, 1808," Cen. Eur. Hist., 6, 1973, 60-82.
5022. HASENCLEVER, Adolf, "Ungedruckte Briefe Theodor von Schöns an den Hallenser Professor Ludwig Heinrich von Jakob (1805-1821)," FBPG, 31, 1919, 345-73.
5023. "HEINRICH Theodor von Schön," Pr. Jbb., 5, 1860, 10-30, 174-88, 264-81.
5024. MAYER, Eduard W., "Politische Erfahrungen und Gedanken Theodors von Schön nach 1815," HZ, 117, 1917, 432-64.
5025. SIMSON, Paul, "Aus der Zeit Theodor von Schöns westpreussischen Oberpräsidium," Pr. Jbb., 109, 1902, 58-72.
5026. THIMME, Friedrich, "Eine Rehabilitierung Theodors von Schön?," FBPG, 23, 1910, 171ff.

Heinrich Friedrich Karl von Stein (1757-1831)

See also entries 3403, 5019

5027. ANRICH, Ernst, "War Stein Romantiker?," HZ, 153, 1935/
       36, 290-305.
5028. BILLY, Robert de, "Le Baron de Stein," Rev. d'hist. dipl.,
       54/55, 1940, 117-28.
5029. BOTZENHART, Erich, "Die Bibliothek des Freiherrn vom
       Stein Zugleich ein Beitrag zur Analyse seiner volkswirt-
       schaftlichen Anschauungen," VSW, 22, 1929, 331-72.
5030. DELBRÜCK, Hans, "Die Ideen Steins über deutsche Ver-
       fassung," Pr. Jbb., 64, 1889, 129-34.
5031. DÖRING, Wolfgang, "Die Entwicklung der wehrpolitischen
       Ideen des Freiherrn vom Stein," WaG, 6, 1940, 15-43.
5032. DRÜNER, Hans, "Der nationale und der universale Gedanke
       bei dem Freiherrn vom Stein," Hist. Vjschr., 22, 1924/
       25, 28-69.
5033. ENNEN, L., ed., "Briefe des Freiherrn vom Stein an den
       Bildhauer Peter Joseph Imhoff in Köln," Ann. Nieder-
       rhein, 28/29, 1876, 1-10.
5034. EPSTEIN, Klaus, "Stein in German Historiography," Hist.
       Theor., 5, 1966, 241-74.
5035. FRIEDRICH, Fritz, "Stein und der Bauernschutz," Vergan-
       genheit und Gegenwart, 29, 1939, 83-94, 140-51.
5036. GEMBRUCH, W., "Krieg und Heerwesen im politischen
       Denken des Freiherrn vom Stein," Militärgesch. Mitt.,
       10, 1971, 27-54.
5037. GNEIST, R., "Die Denkschriften des Freiherrn vom Stein,"
       Pr. Jbb., 37, 1876, 257-80.
5038. HARTUNG, Fritz, "Freiherr vom Stein," ZgesStw., 91,
       1931, 1-22.
5039. HAUSSHERR, Hans, "Stein und Hardenberg," HZ, 190, 1960,
       267-89.
5040. _____, "Steins erste Entscheidung über die französischen
       Kriegstribute," FBPG, 45, 1933, 30-65.
5041. HINTZE, Otto, "Stein und der preussische Staat," HZ, 94,
       1905, 412-46.
5042. KAMNITZER, Heinz, "Stein und das 'Deutsche Comité' in
       Russland 1812/13," Zs. f. Geschw., 1, 1953, 50-92.
5043. KLEIN, Tim, "Der Reichsfreiherr Karl vom Stein," Zeit-
       wende, 7(2), 1931, 97-106.
5044. KLEINSTÜCK, Erwin, "Frankfurt und Stein," Arch. f.
       Frankfurts Gesch., 41, 1953, 79-113.
5045. KRAUEL, R., "Stein während des preussisch-englischen Kon-
       flikts im Jahre 1806," Pr. Jbb., 137, 1909, 429-57.
5046. KÜNTZEL, Georg, "Über das Verhältnis Steins zur franzö-
       sischen Revolution," Schmoll. Jb., 34, 1910, 69-90.
5047. LEHMANN, Max, ed., "Tagebuch des Freiherrn vom Stein
       während des Wiener Kongresses," HZ, 60, 1888, 385-467.
5048. MASUR, Gerhard, "Der Freiherr vom Stein," Zs. f. Pol.,
       22, 1932/33, 454-65.
5049. MOMMSEN, Wilhelm, "Freiherr vom Stein," GiWuU, 8, 1957,

329-41.

5050.   NOACK, Ulrich, "Christentum und Volksstaat in der poli-
        tischen Ethik des Freiherrn vom Stein," HZ, 147, 1933,
        40-52.

5051.   OBENAUS, Herbert, "Verwaltung und ständische Repräsenta-
        tion in den Reformen des Freiherrn vom Stein," Jb. f.
        Gesch. M. O. Dtschl., 18, 1969, 130-79.

5052.   OBERMANN, K., "Uber den Anteil des Freiherrn vom Stein
        an der Vorbereitung der Erhebung von 1813," Wissen-
        schaftliche Annalen, 6, 704-11.

5053.   PRÖSSLER, Helmut, "Die politische Freundschaft zwischen
        Freiherrn vom Stein und Friedrich zu Solms-Laubach von
        1813-1822," Arch. f. hessische Gesch., 26, 1958/61,
        103-38.

5054.   RAUMER, Kurt von, "Der Junge Stein," HZ, 184, 1957,
        497-530.

5055.   RITTER, Gerhard, "Vom jungen Stein," HZ, 148, 1933, 71-
        88.

5056.   ROTHFELS, Hans, "Politik als moralisches Problem,"
        Merkur, 11, 1957, 1105-18.

5057.   SCHMITT, Hans A., "1812: Stein, Alexander I and the
        Crusade against Napoleon," J. Mod. Hist., 31, 1959,
        325-28.

5058.   SCHOFF, Wilhelm, ed., "Briefwechsel zwischen Jacob
        Grimm und dem Freiherrn vom Stein," Pr. Jbb., 238,
        1934, 117-35.

5059.   SCHOTTE, Walther, "Das Erbe Steins," Pr. Jbb., 205,
        1926, 358-68.

5060.   SCHUSTER, Max, "Der Kampf des Reichsfreiherrn vom
        Stein um den konstitutionellen und nationalen Gedanken,"
        Gelbe Hefte, 3, 1927, 840-58.

5061.   SOLL, Karl, "Der Freiherr von und zum Stein und sein
        Wirken als Oberkammerpräsident in Minden für die Wirt-
        schafts- und Sozialstruktur Minden-Ravensberg," Jahresber.
        Hist. Ver. Grafsch. Ravensberg, 16, 1966/67.

5062.   THIEDE, Klaus, "Die Ansichten des Freiherrn vom Stein
        über das Zunftwesen und die Bauernbefreiung," Schmoll.
        Jb., 49, 1925, 1057-74.

5063.   _____, "Freiherr vom Stein und die deutsche Handels-
        politik," Weltwirtsch. Arch., 34, 1931, 212-29.

5064.   ULMANN, Heinrich, "Über eine neue Auffassung des Frei-
        herrn vom Stein," Hist. Vjschr., 13, 1910, 153-67.

5065.   UNRUH, G.-Chr. von, "Die Kreisordnungsentwürfe des Frei-
        herrn vom Stein und seiner Mitarbeiter 1808-1810-1820,"
        Westfäl. Forsch., 21, 1968, 5-41.

5066.   WALLTHOR, A. Hartlieb v., "Stein und Kunth in ihrer
        Bedeutung für die Entwicklung der Wirtschaft Westfalens,"
        Beitr. zur Gesch. Dortmunds und der Grafschaft Mark,
        66, 1970, 45-81.

5067.   _____, "Unbekannte Briefe des Freiherrn vom Steinan
        Caspar Geisberg aus den Jahren 1826 bis 1831," Westf.
        Zs., 107, 1957, 153-68.

5068.   WINTER, Georg, "Das Bild des Freiherrn vom Stein im

Jahre 1931 Ein Literaturbericht, " FBPG, 44, 1932, 385-408.

Ludwig von Vincke (1774-1844)

5069.   BRUNE, F., "Der erste Oberpräsident der Provinz West-
        falen, Frh. Ludwig Vincke, und die evangelische Kirche, "
        Jb. f. Westf. KiG, 65, 1972, 72-112.
5070.   SCHULZE-MARMELING, Wilhelm, "Englische Einflüsse auf
        die Ansichten Ludwig von Vinckes über Wirtschaft und
        Politik, " Westf. Zs., 103/04, 1954, 164-93.
5071.   STEFFENS, Wilhelm, "E. M. Arndt und Vincke Ihre An-
        schauungen über den Bauernstand in den Strömungen ihrer
        Zeit, " Westf. Zs., 91, 1935, 195-279.

1848-1849

See also entries 550, 2048, 2138, 2190, 2225, 2467, 2529,
2564, 2565, 2566, 2598, 3239, 3906, 3907, 3980, 3995,
4003, 4088, 4282, 4283, 4368, 4611, 4718, 4719, 4738,
4739, 4789, 4798, 4800, 4828, 5701

5072.   ADAM, Karl, "Stände und Berufe in Preussen gegenüber der
        nationalen Erhebung des Jahres 1848, " Pr. Jbb., 89, 1897,
        285-308.
5073.   AHÉ, Caesar von der, "Die Berichte über die Flucht des
        Prinzen von Preussen nach England im März 1848, " Mitt.
        d. Ver. f. Gesch., 48, 1931, 119-25.
5074.   BAUMANN, K., "Volkserhebung und Konspiration in der
        pfälzischen Bewegung von 1848/49, " Mitt. des Historischen
        Ver. der Pfalz, 68, 1970, 292-317.
5075.   BECKER, Albert, "Flüchtlingslos Zur Geschichte des ba-
        disch-Pfälzischen Aufstandes von 1849, " ZGORh., 84,
        1931/32, 96-134.
5076.   BECKER, Gerhard, "Antifeudale Petitionen preussischer
        Bauern vom März 1848, " Zs. f. Geschw., 16, 1968, 182-
        97.
5077.   _____, "Die Beschlüsse des zweiten Demokratenkongresses
        1848, " Zs. f. Geschw., 21, 1973, 321-42.
5078.   _____, "Der Kongress der Arbeitervereine der Rhein-
        provinz und Westfalens am 6. Mai 1849, " Beitr. z. Gesch.
        d. dt. Arbeiterbeweg., 10, 1968, 373-83.
5079.   _____, "Die 'soziale Frage' auf dem zweiten demokra-
        tischen Kongress 1848, " Zs. f. Geschw., 15, 1967.
5080.   BELOW, Georg v., ed., "Aus den Frankfurter Parlament
        Briefe des Abgeordneten Ernst v. Saucken-Tarputschen, "
        Deutsche Rundschau, 124(3), 1905, 79-104.
5081.   BENSER, Günter, "Die deutsche Nationalliteratur als Aus-
        druck des revolutionär-demokratischen Bewusstseins vor
        der Revolution von 1848, " Beitr. z. Gesch. d. dt. Ar-
        beiterbeweg., 7, 1965, 445-53.

5082. BERGSTRÄSSER, Ludwig, "Briefe des Präsidenten Lette aus dem Frankfurter Parlament, " Deutsche Rundschau, 45, 1919, 169ff.

5083. _____, "Der erste Entwurf des Verfassungsausschusses der Frankfurter Nationalversammlung über die Abschnitte: Reichsoberhaupt und Reichsrat, " Hist. Vjschr., 16, 1913, 378ff.

5084. _____, "Neue Beiträge zur Geschichte der Berliner Märztage, " Hist. Vjschr., 17, 1914/15, 54-85.

5085. _____, "Parteien von 1848, " Pr. Jbb., 177, 1919, 180-211.

5086. _____, "Die Parteipolitische Lage beim Zusammentritt des Vorparlaments, " Zs. f. Pol., 6, 1913, 594-620.

5087. BERNER, Ernst, "Die Kaiserschriften des Jahres 1888, " FBPG, 2, 1889, 549-93.

5088. BESELER, Hans v., "Aus Georg Beselers Frankfurter Briefen 1848/49, " Deutsche Revue, 37, 1912.

5089. BEYER, H., "Recht, Volk und Obrigkeit in der Schleswig-holsteinischen Erhebung 1848/49, " Jb. f. d. Schleswigsche Geest., 5, 1957, 3ff.

5090. BLECK, W., "Die Posener Frage auf den Nationalversammlungen 1848/49, " Z. d. hist. Ges. f. d. Prov. Posen, 29, 1914, 1ff.

5091. BLEIBER, Helmut, "Bauern und Landarbeiter in der bürgerlich-demokratischen Revolution von 1848/49 in Deutschland, " Zs. f. Geschw., 17, 1969, 289-309.

5092. BÖHM, Jakob, "Die Deutsche Legion im ungarischen Freiheitskampf 1848/49, " Zs. f. MilitärG., 6, 1967, 81-96.

5093. BOLDT, Werner, "Konstitutionelle Monarchie oder parlamentarische Demokratie die Auseinandersetzung um die deutsche Nationalversammlung in der Revolution von 1848, " HZ, 216, 1973, 553-622.

5094. BOYENS, J., "Das Grenzland Schleswig und die deutsche Verfassungsbewegung 1848, " Kieler Bl., 1940, 344ff.

5095. BRANDT, Otto, "Mittelstaatliche Politik im Deutschen Bund nach der Revolution von 1848, " Zs. f. bayer. LG., 2, 1929, 299-318.

5096. "BRIEFE des Abgeordneten zum Frankfurter Parlament S. G. Kerst aus Meseritz, " Zeitschrift f. Geschichte u. Landeskunde Provinz Posen, 2, 1883, 319-69; 3, 1884, 43-73.

5097. BRÜNNERT, Gustav, "Die Revolution in Erfurt im Jahre 1848, " Pr. Jbb., 145, 1911, 474-500.

5098. BRUNNER, H., "Die sog. Garde-du-Corps-Nacht 9/10. April 1848, " Mitt. a. d. Mitgl. d. Ver. f. hess. Gesch., 1908/09, 25ff.

5099. BRUNNER, O., "Die Wiener Abgeordneten zum Frankfurter Vorparlament 1848 und die deutschen Reichskleinodien, " Nachr. Bl. d. Ver. f. Gesch. d. Stadt Wien, 1, 1939, 17ff.

5100. BRUNSCHWIG, Henri, "Propos sur la Révolution de 1848, " Annales, 3, 1948, 129-34.

5101. CHAMMIER-GLISCZINSKI, Frau Generalin v., "Bielefeld im Jahre 1848, " Pr. Jbb., 148, 1912, 435-62.

5102.   COUPE, W. A., "The German Cartoon and the Revolution
         of 1848," Comp. Stud. Soc. Hist., 9, 1966/67, 137-67.
5103.   CROMER, R., "Die Nationalitätenfrage auf den National-
         versammlungen von Frankfurt und Berlin," Nation und
         Staat, 7, 1933/34, 649ff.
5104.   DORPALEN, Andreas, "Die Revolution von 1848 in der
         Geschichtsschreibung der DDR," HZ, 210, 1970, 324-68.
5105.   DROZ, Jacques, "La presse socialiste en Rhénanie pendant
         la révolution de 1848," Ann. Niederrhein, 155/56, 1954,
         184-201.
5106.   _____, "Die religiösen Sekten und die Revolution von
         1848," Arch. f. Sozialgesch., 3, 1963, 109-18.
5107.   _____, "Travaux Récents sur la Révolution de 1848 en
         Allemagne," Rev. d'hist. mod., 1, 1954, 145-55.
5108.   FISCHER, F., "Das Ende der deutschen Nationalversamm-
         lung," Pr. Jbb., 32, 1873, 303-32.
5109.   FLOTTWELL, E., "Briefe aus der Paulskirche," Deutsche
         Revue, 47, 1922, 53ff, 138ff.
5110.   FRAHM, Andrea, "Paulskirche und Volkssouveränität," HZ,
         130, 1924, 210-55.
5111.   GEISEL, K., "Die kurhessischen Petitionen an die Frank-
         furter Nationalversammlung 1848/49," Zs. d. Ver. f.
         hess. Gesch. u. Landeskunde, 81, 1970, 119-79.
5112.   GOLDSMITH, Margaret, "The German Revolution of 1848,"
         Nineteenth Century and After, 130, 1941.
5113.   GOTTFRIED, Paul, "Pessimism and the Revolution of 1848,"
         Rev. Pol., 35, 1973, 193-203.
5114.   GRIEWANK, Karl, "Ursachen und Folgen des Scheiterns der
         Deutschen Revolution von 1848," HZ, 170, 1950, 495-523.
5115.   GRUBE, Walter, "Friedrich Notter und die Revolution von
         1848," Zs. F. Württbg. LG, 25, 1966, 214-73.
5116.   GUNZERT, Walter, "Darmstadt im Jahre 1848," ZGORh.,
         97, 1949, 203-26.
5117.   HAENCHEN, Karl, "Flucht und Rückkehr des Prinzen von
         Preussen 1848," HZ, 154, 1936, 32-95.
5118.   _____, "Der Quellenwert der Nobilingschen Aufzeichnun-
         gen über die Berliner Märzrevolution," FBPG, 52, 1940,
         321-39.
5119.   _____, "Zur revolutionären Unterwühlung Berlins vor den
         Märztagen des Jahres 1848," FBPG, 55, 1943, 83-114.
5120.   HAGENAH, H., "Aus der Geschichte des schleswig-holstein-
         ischen Staatsgrundgesetzes vom 15. September 1848,"
         Nordelbingen, 6, 1927, 437.
5121.   _____, "Der 24. März 1848 in Kiel und seine Bedeutung
         für die deutsche Geschichte," Mitt. d. Ges. f. Kieler
         Stadtgesch., 39, 1936, 145ff.
5122.   _____, "Die Männer der Provisorischen Regierung,"
         Nordelbingen, 2, 1923, 140ff.
5123.   _____, "Revolution und Legitimität in der Erhebung
         Schleswig-Holsteins," Qu. u. Forsch. z. Gesch. Schles-
         wig-Holsteins, 4, 1916, 49ff.
5124.   HAMEROW, T. S., "The Elections to the Frankfurt Parlia-
         ment," J. Mod. Hist., 33, 1961, 15-32.

5125.   _____, "The German Artisan Movement 1848-49," J.
          Cen. Eur. Aff., 21, 1961, 135-52.
5126.   _____, "History and the German Revolution of 1848,"
          AHR, 60, 1954/55, 27-44.
5127.   HAMMEN, Oscar J., "Economic and Social Factors in the
          Prussian Rhineland in 1848," AHR, 54, 1948/49, 825-40.
5128.   HARNACK, Axel von, "Die Paulskirche im Wandel der
          Geschichtsauffassung," Zs. f. Pol., 12, 1922/23, 235-47.
5129.   HAUPTMANN, F., "Der liberale Umschwung in Sachsen im
          März 1848," Meissn.-Sächs. Forsch., 1929, 239ff.
5130.   _____, "Sachsen und Thüringen 1848/49," N. Arch. f.
          sächs. Gesch., 51, 1930, 215ff.
5131.   HAUSLEITER, Otto, "Die Autonomie-Bewegung des Jahres
          1848 im Niederländischen Herzogtum Limburg und ihr
          wahrer soziologischer Charakter Eine Richtigstellung,"
          Rhein. Vtljbll, 14, 1949, 97-137.
5132.   HAWGOOD, J. A., "The Frankfurt Parliament of 1848/49,"
          History, 17, 1932, 147-51.
5133.   HIRSCH, Helmut, "Die beiden Hilgards Ein biographischer
          Beitrag zur Geschichte der achtundvierziger Revolution
          und des Deutschamerikanertums," ZGORh., 98, 1950,
          486-97.
5134.   HOFMANN, Karl, "Der Bauernaufstand des Jahres 1848 im
          badischen Bauland," Neues Archiv f. d. Gesch. d. Stadt
          Heidelberg und der rhein. Pfalz, 5, 1902, 110ff.
5135.   HOPPE, Ruth and Jürgen KUCZYNSKI, "Eine Berufs- bzw.
          auch Klassen- und Schichtenanalyse der Märzgefallenen
          1848 in Berlin," Jb. f. Wgesch., 1964(4), 200-76.
5136.   HUBER, Ernst Rudolf, "Der Volksgedanke in der Revolution
          von 1848," ZgesStw., 99, 1938/39, 393-439.
5137.   HÜSER, Karl, "Der westfälische Kongress für die Sache und
          Rechte der preussischen Nationalversammlung und des
          preussischen Volkes vom 18./19 November 1848 in Mün-
          ster," Westf. Zs., 119, 1969, 121-55.
5138.   HÜTTERMANN, Wilhelm, "Parteipolitisches Leben in West-
          falen vom Beginn der Märzbewegung im Jahre 1848 bis
          zum Einsetzen der Reaktion im Jahre 1849," Westf. Zs.,
          68, 1910, 97-230.
5139.   HUGELMANN, K. G., "Der grossdeutsche Gedanke und die
          Frankfurter Nationalversammlung 1848," Öst. Rundsch.,
          18, 1922, 477ff.
5140.   HUHN, E., "Das Grossherzogtum Sachsen in der Bewegung
          1848/49," Z. d. Ver. f. Thür. Gesch., 27, 1926, 221ff.
5141.   HUNDT, Martin, "Die 17 'Forderungen der Kommunistischen
          Partei in Deutschland' vom März 1848," Beitr. z. Gesch.
          d. dt. Arbeiterbeweg., 10, 1968, 203-36.
5142.   IBLER, H., "Die Wahlen zur Frankfurter Nationalversammlung
          in Österreich 1848," MÖIG, 48, 1934, 103ff.
5143.   JOCHMUS, A. v., "Beitrag zur aktenmässigen Darstellung
          des Deutschen Reichsministeriums von 1849," Ges. Schr.,
          3, 1883.
5144.   KENTENICH, Gottfried, "Aus den nachgelassenen Papieren
          eines vergessenen Frankfurter Parlamentaries," Heidel-

berger Jahrbücher, 14, 1906, 187-214.

5145. KLIEM, Manfred, "Die Rolle der feudaljunkerlichen Reaktion in der Revolution von 1848/49," Zs. f. Geschw., 17, 1969, 310-30.

5146. KLÖTZER, W., "Die Frankfurter Paulskirche-Symbol der deutschen Einheit," Arch. f. Frankfurts Gesch., 51, 1968, 5-22.

5147. KLOPPENBURG, H., "Der Aufruhr in Hildesheim am 17./ 18. April 1849," Alt-Hildesheim, 1919, 25ff.

5148. KÖNIG, Helmut, "Schulpolitische Kämpfe in Thüringer Klein-staaten während der Revolution von 1848 bis 1849," Wiss. Zs. d. Fr.-Sch.-Univ. Jena, 17, 1968, 51-64.

5149. KOHL, D., "Die ersten Reichswahlen in Oldenburg 1848," Old. Jb., 29, 1925, 216ff.

5150. KOLB, Dr., "Aus der Zeit des Frankfurter Parlaments Aufzeichnungen aus dem Nachlass des Abgeordneten Dr. Kolb," Deutsche Revue, 29, 1904.

5151. KOSZYK, Kurt, "Franz Ludwig Sensburg u. d. Münchner 'Vorwärts' von 1848-49," Arch. f. Sozialgesch., 2, 1962, 31-54.

5152. KOTHE, W., "Deutsche Bewegung und preussische Politik im Posener Lande 1848/49," Dt. wiss. Z. f. Polen, 1931 (21).

5153. KUYPERS, Julien, "Wilhelm Wolff und der deutsche Arbei-terverein (1847/48) in Brüssel Ein Fund aus dem bel-gischen Landesarchiv," Arch. f. Sozialgesch., 3, 1963, 103-07.

5154. LANG, W., "Berlin und Frankfurt Mit ungedruckten Briefen aus den Jahren 1848 und 1849," Deutsche Rund-schau, 55, 1888, 332-53; 56, 1888, 47-75.

5155. LANGERMANN, H. v., "Über Abrüstung und Völkerfriedens-kongress 1849 in der Paulskirche zu Frankfurt a. Main," Deutsche Revue, 40, 1915, 134ff.

5156. LAUBERT, Manfred, "Eduard Flottwells Briefe aus der Paulskirche 1848/49," Deutsche Revue, 47, 1922, 53-64, 138-56.

5157. LAUTENSCHLAGER, Friedrich, "Amand Goegg, ein bad-ischer Achtundvierziger Zur Hundertjahrfeier der deutschen Revolution von 1848/49," ZGORh., 96, 1948, 19-38.

5158. LERCHE, Otto, "Die Berliner Synode von 1848/49 Ein Kapitel preussischer Kirchengeschichte," Jb. f. Ber.-Brandenburg. KiG, 38, 1963, 142-76.

5159. LEY, Friedrich, "Frankreich und die deutsche Revolution 1848/49," Pr. Jbb., 213, 1928, 199-216.

5160. LUTZE, Gudrun, "Die Frankfurter Nationalversammlung und die Breslauer Presse," Jb. d. Schles.-Fried.-Wilh. Univ z. Breslau, 5, 1960, 189-203.

5161. MARCKS, Erich, "Die europäischen Mächte und die 48er Revolution," HZ, 142, 1930, 73-87.

5162. MANN, Bernhard, "Das Ende der deutschen Nationalversamm-lung im Jahre 1849," HZ, 214, 1972, 265-309.

5163. _____, "Die Wahlen zur deutschen Nationalversammlung

1848 im Wahlkreis Hall-Gaildorf-Crailsheim," Württem-
bergisch-Franken, 53, 1969, 109-22.

5164. MATTHEISEN, Donald J., "1848: Theory and Practice of
the German juste milieu," Rev. Pol., 35, 1973, 180-92.

5165. _____, "Voters and Parliaments in the German Revolution of 1848: An Analysis of the Prussian Constituent Assembly," Cen. Eur. Hist., 5, 1972, 3-22.

5166. MEERHEIMB, Ferdinand Freiherr von, "Briefe eines preussischen Offiziers aus dem Jahre 1848," Pr. Jbb., 157,
1914, 450-80; 158, 1914, 69-94.

5167. MEINECKE, Friedrich, "The Year 1848 in German History:
Reflections on a Centenary," Rev. Pol., 10, 1948, 475-
92.

5168. MEINERT, Hermann, "Frankfurt und Berlin im Zeichen der
Paulskirche," Arch. f. hessische Gesch., 28, 1963, 417-
36.

5169. MEYERNICK, V., "Rückblick auf die Maitage 1849 in Dres-
den," Jb. f. d. Dt. Armee u. Marine, 104, 1897, 13ff.

5170. MOLDENHAUER, Rüdiger, "Aktenbestand, Geschäftsverfah-
ren und Geschäftsgang der 'Deutschen Verfassungsgebenden
Reichsversammlung' (Nationalversammlung) 1848/49 und
ihrer Ausschüsse," Archiv. Zeitsch., 65, 1969, 47-91.

5171. _____, "Die Petitionen aus der Freien Stadt Frankfurt an
die Deutsche Nationalversammlung 1848/49," Arch. f.
Frankfurts Gesch., 51, 1968, 23-64.

5172. _____, "Die Petitionen aus Oberhessen an die deutsche
Nationalversammlung 1848-1849," Mitt. d. Oberhessischen
Geschichtsvereins, 51, 1966, 75-119.

5173. _____, "Die Petitionen aus den preussischen Saarkreisen
an die deutsche Nationalversammlung 1848/1849," Zs. f.
Gesch. d. Saargegend, 17/18, 1969/70, 38-111.

5174. NÄF, Werner, ed., "Nach der deutschen Revolution von
1848/49 Briefe von Ludwig Pfau und Carl Vogt aus dem
Exil," Zs. f. Schw. Gesch., 12, 1932, 166-209.

5175. NIEBOUR, H., "Die Abgeordneten Steiermarks in der Frankfurter Nationalversammlung," Z. d. Hist. Ver. Steier-
mark, 10, 1912, 247ff.

5176. _____, "Die hannoverschen Abgeordneten zur Nationalversammlung 1848/49," Z. d. Hist. Ver. f. Niedersachsen,
76, 1911, 136ff.

5177. _____, "Die Vertreter der Provinz Posen in der Frankfurter Nationalversammlung," Hist. Monatsbl. f. d.
Prov. Posen, 1911, 65ff.

5178. OBERMANN, Karl, "Die soziale Zusammensetzung der Bürgerwehr in Köln 1848/49," Jb. f. Wgesch., 1970(4), 141-
58.

5179. O'BOYLE, Leonore, "The Democratic Left in Germany,
1848," J. Mod. Hist., 33, 1961, 374-83.

5180. ÖLSNER, L., "Die Wirtschafts- und sozialpolitischen Verhandlungen des Frankfurter Parlaments," Pr. Jbb., 87,
1897, 81-100.

5181. ONCKEN, Hermann, "Zur Genesis der preussischen Revolution von 1848," FBPG, 13, 1900, 123-52.

5182.   "Ein PARLAMENTSALBUM aus der Paulskirche," Deutsche
        Rundschau, 106, 1901, 99-126.
5183.   PASCAL, Roy, "The Frankfort Parliament, 1848 and the
        Drang Nach Osten," J. Mod. Hist., 18, 1946, 108-22.
5184.   PAUR, Theodor, "Briefe aus der Paulskirche," Mitteil a. d.
        Literaturarchiv in Berlin, 16, 1919.
5185.   PELGER, Hans, "Zur demokratischen und sozialen Bewe-
        gung in Norddeutschland im Anschluss an die Revolution
        von 1848," Arch. f. Sozialgesch., 8, 1968, 161-228.
5186.   PERTHES, Otto, "Beiträge zur Geschichte der Märztage
        1848," Pr. Jbb., 63, 1889, 527-43.
5187.   PETERS, Herbert, "Zur 'mobilen Kolonne' des demokraten
        Stockmann im November 1848," Zs. f. MilitärG., 3,
        1964, 483-90.
5188.   PFITZNER, J., "Die grenz- und auslandsdeutsche Bewegung
        1848," HZ, 160, 1939, 308-23.
5189.   PÖLNITZ, Götz Freiherr von, "George P. Phillips Ein
        grossdeutscher Konservativer in der Paulskirche," HZ,
        155, 1936/37, 51-97.
5190.   "PREUSSEN zur Zeit seiner Nationalversammlung," Die
        Gegenwart, 4, 1850, 576-634.
5191.   RACHFAHL, Felix, "Österreich und Preussen im März
        1848," Hist. Vjschr., 6, 1903, 357-86, 503-30; 7, 1904,
        192-240.
5192.   _____, "Zur Berliner Märzrevolution," FBPG, 17, 1904,
        193-236.
5193.   RAPP, Adolf, "Württembergische Politiker von 1848 im
        Kampf um die deutsche Frage," Zs. F. Württbg. LG,
        25, 1916, 572-605.
5194.   RAUCH, Georg von, "Der Widerhall der Revolution von
        1848 im baltischen Deutschtum," Hamb. Mittel- u. ostdt.
        Forsch., 4, 1963, 9-29.
5195.   RAUMER, Kurt von, "Zur deutschen Revolution von 1848,"
        HZ, 148, 1933, 94ff.
5196.   RETHWISCH, C., "Literatur zur deutschen Parlaments-
        geschichte 1848/49," Mitteilungen a. d. hist. Literatur
        der Histor. Gesellschaft Berlin, 9, 1921, 11ff.
5197.   ROBERTSON, Priscilla, "Students on the Barricades: Ger-
        many and Austria 1848," Pol. Sci. Q., 84, 1969, 367-
        79.
5198.   ROSE, Carol, "The Issue of Parliamentary Suffrage at the
        Frankfurt National Assembly," Cen. Eur. Hist., 5, 1972,
        127-49.
5199.   ROTHFELS, Hans, "1848--One Hundred Years After," J.
        Mod. Hist., 20, 1948, 291-319.
5200.   SÄGMULLER, Johannes B., "Der rechtliche Begriff der
        Trennung von Kirche und Staat auf der Frankfurter Na-
        tionalversammlung 1848/1849," Theol. Qu.-Schr., 102,
        1921, 97-133.
5201.   SCHILL, W. F., "Militärische Beziehungen zwischen Preus-
        sen und Baden 1849/50," FBPG, 43, 1930, 290ff.
5202.   SCHMIDT, Max G., "Ein Stammbuch aus dem Frankfurter
        Parlament," Deutsche Revue, 27, 1902, 347-63.

5203.   SCHMIDT, Walter, "Zu einigen Fragen der sozialen Struk-
        tur und der politischen Ideologie in der Zeit des Vormärz
        und der Revolution von 1848/49," Beitr. z. Gesch. d.
        dt. Arbeiterbeweg., 7, 1965, 645-60.
5204.   _____, "Zur Rolle des Proletariats in der deutschen
        Revolution von 1848/49," Zs. f. Geschw., 17, 1969,
        270-88.
5205.   SCHRÖRS, Heinrich, "Kirchliche Bewegungen unter dem
        Kölnischen Klerus im Jahre 1848," Ann. Niederrhein,
        105, 1921, 1-74; 106, 1922, 57-95.
5206.   SCHULZ, Ursula, "Die Abgeordneten der Provinz Schlesien
        im Frankfurter Parlament," Jb. d. Schles.-Fried.-Wilh.
        Univ z. Breslau, 12, 1967, 155-230.
5207.   SCHWARZ, Klaus, "Die Verluste der preussischen Armee
        in der Berliner Märzrevolution 1848," Bär v. Ber., 13,
        1964, 50-67.
5208.   SEPP, I. N., "Erinnerungen an die Paulskirche 1848,"
        Die Grenzboten, 62, 1903, 694-702, 780-86.
5209.   SHORTER, Edward, "Middle-Class Anxiety in the German
        Revolution of 1848," J. Soc. Hist., 2, 1968/69, 189-215.
5210.   SRBIK, Heinrich von, "Die deutsche Einheitsfrage in der
        Frankfurter Nationalversammlung," Hist. Bl., 1, 1921/22,
        353ff.
5211.   STADELMANN, Rudolf, "Das Jahr 1848 und die deutsche
        Geschichte," Deutsche Rundschau, 71, 1948, 99ff.
5212.   STERN, Alfred, "Politische Flüchtlinge in Zürich nach der
        Revolution von 1848 und 1849," Anzeiger f. Schweizerische
        Geschichte, 17, 1919, 337-67.
5213.   SYBEL, Heinrich von, "Aus den Berliner Märztagen 1848,"
        HZ, 63, 1889, 428-53.
5214.   TIDEMANN, Heinrich, "Pastor Rudolf Oulon Ein Beitrag
        zur Geschichte der Märzrevolution in Bremen," Bre-
        misches Jb., 33, 1931, 376-445; 34, 1933, 162-261.
5215.   TRÜBNER, Georg, "Johann Philipp Becker und die Revolu-
        tion 1848," Int. Rev. Soc. Hist., 10, 1965, 410-28.
5216.   ULMANN, H., ed., "Stimmungsberichte aus den letzten
        Tagen der preussischen Nationalversammlung im Novem-
        ber 1848," FBPG, 18, 1905, 585-95.
5217.   VALENTIN, Veit, "Das erste deutsche Parlament und Wir,"
        Deutsche Revolution, 10, 1920.
5218.   _____, "Neue Quellen und Darstellungen zur Geschichte
        der Revolution von 1848-49," Die Geisteswissenschaften,
        1914, 430-33.
5219.   VARRENTRAPP, C., "Meinungen in Kurhessen über das
        deutsche Kaisertum in den Jahren 1848 und 1849," HZ,
        94, 1905, 67-106.
5220.   VITZTHUM, K.-H., "Die soziale Herkunft der Abgeordneten
        der Hamburger Konstituante 1848," Zs. d. Ver. f. ham-
        burg. Gesch., 54, 1968, 51-76.
5221.   WÄTZIG, Alfons and Klaus KITTNER, "Untersuchungen zur
        Rolle der Eisenbahnbauarbeiter und der Einsenbahnarbeiter
        beim Dresdner Maiaufstand 1849," Wiss. Z. Hochschule
        Dresden, 1970(2).

5222.	WEBER, Frank G., "Palmerston and Prussian Liberalism 1848," J. Mod. Hist., 35, 1963, 125-36.
5223.	WEBER, H., "Die Wahlen zur deutschen Nationalversammlung im Wahlbez. Öhringen-Künzelsau, April 1848," Württembergisch-Franken, 53, 1969, 123-32.
5224.	WEBER, Rolf, "Die Beziehungen zwischen Sozialer Struktur und politischen Ideologie des Kleinbürgertums in der Revolution von 1848/49," Zs. f. Geschw., 13, 1965, 1186-93.
5225.	_____, "Emil Ottokar Weller und seine Rolle in der demokratischen- und Arbeiterbewegung in Leipzig 1848," Jb. f. Regionalgesch., 3, 1968, 110-36.
5226.	_____, "Die Entwicklung der sächsischen Arbeitervereine 1848/49," Beitr. z. Gesch. d. dt. Arbeiterbeweg., 10, 1968, 345-72.
5227.	_____, "Samuel Erdmann Tzschirner: Grösse und Grenzen des Führers der Revolution 1848/49 in Sachsen," Letopis, 2, 1970(2).
5228.	_____, "Das Verhältnis der kleinbürgerlichen Demokratie in Sachsen zur polnischen Frage 1848," Zs. f. Geschw., 16, 1968, 855-73.
5229.	WEISS, John, "Karl Marlo, Guild Socialism, and the Revolutions of 1848," Int. Rev. Soc. Hist., 5, 1960, 77-96.
5230.	WENTZCKE, Paul, "Bayerische Stimmen aus der Paulskirche," Archival. Z., 50/51, 1955, 485ff.
5231.	_____, "Friedrich Bassermanns letzte politische Sendung Beiträge zum Verständnis des Endkampfs zwischen Berlin und Frankfurt im Frühjahr 1849," ZGORh., 102, 1954, 319-74.
5232.	_____, "Thüringische Einheitsfragen in der deutschen Revolution von 1848," HZ, 118, 1917, 418-48.
5233.	WERNICKE, Kurt, "Kommunisten und politische Aktivisten in der Berliner Arbeiterbewegung vor, während und nach der Revolution 1848/49," Beitr. z. Gesch. d. dt. Arbeiterbeweg., 10, 1968, 298-344.
5234.	WESENDONCK, Hugo, "Vom ersten deutschen Parlament Erinnerungen," Die Gegenwart, 54, 1898, 54-57, 72-75.
5235.	WOHLEB, Joseph L., "Beiträge zur Geschichte der Revolution von 1848 und 1849 in Baden," ZGORh., 106, 1958, 136-64.
5236.	ZEISE, Roland, "Bauern und Demokratem 1848/49 Zur antifeudalen Bewegung der sächsischen Landbevölkerung in der Revolution vom Sommer 1848 bis zum Vorabend des Dresdner Maiaufstandes," Jb. f. Regionalgesch., 4, 1972, 148-78.
5237.	_____, "Der Sturm auf das Waldenburger Schloss 1848," Zs. f. Geschw., 21, 1973, 343-56.
5238.	_____, "Zur sozialen Struktur und zur Lage der Volksmassen auf dem Lande am Vorabend der Revolution von 1848/49 in Sachsen," Jb. f. Wgesch., 1968(1), 239-73.
5239.	ZERNIN, Gerhard, "Eine Erinnerung an den badischen Aufstand von 1849 und ein Bericht darüber von Dr. J. V. v. Scheffel," Deutsche Revue, 12, 1887, 305ff.
5240.	ZWIEDINECK, H. v., "Österreich und der deutsche Bundes-

staat Ein Beitrag zur deutschen Verfassungsgeschichte
1848-49, " MIÖG, 24, 1903, 283ff.

1848-1871

See also entries 2760, 4404, 4450, 4480, 4489, 4530, 4549,
4566, 4621, 4624

5241. ALLMAYER-BECK, Joh. Christoph, "Das Schichsalsjahr
1866, " GiWuU, 18, 1967, 321-32.
5242. D'AVRIL, Adolphe, "L'Autriche dans la confédération Ger-
manique (1850-1851), " Rev. d'hist. dipl., 1, 1887, 27-60.
5243. BACHMANN, Harald, "Coburgs Weg ins Bismarckreich 1866-
1871, " Jb. Coburger Landesstiftung, 15, 1970.
5244. BAIER, Hermann, "Die politische und wirtschaftliche Lage
im Amtsbezirk Donau-eschingen im Jahre 1852, " ZGORh.,
80, 1928, 87-116.
5245. BARRACLOUGH, Geoffrey, "German Unification. An Essay
in Revision, " Hist. Stud., 4, 1963, 62-81.
5246. BARTEL, Horst, "Die Reichseinigung 1871 in Deutschland--
ihre Geschichte und Folgen, " Zs. f. Geschw., 16, 1968,
1158-67.
5247. BERGSTRÄSSER, Ludwig, "Kritische Studien zur Konflikts-
zeit, " Hist. Vjschr., 19, 1919, 346-76.
5248. BILGER, F., "Grossdeutsche Politik im Lager Radetzkys, "
Hist. Bl., 4, 1931, 3ff.
5249. BOSL, Karl, "Die deutschen Mittelstaaten in der Entscheidung
von 1866, " Zs. f. bayer. LG., 29, 1966, 665-79.
5250. BRANDENBURG, Erich, "Deutsche Einheit, " Hist. Vjschr.,
30, 1935, 757ff.
5251. _____, "Die Verhandlungen über die Gründung des deutschen Reiches 1870, " Hist. Vjschr., 15, 1912, 493-546.
5252. DRAUBACH, Max, "Aus dem neueren Schrifttum zur
Geschichte der deutschen Einheitsbewegung, " H. Jb., 52,
1932, 79-86.
5253. BUKEY, Evan B., "The Exile Government of King George
V of Hannover 1866-71, " Can. J. Hist., 5, 1970, 71-93.
5254. BUSCH, Wilhelm, "Württemberg und Bayern in den Ein-
heitsverhandlungen 1870, " HZ, 109, 1912, 161-90.
5255. DANIELS, Emil, "Die Notverordnung von 1863 und die inneren Vorgänge im preussischen Königshause, " Pr. Jbb.,
226, 1931, 58-76, 176-93.
5256. DEETZ-AROLSEN, Eduard, "Major Albert Deetz, der Abgeordnete für Wittenberg in der Nationalversammlung,
Chef des Centralbureaus des Reichskriegsministerums und
Kommandant von Frankfurt am Main 1848-1854, " Arch. f.
Frankfurts Gesch., 1938, 89-114.
5257. DEHIO, Ludwig, "Die Taktik der Opposition während der Konflikts, " HZ, 140, 1929, 279-347.
5258. DIETRICH, Richard, "Der Preussisch-Sächsische Friedens-
schluss vom 21. Oktober 1866, " Jb. f. Gesch. M. O.
Dtschl., 4, 1955, 109-56.

5259.   DROZ, Jacques, "L'Allemagne et la Révolution Française,"
        RH, 198, 1947, 161-77.
5260.   _____, "L'idée Fédéraliste en Allemagne Autour de
        1860," Rev. d'hist. dipl., 75, 1961, 205-14.
5261.   EASTON, J. C. and Buford ROWLAND, "The Assembly of
        German Princes of 1863," J. Mod. Hist., 14, 1942, 480-
        99.
5262.   EGIDY, B. von, "Die Wahlen im Herzogtum Nassau 1848-
        1952. Ein Beitrag zur Geschichte der politischen Parteien
        am Mittelrhein," Nass. Ann., 82, 1971, 215-306.
5263.   EISEFELD, Gerhard, "Die Anfänge liberaler Parteien in
        Dortmund 1858-1870," Beitr. Gesch. Dortmunds Grafsch.
        Mark, 65, 1969.
5264.   ENGELBERT, G., "Der Beitritt Lippes zum Norddeutschen
        Bund," Lipp. Mitt., 36, 1967, 65-81.
5265.   _____, "Das Jahr 1866 in der deutschen Geschichte,
        unter besonderer Berücksichtigung Lippes und der übrigen
        norddeutschen Kleinstaaten," Lipp. Mitt., 35, 1966, 5-40.
5266.   _____, "Lippe zwischen 1866 und 1871. Vom Norddeut-
        schen Bund zum Deutschen Reich," Lipp. Mitt., 39, 1970,
        137-54.
5267.   ENGEL-JANOSI, Frederic, "Struggle for Austria in Berlin
        and Frankfort 1849-1855," J. Cen. Eur. Aff., 2, 1942,
        34-48.
5268.   ENGELSING, Rolf, "Der Norddeutsche Bund 1867-1871.
        Bericht über eine Ausstellung in Berlin," GiWuU, 22,
        1971, 738-42.
5269.   FABER, Karl-Georg, "Realpolitik als Ideologie Die Bedeu-
        tung des Jahres 1866 für das politische Denken in Deutsch-
        land," HZ, 203, 1966, 1-45.
5270.   FRAHM, Friedrich, "Entstehungs- und Entwicklungsgeschichte
        der preussischen Verfassung (vom März 1848 bis zum
        Januar 1850)," FBPG, 41, 1928, 248-301.
5271.   _____, "Die politische Lage beim Ausbruch des deutsch-
        dänischen Krieges," Hist. Vjschr., 16, 1913, 520-36.
5272.   GEFFEKEN, F. H., "The Unity of Germany," EHR, 6, 1891,
        209-37.
5273.   GOPPEL, Alfons, "Bayern und das Jahr 1866," Zs. f. bayer.
        LG., 29, 1966, 680-88.
5274.   GROBBECKER, H., "Mecklenburg-Strelitz 1848-51," Meck.-
        Strelitz Gesch. Bl., 2, 1924, 77ff.
5275.   GROSS, Reiner, "Die kleinbürgerlich-demokratische Bewegung
        in Sebnitz 1848-1852," Jb. f. Regionalgesch., 1, 1965,
        137-49.
5276.   HAERING, Johannes, "Württemberg unter dem Einfluss der
        Julirevolution," Zs. F. Württbg. LG, 1, 1937, 446-54.
5277.   "HANNOVERS Reactionsjahre," Pr. Jbb., 3, 1859, 505-40.
5278.   HARTUNG, Fritz, "Preussen und die deutsche Einheit,"
        FBPG, 49, 1937, 1-21.
5279.   HASENCLEVER, Adolf, "Zur Geschichte der Neuenburger
        Frage in den Jahren 1856 und 1857," FBPG, 27, 1914,
        517-44.
5280.   HENCHE, Albert, "Der Ausgang der Reaktionszeit in Preus-

sen im Spiegel der nassauischen Gesandtschaftsberichte, "
H. Jb., 58, 1938, 135-49.

5281. HERMAND, Jost, "Zur Literatur der Gründezeit, " Vjschr.
f. Litw., 41, 1967, 202-32.

5282. HESSE, Horst, "Behördeninterne Information über die Volks-
stimmung zur Zeit des liberal-ultramontanen Partei-
kampfes 1868/69, " Zs. f. bayer. LG., 34, 1971, 618-51.

5283. HÖFELE, Karl Heinrich, "Königgrätz und die Deutschen von
1866, " GiWuU, 17, 1966, 393-416.

5284. HÖLZLE, Erwin, "Die Reichsgründung und der Aufstieg der
Weltmächte, " GiWuU, 2, 1951, 132-46.

5285. HOFFMANN, Kurt, "Sturm und Drang in der politischen
Presse Bayerns 1848-1850, " Zs. f. bayer. LG., 3, 1930,
205-66.

5286. JACOBS, Hans Haimar, "Ein grossdeutscher Gedankenaus-
tausch im Jahre 1870   Anton Christ und Alfred von Vi-
venot, " ZGORh., 91, 1938/39, 148-87.

5287. KOEPPEL, Ferdinand, "Baden und die deutsche Entscheidung
des Jahres 1866, " ZGORh., 88, 1935/36, 445-92.

5288. KÖRNER, Hans, "Mit Preussen deutsch! Aus den 1866er
Papieren des Alten Limpurgers Karl Freiherr von Lepel, "
Arch. f. Frankfurts Gesch., 51, 1968, 107-15.

5289. KRAEHE, Enno E., "Austria and the Problem of Reform in
the German Confederation 1851-1863, " AHR, 56, 1950/51,
276-94.

5290. KROPAT, Wolf Arno, "Das liberale Bürgertum in Nassau
und die Reichsgründung (1866-1871), " Nass. Ann., 82,
1971, 307-23.

5291. LACHER, H., "Süddeutschland und die Reichsgründung
(1870/71), " Zs. f. Hohenzollerische Gesch., 6, 1970,
109-27.

5292. LANGE, Karl, "Braunschweig im Jahre 1866, " Hist. Vjschr.,
25, 1929/31, 56-97, 266-302, 561-63.

5293. "Die LEGISLATURPERIODE des Hauses der Abgeordneten
1859-1861, " Pr. Jbb., 8, 1861, 315-402.

5294. LEHMANN, Max, "Der Krieg in West-Deutschland und die
vorangehenden Unterhandlungen des Jahres 1866, " HZ, 22,
1869, 80-147.

5295. MALETTKE, K., "Ein unbekanntes Memorandum der preussischen Botschaft in Paris zum österreichischen Bundesre-
formentwurf von 1863, " Jb. f. Gesch. M. O. Dtschl., 19,
1970, 256-70.

5296. MAYER, Gustav, "Die Trennung der proletarischen von der
bürgerlichen Demokratie in Deutschland (1863-1871), "
Arch. f. d. Gesch. d. Soz., 2, 1911/12, 1-67.

5297. MICHAELIS, Herbert, "Königgrätz   Eine geschichtliche
Wende, " WaG, 12, 1952, 177-202.

5298. MOMMSEN, Wilhelm, "Zur Beurteilung der deutschen Einheitsbewegung, " HZ, 138, 1928, 523-43.

5299. MÜLLER, Karl Alexander von, "Zwei bayerische Denkschrift-
en zur deutschen Frage aus dem Jahr 1867, " Zs. f. bayer. LG., 18, 1955, 490-503.

5300. MÜLLER, Reinhold, "Adolf Friedrich Johann Riedel und die

Reaktion in Preussen, " FBPG, 42, 1929, 274-86.

5301. NAUJOKS, Eberhard, "Württemberg im diplomatischen Kräftespiel der Reichsgründungszeit (1866/70). Zur Problematik der deutschen Politik des Freiherrn von Varnbüler, " Zs. F. Württbg. LG, 30, 1971, 201-40.

5302. NEUBACH, Helmut, "Parteien und Politiker in Oberschlesien zur Bismarckzeit, " Jb. d. Schles.-Fried.-Wilh. Univ z. Breslau, 13, 1968, 193-231.

5303. NEUMANN, Hans, "Franz Ziegler und die Politik der liberalen Oppositionsparteien von 1848-1866, " FBPG, 37, 1925, 271-88.

5304. OBERMANN, Karl, "Die deutsche Einheitsbewegung und die Schillerfeiern 1859, " Zs. f. Geschw., 3, 1955, 705-34.

5305. O'BOYLE, Lenore, "The German Nationalverein, " J. Cen. Eur. Aff., 16, 1957, 333-52.

5306. PAJEWSKI, Janusz, "L'Année 1871 et l'Europe centrale, " Rev. d'hist. mod., 19, 1972, 317-24.

5307. PETRICH, Johannes, "Die Friedensverhandlungen mit den Süddeutschen 1866, " FBPG, 46, 1934, 321-52.

5308. PITZ, Ernst, "Deutschland und Hannover im Jahre 1866, " Niedersächs. Jb. f. LG, 38, 1966, 86-158.

5309. POSCHINGER, Heinrich von, "Handschriften des Geh. Leg. Rats Küpfer über die deutsche Frage in den Jahren 1849 und 1850, " Hist. Vjschr., 5, 1902, 34-47.

5310. _____, "Von der badisch-elsässischen Rheingrenze vor 1870 Aufzeichnungen des badischen Ministers von Frey-dorf, " Pr. Jbb., 121, 1905, 481-503.

5311. "Der PREUSSISCHE Landtag während der Jahre 1851 bis 1857, " Pr. Jbb., 1, 1858, 186-213.

5312. RAPP, Adolf, "Die öffentliche Meinung in Württemberg 1866, " Zs. F. Württbg. LG, 16, 1907, 157-236.

5313. RITTER, Gerhard, "Die Entstehung der Indemnitätsvorlage von 1866, " HZ, 114, 1915, 17-64.

5314. RÖSSLER, Hellmuth, "Das Jahr 1866 und seine Folgen, " Nass. Ann., 77, 1966, 217-32.

5315. ROLOFF, Gustav, "Brünn und Nikolsburg: Nicht Bismarck sondern der König isoliert, " HZ, 136, 1927, 457-501.

5316. ROSENBERG, Hans, "Honoratiorenpolitiker und 'Gross-deutsche' Sammlungsbestrebungen im Reichsgründungs-jahrzehnt, " Jb. f. Gesch. M. O. Dtschl., 19, 1970, 155-233.

5317. RUMPLER, Helmut, "Karl Friedrich Graf Vitzthum von Eckstädts 'Geheimnisse des sächsischen Kabinetts'--ein Beitrag zur nationalpolitischen Publizistik im Jahre 1866, " Arch. f. österr. Gesch., 125, 1966, 208-18.

5318. SCHILL, Wilhelm F., "Baden auf den Dresdener Konferenzen 1850-51, " ZGORh., 83, 1930/31, 505-51.

5319. SCHMIDT, Friedrich, "Bayerns Haltung bei Preussens Kampf um Neuenburg 1856-57, " Zs. f. bayer. LG., 29, 1966, 548-79.

5320. SCHNABEL, Franz, ed., "Aus den Lebenserinnerungen des Dr. med. C. H. Alexander Pagenstecher (1860-1866), " ZGORh., 73, 1919, 227-56.

5321. SCHNEIDER, Eugen, "Württembergs Beitritt zum deutschen

Reich 1870, " Zs. F. Wurttbg. LG, 29, 1920, 121-84.

5322.   SCHOEPS, Hans-Joachim, "Der Frankfurter Fürstentag und
die öffentliche Meinung in Preussen, " GiWuU, 19, 1968,
73-90.

5323.   _____, "Von der Revolution zum Norddeutschen Bund, "
ZRGG, 23, 1971, 260-64.

5324.   STERNE, Margaret, "Frankfurt am Main im Brennpunkt der
preussisch-österreichischen Auseinandersetzung 1865/66, "
Arch. f. Frankfurts Gesch., 43, 1955, 7-86.

5325.   STRUCK, Wolf-Heino, "Das Streben nach bürgerlicher Freiheit und nationaler Einheit in der Sicht des Herzogtums
Nassau Ein Beitrag zur Beurteilung der Entscheidung
von 1866, " Nass. Ann., 77, 1966, 142-216.

5326.   UELSMANN, Erich, "Beiträge zur niederrheinischen Parteigeschichte in besondere zur Neuen Aera und zum Verfassungskonflikt (1858-1863), " Ann. Niederrhein, 109,
1926, 93-144.

5327.   VISCHER, Eduard, "Die deutsche Reichsgründung von 1871
im Urteil schweizerischer Zeitgenossen, " Schw. Zs. f.
Gesch., 1, 1951, 452-84.

5328.   WENTZCKE, Paul, "Nach der Sturmflut der deutschen
Revolution. Aufzeichnungen und Briefe aus dem Nachlass
des Freiherrn Alexander von Soiron (1850-1858), " ZGORh.,
108, 1960, 109-33.

Maximilian II (Bavaria) (1811-1864)

5329.   FRANZ, Eugen, "König Max II von Bayern und seine geheimen politischen Berater, " Zs. f. bayer. LG, 5, 1932,
219-42.

5330.   _____, "Wilhelm von Doenniges und König Max. II in
der Deutschen Frage, " Zs. f. bayer. LG., 2, 1929,
445-76.

5331.   MÜLLER, Karl Alexander v., ed., "Historisch-politische
Denkschriften Sybels für König Maximilian II von Bayern
aus den Jahren 1859-1861, " HZ, 162, 1940, 59-95, 269-
304.

5332.   RALL, Hans, "König Max II von Bayern und die katholische
Kirche, " H. Jb., 74, 1954, 739-47.

5333.   SCHLAICH, H. W., "Die Rechenschaftsberichte der Inneren
Verwaltung unter König Max II. Ein Beitrag zur bayerischen Staats-, Verwaltungs- und Schulpolitik um die
Mitte des 19. Jahrhunderts, " Die Verwaltung, 4, 1971,
31-58.

Karl Schurz (1829-1906)

5334.   CARL Schurz issue, American-German Review, 18, (16),
1952, 1-33.

5335.   ONCKEN, Hermann, "Carl Schurz, Über Demokratie und
Deutschamerikanertum, " HZ, 114, 1915, 302-20.

5336.   RICHTER, Werner, "Carl Schurz," Hochland, 43, 1950/51,
        230-49.
5337.   WILD, Robert, "Lieber, Körner, Schurz, drei grosse
        Deutschamerikaner," Pr. Jbb., 217, 1929, 12-27.

                        Karl Twesten (1820-1870)

        See also entry 4787

5338.   BÄHR, O., "Die Redefreiheit der Volksvertretung und der
        Process Twesten," Pr. Jbb., 21, 1868, 313-25.
5339.   HEYDERHOFF, Julius, "Karl Twestens Wendung zur Politik
        und seine erste politische Broschüre," HZ, 126, 1922,
        242-70.
5340.   TWESTEN, C., "Der preussische Beamtenstaat," Pr. Jbb.,
        18, 1865, 1-39, 109-49.

1871-1914

        See also entries 4367, 4445, 4451, 4487

5341.   ALBRECHT, Willy, "Die Fuchsmühler Ereignisse vom Okto-
        ber 1894 und ihre Folgen für die innere Entwicklung Ba-
        yerns...," Zs. f. bayer. LG, 33, 1970, 307-54.
5342.   BEYERHAUS, Gisbert, "Die Krise des deutschen Liberalis-
        mus und das Problem der 99 Tage," Pr. Jbb., 239,
        1935, 1-19.
5343.   BOSL, Karl, "Gesellschaft und Politik in Bayern vor dem
        Ende der Monarchie," Zs. f. bayer. LG., 28, 1965, 1-
        31.
5344.   BRAUN, Adolf, "Die Reichstagwahlen von 1898 und 1903,"
        Arch. f. Sozialw. u. Sozialpol., 18, 1903, 539-63.
5345.   BRUNSCHWIG, Henri, "L'Allemagne depuis Bismarck,"
        RH, 211, 1954, 317-48.
5346.   _____, "Allemagne moderne et contemporaine de Bis-
        marck a nos jours," RH, 197, 1947, 233-40; 199, 1948,
        81-101.
5347.   BUKEY, E. B., "The Guelph Party in Imperial Germany
        1866-1918," Historian, 35, 1972, 43-60.
5348.   BULMERINCQ, A., "Das allgemeine Stimmrecht und die
        politische Bildung im Deutschen Reich," Schmoll. Jb., 3,
        1879, 665-86.
5349.   CHICKERING, R., "A Voice of Moderation in Imperial Ger-
        many. The 'Verband für Internationale Verständigung'
        1911-1914," J. Contemp. Hist., 8, 1973, 146-54.
5350.   DEUERLEIN, Ernst, "Föderalismus ... VI Das Deutsche
        Reich als Bundesstaat," Das Parlament, 1969, (38-39).
5351.   DORPALEN, Andreas, "The German Conservatives and the
        Parliamentarization of Imperial Germany," J. Cen. Eur.
        Aff., 11, 1951, 184-99.
5352.   _____, "Wilhelmian Germany--A House Divided Against

Itself," J. Cen. Eur. Aff., 15, 1955, 240-47.

5353.   EGELHAAF, Gottlob, "Württemberg in den fünfundzwanzig
        Jahren 1891-1916," Zs. F. Württbg. LG, 25, 1916, 606-
        15.

5354.   ESCHENBURG, Theodor, "Die Daily-Telegraph-Affäre," Pr.
        Jbb., 214, 1928, 199-223.

5355.   FLUCK, B., "Obrigkeitsstaat und Probleme der Demokrat-
        isierung im zweiten Reich," GiWuU, 22, 1971, 462-74.

5356.   FRICKE, D., "Die Affäre Leckert-Lützow-Tausch und die
        Regierungskrise von 1897 in Deutschland," Zs. f. Geschw.,
        8, 1960, 1579-1603.

5357.   GALL, Lothar, "Neuere Untersuchungen zur inneren Ge-
        schichte des Bismarckreiches," ZGORh., 112, 1964, 535-
        50.

5358.   GO., "Die nationalliberale Partei und die 'Ausnahmgesetze,"
        Pr. Jbb., 42, 1878, 224-38.

5359.   HARRIS, James F., "Broadening the Scope: A Computer
        Analysis of the German Reichstag, 1867-1884," Hist.
        Methods Newslett., 1971.

5360.   HARTUNG, Fritz, "Staatsgefüge und Zusammenbruch des
        zweiten Reiches," HZ, 151, 1934/35, 528-44.

5361.   HASENCLEVER, Adolf, "Eduard VII und Deutschland bis
        zum Regierungsantritt Wilhelms II," Pr. Jbb., 235, 1934,
        97-114.

5362.   HENNING, Hansjoachim, "Kriegsvereine in den preussischen
        Westprovinzen. Ein Beitrag zur preussischen Innenpoli-
        tik zwischen 1860 und 1914," Rhein. Vjsbll., 32, 1968,
        430-75.

5363.   HOEGNER, Wilhelm, "Georg von Vollmar--ein bayerischer
        Parlamentarier," Pol. Stud., 15, 1964, 53-64.

5364.   HOHENZOLLERN, Albrecht Prinz v., "Leben und Wirken
        des Prinzen Carl Anton von Hohenzollern," Jb. f. Gesch.
        Kunst d. MRh, 14, 1962, 113-44.

5365.   HOLL, Karl, "Die Darmstädter Reichstagsnachwahl von 1906
        and der 'Fall' Korell," Arch. hess. Gesch. Landesk.,
        27, 1962/67, 121-61.

5366.   JAEGER, Hans, "Unternehmer und Politik in wilhelminischen
        Deutschland," Tradition, 13, 1968, 1-21.

5367.   KÄHLER, Siegfried, "Das preussisch-deutsche Problem seit
        der Reichsgründung," Pr. Jbb., 185, 1921, 26-45.

5368.   KJELLÉN, Rudolf, "Die Koalitionspolitik im Zeitalter 1871-
        1914," Schmoll. Jb., 45, 1921, 1-65, 421-82.

5369.   KLEIN, Fritz, "Das Heranreifen einer politischen Krise in
        Deutschland am Vorabend des 1. Weltkrieges," Zs. f.
        Geschw., 3, 1955, 593-619.

5370.   LAMBI, Ivo N., "The Agrarian-Industrial Front in Bis-
        marckian Politics--1873-1879," J. Cen. Eur. Aff., 20,
        1961, 378-96.

5371.   McCLELLAND, Charles E., "Berlin Historians and German
        Politics," J. Contemp. Hist., 8, 1973, 3-33.

5372.   MUTH, Heinrich, "Jugendpflege und Politik Zur Jugend- und
        Innenpolitik des Kaiserreichs," GiWuU, 12, 1961, 597-
        619.

5373. NIPPERDEY, Thomas, "Interessenverbände und Parteien in
       Deutschland vor dem ersten Weltkrieg," Pol. Vjschr.,
       2, 1961, 262-80.

5374. _____, "Die Organisation der bürgerlichen parteien in
       Deutschland vor 1918," HZ, 185, 1958, 550-602.

5375. O'BOYLE, Lenore, "Liberal Political Leadership in Ger-
       many 1867-1884," J. Mod. Hist., 28, 1956, 338-52.

5376. PHILIPPI, Hans, "Studien zur Geschichte der Beziehungen
       Bayerns zum deutschen Reich 1871-1914," Zs. f. bayer.
       LG., 26, 1963, 323-69.

5377. PIKART, Eberhard, "Der deutsche Reichstag und der Aus-
       bruch des ersten Weltkrieges," Staat, 5, 1966, 47-70.

5378. REINICKE, Brigitte, "Die Reichstagswahlen in Schlesien
       1871-1932," Jb. d. Schles.-Fried.-Wilh. Univ z. Bres-
       lau, 4, 1959, 286-99.

5379. RIEDNER, Otto, "Deutsche Veröffentlichungen zum Kriegs-
       ausbruch," H. Jb., 42, 1922, 57-88.

5380. ROGGE, Helmuth, "Affairen im Kaiserreich," Polit. Mei-
       nung, 8, 1963, 58-72.

5381. _____, "Die Kladderadatschaffäre, Ein Beitrag zur in-
       neren Geschichte des wilhelminischen Reichs," HZ, 195,
       1962, 90-130.

5382. SCHEIDELER, G. U., "Parlament, Parteien und Regierung
       im wilhelminischen Reich 1890-1914," Aus. Pol. u. Zeit-
       gesch., 12, 1971, 16-24.

5383. SCHMIDT, G., "Innenpolitische Blockbildungen in Deutsch-
       land am Vorabend des ersten Weltkrieges," Aus. Pol. u.
       Zeitgesch., 20, 1972, 3-32.

5384. SHEEHAN, James J., "Political Leadership in the German
       Reichstag 1871-1918," AHR, 74, 1968/69, 511-28.

5385. SNELL, John L., "Imperial Germany's Tragic Era, 1888-
       1918: Threshold to Democracy or Foreground of Na-
       zism?," J. Cen. Eur. Aff., 18, 1959, 380-95; 19, 1959,
       57-75.

5386. WEBERSINN, Gerhard, "Thomas Szczeponik," Jb. d. Schles.-
       Fried.-Wilh. Univ z. Breslau, 16, 1971, 159-214.

5387. WEHLER, Hans-Ulrich, "Der Fall Zabern," WaG, 23, 1963,
       27-46.

5388. WERTHEIMER, E. V., "Der Prozess Arnim," Pr. Jbb.,
       222, 1930, 174-33, 274-92.

5389. WESTARP, Graf, "Aus meinen Erinnerungen Revolution von
       unten im letzten Jahrzehnt des Kaiserreiches," Pr. Jbb.,
       234, 1933, 211-25; 235, 1934, 48-64; 236, 1934, 111-30;
       237, 1934, 45-63, 131-47; 238, 1934, 193-214.

Theobald von Bethmann-Hollweg (1856-1921)

5390. ERDMANN, Karl D., "Zur Beurteilung Bethmann Hollwegs,"
       GiWuU, 15, 1964, 525-40.

5391. HILLGRUBER, Andreas, "Riezlers Theorie des kalkulierten
       Risikos und Bethmann Hollwegs politische Konzeption in
       der Julikrise 1914," HZ, 202, 1966, 333-51.

5392.   JARAUSCH, Konrad H., "The Illusion of Limited War:
        Chancellor Bethmann Hollweg's Calculated Risk, July
        1914," Cen. Eur. Hist., 2, 1969, 48-76.
5393.   MOMMSEN, Wolfgang J., "Bethmann Hollweg und die öffent-
        liche Meinung," VjHZG, 17, 1969, 117-59.

Bernhard von Bülow (1849-1919)

See also entry 4295

5394.   DUGGAN, P., "Stimoli di riforma nell 'amministrazione
        prussiana durante la coalizione Buelow 1907-1909," Riv.
        stor. Ital., 81, 1969, 304-42.
5395.   FOTINO, George, "Les Missions de Goluchowski et de
        bülow auprès de Roi Carol Ier de Roumanie," Rev. d'hist.
        dipl., 46, 1932, 275-91.
5396.   FRANK, Walter, "Bernhard von Bülow," HZ, 147, 1933,
        349-67.
5397.   GOOCH, G. P., "Prince Bülow and His Memoirs," History,
        18, 1933, 120-32.
5398.   HALE, Oron James, "Prince von Bülow: His Memoirs and
        his German Critics," J. Mod. Hist., 4, 1932, 261-77.
5399.   HASENCLEVER, Adolf, "Bülows Denkwürdigkeiten," ZgesStw.,
        91, 1931, 126-34.
5400.   LUCKWALDT, Friedrich, "Bernhard Fürst von Bülow," Pr.
        Jbb., 226, 1931, 113-39, 229-52; 227, 1932, 118-42.
5401.   MEISNER, Heinrich O., "Fürst Bülow, der Memoiren-
        schreiber und der Staatsmann," FBPG, 44, 1932, 156-96.
5402.   MORROW, Ian F. D., "The Foreign Policy of Prince von
        Bülow 1898-1909," Hist. J., 4, 1932, 63-93.
5403.   PENNER, C. D., "The Buelow-Chamberlain Recriminations
        of 1901-02," Historian, 5, 1942/43, 97-109.
5404.   SCHMOLLER, Gustav, "Fürst Bülows Politik," Schmoll. Jb.,
        40, 1916, 1609-15.
5405.   THIMME, Friedrich, "Fürst Bülow und Graf Monts Ein
        vervollständigter Briefwechsel," Pr. Jbb., 231, 1933,
        193-219; 232, 1933, 17-34, 97-123, 199-235.
5406.   ZIEKURSCH, Johannes, "Zur Entstehungsgeschichte der
        Denkwürdigkeiten des Fürsten Bülow," FBPG, 44, 1932,
        374-84.

Leo von Caprivi (1831-1899)

See also entry 4486

5407.   DANIELS, Emil, "Prinz Friedrich Karl und Caprivi in der
        Schlacht bei Vionville (16. August 1870)," Pr. Jbb., 218,
        1929, 51-79.
5408.   ROSENTHAL, Harry K., "The Problem of Caprivi's Polish
        Policy," Eur. Stud. Rev., 2, 1972, 255-64.
5409.   SEMPELL, Charlotte, "The Constitutional and Political Prob-

lems of the Second Chancellor, Leo von Caprivi," J. Mod. Hist., 25, 1953, 234-54.

5410. STADELMANN, Rudolf, "Der neue Kurs in Deutschland," GiWuU, 4, 1953, 538-64.

Friedrich III (Germany) (1831-1888)

5411. CURTIUS, Friedrich, "Kaiser Friedrich und das deutsche Volk," Hochland, 23(2), 1925/26, 385-407.
5412. DELBRÜCK, Hans, "Kaiserin Friedrich," Pr. Jbb., 106, 1901, 1-20.
5413. _____, "Persönliche Erinnerungen an den Kaiser Friedrich und sein Haus," Pr. Jbb., 62, 1888, 97-116.
5414. DORPALEN, Andreas, "Emperor Frederick III and the German Liberal Movement," AHR, 54, 1948/49, 1-31.

Chlodwig zu Hohenlohe-Schillingsfürst (1819-1901)

5415. CHROUST, Anton, "Chlodwig Fürst zu Hohenlohe und seine Denkwürdigkeiten," Hochland, 29(2), 1931/32, 220-30.
5416. MEISNER, Heinrich O., "Der Kanzler Hohenlohe und die Mächte seiner Zeit," Pr. Jbb., 230, 1932, 35-50, 131-41.
5417. SALZER, Ernst, "Fürst Chlodwig zu Hohenlohe-Schillingsfürst und die deutsche Frage," Hist. Vjschr., 11, 1908, 40-74.

Friedrich Naumann (1860-1919)

5418. DRUMMOND, Robert J., "Friedrich Naumann," Evan. Q., 11, 1939, 149-52.
5419. EYCK, Erich, "A Great German Liberal," The Contemporary Review, 155, 1939, 320-27.
5420. GÖHRE, Paul, "Erinnerungen an Fr. Naumann," Die Glocke, 5, 1919, 724-31.
5421. HEUSS, Theodor, "Friedrich Naumann und die Innere Mission in Frankfurt," Zeitwende, 22, 1951, 571-78.
5422. HIRSCH, Felix, "Friedrich Naumann," Forum, 106, 1946, 97-102.
5423. LINK, Werner, "Der Nationalverein für das Liberale Deutschland (1907-1918)," Pol. Vjschr., 5, 1964, 422-44.
5424. MAURENBRECHER, Max, "Das religiöse Problem der Gegenwart," Pr. Jbb., 115, 1904, 250-75.
5425. MOMMSEN, Wilhelm, "Friedrich Naumann," Pol. Stud., 6, 1955/56, 17-23.
5426. _____, "Zur Biographie Friedrich Naumanns," HZ, 161, 1939/1940, 539-48.
5427. NAUMANN, Margarete, "Friedrich Naumanns Langenberger Zeit," Die christliche Welt, 43, 1929, 233ff, 283ff.
5428. NÜRNBERGER, Richard, "Imperialismus, Sozialismus und

Christentum bei Friedrich Naumann, " HZ, 170, 1950,
525-48.

5429. RADE, Martin, "Theologische Randglossen zu Naumanns
'Demokratie und Kaisertum', " Zs. f. Theol. u. K., 10,
1900, 489-517.

5430. SCHNABEL, Franz, "Erinnerung an Friedrich Naumann, "
Hochland, 36(1), 1938/39, 437-40.

5431. SCHOEPS, Hans-Joachim, "Friedrich Naumann als politischer Erzieher, " ZRGG, 20, 1968, 3-13.

5432. SHANAHAN, William O., "Friedrich Naumann: A Mirror
of Wilhelmian Germany, " Rev. Pol., 13, 1951, 267-301.

5433. _____, "Liberalism and Foreign Affairs: Naumann and
the Prewar German View, " Rev. Pol., 21, 1959, 188-
223.

5434. STEPHAN, Werner, "Naumann in unserer Zeit, " Liberal,
2, 1960, 3-11.

Wilhelm II (Germany) (1859-1941)

5435. BEALE, Howard, "Theodore Roosevelt, Wilhelm II, und die
deutsch-amerikanischen Beziehungen, " WaG, 15, 1955,
155-87.

5436. BEIN, Alexander, "Erinnerungen und Dokumente über Herzls
Begegnung mit Wilhelm II, " Zs. f. d. Gesch. d. Juden,
2, 1965, 35-52.

5437. BERGHAHN, Volker R., "Zu den Zielen des deutschen
Flottenbaus unter Wilhelm II, " HZ, 210, 1970, 34-100.

5438. BITTNER, Ludwig, "Neue Beiträge zur Haltung Kaiser Wilhelms II in der Faschodafrage, " HZ, 162, 1940, 540-56.

5439. BUCHNER, Max, "Wilhelm II und das katholische Deutschland, " Gelbe Hefte, 5, 1928/29, 189-229.

5440. DORPALEN, Andreas, "Empress Auguste Victoria and the
Fall of the German Monarchy, " AHR, 58, 1952/53, 17-
38.

5441. FAY, Sidney B., "The Kaiser's Secret Negotiations with the
Tsar, 1904-1905, " AHR, 24, 1918/19, 48-72.

5442. GOETZ, W., "Kaiser Wilhelm II. und die deutsche Geschichtsschreibung, " HZ, 179, 1955, 21-44.

5443. GOOCH, G. P., "German Foreign Policy under William II, "
Ger. Life Letters, 3, 1938/39, 1-11.

5444. GSCHLIESSER, Oswald, "Das wissenschaftliche Oeuvre des
ehemaligen Kaisers Wilhelm II, " Arch. f. KuG., 54,
1972, 385-92.

5445. HAAKE, Paul, "Der neue Kurs 1890, " Zs. f. Pol., 15,
1925/26, 320-47.

5446. HELLIGE, H. D., "Wilhelm II. und Walther Rathenau. Ein
Gespräch aus dem Jahre 1900, " GiWuU, 19, 1968, 538-
44.

5447. KANN, Robert A., "Emperor William II and Archduke Francis Ferdinand in their Correspondence, " AHR, 57, 1952/
53, 323-51.

5448. LULVÉS, Jean, "Kaiser Wilhelms II erster Besuch im Vati-

kan 1888, " Gelbe Hefte, 15, 1938/39, 237-44.
5449. _____, "Papst Leos XIII erste Begegnung mit Wilhelm II
       (Oktober 1888) und Frankreichs vatikanische Politik, " Pr.
       Jbb., 225, 1931, 1-14; 226, 1931, 295-312.
5450. RALL, Hans, "Kaiser Wilhelm II, die soziale Frage und die
       Sozialdemokratie, " Gelbe Hefte, 9, 1932/33, 219-34.
5451. RITTHALER, A., "Kaiser Wilhelm II im Kampf um die
       Krone, " Gelbe Hefte, 11, 1934/35, 321-46.
5452. STRIBRNY, Wolfgang, "Kaiser Wilhelm II und die Burg
       Hohenzollern, " ZRGG, 23, 1971, 129-34.
5453. THIELEN, Peter G., "Die Marginalien Kaiser Wilhelms II, "
       WaG, 20, 1960, 249-59.
5454. TOWNSEND, Mary E., "Some Recent Publications Dealing
       with the Reign of William II, " J. Mod. Hist., 3, 1931,
       474-81.
5455. WITTE, Jehan de, "Correspondance entre Guillaume II et
       Nicolas II, " Rev. d'hist. dipl., 39, 1925, 69-75.

Catholic Center Party

See also entries 248, 3384, 5282

5456. DEUERLEIN, Ernst, "Die Bekehrung des Zentrums zur na-
       tionalen Idee, " Hochland, 62, 1970, 432-49.
5457. HOHMANN, Friedrich Gerhard, "Die Soester Konferenzen
       1864-1866.   Zur Vorgeschichte der Zentrumspartei im
       Westfalen, " Westf. Zs., 114, 1964, 293-342.
5458. MARTIN, Hans, "Die Stellung der 'Historisch-Politischen'
       Blätter zur Reichsgründung 1870/71, " Zs. f. bayer. LG.,
       6, 1933, 60-84, 217-45.
5459. NEUBACH, H., "Schlesische Geistliche als Reichstagsab-
       geordnete 1867 bis 1918.   Ein Beitrag zur Geschichte der
       deutschen Zentrumspartei und zur Nationalitätenfrage in
       Oberschlesien, " Arch. für schles. KiG, 26, 1968, 251-
       78.
5460. REISS-VASEK, E., "Zentrum und Sozialpolitik zur Zeit Bis-
       marcks, " Gelbe Hefte, 10, 1933/34, 590-620.
5461. SCHNEE, Heinrich, "Die Zeitung 'Deutschland' (1855-1858)
       ein Beitrag zur Geschichte des politischen Katholizismus
       in Deutschland im 19. Jahrhundert, " H. Jb., 52, 1932,
       477-94.
5462. SILVERMAN, Dan P., "Political Catholicism and Social
       Democracy in Alsace-Lorraine 1871-1914, " Cath. Hist.
       Rev., 52, 1966, 39-65.
5463. ZEENDER, John K., "German Catholics and the Concept of
       an Interconfessional Party 1900-1922, " J. Cen. Eur. Aff.,
       23, 1964, 424-39.

Franz Joseph von Buss (1803-1878)

5464. DORNEICH, J., "Die politische Entwicklung des jungen Buss, "

H. Jb., 45, 1925, 293-307.
5465.   HOSP, Ed., "Briefe von Buss," H. Jb., 48, 1928, 472-88.

Matthias Erzberger (1875-1921)

5466.   EPSTEIN, Klaus, "Erzberger and the German Colonial
        Scandals 1905-1910," EHR, 75, 1959, 637-63.
5467.   _____, "Erzberger's Position in the Zentrumsstreit Be-
        fore World War I," Cath. Hist. Rev., 44, 1958, 1-16.
5468.   ERZBERGER, Matthias, "Die Bedeutung des Zentrums für
        das deutsche Reich," Zs. f. Pol., 2, 1908/09, 212-35.

Joseph Edmund Jörgs (1819-1901)

5469.   DOEBERL, Anton, "Die katholisch-konservative Richtung in
        Bayern und die 'Deutsche Frage' Mit besonderer Berück-
        sichtigung der Haltung E. Jörgs," Gelbe Hefte, 1, 1924/
        25, 1111-35.
5470.   GOLLWITZER, Heinz, "Josef Edmund Jörg," Zs. f. bayer.
        LG., 15, 1949/50, 125ff.

August Reichensperger (1808-1895)

5471.   GRIMM, Hermann, "Der Abgeordnete Reichensperger und
        die deutsche Kunst," Pr. Jbb., 37, 1876, 92-96, 642-50.
5472.   MARTIN, Hortense, "Soziale Anschauungen und Bemühungen
        der Gebrüder Reichensperger und des Freiherrn von
        Thimus um die Mitte des 19. Jahrhunderts," Arch. f.
        mrh. KiG., 7, 1955, 219-34.
5473.   ONCKEN, Hermann, "August Reichensperger," HZ, 88,
        1902, 247-63.

Ludwig Windthorst (1812-1891)

5474.   M., S.M., "A Champion of the Church: Ludwig Windthorst,"
        Irish Monthly, 42, 1914, 515-23.
5475.   RACHFAHL, Felix, "Windthorst und der Kulturkampf," Pr.
        Jbb., 135, 1909, 213-53, 460-90; 136, 1909, 56-73.
5476.   ROSE, Fr. K. A., "Windthorsts Kampf gegen die Sozial-
        demokratie und die Stellung seiner Nachfolger zur dersel-
        ben," Gelbe Hefte, 8, 1931/32, 744-66.
5477.   WOESTE, Ch., "Windthorst," Rev. générale, 69, 435-63.

Social Democratic Party

        See also entries 989, 2220, 2270, 4174

5478.   ADLER, George, "The Evolution of the Socialist Programme in Germany (1863-1890)," Econ. J., 1, 1891, 688-709.

5479.   ARMSTRONG, Sinclair W., "The Internationalism of the
        Early Social Democrats of Germany," AHR, 47, 1941/42,
        245-58.

5480.   _____, "The Social Democrats and the Unification of Ger-
        many 1863-71," J. Mod. Hist., 12, 1940, 485-509.

5481.   ASCHER, Abraham, "Imperialists within German Social
        Democracy Prior to 1914," J. Cen. Eur. Aff., 26, 1961,
        397-422.

5482.   _____. "'Radical' Imperialists Within German Social
        Democracy, 1912-1918," Pol. Sci. Q., 76, 1961, 555-75.

5483.   BARTEL, Horst, "Die historische Rolle der Zeitung 'Der
        Sozialdemokrat' in der Periode des Sozialistengesetzes,"
        Zs. f. Geschw., 4, 1956, 265-90.

5484.   _____, "Der interne Juni-Entwurf zum Erfurter Pro-
        gramm," Int. Rev. Soc. Hist., 12, 1967, 292-302.

5485.   BLANK, R., "Die soziale Zusammensetzung der sozial-
        demokratischen Wählerschaft Deutschlands," Arch. f.
        Sozialw. u. Sozialpol., 20, 1905, 507-50.

5486.   BRACHMANN, Botho, "Russische Sozialdemokraten in Ber-
        lin 1905-1907," Zs. f. Geschw., 6, 1958, 775-96.

5487.   BRAUN, Heinrich, "Zur Lage der deutschen Sozialdemo-
        kratie," Arch. f. Sozialw. u. Sozialpol., 6, 1893, 506-
        20.

5488.   CALKINS, Kenneth R., "The Election of Hugo Haase to the
        Co-Chairmanship of the SPD and the Crisis of Pre-War
        German Social Democracy," Int. Rev. Soc. Hist., 13,
        1968, 174-88.

5489.   CALLESEN, Gerd, "Sozialdemokratie und nationale Frage
        in Nordschleswig um die Jahrhundertwende," Arch. f.
        Sozialgesch., 9, 1969, 267-320.

5490.   ECKERT, Georg, "Der Rechenschaftsbericht der Sozial-
        demokratischen Arbeiter-Partei für den Stuttgarter Par-
        teitag," Arch. f. Sozialgesch., 3, 1963, 497-508.

5491.   FRICKE, Dieter, "The Police Repressions Against Social-
        Democrats in Germany at the End of the 19th Century,"
        Novaya i. Nov. Ist., 4, 1959, 92-102.

5492.   _____, "Der Reichsverband gegen die Sozialdemokratie
        von seiner Gründung bis zu den Reichstagswahlen von
        1907," Zs. f. Geschw., 7, 1959, 237-80.

5493.   _____, "Die sozialdemokratische Parteischule (1906-
        1914)," Zs. f. Geschw., 5, 1957, 229-48.

5494.   GALL, Lothar, "Sozialistengesetz und innenpolitischer
        Umschwung, Baden und die Krise des Jahres 1878,"
        ZGORh., 111, 1963, 473-577.

5495.   GEMKOW, Heinrich, "Dokumente des Kampfes der deutschen
        Sozialdemokratie gegen Bismarcks Kolonialpolitik und
        gegen den Rechtsopportunismus in den Jahren 1884/85,"
        Beitr. z. Gesch. d. dt. Arbeiterbeweg., 1, 1959, 350-68.

5496.   _____, "'Der Sozialismus ist der Friede' Ein sozial-
        demokratisches Flugblatt aus dem Jahre 1895," Beitr. z.
        Gesch. d. dt. Arbeiterbeweg., 4, 1962, 691-704.

5497.   GREBING, Helga, "Die deutsche Sozialdemokratie vor dem

ersten Weltkrieg Die liberalen Anfänge der deutschen
Arbeiterbewegung, " Pol. Stud., 9, 1958, 714-22.

5498. _____, "Hundert Jahre SPD: Zwischen Tradition u.
Fortschritt, " Pol. Stud., 14, 1963, 529-42.

5499. GROH, Dieter, "The 'Unpatriotic Socialists' and the State, "
J. Contemp. Hist., 1, 1966, 151-77.

5500. GÜNTHER, Ernst, "Die revisionistische Bewegung in der
deutschen Sozialdemokratie, " Schmoll. Jb., 29, 1905,
1235-82; 30, 1906, 191-254.

5501. HACKETHAL, Eberhard, "Der Einfluss der Pariser Kommune auf die militärpolitischen Auffassungen in der
deutschen Sozialdemokratie (1871-1875), " Zs. f. MilitärG.,
5, 1966, 645-62.

5502. HARNACK, Agnes, "Die sozialdemokratische Jugendliteratur, "
Pr. Jbb., 153, 1913, 60-70.

5503. HASBACH, W., "Die Unfähigkeit der deutschen Sozialdemokratie zur sozialpolitischen Reformarbeit, " Schmoll. Jb.,
10, 1886, 215-22.

5504. HELLFAIER, Karl-Alexander, "Probleme und Quellen zur
Frühgeschichte der Sozialdemokratie in Westfalen, " Arch.
f. Sozialgesch., 3, 1963, 157-221.

5505. _____, "Die sozialdemokratische Bewegung in Halle/Saale
(1865-1890), " Arch. f. Sozialgesch., 1, 1961, 69-108.

5506. HERRMANN, Ursula, "Der Kampf der Sozialdemokratie gegen
das Dreiklassenwahlrecht in Sachsen in den Jahren 1905/
06, " Zs. f. Geschw., 3, 1955, 856-83.

5507. HERZIG, A., "Die Entwicklung der Sozialdemokratie in
Westfalen bis 1894, " Westf. Zs., 121, 1971, 97-172.

5508. HOSTETTER, Richard, "The S.P.D. and the General Strike
as an Anti-War Weapon, 1905-1914, " Historian, 13,
1950/51, 27-51.

5509. JAFFE, Robert, "Die letzten Reichstagswahlen und die
Zukunft der Sozialdemokratie, " Pr. Jbb., 128, 1907,
300-21.

5510. KOSZYK, Kurt, "Die Presse der Schlesischen Sozialdemokratie, " Jb. d. Schles.-Fried.-Wilh. Univ z. Breslau,
5, 1960, 235-49.

5511. LADEMACHER, Horst, "Zu den Anfängen der deutschen Sozialdemokratie 1863-1878, " Int. Rev. Soc. Hist., 4, 1959,
239-60, 367-93.

5512. LEWINSOHN, Richard, "Die Stellung der deutschen Sozialdemokratie zur Bevölkerungsfrage, " Schmoll. Jb., 46,
1922, 813-59.

5513. LIDTKE, Vernon L., "German Social Democracy and German State Socialism, 1876-1884, " Int. Rev. Soc. Hist.,
9, 1964, 202-25.

5514. LORENZ, Max, "Die Sozialdemokratie und der nationale
Gedanke, " Pr. Jbb., 88, 1897, 302-23.

5515. MAEHL, Wilhelm H., "Recent Literature on the German
Socialists, 1891-1932, " J. Mod. Hist., 33, 1961, 292-
306.

5516. _____, "The Triumph of Nationalism in the German Socialist Party on the Eve of the First World War, " J.

Mod. Hist., 24, 1952, 15-41.
5517. MARKS, Harry J., "The Sources of Reformism in the Social Democratic Party of Germany, 1890-1914," J. Mod. Hist., 11, 1939, 334-56.
5518. MARQUARDSEN, Heinrich, "Das Reichsgesetz vom 31. Mai 1880 betreffend die authentische Erklärung und Gültigkeitsdauer des Gesetzes vom 21. Okt. 1878 gegen die gemeingefährlichen Bestrebungen der Sozialdemokratie," Schmoll. Jb., 5, 1881, 133-60.
5519. MARTIN, Rudolf, "Die Entwicklung des Sozialdemokratismus zum Anarchismus," Pr. Jbb., 61, 1888, 562-91.
5520. MAYER, Eduard W., "Parteikrisen im Liberalismus und in der Sozialdemokratie 1866-1916," Pr. Jbb., 172, 1918, 171-79.
5521. MAYER, Paul, "Die Geschichte des sozialdemokratischen Parteiarchivs und das Schichsal des Marx-Engels-Nachlesses," Arch. f. Sozialgesch., 6/7, 1966/67, 5-198.
5522. MEIRITZ, Heinz, "Joseph Herzfeld, ein Leben für Frieden und Sozialismus," Wiss. Zs. d. Univ Rostock, ges.- und sprachwiss. Reihe, 13, 1964, 361-77.
5523. MICHELS, Robert, "Die deutsche Sozialdemokratie," Arch. f. Sozialw. u. Sozialpol., 23, 1906, 471-556.
5524. _____, "Die deutsche Sozialdemokratie im internationalen Verbande," Arch. f. Sozialw. u. Sozialpol., 25, 1907, 148-231.
5525. NETTL, Peter, "The German Social Democratic Party 1890-1914 as a Political Model," Past and Present, 1965(30), 65-95.
5526. NIEUWENHUIS, Ferdinand Domela, "Der staatssozialistische Charakter der Sozialdemokratie," Arch. f. Sozialw. u. Sozialpol., 28, 1909, 101-45.
5527. NOBBE, Mortiz, "Der Fall des Sozialistengesetzes," Pr. Jbb., 94, 1898, 330-43.
5528. PELGER, Hans, "Zur sozialdemokratischen Bewegung in der Rheinprovinz vor dem Sozialistengesetz," Arch. f. Sozialgesch., 5, 1965, 377-406.
5529. PETERSON, Erich, "Die Bekämpfung der Socialdemokratie," Pr. Jbb., 54, 1884, 395-417.
5530. _____, "Die Entstehung und Bekämpfung der Socialdemokratie," Pr. Jbb., 44, 1879, 268-87.
5531. PÖLS, Werner, "Staat und Sozialdemokratie im Bismarckreich Die Tätigkeit der politischen Polizei beim Polizeipräsidenten in Berlin in der Zeit des Sozialisten-gesetzes 1878-1890," Jb. f. Gesch. M. O. Dtschl., 13/14, 1965, 200-21.
5532. RADLOF, L., "Aus der Entwicklung eines Sozialdemokraten," Pr. Jbb., 163, 1916, 206-21.
5533. ROTHE, Rudolf, "Zum Streit um die Kampfersubvention," Arch. f. Sozialgesch., 1, 1961, 109-18.
5534. RÜMELIN, Obersteuerrat, "Die marxische Dialektik und ihr Einfluss auf die Taktik der Sozialdemokratie," ZgesStw., 50, 1894, 33-59.
5535. SALDERN, Adelheid von, "Die sozialdemokratische Partei

in Göttingen 1890 bis 1914," Göttinger Jb., 18, 1970.
5536.   SCHACHNER, Robert, "Gemeinde und Sozialdemokratie,"
        Arch. f. Sozialw. u. Sozialpol., 23, 1906, 763-85.
5537.   SCHAFFLE, A. E. F., "Die Bekämpfung der Sozialdemo-
        kratie ohne Ausnahmgesetz," ZgesStw., 46, 1890, 201-87.
5538.   SCHMELZER, Georg, "Der berufspädagogischen Bestrebungen
        der sozialdemokratischen Arbeiterjugendbewegung vor dem
        ersten Weltkrieg," Jahrb. f. Erziehungs- u. Schulgesch.,
        9, 1969.
5539.   SCHMIDT, Marianne, "Zur Stellung der sozialdemokratischen
        Führung zum bürgerlichen Wahlrecht (1867-1900)," Ge-
        schichtsunterricht u. Staatsbürgerkunde, 9, 1967, 759-67.
5540.   SCHRODER, Wolfgang and Gustav SEEBER, "Zur Vorbereit-
        ung des Erfurter Programms," Zs. f. Geschw., 14, 1966,
        1117-47.
5541.   SCHÜDDEKOPF, Otto-Ernst, "Der Revolution entgegen: Ma-
        terialien und Dokumente zur Geschichte des linken Flügels
        der deutschen Sozialdemokratie vor dem Ersten Weltkrieg,"
        Arch. f. Sozialgesch., 9, 1969, 451-97.
5542.   SEIDEL, Bruno, "Hundert Jahre sozialdemokratischer Par-
        teitradition," Pol. Vjschr., 5, 1964, 210-21.
5543.   SIMKHOWITSCH, Wladimir Gr., "Die Krisis der Sozial-
        demokratie," Jbb. f. Nationalökon. u. Stat., 72, 1899,
        721-81.
5544.   SNELL, John L., "German Socialists in the Last Imperial
        Reichstag, 1912-1918," Bull. of the Intern. Institute of
        Social Hist., 1952, 196-205.
5545.   THÜMMLER, Heinzpeter, "Zur sozialen Struktur der Aus-
        gewiesenen unter dem Sozialistengesetz (1878 bis 1890),"
        Jb. f. Wgesch., 1971(3), 131-40.
5546.   VETTES, William George, "The German Social Democrats
        and the Eastern Question 1848-1900," American Slavic and
        Eur Review, 17, 86-100.
5547.   VICTOR, Max, "Die Stellung der deutschen Sozialdemokratie
        zu den Fragen der auswärtigen Politik (1869-1914),"
        Arch. f. Sozialw. u. Sozialpol., 60, 1928, 147-79.
5548.   WALTEMATH, Kuno, "Die Sozialdemokratie in Deutschland
        und den anderen grossen Kulturstaaten," Pr. Jbb., 143,
        1911, 45-70.
5549.   _____, "Die Sozialdemokratie in Deutschland und im
        Auslande," Pr. Jbb., 148, 1912, 226-39.
5550.   WEINBERGER, Gerda, "Die deutsche Sozialdemokratie und
        die Kolonialpolitik," Zs. f. Geschw., 15, 1967, 402-23.
5551.   WITTWER, Walter, "Über die Stellung der deutschen Sozial-
        demokratie zur Vaterlandsverteidigung vor dem ersten
        Weltkrieg (1907-1914)," Zs. f. MilitärG., 2, 1903, 280-
        94.

August Bebel (1840-1913)

5552.   ADAMY, Kurt, "Aus August Bebels revolutionärer Parla-
        mentsarbeit," Beitr. z. Gesch. d. dt. Arbeiterbeweg.,

9, 1967, 248-57.

5553. "AUGUST Bebel--Todfeind des Kapitalismus, Vorkämpfer einer marxistischen Arbeiterpolitik," Beitr. z. Gesch. d. dt. Arbeiterbeweg., 2, 1960, 122-34.

5554. BALL, Sidney, "Socialism according to Bebel," Economic Review, 4, 1894, 229-43.

5555. BECKER, Gerhard, ed., "Ein Aufsatz vom August Bebel über die Pariser Kommune," Zs. f. Geschw., 19, 1971, 373-81.

5556. BERTZ, Eduard, "Die Frau und der Sozialismus (Betrachtungen)," Jahrbuch für Sozialwissenschaft und Sozialpolitik, 1/2, 1880, 97-110.

5557. BRUNDIG, Karl and Ursula HERRMANN, "Die Agitationsreise August Bebels durch Thüringen im Juni 1869," Zs. f. Geschw., 18, 1970, 899-912.

5558. DLUBEK, Rolf and Ursula HERRMANN, "Briefe August Bebels an Robert Seidel," Beitr. z. Gesch. d. dt. Arbeiterbeweg., 12, 1970.

5559. FRICKE, Dieter, "August Bebel Heute," Zs. f. Geschw., 11, 1963, 1045-63, 1252-76.

5560. _____, "In der Deutschen Demokratischen Republik wird das Vermächtnis von August Bebel erfüllt. Zu seinem 120. Geburtstag," Zs. f. Geschw., 8, 1960, 277-303.

5561. GEMKOW, Heinrich, "Briefe August Bebels aus den Jahren 1886/1887," Beitr. z. Gesch. d. dt. Arbeiterbeweg., 2, 1960, 135-53.

5562. _____, "Im Kampf um die Gründung der Partei Unveröffentliche Briefe an Bebel und Liebknecht (Juni bis August 1869)," Beitr. z. Gesch. d. dt. Arbeiterbeweg., 12, 1969.

5563. GLUSBERG, M. S., "Die Weltanschauung August Bebels und die heutigen SPD-führer," Dt. Zs. f. Phil., 11, 1963, 1070-85.

5564. HARDEN, Maximilian, "Bebel und Genossen," Die Zukunft, 44, 1903, 495-515; 45, 1903, 1-20, 47-65.

5565. HARDIE, James Keir, "August Bebel," Socialist Review, 11, 1913, 501-04.

5566. LIDTKE, Vernon L., "August Bebel and German Social Democracy's Relation to the Christian Churches," J. Hist. Ideas, 27, 1966, 245-64.

5567. MAYER, Gustav, "Bebels Memoiren," Arch. f. d. Gesch. d. Soz., 2, 1912/13, 441-50.

5568. MEHRING, Franz, "August Bebel Persönliche Erinnerungen," Arch. f. d. Gesch. d. Soz., 4, 1913/14, 304-12.

5569. MICHELS, Robert, "August Bebel," Arch. f. Sozialw. u. Sozialpol., 37, 1913, 671-700.

5570. OBERMANN, Karl, "Zu Bismarcks Verfolgung der polnischen Arbeiterbewegung in den Jahren 1878-1881 und über die Zusammenarbeit deutscher und polnischer Sozialdemokraten. Ein polnisches Flugblatt für August Bebel 1881," Zs. f. Geschw., 4, 1956, 1242-52.

5571. SCHUBARDT, Wolfgang, "August Bebel--ein schöpferischer Marxist," Dt. Zs. f. Phil., 11, 1963, 1061-69.

5572.   THOMAS, Albert, "August Bebel. An Appreciation," Socialist Review, 5, 1910, 175-79.
5573.   WRONA, Vera, "August Bebel und der historische Materialismus," Dt. Zs. f. Phil., 13, 1965, 145-61.
5574.   _____, "Die theoretisch-weltanschauliche Entwicklung August Bebels," Zs. f. Geschw., 16, 1968, 347-62.

Eduard Bernstein (1850-1932)

See also entries 2288, 2427

5575.   BERNSTEIN, Eduard, "Einige Reformversuche im Lohnsystem," Arch. f. Sozialw. u. Sozialpol., 17, 1902, 309-40.
5576.   _____, "Die Entwicklung der Sozialdemokratie von der Sekte zur Partei," Zs. f. Pol., 3, 1909/10, 498-551.
5577.   _____, "The German Elections and the Social Democrats," Contemporary Review, 91, 1907, 479-92.
5578.   _____, "Wie Fichte und Lassalle National Waren," Arch. f. d. Gesch. d. Soz., 5, 1914, 143-62.
5579.   _____, "Zur Litteratur der Gewerkschaftsbewegung in Deutschland," Arch. f. Sozialw. u. Sozialpol., 16, 1901, 379-92.
5580.   MATTHIAS, Erich, "Idéologie et pratique: le faux débat Bernstein-Kautsky," Annales, 19, 1964, 19-30.
5581.   NEUBACH, Helmut, "Von Franz Ziegler bis Eduard Bernstein: Die Vertreter der Stadt Breslau im deutschen Reichstag 1871-1918," Gesch. Landesk., 5, 1969.
5582.   RADCZUN, Günter, "Zum Kampf Eduard Bernsteins gegen die marxistische Lehre vom Staat und von der proletarischen Revolution," Beitr. z. Gesch. d. dt. Arbeiterbeweg., 8, 1966, 446-62.
5583.   VALARCHÉ, Jean, "Edouard Bernstein Marxiste National," Rev. d'hist. econ. soc., 27, 1948, 298-322.

Karl Kautsky (1854-1938)

See also entries 2211, 2398, 5580

5584.   BRILL, Hermann, "Karl Kautsky," Zs. f. Pol., 1, 1954, 211-40.
5585.   KORSCH, Karl, "Die materialistische Geschichtsauffassung Eine Auseinandersetzung mit Karl Kautsky," Arch. f. d. Gesch. d. Soz., 14, 1929, 179-279.
5586.   PLENER, Ulla, "Karl Kautskys Opportunismus in Organisationsfragen (1900-1914) Zur Entstehung des Zentrismus in der deutschen Sozialdemokratie," Beitr. z. Gesch. d. dt. Arbeiterbeweg., 3, 1961, 349-70.
5587.   RATZ, Ursula, "Briefe zum Erscheinen von Karl Kautskys 'Weg zur Macht'," Int. Rev. Soc. Hist., 12, 1967, 432-77.
5588.   _____, "Karl Kautsky und die Abrüstungskontroverse in

der deutschen Sozialdemokratie 1911-12, " Int. Rev. Soc.
Hist., 11, 1966, 197-227.

Karl Liebknecht (1871-1919)

5589.   HERBIG, Erna, "Über Karl Liebknechts Referententätig-
keit, " Beitr. z. Gesch. d. dt. Arbeiterbeweg., 13, 1971,
581-98.

5590.   LASCHITZA, A., "Karl Liebknecht und Rosa Luxemburg
über die Dialektik von Frieden und Sozialismus, " Zs. f.
Geschw., 19, 1971, 1117-38.

5591.   _____, "Rosa Luxemburg und Karl Liebknecht über das
Verhältnis von Demokratie und Sozialismus, " Zs. f.
Geschw., 19, 1971, 861-90.

5592.   LIEBKNECHT, Karl, "Grundzüge einer Marxkritik, " Arch.
f. Sozialw. u. Sozialpol., 46, 1918/19, 605-35.

5593.   RÜCKERT, Otto, "Karl Liebknecht zur Stellung und Rolle
der Arbeiterklasse, " Beitr. z. Gesch. d. dt. Arbeiterbeweg., 14, 1972, 179-92.

5594.   SYRBE, Horst, "Zur nationalen Bedeutung von Karl Liebknechts Schrift 'Militarismus und Antimilitarismus', "
Beitr. z. Gesch. d. dt. Arbeiterbeweg., 3, 1961, 573-
92.

5595.   ULLE, Dieter, "Der theoretisch-philosophische Kampf Karl
Liebknecht gegen die militaristische Ideologie, " Dt. Zs.
f. Phil., 10, 1962, 1371-85.

Wilhelm Liebknecht (1826-1900)

5596.   ALSCHNER, Christian, "Wilhelm Liebknecht als Biblio-
theksbenutzer während seiner Haft in Hubertusburg, "
Beitr. z. Gesch. d. dt. Arbeiterbeweg., 13, 1971, 284-
86.

5597.   BARTEL, Horst, "Wilhelm Liebknecht und das Erfurter
Programm, " Beitr. z. Gesch. d. dt. Arbeiterbeweg., 8,
1966, 974-95.

5598.   HERRMANN, Ursula, "Briefe von Joseph Dietzgen an Wilhelm Liebknecht und die Redaktion des 'Volksstaats', "
Beitr. z. Gesch. d. dt. Arbeiterbeweg., 13, 1971, 241-
53.

5599.   VUILLEUMIER, Marc, "Ein unveröffentlicher Brief Wilhelm
Liebknechts, " Arch. f. Sozialgesch., 4, 1963, 573-77.

5600.   "WILHELM Liebknecht über die Arbeiterbewegung in Deutschland Bericht für die Londoner Konferenz des I Internationale 1865, " Beitr. z. Gesch. d. dt. Arbeiterbeweg., 4,
1962, 942-49.

Rosa Luxemberg (1870-1919)

See also entries 5590, 5591

5601. CARSTEN, F., "Rosa Luxemberg," Contrat Social, 5, 1961, 32-37.

5602. KANCEWICZ, Jan, "Rosa Luxemberg--eine glühende internationalism," Beitr. z. Gesch. d. dt. Arbeiterbeweg., 13, 1971, 398-412.

5603. LASCHITZA, Annelies and Günter RADCZUN, "Zum Wirken Rosa Luxemberg in der deutschen Arbeiterbewegung in den Jahren der ersten Revolution in Russland," Zs. f. Geschw., 19, 1971, 510-38.

5604. _____, "Zum Wirken Rosa Luxembergs in der revolutionären deutschen Arbeiterbewegung," Beitr. z. Gesch. d. dt. Arbeiterbeweg., 13, 1971, 179-97.

5605. LEE, George, "Rosa Luxemberg and the Impact of Imperialism," Econ. J., 81, 1971, 847-62.

5606. SCHMIDT, Giselher, "Rosa Luxemberg zwischen Ost und West," Parlament, 1970(16).

5607. SWEEZY, Paul M., "Rosa Luxemberg's The Accumulation of Capital," Sci. Soc., 31, 1967, 474-85.

5608. TSCHISTJAKOW, W. W., "Der Einfluss der russischen Revolution 1905-1907 auf die Entwicklung der Anschauungen Rosa Luxembergs," Beitr. z. Gesch. d. dt. Arbeiterbeweg., 10, 1968, 617-30.

Franz Mehring (1846-1919)

See also entries 2460, 2461, 2462, 4796, 5568

5609. HELMERT, Heinz, "Franz Mehring und die deutsche Militärgeschichtschreiberg," Zs. f. MilitärG., 2, 1963, 29-40.

5610. MEHRING, Franz, "Aus der Frühzeit der deutschen Arbeiterbewegung F. A. Lange, J. B. v. Schweitzer, W. Lieblmecht, A. Dcbcl," Arch. f. d. Gesch. d. Soz., 1, 1910/11, 101-33.

5611. _____, "Die Pariser Commune 1871," Pr. Jbb., 43, 1879, 275-308, 608-48; 44, 1879, 59-105; 45, 1880, 183-200, 277-312.

5612. _____, "Sozialistische Lyrik--G. Herwegh, F. Freiligrath, H. Heine," Arch. f. d. Gesch. d. Soz., 4, 1913/14, 191-221.

5613. ROMEIN, Jan, "Franz Mehring (1846-1919)," Arch. f. d. Gesch. d. Soz., 13, 1928, 80-103.

5614. SCHLEIFSTEIN, Josef, "Die philosophischen Arbeiten und Anschauungen Franz Mehrings," Dt. Zs. f. Phil., 7, 1959, 5-33.

SCIENCE, MEDICINE, PUBLIC HEALTH

General Studies

5615.   ACKERKNECHT, Erwin H., "Johann Lucas Schoenlein
         1793-1864," J. Hist. Med. Allied Sci., 19, 1964, 131-38.
5616.   ADLER, Francis Heed, "Sketches from the Life of Albrecht
         von Graefe (1828-1870)," Annals Med Hist, 1, 1929, 284-
         90.
5617.   BABINGER, Franz, "Friedrich Eduard Schulz Ein hes-
         sischer Forschungsreisender und Orientalist 1799-1829,"
         Arch. f. hessische Gesch., 8, 1912, 255-75.
5618.   BAST, Theodor H., "Max Johann Sigismund Schultze (1825-
         1874)," Annals Med Hist, 3, 1931, 166-78.
5619.   BÖRNER, Paul, "Die Zukunft der wissenschaftlichen Hygiene
         in Deutschland," Pr. Jbb., 56, 1885, 234-66.
5620.   BONNER, Thomas N., "German Doctors in America--1887-
         1914. Their Views and Impressions of American Life
         and Medicine," J. Hist. Med. Allied Sci., 14, 1959, 1-17.
5621.   BORDEN, Friedrich, "Die deutsche Romantik und die Wis-
         senschaft," Arch. f. KuG., 21, 1931, 44-80.
5622.   BUCHNER, Rudolf, "Die politische und geistige Vorstellungs-
         welt Eduard Buchners (1860-1917)," Zs. f. bayer. LG.,
         26, 1963, 631-45.
5623.   CARLSON, Harold G., "Criticisms of Heredity as a Literary
         Motif with Special Reference to the Newspapers and Peri-
         odicals from 1880-1900," Ger. Rev., 14, 1939, 165-79.
5624.   CASSEDY, James H., "Applied Microscopy and American
         Pork Diplomacy: Charles Wardell Stiles in Germany
         1898-1899," Isis, 62, 1971, 5-20.
5625.   CLARK, Owen E., "The Contributions of J. F. Meckel, the
         Younger to the Science of Teratology," J. Hist. Med.
         Allied Sci., 24, 1969, 310-22.
5626.   CRANEFIELD, Paul F., "The Organic Physics of 1847 and
         the Biophysics of Today," J. Hist. Med. Allied Sci., 12,
         1957, 407-23.
5627.   DIEPGEN, Paul, "Politik und Zeitgeist in der deutschen
         Medizin des 19. Jahrhunderts," H. Jb., 55, 1935, 439-52.
5628.   DITTRICH, Mauritz, "Die Bedeutung von Karl Asmund Ru-
         dolphi (1771-1832) für die Entwicklung der Medizin u.
         Naturwissenschaften im 19. Jahrhundert," Wiss. Zs. der
         Ernst-Moritz-Arndt Universität Greifswald, 16, 1967, 249-
         77.
5629.   DUMITRA, A. P. and R. J. WHITACRE, "Development of

Anesthesia in Germany in the Early Years of the Twentieth Century, " J. Hist. Med. Allied Sci., 1, 1946, 618-34.

5630. FRANKEL, Walter K., "The Introduction of General Anesthesia in Germany, " J. Hist. Med. Allied Sci., 1, 1946, 612-17.

5631. FUCHS, Walther Peter, "Die geschichtliche Gestalt Ferdinand Redtenbachers, " ZGORh., 107, 1959, 205-22.

5632. "Die FÜRSORGE für Epileptische, " Zs. f. Armenwesen, 2, 1865, 109-76.

5633. GRUNDFEST, Harry, "The Different Careers of Gustav Fritsch (1838-1927), " J. Hist. Med. Allied Sci., 18, 1963, 125-29.

5634. HADDA, Siegmund, "Medizinstudent in Breslau am Anfang unseres Jahrhunderts, " Jb. d. Schles.-Fried.-Wilh. Univ. z. Breslau, 14, 1969, 234-74.

5635. HARNDT, Ewald, "Die Stellung der medizinischen Fakultät in der preussischen Friedrich-Wilhelms-Universität zu Berlin als Beispiel für den Wandel des Geisteslebens im 19. Jahrh., " Jb. f. Gesch. M. O. Dtschl., 20, 1971, 134-60.

5636. HOLMES, S. J., "K. E. von Baer's Perplexities over Evolution, " Isis, 37, 1947, 7-14.

5637. HÜPEDEN, Medizinalrath, "Die preussische Medizinalverfassung, ihre Mängel und deren Folgen, " Pr. Jbb., 83, 1896, 466-91.

5638. HUGHES, Thomas Parke, "Technological Momentum in History: Hydrogenation in Germany 1898-1933, " Past and Present, 40, 1969, 106-32.

5639. JARCHO, Saul, "The Contributions of Heinrich and Hermann Berghaus to Medical Cartography, " J. Hist. Med. Allied Sci., 24, 1969, 412-15.

5640. JONES, Oliver P., "Hal Downey's Hematological Training in Germany, 1910-11, " J. Hist. Med. Allied Sci., 27, 1972, 173-86.

5641. KEDROW, B. M., "Die Idee von der Einheit der Welt in den Werken deutscher Naturforscher des 19. Jahrhunderts, " Dt. Zs. f. Phil., 9, 1961, 88-102.

5642. KNAUERHASE, Ramon, "The Compound Steam Engine and Productivity Changes in the German Merchant Marine Fleet, 1871-1887, " J. Econ. Hist., 28, 1968, 390-403.

5643. KNIGHT, D. M., "The Physical Sciences and the Romantic Movement, " Hist. Sci., 9, 1970, 54-75.

5644. KÖHLER, F., "Die Lungentuberkulose des Proletariats, " Pr. Jbb., 139, 1910, 16-49.

5645. KÖHLER, Walther, "Malthus, Ricardo und die Erneuerung der Wissenschaft in Deutschland, " Schmoll. Jb., 35, 1911, 1947-64.

5646. KOSZYK, Kurt, "Aus dem Nachlass Julius Meyers, " Arch. f. Sozialgesch., 8, 1968, 349-63.

5647. "KRANKEN- und Heilpflege im Reich und Preussen, " Zs. f. d. Armenwesen, 9, 1908, 214-21.

5648. LAMMERS, A., "Oeffentliche Gesundheitspflege, " Pr. Jbb.,

32, 1873, 99-109.

5649. LANGE-KOTHE, Irmgard, "Johann Dinnendahl," Tradition, 7, 1962, 32-47, 175-96.

5650. MAULITZ, Russell C., "Schwann's Way: Cells and Crystals," J. Hist. Med. Allied Sci., 26, 1971, 422-37.

5651. MENDELSOHN, Everett, "The Biological Sciences in the Nineteenth Century: Some Problems and Sources," Hist. Sci., 3, 1964, 39-59.

5652. MILLER, Max, "Die Gründungsgeschichte der Naturwissenschaftlichen Fakultät in Tübingen 1859-1863," Zs. F. Württbg. LG, 23, 1964, 189-214.

5653. MOSER, Hugo, "Hermann Fischer und die deutsche Mundartforschung," Zs. F. Württbg. LG, 11, 1952, 225-36.

5654. NAURATZKI, Dr. E., "Die Verplegung Geisteskranter in der Familie mit besonderer Berücksichtigung der Berliner Familienpflege," Zs. f. d. Armenwesen, 5, 1904, 33-45.

5655. PAULSEN, Friedrich, "Die Akademie der Wissenschaften zu Berlin in zwei Jahrhunderten," Pr. Jbb., 99, 1900, 410-53.

5656. PFEIFFER, L., "Die Ausbreitung und der Verlauf der Cholera in Thüringen und Sachsen während der dritten Cholerainvasion 1865-1867," Jbb. f. Nationalökon. u. Stat., 17, 1871, 1-159.

5657. PÖNICKE, Herbert, "Der Anteil Mitteldeutscher an den technischen Errungenschaften des 19. Jahrhunderts," Hamb. Mittel- u. ostdt. Forsch., 3, 1961, 27-94.

5658. _____, "Georg Paul Alexander Petzholdt Ein mitteldeutscher Naturforscher und Lehrer in Russland (1810-1889)," Hamb. Mittel-u. ostdt. Forsch., 2, 1959, 47-70.

5659. REDLICH, Fritz, "The Leaders of the German Steam-Engine Industry During the First Hundred Years," J. Econ. Hist., 4, 1944, 121-48.

5660. RISSE, Guenter B., "Kant, Schelling, and the Early Search for a Philosophical 'Science' of Medicine in Germany," J. Hist. Med. Allied Sci., 27, 1972, 145-58.

5661. RÜTT, A., "Die Orthopädie des 19. Jahrhunderts in Würzburg (von Johann-Georg Heine zu Albert Hoffa)," Mainfränk. Jb., 23, 1971, 117-28.

5662. RUSH, Homer P., "A Biographic Sketch of Arnold Adolf Berthold. An early Experimenter with Ductless Glands," Annals Med Hist, 1, 1929, 208-14.

5663. SARTON, George, "The Discovery of X-rays with a Facsimile reproduction (no. XVIII) of Röntgen's First Account of them published early in 1896," Isis, 26, 1936/37, 349-70.

5664. SCHILLER, J., "Physiology's Struggle for Independence in the First Half of the Nineteenth Century," Hist. Sci., 7, 1968, 64-89.

5665. SCHMANDERER, Eberhard, "Der Einfluss der Chemie auf die Entwicklung des Patentwesens in der Zweiten Hälfte des 19. Jahrhunderts," Tradition, 16, 1971, 144-76.

5666. SEEMANN, H. J., "Eilhard Wiedemann," Isis, 14, 1930, 166-86.

5667. SOURKES, Theodore L., "Mortiz Traube, 1826-1894: His Contribution to Biochemistry, " J. Hist. Med. Allied Sci., 10, 1955, 379-91.
5668. THOMPSON, Silvanus, "Philipp Reis Erfinder des Telephons, " Arch. f. dt. Postgesch., 1963(1), 2-67.
5669. TREUE, Wilhelm, "Die Bedeutung der chemischen Wissenschaft für die chemische Industrie 1770-1870, " Technikgeschichte, 33, 1965, 25-51.
5670. _____, "Erfinder und Unternehmer, " Tradition, 8, 1963, 255-71.
5671. _____, "Ingenieur und Erfinder Zwei sozial- und technikgeschichtliche Probleme, " VSW, 54, 1967, 456-76.
5672. _____, "Max Freiherr von Oppenheim--der Archäologe und die Politik, " HZ, 209, 1969, 37-74.
5673. TROITZSCH, U., "Zu den Anfängen der deutschen Technikgeschichtsschreibung um die Wende von 18. zum 19. Jahrhundert, " Technikgeschichte, 40, 1973, 33-57.
5674. UFFELMANN, Julius, "Ueber Massnahmen und Einrichtungen zum Schutze der Gesundheit der Kinder, " Pr. Jbb., 46, 1880, 351-78.
5675. VALDENAIRE, Arthur, "Das Leben und Wirken des Johann Gottfried Tulla, " ZGORh., 81, 1928/29, 337-64, 588-616; 83, 1930/31, 258-86.
5676. WANKMÜLLER, Armin, "Die Anfänge des Apothekerstudiums in Tübingen, " Zs. F. Württbg. LG, 15, 1956, 298-304.
5677. WELSCH, Fritz, "Zur Herstellung künstlicher Farbstoffe im 19. Jahrhundert und deren Bedeutung für die Entwicklung der Chemie, " Zs. f. Gesch. d. Naturwissenschaften, Technik und Medizin, 1, 1960, 81-103.
5678. WILLIAMS, L. Pearce, "The Physical Sciences in the First Half of the Nineteenth Century: Problems and Sources, " Hist. Sci., 1, 1962, 1-15.

Alexander von Humboldt (1769-1859)

See also entry 4982

5679. ACKERKNECHT, Erwin H., "George Forster, Alexander von Humboldt and Ethnology, " Isis, 46, 1955, 83-95.
5680. "ALEXANDER von Humboldt und sein Einfluss auf die Naturwissenschaft, " Pr. Jbb., 2, 1858, 44-64, 180-209.
5681. BARRETT, Paul H. and Alain F. COREOS, "A Letter from Alexander Humboldt to Charles Darwin, " J. Hist. Med. Allied Sci., 27, 1972, 159-72.
5682. BONJOUR, Edgar, "Briefe Alexander von Humboldts an Johannes von Müller, " Schw. Zs. f. Gesch., 10, 1960, 422-29.
5683. BROWNE, C. A., "Alexander von Humboldt as Historian of Science in Latin America, " Isis, 35, 1944, 134-39.
5684. HAGEN, Victor Wolfgang von, "Was This the Fate of the Library of Alexander von Humboldt?, " Isis, 41, 1950, 164-67.

5685. HARIG, Gerhard, "Alexander von Humboldt--Wissenschaftler
       und Humanist," Dt. Zs. f. Phil., 7, 1959, 253-70.
5686. JAHN, Ilse, "Die anatomischen Studien der Brüder Humboldt
       unter Justus Christian Loder in Jena," Beitr. z. Gesch.
       d. Univ. Erfurt, 14, 1968/69.
5687. KONETZKE, Richard, "Alexander von Humboldt als Ge-
       schichtsschreiber Amerikas," HZ, 188, 1959, 526-65.
5688. SCHIPPERGES, Heinrich, "Alexander von Humboldt und die
       Medizin seiner Zeit," Arch. f. KuG., 41, 1959, 166-82.
5689. SCHRAMM, Percy Ernst, "Alexander von Humboldt--bewun-
       derungswürdig, beneidenswert," Jb. Preussischer Kultur-
       besitz, 1968, 25-40.
5690. SIMON, Karl, "Gottlieb Schick und die Familie Humboldt,"
       Pr. Jbb., 162, 1915, 200-16.
5691. THÉODORIDÈS, J., "Alexandre de Humboldt--observateur
       de la France de Louis-Philippe," Rev. d'hist. dipl., 85,
       1971, 193-380.
5692. "UNE Dépêche D'Alexandre von Humboldt au Roi de Prusse
       Frédéric--Guillaume IV sur la situation politique et so-
       ciale en France," Rev. d'hist. dipl., 80, 1966, 41-45.
5693. VOSSLER, Otto, "Humboldts Idee der Universität," HZ, 178,
       1954, 251-68.

Robert Koch (1843-1910)

5694. SMITH, Theobald, "Koch's Views on the Stability of Species
       among Bacteria," Annals Med Hist, 4, 1932, 524-30.
5695. WEBB, Gerald B., "Robert Koch (1843-1910)," Annals Med
       Hist, 4, 1932, 509-23.

Rudolf Virchow (1821-1902)

5696. DEPPE, Hans-Ulrich, "Rudolf Virchows Kampf um die preus-
       sische Verfassung," Blätter f. deutsche u. internationale
       Politik, 13, 1968, 961-74.
5697. GOLDMAN, Leon, "War and Science--Rudolf Virchow," An-
       nals Med Hist, 8, 1936, 558-61.
5698. KÜMMEL, W., "Rudolf Virchow und der Antisemitismus,"
       Medizinhistorisches Journal, 3, 1968, 165-79.
5699. PRIDAN, Daniel, "Rudolf Virchow and Social Medicine in
       Historical Perspective," Med. Hist., 8, 1964, 274-78.
5700. WILSON, J. Walter, "Virchow's Contribution to the Cell
       Theory," J. Hist. Med. Allied Sci., 2, 1947, 163-78.
5701. WINTER, Kurt, "Rudolf Virchow und die Revolution von
       1848," Zs. f. Geschw., 2, 1954, 844-65.